THE BOOK OF
MAGICAL PSALMS

Part 3

THE BOOK OF MAGICAL PSALMS

Part 3

Shadow Tree Series
Volume 5

Jacobus G. Swart

THE SANGREAL SODALITY PRESS
Johannesburg, Gauteng, South Africa

First edition, 2024
First printing, 2024

Published by The Sangreal Sodality Press
74 Twelfth Street
Parkmore 2196
Gauteng
South Africa
Email: jacobsang@gmail.com

ISBN 978-1-0370-1219-8

Dedicated to Dirk Cloete

"Unbreakable are links of love which faith and friendship forge among all souls discerning one another by the Light within them. Welcome indeed are they that enter with entitlement our closest circles of companionship."

—William G. Gray (*The Sangreal Sacrament*)

Shadow Tree Series

Contents

Illustrations

Hebrew Transliteration

There are transliterations of Hebrew words and phrases throughout this work. In this regard I have employed the following method. The Hebrew vowels are pronounced:

"a" — like "a" in "father";
"e" — like the "e" in "let" or the way the English pronounce the word "Air" without enunciating the "r";
"i" — like the "ee" in "seek";
"o" — like the "o" in "not" or the longer "au" in "naught"; or again like the sound of the word "Awe";
"u" — like the "oo" in "mood";
"ai" — like the letter "y" in "my" or "igh" in "high" or like the sound of the word "eye"; and
"ei" — like the "ay" in "hay."
"ei" — like the "ay" in "hay."

The remaining consonants are as written, except for:

"ch" which is pronounced like the guttural "ch" in the Scottish "Loch" or the equivalent in the German "Ich," and "tz" which sounds like the "tz" in "Ritz" or like the "ts" in "hearts."

In most cases an apostrophe (') indicates a glottal stop which sounds like the "i" in "bit" or the concluding "er" in "father," otherwise it is a small break to separate sections of a word or create a double syllable. For example, I often hear people speak of Daat (Knowledge), sounding one long "ah" between the "D" and the concluding "T." The correct pronunciation is however Da'at, the apostrophe indicating that the term comprises actually two syllables, "dah" and "aht." In this word a quick glottal stop separates the one syllable from the other. As a vowel it is the same sound made when one struggles to find the right word, and say something like "er.....er......er......"

One further rule is that the accent in Hebrew is, more often than not, placed on the last syllable of the word. Of course there are numerous instances which disprove this rule, but it applies almost throughout Hebrew incantations, e.g. those found in Merkavistic literature, etc.

"...... .....but Perele, the Maharal's wife, peace upon her, could not resist making use of Yossele (Yosef) the golem a day before Passover Eve to help her with holiday preparations. Unbeknownst to the Maharal, she motioned to the golem to fetch water and fill up the two large barrels that stood in a special room that had already been cleaned and made ready for Passover...... ....

Introduction

Having reached the culmination of this mammoth study on the magical use of the Biblical Psalms, it is clear that much remains unsaid. It was indeed difficult to decide exactly what to include and exclude in this text, and I simply held to my original intention, which was to ensure that this work is comprehensive and definitive, rather than "complete." In writing works on "Practical Kabbalah," I believe it is especially important to do so with clarity of conscience, and with as much authoritative capability as one can muster, especially in these times when those who are seeking to find their "true being" and a "meaningful existence" in "esotericism," are obliged to wade through an occult minefield on the world wide web. In this regard, my late mentor William G. Gray noted that "unfortunately, the intentions of many would-be guides to the Inner Planes are more like guided missiles aimed at the seeker's wallet. Seldom have so many sharks snapped so eagerly as the unsuspecting plunge into deep occult waters unsupported by anything except a well-inflated money-belt. From mystic supply shops to witch-covens, 'Orders' of this, that, and the other, stretch greedy hands toward the gullible. None but the truly poor in spirit could possibly navigate through such pirate-infested waters and emerge enriched by the experience."[1] My beloved mentor made that observation back in the late 1970's. I am quite certain that if he could witness what is currently transpiring on this side of the styx, he would be dumbstruck at how modern-day seekers after truth are being swamped by a tsunami of trash, which is pandered in the ever so greedy online "occult supermarket" as "the truth and nothing but the truth."

However, that is not my main peeve, and naturally people are perfectly entitled to place their faith and money on whichever "occult altar" grabs their fancy. However, the tragedy for those who wish to share the mysteries of this Sacred Tradition with parties who are genuinely interested in it as a meaningful way of life, is that absolutely nothing is considered sacred on the "occult bandwagon." Thus the Hebrew Divine and Angelic Names of "*Kabbalah Ma'asit*" ("Practical Kabbalah"), which we hold so dear and sacred, are often harnassed willy-nilly for intentions they were not designed for, especially when some of those "intentions" are of the most debased and iniquitous kind. Whilst most of the "Kosher" literature on Jewish Magic is still available in Hebrew only, an English readership intent on distinguishing falsity from truth in the vast arena of "Jewish Magic," can certainly do no better than read the illuminating writings of authors like Rabbi Ariel bar Tzadok.[2]

I am attempting through my own writings to add to this corpus of authentic literature on "Practical Kabbalah," but I readily admit that I am not an absolute "purist." In this regard, as a life-long practitioner of this wonderful Tradition, I find it somewhat difficult to keep myself and my personal experiences out of the picture so to speak. I have been told categorically that the *S'gulot* ("Magical Treasures"/"Remedies") of "*Practical Kabbalah*" do not work for anybody other than a "*Tzadik*," and that they are equally of no use if you *are* a "*Tzadik*." As far as my own person is concerned, I have no rabbinical or "*Tzadik*" pretensions. Yet, having witnessed the effectiveness of the techniques shared in this series of texts on "*Practical Kabbalah*," it is clear that their power is based on the fact that everyone, "sinner" or "saint," create his/her own reality within the condition of the vital "Oneness" of all existence. As said before, "by 'reality' I do not mean the one we *believe* in, but rather the one we actually *express* through our *actions*," and that "the process of 'self-creation' shows us that all life is truly 'One'; that there is no separateness whatsoever; that everything and every dimension is intrinsically interrelated; that there is really no separation between what we perceive to be physical and what we think is spiritual; that all are part of the selfsameness of one great consciousness called אֶהְיֶה (*Ehyeh*—'I am'); and that all possible possibilities exist within us in the 'Eternal Now'."[3]

Thus, when it comes to working the wondrous techniques of "*Practical Kabbalah*," it is absolutely clear to me "that 'magic' is not efficaciously worked 'outwardly,' but rather 'inwardly.' After all, the 'outer' is merely the outward expression of the 'inner'." In this regard, I maintained that "Inner" and "Outer," or "Centre" and "Circumference." are purely and simply "expressions of a great 'Oneness'."[4] I further noted that "as 'separateness' is really an illusion, and since all things are intrinsically related to one another, there are 'expressions of synchronicity' in the 'everywhere,' so to speak, literally patterns of relatedness between everything, even between the grossest aspects of 'materialised spirit' and the most refined 'subtle matter' of the greatly 'Exteriorised One.' One might view these to be 'channels of possibility' existing in the 'Now,' and it is in the 'Wholly Present' where the 'All-Possible-Possibilities' can be arranged into 'miracles'."[5]

Lastly, it is worth stressing again that a "real magical working is the one you perform within. This means that every external ritual expression, should indeed be 'an outer and visible sign of an inner and invisible grace.' Thus, if any part of a magical ritual activity distracts from the 'Centre,' it would have to be modified in such a way so as to maintain the integrity of the balanced 'Inner Centre.' In this regard, if chanting or uttering an incantation aloud is distractive, then you might resort to whispering the said incantation, or even vocalising it in your mind whilst exhaling, as you would when uttering it verbally."[6] In fact, any magical working should be performed from your "Self-centre" where "everything is conjoined, and in which there is no separation between the 'magician,' the 'magic,' and the result. All are part of the selfsameness of one great omni-aware consciousness called 'I am'."[7]

✳✳✳

To those who are studying and practising the material shared in this tome, I again recommend that you consider commencing any study of Kabbalistic material by sitting in a restful, peaceful manner, and then, with eyes shut for a minute or so, to meditate on these words:

"Open my eyes so that I may perceive the wonders of Your teaching."

Whisper the phrase repeatedly and allow yourself to "feel" the meaning of the words you are uttering within the depths of your Self. It is again important not to attempt any mental deliberation on the meaning of the actual words, but to simply repeat them a number of times. As stated previously, it is a good idea to read a section in its entirety, without trying to perceive any specific meaning, then to pause for a few seconds, and afterwards attempt to understand within yourself the general meaning of what was being said. In this way you begin to fulfil an important teaching of *Kabbalah*, which tells you to unite two "worlds"—the inner and the outer within your own Being. By allowing yourself to "feel" the meaning of what you are reading, you learn to surrender to the words. You open yourself, again fulfilling one of the requirements of Kabbalistic study, which is to surrender the "me," the ego, and to remove arrogance and bias. You simply attempt to sense with your being what is being portrayed in the section you are perusing. This act is a serious step on the path of perfecting one's personality, because it stops the expansion of the ego, and increases the chance of obtaining "True Knowledge."

✳✳✳

"*The Book of Magical Psalms*" would not be complete without acknowledging the enormous support from my dear friends, my Companions in the Sangreal Sodality, as well as my many acquaintances who enrich my life in numerous ways, whose encouragement inspire the ongoing expansion of my consciousness, and who continue to fetch the best out of me. In this regard, I wish to express my most profound gratitude to Dirk Cloete to whom I dedicated this volume. There is simply not enough words to express what he means to me. To paraphrase Anais Nin, I can say that Dirk represents a world in me, a world possibly not born until he arrived, and it is only by this meeting that a new world was born. His support and input resulted in the birth of this, the fifth volume in the "Shadow Tree Series" of texts on "*Practical Kabbalah*."

I wish to offer my beloved Gloria my most profound gratitude for the love and care she bestowed on me over the forty-six years of our marriage. As I have said so many times, I owe the well-being of my body, mind, soul and spirit to her. She will always be the love of my life, and I thank her for the joy and laughter I carry in my heart. Acknowledgement is also due to my late mentor, William G. Gray, my Father-Brother, who showed me the way of "Truth and Goodness," and what "common sense" is really all about. I offer my most heartfelt gratitude to my Sangreal Companions and dear friends all over the world, Gidon Fainman, Norma Cosani, Elizabeth Bennet, Geraldine Talbot, Marq and Penny Smith, Ryan Kay, Francois le Roux, Simon O'Regan, Gerhardus Muller, Carlien Steyn, Helene Vogel and Gerrit Viljoen, Dirk Cloete and Sean Smith, Marcus Claridge in England, Hamish Gilbert in Poland, Bence Bodnar, Lukács Gábor, and Dániel Szeretõ in Hungary, Roberto Siqueira Rodrigues in Brazil, Taron Plaza in Japan, Yuriy Fyedin in China, Gil Gier in Israel, and all intimates "whose identities are known unto Omniscience alone."

I again extend my most sincere thanks to Dirk Cloete for reading and correcting this tome, as well as to my dear friend Jonti Mayer who checked and read the transliterations of the Hebrew prayer-incantations shared in this work.

Happy Reading!

Jacobus Swart
Johannesburg
October 2024

. ...Yossele quickly seized the yoke and the two buckets and dashed off to the well to bring water. But no one was around to notice what he was up to....In short, Yossele the golem did not have the faintest idea when to stop fetching water... ... .

Chapter 5
Tzafon — North
The Psalms of David — Book IV

PSALM 90

[1] תפלה למשה איש האלהים אדני מעון אתה
היית לנו בדר ודר

[2] בטרם הרים ילדו ותחולל ארץ ותבל ומעולם
עד עולם אתה אל

[3] תשב אנוש עד דכא ותאמר שובו בני אדם

[4] כי אלף שנים בעיניך כיום אתמול כי יעבר
ואשמורה בלילה

[5] זרמתם שנה יהיו בבקר כחציר יחלף

[6] בבקר יציץ וחלף לערב ימולל ויבש

[7] כי כלינו באפך ובחמתך נבהלנו

[8] שתה עונתינו לנגדך עלמנו למאור פניך

[9] כי כל ימינו פנו בעברתך כלינו שנינו כמו הגה

[10] ימי שנותינו בהם שבעים שנה ואם בגבורת
שמונים שנה ורהבם עמל ואון כי גז חיש ונעפה

[11] מי יודע עז אפך וכיראתך עברתך

[12] למנות ימינו כן הודע ונבא לבב חכמה

[13] שובה יהוה‏אדני‏אהדונהי עד מתי והנחם על עבדיך

[14] שבענו בבקר חסדך ונרננה ונשמחה בכל ימינו

[15] שמחנו כימות עניתנו שנות ראינו רעה

[16] יראה אל עבדיך פעלך והדרך על בניהם

[17] ויהי נעם אדני אלהינו עלינו ומעשה ידינו כוננה
עלינו ומעשה ידינו כוננהו

Transliteration:
[1] *t'filah l'mosheh ish ha'elohim adonai ma'on atah
hayita lanu b'dor vador*
[2] *b'terem harim yuladu vat'cholel eretz v'teivel
umei'olam ad olam atah el*

1

[3] *tasheiv enosh ad daka vatomer shuvu v'nei adam*
[4] *ki elef shanim b'einecha k'yom et'mol ki ya'avor v'ash'murah valaila*
[5] *z'ram'tam sheina yih'yu baboker kechatzir yachalof*
[6] *baboker yatzitz v'chalaf la'erev y'moleil v'yavesh*
[7] *ki chalinu v'apecha uvachamat'cha niv'hal'nu*
[8] *shata avonoteinu l'neg'decha alumeinu lim'or panecha*
[9] *ki chol yameinu panu v'ev'ratecha kilinu shaneinu ch'mo hegeh*
[10] *y'mei sh'noteinu vahem shiv'im shanah v'im big'vurot sh'monim shanah v'roh'bam amal va'aven ki gaz chish vana'ufah*
[11] *mi yodei'a oz apecha uch'yir'at'cha ev'ratecha*
[12] *lim'not yameinu kein hoda v'navi l'vav chochmah*
[13] *shuvah YHVH ad matai v'hinacheim al avadecha*
[14] *sab'einu vaboker chas'decha un'ran'nah v'nis'm'cha b'chol yameinu*
[15] *sam'cheinu kimot initanu sh'not ra'inu ra'ah*
[16] *yeira'eh el avadecha fa'olecha vahadar'cha al b'neihem*
[17] *vihi no'am adonai eloheinu aleinu uma'aseih yadeinu kon'nah aleinu uma'aseih yadeinu kon'neihu*

Translation:

[1] A Prayer of Moses the man of *Elohim*. *Adonai*, Thou hast been our dwelling-place in all generations.
[2] Before the mountains were brought forth, or ever Thou hadst formed the earth and the world, even from everlasting to everlasting, Thou art God.
[3] Thou turnest man to contrition; and sayest: 'Return, ye children of men.'
[4] For a thousand years in Thy sight are but as yesterday when it is past, and as a watch in the night.
[5] Thou carriest them away as with a flood; they are as a sleep; in the morning they are like grass which groweth up.
[6] In the morning it flourisheth, and groweth up; in the evening it is cut down, and withereth.
[7] For we are consumed in Thine anger, and by Thy wrath are we hurried away.
[8] Thou hast set our iniquities before Thee, our secret sins in the light of Thy countenance.

[9] For all our days are passed away in Thy wrath; we bring our years to an end as a tale that is told.

[10] The days of our years are threescore years and ten, or even by reason of strength fourscore years; yet is their pride but travail and vanity; for it is speedily gone, and we fly away.

[11] Who knoweth the power of Thine anger, and Thy wrath according to the fear that is due unto Thee?

[12] So teach us to number our days, that we may get us a heart of wisdom.

[13] Return, *YHVH*; how long? And let it repent Thee concerning Thy servants.

[14] O satisfy us in the morning with Thy mercy; that we may rejoice and be glad all our days.

[15] Make us glad according to the days wherein Thou hast afflicted us, according to the years wherein we have seen evil.

[16] Let Thy work appear unto Thy servants, and Thy glory upon their children.

[17] And let the graciousness of *Adonai* our God be upon us; establish Thou also upon us the work of our hands; yea, the work of our hands establish Thou it.

Psalm 90 is one of eleven psalms, i.e. *Psalms 90–100*, which are said to have been written by Moses. In this regard, the *Midrash on Psalms* tells us that "Moses composed eleven Psalms appropriate to eleven tribes,"[1] to which the great *Rashi* noted that "corresponding to them, he blessed eleven tribes with eleven blessings."[2] In this regard, *Psalm 90* is said to be "appropriate to the tribe of Reuben."[3] As far as the application of the current psalm in Jewish worship is concerned, it should be noted that *Psalm 90* is enunciated during the morning service (*Shacharit*) on the Sabbath and festivals, and it is also recited during the circumambulations (*hakafot*) of תורה שמחת (*Simchat Torah*— "Rejoicing with the *Torah*").[4] We are informed that one of the reasons why the current psalm was included in the Sabbath liturgy is "because it speaks of creation, a concept embodied in the Sabbath, as it is written, 'Before the mountains were born',"[5] and equally that the verse "O satisfy us in the morning with Thy mercy," indicates "the new day of the world to come, when every day will be a Sabbath."[6] As far as its utterance during the "Rejoicing with the *Torah*" (*Simchat Torah*) is concerned, we are told that this is because on this occasion "the portion about the demise of Moses is read."[7]

In Jewish Magic it is said the ninetieth Psalm is recited "to escape a lion."[8] However, whilst the popular published Hebrew version of the *Shimmush Tehillim* references the same application of the current psalm, this text maintains the current psalm should be recited conjointly with *Psalm 91* for the purpose of causing a lion or an evil spirit to flee.[9] We are told the associated Divine Name is שׁדי (*Shadai*), the component letters of which is said to have been derived: שׁ (*Shin*) from ת (*Tav*) in תפלה (*tefila*—"a prayer"): verse 1, the glyph having been transposed by means of the שׁ"ת interchange, i.e. by means of a very obscure cipher called א"ר ב"ק (*Arbak*); ד (*Dalet*) from מ (*Mem*) in מעון (*ma'on*— "dwelling-place"): verse 1, the letters having been converted by means of the דמ"ת interchange, i.e. the ever popular אי"ק בכ"ר (*Ayak Bachar*) cipher; and י (*Yod*) from א (*Alef*) in אתה (*atah*— "Thou"): verse 2, the glyphs having been equally exchanged by means of the אי"ק בכ"ר (*Ayak Bachar*) cipher.[10] We are told that the following prayer-incantation, which includes the mentioned Divine Name, should be recited following the enunciation of the listed two psalms:

יהי רצין מלפניך **אל** שדי הגדול הגבור והנורא
שתדחה רוח רעה מעל [....name of recipient....] ותשלח
לו רפואה שלימה בקרוב ותחזירהו לבריאות ותענה
אותו כמו שענית למשה עבדך בשירה הזות ותעלה
תפלתו לפניך כמו שהיה עולה עשן קטורת לפניך
מעל גבי המזבח אמן אמן אמן סלה סלה סלה סלה

Transliteration:

> *y'hi ratzon mil'fanecha El Shadai hagadol hagibor v'hanora shetid'cheh ru'ach ra'ah mei'al* [....name of recipient....] *v'tish'lach lo r'fu'ah sh'leimah b'karov v'tach'zireihu lib'ri'ot v'ta'aneh oto k'mo shei'anita l'mosheh av'decha b'shirah hazot v'ta'aleh t'filato l'fanecha k'mo shehayah olah ashan k'toret l'fanecha*

mei'al gabei hamiz'bei'ach Omein Omein Omein Selah Selah Selah

Translation:

May it be your will *El Shadai*, the great, mighty, and awesome, to drive away an evil spirit from [....name of recipient....], and speedily send him complete healing, and letting him return to his health. And you shall answer him as you answered Moses, your servant, who prayed this song, and let his prayer rise before you as the fragrance of incense ascended to you from the altar. *Amen Amen Amen Selah Selah Selah.*[11]

Godfrey Selig's presentation of this application of the said two psalms in his popular German/English translation of the *Shimmush Tehillim*, agrees in the main with the standard published Hebrew text, though he added that the psalms could be recited "over a person tormented by an evil spirit, or one afflicted by an incurable disease."[12] Regarding the enunciation of the Divine Name שׁדּי (*Shadai*) with the two psalms, which is said will cause a lion or an evil spirit to flee, Selig wrote "should you accidentally encounter a lion in the forest, or should you be deceived, cheated or plagued by an evil spirit or ghost, then grasp in your mind the name of God (*Schaddei*) and repeat this Psalm, and they will withdraw themselves. But you will be still more secure when such a danger should arise, if you pray the following 91st Psalm in connection with the 90th, at one and the same time."[13]

One source maintains the said psalms could equally be written down as an amulet for the same listed purposes,[14] and in a variant recension of the *Shimmush Tehillim*, the ninetieth Psalm is written conjointly with a prayer-incantation, to be employed as an amulet "against spirits, demons and Lilits." In this regard, we are told that the writing should be located on the person of the individual who is suffering demonic possession.[15] The said prayer-incantation reads:

מיכאל גבריאל רפאל עזרוני וסמכוני ופטרוני מיד
כל רוח ושד ומיד כל רוחין בישׁין דפרחין בעולם
בשם יהוה אלהי עולם אמן אמן אמן סלה סלה סלה

Transliteration:

> *Micha'el Gavri'el Rafa'el az'runi v'sam'chuni upat'runi m'yad kol ru'ach v'sheid um'yad kol ruchin bishin d'par'chin b'olam b'shem YHVH elohei olam Omein Omein Omein Selah Selah Selah.*

Translation:

> *Micha'el Gavri'el Rafa'el* help me, support, and deliver me from the hand of every spirit and demon, and from the hand of all evil spirits that fly around in the world. In the name of *YHVH*, God of the universe, *Amen Amen Amen Selah Selah Selah.*[16]

Regarding the earlier mentioned listing of the current psalm against "Lilits," i.e. sexual demons, I have seen it recommended for protection against all manner of "night spirits," and specifically for protection against *incubi* (male sexual demons), and *succubi* (female sexual demons). It should also be noted that, when it comes to sleep and dreams, *Psalm 90* was recommended against bad or demonic dreams, i.e. nightmares, and equally for insomnia. Also, other than the mentioned application of the current psalm for protection against lions, "unofficial sources" maintained it to be useful against all kinds of savage beasts. Furthermore, besides its employment as a protection against, and to avert attacks from, demonic forces, it is recited against all ghosts, demonic visions, and also for haunted houses. As far as "human evil" is concerned, the ninetieth Psalm is applied against deception, being swindled, and against "bad language," i.e. slander (הרע לשון [*lashon hara*] —"the evil tongue"). Thus it should come as no surprise that *Psalm 90* is employed for protection generally.[17]

On a more positive note, it should be noted that the current psalm has been recommended for enunciation to encourage rainfall during periods of drought, and equally to cause water to be drawn from wells or boreholes. It is also one of the psalms recommended to individuals who are suffering serious or incurable diseases, and is especially employed against plagues.[18] In terms of the latter application, the practitioner is instructed to recite the psalm every morning before leaving his or her home, doing so conjointly with the *Shema*, i.e. the great biblical statement of faith reading:

שמע ישראל יהוה אלהינו יהוה אחד

Transliteration:

sh'ma yis'ra'el YHVH [Adonai] eloheinu YHVH [Adonai] echad

Translation:

Hear O Israel: *YHVH [Adonai]* our God, *YHVH [Adonai]* is One.

The practitioner is further enjoined to focus on the Divine Name כוזו במוכסז כוזו (*Kuzu B'mochsaz Kuzu*),[19] a Divine Name construct which, I noted elsewhere, comprises the Hebrew glyphs succeeding those in the phrase יהוה אלהינו יהוה (*YHVH Eloheinu YHVH*) [*Deuteronomy 6:4*]. This Divine Name is said to be the "severe aspect" of the said biblical phrase, and is claimed to have the power to "awaken the dead."[20] Whilst mentioning "the dead," it should be noted that the ninetieth Psalm is listed for longevity.[21] For serious religionists, the psalm is recited for repentance,[22] and equally when a worshipper considers the greatness of the Divine One compared to the smallness of humankind.

Individual verses from the current psalm are equally employed for magical purposes. In this regard, *Psalm 90:13* is directly aligned with דמב (*Dameb*), the sixty-fifth tri-letter portion of the "Name of Seventy-two Names."[23] It is also worth considering that capitals of the words in *Psalm 90:15–16* reading שנות ראינו רעה יראה אל (*sh'not ra'inu ra'ah yeira'eh el*— "the years wherein we have seen evil, [literally] let God appear"), were conjoined to formulate the Angelic Name שרריאל (*Sharari'el*). Whilst we have no direct indication as to any practical application of this Angelic Name, we are informed that its "secret" pertains to the opening phrase in *Song of Songs 7:3* reading שררך אגן הסהר (*shar'reich agan hasahar*—"Thy navel is like a round goblet").[24]

Be that as it may, particular attention should be paid to *Psalm 90:17*. It is reported that when the Israelites completed the Holy Tarbernacle during their sojourn in the desert, Moses bestowed a blessing upon the people, which is said to be the one listed in the said verse.[25] The twelve Hebrew words of this beautiful verse comprise very pleasant rhythmic and rhyming qualities, and are especially valuable as a magical blessing reading:

ויהי נעם אדני אלהינו עלינו
ומעשה ידינו כוננה עלינו
ומעשה ידינו כוננהו

Transliteration:
> *vihi no'am adonai eloheinu aleinu*
> *uma'aseih yadeinu kon'nah aleinu*
> *uma'aseih yadeinu kon'neihu*

Translation:
> And let the graciousness of *Adonai* our God be upon us;
> establish Thou also upon us the work of our hands;
> yea, the work of our hands establish Thou it.

It has been aptly recommended for recitation when "doing painting, sculpture, crafts, etc."[26] In terms of magical applications, the capitals of the words comprising the seventeenth verse were conjoined in the Divine Name construct ונא אעו יכע ויכ which is included in an amulet employed to reduce fever,[27] and to facilate *Kefitzat ha-Derech* ("Shortening the Way," i.e. magical travel or teleportation).[28] We are informed that the "*Vihi Noam*" verse is considered to be a source of great protection magic, a prayer through which danger and suffering may be turned aside. To avert trouble, there is an old custom of reciting the said verse seven times each night of *Chanukah* (Jewish Festival of Lights), after lighting the candles.[29] It is also customary to write this verse on clean parchment, which is then located behind the entrance of a residence in order to keep it safe from accidents.[30]

I have also seen this verse engraved on rings for amuletic purposes, and it has been employed in the "empowerment," so to speak, of an amulet which is formulated from *Psalm 106:30*. I have addressed this amulet in great detail elsewhere,[31] and will reference it again later in this work. I wish to focus now on the conjoint employment of the two versions of the said amulet shown below, in conjunction with *Psalm 90:17*, as delineated in *Sefer Rafael ha-Malach*:[32]

שדי		קרע			שטן		
וי	פה	וו	והה	וי	יה	עו	מהד
יה	יו	יה	תימ	פי	יה	נו	חהס
עו	נה	פי	עהג	וי	יה	פו	להל
מה	חי	לה	צופ	וי	תה	עו	צהר
די	סה	לו	רהה	הי	מה	נו	פהה

As noted earlier, the ninetieth Psalm is recommended against plagues, and this amulet is likewise employed against plagues and epidemics. The interesting factor here is that the individual constructing the amulet is instructed to cut sprigs of the herb Rue with a golden coin or disc, doing so prior to sunrise on a Wednesday during the period closest to the Full Moon. In this regard, the instruction is to recite *Psalm 90:17* seven times prior to cutting the rue. Some maintain individuals performing this action should enunciate *Psalm 90* in its entirety. Following this action practitioners are advised whilst cutting the herb, to express personal intentions in their mother tongue, saying "I am collecting this herb in honour of 'so and so'." Others insist that the said personal intentions should be expressed in Hebrew, and recommend the use of the following statement:[33]

אנכי לוקט עלי רוטא האלה בשם יהוה אלהי
ישראל לאסותא מן שמיא ולשמירה עבור
[....insert name of recipient....] מן כל פגעים רעים
ומרעין בישין

Transliteration:
> *anochi loket alei ruta ha'eleh b'shem YHVH elohei yisra'el l'asuta min sh'maya ulish'mirah avur* [....insert name of recipient....] *min kol p'ga'im ra'im umar'in bishin*

Translation:
> I am collecting this rue in the name *YHVH*, God of Israel, for healing from heaven and the protection of [....insert name of recipient....] from all bad mishaps and evil doing spirits.

Prior to writing the said amulet, the individual who is set with this task, and whom we are told should be a man, has to fast and be purified by performing the ritual submersion in the waters of a *Mikveh* (Ritual Bath).[34] As I noted elsewhere, the instruction that only a man can write this amulet, has nothing to do with any "prevailing sexism when these instructions were first written down."[35] It pertains to the fact "that in all major religious traditions of the world, Judaism included, women are considered to be 'ritually impure' during *Niddah* (term of menstruation)."[36] As stated, this is "a period when many women experience great hormonal variations and equally great energy fluctuations physically, emotionally and mentally, quite out of sync with their natural disposition. Some might indeed consider such imbalances to have a disadvantageous impact on the flow of 'subtle forces' channelled by an amulet."[37]

When all ritual purity requirements are fulfilled, the amulet is written in *ashurit* (biblical script) on a pure scroll, i.e. a clean sheet of good quality paper. On completion, the rue is rolled into the *Kamea* and located in an appropriately sized, thin leather envelope-like pouch. The item is then worn around the neck of the person for whom the amulet was intended, for the entire length of an epidemic. It is said that no harm will befall this individual, and, God willing, he or she will be spared the disastrous effects of the epidemic.[38]

As far as the application of the ninetieth Psalm in Christian magic is concerned, it is listed in *"Le Livre d'Or"* to be "suitable for acquiring wisdom and knowledge of mechanics."[39] It is enunciated to have success "in all ventures," and to obtain blessings which cannot be reversed, i.e. cannot be "prevented from arriving."[40] It is further said to counteract the kind of spell which blocks relations between a man and his wife, and in this regard we are told that the psalm should be enunciated and written conjointly with the name of a spirit intelligence and a magical sign on linen. This item is then suspended around the neck of the individual requiring this magical healing, and who is expected to recite the psalm twice a day in the morning and evening, actions which are said will ensure that "he will heal."[41]

PSALM 91

[1] יֹשֵׁב בְּסֵתֶר עֶלְיוֹן בְּצֵל שַׁדַּי יִתְלוֹנָן

[2] אֹמַר לַיהֹוָהאדני־יאהדונהי מַחְסִי וּמְצוּדָתִי
אֱלֹהַי אֶבְטַח בּוֹ

[3] כִּי הוּא יַצִּילְךָ מִפַּח יָקוּשׁ מִדֶּבֶר הַוּוֹת

[4] בְּאֶבְרָתוֹ יָסֶךְ לָךְ וְתַחַת כְּנָפָיו תֶּחְסֶה צִנָּה
וְסֹחֵרָה אֲמִתּוֹ

[5] לֹא תִירָא מִפַּחַד לָיְלָה מֵחֵץ יָעוּף יוֹמָם

[6] מִדֶּבֶר בָּאֹפֶל יַהֲלֹךְ מִקֶּטֶב יָשׁוּד צָהֳרָיִם

[7] יִפֹּל מִצִּדְּךָ אֶלֶף וּרְבָבָה מִימִינֶךָ אֵלֶיךָ לֹא
יִגָּשׁ

[8] רַק בְּעֵינֶיךָ תַבִּיט וְשִׁלֻּמַת רְשָׁעִים תִּרְאֶה

[9] כִּי אַתָּה יְהֹוָהאדני־יאהדונהי מַחְסִי עֶלְיוֹן שַׂמְתָּ
מְעוֹנֶךָ

[10] לֹא תְאֻנֶּה אֵלֶיךָ רָעָה וְנֶגַע לֹא יִקְרַב בְּאָהֳלֶךָ

[11] כִּי מַלְאָכָיו יְצַוֶּה לָּךְ לִשְׁמָרְךָ בְּכָל דְּרָכֶיךָ

[12] עַל כַּפַּיִם יִשָּׂאוּנְךָ פֶּן תִּגֹּף בָּאֶבֶן רַגְלֶךָ

[13] עַל שַׁחַל וָפֶתֶן תִּדְרֹךְ תִּרְמֹס כְּפִיר וְתַנִּין

[14] כִּי בִי חָשַׁק וַאֲפַלְּטֵהוּ אֲשַׂגְּבֵהוּ כִּי יָדַע שְׁמִי

[15] יִקְרָאֵנִי וְאֶעֱנֵהוּ עִמּוֹ אָנֹכִי בְצָרָה אֲחַלְּצֵהוּ
וַאֲכַבְּדֵהוּ

[16] אֹרֶךְ יָמִים אַשְׂבִּיעֵהוּ וְאַרְאֵהוּ בִּישׁוּעָתִי

Transliteration:

[1] *yoshev b'seter el'yon b'tzel shadai yit'lonan*
[2] *omar laYHVH mach'si um'tzudati elohai ev'tach bo*
[3] *ki hu yatzil'cha mipach yakush midever havot*
[4] *b'ev'rato yasech lach v'tachat k'nafav tech'seh tzinah
v'socheirah amito*
[5] *lo tira mipachad lailah mechetz ya'uf yomam*
[6] *midever ba'ofel yahaloch miketev yashud tzohorayim*
[7] *yipol mitzid'cha elef ur'vavah miminecha elecha lo
yigash*
[8] *rak b'einecha tabit v'shilumat r'sha'im tir'eh*
[9] *ki atah YHVH mach'si elyon sam'ta m'onecha*

[10] *lo t'uneh eilecha ra'ah v'nega lo yik'rav b'ohalecha*
[11] *ki malachav y'tzaveh lach lish'mor'cha b'chol d'rachecha*
[12] *al kapayim yisa'un'cha pen tigof ba'even rag'lecha*
[13] *al shachal vafeten tid'roch tir'mos k'fir v'tanin*
[14] *ki vi chashak va'afal'tehu asag'vehu ki yada sh'mi*
[15] *yik'ra'eni v'e'eneihu imo anochi v'tzarah achal'tzeihu va'achab'deihu*
[16] *orech yamim as'bi'eihu v'ar'eihu bishu'ati*

Translation:

[1] O thou that dwellest in the covert of the Most High, and abidest in the shadow of *Shadai* [the Almighty];
[2] I will say of *YHVH*, who is my refuge and my fortress, my God, in whom I trust,
[3] That He will deliver thee from the snare of the fowler, and from the noisome pestilence.
[4] He will cover thee with His pinions, and under His wings shalt thou take refuge; His truth is a shield and a buckler.
[5] Thou shalt not be afraid of the terror by night, nor of the arrow that flieth by day;
[6] Of the pestilence that walketh in darkness, nor of the destruction that wasteth at noonday.
[7] A thousand may fall at Thy side, and ten thousand at Thy right hand; it shall not come nigh thee.
[8] Only with thine eyes shalt thou behold, and see the recompense of the wicked.
[9] For thou hast made *YHVH* who is my refuge, even the Most High, thy habitation.
[10] There shall no evil befall thee, neither shall any plague come nigh thy tent.
[11] For He will give His angels charge over thee, to keep thee in all thy ways.
[12] They shall bear thee upon their hands, lest thou dash thy foot against a stone.
[13] Thou shalt tread upon the lion and asp; the young lion and the serpent shalt thou trample under feet.
[14] 'Because he hath set his love upon Me, therefore will I deliver him; I will set him on high, because he hath known My name.

[15] He shall call upon Me, and I will answer him; I will be with him in trouble; I will rescue him, and bring him to honour.
[16] With long life will I satisfy him, and make Him to behold My salvation.'

As in the case of the previous psalm, *Psalm 91* is maintained to have been written by Moses. We are told this psalm "is appropriate to the tribe of Levi, which abode in the Temple courts in the shadow of the Almighty."[1] We are further informed in the *Midrash Tanchuma* that "when Moses went up on the mountain [Sinai], he said this psalm."[2] This is a very important psalm in Jewish liturgies. It is enunciated on *Shabbat* during the morning service (*Shacharit*), and at the conclusion of the Sabbath. It is also recited during festivals, before undertaking journeys, and in all critical situations. It is further incorporated in קְרִיאַת שְׁמַע עַל הַמִּטָּה (*K'ri'at Shema al Hamitah*—the Bedtime Prayer). In this regard, it is customary in some rites to recite the entire psalm, whilst in others only the first nine verses are enunciated during the prayer before retiring at night.[3]

Commonly designated the "antidemonic psalm," the apotropaic qualities of the ninety-first Psalm were acknowledged as far back as the Qumran texts, i.e. the era of the Second Temple.[4] The current psalm has been termed שִׁיר שֶׁל פְּגָעִים (*Shir Shel Pega'im*—"a song against afflictions [evil spirits]") after the phrase in verse 7 reading יִפֹּל מִצִּדְּךָ אֶלֶף (*yipol mitzid'cha elef* —"A thousand may fall at thy side") [*TB Shevuot 15b*]. In this regard, we are informed that this means "the evil spirits will depart when the place is sanctified."[5] It is also termed שִׁיר שֶׁל נְגָעִים (*Shir Shel Nega'im*—"a song against plagues") after the phrase in verse ten reading וְנֶגַע לֹא יִקְרַב בְּאָהֳלֶךָ (*v'nega lo yikrav b'ohalecha*— "neither shall any plague come nigh thy tent") [*TB Shevuot 15b*].[6]

A sharp eyed commentator on the "anti-evil" qualities of the ninety-first Psalm, noted that the letter ז (*Zayin*—"a weapon") is missing in the psalm. This was understood to mean that the individual who recites the psalm with strongly focussed intention and attention, will be saved from all כְּלֵי זַיִן (*k'lei zayin*— "weapons").[7] Another reason behind the incredible powers

attributed to *Psalm 91*, is the inclusion of the Divine Name שׁדי
(*Shadai*—"Almighty") in the current psalm. As noted numerous
times in this series of texts on Jewish Magic, and stated *ad
infinitum* in Jewish literature of both the esoteric and exoteric kind,
"the divine name is the key ingredient in Jewish magical prayer, as
it is in all Jewish prayer."[8] In this regard, it should be noted that in
Psalm 91 the Divine Name שׁדי (*Shadai*— "Almighty") is held to
be of the utmost potency, i.e. it is the protector against evil forces
and misfortune, as indicated in verses 5, 6, 10, 11 and 15. It has
been said that in this mighty Divine Name "all aspects are inherent
and all power lies at his feet."[9] Somewhat more "esoteric" reasons
have also been offered regarding the anti-demonic powers of the
ninety-first Psalm. These pertain to "angelic powers" said to be
hidden inside certain verses. In this regard, we are told in the name
of Eleazer of Worms that in *Psalm 91:4* the words צנה וסחרה
(*tzinah v'socheirah*—"a shield and a buckler"), are the names of
angelic rulers appointed over demonic entities hinted at in the
current psalm. In this regard, we are told that these angels prevent
humans suffering injuries from malevolent forces.[10] However, it is
Psalm 91:11 which is understood to allude "to the protection one
derives from saying the psalm."[11] This verse is said to include the
names of two guardian Spirit Inteligences, of which more anon.

Thus it is the many "anti-evil qualities" which dictate the
extensive use of the current psalm in Jewish liturgies as well as in
Jewish Magic. In this regard, we are informed that "calling the
psalm 'a song against evil occurrences' is on account of the
existing evil spirits that prevail in the air."[12] It was further noted
that, since "the psalm expresses security in God and gives
assurance of Divine protection from dangers and calamities with
which life is beset,"[13] it is appropriate to recite *Psalm 91* on the
Sabbath in order to cleanse the air of evil spirits, and "that all
misfortunes be banished from our midst on the day of rest on the
Sabbath."[14] However, in the *Sefer ha-Zohar* it is said that "as soon
as Sabbath departs, countless forces and companies [evil spirits]
fly, roaming through the world. So the song against maleficent
spirits was instituted to prevent their ruling the holy people."[15]

The version of the ninety-first Psalm which is recited at the
conclusion of the Sabbath is the ever popular "*Vihi No'am
Prayer.*" In this instance the concluding verse of *Psalm 90* is

conjoined with *Psalm 91*, the reason said to be that the current psalm "is a 'psalm of blessing' with which Moses blessed the people of Israel when he completed the construction of the Tabernacle (*Mishkan*)."[16] Additionally, it is further noted that reciting the *Vihi No'am* prayer at the end of the Sabbath "gives expression to the wish, namely, that God may grant us the pleasant portion, that is, 'to be free and independent before all men and to be able to dispose independently over the works of our hands'."[17] We are also informed that the concluding verse of the prayer "is repeated so that the Divine Name is formed in order to serve as a talisman to ward off evil spirits and demons."[18] Thus it is maintained that the "*Vihi No'am*" format of the current psalm, "was officially accepted by Jewish authorities as the charm *par excellence* 'to protect man against demons; nor is this usage to be included in the forbidden category of magical cures'; and it was inserted in the liturgy to serve this purpose."[19]

Here we are again faced by those who would emphasize the "miraculous powers" of the current psalm, but would deny and forbid anything termed "magical." In this regard, I noted previously that "the difference between 'magic' and 'miracle' is merely a question of which side of the fence you are on,"[20] i.e. the "spiritual" or "religious." We are reminded that "the paraphernalia of Jewish prayer includes amulets and sacred scripts—the tefillin and the mezuzah," and that "the 150 psalms that formed the prayerbook of the Second Temple had magical as well as cultic uses."[21] In some Sefardi communities the said "paraphernalia of Jewish prayer" might also include a sword or knife. In this regard it is worth considering the so-called *Tach'did* ceremony, a procedure with decidedly magical overtones, which is still enacted for Jewish boys every night between their birth and circumcision as a protection against evil.[22] The format of the ceremony varies from one community to the next, but in one report we read that "one would walk around the room with a sword at night, especially on the night before the 'Berit Milah' (circumcision), waving the sword as if to kill any present demons, and recite, '*Vihi noam Hashem Elokeinu aleinu umaasei yadeinu konena umaasei yadeinu koneneihu*.' This prayer would be recited as the knife was passed along all the walls, almost as if the would-be demons were clinging to the walls, where they would be destroyed by this sword....It was also common to place a knife under the pillow of the mother and the baby."[23]

It should be noted that the "*Vihi No'am*" version of the ninety-first Psalm is recited before retiring to bed at night, in order "to keep the demons from disturbing one's rest. In fact, such famous rabbinic authorities as Meir of Rothenburg and Jacob Weil made it a point to speak these lines even before taking a nap during the day."[24] The purported dividing line between what is termed "magical" and what is considered "miraculous," blurs even more when we read reports about *Psalm 91* being "recited throughout the ages on various critical occasions."[25] Especially so when we are informed "that during a *Rosh Hashanah* service in the city of Frankfort [i.e. Frankfurt] the shofar refused to function; the remedy employed was to breathe the words of the *Shir shel Pega'im* three times into the wide opening of the ram's horn, whereupon its hoarse notes were restored. Satan had seated himself inside the horn and had impeded its call until dislodged by the charm!"[26]

As in the case of the previous psalm, the *Shir Shel Pega'im* (the psalm against injuries) is enunciated for protection against evil spirits[27] and wild beasts,[28] the latter being mostly designated "lion(s)" in Jewish magical literature.[29] However, we are told that "during the Middle Ages *Psalm 91* was employed at every opportunity, as well as at certain stated times, to obviate the ever-present danger from the evil spirits,"[30] that "it appeared frequently in magical formulas intended to drive off demons and to counteract magic,"[31] and that it "is without a doubt the most frequently cited psalm for defense against illness and demons."[32] In this regard, funerals are understood to be events "when the spirits were unusually active,"[33] and it is at Jewish entombments when the dubitable borderline between Jewish worship and Jewish magic evaporates altogether. Funerary customs vary somewhat amongst the different communities. It is customary in Sefardic tradition to recite *Psalm 91* when exiting the synagogue or a chapel following the funeral service, and mourners would stop three times during the journey to the cemetery, and enunciate the ninety-first Psalm at each stop.[34] Others maintain the ancient custom of halting seven times prior to arriving at the grave, and equally enunciate the current psalm at each stop.[35] The seven stops are said to be "symbolic of the seven times the word הֶבֶל (*hevel*—vanity) occurs in the Book of Ecclesiastes, and also of the seven stages of life."[36]

We are told that in some communities those attending a funeral would also stop seven times when returning from the grave.[37] This custom is said to date back to Talmudic and Geonic times when mourners stopped and sat down seven times on returning home from the cemetary.[38] On this point it should be noted that it is customary to recite the earlier mentioned *Vihi No'am* prayer during the journey home from a funeral, the reason being the belief "that witchcraft can cause the soul to return to the body of the deceased within twelve months," and thus the emphasis that only "the graciousness [pleasantness] of *Adonai* our God be upon us" (*Psalm 90:17*).[39]

All of this is perfectly understandable from a Jewish religious perspective, and yet the number "7" also features in quite a magical manner here, i.e. in terms of dispelling the "evil spirits" who are believed to be swarming the locale of the burial. It is said that those demons were generated from male sexuality, which, we are told, pertains to "man's generative powers" being "held to be a destructive act, through which not the holy, but the 'other side,' obtains progeny."[40] In this regard, any "wasteful ejaculation" is believed to constitute "a terrible flaw in the nature of masculine sexuality."[41] I have addressed this to some extent previously in reference to Rabbi Nachman of Bratslav's *Tikun haK'lali*,[42] and hence I am focusing here only on certain, as it were, "magical customs" in which the current psalm is employed at a gravesite to keep demons at bay, and to dispel them from those who attend a funeral. It is in the light of this that Rabbi Shabbetai Horowitz instructed his sons "while my body is being lowered into the grave, have seven pious and learned men repeat Psalm 91 seven times,"[43] and it is still customary in some Sefardi communities for mourners to circle a grave seven times anticlockwise, whilst reciting the ninety-first Psalm with each circuit.[44]

It has been reported that in Jerusalem until fairly recently, and on occasion still, ten men would perform a circle "dance of death" around the grave prior to the actual burial as they recite the current psalm seven times.[45] It has also been suggested that "as Jews refer to the cemetery in Hebrew as the *Beit HaChayim*, the house of life, so they refer to this dance of death as a dance of life."[46] However, it has also been surmised that this dance around the grave might not be enough to keep the demonic forces at bay, since "they must be placated and dispatched to another place."[47] In this regard, we are told that it is customary amongst some to place "seven tiny pieces of silver" on the abdomen of the corpse. Afterwards "the ten men of the Chevra Kaddisha (Jewish burial society) join hands—careful not to allow for a breach in the circle through which the demons might enter—and recite Psalm 91."[48] The grave is again circled and the current psalm recited seven times. Each circuit is concluded with a special plea to the Divine One. At the conclusion of this action, "the seven tiny pieces of silver are thrown to the wind."[49] There are also reports of the grave of a Jewish saint being circumambulated posthumously. In this regard, we are informed that certain Jewish religionists would recite the *Ana Bechoach Prayer* as well as the ninety-first Psalm whilst circumambulating the resting place of Rabbi Pinchas ben Yair, the father-in-law of Shimon ben Yochai, seven times.[50]

It should be noted that, similarly to *Psalm 90*, the current psalm is employed against all manner of evil,[51] whether it be of the spirit or human kind. In this regard, we find the words of the current psalm intertwined with the *Shema* (*Deuteronomy 6:4*) in both a direct and reversed manner in the Aramaic magical bowls.[52] In the *Shimmush Tehillim* we are told that if the entire psalm is written backwards, i.e. commencing with the concluding word, and ending with the first, and the writing located behind the entrance to the house, one will be saved from every evil.[53] In this instance, the relevant Divine Name to be focused on is אֵל (*EL*), the component glyphs of which are said to have been derived: א [*Alef*] from י [*Yod*] in יְשׁוּעָתִי (*y'shu'ati*—"My salvation"): verse 16, the glyphs having been interchanged by means of the אי"ק בכ"ר (*Ayak Bachar*) cipher; and ל [*Lamed*] from א [*Alef*] in אֹרֶךְ יָמִים (*orech yamim*—"long life"), the letters having been transposed by means of the אל"ב ב"מ (*Albam*) cipher.[54] Whilst Godfrey Selig notes the same Divine Name and its said derivation in his version of the *Shimmush Tehillim*, he makes no reference to the current psalm having to be written in reverse for the said purpose.[55]

It is worth keeping in mind, as I noted elsewhere,[56] that the formulas of the Jewish magical tradition are primarily based on the doctrine regarding the Hebrew alphabet being the primordial creative force behind creation. In this regard, it was said that

Kabbalists "adopted the traditional magical view regarding the capability of linguistic formulas, holy names, and rituals to influence the world."[57] As we know well enough, in mainstream Judaism there are numerous objections against the employment of Hebrew Divine Names for magical purposes. However, the great Joseph Gikatilla, who himself made pronouncements against the use of Divine Names, noted that "it is within the parameters of our historical covenant, however, that those who want their needs fulfilled by employing the Holy Names should try with all their strength to comprehend the meaning of each Name of God as they are recorded in the Torah....One should be aware that all the names mentioned in the Torah are the keys for anything a person needs in the world....Then when he knows the purpose of every Name he will realize the greatness of 'He who spoke and thus the world came into being'....Then he will be close to God and his petitions will be accepted, as it is written: 'I will keep him safe, for he knows my Name. When he calls on me I will answer him' (*Psalm 91:14–15*).... This means that when the time comes he should know the Name that is intrinsically tied to what he needs, then when he calls 'I will answer'."[58]

It is exactly the special procedures and Divine Names "to influence the world," which I am addressing in the "Shadow Tree Series" of texts on *Practical Kabbalah*. As mentioned earlier, the Divine Name associated with *Psalm 91* is שׁדי (*Shadai*), which is listed in one recension of the *Shimmush Tehillim* in a prayer-incantation employed in conjunction with the current psalm to repel מזיקין (*Mazikin*—"harmful spirits").[59] In this regard, an individual who is attacked by injurious spirits or suffering demonic possession, is instructed to recite and write the psalm, which is afterwards suspended on his/her person. The action is concluded with the following prayer-incantation, reading:

ברכיאל שמשיאל יובבאל שדי הצילני מן
המזיקין ומן השדים ומכל מקרה רע ומכל פגע רע

Transliteration:

> *Bar'chi'el Sham'shi'el Yovav'el Shadai hatzileini min hamazikin umin hashedim umikol mik'reh ra umikol pega ra.*

Translation:

> *Bar'chi'el Sham'shi'el Yovav'el Shadai* deliver me from the harmful spirits, and from the demons, from every evil incident, and from every evil calamity.[60]

Psalm 91 is often included in an abbreviated format in Hebrew amulets, as indicated in the following Moroccan amulet which was created to protect the home.[61] The header of the *Kamea* was formulated from the initials of the twelve words in *Psalm 90:17*. As noted earlier, this verse is conjoined with *Psalm 91* in the "*Vihi No'am* prayer." This prayer is clearly intended here, since the Divine Name spiral surrounding the central hexagram, was formulated from the capitals of all the words of the ninety-first Psalm. A similarly constructed abbreviation of *Psalm 121*, of which more anon, is equally incorporated in the Divine Name spiral surrounding the central hexagram:

The said abbreviations read:

ונ״י אע״ו יכ״ע וי״כ ורדפמיאל (*Psalm 90:17*)

יבע בשי אלם ואא בכה ימי מהב ילו (*Psalm 91*)

כתצ ואל תמל מיי מבי מיצ ימא ומא ליר בתו

רתכ אימ עשמ לתא רול יבכ מיל לבד עכי

פתב רעש ותת כוכ בחו אכי שיו עאב אוא יאוב

שלא עאה מיע עמי עשו עמי איל ראי (*Psalm 121*)

שהל יוי שיי שיצ עיי יהל יוב יימ ריא ניי צומ

ועע

The header of this wonderful amulet includes the Angelic Name
רדפמיאל (*Radaf'mi'el*), also called רד פמיאל (*Rad
Pami'el*). We are informed that this Spirit Intelligence protects
women in confinement.[62] Other than this, it is worth noting that the
concluding four letter combination of the Divine Name spiral
אנס״ל, was formulated from the initials of the standard formula
אמן נצח סלה לעולם [ועד] (*Omein Netzach Selah l'olam
[Va'ed]—"Amen*, Enduring [Victory], *Selah*, throughout Eternity
[Forever]"). The six letters comprising the Divine Name
טפטפיה (*Taf'taf'yah*), which I have addressed in some detail
elsewhere,[63] are located externally around the large central
hexagram. The *Digrammaton* י״ה (*Yah*) is positioned in the very
top of the upper triangle, with the Ineffable Name located directly
below in the right and left upper horizontal corners. In the lower
horizontal corners of the hexagram we read right to left the
expression מגן דוד (*Magen David*—"Shield of David").

The Divine Names and words in the very centre of the
hexagram comprise an obscure phrase reading:

באב קבול כסן כסאן כסאבן שמו שדי צורי
אליהו[ן]

Transliteration:
> *Ba'ava Kabul Kesen Kes'an Kes'aban sh'mo Shadai tzuri
> Eliyahu*

Translation:

> *Ba'ava Kabul Kesen Kes'an Kes'aban Shadai* is his name,
> my rock Elijah.[64]

The three letter combination בֵאֲב (*Ba'ava*) comprises the initials of the phrase from *Deuteronomy 28:6* reading בָּרוּךְ אַתָּה בְּבֹאֶךָ (*Baruch atah b'vo'echa*—"Blessed shalt thou be when thou comest in"). This is appropriate to an amulet which is meant to protect a residence. As noted elsewhere, "בֵאֲב (*Ba'ava*) is said to have the power to bring success, i.e. make the occupants of the home successful as per the meaning of the listed verse from whence the Divine Name was derived."[65]

The protective powers of *Psalm 91* also extend to those who are setting out on a journey,[66] who desire to travel in peace, and be protected from robbers. In this regard, travellers are advised to recite the mentioned prayer-incantation seven times, doing so whilst focusing mentally on the Divine/Angelic Name יוֹהַךְ (*Yohach*).[67] This Name is the first of two comprising the Divine Name יוֹהַךְ כַּלַךְ (*Yohach Kalach*), which was formulated from the concluding letters of the seven words of *Psalm 91:11* reading כִּי מַלְאָכָיו יְצַוֶּה לָּךְ לִשְׁמָרְךָ בְּכָל דְּרָכֶיךָ (*ki malachav y'tzaveh lach lish'mor'cha b'chol d'rachecha* —"For He will give His angels charge over thee, to keep thee in all thy ways").[68] This verse, as well as the said associated Divine Name construct, are often engraved on jewellery which function as amulets meant to protect bearers against all manner of evil.[69] As noted elsewhere, it is maintained that the angels referenced in the verse are יוֹהַךְ (*Yohach*) and כַּלַךְ (*Kalach*), two companion guardian Spirit Intelligences.[70]

However, in the current instance the Divine/Angelic Name construct יוֹהַךְ (*Yohach*) is highlighted as the appellative of a unique Spirit Intelligence (angel), and is thus often employed without the accompanying כַּלַךְ (*Kalach*). In fact, this angel is said to be in charge of מִדּוֹת הַדִּין (*Midot haDin*— "Qualities of Judgment"), and is understood to be "appointed over divine vengeance."[71] In light of this, we are informed that the biblical account of ten plagues with which Egypt was afflicted, were brought about by means of the Name יוהך (*Yohach*), which is said to pertain to the sixteen edged "avenging sword" of the Divine One.[72] I wrote previously that "the remarkable powers of the sixteen-edged divine sword" is said to "include the ability to 'diminish the powers of the pestilence and other *mazikin* (malevolent forces)' and the granting of a 'meaningful life'."[73] The singularity of this Divine Name is emphasized by the fact that the Name of the Eternal One (יהו) is contained within it, and thus it is believed that יוהך (*Yohach*) "is empowered to escort, protect and save."[74] In fact, it has been noted that "this Spirit Intelligence, when called upon, will protect us as we journey through life."[75]

I have shared a fairly extensive inventory of the magical applications of this Divine/Angelic Name in previous volumes of the "Shadow Tree Series."[76] There are far too many procedures to convey here in full, or in any great detail, hence I will impart here certain applications which I have found to be most effective for individuals faced with insurmountable difficulties. In this regard, I was taught to utter the Name יוהך (*Yohach*) "seven times in rapid succession as an aid in solving difficult problems."[77] Rabbi Moses Zacutto shared a similar technique in which this Divine Name is incorporated in the following set of Divine/Angelic Names: יוהך טפטפיה צמרכד נצריאל עוזיאל (*Yohach Taf'taf'yah Tzemiroch'da* [or *Tzamar'chad*] *Natzari'el Ozi'el*).[78] These Names, which I noted before pertain to "very potent spirit forces to invoke in difficult situations,"[79] are equally enunciated seven times for the same purpose. In the current instance the action is concluded by enunciating the phrase על צבא על מגן (*al tz'va al magen*—"On the hosts [forces] on the shield") three times.[80]

It is worth noting that the Divine Names צמרכד (*Tzamar'chad*) and טפטפיה (*Taf'taf'yah*) are often conjoined with יוהך (*Yohach*). Listed as one of the seventy names of מטטרון (*Metatron*),[81] the Divine Name טפטפיה (*Taf'taf'yah*) is designated שם המחשבה (*Shem haMach'shavah*—"Name of the Thought"), and is associated with חכמה (*Choch'mah*—"Wisdom"), the latter concept said to be "the source of the mind."[82]

As noted elsewhere, this Divine Name is considered a most potent protective and defensive measure "against the malevolent intentions of both humans and Spirit Intelligences,"[83] hence its affiliation with יוהך (*Yohach*). In this regard, the following prayer-incantation for Divine assistence and protection in the "Forty-two letter Name of God," is particularly useful.[84] It equally includes טפטפיה (*Taf'taf'yah*):

יוהך ישמרני יוהך יצילני בשם **אבגיתץ קרעשטן**
נגדיכש בתרצתג חקבטנע יגלפזק שקוצית
ברוך שם כבוד מלכותו לעולם ועד יוהך טפטפיה

Transliteration:

> *Yohach yish'm'reini Yohach yatzileini b'shem Av'gitatz Karastan Nag'dichesh B't'ratz'tag Chak'vet'na Yag'lef'zok Shakutzit, Baruch Shem K'vod Mal'chuto l'olam va'ed, Yohach Taf'taf'yah*

Translation:

> May *Yohach* protect me, may *Yohach* assist me, in the name *Av'gitatz Karastan Nag'dichesh B't'ratz'tag Chak'vet'na Yag'lef'zok Shakutzit* Blessed be the Name of His glorious Kingdom throughout eternity, *Yohach Taf'taf'yah*.

The association of the Divine Name צמרכד (*Tzamar'chad*) with יוהך (*Yohach*) is perhaps somewhat peculiar, if one considers this Divine Name being delineated "of the Wing (Edge)," which is said to express the beauty of the שכינה (*Sh'chinah*), i.e. the Divine Mother, as well as the fact that it is used "to encourage fertility in women."[85] That is however not its main magical application, since צמרכד, when vocalised "*Tzemiroch'da*," is "mainly employed as a protection against attacks from belligerent beings," and "to bring confusion in the mind of the individual against whom it is directed."[86] This is well illustrated in the following simple amulet, in which the Divine Names combination יוהך צמרכד כוזו (*Yohach Tzamar'chad Kuzu*) is written on deerskin scroll for the very purpose of protection:[87]

This amulet is effectuated by pinning it "to the hem or edge of a garment, which is simply shaken in the direction of whatever possible assailant may come your way."[88] Individuals who might not have had this item handy "during times of mortal danger," were instructed to recite *Psalm 91* over oil, and to anoint themselves with this, as it were, "charged substance." We are told that this is "a palpable way of putting on God's name as 'shield and buckler' against demonic attack."[89] It would seem that in ancient days travel and journeys were reckoned amongst the worst "times of mortal danger." In this regard, the *Vihi No'am* prayer is recited prior to setting out on a journey, and it is said to be good to enunciate the ninety-first Psalm "when one is riding across a bridge," in order "to forestall any accident (for Satan is always on the alert to take advantage of an opportunity to do harm)."[90]

Another possible "mortal danger" which plagued humankind in earlier times, and which still does today even though this phenomenon is now interpreted from psychological perspectives, is the earlier mentioned "demonic possession" or a דיבוק (*Dibuk*), the latter being the malevolent possession of a human by one or more deceased human spirits. As noted elsewhere, I have some misgivings about "demon possession" and "exorcisms," since in my estimation people are more often suffering "*ob*session" rather than "*possession*."[91] Hence I noted that "our obsessions are products of our own personalities, and while some of these are harmless enough, others might turn out to be extremely dangerous and injurious."[92] As said before, "it is only too easy to invent demons where none exist in order to blame some external agency for ones own peculiarities."[93] However, this does not mean that "demonic forces" have no validity. In fact they have as much validity as we do, as I can confirm from several encounters with "demonic possession" as well as exorcism in South Africa.

There is an extensive list in Jewish Magic of specialised procedures to rid an individual of a demon or a דיבוק (*Dibuk*).[94] Naturally I cannot address these fairly complex rituals in any particular detail in this tome, but it should be noted that *Psalm 91* is understood to have the power to expel malevolent forces entirely on its own. In this regard, there is the curious 19th century East European tale of the expulsion of "three witches" from the body of a boy.[95] The saga has it that initially all exorcisms proved ineffective, but that the "witches" were eventually successfully evicted with the repeated recitation of the ninety-first Psalm.[96] However, besides being properly prepared, it has been said that individuals intending "to adjure a spirit who possessed an individual," should be pure and supported, i.e. protected and empowered, by a belt made of leather parchment (deerskin). This special girdle is inscribed with the following Divine Name construct, which was formulated in a highly complex manner from the letters comprising the *Vihi No'am* prayer:[97]

ינו הוה אעו יכע ויכ יבע בשי אלי הוה

מוא אבכ הים ימה ביל וכת צוא לתם למי

ימב ימי צים אום אלי רבת ורת כאי הוה

מעש מלת ארו ליב כמי ללב דעכ י פת ברע

שות תכו כבח ואכ ישי ועא באו איא ובי

וום דוו היו ויי עיו וקי יזר סדן ללך

וון דמל דלך דהו ידב אעה דהא דתן יהו

היה יהם תטך קשא דדה ודל סדב דלר מפץ

הדא אוה ההו תכך ותר שחך איו חיי יהו

היר זיל זרב ווה והו הוו הוה ימי יוה

ללם דול מדו וסל צדת ויח מלב וצפ קדו

אסת נחנ סמי פיח עוד אהק שהפ צלר ילג

עבש שרת החל מעא לען לען קאל צשב רפש גאג
חפד רפת שאש דמק אמנ צחא ומש אית ההי
רהה רכה נהה ייו ותל בונ ייר ויי רגי
ננו סוא ימי ייי בדו יוט ופב מול חרת
רסי חתו בול טהת סום נות שהנ שננ נשנ
ננע ההי עינ יעי ניל הצי בפו ולר במי
לעי והא מכא רמנ פגר עלכ ברש עאע דצנ
אבט וכל ננח רדו ניו ילב יואו

In conclusion, should someone have suffered injury from a demon, that individual could be cured in the following manner. First the residence of the said person is cleaned, and the bedding changed in his/her sleeping chamber, following which the said individual is instructed to lie down on the bed. The exorcist, healer, or "magical practitioner" is instructed to work the healing action by standing adjacent to the sufferer, and to recite *Psalm 91* over him/her "seven times in the correct order, and seven times reversed." It was further said that "it is even better to recite it nine times in the correct order and nine times backwards."[98]

One may well wonder why it should not be possible to preclude destructive forces from entering ones personal existence altogether. After all, we are often told that prevention is better than cure, and yet, everyone knows that living "evil-free" in the realm of mortality is a tall order. As I noted earlier, we are informed that Divine protection can be gained for a year by reciting the *Vihi No'am* prayer seven times at the conclusion of the lighting of each of the eight candles during the "*Festival of Chanukah.*"[99] Some ultra-orthodox worshippers close this daily recitation of the *Vihi No'am* prayer, with the additional enunciation of a single phrase from the seven comprising the *Ana Bechoach* Prayer, concluding on the eight day with the standard blessing accompanying the prayer.[100] I have also noted the recitation of *Psalm 90* in conjunction with the current one for healing purposes. In this regard, it has been reported in the name of Rabbi Isaac Luria, "that in a time of general emergency or advancing plague, the *Vihi Noam* prayer should be prayed seven times every day. And then, after praying it, one should read the verses of Exodus that describe the Israelites in Egypt applying lamb's blood to their doorposts to avert the Angel of Death from their houses during that tenth plague. The Ari's practice suggests that reading the story of the protective doorpost magic can have the same effect as actually doing it."[101]

Godfrey Selig shared the same details in his version of the *Shimmush Tehillim*, stating that "Kabbalists, and especially the celebrated Rabbi Isaac Loria have assured us that in a time of pestilence or general emergency, the Vihi Noam prayer should be prayed seven times daily."[102] To this statement he added details at variance with the said "Lurianic" instruction shared above. Thus he noted that "the figure of the golden candlestick, when it is composed of the forty-one holy and important words and names of this Psalm," should be linked in the mind to the recitations of the *Vihi No'am* prayer.[103] Unfortunately the transliterations of these Names in Selig's publication, are seriously flawed when compared to the Hebrew originals comprising the said "figure of the golden candlestick" shown below:

Corrected transliterations of the said forty-one Names were listed in a modern edition of the so-called *"Sixth and Seventh Books of Moses,"*[104] though they are still flawed in several instances. Whatever the case may be, this set of Divine Names align with several tri-letter combinations of the extensive Divine Name construct of the *Vihi No'am* prayer shared earlier, and which is vowelised in the *Shorshei ha-Shemot*.[105] Selig's flawed version of this Divine Name construct reads:[106]

ואא	אלם	בשי	יבע	ויכ	יכע	אעו	וני
Veaa	*Alm*	*Bichi*	*Iba*	*Wich*	*Ika*	*Aau*	*Veni*

מיי	תמל	יאל	כתצ	ילו	מחב	ימי	בכה
Mii	*Tmol*	*Veal*	*Ktaz*	*Ilu*	*Mehob*	*Imi*	*Becha*

אים	רתכ	בתו	ליר	ומא	ימא	מיצ	מבי
Im	*Retak*	*Betu*	*Lir*	*Uma*	*Ima*	*Miz*	*Mebi*

עכי	לכד	מול	יבכ	רול	לתא	עשמ	פתכ
Aki	*Lakad*	*Mil*	*Ibak*	*Rul*	*Leta*	*Ascham*	*Petash*

עאב	שיו	אכי	בחו	כוב	ותת	רעש	יאוב
Aab	*Schin*	*Aki*	*Bechu*	*Kuck*	*Vetat*	*Raasch*	*Iaub*

אוא

Aua

Selig offers further instruction following the seven enunciations of the *Vihi No'am* prayer, noting that, whilst concentrating on the said Divine Name, "verses 21–28, chapter xii (12), of Exodus" should be enunciated, "and with them keeping in mind the names contained in the 23 and 28th verses, in the following order:

Awal Jahel Ito Huj Husch Aha Imo Vil

As also Vohu, Uha, Bam Bili, Zel, Holo, Vesop, and finally the holy name: Nischaszlas."[107]

In conclusion Selig maintains "And now, he who observes all these things to the very letter, and who can keep in his memory all the letters, points or vowels, he shall be safe from all danger, and shall be as strong as steel, so that no firearms can harm him."[108] It should be noted that neither the action attributed to Isaac Luria, nor everything appended thereto by Godfrey Selig, was listed in any of the primary recensions of the *Sefer Shimmush Tehillim*. Further instructions regarding the recitation of the *Vihi No'am* prayer, as well as additional supplications shared by Selig, are equally nowhere to be found in the said text.

As is the case with all the psalms, *Psalm 91* is employed for a variety of different purposes. In this regard, it has been noted that "a magical recipe to gain release from prison prescribed its daily recitation 72 times, along with other Scriptural selections."[109] Unfortunately the author of this quote did not share the source from whence he gleaned these details. Hence there is difficulty in ascertaining the exact procedure. Be that as it may, the prisoner might have avoided imprisonment altogether, considering the fact that the ninety-first Psalm is employed "to make oneself invisible."[110] Another curious application of the current psalm is its recitation in a divinatory procedure, which in the 19th century was apparently commonly employed "in severe cases of illness" by "Jewish Kabbalists in Jerusalem."[111] The action comprised pouring wax or lead into a vessel filled with water. Whilst pouring, a woman (not the pregnant woman) would recite *Psalms 121* and *91*, whilst another would observe the images forming in the liquid. Depending on the images perceived in the liquid, the latter woman would exclaim "It is a dog," "a cat," etc., these being apparently animals feared by the pregnant woman or patient.[112] We are not informed on how this information is to be applied to aleviate stressful situations or illness, but, as mentioned before, the current psalm is recited in conjunction with *Psalm 90* for the recovery from illness.[113]

Individual verses from the ninety-first Psalm are equally employed for a variety of magical purposes. In this regard, it should be noted that ם'ס (*Sit*), the third tri-letter portion of the *Shem Vayisa Vayet* ("Name of Seventy-two Names"), is directly associated with *Psalm 91:2*.[114] Furthermore, the initials of the opening three words of this verse, were combined in the Divine Name construct ם לא (vocalised *Ileim*), which is said to be very powerful, and is used to give speech to those who are dumb.[115] We are further informed that if you should be approached by individuals who intend striking you with a sword or with any iron tool, you should say three times הוא שופר קורדום אלם (*Ilem Kor'dom Shofar Hu*), and leave immediately.[116]

Psalm 91:3 is indirectly affiliated with ‏דני‎ (*Dani*), the fiftieth portion of the *Shem Vayisa Vayet*.[117] I have earlier addressed this tri-letter portion of the "Name of Seventy-two Names" in terms of its indirect alignment with *Psalm 45:5*.[118] However, in the current instance the said indirect affiliation pertains again to the fact that the numerical value of ‏דני‎ [‏ד‎ = 4 + ‏נ‎ = 50 + ‏י‎ = 10 = 64] is equal to that of ‏נוגה‎ (*nogah*—a "glowing light" [‏נ‎ = 50 + ‏ו‎ = 6 + ‏ג‎ = 3 + ‏ה‎ = 5 = 64]). However, as indicated elsewhere, "the same letter combination could be read *nugah* ('sad' or 'sorrowful')," and "doubling the *gematria* of ‏דני‎ gives us the *gematria* of ‏מפח‎ (*mipach*—a 'snare' or 'trap' [‏מ‎ = 40 + ‏פ‎ = 80 + ‏ח‎ = 8 = 128])." This is believed to be referencing *Psalm 91:3* reading ‏כי הוא יצילך מפח יקוש‎ (*ki hu yatzil'cha mipach yakush*—"That He will deliver thee from the snare of the fowler").[119] Aside from this, the capitals of the words of *Psalm 91:3*, as well as those in the phrase from the fourth verse reading ‏ותחת כנפיו תחסה‎ (*v'tachat k'nafav tech'seh*—"and under His wings shalt thou take refuge"), were conjoined in the Divine Name construct ‏כהימימה וכת‎ which is applied against plagues, and pandemics for that matter.[120] The initials of the four words comprising the concluding phrase of *Psalm 91:10*, which were combined in the Divine Name construct ‏וליב‎, are employed for the same objective.[121]

As noted earlier, the ninety-first Psalm is utilised against evil spirits, but the Divine Name construct ‏לתמלמיי מבימיצ‎, formulated from the capitals of the words comprising *Psalm 91:5-6*, is equally said to be a general protection against evil spirits.[122] We are also informed that "words from Psalm 91 were written on amulets to protect against evil during sleep." In this regard, the great Rashi wrote in his commentary on *TB Shabbat 115b*, that "they would write in the amulet verses to be murmured, like 'Every illness' (Exodus 15:26) and 'You need not fear the terror by night' (Psalms 91:5)."[123] Some parents would combine the capital letters of the four Hebrew words comprising the opening phrase of the fifth verse into the following letter square:

ל	מ	ה	ל
ל	ל	מ	ה
ה	ל	ל	מ
מ	ה	ל	ל

This letter square is inscribed on the front of what is said to be "a tried and tested *Kamea*."[124] The rear of the amulet is imprinted with the initials of the words of *Psalm 91:5–16*, all of which have been arranged into the twenty-one portions of the following Divine Name construct:

לתמל מיימ בימי צימא ומאל ירבת ורתכ
אימע שמלת ארול יבכמ יללב דעכי פתבר
עשות תכוכ בחוא כישי ועאב אואי אוב

As noted elsewhere, this amulet "is suspended around the necks of youngsters who may have to travel around at night, and might require a reinforcement of special protection, and also to ward off bad dreams."[125]

    Psalm 91:5 and *10* are applied conjointly against epilepsy.[126] The concluding letters of the four words comprising the opening phrase of *Psalm 91:5* were formulated into the Divine Name construct ואאדה, which is employed in amulets for protection on the road.[127] The concluding letters of all seven words comprising the said verse, have also been combined into the Divine Name construct אאדהצפם, which was conjoined with the Divine Name construct לתארולייב which was formulated from the capitals of the words comprising *Psalm 91:10*. Both Names are incorporated in a fourfold Divine Name combination reading אתמף לאדם לתארולייב אאדהצפם, which is included in an amulet meant to save a mother from witches. The first two Divine Name constructs in this combination, were respectively derived from the capitals and concluding letters of the first four words of *Proverbs 3:25.*[128] It should also be noted, that the above mentioned Divine Name construct composed from the tenth verse, is also divided into two parts, לְתִאָר וּלִיבָ, which is employed against miscarriage, epilepsy, and plagues.[129]

The tenth and eleventh verse of the current psalm is particularly popular in *Practical Kabbalah*. In this regard, *Psalm 91:10* is often included in Hebrew amulets, which I have addressed in some detail in an earlier volume.[130] However, amongst the material which I have not shared previously is the following Divine Name construct formulated from *Psalm 91:10*, the power of which is said to aid individuals in exiting, or escaping from, dangerous circumstances:[131]

לְיָעָא אָבְלָה תְרָאֵל
אָעֶיךָ נְהַק הֻוָר אָנָב
לְגָב

This eightfold Divine Name construct was produced in a very simple manner. The twenty-eight letters comprising the said verse, were divided into groups of eight letters, which resulted in three groups comprising eight letters, and the remaining portion having four letters. Written in exact order in the standard Hebrew manner from right to left, the first eight are the initials of the eight combinations, with the second eight forming the second letters, the third eight the third letters of the eight combinations, and the remaining four, the concluding letters of the first four letter combinations. The resulting set of letters was further divided into four four-letter, and four three-letter combinations. Two alternating vowel points are employed in vocalising this Divine Name construct, i.e. a *Sh'va* (Hebrew vowel usually indicating a glottal stop—"*uh*"), and a *Patach* (Hebrew vowel "*ah*"). In Kabbalistic doctrine these vowels are respectively associated with גבורה (*Gevurah*—"Might") and חסד (*Chesed*— "Lovingkindness") on the sefirotic Tree. Thus this Divine Name construct reads:

l'ya–'a   'cha–l'ha   t'ra–'la
'a–y'cha   n'hak   h'var   'nav
l'gav

We might also consider another most peculiar application of the tenth verse, which is in a rather unique form of "birth control." We are told that the "Outsiders," i.e. evil forces, attack a man at night to defile him. In this regard, the remedy is for the man to put Galbanum (*Chel'benah*), a putrid–smelling spice, Camphor, and Verbena inside a small bag, which is to be located against his sexual organ at night. I would think this would be enough to drive the hordes of hell into obscurity, but apparently more should be done to ensure absolute safety. Two small, thin leaden plates are engraved with the Divine Name construct לתֿאֹרֿוֹלֿיֿבֿ, which I noted earlier was derived from the tenth verse of the current psalm. With this Divine Name construct facing externally, these plates are located directly against the flesh on both sides of his manhood, and "tightly belted....to keep them fixed and firmly pressed against the body."[132] If that does not keep *Lilit* and every other nocturnal demonic fiend from causing "the heat of desire to rise in his body," nothing will! In fact, I would be surprised if the said individual will be able to sleep at all, considering his nostrils being assaulted with a stench which could awaken the dead!

    Psalm 91:9 is directly associated with חֿעֿם (*Cha'am*), the thirty-eighth tri-letter portion of the "Name of Seventy-two Names."[133] The initials of the words comprising this verse were formulated into the Divine Name construct כֿאֿיֿמֿעֿשֿמֿ, which is employed as a call for help.[134] Be that as it may, as we know well enough, many women need special support when it comes to pregnancies. In this regard, the following Divine Name construct was fashioned from *Psalm 91:10–16* in a fairly complex manner, and which we are told is employed "for everything and every pain." It is especially included in an amulet applied against miscarriages:[135]

$$\text{לבד מיל יבכ רול לתֿא}$$
$$\text{כוב ותֿת רעשֿ פהֿב עכי}$$
$$\text{יֿאֿו אֿוֿא עאֿב שֿיֿו אכֿי בחֿו}$$
$$\text{עתֿי בֿישֿו}$$

The capitals of the words comprising *Psalm 91:11* was equally formulated into the Divine Name construct כמיל לבד, (sometimes vocalised *Ch'mil L'vad*), which is equally employed as a call for help.[136] Considering the "call for help," the current verse is included in the following acclaimed amulet, which is meant to afford a mother and infant special post birth support and protection. The amulet appears .in two formats in the *Sefer Raziel*,[137] of which the following one is the better known:

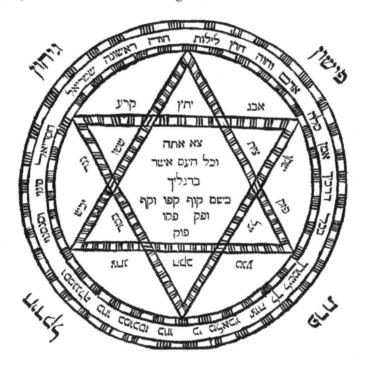

I have addressed this amulet in great detail elsewhere in this series of texts on *Practical Kabbalah*.[138] Regarding the central Divine Name קונף and its permutations, which I have noted pertains etymologically probably to "the principle of opening" and to "produce,"[139] some commentators maintain it to be an abbreviation of קונה ופדה (*koneh u'podeh*—"Creator and Redeemer").[140]

As mentioned earlier, the concluding letters of the words of *Psalm 91:11* were formulated into the Divine Name יוהך כלך, which is used for general protection as well as a call for help.[141] The Divine Name construct יועב, which was formulated from the capitals of four words from the opening phrase of *Psalm 91:15*, specifically יִקְרָאֵנִי וְאֶעֱנֵהוּ עִמּוֹ בְצָרָה (*yikra'eni v'e'eneihu imo v'tzarah*"), and which could be translated "he will call me and answer with him in trouble," is likewise utilised as a call for help.[142]

Very special help is required in dealing with "demonic forces" of the most primeval kind, i.e. the so-called קְלִיפוֹת (*K'lipot*—Demonic "Shards" or "Shells"), these being literally everywhere around and within us. It is not possible here to fully explicate their origin in the chaos and confusion which resulted from the so-called שְׁבִירַת הַכֵּלִים (*Shevirat haKelim*—"shattering of vessels"), which is said to have transpired in the most primordial condition of creation, and which I addressed in some detail elsewhere.[143] Briefly then, Kabbalistic doctrine holds that at the very beginning of the emanation of "Divine Light," the "primordial vessels" meant to contain the light shattered. In this regard, we are told that "when the light becomes too strong, the receptacle disintegrates due to its limited capacity to contain the powerful light."[144] This primordial cosmic disaster resulted in נִצוֹצוֹת (*Nitzotzot*—"Sparks of the Light") becoming enmeshed with the resultant "husks" or "shards" (*K'lipot*), from which ensued the realm of material existence, as well as the סִיתְרָא אָחְרָא (*Sitra Ach'ra*—"Other Side"), i.e. the "realms of evil." The קְלִיפוֹת (*K'lipot*—Demonic "Shards") are directly aligned with the sefirotic Tree, i.e. each sefirotic quality having, as it were, a "demonic counterpart." Thus it has been said that "from the very beginning then, all the Sefirot in the world of the points possessed the capacity to issue evil, so that the source of evil is high indeed, issuing as it does from these exalted degrees."[145] We are informed that within the ranks of the ten "*Sefirot*," it is גְבוּרָה (*Gevurah*—Might), symbolised by the Patriarch Isaac, and associated with the "*K'lipah*" of anger especially, which is the source of great evil, and that this is, as it were, triggered by an imbalance between the *Sefirot* of חֶסֶד (*Chesed*—Lovingkindness) and גְבוּרָה (*Gevurah*—Might). In this regard, we are told that "the linking together of *hesed* and *gevurah* is an infinitely delicate balance. Too much love and the other has no room to exist....But too much power or judgment is even worse. The kabbalists see this *gevurah* aspect of both the divine and human self as fraught with danger, the very birthplace of evil. The *Zohar* tells of a discontent on this 'left,' or *gevurah*, side of God. *Gevurah* becomes impatient with *hesed*, unhappy with its endless casting aside of judgment in the name of love....Rather than doing its job of permitting love to flow in measured ways, *gevurah* seeks out a cosmic moment to rule alone, to hold back the flow of love. In this moment divine power turns to rage or fury; out of it all the forces of evil are born, darkness emerges from the light of God, a shadow of the divine universe that is also manifest in each of us as our ability to do evil."[146]

We are informed that we can control within ourselves the "*K'lipah* on the side of Isaac," i.e. "Anger" or "Rage" associated with *Gevurah* (Might), by means of the "name" of that demonic force which is said to be hidden inside *Psalm 91:12–13*. In this regard, we are told that "our Rabbis of blessed memory said there is one *K'lipah* on the side of Isaac, its name is יְפֵת בָּר עֲשַׁו (*Yipeti Bara Ashava*), and David alluded to it in the said verse."[147] This name was derived from the capitals of the words in the said verses reading יִשָּׁאוּנְךָ פֶּן תִּגֹּף בָּאֶבֶן רַגְלֶךָ עַל שַׁחַל וּפֶתֶן [*yisa'un'cha pen tigof ba'even rag'lecha al shachal vafeten*— "lest thou dash thy foot against a stone; thou shalt tread upon the lion and asp"]. Anyone who recognises the need to deal with the "*K'lipah* of Anger," whether in his/her personal life or elsewhere, is informed that they can cause this demonic force to surrender, have its power cancelled, and fully removed from his or her mind, by reciting the phrases from *Psalm 91:12–13*, whilst being simultaneously tuned into, i.e. focussing mentally on, the said name.[148]

The initials of the words from the phrases in *Psalm 91:15* and *16* reading אֲחַלְּצֵהוּ וַאֲכַבְּדֵהוּ אֹרֶךְ יָמִים אַשְׂבִּיעֵהוּ (*achal'tzeihu va'achab'deihu orech yamim as'bi'eihu*—"I will rescue him, and bring him to honour. With long life will I satisfy him"), were conjoined in the Divine Name construct אואיא which is employed for the purposes of encouraging a long life and salvation in difficult circumstances.[149] The capitals of the first four words of verse 16, or all five comprising this verse, are likewise arranged into Divine Name constructs, respectively איאו[150] and

אָיאוב,[151] which are equally employed for a long life. It is worth keeping in mind, that a long life necessitates good self-preservation. In this regard, consider the Divine Name construct יובב, termed the "Name of Protection," which is said to have been derived from four words in *Psalm 91:15*, i.e. יקראני (*yik'ra'eni*), ואענהו (*v'e'eneihu*), בצרה (*v'tzarah*), and ואכבדדהו (*va'achab'deihu*). Conjointly the words read "He shall call upon Me, and I will answer him in trouble, and bring him to honour."[152] It is also claimed elsewhere that this Divine Name construct was derived from the first four words of *Psalm 91:1*, ישב בסתר עליון בצל (*yoshev b'seter elyon b'tzel*—"O thou that dwellest in the covert of the Most High, and abidest in the shadow"), and that it pertains to מלכות (*Malchut*), the "Kingdom" comprising the whole of existence.[153] Whatever its origins may be, this Divine Name construct inscribed on an amulet, is an effective safeguard, especially when it comes to self-preservation.

Psalm 91 certainly reckons amongst the most diverse psalms in *Practical Kabbalah*. Besides the applications shared above, I have observed this wondrous psalm employed for illness and healing in general; for good sight and hearing; for greater energy; and to sharpen and increase intelligence. Whilst it is recited as a safeguard from harm, especially when in need of Divine aid and support, or Divine Protection, it is particularly useful for protection in perilous situations and in times of trouble. It is recommended for enunciation to the elderly who seek a happy old age and retirement, and to those who are in need of comfort, especially during times of mourning.

As far as the widespread use of *Psalm 91* in Christian Magic is concerned, it was suggested that it "almost certainly grew out of Jewish practice."[154] This psalm is said to be "the most frequently used psalm on early Christian amulets, appearing on papyrus and parchment as well as on pieces of jewelry."[155] It was further noted that the ninety-first Psalm is "quoted in an array of objects or settings from around the ancient world: armbands, medallions, rings, tablets, and inscriptions on door frames, houses, and graves. In smaller objects only the opening verse(s) or a portion thereof may be cited....texts on papyrus or parchment, which afford more space than medallions or rings, either the opening verses or the entire psalm may be transcribed. These may be combined....with gospel *incipits*, the Lord's Prayer, and liturgical acclamations all of which suggest that the artefact had an apotropaic purpose.the opening verses of the psalm may also accompany specific adjurations or petitions."[156]

Magical applications of the Jewish Biblical Psalms found their way into a variety of different cultures over many centuries. Thus we find the syncretistic Greek Magical Papyri from Graeco-Roman Egypt, dating from around 100 BCE to 400 CE, include *Psalm 91:1–2* amongst a set of other paraphrased Jewish and Christian biblical phrases, all of which were incorporated in an incantation to subdue "a fever with shivering fits."[157] However, as in the case of Jewish Magic, the use of the ninety-first Psalm in the Christian variety, is mainly based on the understanding that *Psalm 91* is a "hymn against demons." In this regard, we are informed that in the early centuries of the current era, the ninety-first Psalm was found to have been "inscribed on door lintels of eight ancient houses in Syria and Cyprus and two fifth-century churches in Ravenna, featured on tombs and sarcophagi in the Crimea, frescoed on a wall of the sacred room adjoining the altar of a church near Petra, and interspersed with references to Egyptian astral deities on several early medieval syncretistic magical tablets."[158] It would seem the amuletic use of the current psalm was fairly common in Syria, with the Greek or Syriac text of phrases from the opening two verses of the ninety-first Psalm written on the lintels of Christian homes, sarcophagi, and pendants to be worn around the neck.[159] Amongst the latter, several "utilised images and formulae to repel misfortune from their wearers and, more particularly, the evil eye."[160] Thus these amulets would often incorporate Greek versions of biblical Divine Names, the names of certain Spirit Intelligences, e.g. *Micha'el, Gavri'el*, etc., as well as the opening phrase of the current psalm.[161]

We are informed that "Psalm 91 also proved very popular on amulets and rings among ancient Byzantine Christians. Twenty-five metal armbands and six rings, found scattered around the Roman East dating from the sixth to the twelfth century ce, testify to the wide appeal of such a totemic object."[162] Elsewhere in

Byzantine magical literature we find *Psalm 91:13* listed for anyone wishing "to bind a snake, and any reptile and four-legged animal." In this regard, the individual is instructed to recite the said verse, and, it is said, "the animal will stay put as if dead."[163]

Be that as it may, despite the anti-demonic qualities of the the current psalm having been maintained in the *Glossa Ordinaria*,[164] the most extensively consulted bible commentary in the middle ages, "many medieval and early modern Christian theologians, especially the early Protestants such as Martin Luther and John Calvin, and modern theologians such as Karl Barth cautioned strongly against what they saw as superstitious and magical uses."[165] After all, revered Christian theologians like Isaac of Nineveh and Theodore bar Koni insisted that it was asceticism and virginity which fend off evil.[166] However, when people are beset by plagues and pestilence resulting in mass destruction of their fellow humankind, they are inclined to cast aside the "fundamental sensibilities" of Christian theologians, and happily seek support in the "magical." In this regard Andreas Osiander, a Reformed clergyman living in Nuremberg during the plague of 1533, "heavily criticized the traditional apotropaic understanding of Psalm 91, which had long been seen as curative."[167] On the other hand, Charles Spurgeon, the acclaimed 19th century Baptist preacher, acknowledged the healing powers of the current psalm, noting that "a German physician was wont to speak of it as the best preservative in times of cholera, and in truth, it is a heavenly medicine against plague and pest. He who live in its spirit will be fearless, even if once again London should become a lazar-house, and the grave be gorged with carcases."[168]

This esteemed clergyman would not have foreseen the pandemics which would blight the 20th and 21st centuries, and how these would cause many to praise the "spiritual powers," i.e. the "magical power," of *Psalm 91* as a Divine protection against plague and pestilence.[169] In this regard, one commentator reported that Christians of the more charismatic "Prosperity theology" persuasion, "noted a numerical coincidence, as they juxtaposed Psalm 91 with Covid-19—what some termed a 'palindromic confrontation' of 91 verses 19."[170] He further noted that "the rich array of psalm-related objects, amulets, and memorabilia...now placed far more emphasis on the specific words about plague [in the psalm]," and that "the psalm text, in whole or in part, became a fixture on face masks."[171] Thus the ninety-first Psalm is still maintaining its "magical status" as "a song against evil spirits" and "a song against plagues" in the 21st century, and particularly in the Southern Hemisphere. In this regard, it is said that "even today, the apotropaic understanding of Psalm 91 continues to be exceptionaly popular, especially among communities that desire security, peace, and health. In much of the two-thirds world, belief in personal attacks from evil supernatural forces, magical powers, miraculous healings, and ancestral spirits has not waned amid the secularizing forces of modernity as in much of the northern hemisphere. For many modern African Christians, Psalm 91 offers the promise of spiritual and material peace and access to the divine power that can create the conditions for peace. In one instance, a survivor of the Rwandan massacres claimed that, while attempting to hide from a group of men looking to kill her, she read Psalm 91 and held the Bible open over her chest. According to this survivor, her attackers miraculously could not find her even though she stood in plain sight."[172] The same commentator concluded that "while for many North Americans and Europeans such claims stretch the bounds of credibility, the African reading of Psalm 91 follows much of the text quite closely. YHWH's promised deliverance is not naturalistic; Psalm 91 paints a picture of miraculous salvation (vv. 7, 11-12) that straightforwardly contradicts the realm of physical possibility. For those in the pit of despair, hope in the impossible often offers the only possible hope."[173]

A very different application of the ninety-first Psalm to be found in Christian magical literature, is its enunciation to avert "Spirits" from blocking an individual escaping with "any hidden treasure."[174] In this regard, the said individual is instructed to acquire the plant "Honesty," i.e. Moneywort (*Lunaria Annua*) commonly called "Silver Dollar."[175] The plant is "to be completely pulled up with its roots" whilst reciting *Psalm 91*, as well as the "Name of Seventy-Two Names."[176] We are told that since "Spirits like to look after this herb," this will ensure that "no wicked Spirit can harm you or prevent you from taking your hidden treasure."[177] Other than that, *Psalm 91:1–2* was recommended for recitation "to have God as your guardian"; a curious combination of phrases from verses 3 to 5 was enunciated for protection "against weapons"; verses 11 and 12 in order "to be safe during all journeys"; verses 13 and 14 "to be protected from all beasts and serpents; and verses 15 and 16 "to conserve goods and honours in your life."[178] However, the listed verses are corrupted in several instances. Elsewhere we find *Psalm 91:13* included in a rather bizarre ritual "to prevent a viper from biting you," and to cause "the reptile to spit out its venom."[179]

It has been noted that *Psalm 91* (*Psalm 90* in Christian bibles), "is the most frequently used psalm on early Christian amulets, appearing on papyrus and parchment as well as on pieces of jewelry."[180] Regarding its amuletic applications, it is maintained in "*Le Livre d'Or*" that bearing a written copy of the current psalm on your person, the text having been inscribed "with the blood of a Dove," and perfumed "with roses and wood of aloe," will result in you being "preserved from Demons and protected from all enchantments, from thieves, ferocious beasts and from all manner of men, who lead wicked lives and if you travel by night, you will walk without fear."[181] This is equally recommended to be carried by juveniles, since it is "good against children taking fright."[182]

In conclusion, it should be noted that in the "*Key of Solomon*" the edge of the "*Fifth Pentacle of the Sun*," is inscribed with the eleventh and opening phrase of the twelfth verse. We are told this object serves "to invoke those Spirits who can transport thee from one place unto another, over a long distance and in short time."[183] The same text lists the thirteenth verse imprinted around the outer border of the "*Fifth Pentacle of Mars*," the latter item being used to cause demons to submit to and obey the bearer.[184]

PSALM 92

[1] מזמיר שיר ליום השבת

[2]טוב להדות ליהוה‎אדני‑אהדונהי ולזמר לשמך עליון

[3] להגיד בבקר חסדך ואמונתך בלילות

[4] עלי עשור ועלי נבל עלי הגיון בכנור

[5] כי שמחתני יהוה‎אדני‑אהדונהי בפעלך במעשי ידיך ארנן

[6] מה גדלו מעשיך יהוה‎אדני‑אהדונהי מאד עמקו מחשבתיך

[7]איש בער לא ידע וכסיל לא יבין את זאת

[8] בפרח רשעים כמו עשב ויציצו כל פעלי און להשמדם עדי עד

[9] ואתה מרום לעלם יהוה‎אדני‑אהדונהי

[10] כי הנה איביך יהוה‎אדני‑אהדונהי כי הנה איביך יאבדו יתפרדו כל פעלי און

[11] ותרם כראים קרני בלתי בשמן רענן

[12] ותבט עיני בשורי בקמים עלי מרעים תשמענה אזבני

[13] צדיק כתמר יפרח כארז בלבנון ישגה

[14] שתולים בבית יהוה‎אדני‑אהדונהי בחצרות אלהינו יפריחו

[15] עוד ינובון בשיבה דשנים ורעננים יהיו

[16] להגיד כי ישר יהוה‎אדני‑אהדונהי צורי ולא עולתה בו

Transliteration:
[1] *miz'mor shir l'yom hashabat*
[2] *tov l'hodot laYHVH ul'zamer l'shim'cha elyon*
[3] *l'hagid baboker chas'decha ve'emunat'cha baleilot*
[4] *alei asor va'alei navel alei higayon b'chinor*
[5] *ki simach'tani YHVH b'fo'olecha b'ma'asei yadecha aranein*
[6] *mah gad'lu ma'asecha YHVH m'od am'ku mach'sh'votecha*

[7] *ish ba'ar lo yeida uch'sil lo yavin et zot*

[8] *bif'ro'ach r'sha'im k'mo eisev vayatzitzu kol po'alei aven l'hisham'dam adei ad*

[9] *v'atah marom l'olam YHVH*

[10] *ki hineih oy'vecha YHVH ki hineih oy'vecha yoveida yit'par'du kol po'alei aven*

[11] *va'tarem kir'eim kar'ni baloti b'shemen ra'anan*

[12] *vatabet eini b'shurai bakamim alai m'rei'im tish'ma'nah oz'nai*

[13] *tzadik katamar yif'rach k'erez bal'vanon yis'geh*

[14] *sh'tulim b'veit YHVH b'chatz'rot eloheinu yaf'richu*

[15] *od y'nuvun b'seivah d'sheinim v'ra'ananim yihi'u*

[16] *l'hagid ki yashar YHVH tzuri v'lo av'latah bo*

Translation:

[1] A Psalm, a Song for the Sabbath day.

[2] It is a good thing to give thanks unto *YHVH*, and to sing praises unto Thy name, O Most High;

[3] To declare Thy lovingkindness in the morning, and Thy faithfulness in the night seasons,

[4] With an instrument of ten strings, and with the psaltery; with a solemn sound upon the harp.

[5] For Thou, *YHVH*, hast made me glad through Thy work; I will exult in the works of Thy hands.

[6] How great are Thy works, *YHVH*! Thy thoughts are very deep.

[7] A brutish man knoweth not, neither doth a fool understand this.

[8] When the wicked spring up as the grass, and when all the workers of iniquity do flourish; it is that they may be destroyed for ever.

[9] But Thou, *YHVH*, art on high for evermore.

[10] For, lo, Thine enemies, *YHVH*, for, lo, Thine enemies shall perish: all the workers of iniquity shall be scattered.

[11] But my horn hast Thou exalted like the horn of the wild-ox; I am anointed with rich oil.

[12] Mine eye also hath gazed on them that lie in wait for me, mine ears have heard my desire of the evil-doers that rise up against me.

[13] The righteous shall flourish like the palm-tree; he shall grow like a cedar in Lebanon.
[14] Planted in the house of *YHVH*, they shall flourish in the courts of our God.
[15] They shall still bring forth fruit in old age; they shall be full of sap and richness;
[16] To declare that *YHVH* is upright, my Rock, in whom there is no unrighteousness.

Tradition has it that *Psalm 92*, delineated "a song for the Sabbath day," was first sung by the primordial ancestor Adam. This psalm is essentially a song of praise, regarding which we are told that "this praise was uttered by Adam when he was banished from the Garden of Eden and Sabbath came and defended him."[1] This saga maintains that when the primordial ancestor "sinned," he was "driven out because when God was about to decree his destruction, the Sabbath arrived and brought about his expulsion instead."[2] Thus the Sabbath "became Adam's advocate, saying to the Holy One, blessed be He: 'During the six days of Creation no one suffered punishment. And wilt Thou begin it with me? Is this my holiness? Is this my rest?'" It was noted that "when Adam saw the power of the Sabbath, he was about to sing a hymn in her honor. But the Sabbath said to Adam: 'Dost thou sing a hymn unto me? Let us, I and thou, sing a hymn to the Holy One, blessed be He.' Hence it is said 'It is a good thing to give thanks unto the Lord (*Psalm 92:2*)."[3] This "Divine Sabbath" is one of the personifications of the *Shechinah*, i.e. the Indwelling Presence of the Divine One generally perceived to be the Feminine Aspect of Divinity.[4] I have addressed the *Shechinah-Matronit* in some measure in the previous volumes of this series of texts on Jewish Magic.[5]

Readers may well be confused regarding the stated origins of the current psalm, since it is listed amongst the eleven psalms said to have been composed by Moses. In this regard, it was noted that the primordial ancestor Adam sang *Psalm 92*, but that "it was forgotten throughout all the generations until Moses came and renewed it according to his name, 'A psalm, a song for the Sabbath day,' for the day which is entirely Sabbath and rest in the life of eternity."[6] The statement that Moses renewed the current psalm "according to his own name, 'A psalm, a song for the Sabbath day'," is said to pertain to Moses having "alluded to his own name at the beginning of the psalm." In this regard, we are informed that the capitals of the four words comprising the first verse spell the word לְמֹשֶׁה (*l'Mosheh* —"by Moses").[7] It has been noted that the Ineffable Name (יהוה) appears seven times in the psalm, and this is believed to be "an allusion to the seventh day of creation," i.e. affirming the connection of *Psalm 92* with שַׁבָּת (*Shabbat*— "Sabbath").[8] Furthermore, having been titled "a song for the Sabbath day," with the second verse reading "it is a good thing to give thanks unto *YHVH*, and to sing praises unto Thy name, O Most High," the ninety-second Psalm is attributed to the tribe of Judah.[9] We are told that at his birth the mother of Judah proclaimed "'this time will I praise *YHVH*.'Therefore she called his name Judah [Praise]." (*Genesis 29:35*)

In the days of the Second Temple in Jerusalem, *Psalm 92* was one of the daily psalms sung by the Levites.[10] After the fall of the Temple, the recitation of the daily psalms "was reintroduced to the service, this time in the synagogue."[11] Thus the "Song for the Sabbath Day" is recited during the Friday evening service (*Arvit*) after קַבָּלַת שַׁבָּת (*Kabbalat Shabbat*—"Reception of the Sabbath"), on *Shabbat* during the morning service (*Shacharit*) in פְּסוּקֵי דְזִמְרָא (*Pesukei d'Zimrah*—"Verses of Prayer"), i.e. a set of psalms and biblical verses, and it is also enunciated as the psalm of the day at the conclusion of this service. In the Sefardi rite the ninety-second Psalm is also enunciated during the afternoon prayer service (*Min'chah*).[12] Variant customs arose in different Jewish communities around the globe, as for example in the instance of the Altneuschul synagogue in Prague where it is standard practice to recite the current psalm twice in succession. In this regard, it is said that Rabbi Judah Loew ben Bezalel, the acclaimed "Maharal," whom we are told was a great master of *Practical Kabbalah*, used his knowledge of this Tradition to create his famous "*Golem*." It is reported that he employed this artificial anthropoid as a manservant on six days of the week, but that he would extract the *Shem*, i.e. life-giving Divine Name, from the creature's mouth on a Friday afternoon in order "to let it rest on the Sabbath." Legend has it that "one Friday evening, at twilight, after having completed reciting the psalm, Rabbi Loew became aware that he had forgotten to extract the *Shem*, and the *golem* was running amok, endangering people's lives. The rabbi immediately left the synagogue and pursued the *golem* and hurriedly extracted the *Shem*, whereupon the golem fell to pieces. He then returned to the synagogue and repeated the psalm, a custom that prevails to the present day."[13]

As far as the application of *Psalm 92* in Jewish Magic is concerned, it is recited for longevity,[14] and it is said this psalm should be spoken "before waiting upon high dignitaries."[15] However, the current psalm is primarily listed "to witness great miracles."[16] Elsewhere we are told that great miracles can be affected by reciting the current psalm three times conjointly with *Psalms 94, 23, 20, 24* and *100*.[17] In this regard, the standard published version of the *Shimmush Tehillim* maintains that the enunciation of this psalm will facilitate the ability "to rise to greatness."[18] In a variant recension of this text the ninety-second Psalm is recommended to an individual who wants "to become a lord or a ruler," and in yet another recension it is enunciated by an individual who wishes "to defeat a lord or a ruler."[19]

Whatever may be the primary intention of the practitioner in employing the current psalm, the set of psalms listed above are understood to be good "for ascending to high office."[20] In order to achieve this objective, the practitioner is advised to take a new vessel filled with water, to which is added myrtle and grapevines, and to recite the mentioned set of psalms three times over the liquid,[21] or six times according to a variant recension.[22] This action is followed by the practitioner bathing in the water, and anointing his/her body and face with the same liquid.[23] Variant recensions maintain the concoction should be imbided "three times at night."[24] Be that as it may, in the standard version the magical procedure is concluded with a prayer to the Divine One which is uttered whilst facing north, the result of which is said that "you will see great miracles."[25] It has been suggested to Jewish worshippers to recite *Psalm 92* with a joyous, even ecstatic, mindset.[26] I have found this advice particularly effective in its mentioned magical application. Be that as it may, it should be noted that Godfrey Selig's German/English version of the *Shimmush Tehillim* shares the same details regarding the magical application of *Psalm 92*, to which he appended an additional statement reading "He [the practitioner] will be astonished with his ever-increasing good fortune. He will also, in a wonderful manner, advance from one post of honor to another."[27]

An altogether different application of *Psalm 92* appears in a variant recension of the *Shimmush Tehillim*. In this instance the psalm is recited with the following Divine/Angelic Names twenty-eight times a day for the purpose of being victorious in war: שדיאל ארגיאל מרגיאל נרגיאל עזרירון (*Shadi'el Ar'gi'el Mar'gi'el Nar'gi'el Az'riron*).[28] I have observed the Angelic combination ארגיאל מרגיאל נרגיאל listed conjointly in a magical application of נגד, i.e. the fifth tri-letter portion of the "Forty-two Letter Name of God," for the purpose of creating confusion in the minds of enemies.[29] Whilst mentioning the latter acclaimed Divine Name construct, it is worth noting that *Psalm 92:6* is directly associated with יחו (*Yichu*), the thirty-third tri-letter portion of the "Name of Seventy-two Names."[30] Be that as it may, I have referenced the Divine Name עזרירון (*Az'riron*) elsewhere in terms of its inclusion in two amulets employed to counteract spontaneous abortion.[31] In addition to this, and in line with the recommended recitation of the ninety-second Psalm for attaining high honours, I have seen this psalm recommended to competitive sportsmen. However, *Psalm 92* has also been said to be good to enunciate in order to encourage caution and prudence, and to keep your faith in the Divine One for protection against enemies. It is further recommended for recitation when you encounter the forces of nature.

There is relatively little information about the use of the ninety-second Psalm in Christian magic. In this regard, we find *Psalm 92:11* and *13* employed for a purpose similar to the one shared in *Shimmush Tehillim*, i.e. "to be named for Dignities of this World."[32] Other than that, "*Le Livre d'Or*" shares a technique in which the psalm is written "on a new plate, washed with clean water," and dispensed with "out in the house of your enemy." We are told that following this action "God will prevent him from being able to do you harm."[33]

PSALM 93

[1] יְהֹוָה מֶלֶךְ גֵּאוּת לָבֵשׁ לָבֵשׁ יְהֹוָה
עֹז הִתְאַזָּר אַף תִּכּוֹן תֵּבֵל בַּל תִּמּוֹט
[2] נָכוֹן כִּסְאֲךָ מֵאָז מֵעוֹלָם אָתָּה
[3] נָשְׂאוּ נְהָרוֹת יְהֹוָה נָשְׂאוּ נְהָרוֹת קוֹלָם
יִשְׂאוּ נְהָרוֹת דָּכְיָם
[4] מִקֹּלוֹת מַיִם רַבִּים אַדִּירִים מִשְׁבְּרֵי יָם אַדִּיר
בַּמָּרוֹם יְהֹוָה
[5] עֵדֹתֶיךָ נֶאֶמְנוּ מְאֹד לְבֵיתְךָ נַאֲוָה קֹדֶשׁ יְהֹוָה
לְאֹרֶךְ יָמִים

Transliteration:
[1] *YHVH malach gei'ut laveish laveish YHVH oz hit'azar af tikon teiveil bal timot*
[2] *nachon kis'acha mei'az mei'olam atah*
[3] *nas'u n'harot YHVH nas'u n'harot kolam yis'u n'harot doch'yam*
[4] *mikolot mayim rabim adirim mish'b'rei yam adir bamarom YHVH*
[5] *eidotecha ne'em'nu m'od l'veit'cha na'avah kodesh YHVH l'orech yamim*

Translation:
[1] *YHVH* reigneth; He is clothed in majesty; *YHVH* is clothed, He hath girded Himself with strength; yea, the world is established, that it cannot be moved.
[2] Thy throne is established of old; Thou art from everlasting.
[3] The floods have lifted up, *YHVH*, the floods have lifted up their voice; the floods lift up their roaring.
[4] Above the voices of many waters, the mighty breakers of the sea, *YHVH* on high is mighty.
[5] Thy testimonies are very sure, holiness becometh Thy house, *YHVH*, for evermore.

Psalms 92 and *93* are often addressed conjointly. Being the "song for the Sabbath day," it was said that *Psalm 92*, "functions like the song to a bride as she enters," and that "upon the bride making her debut, the groom appears."[1] Thus *Psalm 92* marks the entry of the

Shechinah, the Divine Queen—"Sabbath Bride," whilst *Psalm 93* extols the majesty of the Most High, the Holy King—"Divine Groom," of whom it is said "*YHVH* reigneth; He is clothed in majesty." It has also been observed that *Psalm 92* itself "begins with the obvious implication of God's kingship, which undergirds the recitation of these psalms,"[2] i.e. the statement that "it is a good thing to give thanks unto *YHVH*, and to sing praises unto Thy name, O Most High."

Regarding the current psalm, we are informed that *Psalm 93*, is the first of the seven so-called "Kingship psalms" (*Psalms 93–99*), and is uttered on a Friday because "on the sixth day....He completed His work of creation and reigned over His creatures." [*TB Rosh Hashanah 31a*] Interestingly enough, as in the case of the previous psalm, it is said *Psalm 93* was enunciated by the primordial ancestor Adam "shortly after he was created toward the end of the sixth day."[3] In this regard, legend has it that the primordial ancestor was of gigantic stature, instilling fear in all the creatures who beheld him, and who consequently prostrate themselves before him in their assumption "that he was their Creator."[4] The saga continues with Adam correcting their erroneous assumption and saying "let us go and adorn in majesty and might, and acclaim as King over us the One who created us."[5] We are told that it was "in that hour Adam opened his mouth and all the creatures answered after him, and they adorned in majesty and might and acclaimed their Creator as King over themselves," as they recited the ninety-third Psalm.[6] It is further said that the association of the current psalm with the primordial ancestor is affirmed by the fact that the *gematria* of the name אדם (*Adam* [א = 1 + ד = 2 + ם = 40 = 45]) aligns with the forty-five words comprising the current psalm.[7]

However, as in the instance of the previous psalm, *Psalm 93*, as well as the succeeding ones up to *Psalm 100*, are claimed to have been penned by Moses. The current psalm is associated with the tribe of Benjamin,[8] and is recited during the Friday morning service (*Shacharit*) as the שיר של יום (*shir shel yom*— "Psalm of the Day"),[9] Friday evening during *Kabbalat Shabbat* ("Reception of the Sabbath"),[10] and equally during the "introductory prayers for the Sabbath and festival morning service."[11] We are told that "in the Frankfurt community, as well as in many congregations up to recent times,"[12] worshippers were reading both *Psalms 92* and *93*, and "that the two Psalms were regarded as constituting a single entity in *Kabbalat Shabbat*."[13]

In Jewish Magic the ninety-third Psalm has been recommended "for support in a law suit."[14] Thus the singular application of the current psalm in the *Shimmush Tehillim* is for the purpose of defeating an opponent in court.[15] In this regard, Selig noted in his German/English version of the *Shimmush Tehillim* that "there is nothing special recorded of this Psalm, other than that it is highly recommended to any one who has a suit with a stern and unjust opponent. The proper use of this Psalm, it is said will surely win him his cause."[16]

As far as the applications of individual verses from the current psalm are concerned, we are told that the magical expression אַדִּיר יִשְׁמְרֵנִי (*Adir yish'm'reini*—"May *Adir* [the Mighty One] protect me"), which is said to have been derived from the phrase אַדִּיר בַּמָּרוֹם יהוה (*adir bamarom YHVH*—"*YHVH* on high is mighty) in *Psalm 93:4*, should be enunciated three times by individuals who find themselves in dangerous circumstances resulting from water,[17] i.e. storms, floods, etc. It is worth noting that the "watery element" is the primary issue in the said verse reading "above the voices of many waters, the mighty breakers of the sea, *YHVH* on high is mighty." In this regard, readers may well be reminded of my references elsewhere to the Divine Name אַדִירִירוֹן (*Adiriron* or *Adir'yaron*),[18] which is employed specifically to calm violent winter storms,[19] but which is used conjointly with *Psalm 29* for the purpose of calming a stormy sea.[20] In conclusion, it is worth noting that the Divine Name combination יְלִי (*Yeli*), the third tri-letter portion of the "Name of Seventy-two Names," is said to be an acronym of the statement in *Psalm 93:5* reading יהוה לְאֹרֶךְ יָמִים (*YHVH l'orech yamim*—"*YHVH* extends forevermore").[21]

I have observed *Psalm 93* being recommended for ailments and difficulties with the ears, heart, and legs. It is further utilised to ensure a safe pregnancy. Besides the mentioned verse enunciated three times to control storms, etc, the current psalm as a whole is also enunciated for protection against floods, as well as the protection of ships at sea. Regarding its use in legal actions, it is worth noting that it is recited against vengeance, in support of judges and tribunals, and for those who are oppressed. In conclusion, the current psalm has also been said to be good for "human sciences."

In Christian magic, according to the *"Livre d'Or,"* the ninety-third Psalm is employed for the purpose of blessing a residence. In this regard, the psalm is recited over "holy water," written down, and the text buried inside the residence, "and all the rats will flee."[22]

PSALM 94

[1] אל נקמות יהוהאדני־אהדונהי אל נקמות הופיע

[2] הנשא שפט הארץ השב גמול על גאים

[3] עד מתי רשעים יהוהאדני־אהדונהי עד מתי רשעים יעלזו

[4] יביעו ידברו עתק יתאמרו כל פעלי און

[5] עמך יהוהאדני־אהדונהי ידכאו ונחלתך יענו

[6] אלמנה וגר יהרגו ויתומים ירצחו

[7] ויאמרו לא יראה יה ולא יבין אלהי יעקב

[8] בינו בערים בעם וכסילים מתי תשכילו

[9] הנטע אזן הלא ישמע אם יצר עין הלא יביט

[10] היסר גוים הלא יוכיח המלמד אדם דעת

[11] יהוהאדני־אהדונהי ידע מחשבות אדם כי המה הבל

[12] אשרי הגבר אשר תיסרנו יה ומתורתך תלמדנו

[13] להשקיט לו מימי רע עד יכרה לרשע שחת

[14] כי לא יטש יהוהאדני־אהדונהי עמו ונחלתו לא יעזב

[15] כי עד צדק ישוב משפט ואחריו כל ישרי לב

[16] מי יקום לי עם מרעים מי יתיצב לי עם פעלי און

[17] לולי יהוהאדני־אהדונהי עזרתה לי כמעט שכנה דומה נפשי

[18] אם אמרתי מטה רגלי חסדך יהוהאדני־אהדונהי יסעדני

[19] ברב שרעפי בקרבי תנחומיך ישעשעו נפשי

[20] היחברך כסא הוות יצר עמל עלי חק

[21] יגודו על נפש צדיק ודם נקי ירשיעו

[22] ויהי יהוהאדני־אהדונהי לי למשגב ואלהי לצור מחסי

[23] וישב עליהם את אונם וברעתם יצמיתם יצמיתם יהוהאדני־אהדונהי אלהינו

Transliteration:

[1] *el n'kamot YHVH el n'kamot hofi'a*

[2] *hinasei shofet ha'aretz hashev g'mul al gei'im*

[3] *ad matai r'sha'im YHVH ad matai r'sha'im ya'alozu*

[4] *yabi'u y'dab'ru atak yit'am'ru kol po'alei aven*

[5] *am'cha YHVH y'dak'u v'nachalat'cha y'anu*

[6] *almanah v'geir yaharogu vitomim y'ratzeichu*

[7] *vayom'ru lo yir'eh Yah v'lo yavin elohei ya'akov*

[8] *binu bo'arim ba'am uch'silim matai tas'kilu*

[9] *hanota ozen halo yish'ma im yotzer ayin halo yabit*

[10] *hayoser goyim halo yochi'ach ham'lamed adam da'at*

[11] *YHVH yodei'a mach'sh'vot adam ki heimah havel*

[12] *ash'rei hagever asher t'yas'renu Yah umitorat'cha t'lamdenu*

[13] *l'hash'kit lo mimei ra ad yikareh larasha shachat*

[14] *ki lo yitosh YHVH amo v'nachalato lo ya'azov*

[15] *ki ad tzedek yashuv mish'pat v'acharav kol yish'rei lev*

[16] *mi yakum li im m'rei'im mi yit'yatzeiv li im po'alei aven*

[17] *lulei YHVH ez'ratah li kim'at shach'nah dumah naf'shi*

[18] *im amar'ti matah rag'li chas'd'cha YHVH yis'adeini*

[19] *b'rov sar'apai b'kir'bi tan'chumecha y'sha'ash'u naf'shi*

[20] *haichov'r'cha kisei havot yotzer amal alei chok*

[21] *yagodu al nefesh tzadik v'dam naki yar'shi'u*

[22] *vay'hi YHVH li l'mis'gav veilohai l'tzur mach'si*

[23] *vayashev aleihem et onam uv'ra'atam yatz'mitem yatz'mitem YHVH eloheinu*

Translation:

[1] Thou God to whom vengeance belongeth, *YHVH*, Thou God to whom vengeance belongeth, shine forth

[2] Lift up Thyself, Thou Judge of the earth; render to the proud their recompense.

[3] How long shall the wicked, *YHVH*, how long shall the wicked exult?

[4] They gush out, they speak arrogancy; all the workers of iniquity bear themselves loftily.

[5] They crush Thy people, *YHVH*, and afflict Thy heritage.

[6] They slay the widow and the stranger, and murder the fatherless.

[7] And they say: '*Yah* will not see, neither will the God of Jacob give heed.'

[8] Consider, ye brutish among the people; and ye fools, when will ye understand?

[9] He that planted the ear, shall He not hear? He that formed the eye, shall He not see?

[10] He that instructeth nations, shall not He correct? even He that teacheth man knowledge?

[11] *YHVH* knoweth the thoughts of man, that they are vanity.

[12] Happy is the man whom Thou instructest, *Yah*, and teachest out of Thy law;

[13] That Thou mayest give him rest from the days of evil, until the pit be digged for the wicked.

[14] For *YHVH* will not cast off His people, neither will He forsake His inheritance.

[15] For right shall return unto justice, and all the upright in heart shall follow it.

[16] Who will rise up for me against the evil-doers? Who will stand up for me against the workers of iniquity?

[17] Unless *YHVH* had been my help, my soul had soon dwelt in silence.

[18] If I say: 'My foot slippeth', Thy mercy, *YHVH*, holdeth me up.

[19] When my cares are many within me, Thy comforts delight my soul.

[20] Shall the seat of wickedness have fellowship with Thee, which frameth mischief by statute?

[21] They gather themselves together against the soul of the righteous, and condemn innocent blood.

[22] But *YHVH* hath been my high tower, and my God the rock of my refuge.

[23] And He hath brought upon them their own iniquity, and will cut them off in their own evil; *YHVH* our God will cut them off.

Psalm 94 is the שִׁיר שֶׁל יוֹם (*shir shel yom*—"Psalm of the Day") on the fourth day of the week, i.e. Wednesday.[1] With its focus on Divine Justice (vengeance), this fearsome psalm, aligned with the tribe of Gad,[2] appears to be the odd one out amongst the seven "enthronement psalms" (*Psalm 93–99*) in which the Divine One is acknowledged as "King." However, we are told that "its address of God as 'judge on earth'....certainly coheres with the portrayal of God in the rest of the collection, especially Psalms 96–99, which mention 'justice'."[3]

Whilst the current psalm does not feature in any prominent manner in Jewish worship, it is certainly well represented in Jewish Magic. We are told that *Psalm 94* is mainly recommended to individuals who are pursued and persecuted by enemies.[4] In this regard, the instruction is to recite the psalm "seven times every day."[5] In the *Shimmush Tehillim* the procedure for finding protection against enemies by means of the ninety-fourth Psalm, is somewhat more complex than merely reciting this psalm. In fact, the said individual is required to recite two psalms, i.e. *Psalm 94* and *92*, after careful preparation. Thus we are informed that one who is oppressed by a "hater," should first purify him or herself, then go outdoors in the open at dawn on a Monday, face North-East, place some incense in his/her mouth (frankincense can be taken orally), then recite the said psalms seven times a day, and it is said "you will see great wonders."[6] A variant recension of the *Shimmush Tehillim* maintains the procedure should be worked whilst facing North, and the incense located on a shoulder.[7] Be that as it may, we are told that the Divine Name אֵל קַנּוֹא טוֹב (*El Kano Tov*—"Good Jealous God") is applicable here, and that the recitation of the said psalms should be concluded with the following prayer-incantation:

יהי רצון מלפניך אֵל קַנּוֹא טוֹב שתשפיל ותכניע
[....insert name of recipient....] אויב וכן הראני נסים
כשם שהכנעת והשפלת את אויבי משה רבינו עליו
השלום כשהתפלל לפניך אלו השירות ותעלה תפלתי
כריח הקטרת מעל המזבח

Transliteration:

> *y'hi ratzon mil'fanecha El Kano Tov shetash'pil v'tach'ni'a* [....insert name of recipient....] *oyeiv v'chein har'eini nisim k'shem shehik'na 'ata v'hish'pal'ta et oy'vei mosheh rabeinu alav hashalom k'shehit'paleil l'fanecha ilu hashirot v'ta'aleh t'filati k'rei'ach hak'toret mei'al hamiz'bei'ach*

Translation:

> May it be your will *El Kano Tov*, to humiliate and subdue [....insert name of recipient....], my enemy, and likewise show me wonders just as you subdued and humbled the enemies of Moses our Master, peace be upon him, when he prayed these songs before you, and let my prayer ascend like the fragrance of incense from the altar.[8]

In his German/English version of the *Shimmush Tehillim*, Godfrey Selig shares some variances in the said magical use of the current psalm. He maintains you should "turn with your face toward the East and West," and whilst reciting the said two psalms "keeping in mind at the same time the holy name Eel Kanno Taf, which signifies great, strong, zealous and good God."[9] His version of the concluding prayer reads "May it please Thee, O great, strong, zealous and good God, to humble my enemy N., son of R., as thou once did the enemies of our great teacher Moses, who rests in peace, and who completed this Psalm to thy glorification. Let my prayer arise to thee as did the sweet smell of incense from the altar of incense, and let me behold thy wonderful power. Amen! Selah!"[10]

Another variant recension of the *Shimmush Tehillim* offers a very different procedure regarding the said application of the ninety-fourth Psalm. In this instance the one seeking to exact retribution on his or her "haters," is instructed to recite *Psalm 94* thirty-two times, and conclude with the following prayer-incantation which incorporates the earlier mentioned Divine Name, with the addition of an Angelic Name:

אל קנוא תוב נקמיאל אתם שמות הקדושים
הנקמו מן השונא הזה אשר הרע בעיני יהוה עשה
על לא [....insert details....] כל ימי חייו ולי הרע

חמס בכפי (*Job 16:17*) על כן תנקמו נקמת השם
ממנו כאשר עשה פינחס בן אלאזר אשר השיב
את חמת השם מעל בני ישראל כן עשו לזה
השונא בשם בורא עולם אמן סלה [....insert name....]

Transliteration:

El Kano Tov Nakami'el atem shemot hak'doshim hinak'mu min hasonei hazeh asher hara b'einei YHVH asah kol y'mei chayav v'li hara [....insert details....] al lo chamas b'chapai (Job 16:17) al kein tin'k'mu nik'mat Hashem mimenu ka'asher asah pin'chas ben el'azar asher heishiv et chamat Hashem mei'al b'nei yis'ra'el ken asu l'zeh [....insert name....] hasonei b'shem borei olam Omein Selah.

Translation:

El Kano Tov Nakami'el, you Holy Names, take revenge on this hater who has done evil in the sight of *YHVH* all the days of his life, and has done evil to me [....insert details....] "although there is no violence in my hands." (*Job 16:17*) Therefore you should take revenge on him with the vengeance of *Hashem*, as did Phinehas the son of Eleazar, who turned away the wrath of *Hashem* against the sons of Israel, so do unto this [....insert name....], the hater, in the Name of the Creator of the world. *Amen Selah.*[11]

The Divine/Angelic Name נקמיאל (*Nakami'el*) could be read "my vengeance is God," and the reference to "Phinehas, the son of Eleazar," pertains to the biblical saga of this individual having turned away a plague, and averted the wrath of the Divine One against the Israelites. (*Numbers 25:11*) Interestingly enough, *Psalm 94.1* and *Numbers 16:46*, respectively referencing Divine vengeance and "the plague," feature likewise in a belligerent magical procedure involving the Divine Name construct יְשַׁהֲקוֹוְֹהָ (*Yishuhakov'vaha*), which was formulated from שֻׁכֹן (*ShuKoVa*), the thirteenth portion of the "Forty-two Letter Name of God" and the Ineffable Name (יִהַוְֹהָ—*YiHaV'Ha*). As mentioned elsewhere, the "governing angel" of שֻׁקֹן (*ShuKoVa*) is נפליאל (*Naf'li'el*), who is supported by the Spirit

Intelligences חֵמָה (*Cheimah* —"rage"); קֶצֶף (*Ketzef*—"anger" or "wrath"); גַבְרִיאֵל (*Gavri'el*); סַמָאֵל (*Sama'el*); יְחִיאֵל (*Yechi'el*); קַפְצִיאֵל (*Kaf'tzi'el*); and רוֹגְזִיאֵל (*Rog'zi'el*— derived from רגז [*Ragaz*], i.e. "to be angry" or "agitated"). These "Spirit Forces" are directly affiliated with "anger," and specifically aligned with the "quality of *Din*," "*Pachad*," or "*Gevurah*," i.e. "Judgment," "Fear," or "Strength (Severity)" on the sefirotic Tree. Thus the most fearsome portion of the "Forty-two Letter Name of God," as well as its conjunction with the Ineffable Name, are said to have the power to increase anger; rebuke whatever needs to be castigated; take revenge; cause anxiety and panic attacks; create fear and strike terror in the heart; drive an individual away from his/her residence; and banish שֵדִים (*Shedim*— Demons). In fact, we are told that the Divine Name combination שְקוּ יִשְהֻקוֹב'והה (*ShuKoVa Yishuhakov'vaha*) will literally shout at the human or "spirit force" against whom it is directed. However, it can equally save an individual from trouble, and, as I noted elsewhere, alleviate distress, mitigate physical onslaughts, and restore peace.[12]

In the current instance, the said Divine Name combination, the associated Spirit Intelligences, and the two biblical verses, are employed to frighten and drive away evil forces of both the human and demonic kind. In this regard, the said Divine Name combination and affiliated Spirit Intelligences are, as I noted elsewhere, "most powerfully invoked on a Monday and a Wednesday, the days when their powers are said to be particularly potent."[13] However, whilst it was clearly indicated that the adjuration should be performed on any of those days, and that it should incorporate the Divine Name combination, the names of the relevant "Spirit Intelligences," and the said two verses, there is no formal adjuration shared in primary Hebrew sources. In fact, it is understood that practitioners should formulate their own. In this regard, I am well aware that most readers of this tome will be unfamiliar with Hebrew, and thus I composed the following fairly simple incantation which is easily enunciated, and can be broadly employed for a variety of related purposes:

אני משביעכם אתם הגבורות העליון נפליאל חמה
קצף גבריאל סמאל יחיאל קפציאל רוגזיאל
בשם שקו ישהקווה הושיעני מפני רשעים זו שדוני
שיתה מורה להם אל נקמות יהוה אל נקמות הופיע
‏[Psalm 94.1]‏ ויאמר משה אל אהרן קח את המחתה
ותן עליה אש מעל המזבח ושים קטרת והולך מהרה
אל העדה וכפר עליהם כי יצא הקצף מלפני יהוה
החל הנגף (Numbers 16:46) שלום יהיה לי אמן נצח
סלה ועד

Transliteration:

> ani mash'bi'achem atem hag'vurot ha'elyon Naf'li'el
> Cheimah Ketzef Gavri'el Sama'el Yechi'el Kaf'tzi'el
> Rog'zi'el b'shem ShuKoVa Yishuhakov'vaha hoshi'eini
> mip'nei r'sha'im zu shaduni shitah morah lahem El
> n'kamot YHVH el n'kamot hofi'a (Psalm 94.1) Vayomer
> Mosheh el Aharon kach et hamach'ta v'ten aleiha esh
> mei'al hamiz'be'ach v'sim k'toret v'holeich m'heirah el
> ha'eidah v'chapeir aleihem ki yatza haketzef milifnei
> YHVH heichel hanagef (Numbers 16:46) shalom yiyeh li,
> Omein Netzach Selah va'ed

Translation:

> I adjure you the Powers of the Almighty, *Nafli'el*,
> *Cheimah*, *Ketzef*, *Gavri'el*, *Sama'el*, *Yechi'el*, *Kaftzi'el*,
> *Rogzi'el*, in the Name *ShuKoVa Yishuhakov'vaha*, save me
> from the face of the wicked who want to oppress me. Teach
> them a lesson. "Thou God to whom vengeance belongeth,
> *YHVH*, Thou God to whom vengeance belongeth, shine
> forth." (*Psalm 94.1*) And Moses said unto Aaron: "Take
> thy fire-pan, and put fire therein from off the altar, and lay
> incense thereon, and carry it quickly unto the congregation,
> and make atonement for them; for there is wrath gone out
> from *YHVH*: the plague is begun." (*Numbers 16:46*) I will
> have peace, *Amen*, victory, *Selah* throughout eternity.

As mentioned previously, it is worth keeping in mind that, whilst
there might indeed be occasions when the severity of physical

circumstances necessitates the use of drastic action, eliciting the aid of powerful "Spirit Forces" for unfair, selfish purposes, or in an irresponsible manner, is likely to cause the magical action to blow up in your face with unexpected repercussions.[14] Be that as it may, it is worth keeping in mind that *Psalm 94:18* is directly aligned with both אֲנִי (*Ani*) and מִיה (*Mih*), the thirty-seventh and forty-eighth tri-letter portions of the "*Shem Vayisa Vayet*," and *Psalm 94:22* is directly associated with הֲרֹה, the fifty-ninth tri-letter portion of the "Name of Seventy-two Names."[15]

I have again observed the current psalm being employed in less "official" sources against paralysis and illness, as well as for healing, in general. The current psalm is also enunciated against divisive individuals and social menaces, as well as for protection in perilous situations and times of trouble. However, in more personal terms, this psalm is recited for forgiveness of errors and transgressions.

It would seem very little use is made of *Psalm 94* in Christian Magic. In this regard we read in the "*Livre d'Or*" that when the current psalm is read every day, "all your enemies will flee," and that it "is also good for the profit of a house or of a mill."[16]

PSALM 95

[1] לכו נרננה ליהוהאהדונהי נריעה לצור ישענו

[2] נקדמה פניו בתודה בזמרות נריע לו

[3] כי אל גדול יהוה אהדונהי ומלך גדול על כל אלהים

[4] אשר בידו מחקרי ארץ ותועפת הרים לו

[5] אשר לו הים והוא עשהו ויבשת ידיו יצרו

[6] באו נשתחוה ונכרעה נברכה לפני יהוה אהדונהי עשנו

[7] כי הוא אלהינו ואנחנו עם מרעיתו וצאן ידו היום אם בקלו תשמעו

[8] אל תקשו לבבכם כמריבה כיום מסה במדבר

[9] אשר נסוני אבותיכם בחנוני גם ראו פעלי

[10] ארבעים שנה אקוט בדור ואמר עם תעי לבב הם והם לא ידעו דרכי

[11] אשר נשבעתי באפי אם יבאון אל מנוחתי

Transliteration:

[1] *l'chu n'ran'nah laYHVH nari'ah l'tzur yish'einu*

[2] *n'kad'mah panav b'todah biz'mirot nari'a lo*

[3] *ki el gadol YHVH umelech gadol al kol elohim*

[4] *asher b'yado mech'k'rei aretz v'to'afo harim lo*

[5] *asher lo hayam v'hu asahu v'yabeshet yadav yatzaru*

[6] *bo'u nish'tachaveh v'nich'ra'ah niv'r'chah lif'nei YHVH oseinu*

[7] *ki hu eloheinu va'anach'nu am mar'ito v'tzon yado hayom im b'kolo tish'ma'u*

[8] *al tak'shu l'vav'chem kim'rivah k'yom masah bamid'bar*

[9] *asher nisuni avoteichem b'chanuni gam ra'u fo'oli*

[10] *ar'ba'im shanah akut b'dor va'omar am to'ei leivav heim v'heim lo yad'u d'rachai*

[11] *asher nish'ba'ti v'api im y'vo'un el m'nuchati*

Translation:

[1] O come, let us sing unto *YHVH*; let us shout for joy to the Rock of our salvation.

[2] Let us come before His presence with thanksgiving, let us shout for joy unto Him with psalms.

[3] For *YHVH* is a great God, and a great King above all gods;

[4] In whose hand are the depths of the earth; the heights of the mountains are His also.

[5] The sea is His, and He made it; and His hands formed the dry land.

[6] O come, let us bow down and bend the knee; let us kneel before *YHVH* our Maker;

[7] For He is our God, and we are the people of His pasture, and the flock of His hand. To-day, if ye would but hearken to His voice!

[8] 'Harden not your heart, as at Meribah, as in the day of Massah in the wilderness;

[9] When your fathers tried Me, proved Me, even though they saw My work.

[10] For forty years was I wearied with that generation, and said: It is a people that do err in their heart, and they have not known My ways;

[11] Wherefore I swore in My wrath, that they should not enter into My rest.

Kabbalat Shabbat ("Reception of the Sabbath") commences with the recitation of *Psalm 95*. This psalm, said to have been penned by Moses, and to be "appropriate to the tribe of Issachar,"[1] invites worshippers to join in joyous song in the presence of the Divine One.[2] Readers might be interested to know that *Kabbalat Shabbat*, a section of the Sabbath liturgy which precedes the Friday evening service (*Arvit*), was introduced into Jewish worship by the Kabbalists in sixteenth century Safed. In this regard, it is worth noting that the custom of these Kabbalists to dress in fine garments, and going out to greet the "Sabbath Bride," was derived from the *Talmud* [*TB Shabbat 35b*].[3] The opening section of the *Kabbalat Shabbat* service, which was introduced by the acclaimed kabbalist Rabbi Moses Cordovero, comprises six psalms, i.e. *Psalms 95–99* and *29*. They are said to be "exuberant in spirit," and representing the six days of Creation, the six working days of the week,[4] as well as the six Shofar (ram's horn) blasts "that were sounded on Friday afternoon to announce the ushering in of the Sabbath" [*TB Shabbat 35b*].[5]

It has been noted that the collective value of the capitals of the opening words of these six psalms [ל = 30 + שׁ = 300 + י = 10 + מ = 40 + י = 10 + מ = 40] is 430, which we are told is equal to the *gematria* of the word נֶפֶשׁ (*Nefesh*—"Soul") [נ = 50 + פ = 80 + שׁ = 300 = 430]. This is said to reference the "additional soul" which Jewish worshippers are said to gain on the Sabbath.[4] In this regard, it has been observed that "one does not have to be a mystic to experience the extra energy, the sense of renewal, and the recovery of meaning and purpose that one gains each Friday night as one welcomes the Sabbath with these psalms."[6] It was further noted that the said six psalms were "associated with the sefirot and with the mystical divine name of Forty-two letters."[7]

In terms of its use in Jewish Magic, we are told that *Psalm 95* is employed "against being betrayed into baptism."[8] It is generally maintained that the current psalm is recited for the purpose of preventing oneself from being "deceived into impurity" by ones fellow city dwellers,[9] and in Judaism "baptism" into a "foreign religion" is certainly viewed as "being led astray into impurity." Whatever may be understood regarding this magical application of the ninety-fifth Psalm, we are told that in the current instance, the relevant Divine Name is אֵל (*El*),[9] which one recension of the *Shimmush Tehillim* maintains to have been derived: א [*Alef*] from אֲשֶׁר נִשְׁבַּעְתִּי (*asher nish'ba'ti*— "Wherefore I swore"): verse 11; and ל (*Lamed*) from לְכוּ נְרַנְּנָה (*l'chu n'ran'nah*—"O come, let us sing"): verse 1.[10] The same recension rephrase the magical use of *Psalm 95* slightly, noting that it is to be employed by individuals who wish to preclude the citizens of their city being seduced into impurity.[11] However, according to Godfrey Selig "the pious believer should pray this Psalm for his erring and unbelieving brethren."[12] He further noted in his German/English version of the *Shimmush Tehillim*, that "the appropriate holy name of God peculiar to this Psalm is Eel, which is, great, strong God, and the letters are found in the words: Eel, verse 4, and Lezur, verse 1."[13] The origins Selig listed for the Divine Name אֵל (*El*), do not appear in any of the manuscripts and other primary sources which I have consulted.

Regarding the said application of *Psalm 95*, a somewhat more demanding procedure is listed in a variant recension of the *Shimmush Tehillim*.[14] In this regard, the practitioner is informed that, "lest the people of his [her] city err in the matter of impurity," he/she should recite the current psalm twenty-six times, each time concluding with the following prayer-incantation:

טהריאל צדקיאל חצילו אנשי העיר הזאת מחטא
נגד השם יתברך ובל יטעו בדבר טומאה זאת ואני
רואה שאחרים טועים על כן תשמרם מלטעות עם
אחרים בשם בוראכם הנכבד והנורא יתברך שמו
לעדי עד ולנצח נצחים

Transliteration:

Tahari'el Tzad'ki'el chatzilu an'shei ha'ir hazot meicheit neged hashem yit'barach ubal yit'u b'davar tum'ah zot v'ani ro'eh sh'acheirim to'im al kein tish'm'reim mil'ta'ot im acheirim b'shem bor'achem hanich'bad v'hanora yit'barach shemo l'adei ad ulanetzach netzachim.

Translation:

Tahari'el Tzad'ki'el save these people of the city from sin against *Hashem*, blessed be He, lest they err in the matter of this impurity, and I see that others err, so you should prevent them from erring with others. In the name of honourable and awesome Creator, blessed be His name, forever and ever, in perpetuity and for all eternity.[15]

In terms of different applications, the ninety-fifth Psalm is recommended to those who wish to express gratitude,[16] and I have seen the current psalm employed against being influenced to indulge misconduct, for the purpose of judgment of people, and to prevent quarrels between couples. On a more positive note, I have observed *Psalm 95* recommended for the protection of gardens, fields, and the earth, as well as to express gratitude to the Divine One. In conclusion, it is worth noting that *Psalm 95:6* is directly aligned with חהו (*Chaho*), the twenty-fourth tri-letter portion of the "Name of Seventy-two Names."[17]

Psalm 95 is put to a very different, and very minimal, use in Christian Magic. We are informed in the "*Livre d'Or*" that this psalm should be read for an invidual who is suffering demonic possession. In this regard, it maintains the current psalm is read "over a new tablet," which is afterwards washed with "holy water and holy oil." The afflicted individual is then anointed with the consecrated substances, and it is said "he will be healed." It was further that the current psalm should be written with a set of magical signs, and to ensure that the "possessee" refrains from eating "billy goat meat."[18]

PSALM 96

[1] שירו ליהוה^{אדני}אהדונהי שיר חדש שירו ליהוה^{אדני}אהדונהי כל הארץ

[2] שירו ליהוה^{אדני}אהדונהי ברכו שמו בשרו מיום ליום ישועתו

[3] ספרו בגוים כבודו בכל העמים נפלאותיו

[4] כי גדול ליהוה^{אדני}אהדונהי ומהלל מאד נורא הוא על כל אלהים

[5] כי כל אלהי העמים אלילים ויהוה^{אדני}אהדונהי שמים עשה

[6] הוד והדר לפניו עז ותפארת במקדשו

[7] הבו ליהוה^{אדני}אהדונהי משפחות עמים הבו ליהוה^{אדני}אהדונהי כבוד ועז

[8] הבו ליהוה^{אדני}אהדונהי כבוד שמו שאו מנחה ובאו לחצרותיו

[9] השתחוו ליהוה^{אדני}אהדונהי בהדרת קדש חילו מפניו כל הארץ

[10] אמרו בגוים יהוה^{אדני}אהדונהי מלך אף תכון תבל בל תמוט ידין עמים במישרים

[11] ישמחו השמים ותגל הארץ ירעם הים ומלאו

[12] יעלז שדי וכל אשר בו אז ירננו כל עצי יער

[13] לפני יהוה^{אדני}אהדונהי כי בא לישפט הארץ ישפט תבל בצדק ועמים באמונתו

Transliteration:

[1] *shiru laYHVH shir chadash shiru laYHVH kol ha'aretz*

[2] *shiru laYHVH bar'chu sh'mo bas'ru miyom l'yom y'shu'ato*

[3] *sap'ru vagoyim k'vodo b'chol ha'amim nif'l'otav*

[4] *ki gadol YHVH um'hulal m'od nora hu al kol elohim*

[5] *ki kol elohei ha'amim elilim vaYHVH shamayim asah*

[6] *hod v'hadar l'fanav oz v'tif'eret b'mik'dasho*

[7] *havu laYHVH mish'p'chot amim havu laYHVH kavod v'oz*

[8] *havu laYHVH k'vod sh'mo s'u min'chah uvo'u l'chatz'rotav*

[9] *hish'tachavu laYHVH b'had'rat kodesh chilu mipanav kol ha'aretz*

[10] *im'ru bagoyim YHVH malach aftikon teiveil bal timot yadin amim b'meisharim*

[11] *yis'm'chu hashamayim v'tageil ha'aretz yir'am hayam um'lo'o*

[12] *ya'aloz sadai v'chol asher bo az y'ran'nu kol atzei ya'ar*

[13] *lif'nei YHVH ki va ki va lish'pot ha'aretz yish'pot teiveil b'tzedek v'amim be'emunato*

Translation:

[1] O sing unto *YHVH* a new song; sing unto *YHVH*, all the earth.

[2] Sing unto *YHVH*, bless His name; proclaim His salvation from day to day.

[3] Declare His glory among the nations, His marvellous works among all the peoples.

[4] For great is *YHVH*, and highly to be praised; He is to be feared above all gods.

[5] For all the gods of the peoples are things of nought; but *YHVH* made the heavens.

[6] Honour and majesty are before Him; strength and beauty are in His sanctuary.

[7] Ascribe unto *YHVH*, ye kindreds of the peoples, ascribe unto *YHVH* glory and strength.

[8] Ascribe unto *YHVH* the glory due unto His name; bring an offering, and come into His courts.

[9] O worship *YHVH* in the beauty of holiness; tremble before Him, all the earth.

[10] Say among the nations: '*YHVH* reigneth.' The world also is established that it cannot be moved; He will judge the peoples with equity.

[11] Let the heavens be glad, and let the earth rejoice; let the sea roar, and the fulness thereof;

[12] Let the field exult; and all that is therein; then shall all the trees of the wood sing for joy;

[13] Before *YHVH*, for He is come; for He is come to judge the earth; He will judge the world with righteousness, and the peoples in His faithfulness.

Psalms 96 is the second of the set of six psalms recited during the introductory section of *Kabbalat Shabbat*. As noted earlier, this is one of the psalms said to have been written by Moses, who aligned it with the tribe of Zebulun.[1] We are told this psalm was sung by King David, when he carried the ark to Jerusalem,[2] and it is worth noting that *Psalms 96–99* have been called "the core of the enthronement collection."[3] In this regard, we are informed that these four psalms "feature the concepts of justice and righteousness," and that "this pair of words summarizes what God will for the world. Because justice and righteousness are what the earthly king was supposed to do."[4] As far as the ninety-sixth Psalm is concerned, the three appearances of the word "sing" in the first two verses of this jubilant psalm, are said "to correspond to the three prayers during which the children of Israel sing praises every day to the Holy One, blessed be He."[5] The phrase "sing unto *YHVH* a new song" corresponds to *Shacharit* (the morning prayer service) "for renewing daily the work of creation," whilst "sing unto *YHVH*, all the earth" pertains to *Min'chah* (the afternoon prayer service), "for all of earth's inhabitants have enjoyed the sun and its light." The third expression reading "Sing unto *YHVH*, bless His name," aligns with *Arvit* (the evening prayer service), "when Israel praises God for bringing evening twilight."[6]

The joy expressed in the current psalm appears to have spilled over in its primary application in Jewish magic. In this regard, this psalm is recommended to those who wish to encourage happiness within their families.[7] Here the relevant Divine Name is said to be יָהּ (*Yah*),[8] which we are told in one recension of the *Shimmush Tehillim*, was derived: י (*Yod*) from שׁ (*Shin*) in שׁירוּ (*shiru*—"sing unto"): verse 1, and ה (*Heh*) from ו (*Vav*) at the end of אֱמוּנָתוֹ (*emunato*—"His faithfulness"): verse 13 through the interchange ה–ו–ז (*He–Vav–Zayin*).[9] Godfrey Selig, who addressed *Psalm 96* and *97* conjointly in his version of the *Shimmush Tehillim*, this being understandable considering the magical application of the two psalms being the same, maintains that the said Divine Name was derived from "Jeschuato [*y'shu'ato*], verse 2, and Hawn [corruption of *havu*], verse 7."[10] This derivation of the said Divine Name again does not appear in any of the primary Hebrew texts which I have consulted. Be that as it may, Selig's version of the said application concludes with the promise that "whosoever will pray these two Psalms three times daily, will cause his family great joy and contentment."[11]

We are told that versions of the *Shimmush Tehillim* dating back to the 14th/15th centuries "added magical formulas against the plague."[12] In this regard, it was noted that "in the fifteenth century Spanish-Jewish version, *Psalm 96* was devoted exclusively to combating the plague which attacked the city."[13] In this regard, we read in one recension of *the Shimmush Tehillim* that "it is good to pray this Psalm on *Rosh Hashanah*,and it is also good to say it during a storm at sea, and three times a day in the days of a plague. And it is good to say it for recurring afflictions."[14]

Besides the magical application of the current psalm to bring contentment and happiness to family members, as well as to combat plagues and epidemics, I have seen it recommended in "unofficial sources" for personal recitation in the synagogue, and *Psalm 96:12* was suggested for enunciation "with walking through the woods."[15] I have personally found the articulation of verses such as these in alignment with everyday living, to greatly increase mindfulness of the eternal Presence of the Divine One. In this regard, it has been noted that "words of Psalms can be valuable tools in refocusing, centering, and quieting oneself, as a kind of Jewish mantra."[16]

It would seem that little is written about the magical use of the ninety-sixth Psalm in Christian magic, and it appears to be employed mainly as a protection against enemies. In this regard, the *"Livre d'Or"* suggests the current psalm to be read "at Vespers" seven times a day over a period of three days, and to copy the psalm with the names of your enemies. The writing is afterwards attached to your arm, and at the conclusion of the action the bearer is instructed to "go forth boldly and make your requests."[17]

PSALM 97

[1] יְהֹוָהאהדונהי מֶלֶךְ תָּגֵל הָאָרֶץ יִשְׂמְחוּ אִיִּים רַבִּים

[2] עָנָן וַעֲרָפֶל סְבִיבָיו צֶדֶק וּמִשְׁפָּט מְכוֹן כִּסְאוֹ

[3] אֵשׁ לְפָנָיו תֵּלֵךְ וּתְלַהֵט סָבִיב צָרָיו

[4] הֵאִירוּ בְרָקָיו תֵּבֵל רָאֲתָה וַתָּחֵל הָאָרֶץ

[5] הָרִים כַּדּוֹנַג נָמַסּוּ מִלִּפְנֵי יְהֹוָהאהדונהי מִלִּפְנֵי
אֲדוֹן כָּל הָאָרֶץ

[6] הִגִּידוּ הַשָּׁמַיִם צִדְקוֹ וְרָאוּ כָל הָעַמִּים כְּבוֹדוֹ

[7] יֵבֹשׁוּ כָּל עֹבְדֵי פֶסֶל הַמִּתְהַלְלִים בָּאֱלִילִים
הִשְׁתַּחֲווּ לוֹ כָּל אֱלֹהִים

[8] שָׁמְעָה וַתִּשְׂמַח צִיּוֹן וַתָּגֵלְנָה בְּנוֹת יְהוּדָה לְמַעַן
מִשְׁפָּטֶיךָ יְהֹוָהאהדונהי

[9] כִּי אַתָּה יְהֹוָהאהדונהי עֶלְיוֹן עַל כָּל הָאָרֶץ מְאֹד
נַעֲלֵיתָ עַל כָּל אֱלֹהִים

[10] אֹהֲבֵי יְהֹוָהאהדונהי שִׂנְאוּ רָע שֹׁמֵר נַפְשׁוֹת
חֲסִידָיו מִיַּד רְשָׁעִים יַצִּילֵם

[11] אוֹר זָרֻעַ לַצַּדִּיק וּלְיִשְׁרֵי לֵב שִׂמְחָה

[12] שִׂמְחוּ צַדִּיקִים בַּיהֹוָהאהדונהי וְהוֹדוּ לְזֵכֶר קָדְשׁוֹ

Transliteration:

[1] *YHVH malach tageil ha'aretz yis'm'chu iyim rabim*
[2] *anan va'arafel s'vivav tzedek umish'pat m'chon kis'o*
[3] *esh l'fanav teileich ut'laheit saviv tzarav*
[4] *hei'iru v'rakav teiveil ra'atah vatacheil ha'aretz*
[5] *harim kadonag namasu milif'nei YHVH milif'nei adon
kol ha'aretz*
[6] *higidu hashamayim tzid'ko v'ra'u chol ha'amim k'vodo*
[7] *yeivoshu kol ov'dei fesel hamit'hal'lim ba'elilim
hish'tachavu lo kol elohim*
[8] *sham'ah vatis'mach tziyon vatageil'nah b'not y'hudah
l'ma'an mish'patecha YHVH*
[9] *ki atah YHVH el'yon al kol ha'aretz m'od na'aleita al
kol elohim*
[10] *ohavei YHVH sin'u ra shomeir naf'shot chasidav
miyad r'sha'im hatzileim*

[11] *or zaru'a latzadik ul'yish'rei leiv sim'chah*
[12] *sim'chu tzadikim baYHVH v'hodu l'zeicher kod'sho*
Translation:

[1] *YHVH* reigneth; let the earth rejoice; let the multitude of isles be glad.

[2] Clouds and darkness are round about Him; righteousness and justice are the foundation of His throne.

[3] A fire goeth before Him, and burneth up His adversaries round about.

[4] His lightnings lighted up the world; the earth saw, and trembled.

[5] The mountains melted like wax at the presence of *YHVH*, at the presence of *YHVH* of the whole earth.

[6] The heavens declared His righteousness, and all the peoples saw His glory.

[7] Ashamed be all they that serve graven images, that boast themselves of things of nought; bow down to Him, all ye gods.

[8] Zion heard and was glad, and the daughters of Judah rejoiced; because of Thy judgments, *YHVH*.

[9] For Thou, *YHVH*, art most high above all the earth; Thou art exalted far above all gods.

[10] O ye that love *YHVH*, hate evil; He preserveth the souls of His saints; He delivered them out of the hand of the wicked.

[11] Light is sown for the righteous, and gladness for the upright in heart.

[12] Be glad in *YHVH*, ye righteous; and give thanks to His holy name.

Psalm 97, the third of the opening six psalms of *Kabbalat Shabbat* recited on Friday evenings, is said to have been assigned to the tribe of Joseph.[1] Elsewhere the psalm is maintained to be appropriate to the Tribes of Ephraim and Manasseh.[2] A single verse from this psalm (*Psalm 97:11*) is of particular importance in Jewish worship, and is recited a number of times at the very start of the service on the eve of *Yom Kippur* (Day of Atonement).[3] Non-Jewish readers might be interested to know that *Yom Kippur* (Day of Atonement) is considered the most holy day in Judaism. This day, the tenth following the start of *Rosh Hashanah* (Jewish

New Year), is believed to be the "Day of Judgement" on which the fate of each individual determined on the Jewish New Year, is sealed for the year ahead.[4] That being said, I align with the axiom that "we are not punished for our sins, but by them."[5] As I noted elsewhere, it is "purely a question of horses and carts, or plain cause and effect, or simply 'if I do this then that will happen,' and taking things from there."[6] Thus the sacred time of the "Day of Atonement" offers one the opportunity to deal with "causes" in an efficient manner, so as to adjust their "effects" effectively. The most meaningful outcome of self-rectification on *Yom Kippur* is expressed in the phrase אוֹר זָרֻעַ לַצַּדִּיק (*or zaru'a latzadik—* "Light is sown for the righteous") from *Psalm 97:11*, which we are told "is taken literally, and a great light is described as descending from heaven on Kol Nidrei, the opening prayer that ushers in Yom Kippur. This light, it is understood, is the divine presence filling the world."[7] Regarding the said biblical phrase, it has been noted that the concluding letters of the three words, i.e. רעק (*Resh/Ayin/Kof*), when "rearranged and supplied with vowels, spell *kara*, 'to rip' or 'to tear'." This is maintained to be "a shorthand reference to the High Holy Day hope that any evil decree that awaits us as the verdict of the day be shredded."[8]

As in the case of the previous psalm, *Psalm 97* is enunciated in Jewish Magic to gladden family memb.ers.[9] The Divine Name associated with the current psalm is likewise יה (*Yah*),[10] which one recension of the *Shimmush Tehillim* maintains to have been derived: י (*Yod*) from יהוה מלך (*YHVH malach—* "YHVH reigneth"): verse 1; and ה (*Heh*) from ע (*Ayin*) in the word עדותיך (*eidotecha—*"thy testimonies"), by means of the ה–ע (*Heh/Ayin*) exchange,[11] i.e. both letters being gutturals are considered interchangeable. Selig, who dealt with *Psalm 96* and *97* conjointly, again shared unverified origins for the said Divine Name, claiming it to be found "in the words, Jismechu, verse 1, and Atta, verse 9."[12] Be that as it may, the following slightly more complex application of the ninety-seventh Psalm for the purpose of pleasing the members of ones family, and for them to accept Divine Will, is shared in a variant recension of the *Shimmush Tehillim*. In this regard, the recitation of the psalm is succeeded by the following prayer-incantation:

ברכיאל שמחיאל רחמיאל שמרו בני משפחתי
מלהיות דואגים ועצבים כאשר ישלח אלהים מה
שחפץ לעשות בעולמו ויקבלו בשמחה ובאהבה
יסורי השם בשם בורא עולם ושחקים

Transliteration:

> *Bar'chi'el Sam'chi'el Rach'mi'el sham'ru b'nei mish'pach'ti mil'hiyot do'agim v'atzavim k'asher yish'lach elohim mah sh'chafetz la'asot b'olamo vikab'lu b'sim'chah ub'ahavah y'sori hashem b'shem borei olam ush'chakim.*

Translation:

> *Bar'chi'el Sam'chi'el Rach'mi'el* keep my family members from being worried and sad when the Divine One (*Elohim*) sends what He desires to do in His universe. And they will receive the tribulations of *Hashem* with joy and love, in the Name of the Creator of the world and heavens.[13]

Other than these applications, the current psalm is recited to express acceptance of Divine Will. It is also worth noting that *Psalm 97:1* is directly associated with הַאא (*Ha'a*), the twenty-sixth tri-letter portion of the "Name of Seventy-two Names,"[14] and the capitals of the seven words comprising *Psalm 97:2* are conjoined in the Divine Name construct עוס צומב, which is included in an amulet to be carried against theft.[15]

The use of the ninety-seventh Psalm in Christian Magic appears to be equally sparse. Furthermore, rather than bringing happiness and pleasure to ones family, the few appearances of this psalm in Christian Magic pertains to malicious intentions. In this regard, the current psalm is referenced in an Arabic Coptic magical manuscript in a procedure to invoke Divine anger against an individual. In this regard, the current psalm is inscribed on wax with an accompanying angry statement. This is done in the name of the said person, following which the inscription is buried inside an unvisited tomb.[16] Elsewhere we find the *Psalm 97* being employed against a wife "whom you hate." In this regard, we are informed in the "*Livre d'Or*," that the individual who holds such sentiments towards his wife, should write the current psalm with a mixture of musk, saffron, rosewater and camphor." The writing is then perfumed with mastic and aloe wood, and buried "in front of her door." Regarding the outcome, we are told "that for which you wish will come to pass."[17] One can only guess at the expected outcome in the mind of the spouse of the unfortunate woman!

PSALM 98

[1] מזמור שירו ליהוה‎אהדונהי שיר חדש כי
נפלאות עשה הושיעה לו ימינו וזרוע

[2] הודיע יהוה‎אהדונהי ישועתו לעיני הגוים
גלה צדקתו

[3] זכר חסדו ואמונתו לבית ישראל ראו כל
אפסי ארץ את ישועת אלהינו

[4] הריעו ליהוה‎אהדונהי כל הארץ פצחו ורננו
וזמרו

[5] זמרו ליהוה‎אהדונהי בכנור בכנור וקול
זמרה

[6] בחצצרות וקול שופר הריעו לפני המלך
יהוה‎אהדונהי

[7] ירעם הים ומלאו תבל וישבי בה

[8] נהרות ימחאו כף יחד הרים ירננו

[9] לפני יהוה‎אהדונהי כי בא לשפט הארץ
ישפט תבל בצדק ועמים במישרים

Transliteration:

[1] *miz'mor shiru laYHVH shir chadash ki nif'la'ot asah hoshi'ah lo y'mino uz'ro'a kad'sho*

[2] *hodi'a YHVH y'shu'ato l'einei hagoyim gilah tzid'kato*

[3] *zachar chas'do ve'emunato l'veit yis'ra'eil ra'u chol af'sei aretz et y'shu'at eloheinu*

[4] *hari'u laYHVH kol ha'aretz pitz'chu v'ran'nu v'zameiru*

[5] *zam'ru laYHVH b'chinor b'chinor v'kol zim'rah*

[6] *bachatzotz'rot v'kol shofar hari'u lif'nei hamelech YHVH*

[7] *yir'am hayam um'lo'o teiveil v'yosh'vei vah*

[8] *n'harot yim'cha'u chaf yachad harim y'raneinu*

[9] *lif'nei YHVH ki va lish'pot ha'aretz yish'pot teiveil b'tzedek v'amim b'meisharim*

Translation:

[1] A Psalm. O sing unto *YHVH* a new song; for He hath done marvellous things; His right hand, and His holy arm, hath wrought salvation for Him.

[2] *YHVH* hath made known His salvation; His righteousness hath He revealed in the sight of the nations. [3] He hath remembered His mercy and His faithfulness toward the house of Israel; all the ends of the earth have seen the salvation of our God. [4] Shout unto *YHVH*, all the earth; break forth and sing for joy, yea, sing praises. [5] Sing praises unto *YHVH* with the harp; with the harp and the voice of melody. [6] With trumpets and sound of the horn shout ye before the King, *YHVH*. [7] Let the sea roar, and the fulness thereof; the world, and they that dwell therein; [8] Let the floods clap their hands; let the mountains sing for joy together; [9] Before *YHVH*, for He is come to judge the earth; He will judge the world with righteousness, and the peoples with equity.

Psalm 98, said to have been dedicated by Moses to the tribe of Naftali,[1] is the fourth psalm recited on Friday evenings during *Kabbalat Shabbat*.[2] In the Sefardic tradition it is enunciated during *Shacharit* (morning prayer service) on *Shabbat*, and in certain Sefardic communities it is one of a special set of ten psalms recited during the Sabbath morning service.[3] These psalms are said to align with the ten *Ma'amarot* (Divine Sayings) "which the Eternal Living Spirit is said to have used in the act of creation,"[4] The current psalm is also one of a set of psalms comprising the זמירות (*Z'mirot*—Hymns ["Verses of Song"]) section pronounced in the Sefardi rite on *Yom Kippur*.[5]

In terms of its magical applications, the ninety-eighth Psalm is utilised to establish peace between one individual and another, e.g. between neighbours, two friends, etc.[6] Elsewhere the current psalm is said to be good "to make peace between enemies,"[7] and Godfrey Selig claims in his German/English version of the *Shimmush Tehillim* that the psalm "should be pronounced in order to establish peace and unity between families."[8] Be that as it may, as in the case of the previous two psalms, the associated Divine Name is in the current instance generally held to be יה (*Yah*),[9] which Selig claims was derived: י (*Yod*) from ישראל (*Yis'ra'el*—"Israel"): verse 3; and ה (*Heh*) from הושיעה (*hoshi'ah*—"salvation"): verse 1.[10] I have yet to verify Selig's claims, which thus far remains unsubstantiated. However, we are informed in a variant recension of the *Shimmush Tehillim* that the relevant Divine Name is הו, which is said to have been derived: ו (*Vav*) from the concluding letter in אלהינו (*Eloheinu*—"our God"): verse 3; and ה (*Heh*) from הריעו ליהוה (*hari'u laYHVH*—"Shout unto *YHVH*"): verse 4.[11]

In a variant recension of the *Shimmush Tehillim* the current psalm is recommend to someone who wishes to relieve the inhabitants of his or her city from a pestilence (plague), which is about to cause great sickness and loss of life "because of the multiplicity of their transgressions."[12] Whilst many would interpreted this statement to mean that a city is being punished by heaven for their sins "Sodom and Gomorrah" style, this is simply a matter of human actions, such as pollution in cities, resulting in the proliferation of life threatening bacteria, germs, and viruses. In the current instance, the recitation of the psalm is succeeded by the following prayer-incantation:

חסדיאל ישריאל חייאל היקלו מעל אנשי העיר
הזאת המגפה אשר חלתה לבוא עליהם וגערו בשטן
המגיף אותם בשם מלך אמ״ץ ורב כח

Transliteration:
> *Chas'di'el Yis'rei'el Chayi'el yikalu mei'al an'shei ha'ir hazot hamageifah asher chal'tah lavo aleihem v'ga'aru b'satan hamagif otam b'shem melech amitz v'rav ko'ach.*

Translation:
> *Chas'di'el Yis'rei'el Chayi'el* relieve the people of this city of the pestilence that is about to make them sick, and rebuke the Satan who contaminated them. In the Name of the courageous and powerful King.[13]

Naturally it should be clearly understood that unhygienic living conditions should be dealt with decisively, so as to minimize reliance on Divine intervention when humans are being punished *by* their sins. However, readers who hold the opinion that the latter application of the current psalm pertains to Divine retribution, should note that *Psalm 98* is equally enunciated for "heavenly mercy."[14] Should disaster strike in the form of a conflagration, something which is so prevalent in current conditions of global warming, the ninety-eighth Psalm is further recommended against fire.[15] It should be noted that the current psalm is also employed "to find peace."[16] In this regard, we are informed that it is a virtue to read *Psalms 96, 97* and *98* regularly after the "*Ribono Shel Olam*" prayer, "if there is no peace in the house."[17] I have addressed the latter prayer in some detail in the first part of "*The Book of Magical Psalms.*"[18] We are told that *Psalm 98* is enunciated to find comfort for one who suffers depression, to request Divine Mercy, and to elicite the loyalty of "good spirits." As far as individual verses from the current psalm are concerned, it should be noted that *Psalm 98:4* is directly affiliated with לחך (*L'hach*), the thirty-fourth tri-letter portion of the "Name of Seventy-two Names."[19]

The application of the ninety-eighth Psalm appears to be very sparse in Christian magic. In this regard, individual verses from the current psalm have been employed in Christian Magic in conjunction with a number of verses from the Jewish and Christian sacred scriptures.[20] Other than this, *Psalm 98* is listed in the "*Livre d'Or*" for the curious purpose of halting "a ship that has its sails to the wind."[21]

PSALM 99

[1] יהוהאדני־יאהדונהי מלך ירגזו עמים ישב כרובים
תנוט הארץ

[2] יהוהאדני־יאהדונהי בציון גדול ורם הוא על כל
העמים

[3] יודו שמך גדול ונורא קדוש הוא

[4] ועז מלך משפט אהב אתה כוננת מישרים
משפט וצדקה ביעקב אתה עשית

[5] רוממו יהוהאדני־יאהדונהי אלהינו והשתחוו להדם
רגליו קדוש הוא

[6] משה ואהרן בכהניו ושמואל בקראי שמו קראים
אל יהוהאדני־יאהדונהי והוא יענם

[7] בעמוד ענן ידבר אליהם שמרו עדתיו וחק נתן
למו

[8] יהוהאדני־יאהדונהי אלהינו אתה עניתם אל נשא היית
להם ונקם על עלילותם

[9] רוממו יהוהאדני־יאהדונהי אלהינו והשתחוו להר קדשו
כי קדוש יהוהאדני־יאהדונהי אלהינו

Transliteration:

[1] *YHVH malach yir'g'zu amim yosheiv k'ruvim tanut ha'aretz*

[2] *YHVH b'tziyon gadol v'ram hu al kol ha'amim*

[3] *yodu shim'cha gadol v'nora kadosh hu*

[4] *v'oz melech mish'pat aheiv atah konan'ta meisharim mish'pat utz'dakah b'ya'akov atah asita*

[5] *rom'mu YHVH eloheinu v'hish'tachavu lahadom rag'lav kadosh hu*

[6] *mosheh v'aharon b'chohanav ush'mu'el b'kor'ei sh'mo korim el YHVH v'hu ya'aneim*

[7] *b'amud anan y'dabeir aleihem sham'ru eidotav v'chok natan lamo*

[8] *YHVH eloheinu atah anitam el nosei hayita lahem v'nokeim al alilotam*

[9] *rom'mu YHVH eloheinu v'hish'tachavu l'har kod'sho ki kadosh YHVH eloheinu*

Translation:
[1] *YHVH* reigneth; let the peoples tremble; He is enthroned upon the cherubim; let the earth quake.
[2] *YHVH* is great in Zion; and He is high above all the peoples.
[3] Let them praise Thy name as great and awful; Holy is He.
[4] The strength also of the king who loveth justice—Thou hast established equity, Thou hast executed justice and righteousness in Jacob.
[5] Exalt ye *YHVH* our God, and prostrate yourselves at His footstool; Holy is He.
[6] Moses and Aaron among His priests, and Samuel among them that call upon His name, did call upon *YHVH*, and He answered them.
[7] He spoke unto them in the pillar of cloud; they kept His testimonies, and the statute that He gave them.
[8] *YHVH* our God, Thou didst answer them; a forgiving God wast Thou unto them, though Thou tookest vengeance of their misdeeds.
[9] Exalt ye *YHVH* our God, and worship at His holy hill; for *YHVH* our God is holy.

Psalm 99 is the fifth psalm recited on Friday evenings at the introduction of *Kabbalat Shabbat*.[1] Attributed to the tribe of Dan,[2] we are told that Palestinian Jews who "reserved specific psalms for all kinds of days," set aside *Psalms 99* and *137* for תשעה באב (*Tisha B'av*—Ninth of Av).[3] This is a day on which a number of great tragedies ensued for the Jewish people, and is commemorated annually as a day of mourning and fasting. The ninety-ninth Psalm is enunciated for a good conscience, and whilst it does not feature in every published version of the *Shimmush Tehillim*, it is recommended in *Practical Kabbalah* to individuals who seek greater religious piety.[4] In this regard, Godfrey Selig noted in his German/English version of the *Shimmush Tehillim*, that "with this Psalm there is no holy name recorded, and all who wish to become really pious are advised to pray it often with proper devotion."[5] In a variant recension it is said that the individual who is seeking to become more devout, should enunciate the current psalm twelve times every day, after each recitation saying:

דרשיאל בקשיאל תנו לי לב לדרוש ולבקש אלהים
ולהאמין בו ובתורתו בשם רוכב ערבות אהגה בה יומם
ולילה אמן נצח סלה

Transliteration:

> *Darashi'el Bak'shi'el tanu li lev lid'rosh ul'vakesh elohim
> ul'ha'amin bo uv'torato b'shem rochev aravot ehegeh bah
> yoman v'lailah Omein Netzach Selah.*

Translation:

> *Darashi'el Bak'shi'el* give me a heart to preach, to ask
> *Elohim*, and to believe in Him, and in His *Torah*. In the
> name of the Rider of *Aravot* [the seventh Heaven (skies)],
> I will ponder this day and night. *Amen* Eternal *Selah*.[6]

The application of *Psalm 99* in Christian Magic appears to be
almost non-existent. The current psalm is listed in the oft-
mentioned *"Livre d'Or,"* in which it is recommended for recitation
in order to "be received honourably." In this regard, the
practitioner is instructed to enunciate the psalm seven times over
water in the morning, afterwards washing his or her face with the
said liquid. We are told this will result in the fulfillment of the said
aim.[7] Other than this, I have seen words from the ninety-ninth
Psalm appearing in a 3rd century magical inscription, i.e. a tablet of
lead found in the extensive necropolis of the ancient city of
Hadrumetum, at the time an important Roman city in North Africa,
in what is now Tunisia. The said inscription comprises a love spell
which incorporates, amongst others, expressions from Jewish and
Christian sacred writ, including corruptions of words from the
current psalm.[8]

PSALM 100

[1] מזמור לתודה הריעו ליהוה‎אדני‏אהדונהי כל הארץ

[2] עבדו את יהוה‎אדני‏אהדונהי בשמחה באו לפניו ברננה

[3] דעו כי יהוה‎אדני‏אהדונהי הוא אלהים הוא עשנו ולו
אנחנו עמו וצאן מרעיתו

[4] באו שעריו בתודה חצרתיו בתהלה הודו לו ברכו
שמו

[5] כי טוב יהוה‎אדני‏אהדונהי לעולם חסדו ועד דר ודר
אמונתו

Transliteration:

[1] *miz'mor l'todah hari'u laYHVH kol ha'aretz*

[2] *iv'du et YHVH b'sim'chah bo'u l'fanav bir'nanah*

[3] *d'u ki YHVH hu elohim hu asanu v'lo anach'nu amo v'tzon mar'ito*

[4] *bo'u sh'arav b'todah chatzeirotav bit'hi'lah hodu lo bar'chu sh'mo*

[5] *ki tov YHVH l'olam chas'do v'ad dor vador emunato*

Translation:

[1] A Psalm of thanksgiving. Shout unto *YHVH*, all the earth.

[2] Serve *YHVH* with gladness; come before His presence with singing.

[3] Know ye that *YHVH* He is *Elohim*; it is He that hath made us, and not we, His people, and the flock of His pasture.

[4] Enter into His gates with thanksgiving, and into His courts with praise; give thanks unto Him, and bless His name.

[5] For *YHVH* is good; His mercy endureth for ever; and His faithfulness unto all generations.

Psalm 100, attributed to the tribe of Asher, is the last of the set of psalms said to have been authored by Moses.[1] Called a "Psalm of Thanksgiving," titled so after the opening two words in the first verse, this psalm is recited every day during the morning prayer service (*Shacharit*), except on *Shabbat*. In this regard it has been suggested that "this weekday *Mizmor L'Todah*, 'Psalm of

Thanksgiving,' originates in the daily *todah* (thanksgiving) sacrifice offered in the Temple. This offering was only made on weekdays, not on Shabbat, explaining why we say Psalm 100 during the week but omit it from our services on Shabbat."[2] However, we are informed that "this psalm provides a key to our day," and indicates the manner in which we should serve the Divine One. This is also a reason given for the recitation of the current psalm "at the very beginning of the morning service and hope we internalize its messages."[3]

As noted earlier, it is said great miracles can be accomplished by reciting *Psalms 92, 94, 23, 20, 24* and *100* three times.[4] Yet, whilst the "Psalm of Thanksgiving" might be considered to be relatively small in size, it is gigantic in its power and impact entirely on its own. We are told that "in this psalm, the psalmist is speaking to an individual who has already experienced an intense private miracle," and thus wishes to express "a volunteer gift of thanks" to the Eternal One for that which transpired in his or her life.[5] In my personal estimation, the hundredth Psalm emphasizes a most important sign of spiritual development, i.e. gratitude. Thus it is recited to express gratitude,[6] and equally to offer praise to the Eternal Living Spirit, as well as to eliminate pride and vanity. However, it is also enunciated for personal ambitions, and to actualize desires in harmony with Divine Will. As in the case of *Psalm 50*, the current psalm is said to support honesty and honest people, and is recited against injustice. We are told it imparts the purity of life, and offers support in dealing with domestic affairs. It is likely that these are the reasons why we are informed in one of the recensions of the *Shimmush Tehillim*, that *Psalm 100* is good for confessing sins.[7] In this regard, the practitioner is instructed to recite this psalm eighteen times whilst fasting, after each recitation saying:

יהי רצון מלפניך יהוה אלהי באתי לפניך יהוה
אלהי להתודות על חטאי חטאתי לפניך יהוה אלהי
[....insert details....] עשיתי ועתה אין לנו מזבח ולא
מקדש להקריב לפניך את קרבנות חובתינו על כן
התעניתי לפניך שתמחול ותסלח ותכפר לכל עונותי
ותקבלני בתשובה שלימה רצוייה לפניך כאמור אנכי

אנכי הוא מוחה פשעיך למעני [*Isaiah 43:25*] וימינך

פשוטה לקבל שבים על כן יהוה אלהי קבלני בתשובה

שלימה ותכפר עונותי ופשעי וקבל ברחמים ורצון

תעניתי וענויי בעבור כבוד שמך הגדול הגבור והנורא

יהו יח ידוי יהוה יהוה שמך יתברך לעולם ועד ויתקדש

אמן סלה

Transliteration:

> *y'hi ratzon mil'fanecha YHVH elohai bati lifanecha YHVH elohai l'hit'vadot al chata'ai chatati l'fanecha YHVH elohai [....insert details....] asiti v'atah ein lanu miz'be'ach v'lo mik'dash l'hak'riv l'fanecha et kor'banot chov'teinu al ken hit'aneiti l'fanecha sh'tim'chol v'tis'lach ut'chafer l'chol avonotai ut'kab'leni b't'shuvah sh'leimah r'tzuyah l'fanecha k'amur anochi anochi hu mocheh f'sha'echa l'ma'ani (Isaiah 43:25) vimin'cha p'shutah l'kabel shavim al ken YHVH elohai kab'le'ni b't'shuvah sh'leimah v't'chaper avonotai up'sha'ai v'kabel b'rachamim uratzon t'aniti v'inuyai b'avur kavod shim'cha hagadol hagibor v'hanora Yaho Yach Yih'vi YHVH shim'cha yit'varach l'olam va'ed v'yit'kadesh Omein Selah.*

Translation:

May it be your will *YHVH* my God, I have come before you *YHVH* my God to confess my transgressions. I have sinned before you *YHVH* my God, and I have done [....insert details....], and now we have no altar and no temple to offer the sacrifices of our duty before you. Therefore I fast before you that you may forgive and pardon, and atone for all my transgressions, and accept my complete repentance which is desired by you, as it is said "I, even I, am He that blotteth out thy transgressions for Mine own sake" (*Isaiah 43:25*), and your right hand is stretched out to receive those who repent. Therefore *YHVH* my God, receive me in complete repentance, and atone for my iniquities and my transgressions, and accept with mercy and kindness my fasting and my penitence, for the sake of the honour of your great, mighty, and awesome name *Yaho Yach Yih'vi YHVH*, sanctified be your Name throughout eternity, and be blessed, *Amen Selah.*[8]

Psalm 100 is further recommended in Jewish Magic for aid in defeating enemies.[9] In this regard, the standard published version of the *Shimmush Tehillim* maintains the psalm should be recited seven times. Godfrey Selig noted in his oft mentioned German/ English version of this text, that "whoever prays it several days successively seven times, will overcome all his enemies."[10] As in the case of *Psalms 96, 97* and *98*, the Divine Name יה (*Yah*) is associated with the current psalm.[11] One manuscript source informs us that this Divine Name was derived: י (*Yod*) from כ (*Kaf*) in טוב כי (*ki tov*—"is good"): verse 5, through the כ–י exchange, these letters being of the same Hebrew phonetic family, i.e. palatals; and ה (*Heh*) from ע (*Ayin*) in עבדו את יהוה (*iv'du et YHVH*— "Serve *YHVH*"): verse 2, again by means of the earlier mentioned ע–ה (*Heh/Ayin*) exchange.[12] Selig claims "the two letters of this holy name are recorded in verse 4, and in "*Aetodah*" [corruption of בתודה—*b'todah*], verse 4."[13] I am sure readers realise by now that much of Selig's statements regarding the magical use of psalms are seriously questionable. Whatever the case may be, a variant recension of the *Shimmush Tehillim* maintains the relevant Divine Name here to be וה (*Vav–Heh*).[14]

Whilst *Psalm 100* is listed in the *Shimmush Tehillim* for recitation in order to conquer or be victorious over enemies, I have seen this psalm recommended for other purposes. These include enunciation against all injustice, pride, vanity, and malice, as well as for protection in times of trouble, and in perilous situations. The current psalm is indicated to be for purity of life, honesty and honest people, and is also recited in support of ambitions, in dealing with domestic affairs, as well as to actualize desires in harmony with Divine Will. It is again one of the psalms recommended to express praise and gratitude. It is further employed against illness and for healing in general. In this regard, Rabbi Nachman of Bratzlav maintained the "Psalm of Thanksgiving" is a virtue for a woman suffering a difficult labour.[15] He substantiated this claim by linking "the screams of a woman in labour with *Psalm 100*." In this regard, he noted that the numerical value of the capitals of the words לתודה מזמור (*miz'mor l'todah*—"Psalm of Thanksgiving" [מ = 40 + ל = 30 =

70]), equals "the 70 screams that precede a birth."[16] I wonder who sat around in the delivery room for the express purpose of determining the exact number of screams emanating from a woman suffering the travails of childbirth! Whether this should be understood literally or interpreted more figuratively, we are further informed that the current psalm comprises קסח ("*KaSaCh*" [168]) letters. Whilst there is no elucidation regarding the importance of this number in this instance, we are told that transposing the Hebrew glyphs representing this number by means of the *Atbash* (א״ת ב״ש) cipher, results in the letters comprising the word חסד (*Chesed*— "Lovingkindness"). This is understood to mean that "through kindness the birth is made easy."[17] Before we focus on the use of the current psalm elsewhere, it should be noted that *Psalm 100:2* is directly associated with עשל (*Eshal*), the forty-seventh tri-letter portion of the "Name of Seventy-two Names."[18]

The hundredth Psalm is employed for a very different purpose in Christian magic. Rather than conquering enemies, or easing childbirth, it is utilised "against a mistress' hate." In this regard, the "*Livre d'Or*" instructs the practitioner to write the current psalm "on a raw eggshell," which is afterwards submerged in a glass of wine. The lady in question is then made to drink this psalm-infused beverage, and it is said "she will love you."[19]

PSALM 101

[1] לדוד מזמור חסד ומשפט אשירה לך יהוה‏אדני‏אהדונהי אזמרה

[2] אשכילה בדרך תמים מתי תבוא אלי אתהלך בתם לבבי בקרב ביתי

[3] לא אשית לנגד עיני דבר בליעל עשה סטים שנאתי לא ידבק בי

[4] לבב עקש יסור ממני רע לא אדע

[5] מלשני בסתר רעהו אותו אצמית גבה עינים ורחב לבב אתו לא אוכל

[6] עיני בנאמני ארץ לשבת עמדי הלך בדרך תמים הוא ישרתני

[7] לא ישב בקרב ביתי עשה רמיה דבר שקרים לא יכון לנגד עיני

[8] לבקרים אצמית כל רשעי ארץ להכרית מעיר יהוה‏אדני‏אהדונהי כל פעלי און

Transliteration:

[1] *l'david miz'mor chesed umish'pat ashirah l'cha YHVH azameirah*

[2] *as'kilah b'derech tamim matai tavo eilai et'haleich b'tom l'vavi b'kerev beiti*

[3] *lo ashit l'neged einai d'var b'liya'al asoh seitim saneiti lo yid'bak bi*

[4] *leivav ikeish yasur mimeni ra lo eida*

[5] *m'losh'ni vaseiter rei'eihu oto atz'mit g'vah einayim ur'chav leivav oto lo uchal*

[6] *einai b'ne'em'nei eretz lashevet imadi holeich b'derech tamim hu yishar'teini*

[7] *lo yeisheiv b'kerev beiti oseih r'miyah doveir sh'karim lo yikon l'neged einai*

[8] *lab'karim atz'mit kol rish'ei aretz l'hach'rit mei'ir YHVH kol po'alei aven*

Translation:

[1] A Psalm of David. I will sing of mercy and justice; unto Thee, *YHVH*, will I sing praises.

[2] I will give heed unto the way of integrity; Oh when wilt Thou come unto me? I will walk within my house in the integrity of my heart.

[3] I will set no base thing before mine eyes; I hate the doing of things crooked; it shall not cleave unto me.

[4] A perverse heart shall depart from me; I will know no evil thing.

[5] Whoso slandereth his neighbour in secret, him will I destroy; whoso is haughty of eye and proud of heart, him will I not suffer.

[6] Mine eyes are upon the faithful of the land, that they may dwell with me; he that walketh in a way of integrity, he shall minister unto me.

[7] He that worketh deceit shall not dwell within my house; he that speaketh falsehood shall not be established before mine eyes.

[8] Morning by morning will I destroy all the wicked of the land; to cut off all the workers of iniquity from the city of *YHVH*.

Psalm 101 is recommended in Jewish Magic against an evil spirit.[1] In this regard, we are informed in the *Shimmush Tehillim* to write the current psalm conjointly with *Psalm 68* on parchment.[2] Selig noted in his German/English version of this text, that the individual who carries the said parchment on his person, "is secure from persecution of evil spirits and vindictive persons."[3] However, the current psalm is listed in a variant recension of the *Shimmush Tehillim* for deliverance "from slanderers and from slander."[4] In this regard, the practitioner is advised to recite the hundred-and-first Psalm five times every day, concluding each recitation with the following prayer-incantation:

אזראל דכריאל סבריאל שתקיאל שמות מלאכים
קדושים שמרוני מכל מלשין ובל יוכל להלשין אותי
ולא לדבר עלי שום לשון הרע בשם שדי שוכן שחקים
אמן נצח סלה

Transliteration:

Ez'ra'el Dach'ri'el Sab'ri'el Shat'ki'el shemot malachim k'doshim sham'runi mikol mal'shin uval yuchal l'hal'shin

*oti v'lo l'daber alai shum lashon hara b'shem Shadai
shochen sh'chakim Omein Netzach Selah.*
Translation:
Ez'ra'el Dach'ri'el Sab'ri'el Shat'ki'el Names of Holy
Angels, save me from every slanderer, so that he cannot
slander me or spread any slander about me. In the Name of
Shadai who lives in the clouds. *Amen* Eternal *Selah.*[5]

It has been suggested that the expression "evil spirit" pertains to a
"dark mood," and thus the current psalm was suggested against a
bad mood. The magical applications of *Psalm 101* are a lot more
diverse in "unofficial sources." In this regard, it has been suggested
against fatigue, insomnia, and despair. It was also recommended
for recitation in days of great adversity, for safety from
persecution, and for the release of prisoners. It is further
enunciated as a support in the diminishing of poverty, and to
acquire food. I have seen the hundred-and-first Psalm employed
for healing purposes, i.e. injuries and damage of every kind,
diseases of the bones, and also for ailments and problems of the
heart. It was also recommended to couples who wish to ensure
conception. Other than that, it is recited for penitence, to affirm a
resolve to act properly between man and Divinity, for the release
of prisoners, and to find peace of soul.

As far as its use in Christian Magic is concerned, *Psalm
101* is listed in the Byzantine magical manuscripts for use against
contempt and enemies. In terms of overcoming enemies, the
practitioner is instructed to recite the current psalm over water, and
then to consume the liquid.[6] Elsewhere in the said manuscripts the
very same procedure is employed for an enemy who "says wicked
things against you."[7] In this regard, the magical action is concluded
with an instruction to "fulfill the Psalm at once,"[8] i.e. to destroy
"whoso slandereth," and to not suffer "whoso is haughty of eye
and proud of heart" (*Psalm 101:5*). Other than this, the current
psalm is referenced in the "*Livre d'Or*" for the purpose of
precluding the picking of grapes from a vineyard without
permission. In this regard, the psalm is copied with a set of magical
characters, which is afterwards buried "in the corners of your
vineyard."[9] Further instruction in the said text maintained the
hundred-and-first Psalm should be written on a glass plate, which

is then washed in holy water. The psalm is subsequently recited seven times over the said liquid, and the action concluded with the magically infused substance consumed by "an enchanted man," who is said "will be healed."[10]

PSALM 102

[1] תפלה לעני כי יעטף ולפני יהוה‎אהדונהי‎אדני‎
ישפך שיחו

[2] יהוה‎אהדונהי‎אדני‎ שמעה תפלתי ושועתי אליך
תבוא

[3] אל תסתר פניך ממני ביום צר לי הטה אלי
אזנך ביום אקרא מהר ענני

[4] כי כלו בעשן ימי ועצמותי כמוקד נחרו

[5] הוכה כעשב ויבש לבי כי שכחתי מאכל לחמי

[6] מקול אנחתי דבקה עצמי לבשרי

[7] דמיתי לקאת מדבר הייתי ככוס חרבות

[8] שקדתי ואהיה כצפור בודד על גג

[9] כל היום חרפוני אויבי מהוללי בי נשבעו

[10] כי אפר כלחם אכלתי ושקוי בבכי מסכתי

[11] מפני זעמך וקצפך כי נשאתני ותשליכני

[12] ימי כצל נטוי ואני כעשב איבש

[13] ואתה יהוה‎אהדונהי‎אדני‎ לעולם תשב וזכרך
לדר ודר

[14] אתה תקום תרחם ציון כי עת לחננה כי בא
מועד

[15] כי רצו עבדיך את אבניה ואת עפרה יחננו

[16] וייראו גוים את שם יהוה‎אהדונהי‎אדני‎ וכל מלכי
הארץ את כבודך

[17] כי בנה יהוה‎אהדונהי‎אדני‎ ציון נראה בכבודו

[18] פנה אל תפלת הערער ולא בזה את תפלתם

[19] תכתב זאת לדור אחרון ועם נברא יהלל יה

[20] כי השקיף ממרום קדשו יהוה‎אהדונהי‎אדני‎ משמים
אל ארץ הביט

[21] לשמע אנקת אסיר לפתח בני תמותה

[22] לספר בציון שם יהוה‎אהדונהי‎אדני‎ ותהלתו בירושלם

[23] בהקבץ עמים יחדו וממלכות לעבד את
יהוה‎אהדונהי‎אדני‎

[24] ענה בדרך כחי קצר ימי

[25] אמר אלי אל תעלני בחצי ימי בדור דורים
שנותיך

[26] לפנים הארץ יסדת ומעשה ידיך שמים

[27] המה יאבדו ואתה תעמד וכלם כבגד יבלו
כלבוש תחליפם ויחלפו

[28] ואתה הוא ושנותיך לא יתמו

[29] בני עבדיך ישכונו וזרעם לפניך יכון

Transliteration:

[1] *t'filah l'ani chi ya'atof v'lif'nei YHVH yish'poch sichu*

[2] *YHVH shim'ah t'filati v'shav'ati eilecha tavo*

[3] *al tas'teir panecha mimeni b'yom tzar li hateih eilai oz'necha b'yom ek'ra maheir aneini*

[4] *ki chalu v'ashan yamai v'atz'motai k'mokeid nicharu*

[5] *hukah cha'eisev vayivash libi ki shachach'ti mei'achol lach'mi*

[6] *mikol an'chati dav'kah atz'mi liv'sari*

[7] *damiti lik'at mid'bar hayiti k'chos choravot*

[8] *shakad'ti va'eh'yeh k'tzipor bodeid al gag*

[9] *kol hayom heir'funi oy'vai m'holalai bi nish'ba'u*

[10] *ki eifer kalechem achal'ti v'shikuvai biv'chi masach'ti*

[11] *mip'nei za'am'cha v'kitz'pecha ki n'satani vatash'licheini*

[12] *yamai k'tzeil natui va'ani ka'eisev ivash*

[13] *v'atah YHVH l'olam teisheiv v'zich'r'cha l'dor vador*

[14] *atah takum t'racheim tziyon ki eit l'chen'nah ki vah mo'eid*

[15] *ki ratzu avadecha et avaneha v'et afarah y'choneinu*

[16] *v'yir'u goyim et shem YHVH v'chol mal'chei ha'aretz et k'vodecha*

[17] *ki vanah YHVH tziyon nir'ah bich'vodo*

[18] *panah el t'filat ha'ar'ar v'lo vazah et t'filatam*

[19] *tikatev zot l'dor acharon v'am niv'ra y'halel Yah*

[20] *ki hish'kif mim'rom kod'sho YHVH mishamayim el eretz hibit*

[21] *lish'mo'a en'kat asir l'fatei'ach b'nei t'mutah*

[22] *l'sapeir b'tziyon shem YHVH ut'hilato birushalam*

[23] *b'hikaveitz amim yach'dav umam'lachot la'avod et YHVH*

[24] *inah vaderech kochi kitzar yamai*
[25] *omar eili al ta'aleini bachatzi yamai b'dor dorim sh'notecha*
[26] *l'fanim ha'aretz yasad'ta uma'aseih yadecha shamayim*
[27] *heimah yoveidu v'atah ta'amod v'chulam kabeged yiv'lu kal'vush tachalifeim v'yachalofu*
[28] *v'atah hu ush'notecha lo yitamu*
[29] *b'nei avadecha yish'konu v'zar'am l'fanecha yikon*

Translation:

[1] A Prayer of the afflicted, when he fainteth, and poureth out his complaint before *YHVH*.

[2] *YHVH*, hear my prayer, and let my cry come unto Thee.

[3] Hide not Thy face from me in the day of my distress; incline Thine ear unto me; in the day when I call answer me speedily.

[4] For my days are consumed like smoke, and my bones are burned as a hearth.

[5] My heart is smitten like grass, and withered; for I forget to eat my bread.

[6] By reason of the voice of my sighing my bones cleave to my flesh.

[7] I am like a pelican of the wilderness; I am become as an owl of the waste places.

[8] I watch, and am become like a sparrow that is alone upon the housetop.

[9] Mine enemies taunt me all the day; they that are mad against me do curse by me.

[10] For I have eaten ashes like bread, and mingled my drink with weeping,

[11] Because of Thine indignation and Thy wrath; for Thou hast taken me up, and cast me away.

[12] My days are like a lengthening shadow; and I am withered like grass.

[13] But Thou, *YHVH*, sittest enthroned for ever; and Thy name is unto all generations.

[14] Thou wilt arise, and have compassion upon Zion; for it is time to be gracious unto her, for the appointed time is come.

[15] For Thy servants take pleasure in her stones, and love her dust.

[16] So the nations will fear the name of *YHVH*, and all the kings of the earth Thy glory;

[17] When *YHVH* hath built up Zion, when He hath appeared in His glory;

[18] When He hath regarded the prayer of the destitute, and hath not despised their prayer.

[19] This shall be written for the generation to come; and a people which shall be created shall praise *Yah*.

[20] For He hath looked down from the height of His sanctuary; from heaven did *YHVH* behold the earth;

[21] To hear the groaning of the prisoner; to loose those that are appointed to death;

[22] That men may tell of the name of *YHVH* in Zion, and His praise in Jerusalem;

[23] When the peoples are gathered together, and the kingdoms, to serve *YHVH*.

[24] He weakened my strength in the way; He shortened my days.

[25] I say: 'O my God, take me not away in the midst of my days, Thou whose years endure throughout all generations.

[26] Of old Thou didst lay the foundation of the earth; and the heavens are the work of Thy hands.

[27] They shall perish, but Thou shalt endure; yea, all of them shall wax old like a garment; as a vesture shalt Thou change them, and they shall pass away;

[28] But Thou art the selfsame, and Thy years shall have no end.

[29] The children of Thy servants shall dwell securely, and their seed shall be established before Thee.'

Titled "a prayer for the afflicted," *Psalm 102* is one of a set of psalms enunciated in the Sefardi rite during the זמירות (*Z'mirot*—Hymns ["Verses of Song"]) section on *Yom Kippur* ("Day of Atonement").[1] It is likewise recited during יום כיפור קטן (*Yom Kippur Katan*—"Little Day of Atonement"), a monthly fast day observed by some Jewish pietists on the day prior to ראש חודש

(*Rosh Chodesh*), i.e. the celebration of the New Moon which marks the first day of the month in Judaism.[2]

As far as magical applications are concerned, we are told that *Psalms 102* and *103* are enunciated in order to have children.[3] In this regard, it was noted in the *Jewish Encyclopedia* that these two psalms are employed "against childlessness."[4] The standard published version of the *Shimmush Tehillim* maintains the current psalm is recited to seek mercy from the Eternal One for a barren (sterile) woman.[5] The associated Divine Name is said to be יה (*Yah*),[6] and we are informed in one recension of the *Shimmush Tehillim* that this Divine Name was derived: י (*Yod*) from the concluding letter in שמעה תפלתי (*shim'ah t'filati*—"hear my prayer"): verse 2; and ה (*Heh*) from the נ (*Nun*) in יכון (*yikon*—"shall be"): verse 29, the glyphs having been interchanged by means of the א"י ק בב"ר (*Ayak Bachar*) cipher.[7] Godfrey Selig, who addressed *Psalms 102* and *103* conjointly in his German/ English version of the *Shimmush Tehillim*, also noted that these psalms "are said to be very good for barren women by the use of which they may receive grace and favour from God."[8] However, he noted the said Divine Name was taken from "*Aneni*" (verse 3), a claim which equally remains unverified.[9]

The current psalm is also said to be good for support "in times of trouble."[10] In this regard, a very different application of *Psalm 102* is shared in a variant recension of the *Shimmush Tehillim*, one which pertains more to individuals seeking clemency from the Divine One on *Yom Kippur* ("Day of Atonement"), and protection from all manner of disaster which might befall them over the coming year. In this regard, we are instructed to recite *Psalm 102* "on the day of fasting," i.e. *Yom Kippur*, conjointly with the following prayer-incantation:

יהי רצון מלפניך אלהים חי מלך עולם שתעשה
שאלתי ותשיב אליך נפשי בשאלתי ובנתיבתי
ובבקשתי והצילני מחרב ומרעב ומדבר ומיגון
ואנחה ומעון ומשטן וממשחית ומכל אויב ואורב
בדרך ומכל מיני פורעניות הבאות המתחדשות
והמתרגשות בעולם בשם הנורא והאיום יה יה יה
יה יה יה יה אמן נצח סלה [repeat the Divine Names]

Transliteration:

> *y'hi ratzon mil'fanecha Elohim Chai melech olam sheta'aseh she'elati v'tashiv eilecha naf'shi b'she'elati uv'n'tivati ub'vakashati v'hatzileini meicherev umira'av umidever umiyagon va'anacha umei'avon umisatan umimash'chit umikol oyeiv v'orev baderech umikol minei pur'aniyot haba'ot hamit'chad'shot v'hamit'rag'shot ba'olam b'shem hanora v'ha'ayom Yah Yah Yah Yah Yah Yah Yah* [repeat the Divine Names] *Omein Netzach Selah*

Translation:

> May it be your will *Elohim Chai* (Living *Elohim*), King of the Universe, to grant my request. and that my soul shall respond to you in my request, and in my path, and in my petition. And deliver me from the sword, and from starvation, and from pestilence, and from grief, and from sighing, and from passing away, and from Satan, and from corruption, and from every enemy and highwayman, and from all kinds of coming calamities renewing and breaking out in the world. In the awesome and terrible name *Yah Yah Yah Yah Yah Yah Yah* [repeat the Divine Names], *Amen* Eternal *Selah*.[11]

Considering the sentiments expressed in this prayer-incantation, I am reminded of אוֹכֵץ (*'v'chitza*), a unique Divine Name construct which is in fact the word תפלה (*t'filah*— "prayer"), the first word of the current psalm, transposed by means of the *Atbash* (א״ת ב״ש) cipher. The vocalisation of the said Divine Name was derived from the initial vowels of the four words in *Psalm 102:1* reading תפלה לעני כי יעטף (*t'filah l'oni chi ya'atof*— "A Prayer of the afflicted, when he fainteth"). This Divine Name construct is also pronounced אוֹכֵץ (*'v'chitzi*), this enunciation having been derived from the concluding four words of the same verse reading ולפני יהוה ישפך שיחו (*v'lif'nei YHVH yish'poch sichu*—"and poureth out his complaint before *YHVH*").[12] We are told the numerical of this Divine Name [א = 1 + ו = 6 + כ = 20 + צ = 90 = 117] is equal to that of the words בן אדני (*Ben Adonai*— "Son of *Adonai*" [ב = 2 + ן = 50 + א = 1 + ד = 4 + נ = 50 + י = 10

= 117]). It is said that the "secret" of אורבץ ('v'chitza) is revealed only to those who know grace and kindness.[13] A Moroccan Jewish friend of mine maintained this Divine Name should be focused on mentally when giving charity. However, it features with other Divine Names in a number of lengthy prayer-incantations included in primary Hebrew texts, and especially in one which was written by Rabbi Chaim Yosef David Azulai for men to find life-partners.[14]

Be that as it may, I have seen *Psalm 102* recommended for recitation against all manner of threats, as well as for protection in perilous situations, and in times of trouble.[15] This psalm is also enunciated for higher officials to deal kindly with the general populace, and it is employed against suffering, affliction, and in support of the afflicted. It is further enunciated against illness, to promote healing, and for the gift of a cure. Interestingly enough, the capitals of the six words comprising *Psalm 102:2* were conjoined in the Divine Name construct ישה ואה, which is employed in amulets against epilepsy, and as a call for help.[16] The current psalm is also recited for the forgiveness of errors and transgressions, and to acquire the loyalty of good spirits.

From all appearances it would seem the current psalm is not particularly popular in Christian magic. However, the "*Livre d'Or*" recommends it to be recited "before leaving the house," which it maintains will cause one to "find only joy and happiness."[17] Other than this, it should be noted that in the "*Key of Solomon*" this psalm is one of nineteen enuciated over the wax from which ritual candles are manufactured, the complete set being *Psalms 8, 15, 22, 46, 47, 49, 51, 53, 68, 72, 84, 102, 110, 113, 126, 130, 131, 133,* and *139.*[18]

PSALM 103

‫[1] לדוד ברכי נפשי את יהו‪ה‬אדני־יאהדונהי וכל‬
‫קרבי את שם קדשו‬

‫[2] ברכי נפשי את יהו‪ה‬אדני־יאהדונהי ואל תשכחי‬
‫כל גמוליו‬

‫[3] הסלח לכל עונכי הרפא לכל תחלואיכי‬

‫[4] הגואל משחת חייכי המעטרכי חסד ורחמים‬

‫[5] המשביע בטוב עדיך תתחדש כנשר נעוריכי‬

‫[6] עשה צדקות יהו‪ה‬אדני־יאהדונהי ומשפטים לכל‬
‫עשוקים‬

‫[7] יודיע דרכיו למשה לבני ישראל עלילותיו‬

‫[8] רחום וחנון יהו‪ה‬אדני־יאהדונהי ארך אפים ורב‬
‫חסד‬

‫[9] לא לנצח יריב ולא לעולם יטור‬

‫[10] לא כחטאינו עשה לנו ולא כעונתינו גמל‬
‫עלינו‬

‫[11] כי כגבה שמים על הארץ גבר חסדו על‬
‫יראיו‬

‫[12] כרחק מזרח ממערב הרחיק ממנו את פשעינו‬

‫[13] כרחם אב על בנים רחם יהו‪ה‬אדני־יאהדונהי על‬
‫יראיו‬

‫[14] כי הוא ידע יצרנו זכור כי עפר אנחנו‬

‫[15] אנוש כחציר ימיו כציץ השדה כן יציץ‬

‫[16] כי רוח עברה בו ואיננו ולא יכירנו עוד‬
‫מקומו‬

‫[17] וחסד יהו‪ה‬אדני־יאהדונהי מעולם ועד עולם על‬
‫יראיו וצדקתו לבנו בנים‬

‫[18] לשמרי בריתו ולזכרי פקדיו לעשותם‬

‫[19] יהו‪ה‬אדני־יאהדונהי בשמים הכין כסאו ומלכותו‬
‫בכל משלה‬

‫[20] ברכו יהו‪ה‬אדני־יאהדונהי מלאכיו גברי כח עשי‬
‫דברו לשמע בקול דברו‬

[21] בַּרְכוּ יהוהאדניאהדונהי כל צבאיו משרתיו עשי
רצונו
[22] בַּרְכוּ יהוהאדניאהדונהי כל מעשיו בכל מקמות
ממשלתו ברכי נפשי את יהוהאדניאהדונהי

Transliteration:

[1] *l'david bar'chi naf'shi et YHVH v'chol k'ravai et shem kod'sho*

[2] *bar'chi naf'shi et YHVH v'al tish'k'chi kol g'mulav*

[3] *hasolei'ach l'chol avoneichi harofei l'chol tachalu'aichi*

[4] *hago'eil mishachat chayaichi ham'at'reichi chesed v'rachamim*

[5] *hamas'bi'a batov ed'yeich tit'chadeish kanesher n'uraichi*

[6] *oseih tz'dakot YHVH umish'patim l'chol ashukim*

[7] *yodi'a d'rachav l'mosheh liv'nei yis'ra'el alilotav*

[8] *rachum v'chanun YHVH erech apayim v'rav chased*

[9] *lo lanetzach yariv v'lo l'olam yitor*

[10] *lo chachata'einu asah lanu v'lo cha'avonoteinu gamal aleinu*

[11] *ki chig'vo'ah shamayim al ha'aretz gavar chas'do al y'rei'av*

[12] *kir'chok miz'rach mima'arav hir'chik mimenu et p'sha'einu*

[13] *k'racheim av al banim richam YHVH al y'rei'av*

[14] *ki hu yada yitz'reinu zachur ki afar anach'nu*

[15] *enosh kechatzir yamav k'tzitz hasadeh kein yatzitz*

[16] *ki ru'ach av'rah bo v'einenu v'lo yakirenu od m'komo*

[17] *v'chesed YHVH mei'olam v'ad olam al y'rei'av v'tzid'kato liv'nei vanim*

[18] *l'shom'rei v'rito ul'zoch'rei pikudav la'asotam*

[19] *YHVH bashamayim heichin kis'o umal'chuto bakol mashalah*

[20] *bar'chu YHVH mal'achav giborei cho'ach osei d'varo lish'mo'a b'kol d'varo*

[21] *bar'chu YHVH kol tz'va'av m'shar'tav osei r'tzono*

[22] *bar'chu YHVH kol ma'asav b'chol m'komot mem'shal'to bar'chi naf'shi et YHVH*

Translation:

[1] A Psalm of David. Bless *YHVH*, O my soul; and all that is within me, bless His holy name.

[2] Bless *YHVH*, O my soul, and forget not all His benefits;

[3] Who forgiveth all thine iniquity; who healeth all Thy diseases;

[4] Who redeemeth Thy life from the pit; who encompasseth thee with lovingkindness and tender mercies;

[5] Who satisfieth thine old age with good things; so that Thy youth is renewed like the eagle.

[6] *YHVH* executeth righteousness, and acts of justice for all that are oppressed.

[7] He made known His ways unto Moses, His doings unto the children of Israel.

[8] *YHVH* is full of compassion and gracious, slow to anger, and plenteous in mercy.

[9] He will not always contend; neither will He keep His anger for ever.

[10] He hath not dealt with us after our sins, nor requited us according to our iniquities.

[11] For as the heaven is high above the earth, so great is His mercy toward them that fear Him.

[12] As far as the east is from the west, so far hath He removed our transgressions from us.

[13] Like as a father hath compassion upon his children, so hath *YHVH* compassion upon them that fear Him.

[14] For He knoweth our frame; He remembereth that we are dust.

[15] As for man, his days are as grass; as a flower of the field, so he flourisheth.

[16] For the wind passeth over it, and it is gone; and the place thereof knoweth it no more.

[17] But the mercy of *YHVH* is from everlasting to everlasting upon them that fear Him, and His righteousness unto children's children;

[18] To such as keep His covenant, and to those that remember His precepts to do them.

[19] *YHVH* hath established His throne in the heavens; and His kingdom ruleth over all.

[20] Bless *YHVH*, ye angels of His, ye mighty in strength, that fulfil His word, hearkening unto the voice of His word. [21] Bless *YHVH*, all ye His hosts; ye ministers of His, that do His pleasure. [22] Bless *YHVH*, all ye His works, in all places of His dominion; bless *YHVH*, O my soul.

Psalm 103, as in the case of the previous psalm, is included in the set of psalms recited in the Sefardi rite during the זמירות (*Z'mirot* —Hymns ["Verses of Song"]) section on *Yom Kippur* ("Day of Atonement),[1] and it is likewise enunciated in Jewish Magic "against childlessness,"[2] as well as for seeking Divine mercy for barren women.[3] The associated Divine Name is said to be אה (*Alef–Heh* [*Aha*]?), and there is no indication as to its derivation in any of the recensions the *Shimmush Tehillim*.[4] As noted earlier, Godfrey Selig addressed *Psalms 102* and *103* conjointly, and whilst he shared the same details found in the standard editions of the said text, the derivations of the Divine Names respectively affiliated with these psalms are not referenced anywhere in its manuscripts or published versions.[5] In fact, in terms of the Divine Name aligned with *Psalm 103*, neither of the two words which Selig listed as the sources, i.e. "taken from the word *Adonai*, verse 12, and from *Sela*, verse 20" [my italics],[6] can be found anywhere in the mentioned verses, or in the entire psalm for that matter.

Be that as it may, the current psalm is employed for the atonement of transgressions, and we are informed in a variant recension of the *Shimmush Tehillim* that those who wish to ask something from their Creator, should enunciate the current psalm with its Divine Name יהו יהו יהו יהו יהו יהו יהו אל חי ונורא וקדוש (*Yaho Yaho Yaho Yaho Yaho Yaho Yaho El Chai v'Nora v'Kadosh*—"*Yaho Yaho Yaho Yaho Yaho Yaho Yaho Living God and Awesome and Holy*"), followed by the following prayer-incantation:

יהי רצון מלפניך שתעניני ברוב רחמיך וחסדיך ועשה
לי אשר נפשי שואלת ומתאוה מעמך שתעשה דבר זה
במהרה ובקרוב זמן תעשה הדבר אמן נצח סלה

Transliteration:

y'hi ratzon mil'fanecha sheta'aneini b'rov rachamecha
v'chas'decha v'aseh li asher naf'shi sho'elet umit'aveh
m'im'cha sheta'aseh davar zeh bim'heirah uv'karov z'man
ta'aseh hadavar Omein Netzach Selah.

Translation:

May it be your will to satisfy me with the abundance of
your mercy and grace, and do for me what my soul asks
and I desire of you. May you execute this task speedily,
and shortly fulfill the matter. *Amen* Eternal *Selah.*[7]

Once again the hundred-and-third Psalm is utilised amongst the
common folk for a variety of purposes. As with *Psalm 72*, the
current one is employed for the "discovery of sources." It is
recommended for the "fruits of the earth," and especially to
gardeners and farmers for the protection of gardens, vines and
vineyards, fields and crops, domestic animals, for the caring of
birds, as well as to ensure good hunting. *Psalm 103* is further
enunciated against severe storm clouds, for protection against
lightning, to ensure good weather, and for the wellbeing of
navigators and seamen. It is recited for protection in perilous
situations and times of trouble, and also to express gratitude. As
noted earlier, this very versatile psalm is recommended to women
who wish to have children,[8] however it is also employed to bring
on menstruation, as well as against illness, and for healing in
general. Interestingly enough, the capitals of the phrase in *Psalm
103:3* reading תחלואיכי לכל הרפא (*harofei l'chol
tachalu'aichi*— "who healeth all Thy diseases"), were formulated
into the Divine Name construct הלהת which is included in amulets
for healing purposes.[9] Other than this, *Psalm 103:19* and *Psalm
103:21* are respectively aligned directly with מבה (*Mivah*) and
כלי (*Keli*), the fifty-fifth and eighteenth tri-letter portions of the
"*Shem Vayisa Vayet.*"[10]

　　As far as the magical uses of the current psalm in Christian
Magic are concerned, *Psalms 103* and *104* are recommended in the
Byzantine magical manuscripts for conjoint application against
"windstorms" or "hailstorms" at sea. The instruction is to write the
two psalms, and place them on the deck of the boat. Following this

action, the psalms and a section of the "Gospel of John" are enunciated, whilst holding a black-hilted knife, and facing the wind, hail and water.[10] On the other hand, the *"Livre d'Or"* assures us that an individual will be healed if the current psalm is recited "seven times over common oil," and the body of the said individual rubbed therewith.[11] Elsewhere we are informed that *Psalm 103:7* and *8* are recited "to receive God's wisdom.[12]

PSALM 104

[1] ברכי נפשי את יהוה‎אדניˉ‎אהדונהי ‎יהוה‎אדניˉ‎אהדונהי‎אדניˉ‎אהדונהי
אלהי גדלת מאד הוד והדר לבשת

[2] עטה אור כשלמה נוטה שמים כיריעה

[3] המקרה במים עליותיו השם עבים רכובו
המהלך על כנפי רוח

[4] עשה מלאכיו רוחות משרתיו אש להט

[5] יסד ארץ על מכוניה בל תמוט עולם ועד

[6] תהום כלבוש כסיתו על הרים יעמדו מים

[7] מן גערתך ינוסון מן קול רעמך יחפזון

[8] יעלו הרים ירדו בקעות אל מקום זה יסדת
להם

[9] גבול שמת בל יעברון בל ישבון לכסות הארץ

[10] המשלח מעינים בנחלים בין הרים יהלכון

[11] ישקו כל חיתו שדי ישברו פראים צמאם

[12] עליהם עוף השמים ישכון מבין עפאים יתנו
קול

[13] משקה הרים מעליותיו מפרי מעשיך תשבע
הארץ

[14] מצמיח חציר לבהמה ועשב לעבדת האדם
להוציא לחם מן הארץ

[15] ויין ישמח לבב אנוש להצהיל פנים משמן
ולחם לבב אנוש יסעד

[16] ישבעו עצי יהוה‎אדניˉ‎אהדונהי ארזי לבנון אשר
נטע

[17] אשר שם צפרים יקננו חסידה ברושים ביתה

[18] הרים הגבהים ליעלים סלעים מחסה לשפנים

[19] עשה ירח למועדים שמש ידע מבואו

[20] תשת חשך ויהי לילה בו תרמש כל חיתו יער

[21] הכפירים שאגים לטרף ולבקש מאל אכלם

[22] תזרח השמש יאספון ואל מעונתם ירבצון

[23] יצא אדם לפעלו ולעבדתו עדי ערב

[24] מה רבו מעשיך יהוה‏אדני‏אהדונהי כלם בחכמה
עשית מלאה הארץ קנינך

[25] זה הים גדול ורחב ידים שם רמש ואין מספר
חיוה קטנות עם גדלות

[26] שם אניות יהלכון לויתן זה יצרת לשחק בו

[27] כלם אליך ישברון לתת אכלם בעתו

[28] תתן להם ילקטון תפתח ידך ישבעון טוב

[29] תסתיר פניך יבהלון תסף רוחם יגועון ואל
עפרם ישובון

[30] תשלח רוחך יבראין ותחדש פני אדמה

[31] יהי כבוד יהוה‏אדני‏אהדונהי לעולם ישמח
יהוה‏אדני‏אהדונהי במעשיו

[32] המביט לארץ ותרעד יגע בהרים ויעשנו

[33] אשירה ליהוה‏אדני‏אהדונהי בחיי אזמרה לאלהי
בעודי

[34] יערב עליו שיחי אנכי אשמח ביהוה‏אדני‏אהדונהי

[35] יתמו חטאים מן הארץ ורשעים עוד אינם ברכי
נפשי את יהוה‏אדני‏אהדונהי הללו יה

Transliteration:

    [1] *bar'chi naf'shi et YHVH YHVH elohai gadal'ta m'od hod v'hadar lavash'ta*

    [2] *oteh or kasal'mah noteh shamayim kay'ri'ah*

    [3] *ham'kareh vamayim aliyotav hasam avim r'chuvo ham'haleich al kan'fei ru'ach*

    [4] *oseh mal'achav ruchot m'shar'tav esh loheit*

    [5] *yasad eretz al m'choneha bal timot olam va'ed*

    [6] *t'hom kal'vush kisito al harim ya'am'du mayim*

    [7] *min ga'arat'cha y'nusun min kol ra'am'cha yeichafeizun*

    [8] *ya'alu harim yeir'du v'ka'ot el m'kom zeh yasad'ta lahem*

    [9] *g'vul sam'ta bal ya'avorun bal y'shuvun l'chasot ha'aretz*

    [10] *ham'shalei'ach ma'yanim ban'chalim bein harim y'haleichun*

    [11] *yash'ku kol chay'to sadai yish'b'ru fera'im tz'ma'am*

[12] *aleihem of hashamayim yish'kon mibein ofa'im yit'nu kol*

[13] *mash'keh harim mei'aliyotav mip'ri ma'asecha tish'ba ha'aretz*

[14] *matz'mi'ach hatzir lab'heimah v'eisev la'avodat ha'adam l'hotzi lechem min ha'aretz*

[15] *v'yayin y'samach l'vav enosh l'hatz'hil panim mishamen v'lechem l'vav enosh yis'ad*

[16] *yis'b'u atzei YHVH ar'zei livanon asher nata*

[17] *asher sham tziporim y'kaneinu chasidah b'roshim beitah*

[18] *harim hag'vohim lay'eilim s'la'im mach'seh lash'fanim*

[19] *asah yarei'ach l'mo'adim shemesh yada m'vo'o*

[20] *tashet choshech vihi lailah bo tir'mos kol chaito ya'ar*

[21] *hak'firim sho'agim lataref ul'vakeish mei'eil och'lam*

[22] *tiz'rach hashemesh yei'aseifun v'el m'onotam yir'batzun*

[23] *yei'tzei adam l'fo'olo v'la'avodato adei arev*

[24] *mah rabu ma'asecha YHVH kulam b'choch'mah asita mal'ah ha'aretz kin'yanecha*

[25] *zeh hayam gadol ur'chav yadayim sham remes v'ein mis'par chayot k'tanot im g'dolot*

[26] *sham oniyot y'haleichun liv'yatan zeh yatzar'ta l'sachek bo*

[27] *kulam eilecha y'sabeirun lateit och'lam b'ito*

[28] *titein lahem yil'kotun tif'tach yad'cha yis'b'un tov*

[29] *tas'tir panecha yibaheilun toseif rucham yig'va'un v'el afaram y'shuvun*

[30] *t'shalach ruchacha yibarei'un ut'chadeish p'nei adamah*

[31] *y'hi ch'vod YHVH l'olam yis'mach YHVH b'ma'asav*

[32] *ha'mabit la'aretz vatir'ad yiga beharim v'ye'eshanu*

[33] *ashirah laYHVH b'chayai azam'rah leilohai b'odi*

[34] *ye'erav alav sichi anochi es'mach baYHVH*

[35] *yitamu hata'im min ha'aretz ur'sha'im od einam bar'chi naf'shi et YHVH hal'lu Yah.*

Translation:

[1] Bless *YHVH*, O my soul. *YHVH* my God, Thou art very great; Thou art clothed with glory and majesty.

[2] Who coverest Thyself with light as with a garment, who stretchest out the heavens like a curtain;

[3] Who layest the beams of Thine upper chambers in the waters, who makest the clouds Thy chariot, who walkest upon the wings of the wind;

[4] Who makest winds Thy messengers, the flaming fire Thy ministers.

[5] Who didst establish the earth upon its foundations, that it should not be moved for ever and ever;

[6] Thou didst cover it with the deep as with a vesture; the waters stood above the mountains.

[7] At Thy rebuke they fled, at the voice of Thy thunder they hasted away—

[8] The mountains rose, the valleys sank down—unto the place which Thou hadst founded for them;

[9] Thou didst set a bound which they should not pass over, that they might not return to cover the earth.

[10] Who sendest forth springs into the valleys; they run between the mountains;

[11] They give drink to every beast of the field, the wild asses quench their thirst.

[12] Beside them dwell the fowl of the heaven, from among the branches they sing.

[13] Who waterest the mountains from Thine upper chambers; the earth is full of the fruit of Thy works.

[14] Who causeth the grass to spring up for the cattle, and herb for the service of man; to bring forth bread out of the earth,

[15] And wine that maketh glad the heart of man, making the face brighter than oil, and bread that stayeth man's heart.

[16] The trees of *YHVH* have their fill, the cedars of Lebanon, which He hath planted;

[17] Wherein the birds make their nests; as for the stork, the fir-trees are her house.

[18] The high mountains are for the wild goats; the rocks are a refuge for the conies.

[19] Who appointedst the moon for seasons; the sun knoweth his going down.

[20] Thou makest darkness, and it is night, wherein all the beasts of the forest do creep forth.

[21] The young lions roar after their prey, and seek their food from God.

[22] The sun ariseth, they slink away, and couch in their dens.

[23] Man goeth forth unto his work and to his labour until the evening.

[24] How manifold are Thy works, *YHVH!* In wisdom hast Thou made them all; the earth is full of Thy creatures.

[25] Yonder sea, great and wide, therein are creeping things innumerable, living creatures, both small and great.

[26] There go the ships; there is leviathan, whom Thou hast formed to sport therein.

[27] All of them wait for Thee, that Thou mayest give them their food in due season.

[28] Thou givest it unto them, they gather it; Thou openest Thy hand, they are satisfied with good.

[29] Thou hidest Thy face, they vanish; Thou withdrawest their breath, they perish, and return to their dust.

[30] Thou sendest forth Thy spirit, they are created; and Thou renewest the face of the earth.

[31] May the glory of *YHVH* endure for ever; let *YHVH* rejoice in His works!

[32] Who looketh on the earth, and it trembleth; He toucheth the mountains, and they smoke.

[33] I will sing unto *YHVH* as long as I live; I will sing praise to my God while I have any being.

[34] Let my musing be sweet unto Him; as for me, I will rejoice in *YHVH*.

[35] Let sinners cease out of the earth, and let the wicked be no more. Bless *YHVH*, O my soul. Hallelujah.

Psalm 104 is enunciated in Ashkenazi tradition after the Sabbath *Min'chah* (Sabbath afternoon prayer service) during the period commencing with the first Sabbath after סוכות (*Sukkot*—"Festival of Booths") and concluding with the first Sabbath prior to the celebration of פסח (*Pesach*—"Passover").[1] We are told that it is recited to make us mindful of the majesty of the Divine One "as revealed in creation."[2] It is further said that due to verse 19 reading "who appointedst the moon for seasons," the current psalm is also vocalised in all liturgies on *Rosh Chodesh* (the New Moon).[3] It is again one of the psalms which Sefardi tradition includes in the *Z'mirot* ("Hymns") section pronounced on *Yom Kippur*.[4]

Individual verses from *Psalm 104* feature equally prominently in Jewish liturgies. In this regard, a set of eighteen verses included in פְּסוּקֵי דְזִמְרָא (*P'sukei D'zimrah*), the "Verses of Song" recited during the morning prayer service (*Shacharit*), commences with *Psalm 104:31*. We are told this verse "was proclaimed by the Angel of the Universe (*Metatron*) when the plant world came forth after its kind" in accordance with the wishes of the Eternal One.[5] Consider also the custom of draping around the shoulders, or covering the head with a טַלִּית (*Talit*), a fringed prayer shawl, which is worn to humble "the heart of man," and cause the wearer to "pray with fear and awe."[6] It is customary to recite *Psalm 104:1–2* whilst examining the fringes of the טַלִּית (*Talit*—"prayer-shawl"), thus ensuring that they are properly separated before wrapping oneself in this special covering.[7]

It is worth noting that the current psalm lists two substances which, since days of yore, were considered to be the most primary as far as human wellbeing and sustenance are concerned, i.e. bread and wine, both of which are of great importance in Jewish worship. We are informed that "wine is a symbol of joy," and "bread serves as a symbol of all the necessaries of life,"[8] sentiments which were affirmed in *Psalm 104:15* telling us that it is "wine that maketh glad the heart of man," and "bread that stayeth man's heart." The great Jewish thinker Franz Rosenzweig eloquently summed up the power of these symbols saying: "Bread and wine are nothing but the ennobled gifts of earth, one is the basis of all the strength of life, the other of all its joy. Both were perfected in the youth of the world and of the people thereon, and neither can ever grow old. Every mouthful of bread, and every sip of wine tastes just as wonderful as the first we ever savored, and certainly no less wonderful than in time immemorial they tasted to those who for the first time harvested the grain for bread and gathered the fruits of the vine."[9] Thus the glorious symbols of bread, wine, together with light, are conjoined in celebrating the Sabbath, the day which "is likened to a bride in whose honor wine should be drunk to make her rejoice."[10]

As far as magical functions are concerned, *Psalm 104* is recommended for recitation when you wish to calm yourself from stress and pressures.[11] However, it is said this psalm is mainly utilised "to be rid of one's enemies,"[12] a statement reiterated in a number of sources in which it is vocalised for the purpose of driving away or distancing oneself from harmful forces.[13] Elsewhere the current psalm is listed "for killing-off pests, things causing harm or demons,"[14] and this application of *Psalm 104* was derived from the *Shimmush Tehillim* in which the current psalm is said to be "good for killing הַמַזִיק (*haMazik*—the injurious spirit [demon])."[15] In this regard, Godfrey Selig wrote in his German/English translation of this text, that "the frequent and earnest prayer of this Psalm is said to be attended with such great power, that through it the Masick may be destroyed."[16] Selig's Hebrew transliteration "*Masick*" is correctly rendered "*Mazik*," a term which is often translated "pest" or "pests" (*Mazikim*). Having understood this application also in a physical sense, the current psalm was recommended for recitation against threats, harmful pests and insects, and also for protection in perilous situations and times of trouble. On a more positive note, I have seen the hundred-and-fourth Psalm, like *Psalm 103*, employed for the "fruits of the earth"; for protection of vines and vineyards; to ensure good crops and good weather, but it is also enunciated for relief from a famine. It is further recommended for recitation when you are out in nature, for success in all manner of commerce, to give praise, and to express gratitude for good fortune. By contrast, *Psalm 104* is employed against ignorance and slavery, and to destroy the influence of the Satan. The latter application aligns with its earlier mentioned use to kill harmful spirits. In conclusion, the current psalm is recommended for recitation during childbirth, against illness and for healing in general, and to promote good health.

It should be noted that individual verses of this psalm are very important in understanding the *Shem Vayisa Vayet*, i.e. the "Name of Seventy-two Names." In this regard, *Psalm 104:16* and *Psalm 104:31* are directly affiliated with יֵזֵל (*Yezel*) and חֲחַשׁ (*Hachash*), i.e. the thirteenth and the fifty-first tri-letter portions of the "*Shem Vayisa Vayet.*[17] *Psalm 104:15* is indirectly aligned with וְהוּ (*Vehu*), the forty-ninth tri-letter portion of "*Name of Seventy-*

two Names." Furthermore, *Psalm 104:1* is indirectly affiliated with פהל (*Pahal*) and פוי (*Poi*), respectively the twentieth and fifty-sixth tri-letter portions of the *"Shem Vayisa Vayet."*[18] *Psalm 104:25* is likewise indirectly affiliated with both הזי (*Hezi*) and מיה (*Mih*), the ninth and forty-eighth tri-letter portions of the said Divine Name construct.[19]

As far as Christian Magic is concerned, and as noted earlier, *Psalms 103* and *104* are employed conjointly against "windstorms" in the Byzantine Christian magical manuscripts.[20] The current psalm is equally utilised in Christian Magic against "enemies that you fear."[21] In this regard, a rather sinister magical procedure involves tying the legs of frogs behind their backs with red silk thread, and then reciting the current psalm over them. Following this action, the unfortunate creatures are located "in a red earthenware vessel" inscribed with magical characters, and the said vessel sealed with clay prior to it being buried in a forgotten tomb.[22] Frogs and red threads feature equally for malignant purposes in Islamic Magic.[23] It saddens me that humans muster so little respect for life on this planet, that they would torture animal creatures to satisfy baleful impulses and carnal cravings. The *"Livre d'Or"* shares a procedure in which *Psalm 104* is fundamentally utilised to coerce an individual to yield to his desires. In this regard the name of the practitioner as well as that of the individual he desires, are written conjointly with those of her parents, and a set of magical characters. The writing is to be done with "the blood of a bat or that of a black hen onto the skin of a nanny-goat."[24] Afterwards the skin is placed in a cooking pot, covered in clay, and burned. The current psalm is recited a number of times as the skin burns, the intention being to magically turn on desire in the recipient for the practitioner.[25] I have abbreviated this procedure, since this book is about the application of the Hebrew biblical Psalms in Jewish Magic, and referencing their use in Christian magical practice is purely for comparative purposes.

PSALM 105

[1] הודו ליהו^{אדני יאהדונהי} קראו בשמו הודיעו בעמים עלילותיו

[2] שירו לו זמרו לו שיחו בכל נפלאותיו

[3] התהללו בשם קדשו ישמח לב מבקשי יהו^{אדני יאהדונהי}

[4] דרשו יהו^{אדני יאהדונהי} ועזו בקשו פניו תמיד

[5] זכרו נפלאותיו אשר עשה מפתיו ומשפטי פיו

[6] זרע אברהם עבדו בני יעקב בחוריו

[7] הוא יהו^{אדני יאהדונהי} אלהינו בכל הארץ משפטיו

[8] זכר לעולם בריתו דבר צוה לאלף דור

[9] אשר כרת את אברהם ושבועתו לישחק

[10] ויעמידה ליעקב לחק לישראל ברית עולם

[11] לאמר לך אתן את ארץ כנען חבל נחלתכם

[12] בהיותם מתי מספר כמעט וגרים בה

[13] ויתהלכו מגוי אל גוי ממלכה אל עם אחר

[14] לא הניח אדם לעשקם ויוכח עליהם מלכים

[15] אל תגעו במשיחי ולנביאי אל תרעו

[16] ויקרא רעב על הארץ כל מטה לחם שבר

[17] שלח לפניהם איש לעבד נמכר יוסף

[18] ענו בכבל רגלו ברזל באה נפשו

[19] עד עת בא דברו אמרת יהו^{אדני יאהדונהי} צרפתהו

[20] שלח מלך ויתירהו משל עמים ויפתחהו

[21] שמו אדון לביתו ומשל בכל קנינו

[22] לאסר שריו בנפשו וזקניו יחכם

[23] ויבא ישראל מצרים ויעקב גר בארץ חם

[24] ויפר את עמו מאד ויעצמהו מצריו

[25] הפך לבם לשנא עמו להתנכל בעבדיו

[26] שלח משה עבדו אהרן אשר בחר בו

[27] שמו בם דברי אתותיו ומפתים בארץ חם

[28] שלח חשך ויחשך ולא מרו את דברו

[29] הפך את מימיהם לדם וימת את דגתם

[30] שרץ ארצם צפרדעים בחדרי מלכיהם

[31] אמר ויבא ערב כנים בכל גבולם

[32] נתן גשמיהם ברד אש להבות בארצם

[33] ויך גפנם ותאנתם וישבר עץ גבולם

[34] אמר ויבא ארבה וילק ואין מספר

[35] ויאכל כל עשב בארצם ויאכל פרי אדמתם

[36] ויך כל בכור בארצם ראשית לכל אונם

[37] ויוציאם בכסף וזהב ואין בשבטיו כושל

[38] שמח מצרים בצאתם כי נפל פחדם עליהם

[39] פרש ענן למסך ואש להאיר לילה

[40] שאל ויבא שלו ולחם שמים ישביעם

[41] פתח צור ויזובו מים הלכו בציות נהר

[42] כי זכר את דבר קדשו את אברהם עבדו

[43] ויוצא עמו בששון ברנה את בחיריו

[44] ויתן להם ארצות גוים ועמל לאמים יירשו

[45] בעבור ישמרו חקיו ותורתיו ינצרו הללו יה

Transliteration:

[1] *hodu laYHVH kir'u vish'mo hodi'u va'amim alilotav*

[2] *shiru lo zam'ru lo sichu b'chol nif'l'otav*

[3] *hit'hal'lu b'shem god'sho yis'mach leiv m'vak'shei YHVH*

[4] *dir'shu YHVH v'uzo bak'shu fanav tamid*

[5] *zich'ru nif'l'otav asher asah mof'tav umish'p'tei fiv*

[6] *zera av'raham av'do b'nei ya'akov b'chirav*

[7] *hu YHVH eloheinu b'chol ha'aretz mish'patav*

[8] *zachar l'olam b'rito davar tzivah l'elef dor*

[9] *asher karat et av'raham ush'vo'ato l'yis'chak*

[10] *vaya'amideha l'ya'akov l'chok l'yis'ra'el b'rit olam*

[11] *leimor l'cha etein et eretz k'na'an chevel nachalat'chem*

[12] *bih'yotam m'tei mis'par kim'at v'garim bah*

[13] *vayit'hal'chu migoi el goi mimam'lacha el am acher*

[14] *lo hini'ach adam l'osh'kam vayochach aleihem m'lachim*

[15] *al tig'u vim'shichai v'lin'vi'ai al tarei'u*

[16] *vayik'ra ra'av al ha'aretz kol mateih lechem shavar*

[17] *shalach lif'neihem ish l'eved nim'kar yoseif*
[18] *inu vakevel rag'lo bar'zel ba'ah naf'sho*
[19] *ad eit bo d'varo im'rat YHVH tz'rafat'hu*
[20] *shalach melech vayatireihu mosheil amim vay'fat'cheihu*
[21] *samo adon l'veito umosheil b'chol kin'yano*
[22] *le'sor sarav b'naf'sho uz'keinav y'chakeim*
[23] *vayavo yis'ra'eil mitz'rayim v'ya'akov gar b'eretz cham*
[24] *vayefer et amo m'od vaya'atzimeihu mitzarav*
[25] *hafach libam lis'no amo l'hit'nakeil ba'avadav*
[26] *shalach mosheh av'do aharon asher bachar bo*
[27] *samu vam div'rei ototav umof'tim b'eretz cham*
[28] *shalach choshech vayach'shich v'lo maru et d'varo*
[29] *hafach et meimeihem l'dam vayamet et d'gatam*
[30] *sharatz ar'tzam tz'far'd'im b'chad'rei mal'cheihem*
[31] *amar vayavo arov kinim b'chol g'vulam*
[32] *natan gish'meihem barad esh lehavot b'ar'tzam*
[33] *vayach gaf'nam ut'einatam vaishabeir eitz g'vulam*
[34] *amar vayavo ar'beh v'yelek v'ein mis'par*
[35] *vayochal kol eisev b'ar'tzam vayochal p'ri ad'matam*
[36] *vayach kol b'chor b'ar'tzam reishit l'chol onam*
[37] *vayotzi'eim b'chesef v'zahav v'ein bish'vatav kosheil*
[38] *samach mitz'rayim b'tzeitam ki nafal pach'dam aleihem*
[39] *paras anan l'masach v'esh l'ha'ir lailah*
[40] *sha'al vayavei s'lav v'lechem shamayim yas'bi'eim*
[41] *patach tzur vayazuvu mayim hal'chu batziyot nahar*
[42] *ki zachar et d'var kod'sho et av'raham av'do*
[43] *vayotzi amo v'sason b'rinah et b'chirav*
[44] *vayitein lahem ar'tzot goyim va'amal l'umim yirashu*
[45] *ba'avur yish'm'ru chukav v'torotav yin'tzoru hal'lu Yah*

Translation:

[1] O give thanks unto *YHVH*, call upon His name; make known His doings among the peoples.

[2] Sing unto Him, sing praises unto Him; speak ye of all His marvellous works.

[3] Glory ye in His holy name; let the heart of them rejoice that seek *YHVH*.

[4] Seek ye *YHVH* and His strength; seek His face continually.

[5] Remember His marvellous works that He hath done, His wonders, and the judgments of His mouth;

[6] O ye seed of Abraham His servant, ye children of Jacob, His chosen ones.

[7] He is *YHVH* our God; His judgments are in all the earth.

[8] He hath remembered His covenant for ever, the word which He commanded to a thousand generations;

[9] The covenant which He made with Abraham, and His oath unto Isaac;

[10] And He established it unto Jacob for a statute, to Israel for an everlasting covenant;

[11] Saying: 'Unto thee will I give the land of Canaan, the lot of your inheritance.'

[12] When they were but a few men in number. Yea, very few, and sojourners in it,

[13] And when they went about from nation to nation, from one kingdom to another people,

[14] He suffered no man to do them wrong, yea, for their sake He reproved kings:

[15] 'Touch not Mine anointed ones, and do My prophets no harm.'

[16] And He called a famine upon the land; He broke the whole staff of bread.

[17] He sent a man before them; Joseph was sold for a servant;

[18] His feet they hurt with fetters, his person was laid in iron;

[19] Until the time that his word came to pass, the word of *YHVH* tested him.

[20] The king sent and loosed him; even the ruler of the peoples, and set him free.

[21] He made him lord of his house, and ruler of all his possessions;

[22] To bind his princes at his pleasure, and teach his elders wisdom.

[23] Israel also came into Egypt; and Jacob sojourned in the land of Ham.

[24] And He increased His people greatly, and made them too mighty for their adversaries.

[25] He turned their heart to hate His people, to deal craftily with His servants.

[26] He sent Moses His servant, and Aaron whom He had chosen.

[27] They wrought among them His manifold signs, and wonders in the land of Ham.

[28] He sent darkness, and it was dark; and they rebelled not against His word.

[29] He turned their waters into blood, and slew their fish.

[30] Their land swarmed with frogs, in the chambers of their kings.

[31] He spoke, and there came swarms of flies, and gnats in all their borders.

[32] He gave them hail for rain, and flaming fire in their land.

[33] He smote their vines also and their fig-trees; and broke the trees of their borders.

[34] He spoke, and the locust came, and the canker-worm without number,

[35] And did eat up every herb in their land, and did eat up the fruit of their ground.

[36] He smote also all the first-born in their land, the first-fruits of all their strength.

[37] And He brought them forth with silver and gold; and there was none that stumbled among His tribes.

[38] Egypt was glad when they departed; for the fear of them had fallen upon them.

[39] He spread a cloud for a screen; and fire to give light in the night.

[40] They asked, and He brought quails, and gave them in plenty the bread of heaven.

[41] He opened the rock, and waters gushed out; they ran, a river in the dry places.

[42] For He remembered His holy word unto Abraham His servant;

[43] And He brought forth His people with joy, His chosen ones with singing.

[44] And He gave them the lands of the nations, and they took the labour of the peoples in possession;
[45] That they might keep His statutes, and observe His laws. Hallelujah.

Ancient Jewish Tradition maintained that King David composed *Psalm 105* and *106* when the Ark of the Covenant was brought into Jerusalem,[1] and a variant of the current psalm was recited by the Levites during the morning sacrifices in the Second Temple in Jerusalem.[2] It has also been suggested that *Psalm 105* and *106* are early versions of the Passover *Haggadah*.[3] In point of fact, the hundred-and-fifth Psalm is recited on the first day of Passover,[4] and, as indicated previously, it is one of ten psalms comprising Rabbi Nachman of Bratslav's הַתִּיקוּן הַכְּלָלִי (*ha-Tikun ha-K'lali*).[5]

Jewish magical literature maintains *Psalm 105* is good to recite against "fourth *kedachat*,"[6] the latter expression having been delineated "quartan ague,"[7] i.e. a fever which occurs every four days. However, some maintain the term קְדַחַת (*Kedachat*) to be referencing "malaria,"[8] and the expression "fourth *Kedachat*" appears to have caused some confusion, with some maintaining it to be a fever which lasts four days,[9] whilst it is said elsewhere to be malaria which recurs a fourth time.[10] Godfrey Selig, who dealt with *Psalms 105* to *107* conjointly in his uncorroborated version of the *Shimmush Tehillim*, maintained that "according to the original writing, it is said, that the 105th Psalm will cure three days' fever."[11] This claim is not verified in the published Hebrew editions which I have perused, or in any of the surviving primary manuscripts of the said text. Whatever the original intention of the author of the *Shimmush Tehillim* may have been regarding the magical use of the hundred-and-fifth Psalm, it is recited today for the purpose of impacting any fever or malaria recurring every four days, or lasting four days.

Selig also maintained the current psalm to be aligned with the Divine Name יָהּ (*Yah*), claiming the latter to have been derived: י (*Yod*) "taken from Lejaikof, verse 7," which is probably יַעֲקֹב (*Ya'akov*—"Jacob"): verse 6; and ה (*Heh*) from הוֹדוּ (*Hodu* —"give thanks"): verse 1.[12] Whilst this statement is not substantiated in any of the primary Hebrew sources, the Ineffable Name (יהוה) features prominently in a variant recension of the *Shimmush Tehillim*. In this regard, an individual suffering the mentioned "fourth *Kedachat*," is instructed to copy *Psalm 105* as well as the following prayer-incantation, and to suspend the writing around his or her neck:

יְהַוֹךָ יֶהְוָהָ יֱהֶוָהָ יְהֶוֶהָ יְהֵוֶהָ יְהַוֶהָ יהוה יהוה שמע אל
עבדך ורפאהו וחזקהו ואמצהו והסר ממני כל החולי
הזה והרחיקהו ממני והצלילהו במעמקי ים לבל יעלה
עוד עלי אמן אמן אמן נצח סלה

Transliteration:

> *YiHaV'Ha YeiH'VaH YeH'VaH YiHeiVeiH' YiHeiVeiHa YiHaVaH' YHVH sh'ma El av'decha ur'feihu v'chaz'keihu v'am'tzeihu v'haseir mimeni kol hacholi hazeh v'har'chikeihu mimeni v'hatzileihu b'ma'amakei yam l'val ya'aleh od alei Omein Omein Omein Netzach Selah.*

Translation:

> *YiHaV'Ha YeiH'VaH YeH'VaH YiHeiVeiH' YiHeiVeiHa YiHaVaH' YHVH*, hear God your servant, and heal him, and strengthen him and fortify him. Turn all this sickness away from me, and remove it from me. Sink it into the depths of the sea, so that it may no longer rise above me. *Amen Amen Amen Eternal Selah*.[13]

As far as the healing properties of the current psalm is concerned, we are told that *Psalm 105:41–45* is good for healing the prostate.[14] Whilst very few verses from the hundred-and-fifth Psalm are employed for magical purposes, it is worth noting that *Psalm 105:1* is directly associated with לאו (*Lav*), the seventeenth tri-letter portion of the "Name of Seventy-two Names."[15] We might also consider the enigmatic Divine Name מיבון (*Meivon*), the origins of which is obscure, but the *gematria* of which [מ = 40 + י = 10 + ב = 2 + ו = 6 + ן = 50 = 108] is said to be equal to that of גיהנם (*Geihinom* —"hell" [ג = 3 + י = 10 + ה = 5 + נ = 50 + ם = 40 = 108]). It is said that this pertains to the fact that this Divine Name teaches a defence of Israel, and saves them from a state of hell.[16] The numerical value of the said Divine Name is also equal to that of the term חמס (*Chamas*— "violence" [ח = 8 + מ = 40 + ס = 60 = 108]), which we are told references the power of the Divine Name to save those who use the said Divine Name from robbery and violence.[17] As an aside, the word חמס (*Chamas*), when used as a verb, means "to rob with violence"). Employed as a noun, the same word references robbery, violence, cruelty, evildoing, and injustice. In this regard we read in the Hebrew Bible that "the earth was corrupt before God, and the earth was filled with חמס (*Chamas*—'violence')." [*Genesis 6:1*] This word appears numerous times in Sacred Writ in reference to violence and being unrighteous, which is rather apt in reference to the terrorist organisation bearing that title. Be that as it may, it was noted that the *gematria* of מיבון (*Meivon*) is equal to that of the word חק (*chak*—"statute" or "rule of law" [ח = 8 + ק = 100 = 8]). In this regard, it is maintained that this "statute" references *Psalm 105:9* and *10* in which we read, "The covenant which He made with Abraham, and His oath unto Isaac; And He established it unto Jacob for a statute, to Israel for an everlasting covenant." A "covenant" was sworn between the Patriarch Abraham and the Divine One, the seal of which is the sign of circumcision. Thus Abraham was circumcised at the age of 100 years, and his son יצחק (*Yitz'chak* [Isaac]), whose name includes חק (*chak*— "statute"), was circumcised at 8 days. In terms of the powers of the said Divine Name, it is said that "the son of the covenant will not see the face of גיהנם (*Geihinom*—'hell')."[18]

In conclusion, it should be noted that *Psalm 105* is again one of the psalms recommended against illness and for healing in general, as well as for protection in times of trouble and perilous situations. It is also said to be good for honesty and honest people, Divine Justice and equality, and to encourage justice for just people. It is further enunciated to express gratitude, and especially to offer thankfulness for good fortune. It is also said to be good to encourage good confidence, as well as humility. The current psalm is further employed against demonic practices, e.g. evil spells, etc.

In terms of the whole of jewry, the current psalm is recommended for "Divine Providence" to be declared through Jewish history.

In Christian Magic the hundred-and-fifth Psalm is recommended in the Byzantine Christian magical manuscripts to those who "are far away" and hated by "all the people there." Individuals who find themselves in such circumstances are advised to "fast for three days and speak the Psalm with a pure heart," and it is maintained they "will have peace with everyone."[21] Other than this application, we are informed that an individual who find themselves imprisoned for an inordinate length of time, should copy *Psalm 105* which is then attached to his or her arm. Following this action, the psalm is recited "during the day," and it is said the incarcerated individual "will be soon delivered."[22] In conclusion, it should be noted that in the *"Key of Solomon" Psalm 105:32–33* are imprinted around the outer borders of the *"Seventh Pentacle of Mars."*[23]

PSALM 106

‫[1] הללו יה הודו ליהוה‪אדני־יאהדונהי‬ כי טוב כי‬
‫לעולם חסדו‬

‫[2] מי ימלל גבורות יהוה‪אדני־יאהדונהי‬ ישמיע כל‬
‫תהלתו‬

‫[3] אשרי שמרי משפט עשה צדקה בכל עת‬

‫[4] זכרני יהוה‪אדני־יאהדונהי‬ ברצון עמך פקדני‬
‫בישועתך‬

‫[5] לראות בטובת בחיריך לשמח בשמחת גויך‬
‫להתהלל עם נחלתך‬

‫[6] חטאנו עם אבותינו העוינו הרשענו‬

‫[7] אבותינו במצרים לא השכילו נפלאותיך‬
‫לא זכרו את רב חסדיך וימרו על ים בים סוף‬

‫[8] ויושיעם למען שמו להודיע את גבורתו‬

‫[9] ויגער בים סוף ויחרב ויוליכם בתהמות‬
‫כמדבר‬

‫[10] ויושיעם מיד שונא ויגאלם מיד אויב‬

‫[11] ויכסו מים צריהם אחד מהם לא נותר‬

‫[12] ויאמינו בדבריו ישירו תהלתו‬

‫[13] מהרו שכחו מעשיו לא חכו לעצתו‬

‫[14] ויתאוו תאוה במדבר וינסו אל בישימון‬

‫[15] ויתן להם שאלתם וישלח רזון בנפשם‬

‫[16] ויקנאו למשה במחנה לאהרן קדוש‬
‫יהוה‪אדני־יאהדונהי‬‬

‫[17] תפתח ארץ ותבלע דתן ותכס על עדת‬
‫אבירם‬

‫[18] ותבער אש בעדתם להבה תלהט רשעים‬

‫[19] יעשו עגל בחרב וישתחוו למסכה‬

‫[20] וימירו את כבודם בתבנית שור אכל עשב‬

‫[21] שכחו אל מושיעם עשה גדלות במצרים‬

‫[22] נפלאות בארץ חם נוראות על ים סוף‬

‫[23] ויאמר להשמידם לולי משה בחירו עמד‬
‫בפרץ לפניו להשיב חמתו מהשחית‬

[24] וימאסו בארץ חמדה לא האמינו לדברו
[25] וירגנו באהליהם לא שמעו בקול
יהואהדונהי
[26] וישא ידו להם להפיל אותם במדבר
[27] ולהפיל זרעם בגוים ולזרותם בארצות
[28] ויצמדו לבעל פעור ויאכלו זבחי מתים
[29] ויכעיסו במעלליהם ותפרץ בם מגפה
[30] ויעמד פינחס ויפלל ותעצר המגפה
[31] ותחשב לו לצדקה לדר ודר עד עולם
[32] ויקציפו על מי מריבה וירע למשה
בעבורם
[33] כי המרו את רוחו ויבטא בשפתיו
[34] לא השמידו את העמים אשר אמר
יהואהדונהי להם
[35] ויתערבו בגוים וילמדו מעשיהם
[36] ויעבדו את עצביהם ויהיו להם למוקש
[37] ויזבחו את בניהם ואת בנותיהם לשדים
[38] וישפכו דם נקי דם בנהם ובנותיהם אשר
זבחו לעצבי כנען ותחנף הארץ בדמים
[39] ויטמאו במעשיהם ויזנו במעלליהם
[40] ויחר אף יהואהדונהי בעמו ויתעב
את נחלתו
[41] ויתנם ביד גוים וימשלו בהם שנאיהם
[42] וילחצום אויביהם ויכנעו תחת ידם
[43] פעמים רבות יצילם והמה ימרו בעצתם
וימכו בעונם
[44] וירא בצר להם בשמעו את רנתם
[45] ויזכר להם בריתו וינחם כרב חסדו
[46] ויתן אותם לרחמים לפני כל שוביהם
[47] הושיענו יהואהדונהי אלהינו וקבצנו
מן הגוים להדות לשם קדשך להשתבח בתהלתך
[48] ברוך יהואהדונהי אלהי ישראל מן העולם
ועד העולם ואמר כל העם אמן הללו יה

Transliteration:

[1] *hal'lu Yah hodu laYHVH ki tov ki l'olam chas'do*

[2] *mi y'maleil g'vurot YHVH yash'mi'a kol t'hilato*

[3] *ash'rei shom'rei mish'pat oseih tz'dakah v'chol eit*

[4] *zoch'reini YHVH bir'tzon amecha pok'deini bishu'atecha*

[5] *lir'ot b'tovat b'chirecha lis'mo'ach b'sim'chat goyecha l'hit'haleil im nachalatecha*

[6] *chatanu im avoteinu he'evinu hir'sha'nu*

[7] *avoteinu v'mitz'rayim lo his'kilu nif'l'otecha lo zach'ru et rov chasadecha vayam'ru al yam b'yam suf*

[8] *vayoshi'eim l'ma'an sh'mo l'hodi'a et g'vurato*

[9] *vayig'ar b'yam suf vayecherav vayolicheim bat'homot kamid'bar*

[10] *vayoshi'eim miyad sonei vayig'aleim miyad oyeiv*

[11] *vay'chasu mayim tzareihem echad meihem lo notar*

[12] *vaya'aminu vid'varav yashiru t'hilato*

[13] *miharu shach'chu ma'asav lo chiku la'atzato*

[14] *vayit'avu ta'avar bamid'bar vay'nasu el bishimon*

[15] *vayitein lahem she'elatam vaishalach razon b'naf'sham*

[16] *vaikan'u l'mosheh bamachaneh l'aharon k'dosh YHVH*

[17] *tif'tach eretz vativ'la datan vat'chas al adat aviram*

[18] *vativ'ar eish ba'adatam lehavah t'laheit r'sha'im*

[19] *ya'asu eigel b'choreiv vayish'tachavu l'maseichah*

[20] *vayamiru et k'vodam b'tav'nit shor ocheil eisev*

[21] *shach'chu el moshi'am oseh g'dolot b'mitz'rayim*

[22] *nif'la'ot b'eretz cham nora'ot al yam suf*

[23] *vayomer l'hash'midam lulei mosheh v'chiro amad baperetz l'fanav l'hashiv chamato meihash'chit*

[24] *vayim'asu b'eretz chem'dah lo he'eminu lid'varo*

[25] *vayeirag'nu v'oholeihem lo sham'u b'kol YHVH*

[26] *vayisa yado lahem l'hapil otam bamid'bar*

[27] *ul'hapil zar'am bagoyim ul'zarotam ba'aratzot*

[28] *vayitzam'du l'va'al p'or vayoch'lu ziv'chei meitim*

[29] *vayach'isu b'ma'al'leihem vatif'rotz bam mageifah*

[30] *vaya'amod pin'chas vay'faleil vatei'atzar hamageifah*

[31] *vateichashev lo litz'dakah l'dor vador ad olam*

[32] *vayak'tzifu al mei m'rivah vayeira l'mosheh ba'avuram*

[33] *ki him'ru et rucho vay'vatei bis'fataf*

[34] *lo hish'midu et ha'amim asher amar YHVH lahem*

[35] *vayit'ar'vu vagoyim vayil'm'du ma'aseihem*

[36] *vaya'av'du et atzabeihem vayih'yu lahem l'mokeish*

[37] *vayiz'b'chu et b'neihem v'et b'noteihem lasheidim*

[38] *vayish'p'chu dam naki dam b'neihem uv'noteihem asher zib'chu la'atzabei ch'na'an vatechenaf ha'aretz badamim*

[39] *vayit'm'u v'ma'aseihem vayiz'nu b'ma'al'leihem*

[40] *vayichar af YHVH b'amo vay'ta'eiv et nachal'to*

[41] *vayit'neim b'yad goyim vayim'sh'lu vahem son'eihem*

[42] *vayil'chatzum oy'veihem vayikan'u tachat yadam*

[43] *p'amim rabot yatzileim v'heimah yam'ru va'atzatam vayamoku ba'avonam*

[44] *vayar batzar lahem b'shom'o et rinatam*

[45] *vayiz'kor lahem b'rito vayinacheim k'rov chasadav*

[46] *vayitein otam l'rachamim lif'nei kol shoveihem*

[47] *hoshi'einu YHVH eloheinu v'kab'tzeinu min hagoyim l'hodot l'shem kod'shecha l'hish'tabei'ach bit'hilatecha*

[48] *baruch YHVH elohei yis'ra'el min ha'olam v'ad ha'olam v'amar kol ha'am omein hal'lu Yah*

Translation:

[1] Hallelujah. O give thanks unto *YHVH*; for He is good; for His mercy endureth for ever.

[2] Who can express the mighty acts of *YHVH*, or make all His praise to be heard?

[3] Happy are they that keep justice, that do righteousness at all times.

[4] Remember me, *YHVH*, when Thou favourest Thy people; O think of me at Thy salvation;

[5] That I may behold the prosperity of Thy chosen, that I may rejoice in the gladness of Thy nation, that I may glory with Thine inheritance.

[6] We have sinned with our fathers, we have done iniquitously, we have dealt wickedly.

[7] Our fathers in Egypt gave no heed unto Thy wonders; they remembered not the multitude of Thy mercies; but were rebellious at the sea, even at the Red Sea.

[8] Nevertheless He saved them for His name's sake, that He might make His mighty power to be known.

[9] And He rebuked the Red Sea, and it was dried up; and He led them through the depths, as through a wilderness.

[10] And He saved them from the hand of him that hated them, and redeemed them from the hand of the enemy.

[11] And the waters covered their adversaries; there was not one of them left.

[12] Then believed they His words; they sang His praise.

[13] They soon forgot His works; they waited not for His counsel;

[14] But lusted exceedingly in the wilderness, and tried God in the desert.

[15] And He gave them their request; but sent leanness into their soul.

[16] They were jealous also of Moses in the camp, and of Aaron the holy one of *YHVH*.

[17] The earth opened and swallowed up Dathan, and covered the company of Abiram.

[18] And a fire was kindled in their company; the flame burned up the wicked.

[19] They made a calf in Horeb, and worshipped a molten image.

[20] Thus they exchanged their glory for the likeness of an ox that eateth grass.

[21] They forgot God their saviour, who had done great things in Egypt;

[22] Wondrous works in the land of Ham, terrible things by the Red Sea.

[23] Therefore He said that He would destroy them, had not Moses His chosen stood before Him in the breach, to turn back His wrath, lest He should destroy them.

[24] Moreover, they scorned the desirable land, they believed not His word;

[25] And they murmured in their tents, they hearkened not unto the voice of *YHVH*.

[26] Therefore He swore concerning them, that He would overthrow them in the wilderness;

[27] And that He would cast out their seed among the nations, and scatter them in the lands.

[28] They joined themselves also unto Baal of Peor, and ate the sacrifices of the dead.

[29] Thus they provoked Him with their doings, and the plague broke in upon them.

[30] Then stood up Phinehas, and wrought judgment, and so the plague was stayed.

[31] And that was counted unto him for righteousness, unto all generations for ever.

[32] They angered Him also at the waters of Meribah, and it went ill with Moses because of them;

[33] For they embittered his spirit, and he spoke rashly with his lips.

[34] They did not destroy the peoples, as *YHVH* commanded them;

[35] But mingled themselves with the nations, and learned their works;

[36] And they served their idols, which became a snare unto them;

[37] Yea, they sacrificed their sons and their daughters unto demons,

[38] And shed innocent blood, even the blood of their sons and of their daughters, whom they sacrificed unto the idols of Canaan; and the land was polluted with blood.

[39] Thus were they defiled with their works, and went astray in their doings.

[40] Therefore was the wrath of *YHVH* kindled against His people, and He abhorred His inheritance.

[41] And He gave them into the hand of the nations; and they that hated them ruled over them.

[42] Their enemies also oppressed them, and they were subdued under their hand.

[43] Many times did He deliver them; but they were rebellious in their counsel, and sank low through their iniquity.

[44] Nevertheless He looked upon their distress, when He heard their cry;

[45] And He remembered for them His covenant, and repented according to the multitude of His mercies.

[46] He made them also to be pitied of all those that carried them captive.

[47] Save us, *YHVH* our God, and gather us from among the nations, that we may give thanks unto Thy holy name, that we may triumph in Thy praise.

[48] Blessed be *YHVH*, the God of Israel, from everlasting even to everlasting, and let all the people say: 'Amen.' Hallelujah.

Psalm 106 concludes the fourth Book of Psalms. As mentioned earlier, *Psalm 105* and *106* are believed to be early versions of the Passover *Haggadah*,[1] and the hundred-and-sixth Psalm is recited on the second day of פֶסַח (*Pesach*—"Passover").[2] Other than this, selected verses from the current psalm are incorporated in Jewish liturgies.[3] Whilst the use of this psalm appears to be somewhat minimal in Jewish worship, it features fairly prominently in Jewish Magic. In this regard, *Psalm 106* is said in the *Shimmush Tehillim* to be good for "a third *Kedachat*,"[4] which is depicted "tertian ague," i.e. a fever or a kind of malaria "which recurs every third day."[5] However, some maintain this to be a fever which lasts three days,[6] or malaria which recurs a third time.[7] It is said the Divine Name וָה (*Vav–Heh*) is associated with this psalm,[8] which one recension of the *Shimmush Tehillim* maintains was derived: ו (*Vav*) from the concluding letter of הוֹדוּ (*Hodu*—"give thanks"): verse 1; and ה (*Heh*) from the concluding glyph of the expression הַלְלוּ יָהּ ("*Hallelujah*"): verse 48.[9]

In some of the published Hebrew editions of the *Shimmush Tehillim* it is maintained that the current psalm is good to recite for "perpetual fever," and it is said the affiliated Divine Name is יָהּ (*Yah*).[10] In his German/English version of this text, Godfrey Selig maintains *Psalm 106* "will cure the four days' fever," and that the Divine Name יָהּ (*Yah*) is associated with the current psalm. In this regard, he maintains this Divine Name to have been derived: י (*Yod*) from זָכְרֵנִי (*zoch'reini*—"remember me"): verse 2; and ה (*Heh*) from תְּהִלָּתוֹ (*t'hilato*—"His praise"): verse 2.[11] Once again I have to date found no verification of these claims in any of the existing primary sources. However, in terms of its standard application against "a three day fever," one recension of the *Shimmush Tehillim* maintains it is good to write the current psalm both in regular as well as in reverse order. This is done in the Name יָהּ אכתיאל (*Yah Achat'ri'el*), which is employed in conjunction with the following prayer-incantation:

[....name of recipient....] יה אכתריאל רפא נא לזה

והסר ממנו הקדחת השלישית הזאת ולא תוכל עוד

לגעת בו ולא באחד ממאתיים וארבעים ושמונה

איברים שבו בשם נוטה שמים כיריעה (*Psalm 104:2*)

ויתלה בזרועו השמאלית יפה ונאה אמן נצח סלה

Transliteration:

> *Yah Achat'ri'el r'fa na l'zeh* [....name of recipient....]
> *v'haseir mimenu hakadachat hash'lishit hazot v'lo tuchal*
> *od laga'at bo v'lo b'echad mimatayim v'ar'ba'im*
> *ush'monah eivarim shebo b'shem noteh shamayim*
> *kay'ri'ah* (*Psalm 104:2*). *Omein Netzach Selah.*

Translation:

> *Yah Achat'ri'el* please heal this [....name of recipient....],
> and remove this three days fever from him, and it should
> no longer be able to strike him down, and not one of the
> 248 limbs that are within him. In the name "who stretchest
> out the heavens like a curtain" (*Psalm 104:2*). *Amen*
> Eternal *Selah*.

The writing is afterwards suspended on the left arm of the one
suffering the fever.[12]

As far as the use of individual verses for magical purposes
are concerned, it is worth noting that another וה (*Vav–Heh*)
Divine Name construct was formulated from the initials of the
concluding two words of *Psalm 106:30* reading ותעצר המגפה
(*vatei'atzar hamageifah*—"and so the plague was stayed"), and
was employed in amulets against the plague.[13] However, the entire
verse comprising five words of exactly five letters each, is one of
the most popular in *Practical Kabbalah*, and, as I noted elsewhere,
"is employed in the form of a 'word square,' as an amulet for a
variety of important purposes as far as basic human survival on this
planet is concerned."[14] In this regard, the said word square is
employed to keep one from all of the baneful forces one may
encounter in ones life, i.e. diseases, the evil eye, evil spirits, and
even from being stoned to death, this construct features mainly in
amulets pertaining to protection against plagues and epidemics.[15]
As indicated below, the word square appears in mainly two
formats:

ד	מה	עו	יה	יי
ס	חה	נו	יה	פי
ל	לה	פו	יה	וי
ר	צה	עו	תה	יי
ה	פה	גו	מה	חי

ה	וה	וו	פה	יי
מ	תי	יה	יו	יה
ג	עה	פי	נה	עו
פ	צו	לה	חי	מה
ה	רה	לו	סה	די

As indicated, twenty letters from this verse are individually conjoined with single letters of the Ineffable Name, and this is accomplished in two ways. As I noted elsewhere, "in the first version the letter י (*Yod*) is aligned with the initials of the five words comprising the said verse; the first ה (*Heh*) of the Explicit Name with the second letter of each word; the letter ו (*Vav*) with the third; and the concluding ה (*Heh*) with the fourth letter of each word. The concluding letter of the five words is left 'unsupported' by the Ineffable Name. In the second version, the four glyphs comprising the *Tetragrammaton* are simply added in exact marching order to the first twenty letters of the verse."[16] The word square is applied in a number of ways, and I have seen a variety of application of this amulet ranging from the most basic to quite complex.[17] The least complicated application is to simply copy it on parchment, or a clean sheet of paper, with a subscript delineating its purpose. In this regard, a number of examples are located in the Wellcome Collection. and the following *Kamea* is one of the simplest in the said collection:[18]

וי	פה	וו	וה	ה
יה	יו	יה	תי	מ
עו	נה	פי	עה	ג
מה	חי	לה	צו	פ
די	סה	לו	רה	ה

שמירה והגנה ל....[פב״פ.....] מדבר
וממגפה ומאבן נגף מו״ע א״ס

The format of the *Kamea* comprises the word square drawn on the upper portion of a piece of deerskin parchment, with the subscript delineating its protective purposes, and including the name of the owner, located directly below. Since the amulet was meant to be carried on the person of the individual for whom it was created, it was located in a slightly larger square leather envelope. As noted elsewhere, "you could employ the exact inscription, and simply insert your own name, or that of the intended bearer of the amulet, in the space marked פב״פ [*Ploni ben Ploni*]. This is the standard manner in Jewish magical texts of saying 'so and so,' in order to indicate where you should insert your own name, or that of the individual for whom the amulet is intended."[19] The abbreviations at the end, refer to an expression sometimes used in protection *Kameot* reading מעתה ועד עולם אמן סלה. The inscription below the word square reads:

שמירה והגנה ל[....name of the recipient....] מדבר
וממגפה ומאבן מעתה ועד עולם אמן סלה

Transliteration:
> Sh'mirah v'haganah l'[....name of the recipient....] mideber u'mimagefah umi'aven negef mei'atah v'ad olam Omein Selah.

Translation:
> Protection and safety for [....name of the recipient....] from pestilence and from plagues, and from being stoned, from now unto eternity *Amen Selah.*

As can be expected, there are yet more complex presentations of this amulet, as can be seen in the following *Kamea* listed amongst a set of magical recipes in an anonymous magical manuscript in the Wellcome Collection:[20]

אגלא אהיה ילאל

מה	עו	יה	וי
חה	נה	יה	פי
לה	פו	יה	וי
צה	עו	תה	וי
פה	גי	מא	הי

אבגיתץ קרע שטן שדי

אכתריאל שמריאל ישמור הנושא קמיע
זו ממגיפה ומדבר ומכל חולי ומעין
הרע ומרוח רע מעתה ועד עולם אמן
וכן יהי רצון

Transliterated the concluding prayer-incantation reads:

Achatri'el Sham'ri'el yish'mor hanose kamia zo mimagefah umideber umikol choli umi'ayin hara umiru'ach ra me'atah v'ad olam Omein v'chen y'hi ratzon

Translation:

Achatri'el Shamri'el protect the carrier of this amulet from plagues and pestilence, and from all disease, and from the evil eye, and from evil spirits, from now unto eternity *Amen* and thus be it so willed.

The five concluding letters of the words employed in formatting the *Kamea*, are located external to the actual word square, and the entire construct is encircled with Divine and Angelic Names:

(Top) *Agala'a Eh'yeh Yelel*
(Bottom) *Avgitatz K'ra Satan Shadai*
(Right) *Ori'el Eh'yeh*
(Left) *Nuri'el Eh'yeh*

I have addressed these Divine/Angelic Names in fair detail in previous volumes.[21] Conjoining the letters of the five words comprising *Psalm 106:30* with the four glyphs of the Ineffable Name, also resulted in five unique Divine Name constructs incorporated in the following חותם (*chotam*—"magical seal"):

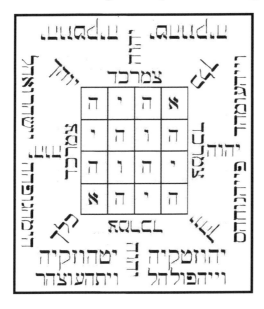

The said four Divine Name constructs are:

(Right) וייהעומהד פייהנוחהם

(Lower Bottom) וייהפולהל ויתהעוצהר

(Left) הימהגופהה

The second Divine Name construct on the left reading יישהרואהל, was formulated from the word ישראל intertwined with the Ineffable Name.[22] As noted elsewhere, "it has been suggested that the name of the individual requiring the support of this amulet, should be conjoined with the four letters of the

Ineffable Name in the same manner, and included in lieu of the latter concluding Divine Name combination. Whilst I am not sure how 'kosher' this recommendation is, it will certainly personalise the *Kamea* in a most powerful manner."[23] Whatever the case may be, this magical seal feature in a number of amulets, including the following one formulated for the alleviation of plagues, smallpox, chicken-pox, measels, etc.:

This amulet commences with the following prayer-incantation which should be written at the top of the scroll or page:

יהי רצון מלפניך יהוה אלהי ואלהי אבותי עשה למען
קדושת שמותיך אנקתם פסתם פספסים דיונסים
אבגיתץ קרעשטן נגדיכש בטרצתג חקבטנע
יגלפזק שקוצית ובזכות שם עשציי שתחום ותחמול
ותחון ותגן אל [....name of the recipient....] נושא קמיע זה
עליו מכל מרעין בישין ומחולי אבעבועות אמן נצח
סלה ועד

Transliteration:

> *Y'hi ratzon milfanecha YHVH Elohai v'Elohei avotai aseh l'ma'an k'dushat sh'motecha Anaktam Pastam Paspasim Dionsim Av'gitatz Karastan Nag'dichesh Batratz'tag Chak'vet'na Yag'lef'zok Shakutzit v'biz'chut shem Ashtzei shetachus v'tach'mol v'tachon v'tagen al [....name of the recipient....] nose kame'a zeh alav m'chol mere'in b'ishin um'cholei aba'abu'ot Omein Netzach Selah va'ed.*

Translation:

> May it be your will *YHVH* my God, and God of my fathers, act for the sake of the holiness of Your Names, *Anaktam Pastam Paspasim Dionsim, Av'gitatz Karastan Nag'dichesh Bat'ratz'tag Chak'vet'na Yag'lef'zok Shakutzit,* and in the merit of the Name *Ashtzei,* to spare and have mercy and pity and protect [.....name of the recipient.....], the bearer of this amulet, from all evil doers and bad spirits, and the illness of pox, *Amen,* Enduring, *Selah* throughout eternity.[24]

Below the prayer-incantation is the *Kamea* construct proper, which includes a set of Divine Names which I have addressed in some detail in a previous volume in this series of texts on Jewish Magic.[25] The amulet is completed with the following written adjuration, which repeats some of the sentiments expressed in the opening prayer-incantation:

[....name of recipient....] אסותא מן שמיא תיהוי ל
נושא קמיע זהעליו מעין הרע ומכל מרעין בישין
ומחולי אבעבועות ומכל מיני חולאים ומבכיה
בעגלא ברחמי שמייא מאן דאמר והוה עלמא אמן
נצח סלה ועד

Transliteration:

> *Asuta min sh'maya tihavi l'[....name of recipient....] nose
> kamea zeh alav m'ayin ha'ra v'm'kol mera'in b'ishin
> v'micholi aba'abu'ot um'kol minei chola'im umib'chiyah
> ba'agala b'rachamei sh'maya me'ein d'amar vahava alma
> Omein Netzach Selah va'ed.*

Translation:

> May there be Healing from Heaven for [.....name of
> recipient.....], the bearer of this amulet, from the Evil Eye,
> and from all evil doers and bad spirits, and the sickness of
> pox, and from all bad illness and from all lamentation
> speedily, with mercy from heaven and who speaks unto
> eternity *Amen*, Enduring, *Selah* throughout eternity.[26]

Whilst *Psalm 106* is recommended against fevers, I have noticed
it being enunciated in "unofficial sources" against diseases of the
spine. It is further used against disaster generally, especially those
of the unforseen kind, and is also recited against ignorance and
despair, as well as to receive grace and mercy. It is employed for
"discoveries," and is vocalised for the wellbeing of navigators and
seamen. In this regard, this psalm is uttered against storms in
general, and against sea-sickness for that matter. The current psalm
is further said to be good for the home, a good wind, and the "fruits
of the earth," hence it is voiced for the protection of vines and
vineyards, gardens, fields, and domestic animals. In conclusion, it
should be noted that *Psalm 106:2* is directly affiliated with ילדה
(*Yelah*), the forty-fourth tri-letter portion of the "Name of Seventy-
two Names."[27]

It would seem the hundred-and-sixth Psalm is not
particularly popular in Christian Magic. However, similar to the
employment of this psalm in Jewish Magic, *Psalm 106:4* is recited
against malaria.[28] Other than that, the current psalm was

recommended for recitation "to sink a sailing ship." In this regard, the psalm is recited seven times over salt, following which it is said the vessel will sink when the salt is cast "where the sails have been spread."[29]

. ...Because no one told him to stop, he kept on bringing water and pouring it into the barrels, even though they were already full....When members of the household noticed the water suddenly gushing on the floor of the house, they became frightened and astounded. 'Water! Water!" they began shouting... ... .

Chapter 6
Ma'arav — West
The Psalms of David — Book V

PSALM 107

[1] הדו ליהוה‎אדני‎יאהדונהי כי טוב כי לעולם חסדו

[2] יאמרו גאולי יהוה‎אדני‎יאהדונהי אשר גאלם מיד צר

[3] ומארצות קבצם ממזרח וממערב מצפון ומים

[4] תעו במדבר בישימון דרך עיר מושב לא מצאו

[5] רעבים גם צמאים נפשם בהם תתעטף

[6] ויצעקו אל יהוה‎אדני‎יאהדונהי בצר להם
ממצוקותיהם יצילם

[7] וידריכם בדרך ישרה ללכת אל עיר מושב

[8] יודו ליהוה‎אדני‎יאהדונהי חסדו ונפלאותיו לבני
אדם

[9] כי השביע נפש שקקה ונפש רעבה מלא טוב

[10] ישבי חשך וצלמות אסירי עני וברזל

[11] כי המרו אמרי אל ועצת עליון נאצו

[12] ויכנע בעמל לבם כשלו ואין עזר

[13] ויזעקו אל יהוה‎אדני‎יאהדונהי בצר להם
ממצקותיהם יושיעם

[14] יוציאם מחשך וצלמות ומוסרותיהם ינתק

[15] יודו ליהוה‎אדני‎יאהדונהי חסדו ונפלאותיו לבני
אדם

[16] כי שבר דלתות נחשת ובריחי ברזל גדע

[17] אולים מדרך פשעם ומעונתיהם יתענו

[18] כל אכל תתעב נפשם ויגיעו עד שערי מות

[19] ויזעקו אל יהוה‎אדני‎יאהדונהי בצר להם
ממצקותיהם יושיעם

[20] ישלח דברו וירפאם וימלט משחיתותם

[21] יודו ליהוה‎אהדנ‎יה‎אהדונהי חסדו ונפלאותיו לבני אדם

[22] ויזבחו זבחי תודה ויספרו מעשיו ברנה

[23] יורדי הים באניות עשי מלאכה במים רבים

[24] המה ראו מעשי יהוה‎אהדנ‎יה‎אהדונהי ונפלאותיו במצולה

[25] ויאמר ויעמד רוח סערה ותרומם גליו

[26] יעלו שמים ירדו תהומות נפשם ברעה תתמוגג

[27] יחוגו וינועו כשכור וכל חכמתם תתבלע

[28] ויצעקו אל יהוה‎אהדנ‎יה‎אהדונהי בצר להם וממצוקתיהם יוציאם

[29] יקם סערה לדממה ויחשו גליהם

[30] וישמחו כי ישתקו וינחם אל מחוז חפצם

[31] יודו ליהוה‎אהדנ‎יה‎אהדונהי חסדו ונפלאותיו לבני אדם

[32] וירוממוהו בקהל עם ובמושב זקנים יהללוהו

[33] ישם נהרות למדבר ומצאי מים לצמאון

[34] ארץ פרי למלחה מרעת יושבי בה

[35] ישם מדבר לאגם מים וארץ ציה למצאי מים

[36] ויושב שם רעבים ויכוננו עיר מושב

[37] ויזרעו שדות ויטעו כרמים ויעשו פרי תבואה

[38] ויברכם וירבו מאד ובהמתם לא ימעיט

[39] וימעטו וישחו מעצר רעה ויגון

[40] שפך בוז על נדובים ויתעם בתהו לא דרך

[41] וישגב אביון מעוני וישם כצאן משפחות

[42] יראו ישרים וישמחו וכל עולה קפצה פיה

[43] מי חכם וישמר אלה ויתבוננו חסדי יהוה‎אהדנ‎יה‎אהדונהי

Transliteration:

[1] *hodu laYHVH ki tov ki l'olam chas'do*

[2] *yom'ru g'ulei YHVH asher g'alam miyad tzar*

[3] *umei'aratzot kib'tzam mimiz'rach umima'arav mitzafon umiyam*

[4] *ta'u vamid'bar bishimon darech ir moshav lo matza'u*

[5] *r'eivim gam tz'mei'im naf'sham bahem tit'ataf*

[6] *vayitz'aku el YHVH batzar lahem mim'tzukoteihem yatzileim*

[7] *vayad'richeim b'derech y'sharah lalechet el ir moshav*

[8] *yodu laYHVH chas'do v'nif'l'otav liv'nei adam*

[9] *ki his'bi'a nefesh shokeikah v'nefesh r'eivah milei tov*

[10] *yosh'vei choshek v'tzal'mavet asirei oni uvar'zel*

[11] *ki him'ru im'rei el va'atzat el'yon na'atzu*

[12] *vayach'na be'amal libam kash'lu v'ein ozeir*

[13] *vayiz'aku el YHVH batzar lahem mim'tzukoteihem yoshi'eim*

[14] *yotzi'eim meichoshech v'tzal'mavet umos'roteihem y'nateik*

[15] *yodu laYHVH chas'do v'nif'l'otav liv'nei adam*

[16] *ki shibar dal'tot n'choshet uv'richei var'zel gidei'a*

[17] *evilim miderech pish'am umei'avonoteihem yit'anu*

[18] *kol ochel t'ta'eiv naf'sham vayagi'u ad sha'arei mavet*

[19] *vayiz'aku el YHVH batzar lahem mim'tzukoteihem yoshi'eim*

[20] *yish'lach d'varo v'yir'pa'eim vimaleit mish'chitotam*

[21] *yodu laYHVH chas'do v'nif'l'otav liv'nei adam*

[22] *v'yiz'b'chu ziv'chei todah visap'ru ma'asav b'rinah*

[23] *yor'dei hayam bo'oniyot osei m'lachah b'mayim rabim*

[24] *heimah ra'u ma'asei YHVH v'nif'l'otav bim'tzulah*

[25] *vayomer vaya'ameid ru'ach s'arah vat'romeim galav*

[26] *ya'alu shamayim yeir'du t'homot naf'sham b'ra'ah tit'mogag*

[27] *yachogu v'yanu'u kashikor v'chol choch'matam tit'bala*

[28] *vayitz'aku el YHVH batzar lahem umim'tzukoteihem yotzi'eim*

[29] *yakeim s'arah lid'mamah vayecheshu galeihem*

[30] *vayis'm'chu chi yish'toku vayan'cheim el m'choz chef'tzam*

[31] *yodu laYHVH chas'do v'nif'l'otav liv'nei adam*

[32] *virom'muhu bik'hal am uv'moshav z'keinim y'hal'luhu*

[33] *yaseim n'harot l'mid'bar umotza'ei mayim l'tzima'on*

[34] *eretz p'ri lim'leichah meira'at yosh'vei vah*
[35] *ya'seim mid'bar la'agam mayim v'eretz tziyah l'motza'ei mayim*
[36] *vayoshev sham r'eivim vaichon'nu ir moshav*
[37] *vayiz'r'u sadot vayit'u ch'ramim vaya'asu p'ri t'vu'ah*
[38] *vaivar'cheim vayir'bu m'od uv'hem'tam lo yam'it*
[39] *vayim'atu vayashochu mei'otzer ra'ah v'yagon*
[40] *shofeich buz al n'divim vayat'eim b'tohu lo darech*
[41] *vaisageiv ev'yon mei'oni vayasem katzon mish'pachot*
[42] *yir'u y'sharim v'yis'machu v'chol av'lah kaf'tzah pi'ah*
[43] *mi chacham v'yish'mor eileh v'yit'bon'nu chas'dei YHVH*

Translation:

[1] O give thanks unto *YHVH*, for He is good, for His mercy endureth for ever.'
[2] So let the redeemed of *YHVH* say, whom He hath redeemed from the hand of the adversary;
[3] And gathered them out of the lands, from the east and from the west, from the north and from the sea.
[4] They wandered in the wilderness in a desert way; they found no city of habitation.
[5] Hungry and thirsty, their soul fainted in them.
[6] Then they cried unto *YHVH* in their trouble, and He delivered them out of their distresses.
[7] And He led them by a straight way, that they might go to a city of habitation.
[8] Let them give thanks unto *YHVH* for His mercy, and for His wonderful works to the children of men!
[9] For He hath satisfied the longing soul, and the hungry soul He hath filled with good.
[10] Such as sat in darkness and in the shadow of death, being bound in affliction and iron—
[11] Because they rebelled against the words of *El*, and contemned the counsel of the Most High.
[12] Therefore He humbled their heart with travail, they stumbled, and there was none to help—
[13] They cried unto *YHVH* in their trouble, and He saved them out of their distresses.

[14] He brought them out of darkness and the shadow of death, and broke their bands in sunder.

[15] Let them give thanks unto *YHVH* for His mercy, and for His wonderful works to the children of men!

[16] For He hath broken the gates of brass, and cut the bars of iron in sunder.

[17] Crazed because of the way of their transgression, and afflicted because of their iniquities—

[18] Their soul abhorred all manner of food, and they drew near unto the gates of death—

[19] They cried unto *YHVH* in their trouble, and He saved them out of their distresses;

[20] He sent His word, and healed them, and delivered them from their graves.

[21] Let them give thanks unto *YHVH* for His mercy, and for His wonderful works to the children of men!

[22] And let them offer the sacrifices of thanksgiving, and declare His works with singing.

[23] They that go down to the sea in ships, that do business in great waters—

[24] These saw the works of *YHVH*, and His wonders in the deep;

[25] For He commanded, and raised the stormy wind, which lifted up the waves thereof;

[26] They mounted up to the heaven, they went down to the deeps; their soul melted away because of trouble;

[27] They reeled to and fro, and staggered like a drunken man, and all their wisdom was swallowed up—

[28] They cried unto *YHVH* in their trouble, and He brought them out of their distresses.

[29] He made the storm a calm, so that the waves thereof were still.

[30] Then were they glad because they were quiet, and He led them unto their desired haven.

[31] Let them give thanks unto *YHVH* for His mercy, and for His wonderful works to the children of men!

[32] Let them exalt Him also in the assembly of the people, and praise Him in the seat of the elders.

[33] He turneth rivers into a wilderness, and watersprings into a thirsty ground;

[34] A fruitful land into a salt waste, for the wickedness of them that dwell therein.

[35] He turneth a wilderness into a pool of water, and a dry land into watersprings.

[36] And there He maketh the hungry to dwell, and they establish a city of habitation;

[37] And sow fields, and plant vineyards, which yield fruits of increase.

[38] He blesseth them also, so that they are multiplied greatly, and suffereth not their cattle to decrease.

[39] Again, they are minished and dwindle away through oppression of evil and sorrow.

[40] He poureth contempt upon princes, and causeth them to wander in the waste, where there is no way.

[41] Yet setteth He the needy on high from affliction, and maketh his families like a flock.

[42] The upright see it, and are glad; and all iniquity stoppeth her mouth.

[43] Whoso is wise, let him observe these things, and let them consider the mercies of *YHVH*.

Psalm 107 is recited in the Sefardic tradition on *Pesach* (Passover) prior to *Arvit* (the evening prayer service). We are told it is enunciated at this time due to the fact that "the entire psalm concerns itself with the redemption of the Israelites from Egypt."[1] However, it is said that the hundred-and-seventh Psalm primarily "serves as the basis for the four categories of persons who offer thanksgiving"[2] when they recite הגומל ברכת (*Bir'kat Hagomeil* —"The Blessing of Thanksgiving").[3] This unique benediction derives from the statement in the *Talmud* informing us that "Rab Judah said in the name of Rab: There are four [classes of people] who have to offer thanksgiving: those who crossed the sea, those who have traversed the wilderness, one who has recovered from illness, and a prisoner who has been set free." [*TB Berachot 54b*] The said four categories are referenced in *Psalm 107*, and thus this psalm is considered the basis of "The Blessing of Thanksgiving." In this regard, verses 23–31 are said to reference those who "go down to the sea in ships"; 4–8 those who "wandered in the wilderness"; 17–21 those who are "healed"; and verses 10–15 pertains to those who were "bound in affliction and iron."[4]

We are further informed that the expression חיים (*chayim* —"life"/"living") from the phrase in the *Amidah* prayer reading וכל החיים יודוך סלה (*v'chol hachayim yoducha selah* —"and all living beings will give thanks to You, *Selah*"), is an anagram alluding to the said four categories, i.e. ח (*Chet*)—חבוש (*chavush* —"prisoner"); י (*Yod*)—יסורים (*yesurim*—"suffering"); י (*Yod*) —ים ("sea"); and מ ("*Mem*")—מדבר ("wilderness").[5] In ancient days when people worshipped in the Temple in Jerusalem, individuals who "escaped peril or recovered from illness," would bring thanksgiving offerings to be sacrificed in the sacred precinct. Today the *Bir'kat Hagomeil* ("The Blessing of Thanksgiving") is uttered in lieu of the thanksgiving sacrifice, by those who have undertaken an extensive journey, or have narrowly escaped danger. Women are also expected to recite this special thanksgiving blessing after recovery from illness, and equally after giving birth.[6] As the "Blessing of Thanksgiving" is based on *Psalm 107*, this psalm is recommended to those who seek heavenly mercy, as well as to express gratitude.[7]

It should be noted that, whilst some of the published editions of the *Shimmush Tehillim* do not include the current psalm, in those in which it is listed, this psalm is said to be good for individuals who suffer chronic *kedachat*,[8] i.e. continuous fever,[9] stubborn malaria,[10] or "the daily fever" according to Godfrey Selig.[11] The Divine Name יה (*Yah*) is said to be associated with the hundred-and-seventh Psalm, and we are informed in one recension of the *Shimmush Tehillim* that the component glyphs of this Divine Name were derived: י (*Yod*) from יאמרו (*yom'ru*— "they will say"): verse 2; and ה (*Heh*) from the concluding letter of the expression חסדי יהוה (*chas'dei YHVH*— "mercies of *YHVH*"): verse 43.[12] Be that as it may, in his ever popular German/English translation of the *Shimmush Tehillim*, Selig maintains the following origination of the said Divine Name: י (*Yod*) from ישלח (*yish'lach* —"He sent"): verse 20; and ה (*Heh*) from ברנה (*b'rinah*—"with singing"): verse 22.[13]

In a variant recension of the *Shimmush Tehillim* the current psalm is said to be good against "a two-day fever." In this regard, *Psalm 107* should be copied on deerskin parchment conjointly with the following prayer-incantation:

שדי שדישדישדישדישדישד שלח רפואה לזה

[....name of recipient....] רפואה שלימה בקירוב זמן

אמן נצח סלה

Transliteration:

> *Shadai Shadai Shadai Shadai Shadai Shadai Shadai*
> *sh'lach na r'fu'ah l'zeh* [....name of recipient....] *r'fu'ah*
> *sh'leimah b'kiruv z'man Omein Netzach Selah.*

Translation:

> *Shadai Shadai Shadai Shadai Shadai Shadai Shadai,*
> please send healing to this [....name of recipient....] full
> healing speedily. *Amen* Eternal *Selah.*

The writing is afterwards attached to the right arm of the sufferer.[14]
The left arm features equally in a different magical procedure
pertaining to the current psalm. In this regard, the following Divine
Name construct is written directly on the left arm:

$$\text{וַאֶי בַּלָמִי וּלְהָרַסֶסֶם}$$

The first seven glyphs of the Divine Name construct are the
capitals of the seven words comprising *Psalm 107:6*, and the last
seven are the concluding letters of the said seven words. It is said
to be good for an individual who observes a strict religious fast, i.e.
one in which the worshipper is expected to abstain altogether from
imbibing any food or beverages. Should the said individual
become seriously distressed due to this action, he/she is advised to
write this Divine Name construct on his/her left arm.[15]

As far as the use of single verses from the current psalm are
concerned, the glyphs comprising *Psalm 107:29–30* were
formulated into the following Divine Name construct, which is
employed to calm violent storms at sea:

$$\text{יִיחֶ קֶוַשׁ מֶהוּ סְמֶג עָמֶל}$$
$$\text{רְדִי הָלְהֶם וַנֶח יַיֶם שׁוּא}$$
$$\text{מוּל חֹקֶם וַתֹח כֹּשׁוּ יִיז}$$
$$\text{חֶפֶצָם}$$

To affect its purpose, the Divine Name construct is copied on deerskin parchment, and suspended on the mast of a ship. The said verses are then read sixteen times, and the Divine Names enunciated, which we are informed will result in calming the angry ocean.[16] The Divine Name construct, which is maintained to have been derived "from the Kabbalah" of the great 13th century Kabbalist Eleazar ben Yehudah ben Kalonymus of Worms,[17] was constructed by means of the previously mentioned popular *Serugin* (trellis) method of conjoining letters of Biblical verses.[18] In the current instance, the first seven letters of verse 29 comprise the capitals of the first six tri-letter and one four-letter combinations, the second group of seven glyphs the second letters written in reverse order, the third set of seven letters the third letters of the Divine Name construct, again written in direct order, and the concluding letter of this verse the fourth glyph of the seventh combination. The same formula was applied with the letters of verse 30, in order to compose the second set of eight tri-letter combinations. The final four-letters of the Divine Name construct is the concluding word of this verse.[19]

Whilst the current psalm is employed against chronic or incurable fever, or just a one-day or two-day fever, I have also seen *Psalm 107* being enunciated against paralysis; all manner of illness; and for healing in general. In fact, it is recommended for all kinds of trouble and distress; against enemies; and for protection in perilous situations, and in times of trouble. On a more positive note, it should be noted that the current psalm is also suggested to those who are seeking to establish alliances, and who wish to express grateful thanks for Divine Providence.

As in the case of the previous psalm, it would seem little use is made of the hundred-and-seventh Psalm in Christian Magic. However, we are informed that an individual who desires his or her imprisoned enemy to remain incarcerated for an extended period of time, should visit the prison and enunciate the current psalm in front of the said adversary whom we are told "will not get out of there for a long time."[20] Lastly, it is worth noting that *Psalm 107:16* is engraved in the "*Key of Solomon*" on the "*First Pentacle of the Moon*."[21]

PSALM 108

[1] שיר מזמור לדוד

[2] נכון לבי אלהים אשירה ואזמרה אף כבודי

[3] עורה הנבל וכנור אעירה שחר

[4] אודך בעמים יהוה ואזמרך בלאמים

[5] כי גדול מעל שמים חסדך ועד שחקים אמתך

[6] רומה על שמים אלהים ועל כל הארץ כבודך

[7] למען יחלצון ידידיך הושיעה ימינך וענני

[8] אלהים דבר בקדשו אעלוזה אחלקה שכם ועמק
סכות אמדד

[9] לי גלעד לי מנשה ואפרים מעוז ראשי יהודה
מחקקי

[10] מואב סיר רחצי על אדום אשליך נעלי עלי
פלשת אתרועע

[11] מי יבלני עיר מבצר מי נחני עד אדום

[12] הלא אלהים זנחתנו ולא תצא אלהים בצבאתינו

[13] הבה לנו עזרת מצר ושוא תשועת אדם

[14] באלהים נעשה חיל והוא יבוס צרינו

Transliteration:

[1] *shir miz'mor l'david*

[2] *nachon libi elohim ashirah va'azam'rah af k'vodi*

[3] *urah haneivel v'chinor a'irah shachar*

[4] *od'cha ba'amim YHVH va'azamer'cha bal'umim*

[5] *ki gadol mei'al shamayim chas'decha v'ad sh'chakim amitecha*

[6] *rumah al shamayim elohim v'al kol ha'aretz k'vodecha*

[7] *l'ma'an yeichal'tzun y'didecha hoshi'ah y'min'cha va'aneini*

[8] *elohim diber b'kod'sho e'lozah achal'kah sh'chem v'eimek sukot amadeid*

[9] *li gil'ad li m'nasheh v'ef'rayim ma'oz roshi y'hudah m'chok'ki*

[10] *mo'av sir rach'tzi al edom ash'lich na'ali alei f'leshet et'ro'a*

[11] *mi yovileini ir miv'tzar mi nachani ad edom*

[12] *halo elohim z'nach'tanu v'lo teitzei elohim b'tziv'oteinu*

[13] *havah lanu ez'rat mitzar v'shav t'shu'at adam*

[14] *beilohim na'aseh chayil v'hu yavus tzareinu*

Translation:

[1] A Song, a Psalm of David.

[2] My heart is steadfast, *Elohim*; I will sing, yea, I will sing praises, even with my glory.

[3] Awake, psaltery and harp; I will awake the dawn.

[4] I will give thanks unto Thee, *YHVH*, among the peoples; and I will sing praises unto Thee among the nations.

[5] For Thy mercy is great above the heavens, and Thy truth reacheth unto the skies.

[6] Be Thou exalted, *Elohim*, above the heavens; and Thy glory be above all the earth.

[7] That Thy beloved may be delivered, save with Thy right hand, and answer me.

[8] *Elohim* spoke in His holiness, that I would exult; that I would divide Shechem, and mete out the valley of Succoth.

[9] Gilead is mine, Manasseh is mine; Ephraim also is the defence of my head; Judah is my sceptre.

[10] Moab is my washpot; upon Edom do I cast my shoe; over Philistia do I cry aloud.

[11] Who will bring me into the fortified city? Who will lead me unto Edom?

[12] Hast not Thou cast us off, *Elohim*? and Thou goest not forth, *Elohim*, with our hosts?

[13] Give us help against the adversary; for vain is the help of man.

[14] Through *Elohim* we shall do valiantly; for He it is that will tread down our adversaries.

Psalm 108 does not feature in any Jewish liturgies that I am aware of, but fine use is made of it in *Practical Kabbalah* in which we are told that it is good for success.[1] To affect this aim, it was suggested the psalm should be written as an amulet.[2] We are informed in the *Shimmush Tehillim* that anyone seeking success, should copy the current psalm, locate it behind the entrance of his or her residence, and it is said "you will succeed."[3] In terms of the desired outcome, Godfrey Selig notes in his German/English version of the *Shimmush Tehillim* that "your going and coming will be blessed, and you will be successful in all your business transactions."[4] There is a Divine Name associated with the psalm, but there is some confusion as to exactly what it is supposed to be. In some published versions of the *Shimmush Tehillim* the Divine Name is indicated to be ‏וֹן‎ (*Vav–Nun*), the glyphs said to have been derived: ‏ו‎ (*Vav*) from ‏צָרֵינוּ‎ (*tzareinu*—"our adversaries"): the concluding word of the psalm (verse 14); and ‏נ‎ (*Nun*) from ‏נָכוֹן‎ (*nachon*— "steadfast"): verse 2, "by means of letters ‏הנך‎ (*Heh–Nun–Kaf*)," i.e. the ‏אי"ק בכ"ר‎ (*Ayak Bachar*) cipher.[5] In terms of the current Divine Name, it would seem there is no need for the letter exchange afforded by the said cipher, since the selected words both conclude with the ‏נ–ו‎ (*Vav–Nun*) combination. However, the matter is resolved in a different recension of the *Shimmush Tehillim*, in which it is noted that the relevant Divine Name is ‏וה‎ (*Vav–Heh*), which it maintains originated from the same Hebrew terms. In this instance, the letter ‏ה‎ (*Heh*) is indicated to have been derived from ‏נ‎ (*Nun*) in ‏נָכוֹן‎ (*nachon*—"steadfast"): verse 2, by means of the said ‏ה–נ–ך‎ (*Heh–Nun–Kaf*) interchange.[6] In his very flawed version of the *Shimmush Tehillim*, Selig makes the unsubstantiated claim that the "proper holy name" of the hundred-and-eighth Psalm is "*Vi*," i.e. ‏וי‎ (*Vav–Yod*), which he noted are two letters from the Ineffable Name "in which Kabbalists seek through its many divisions, great secrets."[7] He likewise shares the earlier listed two Hebrew terms to be the sources of the Divine Name.

The current psalm is employed in a variant recension of the *Shimmush Tehillim* to save an individual from serious illness. In this regard, the words of *Psalm 108* are written down in direct and in reverse order. This is done in conjunction with the Divine Name ‏אֵל שַׁדַי‎ (*El Shadai*). The action is concluded by adding the following prayer-incantation, and then suspending the entire writing around the neck of the sufferer. The prayer-incantation reads:

[....name of recipient....] אַרְגִי מַרְגִי אַרְגִי מַרְגִי הַצִּיל
הַחוֹלֶה וְעָזְרֵיהוּ וְסָמְכֵהוּ וּפַלְּטֵהוּ בַּעֲגָלָא וּבִזְמָן קָרִיב
אָמֵן נֶצַח סֶלָה

Transliteration:

Ar'gi Mar'gi Ar'gi Mar'gi hatzil [....name of recipient....] hacholeh v'az'reihu v'sam'cheihu upal'teihu b'agala u'viz'man kariv Omen Netzach Selah.

Transliteration:

Ar'gi Mar'gi Ar'gi Mar'gi save [....name of recipient....], the sick, and help him, sustain and save him, suddenly and shortly. *Amen* Eternal *Selah.*[8]

Whilst they are quite rarely employed in Jewish Magic, I have observed the enigmatic Divine Names מַרְגִי אַרְגִי (*Argi Margi*) included with other Divine Names in a somewhat different format, i.e. אַרְגִי נַרְגִי סַרְגִי אַגָף נָגָף שָׁגָף (*Ar'gi Nar'gi Sar'gi 'gaf N'gaf Sh'gaf*), for the purpose of שְׁאֵלַת חֲלוֹם (*she'elat chalom*— "dream questioning").[9]

In terms of different applications, we are informed that *Psalm 108* is enunciated "to have happiness in one's house,"[10] and it is likewise recommended to those who wish to express gratitude.[11] Other than this, I have observed the current psalm recommended specifically for financial success, i.e. success in business, as well as in general, and in all endeavours. In this regard, it is recited for your coming and going to be blessed. It is also employed to ensure a safe pregnancy, and to express gratitude for good fortune. This psalm is further enunciated against lies; and equally against, as well as to be saved from, defamation, slander, and gossip. It is one of the psalms said to offer support in moments of incredulity, i.e. disbelief.

The application of the the hundred-and-eighth Psalm is again sparse in Christian Magic. The Byzantine Christian magical manuscripts suggests that an individual who resides in a far away land, and who is hated by the citizens, should write the psalm and bury it beneath the entrance of his/her residence. The said individual is further advised to recite the psalm "over water from a spring that no sunlight sees," and to wash his or her face and hands, afterwards disposing of the used liquid at the entrance of the residence.[12] Other than this, we are told in the *"Livre d'Or"* that those who "wish to approach a Prince or a King," should recite *Psalm 108* seven times before entering into the presence of the overlord, and they will have nothing to fear.[13]

PSALM 109

[1] למנצח לדוד מזמור **אלהי** תהלתי אל תחרש

[2] כי **פי** רשע ופי מרמה עלי פתחו דברו אתי לשון שקר

[3] ודברי שנאה סבבוני וילחמוני חנם

[4] תחת **אהבתי** ישטנוני ואני תפלה

[5] וישימו עלי רעה תחת טובה ושנאה תחת **אהבתי**

[6] הפקד עליו רשע ושטן יעמד על ימינו

[7] בהשפטו יצא רשע ותפלתו תהיה לחטאה

[8] יהיו ימיו מעטים פקדתו יקח **אחר**

[9] יהיו בניו יתומים ואשתו אלמנה

[10] ונוע ינועו בניו ושאלו ודרשו מחרבותיהם

[11] ינקש נושה לכל **אשר** לו ויבזו זרים יגיעו

[12] **אל** יהי לו משך חסד ואל יהי חונן ליתומיו

[13] יהי אחריתו להכרית בדור **אחר** ימח שמם

[14] יזכר עון **אבתיו** אל **יהוה**אדניאהדונהי וחטאת אמו אל תמח

[15] יהיו נגד **יהוה**אדניאהדונהי תמיד ויכרת מארץ זכרם

[16] יען אשר **לא** זכר עשות חסד וירדף **איש** עני ואביון ונכאה לבב למותת

[17] וי**אהב** קללה ותבואהו ולא חפץ בברכה ותרחק ממנו

[18] וילבש קללה כמדו ותבא כמים בקרבו וכשמן בעצמותיו

[19] תהי לו כבגד יעטה ולמזח תמיד יחגרה

[20] זאת פעלת שטני מאת **יהוה**אדניאהדונהי והדברים רע על נפשי

[21] ואתה **יהוה**אדניאהדונהי אדני עשה אתי למען שמך כי טוב חסדך הצילני

[22] כי עני ואביון **אנכי** ולבי חלל בקרבי

[23] כצל כנטותו נהלכתי ננערתי כארבה

[24] ברכי כשלו מצום ובשרי כחש משמן

[25] ואני הייתי חרפה להם יראוני יניעון ראשם

[26] עזרני יהוה‎אהדונהי אלהי הושיעני כחסדך

[27] וידעו כי ידך זאת אתה יהוה‎אהדונהי עשיתה

[28] יקללו המה ואתה תברך קמו ויבשו ועבדך
ישמח

[29] ילבשו שוטני כלמה ויעטו כמעיל בשתם

[30] אודה יהוה‎אהדונהי מאד בפי ובתוך רבים
אהללנו

[31] כי יעמד לימון אביון להושיע משפטי נפשו

Transliteration:

[1] *lam'natzei'ach l'david miz'mor elohei t'hilati al techerash*

[2] *ki fi rasha ufi mir'mah alai patachu dib'ru iti l'shon shaker*

[3] *v'div'rei sin'ah s'vavuni vayilachamuni chinam*

[4] *tachat ahavati yis't'nuni va'ani t'filah*

[5] *vayasimu alai ra'ah tachat tovah v'sin'ah tachat ahavati*

[6] *haf'keid alav rasha v'satan ya'amod al y'mino*

[7] *b'hishaf'to yeitzei rasha ut'filato tih'yeh lachata'ah*

[8] *yih'yu yamav m'atim p'kudato yikach acher*

[9] *yih'yu vanav y'tomim v'ish'to al'manah*

[10] *v'no'a yanu'u vanav v'shi'eilu v'dar'shu meichor'voteihem*

[11] *y'nakeish nosheh l'chol asher lo v'yavozu zarim y'gi'o*

[12] *al y'hi lo mosheich chased v'al y'hi chonein litomav*

[13] *y'hi acharito l'hach'rit b'dor acheir yimach sh'mam*

[14] *yizacheir avon avotav el YHVH v'chatat imo al timach*

[15] *yih'yu neged YHVH tamid v'yach'reit mei'eretz zich'ram*

[16] *ya'an asher lo zachar asot chased vayir'dof ish ani v'ev'yon v'nich'eih leivav l'moteit*

[17] *vaye'ehav k'lalah vat'vo'eihu v'lo chafetz biv'rachah vatir'chak mimenu*

[18] *vayil'bash k'lalah k'mado vatavo chamayim b'kir'bo v'chashemen b'atz'motav*

[19] *t'hi lo k'veged ya'teh ul'meizach tamid yach'g'reha*

[20] *zot p'ulat sot'nai mei'eit YHVH v'hadov'rim ra al naf'shi*

[21] *v'atah YHVH adonai aseih iti l'ma'an sh'mecha ki tov chas'd'cha hatzileini*

[22] *ki ani v'ev'yon anochi v'libi chalal b'kir'bi*

[23] *k'tzeil kin'toto nehelach'ti nin'ar'ti ka'ar'beh*

[24] *bir'kai kash'lu mitzom uv'sari kachash mishamen*

[25] *va'ani hayiti cher'pah lahem yir'uni y'ni'un rosham*

[26] *oz'reini YHVH elohai hoshi'eini ch'chas'decha*

[27] *v'yeid'u ki yad'cha zot atah YHVH asitah*

[28] *y'kal'lu heimah v'atah t'vareich kamu vayeivoshu v'av'd'cha yis'mach*

[29] *yil'b'shu sot'nai k'limah v'ya'atu cham'il bosh'tam*

[30] *odeh YHVH m'od b'fi uv'toch rabim ahal'lenu*

[31] *ki ya'amod limin ev'yon l'hoshi'a mishof'tei naf'sho*

Translation:

[1] For the Leader. A Psalm of David. O God of my praise, keep not silence;

[2] For the mouth of the wicked and the mouth of deceit have they opened against me; they have spoken unto me with a lying tongue.

[3] They compassed me about also with words of hatred, and fought against me without a cause.

[4] In return for my love they are my adversaries; but I am all prayer.

[5] And they have laid upon me evil for good, and hatred for my love:

[6] Set Thou a wicked man over him; and let an adversary stand at his right hand.

[7] When he is judged, let him go forth condemned; and let his prayer be turned into sin.

[8] Let his days be few; let another take his charge.

[9] Let his children be fatherless, and his wife a widow.

[10] Let his children be vagabonds, and beg; and let them seek their bread out of their desolate places.

[11] Let the creditor distrain all that he hath; and let strangers make spoil of his labour.

[12] Let there be none to extend kindness unto him; neither let there be any to be gracious unto his fatherless children.

[13] Let his posterity be cut off; in the generation following let their name be blotted out.

[14] Let the iniquity of his fathers be brought to remembrance unto *YHVH*; and let not the sin of his mother be blotted out.

[15] Let them be before *YHVH* continually, that He may cut off the memory of them from the earth.

[16] Because that he remembered not to do kindness, but persecuted the poor and needy man, and the broken in heart he was ready to slay.

[17] Yea, he loved cursing, and it came unto him; and he delighted not in blessing, and it is far from him.

[18] He clothed himself also with cursing as with his raiment, and it is come into his inward parts like water, and like oil into his bones.

[19] Let it be unto him as the garment which he putteth on, and for the girdle wherewith he is girded continually.'

[20] This would mine adversaries effect from *YHVH*, and they that speak evil against my soul.

[21] But Thou, *YHVH Adonai*, deal with me for Thy name's sake; because Thy mercy is good, deliver Thou me.

[22] For I am poor and needy, and my heart is wounded within me.

[23] I am gone like the shadow when it lengtheneth; I am shaken off as the locust.

[24] My knees totter through fasting; and my flesh is lean, and hath no fatness.

[25] I am become also a taunt unto them; when they see me, they shake their head.

[26] Help me, *YHVH* my God; O save me according to Thy mercy;

[27] That they may know that this is Thy hand; that Thou, *YHVH*, hast done it.

[28] Let them curse, but bless Thou; when they arise, they shall be put to shame, but Thy servant shall rejoice.

[29] Mine adversaries shall be clothed with confusion, and shall put on their own shame as a robe.

[30] I will give great thanks unto *YHVH* with my mouth; yea, I will praise Him among the multitude;

[31] Because He standeth at the right hand of the needy, to save him from them that judge his soul.

Delineated "the most vindictive,"[1] *Psalm 109* is not employed in Jewish worship. However, it is said that this psalm, "especially verse 6, is useful in performing exorcisms when recited in reverse."[2] According to Rabbi Chaim Vital of Lurianic fame, the said verse "represents King David's curse against 'the wicked that the Blessed Holy One should appoint a wicked soul over him, to penetrate and to harm him'."[3] In this regard, it has been suggested that the said verse "represent a classic case of 'blaming the victim.' As a punishment for wickedness, the victim is invaded by foreign spirits and is subjected to the attendant suffering entailed by their penetration."[4] However, this state of affairs was also understood to be a rectification, and thus it has been said that "counter-intuitively, this verse, which seems to be a command to appoint this wicked soul over him, here alludes to its rectification...." In this regard, Rabbi Vital perceived *Psalm 109:6* to be "an example of how 'with what God crushes, he heals'."[5]

Here the fundamental "curing" of the "demonic problem" appears to involve a kind of "magical homoeopathy," i.e. a spiritual "like cures like," which is plainly an expression of the doctrine of sympathetic magic in a different garb. Whatever the case may be, in the current instance the exorcism is quite a complex affair, incorporating contemplations of Divine Names and unique mystico-magical formulae, i.e. *Kavvanot*, which are to be enacted prior to the actual act of expelling a demonic force from the possessee. Reading the pulse "as an indicator of ailments of the soul,"[6] it is said the exorcist is located "behind the possessed, holding the arms of the victim by the wrists while engaged in pulse-based diagnosis."[7] Having arrived at some sort of a verdict, "while still gripping the possessed from behind, the exorcist recites Psalm 109, verse 6, into his or her ear....This verse is said forward and then backward....The verse is also permuted numerically, and its posterior and anterior acrostics contemplated."[8]

It is impossible to share the full exorcism procedure in the limited number of pages afforded by this tome, hence we will turn our attention to the uses made of *Psalm 109* in *Practical Kabbalah*. In this regard, we are told in the *Jewish Encyclopedia* the current psalm is used "against enemies."[9] However, in Jewish Magic it is in fact mainly employed against one who hates and oppresses you,[10] or "if an enemy pursues you."[11] In this regard, we are informed in the *Shimmush Tehillim* that if a person is oppressed by a hater, that individual should take mustard which, it would seem, should be placed inside a new vessel which is filled with wine,[12] "new sparkling wine" according to Godfrey Selig.[13] Some versions of the said text maintain the "new vessel" should be filled with spring water.[14] The current psalm is then recited over the liquid substance for a period of three days, following which it is dispensed at the gate of the enemy. As might be expected, the wine/water is, as it were, infused with the malevolence expressed in the psalm, and hence the *Shimmush Tehillim* advises the practitioner to ensure that not a drop of the said liquid substance is spilled on his or her person.[15]

The Divine Name to concentrate on whilst reciting the hundred-and-ninth Psalm is indicated to be אֵל (*El*), the glyphs of which were said in most of the published editions of the *Shimmush Tehillim* to have been derived: א (*Alef*) from אֲהַלְלֶנּוּ (*ahal'lenu*—"I will praise Him"): verse 30; and ל from כִּי יַעֲמֹד לִימִין אֶבְיוֹן (*ki ya'amod limin ev'yon*—"Because He standeth at the right hand of the needy"): verse 31.[16] However, some recensions of this text maintains the Divine Name to originate: א (*Alef*) from אֱלֹהֵי (*Elohei*—"God"): verse 1; and ל from כִּי יַעֲמֹד (*ki ya'amod*—"Because He standeth"): verse 31, by means of the practice of exchanging one glyph with the succeeding one in the Hebrew alphabet, i.e. the letters ל–כ (*Kaf–Lamed*) in the current instance.[17] While Selig expresses virtually the same origins of the said Divine Name in his German/English translation of the *Shimmush Tehillim*, he maintains the letter א (*Alef*) is derived from אֱלֹהִים (*Elohim*) in verse 3.[18] Since this Divine Name does not feature in the said verse, or for that matter anywhere else in the current psalm, I presume he was in all likelihood referencing the term אֱלֹהֵי (*Elohei*) in verse 1.

A variant recension of the *Shimmush Tehillim* maintains that an individual who is oppressed by a "hater," should recite *Psalm 109* as well as the following prayer-incantation, doing so twelve times in the synagogue:

צבא צבא צבא צבא שר צבא מעלה הצילני מן יד
האויב הזה אשר הוא צורר אותי בשם שוכן שחקים
אמן אמן אמן

Transliteration:

*Tz'va Tz'va Tz'va Tz'va Sar Tz'va Ma'lah hatzileini min
yad ha'oyeiv hazeh asher hu tzoreir oti b'shem shochen
sh'chakim Omein Omein Omein*

Translation:

Tz'va Tz'va Tz'va Tz'va Sar Tz'va Ma'lah [Hosts Hosts
Hosts Hosts Prince of the Heavenly Hosts], deliver me
from the hand of this enemy who afflicts me, in the name
of the One dwelling in the skies. *Amen Amen Amen.*[19]

Besides its use against mighty enemies, and as a protection from
harm,[20] I have seen the current psalm recommended for protection
in times of trouble and perilous situations, and also against illness,
as well as for healing in general. Several verses from this psalm are
also individually applied for magical purposes. In this regard, the
seven words of *Psalm 109:6*, read both in direct and reverse order,
and enunciated with the vowel points associated with the first
seven *sefirot*, i.e. from *Keter* (Crown) to *Yesod* (Foundation), were
formulated into the following Divine Name construct:

הַפְקֵד עָלָיו רֶשַׁע וְשָׂטָן יַעֲמֹד עַל יְמִינוֹ
וְנִימָי לַע דֶּוּמֵעִי נֶטֶשֶׁו עֶשֶׂר וִילֵע דְּקִפֵּה

Transliterated this Divine Name construct reads: *hafakada alayava
reishei'ei vesetene y''m'v'd' olo yimiyinivi vanayamaya la'a
deiveimei'eiyei netesheve 'sh'r' voyolo'o dikifihi*. It is recited for
protection against plagues and epidemics.[21] It should be noted that
verses from the current psalm are also employed to empower and
heal those who find themselves in poor health. In this regard, the
letters of *Psalm 109:18* were intertwined without vowels in the
composition of the following Divine Name construct:[22]

וים ימבו לככי בארת שבבו
קתום לווץ לוכע הדשב כממן

In the current instance, the first ten letters comprise the initials of the ten letter combinations, whilst the second group of ten, written in reverse, defines the second letters. In turn, the third set of ten letters, written in direct order, constitutes the third letters, and the remaining nine, written again in reverse, comprise the concluding letters of the nine four-letter combinations. The very same procedure was applied with *Psalm 109:19*, in order to create the following Divine Name construct which is likewise employed for the purpose of empowering and healing the sick:[23]

תחת הזמ ימי ללד ווי כהח בטג גער דיה

These two Divine Name constructs are considered to be particularly powerful, when employed in conjunction with a Divine Name construct formulated from the portion of *Numbers 5:21* reading:

יתן יהוה אותך לאלה ולשבעה בתוך עמך בתת יהוה
את ירכך נפלת ואת בטנך צבה

Transliteration:
> *Yitein YHVH otach l'alah v'lish'vu'ah b'toch ameich b'teit YHVH et y'reicheich nofelet v'et bit'neich tzavah.*

Translation:
> *YHVH* make thee a curse and an oath among thy people, when *YHVH* doth make thy thigh to fall away, and thy belly to swell.

Applying again the same formula utilised in the construction of the Divine Names derived from *Psalm 109:18* and *19*, the following Divine Name construct was formulated from the earlier mentioned verse in the biblical *Book of Numbers*:[24]

יָאֶת תֶּהִי נָוֶר יְהֹר הֹיֵכ וְתֹנ
הֹתֶפ אֹבֶּל וּכֵת תָּמֶו כְּעֵא לְכֵת
אוּב לְתֹמ הֹבֶנ וְהֵכ לְעֹצ שֶׁבְבָה

It is interesting that practitioners are explicitly instructed to write the Divine Name constructs formulated from *Psalm 109:18* and *19* without vowel-points, whilst in the current instance the Hebrew glyphs are copied with vowels,[25] almost as if it is expected that the letters would be vocalised mentally during the construction of the Divine Name. However, each of the letter-combinations created from *Numbers 5:21* is subsequently interwoven with the four letters of the Divine Name אדני (*Adonai*), resulting in the following array:[26]

אידאנתי אתדהניי אנדוונרי אידהנכי
אהדיינכי אודתנני אהדתנפי אאדבנלי
אודכנתי אתדמנוי אכדע012 אלדכנתי
אאדונבי אלדתנטי אהדבנני אודהנכי
אלדענצי אשדבנביה

It has been suggested that the Divine Name constructs created from *Psalm 109:18* and *19* should equally be conjoined with the Divine Name אדני (*Adonai*).[27] Whatever the case may be, having written down the array of Sacred Names, it is afterwards carried as an amulet on the person of the one needing to be empowered and healed.

It should be noted that *Psalm 109:7* is likewise used for magical purposes. In this regard, the emboldened letters in this verse reading בְּהִשָּׁפְטוֹ יֵצֵא רָשָׁע וּתְפִלָּתוֹ תִּהְיֶה לַחֲטָאָה (when he is judged, let him go forth condemned; and let his prayer be turned into sin), were conjoined in the construction of the Divine Name construct פְּלָלְ (*F'la'la*), which is employed to win a lawsuit. Its power is enacted by staring hard in the face of the witnesses in court, whilst mentally uttering the said Divine Name construct, and it is said winning is assured.[28] In conclusion, it should be noted that *Psalm 109:30* is directly affiliated with מִיה (*Mih*), the forty-eighth tri-letter portion of the "Name of Seventy-two Names."[29]

It would seem the application of the hundred-and-ninth Psalm against enemies in Jewish Magic, was absorbed directly into

Christian magic. In this regard, we find details in a Coptic text pertaining to destroying a victim by burying bath water and wild mustard at the entrance of his/her residence.[30] Whilst there is no reference to *Psalm 109* in this instance, we are told that this magical action "is clearly echoed in a Syriac Psalter found at the Syrian Monastery in the Wadi Natrun to which a note was added instructing the reader to put mustard-seed and water in a new pot and read the psalm (109) over it for three days, and then pour it out before the door of the enemy, thereby killing him."[31] Elsewhere we find *Psalm 109:1–20* written down, washed in the bathwater of a woman who bathed on a Saturday, and the now baneful substance sprinkled in the house of an enemy. It was said "the memory of him will be erased from the surface of the Earth."[32] In conclusion, it should be noted that *Psalm 109:18* is inscribed on the surrounding border of the "*Fourth Pentacle of Saturn*" in the "*Key of Solomon.*"[33]

PSALM 110

[1] לדוד מזמור נאם יהוה‏ אדני שב לימיני עד אשית איביך הדם לרגליך

[2] מטה עזך ישלח יהוה‏ מציון רדה בקרב איביך

[3] עמך נדבת ביום חילך בהדרי קדש מרחם משחר לך טל ילדתיך

[4] נשבע יהוה‏ ולא ינחם אתה כהן לעולם על דברתי מלכי צדק

[5] אדני על ימינך מחץ ביום אפו מלכים

[6] ידין בגוים מלא גויות מחץ ראש על ארץ רבה

[7] מנחל בדרך ישתה על כן ירים ראש

Transliteration:

[1] *l'david miz'mor n'um YHVH ladoni sheiv limini ad ashit oy'vecha hadom l'rag'lecha*

[2] *mateih uz'cha yish'lach YHVH mitziyon r'deih b'kerev oy'vecha*

[3] *am'cha n'davot b'yom cheilecha b'had'rei kodesh meirechem mish'char l'cha tal yal'dutecha*

[4] *nish'ba YHVH v'lo yinacheim atah chohein l'olam al div'rati mal'ki tzedek*

[5] *adonai al y'min'cha machatz b'yom apo m'lachim*

[6] *yadin bagoyim malei g'viyot machatz rosh al eretz rabah*

[7] *minachal baderech yish'teh al kein yarim rosh*

Translation:

[1] A Psalm of David. *YHVH* saith unto my lord: 'Sit thou at My right hand, until I make thine enemies thy footstool.'

[2] The rod of Thy strength *YHVH* will send out of Zion: 'Rule thou in the midst of thine enemies.'

[3] Thy people offer themselves willingly in the day of thy warfare; in adornments of holiness, from the womb of the dawn, thine is the dew of thy youth.

[4] *YHVH* hath sworn, and will not repent: 'Thou art a priest for ever after the manner of Melchizedek.'

[5] *Adonai* at thy right hand doth crush kings in the day of His wrath.

[6] He will judge among the nations; He filleth it with dead bodies, He crusheth the head over a wide land.
[7] He will drink of the brook in the way; therefore will he lift up the head.

Psalm 110, whilst not as wrathful as the previous psalm, equally does not feature in Jewish worship. However, contrary to the magical application of *Psalm 109* in seeking the destruction of an enemy, the current psalm is employed in Jewish Magic "to make peace."[1] In this regard, it is noted in the *Shimmush Tehillim* that the current psalm is enunciated "so that your haters can make peace with you,"[2] i.e. it is used to reconcile with enemies.[3] Godfrey Selig, maintains in his German/English version of the *Shimmush Tehillim*, that the frequent use of the current psalm "in the form of a prayer," will aid an individual to "compel all enemies and opposers to bow to him and beg for quarters and peace."[4] In a contemporary edition of this text we read that by reciting the current psalm as a prayer, "a man may compel all enemies and adversaries to grovel, ask for forgiveness, and make peace."[5]

All sources agree that the Divine Name associated with *Psalm 110* is יָהּ (*Yah*).[6] In one recension of this text it is said this Divine Name was derived: י (*Yod*) from מ (*Mem*) in מנחל בדרך (*minachal baderech*—"of the brook in the way"): verse 7, by means of the י–מ (*Yod–Mem*) interchange, i.e. by means of the ever popular א״ת ב״ש (*Atbash*) cipher; and ה (*Heh*) from נ (*Nun*) in נאם יהוה לאדני (*n'um YHVH ladoni*—"YHVH saith unto my lord"): verse 1, through the ה–נ–כ (*Heh–Nun–Kaf*) interchange, i.e. the א״י ק בכ ר״ך (*Ayak Bachar*) cipher.[7]

A variant recension of the *Shimmush Tehillim* included a much larger procedure pertaining to the use of the current psalm, for the purpose of establishing peace with enemies. In this instance the practitioner is instructed to fast for four days, recite *Psalm 110* twenty times on the fifth day, and conclude with the following prayer-incantation:

שוכן שחקים עני ממעון קדשך והשלים אויבי לנגדי
וכאשר תשלום ברצות יהוה דרכי איש גם אויביו

יֹשֵׁלם אֹתוֹ בֶּן יְהוָה אֱלֹהֵינוּ אֱלֹהֵי (*Proverbs 16:7*)
צְבָאוֹת תִּרְצֶה דַרְכִי וְהַצְלִיחֵנִי בְּכָל מַעֲשַׂי וְהַשְׁלִים
לִי אוֹיְבִי בִּמְהֵרָה וּבְקָרוֹב זְמָן אָמֵן אָמֵן אָמֵן נֶצַח
סֶלָה

Transliteration:

Shochen sh'chakim aneini mima'on kod'sh'cha v'hash'lim oy'vai l'neg'di uk'asher tash'lim bir'tzot YHVH dar'chei ish gam oy'vav yash'lim ito (Proverbs 16:7) kein YHVH Eloheinu Elohei tz'va'ot tir'tzeh dar'kai v'hatz'licheini b'chol ma'asai v'hash'lim li oy'vai bim'heira uv'kirov z'man Omein Omein Omein Netzach Selah.

Translation:

Dweller in the Skies, answer me from the tabernacle of your holiness. Let my enemy make peace with me as you make peace. "When a man's ways please *YHVH*, He maketh even his enemies to be at peace with him." (*Proverbs 16:7*) So *YHVH* our God, God of hosts, be pleased with my ways, and make all my deeds prosper. and let my enemy make peace with me, speedily and forthwith. *Amen Amen Amen* Eternal *Selah*.[8]

Regarding the use of single verses from the current psalm for magical purposes, *Psalm 110:4* is especially important. The curious Divine Name construct יִּיק הֹנֵם was formulated from this verse, i.e. the first three glyphs from the concluding letters of the three words reading דִּבְרָתִי מַלְכִּי צֶדֶק (*div'rati mal'ki tzedek*—"the manner of Melchizedek"), and the second three from the concluding letters of the phrase אַתָּה כֹהֵן לְעוֹלָם (*atah chohein l'olam*—"Thou art a priest for ever").[9] The first listed phrase having been translated elsewhere "order of Melchizedek," led to the mistaken notion, which was espoused mainly in 20th/21st century western occult enclaves, that there was a literal spiritual brotherhood of the Hermetic variety, with the enigmatic Melchizedek as its "grand master." It would seem that those who promulgated this notion, did not bother to check the original Hebrew scriptures.

Be that as it may, great meaning was derived from investigating the numerical associations (*Gematria*) of the current

Divine Name construct with other Divine Names. In this manner, three names, i.e. אֶהְיֶה (*Eh'yeh*—"I am"), אֱלֹהִים (*Elohim*), and אֲדֹנָי (*Adonai*), are said to be hinted at in *Psalm 110:4*, and are thus closely associated with the said Divine Name construct.[10] This led to a claim that the statement in the said verse reading "Thou art a priest," alluded to the quality of חֶסֶד (*Chesed*— "Lovingkindness") on the sefirotic Tree.[11]

It should be noted, that the concluding letters of the first four words of the said verse reading נשבע יהוה ולא ינחם (*nish'ba YHVH v'lo yinacheim*— "*YHVH* hath sworn, and will not repent*"*), were likewise formulated into a Divine Name construct, specifically עַהֵאָם. The vowels employed in its enunciation are those of the capitals of the said four words.[12] We are told its "secret" is revealed in the יִחוּדִים (*Yichudim*—Unification-meditations) of Rabbi Isaac Luria,[13] and by means of which the worshipper can reach "a transcended state of awareness, and be afforded the opportunity to tap into powerful spiritual currents."[14] This Divine Name was also converted by means of the אָת בַּ"ש (*Atbash*) cipher into the Divine Name construct זַצְתִי. The numerical value of this Divine Name construct [ז = 7 + צ = 90 + ת = 400 + י = 10 = 507] is equal to that of אבג יתצ (*Avige Yatotzi*) [א = 1 + ב = 2 + ג = 3 + י = 10 + ת = 400 + צ = 90 + *kolel* = 507].[15] The latter Divine Name is therefore said to comprise the first two tri-letter portions of the "Forty-two Letter Name of God,"[16] and we are informed that by the Divine Name אבג יתצ (*Avige Yatotzi*) "laws are broken and destroyed."[17]

Whilst the Divine Name constructs formulated from *Psalm 110:4* are said to afford the chance of accessing "powerful spiritual currents," a Divine Name construct comprising the capitals of the nine words of *Psalm 110:6*, יבא אמ גמר עאר, is included in amulets for protection against harmful spirit forces.[18] Other than that, the initials of the first six words of *Psalm 110:7*, are conjoined in the Divine Name construct מבי עבי which is carried for safety at sea.[19] In conclusion, besides being employed to establish peace with enemies, *Psalm 110* is one of the psalms suggested for protection in perilous situations and times of trouble, as well as for Divine Justice and equality. It is also enunciated for illness and healing in general, and, curiously enough, is recommended to acquire the gift of speech.

The Byzantine Christian magical manuscripts delineates the current psalm to be "useful in magic." In this regard, individuals who "wish to assume a position of power," or desire "to get power and be honored by all," are advised to "write and carry" the current psalm.[20] Elsewhere in the same manuscripts, we are informed that "a curse and an evil hour or encounter," may be repelled from an individual by taking water and "holy oil from Saint Elisha and Elijah," as well as a number of other "saint oils," and placing these substances inside a brass container, which is left under the stars. At sunrise these substances are located in a high quality pot with a bit of seawater added. The pot is boiled well, and *Psalm 110* repeated over it three times, at the conclusion of which the cursed individual is washed with the liquid. The instruction concludes "likewise write the Psalm and carry (it) as your ensign and you will be released from every evil."[21]

Elsewhere we find the instruction to write the first three verses of the current psalm, and to tie it to "the right thigh of a pregnant woman," and it is said she will give birth forthwith.[22] The hundred-and-tenth Psalm is also listed in the "*Key of Solomon*" as one in a set of nineteen, i.e. *Psalms 8, 15, 22, 46, 47, 49, 51, 53, 68, 72, 84, 102, 110, 113, 126, 130, 131, 133,* and *139,* which are recited over the wax from which ritual candles are made.[23] Also in the "*Key of Solomon*," *Psalm 110:5* is written around the outer circumference of the "*Fourth Pentacle of Mars.*"[24]

PSALM 111

[1] הללו יה אודה יהוהֲֲֵֵיאהדונהי בכל לבב בסוד ישרים ועדה

[2] גדלים מעשי יהוהֲֲֵֵיאהדונהי דרושים לכל חפציהם

[3] הוד והדר פעלו וצדקתו עמדת לעד

[4] זכר עשה לנפלאותיו חנון ורחום יהוהֲֲֵֵיאהדונהי

[5] טרף נתן ליראיו יזכר לעולם בריתו

[6] כח מעשיו הגיד לעמו לתת להם נחלת גוים

[7] מעשי ידיו אמת ומשפט נאמנים כל פקודיו

[8] סמוכים לעד לעולם עשוים באמת וישר

[9] פדות שלח לעמו צוה לעולם בריתו קדוש ונורא שמו

[10] ראשית חכמה יראת יהוהֲֲֵֵיאהדונהי שכל טוב לכל עשיהם תהלתו עמדת לעד

Transliteration:

[1] *hal'lu Yah odeh YHVH b'chol leivav b'sod y'sharim v'eidah*

[2] *g'dolim ma'asei YHVH d'rushim l'chol chef'tzeihem*

[3] *hod v'hadar po'olo v'tzid'kato omedet la'ad*

[4] *zeicher asah l'nif'l'otav chanun v'rachum YHVH*

[5] *teref natan lirei'av yiz'kor l'olam b'rito*

[6] *ko'ach ma'asav higid l'amo lateit lahem nachalat goyim*

[7] *ma'asei yadav emet umish'pat ne'emanim kol pikudav*

[8] *s'muchim la'ad l'olam asuyim be'emet v'yashar*

[9] *p'dut shalach l'amo tzivah l'olam b'rito kadosh v'nora sh'mo*

[10] *reishit choch'mah yir'at YHVH seichel tov l'chol oseihem t'hilato omedet la'ad*

Translation:

[1] Hallelujah. I will give thanks unto *YHVH* with my whole heart, in the council of the upright, and in the congregation.

[2] The works of *YHVH* are great, sought out of all them that have delight therein.

[3] His work is glory and majesty; and His righteousness endureth for ever.

[4] He hath made a memorial for His wonderful works; *YHVH* is gracious and full of compassion.

[5] He hath given food unto them that fear Him; He will ever be mindful of His covenant.

[6] He hath declared to His people the power of His works, in giving them the heritage of the nations.

[7] The works of His hands are truth and justice; all His precepts are sure.

[8] They are established for ever and ever, they are done in truth and uprightness.

[9] He hath sent redemption unto His people; He hath commanded His covenant for ever; Holy and awful is His name.

[10] The fear of *YHVH* is the beginning of wisdom; a good understanding have all they that do thereafter; His praise endureth for ever.

Psalm 111 and *112* have been delineated "twin psalms."[1] Both commence with the term *"Hallelujah,"* and both are acrostic poems in which the twenty-two phrases of around three or four words each, commence respectively with letters of the Hebrew alphabet listed in alphabetical order. Furthermore, the message expressed in the concluding verse of *Psalm 111*, i.e. "the fear of *YHVH* is the beginning of wisdom; a good understanding have all they that do thereafter; His praise endureth for ever," is further highlighted and personalised in the first verse of *Psalm 112* reading "happy is the man that feareth *YHVH*, that delighteth greatly in His commandments."[2] It has been noted that related phrases are in the exact same position in each of these two psalms. In this regard, we are reminded that the phrase in *Psalm 111:3* commencing with the letter ו (*Vav*), "refer to God's righteousness enduring forever," whilst in *Psalm 112:3* the phrase which likewise starts with the same letter, "refers to human righteousness enduring forever."[2] Similarly, we find the phrase in *Psalm 111:3* commencing with the letter ח (*Chet*), "refers to God being 'gracious and merciful'," whilst the phrase commencing with the same letter in *Psalm 112:4*, "uses the same formula, whilst implying that humans should emulate this too."[3] The difference between the two psalms is said to be "brought out in these two correspondences: Psalm 111 is more concerned about God's righteousness, whilst Psalm 112 is more interested in how humans can live righteously."[4] As things go, one of the most popular biblical expressions, one which is regularly uttered with great gusto in both Judaism and Christianity, is the opening phrase in *Psalm 111:10* (reiterated in *Proverbs 9:10*) reading "the fear of the Lord is the beginning of wisdom," which I noted elsewhere "is simply a reminder of the awe the 'Work of Creation,' the infinite manifestation of the Almighty, inspires in us."[5]

As far as the recitation of *Psalms 111* and *112* in mainstream Jewish worship is concerned, it is said that some recite these two psalms during the third Sabbath meal.[6] It is also customary amongst most *Chasidim* to enunciate *Psalms 111* and *112* prior to returning the Torah scrolls to the ark during the Saturday afternoon service.[7] It should be noted that *Psalm 111* is also enunciated by *Sefardim* on *Shabbat* during *Min'chah* (Sabbath afternoon prayer service). It is said the reason for this is the phrase in verse 4 reading זכר עשה לנפלאותיו (*zeicher asah l'nif'l'otav* —"He hath made a memorial for His wonderful works").[8]

Psalm 111 is employed in Jewish Magic for the purpose of gaining many "lovers," i.e. friends who love you.[9] In this regard, Godfrey Selig stated in his German/English version of the *Shimmush Tehillim* that "through praying the 111th Psalm a man may acquire many friends without the necessity of keeping constantly in mind any special holy name."[10] One recension of the *Shimmush Tehillim* maintains that those who wish to have multiple friends, should recite the psalm, as well as the following accompanying prayer, eight times a day:

נורא ואדיר אמיץ כח שתתנני לחן לחסד ולרחמים
ולאהבה בעיניך ובעיני כל רואי בענין שירבו לי
אוהבים מבלי מספר שכל רואי יאשרוני ואשא חן
וחסד לפניהם אמן נצח סלה

Transliteration:

Nora v'Adir Amitz Ko'ach shetit'nuni l'chein ul'chesed ul'rachamim ul'ahavah b'eineicha ub'einei kol ro'ai b'in'yan sheyar'bu li ohavim mib'li mis'par sh'kol ro'ai y'ash'runi v'esa chen v'chesed l'faneihem Omein Netzach Selah.

Translation:

Awesome and Mighty, Courageous Power, grant me grace, and kindness, and compassion, and love in your eyes, and in the eyes of all who see me in this matter, so that I may have countless friends, that everyone who sees me will count me fortunate, and I will carry favour and kindness with them. *Amen* Eternal *Selah.*[11]

The current psalm was also recommended "for success,"[12] and, curiously enough, to be freed speedily from incarceration. In this regard, we are informed that reciting *Psalm 111* seven times over olive oil, and then having the prisoner rub the substance on his or her face, will ensure a speedy release from prison. Further instruction has it that the psalm should be copied, and tied to the arm.[13] It is worth noting that the capitals of all the words in this psalm were employed in the composition of the following Divine Name construct:

הָאִי בְּלֵ בְּ יָוֹגְ מַיְד לְחֵה וְפֻוּ עֲלֵ זְ עָלֵ חַ
וְיֵט נָלֵי לְבְכֵ מֵהֶל לְלָנַ גָמֵי אָוּנ כְּפֵס
לָלֵע בֻוֹפֵ שָׁלֵצ לְבְקָן וְשֵׁר חַיְי שֶׁטֵל
עֹת עַל

In the current instance the said initials were arranged, in direct order, into twenty-three tri-letter and two bi-letter combinations. The power of this Divine Name construct is said to be in its ability to cure a child who is crying incessantly. In this regard, recite *Psalm 111* directly in the ear of the infant. Following this action, create an amulet by writing down the Divine Name construct, i.e. copying the component Hebrew glyphs with their relevant vowels, and conclude by inserting the following prayer incantation:

מִן [....name of infant....]'לִ שלמה רפוּאה שתשלחו
הבכי ומן הכעס ומן החמה שיש בו אמן כן יהי
רצון ויתרפא בעזרת השם

Transliteration:

> *Shetish 'l'chu r'fu'ah sh'leimah l'*[....name of infant....] *min habechi umin haka'as umin hachamah sheyeish bo Omein kein y'hi ratzon v'yit'rapei b'ez'rat Hashem.*

Translation:

> May you send complete healing to [....name of infant....] from the crying, and from the anger, and from the heat that is in him. *Amen*, yes, be it so willed, and he will be healed with the help of the Divine One.[14]

It goes without saying that this amulet should be located on the person of the juvenile. If the said amulet appears somewhat complex, it is worth considering that the capitals of the opening phrase of *Psalm 111:1* reading הללו יה **אודה** יהוה בכל לבב (*hal'lu Yah odeh YHVH b'chol leivav*—"Hallelujah. I will give thanks unto *YHVH* with my whole heart"), were conjoined in the Divine Name construct האי'בבל, which fulfills the same function when suspended on the crying infant.[15] In conclusion it is worth noting that *Psalm 111:10* is indirectly affiliated with לכב (*Lekav*), the thirty-first portion of the "Name of Seventy-two Names."[16] As with the previous psalms, the current one is likewise employed for a variety of other purposes. In this regard, it is not only recited to have more friends, but equally for oneself to set a good example for others. It is further enunciated against jealousy and resentment, and to encourage justice for just people. *Psalm 111* is also one of the psalms recommended for recitation when visiting the grave of a loved one.

We are informed in the Byzantine Christian magical manuscripts that *Psalm 111* "is a confession from the heart," and that if you have an enemy who "slanders you and speaks groundlessly and falsely against you," that you can overcome him or her by reciting the current psalm three times in the morning, and by writting it "on a glass vessel," which is afterwards washed with rose oil and your face anointed with the oil.[17] By contrast, we are told elsewhere that enunciating this psalm on the property "where you wish to build," will ensure that "the place will be blessed."[18]

PSALM 112

[1] הללו יה אשרי איש ירא את יהוה‏אדני‏אהדונהי
במצותיו חפץ מאד

[2] גבור בארץ יהיה זרעו דור ישרים יברך

[3] הון ועשר בביתו וצדקתו עמדת לעד

[4] זרח בחשך אור לישרים חנון ורחום וצדיק

[5] טוב איש חונן ומלוה יכלכל דבריו במשפט

[6] כי לעולם לא ימוט לזכר עולם יהיה צדיק

[7] משמועה רעה לא יירא נכון לבו בטח
ביהוה‏אדני‏אהדונהי

[8] סמוך לבו לא יירא עד אשר יראה בצריו

[9] פזר נתן לאביונים צדקתו עמדת לעד קרנו
תרום בכבוד

[10] רשע יראה וכעס שניו יחרק ונמס תאות
רשעים תאבד

Transliteration:

[1] *hal'lu Yah ash'rei ish yarei et YHVH b'mitz'votav chafeitz m'od*

[2] *gibor b'aretz yih'yeh zar'o dor y'sharim y'vorach*

[3] *hon va'osher b'veito v'tzid'kato omedet la'ad*

[4] *zarach bachoshech or lay'sharim chanun v'rachum v'tzadik*

[5] *tov ish chonein umal'veh y'chal'keil d'varav b'mish'pat*

[6] *ki l'olam lo yimot l'zeicher olam yih'yeh tzadik*

[7] *mish'mu'ah ra'ah lo yira nachon libo batu'ach baYHVH*

[8] *samuch libo lo yira ad asher yir'eh v'tzarav*

[9] *pizar natan la'ev'yonim tzid'kato omedet la'ad kar'no tarum b'chavod*

[10] *rasha yir'eh v'cha'as shinav yacharok v'namas ta'avat r'sha'im toveid*

Translation:

[1] Hallelujah. Happy is the man that feareth *YHVH*, that delighteth greatly in His commandments.

[2] His seed shall be mighty upon earth; the generation of the upright shall be blessed.

[3] Wealth and riches are in his house; and his merit endureth for ever.

[4] Unto the upright He shineth as a light in the darkness, gracious, and full of compassion, and righteous.

[5] Well is it with the man that dealeth graciously and lendeth, that ordereth his affairs rightfully.

[6] For he shall never be moved; the righteous shall be had in everlasting remembrance.

[7] He shall not be afraid of evil tidings; his heart is stedfast, trusting in *YHVH*.

[8] His heart is established, he shall not be afraid, until he gaze upon his adversaries.

[9] He hath scattered abroad, he hath given to the needy; his righteousness endureth for ever; his horn shall be exalted in honour.

[10] The wicked shall see it, and be vexed; he shall gnash with his teeth, and melt away; the desire of the wicked shall perish.

As noted earlier, *Psalm 112* is an acrostic poem which has been delineated the "twin psalm" of *Psalm 111*. Since I have already addressed the current psalm in conjunction with the previous one, I will focus on the practical applications of the hundred-and-twelfth Psalm, which we are told is enunciated to achieve success in all endeavours.[1] However, the *Shimmush Tehillim* recommends this psalm to increase your personal strength,[2] which has been variously interpreted to mean that one becomes strong and powerful,[3] "increasing one's courage,"[4] or to overcome someone with your own powers.[5] In Godfrey Selig's version of this text we are told that by praying the current psalm, "a man will increase in might and power from time to time."[5]

Be that as it may, a variant recension of the *Shimmush Tehillim* maintains that those who wish to become empowered, or to increase their strength, should recite *Psalm 112* twenty-nine times, and after each time enunciate the following prayer-incantation:

צור צור צור אלהי עולם אתה הוא גבור וגדול
וחזק ולך הגדולה והגבורה והכל בידך ואתה הוא

ושנותיך לא יתמו (Psalm 102:28) ואתה הוא שנאמר
עליך יהוה איש מלחמה יהוה שמו (Exodus 15:3)
האל הגדול הגבור והנורא (Nehemiah 9:32) יצא
דבר מלפניך שאתגבר על גבורתי ואתחזק על חוזק
גופי כי אתה אזור בגבורה ואמיץ כח בעבור שמך
חזקני ואמצני בכחי ובגבותי בעבר שמך הגדול
הגבור הנכבד והנורא צור צור צור צור צור אמן נצה
סלה

Transliteration:

Tzur Tzur Tzur Elohei olam atah hu gibor v'gadol v'chazak ul'cha hag'dulah v'hag'vurah v'hakol b'yad'cha v'atah hu ush'notecha lo yitamu (Psalm 102:28) v'atah hu shene'emar alecha YHVH ish mil'chamah YHVH sh'mo (Exodus 15:3) ha'el hagadol hagibor v'hanora (Nehemiah 9:32) yeitzei davar mil'fanecha sh'et'gaber al g'vurotai v'et'chazek al chozek gufi ki atah ezor big'vurah v'amitz ko'ach ba'avur shim'cha chaz'keini v'am'tzeini b'kochi ubig'votai ba'avur shim'cha hagadol hagibor hanich'bad v'hanora Tzur Tzur Tzur Tzur Omein Netzach Selah.

Translation:

Tzur Tzur Tzur [Rock Rock Rock], Eternal God, you are mighty, great and strong, and yours is the greatness and the power, and everything is in your hands. "But Thou art the selfsame, and Thy years shall have no end." (*Psalm 102:28*) And you are the same, for it is said of you "*YHVH is a man of war, YHVH is his name,*" (*Exodus 15:3*) "the great, the mighty, and the awful God." (*Nehemiah 9:32*) Let a word go before you, so that I may become stronger in my power, and empowered in the strength of my body, for you are girded with strength, courage and power. For the sake of your name boldster and encourage me in my power and in my strength, for the sake of your great, mighty, honoured and awesome name *Tzur Tzur Tzur Tzur Amen Eternal Selah.*[6]

Other than the listed applications, *Psalm 112* is enunciated for the protection of paupers and beggars; to encourage humility; and in praise of righteousness. This psalm is further employed to counteract sterility; ensure conception; and is again one of the psalms recommended for recitation when visiting the graves of loved ones.

It seems little use is made of the current psalm in Christian Magic. In this regard, there is a most belligerent application of *Psalm 112:1–8* listed in the *"Livre d'Or,"* in which the psalm is read over "powdered swallow" for three days, for the purpose of slaying an enemy and all his kin.[7] The current psalm is utilised for much more benevolent reasons in the *"Key of Solomon,"* where *Psalm 112:3* features in both the second and fourth *"Pentacle of Jupiter."*[8]

PSALM 113

[1] הללו יה הללו עבדי יהוהאדני־אהדונהי הללו
את שם יהוהאדני־אהדונהי

[2] יהי שם יהוהאדני־אהדונהי מברך מעתה ועד
עולם

[3] ממזרח שמש עד מבואו מהלל שם
יהוהאדני־אהדונהי

[4] רם על כל גוים יהוהאדני־אהדונהי על השמים
כבודו

[5] מי כיהוהאדני־אהדונהי אלהינו המגביהי לשבת

[6] המשפילי לראות בשמים ובארץ

[7] מקימי מעפר דל מאשפת ירים אביון

[8] להושיבי עם נדיבים עם נדיבי עמו

[9] מושיבי עקרת הבית אם הבנים שמחה הללו יה

Transliteration:

[1] *hal'lu Yah hal'lu av'dei YHVH hal'lu et shem YHVH*
[2] *y'hi shem YHVH m'vorach mei'atah v'ad olam*
[3] *mimiz'rach shemesh ad m'vo'o m'hulal shem YHVH*
[4] *ram al kol goyim YHVH al hashamayim k'vodo*
[5] *mi kaYHVH eloheinu hamag'bihi lashavet*
[6] *hamash'pili lir'ot bashamayim uva'aretz*
[7] *m'kimi mei'afar dal mei'ash'pot yarim ev'yon*
[8] *l'hoshivi im n'divim im n'divei amo*
[9] *moshivi akeret habayit eim habanim s'meichah hal'lu Yah*

Translation:

[1] Hallelujah. Praise, O ye servants of *YHVH*, praise the name of *YHVH*.
[2] Blessed be the name of *YHVH* from this time forth and for ever.
[3] From the rising of the sun unto the going down thereof *YHVH*'s name is to be praised.
[4] *YHVH* is high above all nations, His glory is above the heavens.
[5] Who is like unto *YHVH* our God, that is enthroned on high,

[6] That looketh down low upon heaven and upon the earth?

[7] Who raiseth up the poor out of the dust, and lifteth up the needy out of the dunghill;

[8] That He may set him with princes, even with the princes of His people.

[9] Who maketh the barren woman to dwell in her house as a joyful mother of children. Hallelujah.

Psalm 113 is the first of a set of six psalms, i.e. *Psalms 113–118*, collectively termed *Halel Mitz'ri* ("Egyptian *Halel* (Praise)." Deriving this title from the opening phrase of *Psalm 114* reading בצאת ישראל ממצרים (*b'tzeit yis'ra'el mimitz'rayim* —"When Israel came forth out of Egypt"), these psalms are recited both in the synagogue and during the *Seder*, i.e. the religious meal over *Pesach* (Passover), i.e. the festival when we celebrate the journey of the Israelites from slavery to freedom.[1] We are told that "the critical moment of liberation for God's people from their slavery in Egypt under Pharaoh was Passover night,"[2] and it is said that *Psalms 113—118* were "recited in Temple times, during the sacrifice of the Passover offerings."[3] Today *Psalms 113* and *114* are enunciated before the Passover meal, and the remaining four at the conclusion of the meal.[4] As indicated by the term הלל (*halel*), the said psalms are all about "praise," regarding which we are told that "reliving the journey from enslavement to freedom" over the Festival of *Pesach* (Passover), "leads naturally to praise of God, who freed us."[5]

Several terms are employed to express "praise" in the many versions of the הגדה (*Hagadah*), the text delineating the order of the Passover *Seder*. Whilst these terms vary a lot, one commentator maintains the following seven are employed to express praise or honour: להודות (*l'hodot*"); להלל (*l'haleil*); לשבח (*l'shabei'ach*); לפאר (*l'fa'eir*); לרומם (*l'romeim*); להדר (*l'hadeir*); and לקלס (*l'kaleis*). They are said to "correspond to the seven heavens," and "to the seven 'shepherds' of Israel,"[6] i.e. the seven *Ush'pizin* ("Holy Guests"): Abraham, Isaac, Jacob, Moses, Aaron, Joseph, and David, whom I have referenced elsewhere.[7] It should be noted that *Psalms 113–118* are also enunciated during the festivals of *Chanukah* (Festival of Lights),

Sukkot (Festival of Booths), *Shavuot* (Festival of Weeks), and on *Rosh Chodesh*, the monthly celebration of the New Moon.[8]

Psalm 113 is recommended in Jewish Magic against heresy.[9] In this regard, one source notes the current psalm is employed "to secure the removal of idolatry."[10] The standard published Hebrew edition of the *Shimmush Tehillim* succinctly described it to be "good to destroy idolatry."[11] Godfrey Selig noted in his more wordy German/English version of the *Shimmush Tehillim* that "by praying [this psalm] devoutly it is possible to check growing heresy and infidelity."[12] Yet the "wordiest" instruction on the magical use of *Psalm 113* appears in a variant recension of the *Shimmush Tehillim*, in which we are informed that a person who wishes to destroy idolatry should fast three days. Then, on the third day, the said individual is advised to "cry out" the psalm three times, each time concluding with the following prayer-incantation:

מלכי ואלהי שמע שועתי והקשיב זעקתי והאזין
תפלתי וראה במרירות נפשי ובמר רוחי והשפיל
והכניע ואבד עבודה זרה בשם יה יה אל שדי
הנראה למשה רבינו עליו השלום באש הסנה יהיה
הדבר הזה במהרה ובקירוב זמן בעגלא ובזמן קריב
אמן נצח סלה

Transliteration:
> *Mal'ki veilohai sh'ma shiva'ti v'hag'shiv za'ak'ti v'ha'azin t'filati ur'eih b'm'rirut naf'shi ub'mar ruchi v'hash'pil v'hich'ni'a v'avad avodah zarah b'shem Yah Yah El Shadai hanir'eh l'mosheh rabeinu alav hashalom b'esh has'neh yih'yeh hadavar hazeh bim'heirah ub'kirov z'man ba'agala uviz'man kariv Omein Netzach Selah.*

Translation:
> My King and my God, hear my cry, and answer my call, and give ear to my prayer, and see the bitterness of my soul and the bitterness of my spirit. And debase, and subjugate, and eradicate idolatry, in the name *Yah Yah El Shadai*, who appeared to Moses our Teacher, peace be upon him, in the fire of the thorn bush, this issue will happen speedily and some time soon, fast, and in a brief period. *Amen* Eternal *Selah*.[13]

Whilst *Psalm 113* is primarily uttered against blasphemy, I have seen it recommended for the atonement of transgressions, and to declare the greatness of the Divine One. Secular minded readers, who might find these applications somewhat disappointing, should note that this psalm is also recommended for a variety of different purposes. In this regard, it is again one of the psalms which is recited against despair; to increase in might and power; as well as to encourage humility. It is further employed for diseases of, or problems with, the ears, eyes, hands, legs, mouth, nose, and throat. It is also enunciated for the protection of children; in support of the elderly; and for a natural death. It is further considered useful in the raising of cattle and livestock, and for protection against floods. As far as "healing activities in nature is concerned," we are told that *Psalm 113:3* is beneficial for those who like "joining in sunrises or sunsets."[14] In conclusion, it has been noted that *Psalm 113:2* is directly associated with יִּל (*Yeyil*), the fifty-eighth tri-letter portion of the "Name of Seventy-two Names."[15]

    Psalm 113 is applied for very different purposes in Christian magic. The Byzantine Christian magical manuscripts list the current psalm in conjunction *Psalm 114* to counteract potential drunkenness after an individual was coaxed into consuming a lot of alcohol. In this regard, the said individual is instructed to repeat these psalms over a cup of wine, which is to be consumed with "five or three bitter almonds and cabbage-stem with the flower if available."[16] Talking of almonds reminds me of a very different application of the current psalm in the second part of *"The Book of Abramelin the Mage,"* with specific reference to a recently discovered German manuscript titled *"Extract from some magical experiments of Ramon Llull but, more so, from Part II of the book by Abraham of Worms."*[17] In this regard, *Psalm 113* is enunciated seven times over a glass of almond milk to counteract infertility. It is said this beverage should be prepared by the practitioner in person, and a little incense sprinkled over it. This substance is afterwards consumed on an empty stomach by the barren woman, and the action repeated every morning for a period of seven days. Additionally the said woman has to carry an amulet constructed from gold, silver, or pure wax, with verse two of the current psalm inscribed on one side, and verse 9 on the other.[18] Elsewhere in the same text it is suggested that the married couple should both consume the said milk every morning and evening over the period of seven days.[19]

The *"Livre d'Or"* maintains the psalm should be read over "holy water," which is afterwards sprinkled seven times over the residence of the practitioner, and it is said that "all that you will receive will be profitable."[20] The same source maintains this psalm to be "very good written down," and located "in a stable for the protection of sheep, cattle and goats."[21] *Psalm 113:7* and *8* are listed elsewhere for the purpose of rising "out of poverty and to be raised up in honours and riches."[22] The current psalm is also one of the earlier mentioned set of nineteen listed in the *"Key of Solomon,"* i.e. *Psalms 8, 15, 22, 46, 47, 49, 51, 53, 68, 72, 84, 102, 110, 113, 126, 130, 131, 133,* and *139*, which are enunciated over the wax from which ritual candles are manufactured.[23] In the same text *Psalm 113:7* is said to be inscribed around the perimeter of the *"Seventh Pentacle of Jupiter."*[24]

PSALM 114

[1] בצאת ישראל ממצרים בית יעקב מעם לעז

[2] היתה יהודה לקדשו ישראל ממשלותיו

[3] הים ראה וינס הירדן יסב לאחור

[4] ההרים רקדו כאילים גבעות כבני צאן

[5] מה לך הים כי תנוס הירדן תסב לאחור

[6] ההרים תרקדו כאילים גבעות כבני צאן

[7] מלפני אדון חולי ארץ מלפני אלוה יעקב

[8] ההפכי הצור אגם מים חלמיש למעינו מים

Transliteration:

[1] *b'tzeit yis'ra'el mimitz'rayim beit ya'akov mei'am lo'eiz*

[2] *hay'tah y'hudah l'kod'sho yis'ra'el mam'sh'lotav*

[3] *hayam ra'ah vayanos hayar'dein yisov l'achor*

[4] *heharim rak'du ch'eilim g'va'ot kiv'nei tzon*

[5] *mah l'cha hayam ki tanus hayar'dein tisov l'achor*

[6] *heharim tir'k'du ch'eilim g'va'ot kiv'nei tzon*

[7] *milif'nei adon chuli aretz milif'nei elo'ah ya'akov*

[8] *hahof'chi hatzur agam mayim chalamish l'ma'y'no mayim*

Translation:

[1] When Israel came forth out of Egypt, the house of Jacob from a people of strange language;

[2] Judah became His sanctuary, Israel His dominion.

[3] The sea saw it, and fled; the Jordan turned backward.

[4] The mountains skipped like rams, the hills like young sheep.

[5] What aileth thee, O thou sea, that thou fleest? thou Jordan, that thou turnest backward?

[6] Ye mountains, that ye skip like rams; ye hills, like young sheep?

[7] Tremble, thou earth, at the presence of the Lord, at the presence of the God of Jacob;

[8] Who turned the rock into a pool of water, the flint into a fountain of waters.

Psalm 114 is the second of the set of "Egyptian *Halel*" psalms, this designation having been derived, as noted earlier, from the opening phrase of this psalm reading "when Israel came forth out of Egypt." It is worth keeping in mind that the *"Hallel Mitz'ri"* psalms share the characteristic הללו יה (*hal'lu Yah*—*"Hallelujah* [Praise *Yah*]"*) in the opening and/or concluding statement, except for *Psalm 114* and *118* in which this proclamation is absent. It was suggested that the concluding *"Hallelujah"* of *Psalm 113:9* should be the opening declaration of the current psalm.[1] However, it has also been said that since the *"Hallelujah"* exclamation is absent in *Psalm 118* as well, the concluding psalm of the "Egyptian *Halel*" set, "the seemingly missing 'hallelujah' in Psalm 114 need not be viewed as problematic."[2] It was further suggested that *Psalm 113* should "be read as an introduction to Psalm 114."[3] Whatever the case may be, the current psalm is, as mentioned earlier, recited during the three "Pilgrim Festivals," as well as during *Chanukah*, as well as on *Rosh Chodesh*.[4]

    Psalm 114 is said in *Practical Kabbalah* to be good for those who are buying and selling.[5] In other words, it is recited for good fortune in business.[6] In this regard, the *Shimmush Tehillim* maintains success can be assured if this psalm is written in the shop, or locale from whence business is conducted.[7] Godfrey Selig extensively enlarged the succinct instruction in the primary text, saying "if you desire success in your trade or business, write this Psalm with its appropriate holy name upon clean parchment, and carry it about your person constantly in a small bag prepared especially for this purpose."[8] In the regular Hebrew editions of the *Shimmush Tehillim* the associated Divine Name is said to be אה (*Alef–Heh*), with no indications of its derivation.[9] Selig stated that this Divine Name, vocalised *"Aha,"* pertains to the Divine Names אדני (*Adonai*) and the Ineffable Name (יהוה), and he further noted that it was derived: א (*Alef*) from ישראל (*Yis'ra'el*—"Israel"): verse 1; and ה (*Heh*) from יהודה (*Yehudah*—"Judah"): verse 2.[10] In this regard, there is once again no evidence in primary sources to support these claims. However, a different recension of the *Shimmush Tehillim* maintains the Divine Name to be וה (*Vav–Heh*).[11]

    In yet another recension of the *Shimmush Tehillim*, the current psalm is recommended to those who intend travelling away from their place of residence. In this instance, the practitioner is instructed to recite the psalm three times, each time ending with the following prayer-incantation:

שדי שדי שדי אל אלהים הצילני נא והוציאני
מן העיר הזאת לשלום ולחיים ולטובה ולברכה
ולהצלחה והשקט ובמצה בשם יהוה אלהי ישראל
אלהי עולם ישר אורחותי אמן נצח סלה

Transliteration:

> *Shadai Shadai Shadai El Elohim hatzileini na v'hotzi'ani min ha'ir hazot l'shalom ul'chayim ul'tovah v'liv'rachah ul'hatz'lacha v'hash'ket ubit'chah b'shem YHVH Elohei yis'ra'el Elohei olam yishar or'chotai Omein Netzach Selah.*

Translation:

> *Shadai Shadai Shadai El Elohim,* please save me, and bring me out of this city in peace, for life, for good, for blessing and for success, and calmness and safety. In the name of *YHVH* God of Israel, Eternal God, straighten my ways. *Amen Eternal Selah.*[12]

As far as employing *Psalm 114* for success is concerned, all the letters of this psalm were combined in the following Divine Name construct for this very purpose:[13]

בצא תיש ראל ממצ רים בית יעק
במע סלע זהי תהי הוד הלק דשו ישר
אלם משל ותי והי סרא הוי נסה ירד
ויס בלא חור ההר יסר קדו כאי לים
גבע ותכ בני צאן מהל דהי סכי תנו
סהי רדן תסב לאח ורה הדי סתר קדו
כאי לים גבע ותכ בני צאן מלפ ניא
דון חול יאר זמל פני אלו היע קבה
הפכ יהצ ורא גסמ יסח למי שלמ עינ
ומים

This Divine Name construct was formulated by simply combining all the letters of the current psalm, and then dividing them into seventy-one three-letter combinations, and a concluding four-letter combination, i.e. a total of seventy-two letter combinations. Whether intentional or not, it is tempting to find a hidden meaning in this number. After all, seventy-two is the *gematria* of חסד [ח = 8 + ס = 60 + ד = 4 = 72] (*Chesed*), the *sefirah* of "lovingkindness" on the sefirotic Tree, which is said to comprise the "seventy-two bridges that come from the water of *Chesed haGedolah* (great loving-kindness),"[14] and which are further said to be termed "the Seventy-two Holy Names."[15] In this regard the expansive quality of the "loving-kindness" of *Chesed* associated with the planet Jupiter, is well aligned with this Divine Name construct, which was formulated to be carried as an amulet by those who seek success in all their endeavours.[16] Be that as it may, if practitioners should again find copying the said Divine Name construct to be somewhat cumbersome, they could simply write ב״ים. This Divine Name construct comprises the initials of the first three words of the current psalm reading בצאת ישראל ממצרים (*b'tzeit yis'ra'el mimitz'rayim*—"When Israel came forth out of Egypt"), which is considered equally good as an amulet for success in business.[17]

Psalm 114 has also been recommended for success in general; to express gratitude for good fortune; to give praise, as well as for love of the Divine One. It is further enunciated to ensure a safe pregnancy; for the protection of children; and against diseases in general. It is also enunciated to encourage humility, and for support in dealing with internal desolation. In this regard, I have benefited greatly from reciting both *Psalms 113* and *114*, respectively against feelings of despair and dark depression, following the passing of a loved one.

In Christian magic we find the current psalm used for a purpose entirely at odds with its very positive application in *Practical Kabbalah*. In this regard, *Psalm 114* is employed to preclude fishermen from catching any fish. To affect this result, the psalm is recited over holy water which is afterwards spilled in the targeted fishermen's boats.[18]

PSALM 115

‎[1] לא לנו יהוה‎אהדונהי‎ לא לנו כי לשמך תן כבוד על חסדך על אמתך

‎[2] למה יאמרו הגוים איה נא אלהיהם

‎[3] ואלהינו בשמים כל אשר חפץ עשה

‎[4] עצביהם כסף וזהב מעשה ידי אדם

‎[5] פה להם ולא ידברו עינים להם ולא יראו

‎[6] אזנים להם ולא ישמעו אף להם ולא יריחון

‎[7] ידיהם ולא ימישון רגליהם ולא יהלכו לא יהגו בגרונם

‎[8] כמוהם יהיו עשיהם כל אשר בטח בהם

‎[9] ישראל בטח ביהוה‎אהדונהי‎ עזרם ומגנם הוא

‎[10] בית אהרן בטחו ביהוה‎אהדונהי‎ עזרם ומגנם הוא

‎[11] יראי יהוה‎אהדונהי‎ בטחו ביהוה‎אהדונהי‎ עזרם ומגנם הוא

‎[12] יהוה‎אהדונהי‎ זכרנו יברך יברך את בית ישראל יברך את בית אהרן

‎[13] יברך יראי יהוה‎אהדונהי‎ הקטנים עם הגדלים

‎[14] יסף יהוה‎אהדונהי‎ עליכם עליכם ועל בניכם

‎[15] ברוכים אתם ליהוה‎אהדונהי‎ עשה שמים וארץ

‎[16] השמים שמים ליהוה‎אהדונהי‎ והארץ נתן לבני אדם

‎[17] לא המתים יהללו יה ולא כל ירדי דומה

‎[18] ואנחנו נברך יה מעתה ועד עולם הללו יה

Transliteration:

[1] *lo lanu YHVH lo lanu ki l'shim'cha tein kavod al chas'd'cha al amitecha*

[2] *lamah yom'ru hagoyim ayeih na eloheihem*

[3] *veiloheinu vashamayim kol asher chafeitz asah*
[4] *atzabeihem kesef v'zahav ma'aseih y'dei adam*
[5] *peh lahem v'lo y'dabeiru einayim lahem v'lo yir'u*
[6] *oz'nayim lahem v'lo yish'ma'u af lahem v'lo y'richun*
[7] *y'deihem v'lo y'mishun rag'leihem v'lo y'haleichu lo
yeh'gu big'ronam*
[8] *k'mohem yih'yu oseihem kol asher botei'ach bahem*
[9] *yis'ra'eil b'tach baYHVH ez'ram umaginam hu*
[10] *beit aharon bit'chu vaYHVH ez'ram umaginam hu*
[11] *yir'ei YHVH bit'chu vaYHVH ez'ram umaginam hu*
[12] *YHVH z'charanu y'vareich y'vareich et beit yis'ra'el
y'vareich et beit aharon*
[13] *y'vareich yir'ei YHVH hak'tanim im hag'dolim*
[14] *yoseif YHVH aleichem aleichem v'al b'neichem*
[15] *b'ruchim atem laYHVH oseih shamayim va'aretz*
[16] *hashamayim shamayim laYHVH v'ha'aretz natan
liv'nei adam*
[17] *lo hameitim y'hal'lu Yah v'lo kol yor'dei dumah*
[18] *va'anach'nu n'vareich Yah mei'atah v'ad olam hal'lu
Yah*

Translation:

[1] Not unto us, *YHVH*, not unto us, but unto Thy name give glory, for Thy mercy, and for Thy truth's sake.

[2] Wherefore should the nations say: 'Where is now their God?'

[3] But our God is in the heavens; whatsoever pleased Him He hath done.

[4] Their idols are silver and gold, the work of men's hands.

[5] They have mouths, but they speak not; eyes have they, but they see not;

[6] They have ears, but they hear not; noses have they, but they smell not;

[7] They have hands, but they handle not; feet have they, but they walk not; neither speak they with their throat.

[8] They that make them shall be like unto them; yea, every one that trusteth in them.

[9] O Israel, trust thou in *YHVH*! He is their help and their shield!

[10] O house of Aaron, trust ye in *YHVH*! He is their help and their shield!

[11] Ye that fear *YHVH*, trust in *YHVH*! He is their help and their shield.

[12] *YHVH* hath been mindful of us, He will bless—He will bless the house of Israel; He will bless the house of Aaron.

[13] He will bless them that fear *YHVH*, both small and great.

[14] *YHVH* increase you more and more, you and your children.

[15] Blessed be ye of *YHVH* who made heaven and earth.

[16] The heavens are the heavens of *YHVH*; but the earth hath He given to the children of men.

[17] The dead praise not *Yah*, neither any that go down into silence;

[18] But we will bless *Yah* from this time forth and for ever. Hallelujah

Psalm 115 is the third of the "Egyptian *Halel* Psalms," and the first of the set of four recited at the conclusion of the Passover meal.[1] There have been some conjecture regarding the current psalm and the previous one being considered to be a single unit.[2] In this regard, it has been noted that in some of the older Hebrew scriptures, e.g. *Aleppo Codex* (925 C.E.) and *Codes Lenigradensis* (1008 C.E.), as well as in an early fragment from the Cairo Genizah, which includes a list of the opening and closing fragments of all the biblical psalms,[3] *Psalms 114* and *115* are conjoined into a single psalm.[4] The same arrangement can be found in the Greek Septuagint (3rd century B.C.E.),[5] and in the Latin Vulgate (*Biblia Vulgata* [4th century C.E.]).[6] However, there were several textual variances of the Hebrew scriptures dating as far back as the Qumran texts, and it is fairly well acknowledged that there were parallel developments in the formulation of the Hebrew Psalter.[7] Besides, in the *Biblia Hebraica Stuttgartensia*, considered the most definitive of the Hebrew Scriptures, the said psalms are listed separate.[8] In fact, it is worth keeping in mind that until the 16th century, there were no concensus in the medieval texts regarding the arrangement of the Hebrew Psalms,[9] but this issue appears to have been resolved following the publication in 1525 of the *"Second Edition of the Rabbinic Bible"* with *Masorah*, edited by Jacob ben Chayim,[10] which includes the standard division of the hundred and fifty psalms, and which remained the most authoritative version of the Hebrew Bible until the appearance of *Biblia Hebraica* in 1937.[11]

Whatever the supposed "correct arrangement" of the Hebrew psalms may be, it is perfectly clear that the *Shimmush Tehillim*, and the uses of psalms in Jewish Magic generally, are based on the hundred-and-fifty psalms as they appear in the standard, readily available Hebrew Bible. In this regard, *Psalm 115*, in addressing the folly of idolatry, is setting the tone of its magical application, i.e. affording support "when arguing with heretics,"[12] "to be victorious in debate,"[13] or in the words of the *Shimmush Tehillim*, "this psalm is good when entering into a religious dispute against idolaters."[14] Godfrey Selig again embelished this application slightly in his German/English translation of this text, saying "if you are determined to dispute with infidels, heretics, and scoffers at religion, pray this Psalm devoutly beforehand."[15] This application is somewhat different in a variant recension of the *Shimmush Tehillim*, which addressed the issue of entering into a public dispute with Christian priests, a matter which in days of yore could result in violent retribution. In this instance, we are told that individuals who are obliged to meet with גלחים (*galachim*—"shaven heads"), i.e. a reference to the tonsured heads of Christian monks and priests, should fast, and recite *Psalm 115* sixty times with its associated Divine Name. This action is concluded by enunciating the following prayer-incantation:

אמון אמון אמון סל סל צור אלהי עולם עזרני
ליעד עם אלו הגלחים [....insert names of priests...]
והשב גמולם להם בראשם על הרעה אשר עשו פעמים
רבות וקלקל מחשבותם ולא יוכלו ליעד נגדי בשם
יהוה אלהי ישראל אמן נצח סלה

Transliteration:
Eimun Eimun Eimun Sal Sal Tzur Elohei olam az'reini l'ya'ad im eilu hagal'chim [....insert names of priests...]

> *v'hashev g'mulam lahem b'rosham al hara'ah asher asu pa'amim rabot v'kil'keil mach'shavotam v'lo yoch'lu l'ya'ed neg'di b'shem YHVH Elohei yis'ra'el Omein Netzach Selah.*

Translation:

> *Eimun Eimun Eimun Sal Sal Tzur* ["Faith Faith Faith Containment (Basket) Containment Rock"], Eternal God, help me in meeting these priests [....insert names of priests...], and repay them on their heads for their deeds, for the evil they have done many times, and ruin their thoughts so that they will not be able to act against me. In the name of *YHVH* God of Israel. *Amen* Eternal *Selah*.[16]

Other than the listed uses of the current psalm to counteract idolatry, and to have success in arguments with idolaters, or, for that matter, when disputing with the unfaithful and non-believers, I have observed the hundred-and-fifteenth Psalm recommended in less official sources for recitation against lies, and to strengthen faith.

As far as individual verses are concerned, it should be noted that the initials of the words comprising the phrase in *Psalm 115:11* reading יִרְאֵי יהוה בִּטְחוּ בַיהֹוָה (*yir'ei YHVH bit'chu vaYHVH* —"Ye that fear *YHVH*, trust in *YHVH*"), were combined in the Divine Name construct יִּבְב, which is employed in amulets as a call for help.[17] The said verse is also directly affiliated with יִּז (*Yeyiz*), the fortieth tri-letter portion of the "*Shem Vayisa Vayet.*"[18]

Psalm 115:12 is utilised for a very interesting purpose in Jewish Magic. In this regard, the letters comprising this verse were conjoined in the following Divine Name construct, which we are told married couples are obliged to recite prior to sexual union, in order to ensure that they will engender pure and holy offspring "who would have the power to bring to light pure deeds":[19]

$$
\text{יַן הַר וַה הַא זַת כֹּי רַב}
$$
$$
\text{נַת וַא יַן בַר רַב כֹּי יַל}
$$
$$
\text{בָּא רַר כַשׁ אַי תַת יַב}
$$

Vocalised *YaN' HaR' VaH' Ha' ZaT' ChaY' RaB' NaT' Va' YaCh' VaR' RaB' ChaY' YaL' Va' RaR' ChaSh' AY' TaT' YaV'*, this Divine Name construct was formulated by dividing the forty letters into two groups. The first group of twenty, written in exact order of appearance in the said verse, is conjoined with the second set of twenty written in reverse order. The two vowels employed in the enunciation of each of the two-letter combinations, are respectively aligned with חֶסֶד (*Chesed*) and גְּבוּרָה (*Gevurah*) on the sefirotic Tree. This is therefore a magical action to balance the forces of "mercy" and "might" prior to engaging in the act of procreation.

It would seem that little use is made of *Psalm 115* in Christian Magic. However, the *"Livre d'Or"* offers instruction on writing this psalm, and perfuming the written text with certain fragrant resins, doing so during a certain astrological configuration. The writing is afterwards tied to the right arm of an infant, and it is said "he will be delivered from all manner of sicknesses and perils."[20]

PSALM 116

[1] אהבתי כי ישמע יהוה‎אהדונהי את קולי
תחנוני

[2] כי הטה אזנו לי ובימי אקרא

[3] אפפוני חבלי מות ומצרי שאול מצאני צרה
ויגון אמצא

[4] ובשם יהוה‎אהדונהי אקרא אנה יהוה‎אהדונהי
מלטה נפשי

[5] חנון יהוה‎אהדונהי וצדיק ואלהינו מרחם

[6] שמר פתאים יהוה‎אהדונהי דלתי ולי יהושיע

[7] שובי נפשי למנוחיכי כי יהוה‎אהדונהי גמל
עליכי

[8] כי חלצת נפשי ממות את עיני מן דמעה את
רגלי מדחי

[9] אתהלך לפני יהוה‎אהדונהי בארצות החיים

[10] האמנתי כי אדבר אני עניתי מאד

[11] אני אמרתי בחפזי כל האדם כזב

[12] מה אשיב ליהוה‎אהדונהי כל תגמולוהי עלי

[13] כוס ישועות אשא ובשם יהוה‎אהדונהי אקרא

[14] נדרי ליהוה‎אהדונהי אשלם נגדה נא לכל עמו

[15] יקר בעיני יהוה‎אהדונהי המותה לחסידיו

[16] אנה יהוה‎אהדונהי כי אני עבדך אני עבדך
בן אמתך פתחת למוסרי

[17] לך אזבח זבח תודה ובשם יהוה‎אהדונהי
אקרא

[18] נדרי ליהוה‎אהדונהי אשלם נגדה נא לכל עמו

[19] בחצרות בית יהוה‎אהדונהי בתוככי ירושלם
הללו יה

Transliteration:
[1] *ahav'ti ki yish'ma YHVH et koli tachanunai*
[2] *ki hitah oz'no li uv'yamai ek'ra*
[3] *afafuni chev'lei mavet um'tzarei sh'ol m'tza'uni tzarah*
v'yagon em'tza

[4] *uv'shem YHVH ek'ra anah YHVH mal'tah naf'shi*
[5] *chanun YHVH v'tzadik veiloheinu m'racheim*
[6] *shomeir p'ta'im YHVH daloti v'li y'hoshi'a*
[7] *shuvi naf'shi lim'nuchaichi ki YHVH gamal alaichi*
[8] *ki chilatz'ta naf'shi mimavet et eini min dim'ah et rag'li midechi*
[9] *et'haleich lif'nei YHVH b'ar'tzot hachayim*
[10] *he'eman'ti ki adabeir ani aniti m'od*
[11] *ani amar'ti v'chof'zi kol ha'adam kozeiv*
[12] *mah ashiv laYHVH kol tag'mulohi alai*
[13] *kos y'shu'ot esa uv'shem YHVH ek'ra*
[14] *n'darai laYHVH ashaleim neg'dah na l'chol amo*
[15] *yakar b'einei YHVH hamav'tah lachasidav*
[16] *anah YHVH ki ani av'decha ani av'd'cha ben amatecha pitach'ta l'moseirai*
[17] *l'cha ez'bach zevach todah uv'shem YHVH ek'ra*
[18] *n'darai laYHVH ashaleim neg'dah na l'chol amo*
[19] *b'chatz'rot beit YHVH b'tocheichi y'rushalam ha'lu Yah*

Translation:

[1] I love that *YHVH* should hear my voice and my supplications.

[2] Because He hath inclined His ear unto me, therefore will I call upon Him all my days.

[3] The cords of death compassed me, and the straits of the nether-world got hold upon me; I found trouble and sorrow.

[4] But I called upon the name of *YHVH*: 'I beseech thee, *YHVH*, deliver my soul.'

[5] Gracious is *YHVH*, and righteous; yea, our God is compassionate.

[6] *YHVH* preserveth the simple; I was brought low, and He saved me.

[7] Return, O my soul, unto Thy rest; for *YHVH* hath dealt bountifully with thee.

[8] For thou hast delivered my soul from death, mine eyes from tears, and my feet from stumbling.

[9] I shall walk before *YHVH* in the lands of the living.

[10] I trusted even when I spoke: 'I am greatly afflicted.'

[11] I said in my haste: 'All men are liars.'

[12] How can I repay unto *YHVH* all His bountiful dealings toward me?

[13] I will lift up the cup of salvation, and call upon the name of *YHVH*.

[14] My vows will I pay unto *YHVH*, yea, in the presence of all His people.

[15] Precious in the sight of *YHVH* is the death of His saints.

[16] I beseech Thee, *YHVH*, for I am Thy servant; I am Thy servant, the son of Thy handmaid; Thou hast loosed my bands.

[17] I will offer to thee the sacrifice of thanksgiving, and will call upon the name of *YHVH*.

[18] I will pay my vows unto *YHVH*, yea, in the presence of all His people;

[19] In the courts of *YHVH*'s house, in the midst of thee, O Jerusalem. Hallelujah.

Psalm 116 is the fourth of the "Egyptian *Halel* Psalms," which we noted earlier are enunciated over the Pilgrim Festivals, *Chanukah* and on *Rosh Chodesh* (New Moon). However, it is worth noting that during the concluding six days of *Pesach* (Passover), and also on *Rosh Chodesh*, a "Half *Halel*" is read which means that the previous and current psalm are abbreviated, i.e. the first eleven verses of both of these psalms are omitted.[1] Amongst the reasons given for this reduction on the "New Moon," is that both psalms are about joyous praise of the Ineffable One, whilst the arrival of the New Moon is understood to be a solemn "day of forgiveness and atonement for sins that may bring epidemics, especially upon children."[2] Thus it is considered more appropriate on the said occasions, to commence reading *Psalms 115* and *116* at the twelfth verse in which we acknowledge the Divine One having been "mindful of us," and also consider how we might repay the Eternal One for all the "bountiful dealings" bestowed on us.

Regarding the performance of personal acts of spiritual rectification in order to forestall epidemics besetting the community, we are informed in Jewish Magic that whoever enunciates this psalm regularly, will not die a strange,[3] violent,[4] unusual,[5] unatural, or a sudden death.[6] In this regard, Godfrey Selig noted that "whoever prays this Psalm daily with devotion, trusting fully in God, will be safe from violent death, neither will he be overtaken by a sudden death."[7] However, in a variant recension of the *Shimmush Tehillim* the current psalm is listed for the purpose of atonement, which I referenced in terms of *Rosh Chodesh*. In this regard, we are informed that those who wish to repent should fast for five days, following which *Psalm 116* is recited on the sixth day, and the action concluded with the following prayer-incantation:

אוי לי כי נדדתי ממך שוד שוד לי כי פשעתי בך וגרשוני
עונותי מהסתפח בנחלת יהוה (*I Samuel 26:19*) והשיגוני
רעות רבות וצרות וקשות ולא בקשתיך בכל זאת עתה
תשיגני כלמתי ואשמתי תלאה פגעה לימי השחרות
אחר שיבה זרקה בי גם ניחמתי כי צדק יעצוני
רעיוני אפלה נא ביד יהוה (*I Chronicles 21:13*) כי
אתה קרוב לכל קוראיך ונדרש לכל דורשיך רצה
תשובת שבים ורפא תשובת שובבים שאוכל לעמוד
לפניך ומשוך לבי לרצוניך וקרבני לברית ולחוק
ואל אשתחוה מרחוק זה הוידוי מצאתי שאשאו אליהו
הנביא זכרונו לברכה

Transliteration:

> *Oi li ki nadad'ti mim'cha shod li ki pash'ati b'cha v'geir'shuni avonotai meihis'tapei'ach b'nachalat YHVH (I Samuel 26:19) v'hishiguni ra'ot rabot v'tzarot v'kashot v'lo bakash'ticha b'chol zot atah tashigeini kalam'ti vasham'ti til'eh pig'ah liyamai hashach'rut achar seivah zar'ka bi gam nich'mati ki tzedek ya'atzuni ra'ayonai ef'lah na b'yad YHVH (I Chronicles 21:13) ki atah karov l'chol kor'echa v'nid'rash l'chol dor'shecha r'tzeih t'shuvat shavim v'rofei t'shuvat shov'vim sh'uchal l'amod lif'neicha um'shoch libi l'r'tzonecha v'kar'veini l'b'rit v'l'chok v'el esh'tachaveh meirachok zeh havidui matzati she'asa'o eiliyahu hanavi zich'rono liv'racha.*

Translation:

> Woe is me! I have strayed. Desolation is upon me, for I
> have transgressed against you. And my misdeeds have
> driven me out, "that I should not cleave unto the
> inheritance of YHVH." (*I Samuel 26:19*) And many evils,
> and troubles, and severe hardships have overtaken me, and
> I have not queried you about any of these. Now my shame
> and guilt reach me. Hardship has met my black days after
> gray hair are here and there upon me. I too was comforted,
> for justice will be advised to me, and is my council. "Let
> me fall now into the hand of *YHVH*," (*I Chronicles 21:13*)
> because you are close to all those who call you, and let all
> those who are looking for you find you. Accept the
> repentance of those who repent, and heal the repentance of
> the backsliders, so that I may stand before you. Draw my
> heart to your will, and near to the covenant and the law,
> and I will not prostrate myself from afar. This confession
> have I found, which was spoken by the prophet Elijah of
> blessed memory.[8]

There is again greater magical use made of *Psalm 116* in unlisted
oral sources. Thus, besides its application against unusual or
unexpected deaths, the current psalm is recited for illness and
healing in general, and for protection when individuals find
themselves in perilous situations and times of trouble. This psalm
is also recommended to those who seek to express gratitude to the
Divine One.[9] Single verses from this psalm are equally employed
in *Practical Kabbalah*. In this regard, *Psalm 116:6* is included in
amulets meant to protect mothers against miscarriage, and
premature delivery.[10] The capitals of the three words in *Psalm
116:9* reading יהוה לפני אתהלך (*Et'halech lifnei YHVH*—"I
shall walk before *YHVH*") were conjoined in the Divine Name
construct אלי, which is often included in *Shiviti* plaques and
amulets.[11] It is worth noting that *Psalm 116:14* is directly affiliated
with ורש (*Vesher*), the thirty-second tri-letter portion of the
"Name of Seventy-two Names."[12]

I have not seen much use made of the hundred-and-
sixteenth Psalm in Christian Magic, and the applications which I
have perused are very different from the use of this psalm in

Jewish Magic. One source instructs the psalm to be read seven times over wine, in order to preclude getting drunk when consumed, and it is further noted that those who drink it will be healed if they should happen to be ill. The same source maintains that those intending "to approach a Prince or enter into a Council chamber," should recite the current psalm, and copy it with a set of magical characters to be carried on their persons, which will ensure what they seek will be granted.[13] In conclusion, it should be noted that in the *"Key of Solomon"* the concluding phrase of *Psalm 116* verse 16, and the whole of verse 17, are inscribed on the parameter of the *"Seventh Pentacle of the Sun."*[14]

PSALM 117

[1] הללו את יהוﬠ‎אהﬞﬞﬞﬞﬞﬞﬞﬞﬞﬞﬞﬞﬞﬞﬞﬞﬞﬞﬞﬞﬞﬞﬞﬞ‎אהﬞﬞﬞﬞﬞﬞﬞﬞﬞﬞ‎ﬠﬞﬞﬞﬞﬞﬞﬞﬞﬞ‎ﬠﬞﬞﬞﬞﬞﬞﬞ‎ כל גוים שבחוהו
כל האמים
[2] כי גבר עלינו חסדו ואמת יהוﬠ‎אהﬞﬞﬞﬞﬞﬞﬞﬞﬞﬞﬞﬞﬞﬞﬞﬞﬞﬞﬞﬞﬞﬞﬞ
לעולם הללו יה

Transliteration:
[1] *hal'lu et YHVH kol goyim shab'chuhu kol ha'umim*
[2] *ki gavar aleinu chas'do ve'emet YHVH l'olam hal'lu Yah*

Translation:
[1] O praise *YHVH*, all ye nations; laud Him, all ye peoples.
[2] For His mercy is great toward us; and the truth of *YHVH* endureth for ever. Hallelujah.

Psalm 117, comprising just two verses, is the shortest in the Psalter. It is the fifth of the "Egyptian *Halel* Psalms," and the third read whilst imbibing the fourth cup of wine at the conclusion of the Passover meal.[1] It has been suggested that this psalm should be linked to *Psalm 116*, but "the consensus of the textual evidence is that Psalm 117 should be read as a discrete psalm with a simple yet powerful statement about the relationship between a believing community and its God."[2]

Considering the size of the current psalm, it should come as no surprise that in official sources its magical application is equally brief. In this regard, we are informed that *Psalm 117* is employed against slander.[3] In other words, it is good for individuals who are wrongly accused,[4] or slandered falsely.[5] One commentator on the *Shimmush Tehillim* noted that this psalm is for "protection against one who informed on you without basis,"[6] such situations having been quite common under the"hell-fire-and-brimstone" control medieval Christianity held over all and sundry. It is yet still common today in the oppressive, fear-based laws of cults and ultra-fundamentalist religions, as well as in the repressive governance of communist regimes, and dictatorships. Be this as it may, this is one instance in which Godfrey Selig's entry on the magical application of this psalm in his German/English version of the *Shimmush Tehillim*, is entirely at odds with all the available primary Hebrew versions of that text. Thus he wrote "Did you make a vow to obtain a certain commandment or perform a good work, and fail in the performance of them through forgetfulness or carelessness, as soon as you recollect your remissness pray this Psalm with a broken and contrite heart."[7] This statement is clearly the source behind the recommendation of *Psalm 117* to those who failed to fulfill a commitment of charity, and it being suggested to individuals who seek forgiveness of errors and transgressions. However, the current psalm is also enunciated to acknowledge the infinite goodness of the Divine One, and to give praise.

The hundred-and-seventeenth Psalm appears to be again of limited use in Christian Magic. We are told that "St Augustine says that it is good for destroying idleness of lazy people, so that they may take pleasure in work."[8] In alignment with the application listed in the *Shimmush Tehillim*, the *"Livre d'Or"* maintains this psalm to be good for individuals who are being persecuted whilst they are innocent, as well as for prisoners. In this regard, a magical character and the name of a Spirit Intelligence are copied on parchment, and the psalm recited with the name of the said "Intelligence." The action is concluded with an associated prayer.[9] Other than these applications, the current psalm is recited in the *"Key of Solomon"* prior to "cutting the reed."[10] In this regard, it is further enunciated in conjunction with *Psalms 72* and *124* over an associated parchment to ensure its "efficacy and strength."[11] The same text lists *Psalm 117* amongst a set of seven psalms, i.e. *Psalms 15, 131, 137, 117, 67, 68*, and *127*, which is recited whilst being dressed in ritual garments.[12]

PSALM 118

[1] הודו ליהוהאדניאהדונהי כי טוב כי לעולם חסדו

[2] יאמר נא ישראל כי לעולם חסדו

[3] יאמרו נא בית אהרן כי לעולם חסדו

[4] יאמרו נא יראי יהוהאדניאהדונהי כי לעולם חסדו

[5] מן המצר קראתי יה ענני במרחב יה

[6] יהוהאדניאהדונהי לי לא אירא מה יעשה לי אדם

[7] יהוהאדניאהדונהי לי בעזרי ואני אראה בשנאי

[8] טוב לחסות ביהוהאדניאהדונהי מבטח באדם

[9] טוב לחסות ביהוהאדניאהדונהי מבטח בנדיבים

[10] כל גוים סבבוני בשם יהוהאדניאהדונהי כי
אמילם

[11] סבוני גם סבבוני בשם יהוהאדניאהדונהי כי
אמילם

[12] סבוני כדבורים דעכו כאש קוצים בשם
יהוהאדניאהדונהי כי אמילם

[13] דחה דחיתני לנפל ויהוהאדניאהדונהי עזרני

[14] עזי וזמרת יה ויהי לי לישועה

[15] קול רנה וישועה באהלי צדיקים ימין
יהוהאדניאהדונהי עשה חיל

[16] ימין יהוהאדניאהדונהי רוממה ימין יהוהאדניאהדונהי
עשה חיל

[17] לא אמות כי אחיה ואספר מעשי יה

[18] יסר יסרני יה ולמות לא נתנני

[19] פתחו לי שערי צדק אבא בם אודה יה

[20] זה השער ליהוהאדניאהדונהי צדיקים יבאו בו

[21] אודך כי עניתני ותהי לי לישועה

[22] אבן מאסו הבונים היתה לראש פנה

[23] מאת יהוהאדניאהדונהי היתה זאת היא נפלאת
בעינינו

[24] זה היום עשה יהוהאדניאהדונהי נגילה ונשמחה
בו

[25] אָנָּא יְהֹוָהאהדונהיאדנ־י הוֹשִׁיעָה נָּא אָנָּא יְהֹוָהאדנ־יאהדונהי
הַצְלִיחָה נָּא

[26] בָּרוּךְ הַבָּא בְּשֵׁם יְהֹוָהאדנ־יאהדונהי בֵּרַכְנוּכֶם
מִבֵּית יְהֹוָהאדנ־יאהדונהי

[27] אֵל יְהֹוָהאדנ־יאהדונהי וַיָּאֶר לָנוּ אִסְרוּ חַג בַּעֲבֹתִים
עַד קַרְנוֹת הַמִּזְבֵּחַ

[28] אֵלִי אַתָּה וְאוֹדֶךָּ אֱלֹהַי אֲרוֹמְמֶךָּ

[29] הוֹדוּ לַיהֹוָהאדנ־יאהדונהי כִּי טוֹב כִּי לְעוֹלָם חַסְדּוֹ

Transliteration:

[1] *hodu laYHVH ki tov ki l'olam chas'do*
[2] *yomar na yis'ra'el ki l'olam chas'do*
[3] *yom'ru na veit aharon ki l'olam chas'do*
[4] *yom'ru na yir'ei YHVH ki l'olam chas'do*
[5] *min hameitzar karati Yah anani vamer'chav Yah*
[6] *YHVH li lo ira mah ya'aseh li adam*
[7] *YHVH li b'oz'rai va'ani er'eh b'son'ai*
[8] *tov lachasot baYHVH mib'to'ach ba'adam*
[9] *tov lachasot baYHVH mib'to'ach bin'divim*
[10] *kol goyim s'vavuni b'shem YHVH ki amilam*
[11] *sabuni gam s'vavuni b'shem YHVH ki amilam*
[12] *sabuni chid'vorim do'achu k'esh kotzim b'shem YHVH ki amilam*
[13] *dachoh d'chitani lin'pol vaYHVH azarani*
[14] *ozi v'zim'rat Yah vay'hi li lishu'ah*
[15] *kol rinah vishu'ah b'oholei tzadikim y'min YHVH osah chayil*
[16] *y'min YHVH romeimah y'min YHVH osah chayil*
[17] *lo amut ki ech'yeh va'asapeir ma'asei Yah*
[18] *yasor yis'rani Yah v'lamavet lo n'tanani*
[19] *pit'chu li sha'arei tzedek avo vam odeh Yah*
[20] *zeh hasha'ar laYHVH tzadikim yavo'u vo*
[21] *od'cha ki anitani vat'hi li lishu'ah*
[22] *even ma'asu habonim hay'tah l'rosh pinah*
[23] *mei'eit YHVH hay'tah zot hi nif'lat b'eineinu*
[24] *zeh hayom asah YHVH nagilah v'nis'm'chah vo*
[25] *ana YHVH hoshi'ah na ana YHVH hatz'lichah na*
[26] *baruch haba b'shem YHVH beirach'nuchem mibeit YHVH*

[27] *el YHVH vaya'er lanu is'ru chag ba'avotim ad kar'not hamiz'bei'ach*

[28] *eili atah v'odeka elohai arom'meka*

[29] *hodu laYHVH ki tov ki l'olam chas'do*

Translation:

[1] 'O give thanks unto *YHVH*, for He is good, for His mercy endureth for ever.'

[2] So let Israel now say, for His mercy endureth for ever,

[3] So let the house of Aaron now say, for His mercy endureth for ever.

[4] So let them now that fear *YHVH* say, for His mercy endureth for ever.

[5] Out of my straits I called upon *Yah*; He answered me with great enlargement.

[6] *YHVH* is for me; I will not fear; what can man do unto me?

[7] *YHVH* is for me as my helper; and I shall gaze upon them that hate me.

[8] It is better to take refuge in *YHVH* than to trust in man.

[9] It is better to take refuge in *YHVH* than to trust in princes.

[10] All nations compass me about; verily, in the name of *YHVH* I will cut them off.

[11] They compass me about, yea, they compass me about; verily, in the name of *YHVH* I will cut them off.

[12] They compass me about like bees; they are quenched as the fire of thorns; verily, in the name of *YHVH* I will cut them off.

[13] Thou didst thrust sore at me that I might fall; but *YHVH* helped me.

[14] *Yah* is my strength and song; and He is become my salvation.

[15] The voice of rejoicing and salvation is in the tents of the righteous; the right hand of *YHVH* doeth valiantly.

[16] The right hand of *YHVH* is exalted; the right hand of *YHVH* doeth valiantly.

[17] I shall not die, but live, and declare the works of *Yah*.

[18] *Yah* hath chastened me sore; but He hath not given me over unto death.

[19] Open to me the gates of righteousness; I will enter into them, I will give thanks unto *Yah*.

[20] This is the gate of *YHVH*; the righteous shall enter into it.

[21] I will give thanks unto Thee, for Thou hast answered me, and art become my salvation.

[22] The stone which the builders rejected is become the chief corner-stone.

[23] This is *YHVH*'s doing; it is marvellous in our eyes.

[24] This is the day which *YHVH* hath made; we will rejoice and be glad in it.

[25] We beseech Thee, *YHVH*, save now! We beseech Thee, *YHVH*, make us now to prosper!

[26] Blessed be he that cometh in the name of *YHVH*; we bless you out of the house of *YHVH*.

[27] *YHVH* is God, and hath given us light; order the festival procession with boughs, even unto the horns of the altar.

[28] Thou art my God, and I will give thanks unto Thee; Thou art my God, I will exalt Thee.

[29] O give thanks unto *YHVH*, for He is good, for His mercy endureth for ever.

Psalm 118 concludes the set of six "Egyptian *Halel* Psalms," which we are told "constitutes the heart of Jewish worship."[1] In this regard, we are reminded that "Psalm 113 speaks of the majesty and mercy of the Lord; Psalm 114, retells the story of the Exodus; Psalm 115 promises blessing; Psalm 116, gives thanks to the Lord for providing us with freedom; Psalm 117 exhorts the nations to praise Him; Psalm 118 is a beautiful song of thanksgiving."[2] As noted previously, the term "*Hallelujah*" is absent in this "*Halel* psalm," as it is in *Psalm 114*, but the current psalm plays an important role in Jewish liturgies, with its opening and concluding verse reading "O give thanks unto *YHVH*, for He is good, for His mercy endureth for ever," having been "well known in the days of Ezra, Jeremiah, and in Solomon's Temple."[3] It is said that the opening phrase of the said verse, reiterated in *2 Chronicles 5:13*, "was on the lips of the Levites."[4] We are further informed that following the victory at Emmaus during the Maccabean Revolt

(167 B.C.E.), the Jewish army "returned home and sang a song of thanksgiving and gave praise unto heaven because He is good, because His mercy endureth forever" [*Psalm 118:1/29*].[5]

It has been noted that "this refrain became a favorite in the mouths of the people and the custom grew to repeat it after the leader."[6] This is a reference to the responsive liturgical recitation of *Psalm 118* in the synagogue, i.e. it is customary to enunciate the first four verses of the psalm in, as it were, a statement and response manner, meaning that the pronunciation of each verse is an interaction between the שְׁלִיחַ צִבּוּר (*Shali'ach Tzibur*— "Prayer Leader" [literally "a public messenger"]) and the worshippers. In this regard, each of the concluding nine verses of the current psalm are recited twice, first by the *Shali'ach Tzibur* and then by the congregation.[7] However, customs do vary within different Jewish communities. It was noted "that repeating the verses is only a *minhag* (custom),"[8] and that this "is done mainly to beautify the reading of *Hallel* and give praises to God and thank Him in song for His great kindness that He did in the past and continues to do."[9] Thus we are reminded that the "*Halel* Psalms" should be "recited with much enthusiasm in song and with sweet voice."[10]

Some attention should be paid to *Psalm 118:25*, since it features prominently in both Jewish worship and Jewish Magic, and it is also the source of an "oddity" in the Christian bible, i.e. the reported "triumphal entry into Jerusalem" of the Christian saviour on the back of a donkey. This verse is recited with *Psalm 20:10*, at the commencement of the seven הַקָּפוֹת (*hakafot*— "circumambulations") during the previously mentioned wonderful הוֹשַׁעְנָא רַבָּא (*Hoshanah Rabah*—"Great Supplication"), and on שִׂמְחַת תּוֹרָה (*Simchat Torah*— "Rejoicing with the *Torah*").[11] At the beginning of the *Hakafot* ("circuits"), the prayer leader and worshippers chant the said verses responsively, saying "We beseech Thee, *YHVH*, save now! We beseech Thee, *YHVH*, make us now to prosper!" [*Psalm 118:25*]; "Save, *YHVH*; let the King answer us in the day that we call." [*Psalm 20:10*]. Each of the seven circuits is completed with *Psalm 118:16*.[12]

The mentioned "oddity" in the Christian Bible pertains to the appearance of the term "*Hosanna*," which we are told were uttered by the populace who purportedly were waving palm branches and shouting "Hosanna to the Son of David....Hosanna in the highest," as the Christian saviour made his "triumphal entry into Jerusalem" prior to the celebration of Passover. There were suggestions that the palm branches carried by the worshippers pertained to the festival of *Sukkot* (Festival of Booths). In this regard, the timing is out since *Sukkot* is held in autumn, whilst *Pesach* (Passover) occurs in Spring. However, the said "oddity" pertains to the meaning of the word "Hosanna" which Christians maintained, until fairly recently, to be a declaration of the "highest praise." It should be noted that the said expression was derived from the Hebrew expression נא הושיעה (*hoshi'ah na*) in *Psalm 118:25*, the plain meaning of which is simply "please save" without any reference to "praise." Some attempts were made by Christian commentators to reinterpret the word "hosannah," claiming it to mean both "praise" and "save us." Interestingly enough, the term הושענא (*"Hoshana"*), pronounced *"Hosha'ana"* in the Sefardic tradition, should be read as two words, נא הושע (*hosha na*). We are informed that "because of the manner of pronouncing the two words as one, the sages used the contracted form, *Hoshana*."[13] The expression indeed features prominently in the *Sukkot* service. In this regard, the Ashkenazic rite includes a truly magical liturgical poem comprised of four verses,[14] which was recommended to me in my remote youth for support in times of stress. I have memorised it, and still use to this very day. Written in alphabetical order, each verse includes the expression *Hosha Na* ("Save, we beseech Thee"), as indicated below:

הושע נא   למענך אלהינו   הושע נא

הושע נא   למענך בוראנו   הושע נא

הושע נא   למענך גואלנו   הושע נא

הושע נא   למענך דורשנו   הושע נא

Transliteration:

hosha na	*l'ma'an'cha Eloheinu*	*hosha na*
hosha na	*l'ma'an'cha Bor'einu*	*hosha na*
hosha na	*l'ma'an'cha Go'aleinu*	*hosha na*
hosha na	*l'ma'an'cha Dor'einu*	*hosha na*

Translation:

Please save	for Your sake, our God;	please save
Please save	for Your sake, our Creator;	please save
Please save	for Your sake, our Redeemer;	please save
Please save	for Your sake, you seek us;	please save

As far as its magical applications are concerned, *Psalm 118* is recited for support when responding to an "*epikurus*," i.e. an Epicurean, this appellative being a reference to a hedonist. However, in the current instance it indicates a heretic,[15] disbeliever,[16] or a scoffer.[17] In this regard, Godfrey Selig informs us in his German/English version of the *Shimmush Tehillim* that "if you pray this Psalm often and devoutly, you will be able to silence all free-thinkers, scoffers of religion and heretics, who labor to lead you astray."[18] There is no indication in any version of the *Shimmush Tehillim* that I am aware of, in which this psalm is said to be good to silence "free thinkers." Whatever the case may be, a variant recension of this text maintains this psalm to be enunciated to turn a heretic to repentance. In this instance, the said apostate who wishes to "return," is instructed to recite the current psalm with the following prayer-incantation:

רחום רחום רחום תן לי לב ונפש וגבורה להשיב
לזה הרשע כמשפט ואל אכשל ולא יוכל להשיב
אחר דברי אמן אמן אמן נצח סלה

Transliteration:

Rachum Rachum Rachum ten li lev v'nefesh ug'vurah l'hashiv l'zeh harasha k'mish'pat v'al ekashel v'lo yuval l'hashiv achar d'varai Omein Omein Omein Netzach Selah

Translation:

Rachum Rachum Rachum [Compasionate Compasionate Compasionate] give me heart, and soul, and strength to turn this wicked one according to the law, and I shall not stumble, and he shall not be able to reply to my words. *Amen Amen Amen* Eternal *Selah.*[19]

The *Shimmush Tehillim* further maintains the current psalm to be good for appearing before a judge.[20] In this regard, we are told that anyone who wishes to appear before a judge or before uthorities, should meet with a companion at the court, where the said friend should recite this psalm with an associated prayer-incantation, doing so prior to the said individual making his/her appearance before the judge:

חנון חנון חנון יהוה **אשר** היה והווה ויהיה

לעולם ועד מלפניך יצא דבר שתשמע אלי ותתן

[....name of recipient....] חברי לחן לחסד ולרחמים

בעיני כל רואיו ובעיני השרים והשופטים שלא

יוכלו לסור מדבריו ימין ושמאל **אמן** אמן נצח סלה

Transliteration:

Chanun Chanun Chanun YHVH asher hayah v'hoveh v'yih'yeh l'olam va'ed mil'fanecha yeitzei davar sh'tish'ma eilai v'titein [....name of recipient....] *chaveiri l'chen l'chesed ul'rachamim b'einei kol ro'av uv'einei hasarim v'hashof'tim sh'lo yoch'lu lasur mid'varav yamin ush'mol Omein Omein Netzach Selah.*

Translation:

Chanun Chanun Chanun [Merciful (Gracious) Merciful Merciful] *YHVH* that was, is, and will be forever and ever. A word go forth from you, that you should hear, and give [....name of recipient....], my companion, grace, mercy, and compassion in the eyes of all who see him, and in the eyes of princes and judges, lest they stray from his words right and left. *Amen Amen* Eternal *Selah.*[21]

That is the extent of the practical applications of *Psalm 118* listed in the *Shimmush Tehillim.* However, this psalm is again employed for a wide range of magical purposes in "unofficial sources," i.e. it is listed against paralysis; for injuries and physical damage of every kind; as well as for illness and healing in general. The psychological impact of this psalm is recognised in the fact that it is employed against vanity and pride; to bring discipline; and to act against despair. This psalm is said to preserve the purity of life, is recited to sharpen and increase intelligence, and is one of the psalms believed to be good for human sciences. It is further enunciated for the infinite goodness of the Divine One, and to increase fear and love of the Eternal One. As intimated earlier, it is employed to elicit support in responding to, and have success in, arguments with non-believers, as well as to silence heretics. However, it is also recited when facing spiritual troubles, and hence it is understood to be good against, as well as to be saved from, malice, defamation, slander, gossip, and to find protection in perilous situations and in times of trouble. The current psalm is also one of the many vocalised for forgiveness of errors and transgressions.

Several verses from this psalm are equally employed in Jewish Magic. In this regard, the capitals of the concluding four words of *Psalm 118:6* reading אדם לי יעשה מה (*mah ya'aseh li adam*—"what can man do unto me?"), were formulated into the Divine Name construct מָיְלָא (*May'la*). It is inscribed with the Divine Name צמרכד (*Tzamar'chad* or *Tzemiroch'da*) on a ring or small tablet to be worn or carried as an amulet.[22] I have addressed the latter Divine Name in fair detail elsewhere.[23] The purpose of this amulet is clearly for the bearer to be protected from any baneful effects engendered by his or her fellow humankind. Interestingly enough, all the letters comprising *Psalm 118:6–7* were conjoined in the following Divine Name construct which is equally employed for protection:[24]

$$\text{יְמַהֲנִ הֲהֹוִי וְיַהָא הָעֲלַר}$$
$$\text{לְשִׁיא יְהִבָה לֹלֹעֹב אִיזֹש}$$
$$\text{אָאֲרַנ יְדִיא רְמֹוִי אִיא}$$

If it is vocalised, this Divine Name construct would read *Y'MaHaNi HaH'V'Y' V'YaHa'E Ha'ALiR' LiSheY'E Y'H'V'H' LoLi'OV' 'Y'Z'Sho I'ARaN' Y'DaY'A RaM'VaY' IY'A*. In this instance, the initials of the twelve portions of this Divine Name construct comprise the first twelve glyphs of verse six, and the remaining eleven characters of this verse the second letters of the eleven four-letter combinations. The second letter of the concluding tri-letter combination, is the initial of verse seven. The second to thirteenth letters of the latter verse are the third glyphs of the twelve letter combinations, and the remaining eleven letters of the said verse, are the concluding glyphs of the eleven four-letter formulations. All the characters of the said verses were located in exact order within this Divine Name construct, which is likely meant to be enunciated, considering the inclusion of vowel points. However, in my estimation, it could equally be written down, and carried as an amulet for the said purpose of safeguarding the bearer.

It should be noted that selected glyphs from certain words in *Psalm 118:9–11* were conjoined in the following Divine Name construct comprising three bi-letter combinations: ‏נֶס מֶס טֶס‎ (*Toso Mis' Nis'*). The three bi-letter combinations were derived: ‏טֶס‎ (*Tet–Samech*) from the expression ‏טוֹב לַחֲסוֹת‎ (*Tov lachasot* —"It is better to take refuge"): verse 9; the ‏מֶס‎ (*Mem– Samech*) combination from ‏גּוֹיִם סְבָבוּנִי‎ (*goyim s'vavuni* —"nations [en]compass me"): verse 10; and the concluding ‏נֶס‎ (*Nun–Samech*) from the phrase ‏סַבּוּנִי גַם סְבָבוּנִי‎ (*sabuni gam s'vavuni*—"they compass me about, yea, they compass me about"): verse 11.[25] As readers probably guessed, this Divine Name construct is likewise said to have the power of protection. In this regard, Jewish individuals who are leaving their homes, are advised to say the Divine Name ‏שַׁדַּי‎ (*Shadai*) whilst touching the *Mezuzah*, i.e. the religious item affixed to the entrances of Jewish homes, and which is said to have "retained its original significance as an amulet despite rabbinic efforts to make it an exclusively religious symbol."[26] Afterwards the three bi-letter portions of the Divine Name construct are enunciated mentally, and succeeded by uttering the following prayer-incantation:

‏רבון כול העולמים יהי רצון מילפניך שתעמוד לי‎
‏ולכל יוצאי יריכי בסתר רחמיך ובצל כנפיך שלא‎
‏תוכל שום בריה לא מן העליונים ולא מן התחתונים‎
‏להזיקני לא בגופי ולא בנפשי מעתה ועד עולם אמן‎
‏אמן אמן סלה סלה סלה‎

Transliteration:

Ribon kol ha'olamim y'hi ratzon mil'fanecha sh'ta'amod li v'l'kol yotz'ei yer'chai b'seiter rachameicha ub'tzel k'nafeicha shalo tuchal shum b'riyah lo min ha'el'yonim v'lo min hatach'tonim l'hazikeni lo b'gufi v'lo b'naf'shi mei'atah v'ad olam Omein Omein Omein Selah Selah Selah.

Translation:

> Master of all the worlds, may it be your will that you stand
> by me, and hide all my descendants in the sanctuary of
> your mercy, and in the shadow of your wings, that no
> creature, neither from above nor from below, will be able
> to harm me either in my body or in my soul, from now on
> and forever *Amen Amen Amen Selah Selah Selah.*[27]

In terms of other verses from the current psalm which features in
Jewish Magic, it is worth noting that the initials of the seven words
comprising *Psalm 118:14* were formulated into the Divine Name
construct עוייולל, which is included in an amulet which is said
to save the bearer from trouble.[28] The letters קקש, which is one
of the names of the childkiller demoness *Lilit*, were selected from
the fifteenth verse of the current psalm, to include in an amulet for
"protection of the newborn."[29] There are also twin Divine Name
constructs אַיְהָ֖ן אַיְהֹ֖ן (*Ay'hona Ay'hana*), which were
formulated respectively from the capitals of the words comprising
the two popular phrases of *Psalm 118:25*. They are added to the
bottom of amulets, to further empower the purpose of relevant
amulets.[30] It is worth noting that *Psalm 118:16* and *24* are
respectively affiliated directly with רההע (*Reho*) and מלה
(*Melah*) , the thirty-ninth and twenty-third tri-letter portions of the
"Name of Seventy-two Names."[31] The sixty-first and sixtieth tri-
letter portions of the "Name of Seventy-two Names," ומב (*Umab*)
and מצר (*Metzer*), are respectively indirectly associated with
Psalm 118:5 and *16*.[32] Lastly, it was suggested to those who are
seeking healing for their souls in nature, to recite *Psalm 118:22*
"when handling or exploring rocks."[33]

I have again found very few details on the use of the
current psalm in Christian Magic. However, we are informed in the
"*Livre d'Or*" that those who have lost the key to a residence,
should read this psalm seven times, and it is said "the room or
house will all be opened immediately."[34]

PSALM 119

א

[1] **אשרי** תמימי דרך ההלכים בתורת יהוה‎אדני‎אהדונהי

[2] **אשרי** נצרי עדתיו בכל לב ידרשוהו

[3] **אף** לא פעלו עולה בדרכיו הלכו

[4] **אתה** צויתה פקדיך לשמר מאד

[5] **אחלי** יכנו דרכי לשמר חקיך

[6] **אז** לא אבוש בהביטי אל כל מצותיך

[7] **אודך** בישר לבב בלמדי משפטי צדקך

[8] **את** חקיך אשמר אל תעזבני עד מאד

ב

[9] **במה** יזכה נער את ארחו לשמר כדברך

[10] **בכל** לבי דרשתיך אל תשגני ממצותיך

[11] **בלבי** צפנתי אמרתך לבען לא אחטא לך

[12] **ברוך** אתה יהוה‎אדני‎אהדונהי למדני חקיך

[13] **בשפתי** ספרתי כל משפטי פיך

[14] **בדרך** עדותיך ששתי כעל כל הון

[15] **בפקודיך** אשיחה ואביטה ארחתיך

[16] **בחקתיך** אשתעשע לא אשכח דברך

ג

[17] **גמל** על עבדך אחיה ואשמרה דברך

[18] **גל** עיני ואביטה נפלאות מתורתך

[19] **גר** אנכי בארץ אל תסתר ממני מצותיך

[20] **גרסה** נפשי לתאבה אל משפטיך בכל עת

[21] **גערת** זדים ארורים השגים ממצותיך

[22] **גל** מעלי חרפה ובוז כי עדתיך נצרתי

[23] **גם** ישבו שרים בי נדברו עבדך ישיח בחקיך

[24] **גם** עדתיך שעשעי אנשי עצתי

ד

[25] **דבקה** לעפר נפשי חיני כדברך

[26] **דרכי** ספרתי ותענני למדני חקיך

[27] **דרך** פקודיך הבינני ואשיחה בנפלאותיך

[28] דלפה נפשי מתוגה קימני כדברך

[29] דרך שקר הסר ממני ותורתך חנני

[30] דרך אמונה בחרתי משפטיך שויתי

[31] דבקתי בעדותיך יהו‎אהדונהי אל תבישני

[32] דרך מצותיך ארוץ כי תרחיב לבי

ה

[33] הורני יהו‎אהדונהי דרך חקיך ואצרנה עקב

[34] הבינני ואצרה תורתך ואשמרנה בכל לב

[35] הדריכני בנתיב מצותיך כי בו חפצתו

[36] הט לבי אל עדותיך ואל אל בצע

[37] העבר עיני מראות שוא בדרכך חיני

[38] הקם לעבדך אמרתך אשר ליראתך

[39] העבר חרפתי אשר יגרתי כי משפטיך טובים

[40] הנה תאבתי לפקדיך בצדקתך חיני

ו

[41] ויבאני חסדך יהו‎אהדונהי תשועתך כאמרתך

[42] ואענה חרפי דבר כי בטחתי בדברך

[43] ואל תצל מפי דבר אמת עד מאד כי למשפטך יחלתי

[44] ואשמרה תורתך תמיד לעולם ועד

[45] ואתהלכה ברחבה כי פקדיך דרשתי

[46] ואדברה בעדתיך נגד מלכים ולא אבוש

[47] ואשתעשע במצותיך אשר אהבתי

[48] ואשא כפי אל מצותיך אשר אהבתי ואשיחה בחכיך

ז

[49] זכר דבר לעבדך על אשר יחלתני

[50] זאת נחמתי בעניי כי אמרתך חיתני

[51] זדים הליצני עד מאד מתורתך לא נטיתי

[52] זכרתי משפטיך מעולם יהו‎אהדונהי ואתנחם

[53] זלעפה אחזתני מרשעים עזבי תורתך

[54] זְמִרוֹת הָיוּ לִי חֻקֶּיךָ בְּבֵית מְגוּרָי

[55] זָכַרְתִּי בַלַּיְלָה שִׁמְךָ יְהוָֹהֱאֱלֹהִיםֶיאֲהֹדוֹנָהי וָאֶשְׁמְרָה תּוֹרָתֶךָ

[56] זֹאת הָיְתָה לִּי כִּי פִקֻּדֶיךָ נָצָרְתִּי

ח

[57] חֶלְקִי יְהוָֹהֱאֱלֹהִיםֶיאֲהֹדוֹנָהי אָמַרְתִּי לִשְׁמֹר דְּבָרֶיךָ

[58] חִלִּיתִי פָנֶיךָ בְכָל לֵב חָנֵּנִי כְּאִמְרָתֶךָ

[59] חִשַּׁבְתִּי דְרָכָי וָאָשִׁיבָה רַגְלַי אֶל עֵדֹתֶיךָ

[60] חַשְׁתִּי וְלֹא הִתְמַהְמָהְתִּי לִשְׁמֹר מִצְוֹתֶיךָ

[61] חֶבְלֵי רְשָׁעִים עִוְּדֻנִי תּוֹרָתְךָ לֹא שָׁכָחְתִּי

[62] חֲצוֹת לַיְלָה אָקוּם לְהוֹדוֹת לָךְ עַל מִשְׁפְּטֵי צִדְקֶךָ

[63] חָבֵר אָנִי לְכָל אֲשֶׁר יְרֵאוּךָ וּלְשֹׁמְרֵי פִּקּוּדֶיךָ

[64] חַסְדְּךָ יְהוָֹהֱאֱלֹהִיםֶיאֲהֹדוֹנָהי מָלְאָה הָאָרֶץ חֻקֶּיךָ לַמְּדֵנִי

ט

[65] טוֹב עָשִׂיתָ עִם עַבְדְּךָ יְהוָֹהֱאֱלֹהִיםֶיאֲהֹדוֹנָהי כִּדְבָרֶךָ

[66] טוּב טַעַם וָדַעַת לַמְּדֵנִי כִּי בְמִצְוֹתֶיךָ הֶאֱמָנְתִּי

[67] טֶרֶם אֶעֱנֶה אֲנִי שֹׁגֵג וְעַתָּה אִמְרָתְךָ שָׁמָרְתִּי

[68] טוֹב אַתָּה וּמֵטִיב לַמְּדֵנִי חֻקֶּיךָ

[69] טָפְלוּ עָלַי שֶׁקֶר זֵדִים אֲנִי בְּכָל לֵב אֶצֹּר פִּקּוּדֶיךָ

[70] טָפַשׁ כַּחֵלֶב לִבָּם אֲנִי תּוֹרָתְךָ שִׁעֲשָׁעְתִּי

[71] טוֹב לִי כִי עֻנֵּיתִי לְמַעַן אֶלְמַד חֻקֶּיךָ

[72] טוֹב לִי תוֹרַת פִּיךָ מֵאַלְפֵי זָהָב וָכָסֶף

י

[73] יָדֶיךָ עָשׂוּנִי וַיְכוֹנְנוּנִי הֲבִינֵנִי וְאֶלְמְדָה מִצְוֹתֶיךָ

[74] יְרֵאֶיךָ יִרְאוּנִי וְיִשְׂמָחוּ כִּי לִדְבָרְךָ יִחָלְתִּי

[75] יָדַעְתִּי יְהוָֹהֱאֱלֹהִיםֶיאֲהֹדוֹנָהי כִּי צֶדֶק מִשְׁפָּטֶיךָ וֶאֱמוּנָה עִנִּיתָנִי

[76] יְהִי נָא חַסְדְּךָ לְנַחֲמֵנִי כְּאִמְרָתְךָ לְעַבְדֶּךָ

[77] יְבֹאוּנִי רַחֲמֶיךָ וְאֶחְיֶה כִּי תוֹרָתְךָ שַׁעֲשֻׁעָי

[78] יֵבֹשׁוּ זֵדִים כִּי שֶׁקֶר עִוְּתוּנִי אֲנִי אָשִׂיחַ בְּפִקּוּדֶיךָ

[79] ישובו לי יראיך וידעי עדתיך

[80] יהי לבי תמים בחקיך למען לא אבוש

כ

[81] כלתה לתשועתך נפשי לדברך יחלתי

[82] כלו עיני לאמרתך לאמר מתי תנחמני

[83] כי הייתי כנאד בקיטור חקיך לא שכחתי

[84] כמה ימי עבדך מתי תעשה ברדפי משפט

[85] כרו לי זדים שיחות אשר לא כתורתך

[86] כל מצותיך אמונה שקר רדפוני עזרני

[87] כמעט כלוני בארץ ואני לא עזבתי פקדיך

[88] כחסדך חיני ואשמרה עדות פיך

ל

[89] לעולם יהוהאדני־אהדונהי דברך נצב בשמים

[90] לדר ודר אמונתך כוננת ארץ ותעמד

[91] למשפטיך עמדו היום כי הכל עבדיך

[92] לולי תורתך שעשעי אז אבדתי בעניי

[93] לעולם לא אשכח פקודיך כי בם חייתני

[94] לך אני הושיעני כי פקודיך דרשתי

[95] לי קוו רשעים לאבדני עדתיך אתבונן

[96] לכל תכלה ראיתי קץ רחבה מצותך מאד

מ

[97] מה אהבתי תורתך כל היום היא שיחתי

[98] מאיבי תחכמני מצותך כי לעולם היא לי

[99] מכל מלמדי השכלתי כי עדותיך שיחה לי

[100] מזקנים אתבונן כי פקודיך נצרתי

[101] מכל ארח רע כלאתי רגלי למען אשמר דברך

[102] ממשפטיך לא סרתי כי אתה הורתני

[103] מה נמלצו לחכי אמרתך מדבש לפי

[104] מפקודיך אתבונן על כן שנאתי כל ארח שקר

נ

[105] נר לרגלי דברך ואור לנתיבתי

[106] נשבעתי ואקימה לשמר משפטי צדקך

[107] נעניתי עד מאד יהוה‎אהדונהי חיני כדברך

[108] נדבות פי רצה נא יהוה‎אהדונהי ומשפטיך
למדני

[109] נפשי בכפי תמיד ותורתך לא שכחתי

[110] נתנו רשעים פח לי ומפקודיך לא תעיתי

[111] נחלתי עדותיך לעולם כי ששון לבי המה

[112] נטיתי לבי לעשות חקיך לעולם עקב

ס

[113] סעפים שנאתי ותורתך אהבתי

[114] סתרי ומגני אתה לדברך יחלתי

[115] סורו ממני מרעים ואצרה מצות אלהי

[116] סמכני כאמרתך ואחיה ואל תבישני משברי

[117] סעדני ואושעה ואשעה בחקיך תמיד

[118] סלית כל שוגים מחקיך כי שקר תרמיתם

[119] סגים השבת כל רשעי ארץ לכן אהבתי
עדתיך

[120] סמר מפחדך בשרי וממשפטיך יראתי

ע

[121] עשיתי משפט וצדק בל תניחני לעשקי

[122] ערב עבדך לטוב אל עשקני זדים

[123] עיני כלו לישועתך ולאמרת צדקך

[124] עשה עם עבדך כחסדך וחקיך למדני

[125] עבדך אני הבונני ואדעה עדתיך

[126] עת לעשות ליהוה‎אהדונהי הפרו תורתך

[127] על כן אהבתי מצותיך מזהב ומפז

[128] על כן כל פקודי כל ישרתי כל ארח שקר
שנאתי

פ

[129] פלאות עדותיך על כן נצרתם נפשי

[130] פתח דבריך יאיר מבין פתיים

[131] פערתי ואשאפה כי למצותיך יאבתי

[132] פנה אלי וחנני כמשפט לאהבי שמך

[133] פעמי הכן באמרתך ואל תשלט בי כל און

[134] פדני מעשק אדם ואשמרה פקודיך

[135] פניך האר בעבדך ולמדני את חקיך

[136] פלגי מים ירדו עיני על לא שמרו תורתך

צ

[137] צדיק אתה ליהוﬣﬡﬣﬢﬡﬨﬠﬣﬤﬡﬨﬣ ﬩ﬨﬡ﬩﬩ﬡﬨﬢﬡ﬩﬩ﬡﬨﬣﬡﬨﬥﬨﬢﬣ וישר משפטיך

[138] צוית צדק עדתיך ואמונה מאד

[139] צמתתני קנאת כי שכחו דבריך צרי

[140] צרופה אמרתך מאד ועבדך אהבה

[141] צעיר אנכי ונבזה פקדיך לא שכחתי

[142] צדקתך צדק לעולם ותורתך אמת

[143] צר ומצוק מצאוני מצותיך שעשעי

[144] צדק עדותיך לעולם הבינני ואחיה

ק

[145] קראתי בכל לב ענני יהוﬣﬡﬣﬢﬡﬨﬠﬣﬤﬡﬨﬣ חקיך אצרה

[146] קראתיך הושיעני ואשמרה עדתיך

[147] קדמתי בנשף ואשועה לדבריך יחלתי

[148] קדמו עיני אשמרות לשיח באמרתך

[149] קולי שמעה כחסדך יהוﬣﬡﬣﬢﬡﬨﬠﬣﬤﬡﬨﬣ כמשפטך חיני

[150] קרבו רדפי זמה מתורתך רחקו

[151] קרוב אתה יהוﬣﬡﬣﬢﬡﬨﬠﬣﬤﬡﬨﬣ וכל מצותיך אמת

[152] קדם ידעתי מעדתיך כי לעולם יסדתם

ר

[153] ראה עניי וחלצני כי תורתך לא שכחתי

[154] ריבה ריבי וגאלי לאמרתך חיני

[155] רחוק מרשעים ישועה כי חקיך לא דרשו

[156] רחמיך רבים יהוﬣﬡﬣﬢﬡﬨﬠﬣﬤﬡﬨﬣ כמשפטיך חיני

[157] רבים רדפי וצרי מעדותיך לא נטיתי

[158] ראיתי בגדים ואתקוטטה אמרתך לא שמרו

[159] רְאֵה כִּי פִקּוּדֶיךָ אָהָבְתִּי יְהֹוָהאהדונהיאדני כְּחַסְדְּךָ חַיֵּנִי

[160] רֹאשׁ דְּבָרְךָ אֱמֶת וּלְעוֹלָם כָּל מִשְׁפַּט צִדְקֶךָ

שׁ

[161] שָׂרִים רְדָפוּנִי חִנָּם וּמִדְּבָרְךָ פָּחַד לִבִּי

[162] שָׂשׂ אָנֹכִי עַל אִמְרָתֶךָ כְּמוֹצֵא שָׁלָל רָב

[163] שֶׁקֶר שָׂנֵאתִי וַאֲתַעֵבָה תּוֹרָתְךָ אָהָבְתִּי

[164] שֶׁבַע בַּיּוֹם הִלַּלְתִּיךָ עַל מִשְׁפְּטֵי צִדְקֶךָ

[165] שָׁלוֹם רָב לְאֹהֲבֵי תוֹרָתֶךָ וְאֵין לָמוֹ מִכְשׁוֹל

[166] שִׂבַּרְתִּי לִישׁוּעָתְךָ יְהֹוָהאהדונהיאדני וּמִצְוֹתֶיךָ עָשִׂיתִי

[167] שָׁמְרָה נַפְשִׁי עֵדֹתֶיךָ וָאֹהֲבֵם מְאֹד

[168] שָׁמַרְתִּי פִקּוּדֶיךָ וְעֵדֹתֶיךָ כִּי כָל דְּרָכַי נֶגְדֶּךָ

ת

[169] תִּקְרַב רִנָּתִי לְפָנֶיךָ יְהֹוָהאהדונהיאדני כִּדְבָרְךָ הֲבִינֵנִי

[170] תָּבוֹא תְּחִנָּתִי לְפָנֶיךָ כְּאִמְרָתְךָ הַצִּילֵנִי

[171] תַּבַּעְנָה שְׂפָתַי תְּהִלָּה כִּי תְלַמְּדֵנִי חֻקֶּיךָ

[172] תַּעַן לְשׁוֹנִי אִמְרָתֶךָ כִּי כָל מִצְוֹתֶיךָ צֶּדֶק

[173] תְּהִי יָדְךָ לְעָזְרֵנִי כִּי פִקּוּדֶיךָ בָחָרְתִּי

[174] תָּאַבְתִּי לִישׁוּעָתְךָ יְהֹוָהאהדונהיאדני וְתוֹרָתְךָ שַׁעֲשֻׁעָי

[175] תְּחִי נַפְשִׁי וּתְהַלְלֶךָּ וּמִשְׁפָּטֶךָ יַעְזְרֻנִי

[176] תָּעִיתִי כְּשֶׂה אֹבֵד בַּקֵּשׁ עַבְדֶּךָ כִּי מִצְוֹתֶיךָ לֹא שָׁכָחְתִּי

Transliteration:

Alef

[1] *ash'rei t'mimei darech hahol'chim b'torat YHVH*

[2] *ashrei notz'rei eidotav v'chol leiv yid'r'shuhu*

[3] *af lo fa'alu av'lah bid'rachav halachu*

[4] *atah tzivitah fikudecha lish'mor m'od*

[5] *achalai yikonu d'rachai lish'mor chukecha*

[6] *az lo eivosh b'habiti el kol mitz'votecha*

[7] *od'cha b'yosher leivav b'lom'di mish'p'tei tzid'kecha*

[8] *et chukecha esh'mor al ta'az'veini ad m'od*

Bet

[9] *bameh y'zakeh na'ar et or'cho lish'mor kid'varecha*

[10] *b'chol libi d'rash'ticha al tash'geini mimitz'votecha*

[11] *b'libi tzafan'ti im'ratecha l'ma'an lo echeta lach*

[12] *baruch atah YHVH lam'deini chukecha*

[13] *bis'fatai sipar'ti kol mish'p'tei ficha*

[14] *b'derech eidotecha sas'ti k'al kol hon*

[15] *b'fikodecha asichah v'abitah or'chotecha*

[16] *b'chukotecha esh'ta'asha lo esh'kach d'varecha*

Gimel

[17] *g'mol al av'd'cha ech'yeh v'esh'm'rah d'varecha*

[18] *gal einai v'abitah nif'la'ot mitoratecha*

[19] *geir anochi va'aretz al tas'teir mimeni mitz'votecha*

[20] *gar'sah naf'shi l'ta'avah el mish'patecha v'chol eit*

[21] *ga'ar'ta zeidim arurim hashogim mimitz'votecha*

[22] *gal mei'alai cher'pah vavuz ki eidotecha natzar'ti*

[23] *gam yash'vu sarim bi nid'baru av'd'cha yasi'ach b'chukecha*

[24] *gam eidotecha sh'ashu'ai an'shei atzati*

Dalet

[25] *dav'kah le'afar naf'shi chayeini kid'varecha*

[26] *d'rachai sipar'ti vata'aneini lam'deini chukecha*

[27] *derech pikudecha havineini v'asichah b'nif'l'otecha*

[28] *dal'fah naf'shi mitugah kay'meini kid'varecha*

[29] *derech sheker haseir mimeni v'torat'cha choneini*

[30] *derech emunah vachar'ti mish'patecha shiviti*

[31] *davak'ti v'eidotecha YHVH al t'visheini*

[32] *derech mitz'votecha arutz ki tar'chiv libi*

Heh

[33] *horeini YHVH derech chukecha v'etz'renah eikev*

[34] *havineini v'etz'rah toratecha v'esh'm'renah v'chol leiv*

[35] *had'richeini bin'tiv mitz'votecha ki vo chafatz'ti*

[36] *hat libi el eidotecha v'al el batza*

[37] *ha'aveir einai meir'ot shav bid'rachecha chayeini*

[38] *hakeim l'av'd'cha im'ratecha asher l'yir'atecha*

[39] *ha'aveir cher'pati asher yagor'ti ki mish'patecha tovim*

[40] *hineih ta'av'ti l'fikudecha b'tzid'kat'cha chayeini*

Vav

[41] *vivo'uni chasadecha YHVH t'shu'at'cha k'im'ratecha*

[42] *v'e'eneh chor'fi davar ki vatach'ti bid'varecha*
[43] *v'al tatzeil mipi d'var emet ad m'od ki l'mish'patecha yichal'ti*
[44] *v'esh'm'rah torat'cha tamid l'olam va'ed*
[45] *v'et'hal'cha var'chavah ki fikudecha darash'ti*
[46] *va'adab'rah v'eidotecha neged m'lachim v'lo eivosh*
[47] *v'esh'ta'asha b'mitz'votecha asher ahav'ti*
[48] *v'esa chapai el mitz'votecha asher ahav'ti v'asichah v'chukecha*

Zayin

[49] *z'chor davar l'av'decha al asher yichal'tani*
[50] *zot nechamati v'oni ki im'rat'cha chiyat'ni*
[51] *zeidim helitzuni ad m'od mitorat'cha lo natiti*
[52] *zachar'ti mish'patecha mei'olam YHVH va'et'necham*
[53] *zal'afah achazat'ni meir'sha'im oz'vei toratecha*
[54] *z'mirot hayu li chukecha b'veit m'gurai*
[55] *zachar'ti valailah shim'cha YHVH va'esh'm'rah toratecha*
[56] *zot hay'tah li ki fikudecha natzar'ti*

Chet

[57] *chel'ki YHVH amar'ti lish'mor d'varecha*
[58] *chiliti fanecha v'chol leiv choneini k'im'ratecha*
[59] *chishav'ti d'rachai va'ashivah rag'lai el eidotecha*
[60] *chash'ti v'lo hit'mah'mah'ti lish'mor mitz'votecha*
[61] *chev'lei r'sha'im iv'duni torat'cha lo shachach'ti*
[62] *chatzot lailah akum l'hodot lach al mish'p'tei tzid'kecha*
[63] *chaveir ani l'chol asher y'rei'ucha ul'shom'rei pikudecha*
[64] *chas'd'cha YHVH mal'ah ha'aretz chukecha lam'deini*

Tet

[65] *tov asita im av'd'cha YHVH kid'varecha*
[66] *tuv ta'am vada'at lam'deini ki v'mitz'votecha he'eman'ti*
[67] *terem e'eneh ani shogeig v'atah im'rat'cha shamar'ti*
[68] *tov atah umeitiv lam'deini chukecha*
[69] *taf'lu alai sheker zeidim ani b'chol leiv etzor pikudecha*
[70] *tafash kacheilev libam ani torat'cha shi'asha'ti*

[71] *tov li chi uneiti l'ma'an el'mad chukecha*
[72] *tov li torat picha mei'al'fei zahav vachasef*
Yod
[73] *yadecha asuni vaichon'nuni havineini v'el'm'dah mitz'votecha*
[74] *y'rei'echa yir'uni v'yis'machu ki lid'var'cha yichal'ti*
[75] *yada'ti YHVH ki tzedek mish'patecha ve'emunah initani*
[76] *y'hi na chas'd'cha l'nachameini k'im'rat'cha l'av'decha*
[77] *y'vo'uni rachamecha v'ech'yeh ki torat'cha sha'ashu'ai*
[78] *yeivoshu zeidim ki sheker iv'tuni ani asi'ach b'fikudecha*
[79] *yashuvu li y'rei'echa v'yod'ei eidotecha*
[80] *y'hi libi tamim b'chukecha l'ma'an lo eivosh*
Kaf
[81] *kal'tah lit'shu'at'cha naf'shi lid'var'cha yichal'ti*
[82] *kalu einai l'im'ratecha leimor matai t'nachameini*
[83] *ki hayiti k'nod b'kitor chukecha lo shachach'ti*
[84] *kamah y'mei av'decha matai ta'aseh v'rod'fai mish'pat*
[85] *karu li zeidim shichot asher lo ch'toratecha*
[86] *kol mitz'votecha emunah sheker r'dafuni oz'reini*
[87] *kim'at kiluni va'aretz va'ani lo azav'ti fikudecha*
[88] *k'chas'd'cha chayeini v'esh'm'rah eidut picha*
Lamed
[89] *l'olam YHVH d'var'cha nitzav bashamayim*
[90] *l'dor vador emunatecha konan'ta eretz vata'amod*
[91] *l'mish'patecha am'du hayom ki hakol avadecha*
[92] *lulei torat'cha sha'ashu'ai az avad'ti v'on'yi*
[93] *l'olam lo esh'kach pikudecha ki vam chiyitani*
[94] *l'cha ani hoshi'eini ki fikudecha darash'ti*
[95] *li kivu r'sha'im l'ab'deini eidotecha et'bonan*
[96] *l'chol tich'lah ra'iti keitz r'chavah mitz'vat'cha m'od*
Mem
[97] *mah ahav'ti toratecha kol hayom hi sichati*
[98] *mei'oy'vai t'chak'meini mitz'votecha ki l'olam hi li*
[99] *mikol m'lam'dai his'kal'ti ki eidotecha sichah li*

[100] *miz'keinim et'bonan ki fikutecha natzar'ti*

[101] *mikol orach ra kaliti rag'lai l'ma'an esh'mor d'varecha*

[102] *mimish'patecha lo sar'ti ki atah horeitani*

[103] *mah nim'l'tzu l'chiki im'ratecha mid'vash l'fi*

[104] *mipikudecha et'bonan al kein saneiti kol orach shaker*

Nun

[105] *ner l'rag'li d'varecha v'or lin'tivati*

[106] *nish'ba'ti va'akayeimah lish'mor mish'p'tei tzid'kecha*

[107] *na'aneiti ad m'od YHVH hayeini chid'varecha*

[108] *nid'vot pi r'tzeih na YHVH umish'patecha lam'deini*

[109] *naf'shi v'chapi tamid v'torat'cha lo shachach'ti*

[110] *nat'nu r'sha'im pach li umipikudecha lo ta'iti*

[111] *nachal'ti eidotecha l'olam ki s'son libi heimah*

[112] *natiti libi la'asot chukecha l'olam eikev*

Samech

[113] *sei'afim saneiti v'torat'cha ahav'ti*

[114] *sit'ri umagini atah lid'var'cha yichal'ti*

[115] *suru mimeni m'rei'im v'etz'rah mitz'vot elohai*

[116] *som'cheini ch'im'rat'cha v'ech'yeh v'al t'visheini misiv'ri*

[117] *s'adeini v'ivashei'ah v'esh'ah v'chukecha tamid*

[118] *salita kol shogim meichukecha ki sheker tar'mitam*

[119] *sigim hish'bata chol rish'ei aretz lachein ahav'ti eidotecha*

[120] *samar mipach'd'cha v'sari umimish'patecha yareiti*

Ayin

[121] *asiti mish'pat vatzedek bal tanicheini l'osh'kai*

[122] *arov av'd'cha l'tov al ya'ash'kuni zeidim*

[123] *einai kalu lishu'atecha ul'im'rat tzid'kecha*

[124] *aseih im av'd'cha ch'chas'decha v'chukecha lam'deini*

[125] *av'd'cha ani havineini v'eid'ah eidotecha*

[126] *eit la'asot laYHVH heifeiru toratecha*

[127] *al kein ahav'ti mitz'votecha mizahav umipaz*

[128] *al kein kol pikudei chol yishar'ti kol orach sheker saneiti*

Peh

[129] p'la'ot eidotecha al kein n'tzaratam naf'shi

[130] peitach d'varecha ya'ir meivin p'tayim

[131] pi fa'ar'ti va'esh'afah ki l'mitz'votecha ya'av'ti

[132] p'nei eilai v'choneini k'mish'pat l'ohavei sh'mecha

[133] p'amai hachein b'im'ratecha v'al tash'let bi chol aven

[134] p'deini mei'oshek adam v'esh'm'rah pikudecha

[135] panecha ha'eir b'av'decha v'lam'deini et chukecha

[136] pal'gei mayim yar'du einai al lo sham'ru toratecha

Tzade

[137] tzadik atah YHVH v'yashar mish'patecha

[138] tzivita tzedek eidotecha ve'emunah m'od

[139] tzim'tat'ni kin'ati ki shach'chu d'varecha tzarai

[140] tz'rufah im'rat'cha m'od v'av'd'cha aheivah

[141] tza'ir anochi v'niv'zeh pikudecha lo shachach'ti

[142] tzid'kat'cha tzedek l'olam v'torat'cha emet

[143] tzar umatzok m'tza'uni mitz'votecha sha'ashu'ai

[144] tzedek eidotecha l'olam havineini v'ech'yeh

Kof

[145] karati v'chol leiv aneini YHVH chukecha etzorah

[146] k'raticha hoshi'eini v'esh'm'rah eidotecha

[147] kidam'ti vaneshef va'ashavei'ah lid'var'cha yichal'ti

[148] kid'mu einai ash'murot lasi'ach b'im'ratecha

[149] koli shim'ah ch'chas'decha YHVH k'mish'patecha chayeini

[150] kar'vu rod'fei zimah mitorat'cha rachaku

[151] karov atah YHVH v'chol mitz'votecha emet

[152] kedem yada'ti mei'eidotecha ki l'olam y'sad'tam

Resh

[153] r'eih on'yi v'chal'tzeini ki torat'cha lo shachach'ti

[154] rivah rivi ug'aleini l'im'rat'cha chayeini

[155] rachok mei'r'sha'im y'shu'ah ki chukecha lo darashu

[156] rachamecha rabim YHVH k'mish'patecha chayeini

[157] rabim rod'fai v'tzarai mei'eidotecha lo natiti

[158] ra'iti vog'dim va'et'kotatah asher im'rat'cha lo shamaru

[159] r'eih ki fikudecha ahav'ti YHVH k'chas'd'cha chayeini

[160] rosh d'var'cha emet ul'olam kol mish'pat tzid'kecha

Shin

[161] *sarim r'dafuni chinam umid̦'var'cha pachad libi*

[162] *sas anochi al im'ratecha k'motzei shalal rav*

[163] *sheker saneiti va'ata'eivah torat'cha ahav'ti*

[164] *sheva bayom hilal'ticha al mish'p'tei tzid'kecha*

[165] *shalom rav l'ohavei toratecha v'ein lamo mich'shol*

[166] *sibar'ti lishu'at'cha YHVH umitz'votecha asiti*

[167] *sham'rah naf'shi eidotecha va'ohaveim m'od*

[168] *shamar'ti fikudecha v'eidotecha ki chol d'rachai neg'decha*

Tav

[169] *tik'rav rinati l'fanecha YHVH kid'var'cha havineini*

[170] *tavo t'chinati l'fanecha k'im'rat'cha hatzileini*

[171] *taba'nah s'fatai t'hilah ki t'lam'deini chukecha*

[172] *ta'an l'shoni im'ratecha ki chol mitz'votecha tzedek*

[173] *t'hi yad'cha l'oz'reini ki fikudecha vachar'ti*

[174] *ta'av'ti lishu'at'cha YHVH v'torat'cha sha'ashu'ai*

[175] *t'hi naf'shi ut'hal'leka umish'patecha ya'z'runi*

[176] *ta'iti k'seh oveid bakeish av'decha ki mitz'votecha lo shachach'ti*

Translation:

Alef

[1] Happy are they that are upright in the way, who walk in the law of *YHVH*.

[2] Happy are they that keep His testimonies, that seek Him with the whole heart.

[3] Yea, they do no unrighteousness; they walk in His ways.

[4] Thou hast ordained Thy precepts, that we should observe them diligently.

[5] Oh that my ways were directed to observe Thy statutes!

[6] Then should I not be ashamed, when I have regard unto all Thy commandments.

[7] I will give thanks unto Thee with uprightness of heart, when I learn Thy righteous ordinances.

[8] I will observe Thy statutes; O forsake me not utterly.

Bet

[9] Wherewithal shall a young man keep his way pure? By taking heed thereto according to Thy word.

[10] With my whole heart have I sought Thee; O let me not err from Thy commandments.

[11] Thy word have I laid up in my heart, that I might not sin against Thee.

[12] Blessed art Thou, *YHVH*; teach me Thy statutes.

[13] With my lips have I told all the ordinances of Thy mouth.

[14] I have rejoiced in the way of Thy testimonies, as much as in all riches.

[15] I will meditate in Thy precepts, and have respect unto Thy ways.

[16] I will delight myself in Thy statutes; I will not forget Thy word.

Gimel

[17] Deal bountifully with Thy servant that I may live, and I will observe Thy word.

[18] Open Thou mine eyes, that I may behold wondrous things out of Thy law.

[19] I am a sojourner in the earth; hide not Thy commandments from me.

[20] My soul breaketh for the longing that it hath unto Thine ordinances at all times.

[21] Thou hast rebuked the proud that are cursed, that do err from Thy commandments.

[22] Take away from me reproach and contempt; for I have kept Thy testimonies.

[23] Even though princes sit and talk against me, thy servant doth meditate in Thy statutes.

[24] Yea, Thy testimonies are my delight, they are my counsellors.

Dalet

[25] My soul cleaveth unto the dust; quicken Thou me according to Thy word.

[26] I told of my ways, and Thou didst answer me; teach me Thy statutes.

[27] Make me to understand the way of Thy precepts, that I may talk of Thy wondrous works.

[28] My soul melteth away for heaviness; sustain me according unto Thy word.

[29] Remove from me the way of falsehood; and grant me Thy law graciously.

[30] I have chosen the way of faithfulness; Thine ordinances have I set before me.

[31] I cleave unto Thy testimonies; *YHVH*, put me not to shame.

[32] I will run the way of Thy commandments, for Thou dost enlarge my heart.

Heh

[33] Teach me, *YHVH*, the way of Thy statutes; and I will keep it at every step.

[34] Give me understanding, that I keep Thy law and observe it with my whole heart.

[35] Make me to tread in the path of Thy commandments; for therein do I delight.

[36] Incline my heart unto Thy testimonies, and not to covetousness.

[37] Turn away mine eyes from beholding vanity, and quicken me in Thy ways.

[38] Confirm Thy word unto Thy servant, which pertaineth unto the fear of Thee.

[39] Turn away my reproach which I dread; for Thine ordinances are good.

[40] Behold, I have longed after Thy precepts; quicken me in Thy righteousness.

Vav

[41] Let Thy mercies also come unto me, *YHVH*, even Thy salvation, according to Thy word;

[42] That I may have an answer for him that taunteth me; for I trust in Thy word.

[43] And take not the word of truth utterly out of my mouth; for I hope in Thine ordinances;

[44] So shall I observe Thy law continually for ever and ever;

[45] And I will walk at ease, for I have sought Thy precepts;

[46] I will also speak of Thy testimonies before kings, and will not be ashamed.

[47] And I will delight myself in Thy commandments, which I have loved.

[48] I will lift up my hands also unto Thy commandments, which I have loved; and I will meditate in Thy statutes.
Zayin
[49] Remember the word unto Thy servant, because Thou hast made me to hope.
[50] This is my comfort in my affliction, that Thy word hath quickened me.
[51] The proud have had me greatly in derision; yet have I not turned aside from Thy law.
[52] I have remembered Thine ordinances which are of old, *YHVH*, and have comforted myself.
[53] Burning indignation hath taken hold upon me, because of the wicked that forsake Thy law.
[54] Thy statutes have been my songs in the house of my pilgrimage.
[55] I have remembered Thy name, *YHVH*, in the night, and have observed Thy law.
[56] This I have had, that I have kept Thy precepts.
Chet
[57] My portion is *YHVH*, I have said that I would observe Thy words.
[58] I have entreated Thy favour with my whole heart; be gracious unto me according to Thy word.
[59] I considered my ways, and turned my feet unto Thy testimonies.
[60] I made haste, and delayed not, to observe Thy commandments.
[61] The bands of the wicked have enclosed me; but I have not forgotten Thy law.
[62] At midnight I will rise to give thanks unto Thee because of Thy righteous ordinances.
[63] I am a companion of all them that fear Thee, and of them that observe Thy precepts.
[64] The earth, *YHVH*, is full of Thy mercy; teach me Thy statutes.
Tet
[65] Thou hast dealt well with Thy servant, *YHVH*, according unto Thy word.
[66] Teach me good discernment and knowledge; for I have believed Thy commandments.

[67] Before I was afflicted, I did err; but now I observe Thy word.

[68] Thou art good, and doest good; teach me Thy statutes.

[69] The proud have forged a lie against me; but I with my whole heart will keep Thy precepts.

[70] Their heart is gross like fat; but I delight in Thy law.

[71] It is good for me that I have been afflicted, in order that I might learn Thy statutes.

[72] The law of Thy mouth is better unto me than thousands of gold and silver.

Yod

[73] Thy hands have made me and fashioned me; give me understanding, that I may learn Thy commandments.

[74] They that fear Thee shall see me and be glad, because I have hope in Thy word.

[75] I know, *YHVH*, that Thy judgments are righteous, and that in faithfulness Thou hast afflicted me.

[76] Let, I pray Thee, Thy lovingkindness be ready to comfort me, according to Thy promise unto Thy servant.

[77] Let Thy tender mercies come unto me, that I may live; for Thy law is my delight.

[78] Let the proud be put to shame, for they have distorted my cause with falsehood; but I will meditate in Thy precepts.

[79] Let those that fear Thee return unto me, and they that know Thy testimonies.

[80] Let my heart be undivided in Thy statutes, in order that I may not be put to shame.

Kaf

[81] My soul pineth for Thy salvation; in Thy word do I hope.

[82] Mine eyes fail for Thy word, saying: 'When wilt Thou comfort me?'

[83] For I am become like a wine-skin in the smoke; yet do I not forget Thy statutes.

[84] How many are the days of Thy servant? When wilt Thou execute judgment on them that persecute me?

[85] The proud have digged pits for me, which is not according to Thy law.

[86] All Thy commandments are faithful; they persecute me for nought; help Thou me.

[87] They had almost consumed me upon earth; but as for me, I forsook not Thy precepts.

[88] Quicken me after Thy lovingkindness, and I will observe the testimony of Thy mouth.

Lamed

[89]For ever, *YHVH*, Thy word standeth fast in heaven.

[90] Thy faithfulness is unto all generations; Thou hast established the earth, and it standeth.

[91] They stand this day according to Thine ordinances; for all things are Thy servants.

[92] Unless Thy law had been my delight, I should then have perished in mine affliction.

[93] I will never forget Thy precepts; for with them Thou hast quickened me.

[94] I am Thine, save me; for I have sought Thy precepts.

[95] The wicked have waited for me to destroy me; but I will consider Thy testimonies.

[96] I have seen an end to every purpose; but Thy commandment is exceeding broad.

Mem

[97] O how love I Thy law! It is my meditation all the day.

[98] Thy commandments make me wiser than mine enemies: for they are ever with me.

[99] I have more understanding than all my teachers; for Thy testimonies are my meditation.

[100] I understand more than mine elders, because I have keep Thy precepts.

[101] I have refrained my feet from every evil way, in order that I might observe Thy word.

[102] I have not turned aside from Thine ordinances; for Thou hast instructed me.

[103] How sweet are Thy words unto my palate! yea, sweeter than honey to my mouth!

[104] From Thy precepts I get understanding; therefore I hate every false way.

Nun

[105] Thy word is a lamp unto my feet, and a light unto my path.

[106] I have sworn, and have confirmed it, to observe Thy righteous ordinances.

[107] I am afflicted very much; quicken me, *YHVH*, according unto Thy word.

[108] Accept, I beseech Thee, the freewill-offerings of my mouth, *YHVH*, and teach me Thine ordinances.

[109] My soul is continually in my hand; yet have I not forgotten Thy law.

[110] The wicked have laid a snare for me; yet went I not astray from Thy precepts.

[111] Thy testimonies have I taken as a heritage for ever; for they are the rejoicing of my heart.

[112] I have inclined my heart to perform Thy statutes, for ever, at every step.

Samech

[113] I hate them that are of a double mind; but Thy law do I love.

[114] Thou art my covert and my shield; in Thy word do I hope.

[115] Depart from me, ye evildoers; that I may keep the commandments of my God.

[116] Uphold me according unto Thy word, that I may live; and put me not to shame in my hope.

[117] Support Thou me, and I shall be saved; and I will occupy myself with Thy statutes continually.

[118] Thou hast made light of all them that err from Thy statutes; for their deceit is vain.

[119] Thou puttest away all the wicked of the earth like dross; therefore I love Thy testimonies.

[120] My flesh shuddereth for fear of Thee; and I am afraid of Thy judgments.

Ayin

[121] I have done justice and righteousness; leave me not to mine oppressors.

[122] Be surety for Thy servant for good; let not the proud oppress me.

[123] Mine eyes fail for Thy salvation, and for Thy righteous word.

[124] Deal with Thy servant according unto Thy mercy, and teach me Thy statutes.

[125] I am Thy servant, give me understanding, that I may know Thy testimonies.

[126] It is time for *YHVH* to work; they have made void Thy law.

[127] Therefore I love Thy commandments above gold, yea, above fine gold.

[128] Therefore I esteem all Thy precepts concerning all things to be right; every false way I hate.

Peh

[129] Thy testimonies are wonderful; therefore doth my soul keep them.

[130] The opening of Thy words giveth light; it giveth understanding unto the simple.

[131] I opened wide my mouth, and panted; for I longed for Thy commandments.

[132] Turn Thee towards me, and be gracious unto me, as is Thy wont to do unto those that love Thy name.

[133] Order my footsteps by Thy word; and let not any iniquity have dominion over me.

[134] Redeem me from the oppression of man, and I will observe Thy precepts.

[135] Make Thy face to shine upon Thy servant; and teach me Thy statutes.

[136] Mine eyes run down with rivers of water, because they observe not Thy law.

Tzade

[137] Righteous art Thou, *YHVH*, and upright are Thy judgments.

[138] Thou hast commanded Thy testimonies in righteousness and exceeding faithfulness.

[139] My zeal hath undone me, because mine adversaries have forgotten Thy words.

[140] Thy word is tried to the uttermost, and Thy servant loveth it.

[141] I am small and despised; yet have I not forgotten Thy precepts.

[142] Thy righteousness is an everlasting righteousness, and Thy law is the truth.

[143] Trouble and anguish have overtaken me; yet Thy commandments are my delight.

[144] Thy testimonies are righteous for ever; give me understanding, and I shall live.

Kof

[145] I have called with my whole heart; answer me, *YHVH*; I will keep Thy statutes.

[146] I have called Thee, save me, and I will observe Thy testimonies.

[147] I rose early at dawn, and cried; I hoped in Thy word.

[148] Mine eyes forestalled the night-watches, that I might meditate in Thy word.

[149] Hear my voice according unto Thy lovingkindness; quicken me, *YHVH*, as Thou art wont.

[150] They draw nigh that follow after wickedness; they are far from Thy law.

[151] Thou art nigh, *YHVH*; and all Thy commandments are truth.

[152] Of old have I known from Thy testimonies that Thou hast founded them for ever.

Resh

[153] O see mine affliction, and rescue me; for I do not forget Thy law.

[154] Plead Thou my cause, and redeem me; quicken me according to Thy word.

[155] Salvation is far from the wicked; for they seek not Thy statutes.

[156] Great are Thy compassions, *YHVH*; quicken me as Thou art wont.

[157] Many are my persecutors and mine adversaries; yet have I not turned aside from Thy testimonies.

[158] I beheld them that were faithless, and strove with them; because they observed not Thy word.

[159] O see how I love Thy precepts; quicken me, *YHVH*, according to Thy lovingkindness.

[160] The beginning of Thy word is truth; and all Thy righteous ordinance endureth for ever.

Shin

[161] Princes have persecuted me without a cause; but my heart standeth in awe of Thy words.

[162] I rejoice at Thy word, as one that findeth great spoil.

[163] I hate and abhor falsehood; Thy law do I love.

[164] Seven times a day do I praise Thee, because of Thy righteous ordinances.

[165] Great peace have they that love Thy law; and there is no stumbling for them.

[166] I have hoped for Thy salvation, *YHVH*, and have done Thy commandments.

[167] My soul hath observed Thy testimonies; and I love them exceedingly.

[168] I have observed Thy precepts and Thy testimonies; for all my ways are before Thee.

Tav

[169] Let my cry come near before Thee, *YHVH*; give me understanding according to Thy word.

[170] Let my supplication come before Thee; deliver me according to Thy word.

[171] Let my lips utter praise: because Thou teachest me Thy statutes.

[172] Let my tongue sing of Thy word; for all Thy commandments are righteousness.

[173] Let Thy hand be ready to help me; for I have chosen Thy precepts.

[174] I have longed for Thy salvation, *YHVH*; and Thy law is my delight.

[175] Let my soul live, and it shall praise Thee; and let Thine ordinances help me.

[176] I have gone astray like a lost sheep; seek Thy servant; for I have not forgotten Thy commandments.

Psalm 119, titled אלפא ביתא (*Alfa Beta*), or תמניא אפין (*T'man'ya Apin*—"eightfold") in the *Talmud* [*TB Berachot 4b*], is a mammoth acrostic psalm comprising one hundred and seventy-six verses divided into twenty-two stanzas. Each of these stanzas is composed of eight verses, and all twenty-two are arranged in exact alphabetical order. In Sefardic rites *Psalm 119* is recited at sundown on Saturdays at the close of the Sabbath.[2] This psalm is traditionally read over *Shavuot* (Festival of Weeks), and a number of verses were introduced into Jewish worship by the *Ari*, the remarkable Rabbi Isaac Luria of kabbalah fame.[3] In this regard, *Psalm 118:5* and *Lamentations 3:56* are conjoined with *Psalm*

119:160, 122, 162, 66 and *108*, for recitation prior to blowing the
שׁופָר (*Shofar*—Ram's Horn) on *Rosh Hashanah* (Jewish New
Year) in Ashkenazic and certain Sefardic liturgies.[4] Excluding the
first verse, the capitals of the remaining verses spell קְרַע שָׂטָן
(*K'ra Satan*—"tear Satan"),[5] a Divine Name construct which I
have addressed elsewhere in some detail,[6] and which features
prominently in both the religious and magical uses of the current
psalm. Other than this, it should be noted that verses *89* to *91* of
the current psalm are enunciated on the second day of the New
Year.[7]

Psalm *119* plays a prominent role in Jewish life from the
cradle to the grave. In this regard, as far as childbirth is concerned,
we are told there are two "Spirit Intelligences" who govern those
who are suffering a crisis, i.e. אַהֲרִיאֵל (*Ahari'el*) and בְּרָהִיאֵל
(*Barahi'el*), and who are called upon when a woman is in labour.
However, their names are never uttered audibly. Hence they are
called upon by spelling their names with the associated verses from
the current psalm.[8] Following the birth, we are informed that "in
one naming ceremony, verses are selected from that psalm so that
the first letters of the selected passages spell the baby's name."[9]
Verses from this psalm are also enunciated during בְּרִית מִילָה
(*B'rit Milah*), the ceremony of circumcision,[10] and the current
psalm plays a particularly important role in prayers for the sick, the
deceased, at funerals, during the period of mourning, as well as at
the dedication of tombstones.[11] Regarding saying prayers for an
individual whose health is adversely afflicted, we are informed that
"depending upon local custom, the name of a gravely ill person
may be changed during this prayer in accordance with the
statement of the rabbis that a change of name cancels one's
doom."[12] Others would follow the custom of "saying specific
psalms on behalf of a person who is seriously ill," then vocalise the
verses in the current psalm "that begin with the letters of the sick
person's name, followed by those verses with the initial letters of
the words קְרַע שָׂטָן (*K'ra Satan*—'destroy Satan')."[13] I have
addressed the latter custom to some extent earlier in the first part
of "*The Book of Magical Psalms.*"[14] We are reminded that "when
spelling out the person's name in the psalm, it is a plea for the
person to recover."[15]

Should the said individual succumb to his or her illness, we are informed that in Sefardic tradition "spelling out the letters of the name of a deceased person in the psalm is practiced at the cemetery," also during the period of mourning, and again at the dedication of a tombstone.[16] Some would conclude the recitation with the verses from *Psalm 119* which spell the word נשמה (*Neshamah*—the "Spirit Self"), or again with the magical expression קרע שטן (*K'ra Satan*—"tear Satan").[17] Be that as it may, we are told that "the saintly mystics taught that we must observe the anniversary of the death of a parent even for one hundred years because of its auspicious nature and benefit to the soul of the deceased."[18] In this regard, it has been noted that "it is most appropriate to recite psalms at the gravesite, and again that "one can recite the verses of Psalm 119 beginning with the letters that spell the name of the deceased and the word *neshamah* (soul)."[19]

In terms of the magical uses of the current psalm, we are told that *Psalm 119* "has protective uses for every letter-verse."[20] However, it will be noticed that the various recensions of the *Shimmush Tehillim* focus mainly on the twenty-two divisions of the current psalm, and do not offer a lot of details on the magical application of *Psalm 119* as a whole. Yet there are relevant practices which did not find their way into the pages of that remarkable tome. In this regard, the *Jewish Encyclopedia* maintains this psalm to be "valuable for preachers," for recitation "when one is in deep perplexity," and "against dizziness."[21] The same source recommends the current psalm for recitation "on taking children to school," and "to sharpen the intellect."[22] In this regard, I have seen *Psalm 119* recommended to those who wish to commit themselves to intense *Torah* study, i.e. "Opening the Heart," and it is also enunciated when undertaking a journey, as well as to find favour.[23]

The current psalm is also employed for protection in perilous situations and times of trouble, i.e. protection from harm;[24] against bad language (slander); and especially against the "Evil Inclination," the latter being basically the "desire to receive." In this regard, we are informed that those who wish to control the said "inclination," should read *Psalm 119* over the seven days of the week in the following manner:

Day 1–letters א to ג (verses 1–24)
Day 2–letters ד to ו (verses 25–48)
Day 3–letters ז to ט (verses 49–72)
Day 4–letters י to ל (verses 73–96)
Day 5–letters מ to ס (verses 97–120)
Day 6–letters ע to צ (verses 121–144)
Day 7–letters ק to ת (verses 145–176).[25]

From what has been said thus far, it is clear that *Psalm 119* is enunciated in normative Judaism mostly for the sick, and the deceased. In this regard, we have noted the custom of spelling the names of individuals with verses from the current psalm. However, this popular procedure is applied in a number of different ways in Jewish Magic where, amongst others, it is employed for protection of a new residence against demonic forces; to maintain peace in the home; and even to improve sexual relations between a husband and wife. We are told that an individual who is moving into a new dwelling could keep pestilent spirits away from the house by reciting the verses which spell מישער (*Misha'ar*), The latter term is the name of a "Demonic Power" who is said to reside in a new home, who is in charge of the "sword of the house," can cause major problems for the occupants, delays in earning a livelihood, and whose design it is to destroy homes.[26] Hence, it is believed that the negative energy in the new residence can be changed to a positive one, by focusing on this impure power during the recitation of the said verses from *Psalm 119* in conjunction with the whole of *Psalm 30*.[27] Additionally, it has been suggested to locate a knife or a sword inside the house.[28]

   Be that as it may, we are further informed that peace, harmony, domestic bliss, and good marital relations, can be maintained in the home, by reciting the entire day those verses from the current psalm which spell the words שלום בית (*Shalom Bayit*—"Peace of the Home"). It is said that those who work this daily recitation can ask for, and receive, "whatever is required."[29] However, most people who have to live and earn a livelihood in the hustle and bustle of modern city life, would find it virtually impossible to maintain this recitation "the entire day."

In this regard, I have found it particularly effective to recite the said verses once early in the morning, and once at night. As far as the stated "marital relations" are concerned, it is said that Rabbi Yitzchak Kaduri, the acclaimed 20th century Kabbalist, maintained that an individual could improve sexual relations with his/her marriage partner, by reciting the verses in *Psalm 119* which align with the letters of the name of the latter individual and his/her mother.[30]

Being the largest psalm in the Hebrew Bible, the verses of which are magically employed for a great variety of purposes, the anonymous author of the *Shimmush Tehillim* paid special attention to the magical applications of the twenty-two eightfold components of *Psalm 119*. These appear to be directly aligned in several instances with the distinctive divisions of the Hebrew alphabet, and their respective associated bodily parts as delineated in two versions of the *Sefer Yetzirah*, i.e. the "Long" and "Saadyan."[31] Regarding the seven so-called "Double Letters," this appellative referring to the fact that these Hebrew glyphs have double enunciations, we notice for example the following six *Sefer Yetzirah/Shimmush Tehillim* alignments:

Double Letter	Physical Attribution	
	Sefer Yetzirah	*Shimmush Tehillim*
ג *(Gimel)*	Right Eye	Against ailments of the right eye
ד *(Dalet)*	Left Eye	To heal an injured left eye
כ *(Kaf)*	Right Nostril	For boils on the right side of nose
פ *(Peh)*	Left Nostril	For boils on the left side of nose
ר *(Resh)*	Right Ear	To heal boils in the right ear
ת *(Tav)*	Left Ear	To cure sores in the left ear

The magical "treatments" of several of the remaining glyphs in the *Shimmush Tehillim*, equally agree with the letter/limb attributions of the *Sepher Yetzirah*. Furthermore, as far as those letters which do not appear to be in full alignment in the said texts, one might argue that they are perhaps affiliated in more indirect ways. For example, an acquaintance of mine observed that "the verses starting with the letter *Bet* (ב) are not said [in the *Sefer Yetzirah*] to treat mouth pains, but rather to assist memory and study— possibly the connection is language and verbal abilities required to study and of which the mouth is a tool."[32] Whatever the cross-pollination between the listed texts may be, we are offered the following details regarding the magical applications of the twenty-two eightfold divisions of *Psalm 119*:

א (*Alef*) Verses 1–8: These verses are recommended against trembling of the body, shaking of limbs, or, according to one source, for "protection against fright."[33] In this regard, it is said this set of eight verses should be recited twice (six times according to a different recension of the *Shimmush Tehillim*) over the sorely afflicted individual.[34] Godfrey Selig noted in his German/English version of the *Shimmush Tehillim*, that "the eight verses of this letter, which all begin with *Alef*, should be pronounced over a man whose limbs shake and quiver, and if this be done in a low and even tone of voice, he will be relieved."[35] As one has come to expect from Selig's writing, there is once again no reference to the necessity of a "low and even tone of voice" to be found in any of the primary recensions of the *Shimmush Tehillim*.

We are further told that this portion of the hundred-and-nineteenth Psalm should be recited by one who wishes to keep and fulfill promises, perform a *Mitzvah*, i.e. fulfill a religious commandment, or a good deed.[36] Selig felt it necessary to rework this simple instruction in such a manner, that the original intention of fulfilling a *Mitzvah* is lost. Thus he wrote "if any one has made a vow, which has become burdensome to fulfill, it will be easy for him to keep his promise."[37] In a variant recension of this text we find the said recitation of the listed verses concluded with the following prayer incantation:

יהי רצון מלפניך צורי אלהי עולם שתתן לי יכולת
לעשות מצוה [....title and description of the *Mitzvah*....]
ויפרש שם המצוה ולא יעכבני ולא יבטלני שום דבר
אמן נצח סלה

Transliteration:

> *Y'hi ratzon mil'fanecha tzuri Elohei olam sh'titen li*
> *y'cholet la'asot mitz'vah* [....title and description of the
> *Mitzvah*....] *vifaresh shem hamitz'vah v'lo ya'ak'veini v'lo*
> *yivat'luni shum davar Omein Netzach Selah.*

Translation:

> May it be your will my rock, eternal God, that you grant
> me the ability to fulfill a *Mitzvah* [....title and description of
> the *Mitzvah*....], and nothing will delay me and nothing
> impede me. *Amen* Eternal *Selah.*[38]

ב (*Bet*) Verses 9–16: The second eightfold segment of the
current psalm is enunciated "to not lose memory."[39] It is listed
in the *Shimmush Tehillim* against forgetfulness,[40] or, according to
one translator, as an aid "in remembering his learning."[41] In this
regard, variant versions of this text maintain this section should be
recited three or four times a day,[42] and in one recension the
recitation is concluded with a prayer-incantation. In this regard, we
are informed that "you will be accepted" if you recite this portion
of *Psalm 119* three times each day, and conclude by saying:

יהי רצון מלפניך אהו מלך עולמים שתסיר ממני
ומלבי כל שכחה ולא אשכח עוד למודי בשמך הגדול
הגבור והנורא אמן נצח סלה

Transliteration:

> *Y'hi ratzon mil'fanecha Aheivah melech olamim sh'tasir*
> *mimeini umilibi kol shik'chah v'lo esh'kach od limodi*
> *b'shim'cha hagadol hagibor v'hanora Omein Netzach*
> *Selah.*

Translation:

> May it be your will *Aheivah*, King of the universe, that you
> turn all forgetfulness away from me and from my heart,
> and may I no longer forget my studies in your great,
> mighty, and awesome name. *Amen* Eternal *Selah.*[43]

The curious Divine Name אֱהֶיָה (*Aheiva*) is listed elsewhere, and
is said to have the power to improve memory.[44] In this regard, the
practitioner is instructed to recite *Psalm 119:9* three times, though

I suspect this pertains to the entire eightfold section. Each enunciation is concluded with the following prayer-incantation, which is virtually the same as the one listed above:

יהי רצון מלפניך יהוה אלהי ואלהי אבותי בשם
אָהֶוָ מלך העולמים שתסיר כל שכחה מליבי ולא
אשכח עוד לימודי בשם הנורא

Transliteration:
> *Y'hi ratzon mil'fanecha YHVH Elohai v'Elohei avotai b'shem Aheiva melech ha'olamim shetasir kol shik'chah milibi v'lo esh'kach od limudi b'shem hanora.*

Translation:
> May it be your will *YHVH* my God, and God of my fathers, in the Name *Aheiva*, King of the universe, that you will remove all forgetfulness from my heart, and I will no longer forget my studies, in the awesome name.[45]

There is yet further instructions regarding the use of the current eightfold portion of *Psalm 119* to encourage good recollection. In this regard, the practitioner is instructed to taste *Havdalah* wine, i.e. the wine which is blessed and consumed at the conclusion of the Sabbath, and then recite this section of the psalm. This action is concluded by saying:

יהי רצון מלפניך יהוה אלהי ואלהי אבותי שתישלח לי
את אליהו הנביא אשר שמך בקרבו ורמוז באותיותיו
ויפתח את לבבי בתורה במקרא במשנה בתלמוד באגדה
ובכל פסרי הפוסקים שלא אשכח דבר מכל מה שאני
שונה ולומד מעתה ועד עולם אמן כן יהי רצון

Transliteration:
> *Y'hi ratzon mil'fanecha YHVH Elohai v'Elohei avotai shetish'lach li et eiliyahu hanavi asher shim'cha b'kir'bo v'ramuz b'otiotav v'yif'tach et l'vavi b'torah b'mik'ra b'mishna b'talmud b'agadah ub'chol sif'rei hapos'kim sh'lo esh'kach davar mikol mah she'ani shoneh v'lomeid mei'atah v'ad olam Omein kein y'hi ratzon.*

Translation:

> May it be your will *YHVH*, my God and God of my father, to send me Elijah the prophet who bears your name within him, as implied by his letters [of his name], and who will open my heart to the Torah, the Bible, the Mishnah, the *Talmud*, the *Agadah*, and all the books of the arbitrators (scholars of Jewish Law), that I will not forget anything which is unfamiliar and learnt, from now unto eternity *Amen*, be it so willed.[46]

Magical procedures for פתיחת הלב (*Petichat haLev*—"Opening of the Heart"), i.e. "awakening/sharpening one's intellect"[47] for the purpose of studying and comprehending sacred writ, are quite common in Jewish Magic. In terms of employing the current eightfold segment of *Psalm 119* for this purpose, the *Shimmush Tehillim* instructs the practitioner to boil and peel an egg, then copy on it the current eight verses of *Psalm 119*, including *Deuteronomy 33:4* reading:

תורה צוה לנו משה מורשה קהלת יעקב

Transliteration:

> *Torah tzivah lanu mosheh morashah k'hilat ya'akov*

Translation:

> Moses commanded us a law, an inheritance of the congregation of Jacob.

as well as *Joshua 1:8* reading:

לא ימוש ספר התורה הזה מפיך והגית בו יומם ולילה
למען תשמר לעשות ככל הכתוב בו כי אז תצליח את
דרכך ואז תשכיל

Transliteration:

> *Lo yamush seifer hatorah hazeh mipicha v'hagita bo yomam valailah l'ma'an tish'mor la'asot k'chol hakatuv bo ki az tatz'li'ach et d'rachecha v'az tas'kil*

Translation:

> This book of the law shall not depart out of thy mouth, but thou shalt meditate therein day and night, that thou mayest observe to do according to all that is written therein; for

then thou shalt make thy ways prosperous, and then thou shalt have good success.[48]

"Opening the Heart" procedures requiring passages to be written on peeled boiled eggs are not uncommon in *Practical Kabbalah*. However, considering the size of the inscription, it will fit the surface of an ostrich egg, but definitely not the egg of a chicken. Be that as it may, this action is concluded by uttering the following prayer-incantation, which in the standard published version of the *Shimmush Tehillim* reads:

פניאל שובניאל מופיאל פתח לבי בתורתיך וכל
מה שאני לומד אהיה זוכר

Transliteration:
Pani'el Shov'ni'el Mupi'el p'tach libi b'toratecha v'chol mah she'ani lomeid eh'yeh zocher.

Translation:
Pani'el Shov'ni'el Mupi'el, open my heart to your Torah, and everything I learn I will remember.

We are told this should be done at the conclusion of a fast on a Thursday during *Min'chah* (the afternoon prayers), following which the egg is consumed whole, and the action completed with the enunciation of *Psalm 119:9–12* three times.[49] A different recension of the *Shimmush Tehillim* maintains the associated three Divine/Angelic Names to be חפניאל שובניאל סופיאל (*Chaf'ni'el Shov'ni'el Sofi'el*).[50] Godfrey Selig's version maintains eight verses from *Joshua 1* should be included, and he references two angelic appellatives which are nowhere to be found in any primary source of the *Shimmush Tehillim*. not even a master of microcalligraphy would be able to inscribe the surface of an egg with the mass of details he lists in his German/English offering of the *Shimmush Tehillim*. In this regard, he wrote "it is said that through the second division from the ninth to the sixteenth verse, a man may obtain a good memory, an open heart, desirous to learn, and an extended intelligence. Whosoever desires to attain this must begin as follows: Remove from a hard-boiled egg the shell deftly and cleanly, so that the inside shall remain uninjured, and write upon it the above eight verses as well as the fourth verse of *Deuteronomy 33*, and eight verses of *Joshua 1*, and also the holy name of the angels *Chosniel, Schrewniel*, and *Mupiel*. The translation of these three angel-names it is not necessary to know, because they must not be pronounced, but since it will be of interest to the reader to know the meaning of them, it will not be superfluous to give them here. *Chosniel* signifies Cover, or overshadow me, mighty God! (namely, with the spirit of wisdom and knowledge). *Schrewniel*, turn me, again, mighty God! that is, change me, convert me into a better man or woman, as David once said, 'Create in me, oh God,' etc. *Mupiel* means: Out of the mouth of the mighty God (namely, let me attend upon the decrees of thy laws, as if I heard and received them from the mouth of God himself). Finally, the following must also be written upon the egg: Open and enlarge my heart and understanding, that I may hear and comprehend everything that I read, and that I may never forget it. All this must be done on a Thursday evening, after fasting the entire day, and then the egg must be inserted whole into the mouth, and when it is eaten, the four first verses of this division must be repeated three times in succession."[51]

ג (*Gimel*) Verses 17–24: This portion of *Psalm 119* is enunciated (whispered) "for the right eye,"[52] or, in the words of one source, "against the weakness of the right eye."[53] Another source maintains it is "for one who has illness in the right eye (catarrh)."[54] According to the *Shimmush Tehillim*, this section of the current psalm is whispered seven times (five according to one recension) over the indisposed right eye.[55] Selig limited the current magical application to the "injured eye of a friend," with no reference to which eye is being granted this magical support. Thus he wrote "the division of the third letter, should be prayed seven times in succession, in a low, solemn tone and with full confidence in the omnipotence of God, over the seriously injured eye of a friend, so that the pain may cease and the eye restored.[56]

A variant recension of the *Shimmush Tehillim* offers an additional use of the current eight verses, noting that anyone wishing to confess his iniquities publically, should recite the said verses ten times.[57] In this regard, it is interesting that *Psalm 119:18* was arranged into the following Divine Name construct, which is employed for the purpose of correcting the יֵצֶר הָרַע (*Yetzer Hara* —"Evil Inclination") which the bearer might have suffered from prior to studying Kabbalah:

גִבֵת לְיִם עֵטַת יְהוּ
נֵגָר יְפָת וְלָךְ אַאוֹ

This Divine Name construct was formulated from the twenty-four glyphs of the said verse, arranged by means of the earlier mentioned *Serugin* (trellis) method into eight tri-letter combinations. The first eight glyphs of the verse comprise the eight capitals of the said tri-letter combinations, and the second eight the central glyphs. The eight combinations were completed by placing the first of the concluding eight letters at the very end, thus completing the last tri-letter combination first, then continue by adding the remaining seven glyphs in direct order from the first to the seventh letter combination.[58]

The same verse was also formulated into the Divine Name construct גֵעַוְנְמָ (*Ga'eiv'nimi*), which is said to have the power of "opening the heart," i.e. to sharpen the intellect. It is applied by reciting *Psalm 119:18* three times in the morning on an empty stomach, and then copying the five letters of the Divine Name construct respectively on the five nails of your hand. Afterwards, kiss your inscribed nails, and say whilst smiling:

ונחה עליו רוח יהוה רוח חכמה גֵעַ ובינה רוח
עצה וגבורה רוח דעת ויראת יהוה (*Isaiah 11:2*)
וְנְמָ ואהיה אצלו אמון ואהיה שעשועים יום יום
משחקת לפניו בכל עת : משחקת בתבל ארצו
ושעשעי את בני אדם (*Proverbs 8:30–31*)

Transliteration:

v'nachah alav ru'ach YHVH ru'ach choch'mah Ga'ei uvinah ru'ach eitza ug'vurah ru'ach da'at v'yir'at YHVH (Isaiah 11:2)
V'nimi va'eh'yeh etz'lo amon va'eh'yeh sha'ashu'im yom yom m'sacheket l'fanav b'chol eit m'sacheket b'teiveil ar'tzo v'sha'ashu'ai et b'nei adam (Proverbs 8:30–31)

Translation:

>And the spirit of *YHVH* shall rest upon him, the spirit of
>wisdom *Ga'ei* and understanding, the spirit of counsel and
>might, the spirit of knowledge and of the fear of *YHVH*.
>(*Isaiah 11:2*)
>*V'nimi*, then I was by Him, as a nursling; and I was daily
>all delight, playing always before Him; Playing in His
>habitable earth, and my delights are with the sons of men.
>(*Proverbs 8:30–31*).[59]

Elsewhere, in a variant recension of the *Shimmush Tehillim*, it is
noted that "if you want a good plan to fall into your heart," you
should recite this eightfold division of the current psalm seven
times, "and a good plan will fall into your heart."[60] On the other
hand, if you need to face anyone with a demand, it is said the
Divine Name יה יה (*Yah Yah*) has the power to fulfill demands.
In this regard, *Psalm 119:20* is enunciated seven times, and this
action concluded with the following prayer-incantation:

יהי רצון מלפניך יה יה השם הגדול והקדוש והנורא
שתהיה עם פי והורני אשר אדבר וצוה למלאכיך
יפיפיה שר התורה שיהיה עם פי

Transliteration:

>*Y'hi ratzon mil'fanecha Yah Yah hashem hagadol
>v'hakadosh v'hanora she'tih'yeh im pi v'horeini asher
>adaber v'tza'veih l'mal'achecha Y'fifiyah sar hatorah
>sh'yih'yeh im pi.*

Translation:

>May it be your will *Yah Yah*, the great and holy and
>awesome Name, to be with my mouth, and teach me that
>which I will speak, and command your beautiful angels,
>*Y'fifiyah*, the Prince of the Torah, to be with my mouth.

Repeat the Angelic Name יפיפיה (*Y'fifiyah*) until you lose count,
and forthwith begin to make the demand. It is said that in this
manner this unique "Spiritual Intelligence" will place words in
your mouth, and arrange them on your tongue. The practitioner is
exhorted to practise by repeating the Divine/Angelic Names

verbally so as not to forget them, and it is said things will be brought before you which you have never seen before.[61]

ד (*Dalet*) Verses 25–32: These eight verses are enunciated to alleviate pain in, and promote recovery of, the left eye.[62] Another source noted this section of the current psalm to be "for one who has illness in the left eye (catarrh),"[63] and one recension of the *Shimmush Tehillim* maintains it should be whispered five times over the afflicted eye.[64] It is further recited seven times when it is difficult to deal with advice or come to a decision. It is also said to be beneficial for preaching to crowds,[65] or when speaking in public.[66] In the latter instance it is enunciated ten times. As expected, Selig has a lot more to say in his German/English version of this text. Thus he noted "by the earnest praying of this division, a painful injury of the left eye can be cured in the first place..., and in the second place, if a man is engaged in a lawsuit, or is vexed by a change of occupation, or residence, or if he desires to make an advantageous selection, or make a resolution, he should repeat these eight times in succession. On the other hand, however, if a man must avail himself of the advice and assistance of many persons in order to accomplish an undertaking successfully, he should repeat this division ten times."[67] As we have seen again and again, much of the statements he make in the name of the *Shimmush Tehillim* is absent in the original text. I have seen the current eight verses recommended for success in a lawsuit, and a variant recension of the *Shimmush Tehillim* stated that this portion of *Psalm 119* should be vocalised nine times, in order to avoid being dismissed from your work, and to find employment in any business. In this regard, the action is concluded with the following prayer incantation:

ברכיאל מעשיאל ונתניאל עזרוני לעשות מלאכתי
זאת ואל יבטלוני אנשים בשם בורא עולם במדת רחמים
אמן נצח לסה

Transliteration:
> *Bar'ki'el Ma'asi'el uNatani'el az'runi la'asot mal'ach'ti zot v'al yivat'luni anashim b'shem borei olam b'midat rachamim Omein Netzach Selah.*

Translation:

> *Bar'ki'el Ma'asi'el* and *Natani'el*, help me to do this my job, and the people shall not dismiss me. In the name of the One who creates the world with the measure of mercy. *Amen* Eternal *Selah*.[68]

ה (*Heh*) Verses 33–40: This section of the current psalm is recommended against temptation.[69] In the *Shimmush Tehillim* it is listed as a protection against sinning,[70] and a variant recension of this text maintains it should be used when impure ideas enter your mind.[71] In this regard, we are informed that one should recite this portion of the current psalm, or say mentally, i.e. think, the Ineffable Name, vocalised יְהֹוֹוֹ (*YooHooVooHoo*), in your heart.[72] However, to affect protection against sinning, the *Shimmush Tehillim* instructs the practitioner to write the said eight verses on deerskin, which is to be worn as an amulet.[73] The said variant of this text further maintains these verses should also be spoken fifteen or twenty-one times,[74] and in yet another recension it is claimed the said verses should be recited eighteen times to nullify the evil instinct.[75] As usual, Godfrey Selig greatly expanded these details in his version of the *Shimmush Tehillim*, stating that "the division of the letter *Heh*, is said to make people refrain from committing sins. A sinful being, who has become so much accustomed to commit sin and vice, that he cannot refrain from them, notwithstanding his best resolutions, should write these eight verses upon parchment prepared from a clean deer skin, (or cause them thus to be written,) place it in a bag prepared for this purpose and hang it around his neck, so that he will carry it continually upon his breast."[76]

In an alternative recension of the *Shimmush Tehillim* the said verses are employed for the oft mentioned "opening the heart." In this regard, the practitioner is instructed to write the said verses on leaves of a thorn bush, following which the writing is blotted out by being covered with honey. The honey is afterwards consumed, and the action concluded with the following prayer-incantation:

פתחיאל רפאל ענאל יה יהו טרפיאל שתפתחו
לבי וכליותי יהוה יהוה יהוה יהוה יהוה יהוה
יהוה יהי רצון מלפניך שתפתח לבי וכליותי ללמוד
כל חכמה וכל תורה ודבר הלכה אמן

Transliteration:

Petachi'el Rafa'el Ana'el Yah Yaho Tar'pi'el sh'tif't'chu libi v'kil'yotai YHVH YHVH YHVH YHVH YHVH YHVH YHVH y'hi ratzon mil'fanecha sh'tif'tach libi v'kil'yotai lil'mod kol choch'mah v'chol Torah v'davar halachah Omein.

Translation:

Petachi'el Rafa'el Ana'el Yah Yeho Tar'pi'el, that you may open my heart and my kidneys. *YHVH YHVH YHVH YHVH YHVH YHVH YHVH*, may it be your will to open my heart and kidneys [mind] to learn every wisdom, every *Torah*, and everything of *Halacha* (religious legal pronouncements) *Amen.*[77]

In conclusion, it should be noted that *Psalm 119:33* is recited to increase personal מזל (*Mazal*—"luck"/"good fortune"). In this regard, the practitioner should recite the said verse seven times, and conclude with this brief prayer-incantation:

יהי רצון בזכות השם הקם מקה יקים יהוה מזלי
לטובה ולברכה

Transliteration:

Y'hi ratzon biz'chut hashem Heh–Kof–Mem Mem–Kof–Heh yakim YHVH mazali l'tovah v'liv'rachah

Translation:

May it be your will in the merit of the Name *Heh–Kof–Mem Mem–Kof–Heh*, to let my fortune (luck) ascend *YHVH* for good and a blessing.

The letter combination הקם (*Heh–Kof–Mem*) is in fact the sixteenth tri-letter portion of the "Name of Seventy-two Names," which we are told is recited in direct and reverse order in order to strengthen the power of this magical procedure.[78]

ר (*Vav*) Verses 41–48: It would seem there is some confusion as to the exact magical impact of the current set of eight verses. All agree it revolves around fear and rulers. In this regard we are told it is recounted "to intimidate a ruler,"[79] whilst another expresses the opinion that it is employed "to inspire fear of a governor."[80] Another source is of the opinion that this eightfold portion of *Psalm 119* is recited "to threaten a governor,"[81] whilst one recension of the *Shimmush Tehillim* recommends it to those who have "to go before a king or a lordship."[82] However, the opinion held in the standard published version of this text, is that this section of the current psalm is enunciated to inspire anger in a ruler against an individual.[83] In this regard, the practitioner is instructed to recite it over water, and to have the said individual drink it.[84] However, a variant recension of the *Shimmush Tehillim* maintains the said verses should be recited twenty-one times.[85]

Other than the statement that this section should be pronounced over water, Selig's notion on the magical use of these verses in his German/English version of the said text, is entirely at odds with everything said thus far. Thus he advises the verses to be spoken "properly over water," and then given "to your servant or dependent to drink, and then your rule and power over him will become easy and agreeable, and he will serve you willingly."[86] Whilst none of this features anywhere in the *Shimmush Tehillim*, it should be noted that variant views on the magical applications of biblical psalms are prevalent throughout the different recensions of this text. Thus we are informed in one recension that the current eight verses are employed "for mercy and to be saved from every affliction." In this regard, the practitioner is instructed to write the verses on "kosher parchment,"[87] i.e. deerskin, but a clean sheet of paper will suffice equally well. Be that as it may, the following prayer-incantation is included in the writing after the psalm:

חי חי אמון סלה סלה סלה סלה סלה סלה יהו יהו

יהו יהו יהו יהו יהו יהו ליש ועת בקו יתי יהוה

ואע שב חנח מיני יהוה הצדיק שתצילני מכל

צרה אמן

Transliteration:

Chai Chai Eimun Selah Selah Selah Selah Selah Yaho Yaho Yaho Yaho Yaho Yaho Yaho Layish V'at K'kav Yatai YHVH Va'a Shav Chanach Mini YHVH hatzadik sh'tatzileini mikol tzarah Omein.

Translation:

Chai Chai Eimun Selah Selah Selah Selah Selah Yehu Yehu Yehu Yehu Yehu Yehu Yehu Layish V'at K'kav Yatai YHVH V'a Shav Ch'nach Mini YHVH, the righteous, deliver me from every affliction *Amen.*[88]

The first three Divine Names read "Life Life Faith," and the suceeding Divine Name construct ליש ועת בכו יתי יהוה (*Layish V'at K'kav Yatai YHVH*) was derived from *Genesis 49:18* reading לישועתך קויתי יהוה (*Lishu'at'cha kiviti YHVH*—"I wait for Thy salvation *YHVH*").[89] The concluding portion of the Divine Name construct ואע שב חנח מיני יהוה (*V'a Shav Ch'nach Mini YHVH*) was formulated from *Genesis 6:8* reading ונח מצא חן בעיני יהוה (*v'no'ach matza chen b'einei YHVH*— "But Noah found grace in the eyes of *YHVH*"). However, this portion of the Divine Name construct appears to be flawed. The version which is in line with the glyphs of the said verse, was shared by Moses Zacutto in his mammoth *Shorshei Hashemot*. It reads ואע נצב חנח מיני יהוה (*V'a N'tzav Ch'nach Mini YHVH*), and is employed for the purpose of acquiring Divine Grace.[90]

The action of writing down the current verses and related prayer-incantation, is followed by the inclusion of the "Name of Seventy-two Names." In this regard, the said recension of the *Shimmush Tehillim* lists the first three tri-letter portions of the said Divine Name.[91] However, it would seem the whole "*Shem Vayisa Vayet*" is meant, in the same way as the customary statement "ABC" is a reference to the whole alphabet. Whatever the case may be, for easy access I include here the entire "Name of Seventy-two Names":

והו ילי סיט עלם מחש ללה אכא כהת הזי אלד
לאו ההע יזל מבה הרי הקם לאו כלי לוו פהל
נלך ייי מלה חהו נתה האא ירת שאה ריי אום
לכב ושר יחו להח כוק מנד אני חעם רהע ייז
ההה מיך וול ילה סאל ערי עשל מיה והו דני
החש עמם ננא נית מבה פוי נמם ייל הרח מצר
ומב יהה ענו מחי דמב מנק איע חבו ראה יבם
היי מום

The complete writing is afterwards wrapped in wax, which we are told will be beneficial.[92] In conclusion, I have seen the current eight verses recommended against making erroneous decisions.

ז (*Zayin*) Verses 49–56: This set of eight verses is said to be "for the spleen,"[93] "against spleen pain,"[94] or "for one who has illnesses associated with the spleen."[95] In this regard, the practitioner is instructed to write these verses on the body directly over the locale of the spleen with the Angelic Name רפאל (*Rafa'el*).[96] This is the appellative of the acclaimed "Spirit Intelligence" whose name means "God has healed." The current verses are also utilised to disengage from evil undertakings, and as a "protection against evil counsel."[97] It is said that if you should be tempted by a bad plan, you should recite these verses eighteen times,[98] or twenty-eight times according to a different version of the *Shimmush Tehillim*.[99] Of course, Godfrey Selig could not be expected to be satisfied with such simple instructions in his version of this text. Thus he elaborated the original instructions extensively, noting that "to the seventh division, two different effects are ascribed. It is said, for example: If one of your friends or acquaintances is afflicted with melancholy, or becomes splenetic, or has severe stitching in the side, write this division, with the holy name *Rafael*, which signifies, heal, mighty God, properly upon a small piece of clean parchment, and bind it upon the patient where the spleen is situated. If you have been led into an undertaking that promises evil results, through the misrepresentations of evil counsellors, repeat this division eighteen times, and you will find means to withdraw from the undertaking

without injury to yourself."[100] I have also observed the current
eight verses recommended elsewhere against melancholy.

As we have seen, differences, from relatively minor to the
most major kind, can be found in the various recensions of the
Shimmush Tehillim. In this regard, we are informed in one version
of this text that the current eightfold portion of *Psalm 119*, should
be enunciated eighteen times in order to "not be afraid of
anyone."[101] The same recension recommends this section against
diseases of the teeth and eyes. In this regard, it instructs the
practitioner to utter the eight verses over white wine and olive oil,
and to conclude by reciting the following prayer-incantation:

יהיה יהיה יהיה יהיה יהיה יהיה יהיה יהיה אוריאל
רפאל אורפניאל אל חי מלך עולם יהי רצון
מלפניך שיקל החולי הזה מעלי לבל יקשה עלי יותר
בשם הנוטה כדוק שמים (*Isaiah 40:22*) אמן נצח סלה

Transliteration:

> *Yih'yeh Yih'yeh Yih'yeh Yih'yeh Yih'yeh Yih'yeh Yih'yeh
> Ori'el Rafa'el Or'pani'el El Chai melech olam y'hi ratzon
> mil'fanecha sheyakel hacholi hazeh m'alai l'val yak'she
> alai yoter b'shem hanoteh chadok shamayim (Isaiah 40:22)
> Omein Netzach Selah*

Translation:

> *Yih'yeh Yih'yeh Yih'yeh Yih'yeh Yih'yeh Yih'yeh Yih'yeh
> Ori'el Rafa'el Or'pani'el El Chai,* King of the universe,
> may it be your will that this sickness be lifted from me, lest
> it become more difficult. In the Name of the One "that
> stretcheth out the heavens as a curtain" (*Isaiah 40:22*).
> *Amen* Eternal *Selah.*[102]

Psalm 119:49 was recommended for recitation prior to study,[103]
and the following Divine Name construct was derived from the
opening three words of this verse reading זכר דבר לעבדך
(*z'chor davar l'av'decha*—"Remember the word unto Thy
servant"). In harmony with the sentiment expressed in this verse,
the said Divine Name construct is said to hold the power of
"remembrance" (memory):

זְדַל רְרַךְ זְרַד רְלַךְ

The first tri-letter portion was derived from the capitals, and the second portion from the concluding glyphs, of the first three words of the said verse. The remaining two tri-letter portions are permutations of the letters comprising the first two tri-letter combinations. Vocalised *Z'dal' R'rach' Z'r'da Ral'ch'*, the two vowels employed pertain to the enunciation of the first three glyphs in the said verse.[104] They are also respectively aligned with גבורה (*Gevurah*) and חסד (*Chesed*) on the Sefirotic Tree.

ח (*Chet*) Verses 57–64: These verses were recommended "against stomach pain,"[105] with specific reference to the upper abdomen.[106] I have also seen this portion of *Psalm 119* recommended for intestinal problems in general, as well as for pains in the upper body. However, the *Shimmush Tehillim* advises those who suffer from a problematic or painful upper stomach, to recite the current eight verses seven times over wine, and then to consume the liquid.[107] Selig similarly maintains the current eight verses should be recited seven times over wine, but in his estimation it should be given to "a sick person who has severe pains in the upper part of the body, to drink of it, and he will soon find relief."[108]

A variant recension of the *Shimmush Tehillim* recommends these verses to an individual who seeks to keep his or her vows (commitments), study *Torah*, as well as to be able to retain the knowledge learned. In this regard, the practitioner is instructed to recite the eight verses eight times, and then conclude with the following prayer-incantation:

אהיה אהיה יהוה צבאות שמעני ותן לי לב טהור
וחכם ללמוד תורתיך ותן לי הזמנות טובות לשלם
נדרי אשר אני נודר ואשר אני חייב לפניך בשם
יהוה אלהי ישראל אלהי הצבאות יתברך ויתעלה
אמן נצח סלה

Transliteration:

Eh'yeh Eh'yeh YHVH Tz'va'ot sh'ma'uni v'ten li lev tahor v'chacham lil'mod torat'cha v'ten li haz'manot tovot l'shalem nedarai asher ani noder v'asher ani chayav l'fanecha b'shem YHVH elohei yis'ra'el elohei hatz'va'ot yit'barach v'yit'aleh Omein Netzach Selah.

Translation:

> *Eh'yeh Eh'yeh YHVH Tz'va'ot* ("I am I am *YHVH* of Hosts") hear me, and give me a pure and wise heart to learn your *Torah*, and grant me good preparations to fulfill my vows that I made and pledged to you. Blessed and exalted be he in the name of the Lord, the God of Israel, the God of hosts. *Amen* Eternal *Selah*.[109]

ט (*Tet*) Verses 65–72: This section is recited for illness, weakness of, or pain in the kidneys.[110] In this regard, we are informed in the *Shimmush Tehillim* that the current eight verses should be enunciated seven times over the left kidney,[111] or both kidneys according to a different recension of this text.[112] Selig is of the opinion in his German/English translation of this text, that "the division of the letter *Teth*, is an easy, quick, and tried remedy to cure the severest case of kidney or liver complaints, or to take away pain in the hips. Pronounce these eight verses properly, specially, and reverently over the sick person and he will convalesce."[113] I have personally witnessed this section recited for hip and liver problems with great success. Be that as it may, a variant recension of the *Shimmush Tehillim* maintains that anyone wishing to have his or her prayer accepted, should recite these eight verses seventeen times during a fast, and conclude with the following prayer-incantation:

יהו יהו אל שדי חי אמון אמיץ שמע קול תפלתי
ועשה בקשתי וענה עתירתי וענני ברחמיך הרבים
אמן נצח סלה

Transliteration:

> *Yaho Yaho El Shadai Chai Eimun Amitz sh'ma kol t'filati va'aseih bakashati v'aneih atirati v'aneini b'rachamecha harabim Omein Netzach Selah.*

Translation:

> *Yaho Yaho El Shadai Chai Eimun Amitz* (Brave One), hear my prayerful voice, and grant my request, answer my supplication, and answer me with Your abundant mercy. *Amen* Eternal *Selah*.[114]

As far as individual verses are concerned, we are informed that the earlier mentioned Divine/Angelic Name טפטפיה (*Taf'taf'yah* [also vocalised *Tef'tef'yah*, *Tef'taf'yah*, *Tif'tuf'yah* and *Tafitofeiho*]), which is said to be one of the seventy names of the archangel *Metatron*, was derived from the first two letters of the first words of verses *69* and *70*, as well as verse *76* of the י (*Yod*) portion of the current psalm.[115] As noted elsewhere, "*Taf'taf'yah* is considered amongst the most potent Sacred Names, certainly one which, in combination with the 'Shield of David' (hexagram), was amongst the most popular protective magical charms of the mediaeval world."[116] I have addressed this Divine Name in previous volumes,[117] and it would take far too much space to repeat that material here. However, it is worth keeping in mind that this Divine/Angelic Name, termed the "Name of the Thought,"[118] is considered particularly efficacious in procedures requiring visualisation. In this regard, Moses Zacutto recommends it should be visualised in the "colour of blood (red) in front of your enemies" as a potent protective device.[119] A dear acquaintance of mine, Rabbi Yosef Cohen, alerted me to a similar envisioning of the Divine Name *Taf'taf'yah* in Chaim Vital's *Sefer haPe'ulot* ("*The Book of Actions*").[120] In this instance, it is the Ineffable Name which is "engraved in red" on the forehead of the "angel *Taf'taf'yah*." The appropriate section of the said work reads (Rabbi Cohen's translation): "I have heard from one who tested it, for all times of duress and danger to have *kavana* that the angel named *Taftafiyah* is standing on your right side holding a flaming sword in his right hand and a bow in his left, and the Tetragrammaton engraved in red letters upon his forehead."[121]

As noted elsewhere, on a more spiritual level the Divine Name *Taf'taf'yah* is pronounced to banish negative and disturbing thoughts during prayers or meditation. In this instance the Divine Name is vocalised *Tif'tuf'yah*, and it is said the vowels employed were derived from the phrase שופטים ושפטו הרי טפטף (*shof'tim v'shaf'tu harei tif'tuf*), which can be translated "they judged the dripping mountains." The latter expression is said to refer to the mass of frustrating forces who are negatively impacting the mind of the worshipper or meditator.[122]

ℸ (*Yod*) Verses 73–80: This eightfold portion of *Psalm 119* is recommended to individuals who wish to be viewed favourably or find mercy.[123] According to the *Shimmush Tehillim* these verses should be recited during *Shacharit* (Morning Prayer Service).[124] In this regard, Selig wrote "would you find grace and favor with God and man, pray at the close of each morning prayer the division of this letter, trusting fully in the mercy and grace of God, and your prayer will be heard."[125] Elsewhere we are told these verse are said "to ward off suspicion,"[126] and a variant recension of the *Shimmush Tehillim* maintains that anyone who wishes to be worthy of the *Torah*, or be cured of an illness, should recite these eight verses every day twenty-six times, and then conclude with the following prayer-incantation:

רפאל צדקיאל חזקיאל חכמיאל אתם המלאכים
הקדושים תנו לי חלק טוב בתורה ובמצוות ותנו
רפואה לחליי ולמכאובי ככתוב רפאני יהוה וארפא
הושיעני ואושעה כי תהלתי אתה (*Jeremiah 17:14*)
אמן נצח סלה

Transliteration:

> *Rafa'el Tzad'ki'el Chez'ki'el (Chazaki'el) Choch'mi'el atem hamal'achim hak'doshim t'nu li chelek tov b'torah ub'mitz'vot ut'nu r'fu'ah l'chol'yi ul'mach'ovi k'katuv r'fa'eini YHVH v'eirafei hoshi'eini v'ivashei'ah ki t'hilati atah (Jeremiah 17:14) Omein Netzach Selah.*

Translation:

> *Rafa'el Tzad'ki'el Chez'ki'el (Chazaki'el) Choch'mi'el*, you holy angels, give me a fair share of the *Torah* and the *Mitz'vot*. Grant healing for my sickness and for my pain, as it is written "Heal me *YHVH*, and I shall be healed; save me, and I shall be saved; for Thou art my praise." (*Jeremiah 17:14*) *Amen* Eternal *Selah*.[127]

In conclusion, it is worth noting that כהת (*Kahet*), the eighth tri-letter portion of the "Name of Seventy-two Names," is directly affiliated with *Psalm 119:75*.[128]

ℶ (*Kaf*) Verses 81–88: These eight verses are recited for the right nostril,[129] i.e. "to clear the right nostril,"[130] or, according to one commentator, "for one who has a swollen/blocked right nostril (sinusitis?)."[131] Regarding this condition, I can personally vouch for the efficacy of these verses in relieving sinusitis. According to the *Shimmush Tehillim* an individual who wants "to blow through the right nostril," should recite the said verses ten times.[132] Godfrey Selig again elaborated on these details with much more than a single word in edgeways. Thus he noted that "if one of yours has a dangerous sore, or a burning swelling on the right side of the nose, pray the eight verses of this division, ten times, in a low and conjuring voice, over the sore, and you will perceive to your astonishment and joy, that the otherwise incurable sore will be healed."[133] However, I have further observed this portion of the current psalm recommended in unofficial sources, i.e. amongst the common folk, for pain, swelling, and other medical issues pertaining to the entire nose.

A variant recension of the *Shimmush Tehillim* informs those who wish to fulfill what they hope for, or avert evil machinations against their persons, should recite this section of the current psalm eight times, and then conclude with the following prayer-incantation:

ברקיאל עזריאל חפציאל האזינו ושמעו תפלתי
ותזכוני לעשות דבר זה ויפרש שאלתו וכמו כן עצות
רעות מעלי ככתוב עצו עצה ותופר דברו דבר ולא
יקום כי עמנו אל (*Isaiah 8:10*) בשם יהוה אלהי ישראל
אמן אמן אמן צנח סלה

Transliteration:

Bar'ki'el Az'ri'el Cheifetzi'el ha'azinu ush'mav t'filati ut'zakuni la'asot davar zeh v'yaf'reish she'elato uk'mo chen etzot ra'ot me'alai k'katuv utzu eitzah v'tufar dab'ru davar v'lo yakum ki imanu el (Isaiah 8:10) b'shem YHVH elohei Yis'ra'el Omein Omein Omein Netzach Selah.

Translation:

Bar'ki'el Az'ri'el Cheifetzi'el, answer and hear my prayer, and let me accomplish this matter, and he shall take back his request, and also the evil plans upon me, as it is written "take counsel together, and it shall be brought to nought; speak the word, and it shall not stand; for God is with us." (*Isaiah 8:10*) In the name of *YHVH*, God of Israel. *Amen Amen Amen* Eternal *Selah*.[134]

(*Lamed*) Verses 89–96: We are told this portion of the current psalm is for sweetening or nullifying negative judgement,[135] i.e. to find favour with a judge, and it was suggested to recite these verses "before going to court."[136] In the *Shimmush Tehillim* it is said that enunciating the eight verses after *Min'chah* (the afternoon prayers), will secure victory in a legal action.[137] In this regard, Godfrey Selig noted that "if you are summoned to appear personally before the Judge in a lawsuit, pray on the preceding day, just after the evening prayer, the division of the letter *Lamed*, and you will obtain a favorable hearing, and will be permitted to leave the court justified."[138] According to a variant recension of the *Shimmush Tehillim*, "if you wish to keep the words of your mouth, and be victorious in court," you should recite this portion of *Psalm 119*, as well as the following associated prayer-incantation twenty times. The latter reads:

יהוה אלהי זכיני לקיים דברי פי ואל אשקר בשם
ואל יצא מפי דבר שקר אמן וזכיני בדיני לפניך אמן
נצח סלה

Transliteration:
YHVH elohai zakeini l'kayeim div'rei pi v'al ashaker b'shem v'al yeitzei m'pi d'var sheker Omein v'zakeini b'dini l'fanecha Omen Netzach Selah.
Translation:
YHVH my God, privilege me to keep the words of my mouth, and not lie in the name. Let no false word come from mouth *Amen*, and privilege me in my trial before you. *Amen* Eternal *Selah*.[139]

(*Mem*) Verses 97–104: This section is said to be for the right hand.[140] It was noted that it is enunciated "for a weakness of the right hand,"[141] and for pain in or an ailment of the right hand, as well as the right arm for that matter. The *Shimmush Tehillim* suggests that the current eight verses should be whispered over the hand seven times (or ten times in a variant recension) over a period of three days.[142] Selig maintained, with some elaboration, that "for pain in the limbs, and especially for paralysis in the right arm or hand, a man should pray this division, seven times for three successive days, in a low conjuring voice, over the affected arm, and the pain will cease and the arm will be healed."[143]

נ (*Nun*) Verses 105–112: We are informed these eight verses are recited before going out on the road,[144] i.e. "before going on a journey or trip."[145] In this regard, it is noted in the *Shimmush Tehillim* that one should enunciate the said verses as one sets out, in order to be spared from any trouble,[146] and to travel in safety. As expected, Selig inflated and altered these brief instructions, saying, "have you a mind to travel, pray this division, which begins with the words: 'For thy word is a lamp to my feet,' a few days previous to starting upon your journey, each time after the morning and evening prayer, and you will accomplish your journey safely and will prosper in your avocation."[147] On quite a different note, we are informed in a variant recension of the *Shimmush Tehillim* that one who wishes not to forget what he learned, and who do not want to be interrupted in his *Torah* studies, should recite this section six times with the following prayer incantation:

נוריאל דלריאל אתם שמות הקדושים הצילוני
שלא אתבטל מללמוד תורה בשם שומר ישראל
ברוך שומר עמו ישראל לעד אמן אמן אמן נצח סלה

Transliteration:
> *Nuri'el Dal'ri'el atem shemot hak'doshim hatziluni sh'lo et'batel m'lil'mod torah b'shem shomer yis'ra'el baruch shomer amo yis'ra'el l'ad Omein Omein Omein Netzach Selah.*

Translation:
> *Nuri'el Dal'ri'el*, you holy names, save me from being interrupted in learning the *Torah*. In the name of the Keeper of Israel, blessed be the Keeper of his people Israel forever. *Amen Amen Amen* Eternal *Selah*.[148]

To encourage a good memory, a simpler magical application listed elsewhere instructs the practitioner to say *Psalm 119:105* seven times every day,[149] and finally it is worth noting that *Psalm 119:108* is directly affiliated with בֿהל (*Pahal*), the twentieth tri-letter portion of the "*Shem Vayisa Vayet*."[150]

ס (*Samech*) Verses 113–120: This set of eight verses is recited when an individual intends to petition for anything which is required,[151] i.e. necessities. In this regard, the *Shimmush Tehillim* notes "if you have a request, pray this and then ask (for whatever you want)."[152] Selig interpreted this one-liner statement to read "if you have a favor to ask of a superior, pray, before presenting your petition, or before you attempt to ask the favor verbally, the eight verses of the letter *Samech*, and you will not go away unheard.[153] Be that as it may, a variant recension of the *Shimmush Tehillim* recommends the current eightfold section of *Psalm 119* to those who seek to be saved from the evil eye, as well as for teaching *Torah* to others. The said verses are enunciated seven times, and the action concluded with the following prayer-incantation:

יה מלך מלכי המלכים הקדוש ברוך הוא יהי רצון
מלפניך שאזכה ללמד תורה לאחרים בשם צור
מלך עולם והצילני מעין הרע ומלשין הרע תסתירני
בסתר פניך מרוכסי איש תצפניני בסוכה מריב לשונות
אמן אמן אמן נצח סלה (*Psalm 31:21*)

Transliteration:
> *Yah melech mal'chei ham'lachim hakadosh baruch hu y'hi ratzon mil'fanecha sh'ez'keih l'lameid torah la'acheirim b'shem Tzur Melech Olam v'hatzileini mei'eyin hara umi'lashon hara tas'tireini b'seiter panecha meiruch'sei ish titz'p'neini b'sukah meiriv l'shonot (Psalm 31:21) Omein Omein Omein Netzach Selah.*

Translation:
> *Yah* King of the king of kings, the Holy One, blessed be He, may it be your will that I shall be worthy to teach *Torah* to others, in the name of Rock Eternal King, and save me from the evil eye and from slander. "Thou hidest me in the covert of Thy presence from the plottings of man;

Thou concealest me in a pavilion from the strife of tongues." (*Psalm 31:21*) *Amen Amen Amen* Eternal *Selah.*[154]

The text of *Psalm 31:21* was adjusted to read with first person singular pronouns.

ע (*Ayin*) Verses 121–128: We are informed this portion of the current psalm is "for the left hand,"[155] "for a weakness of the left hand,"[156] or for an individual who suffers pain in the left hand,[157] or in the left arm. The *Shimmush Tehillim* stated the current eight verses should be whispered over the afflicted hand seven times (ten times according to a variant recension), doing so over three days.[158] For once Selig's German/English version of this text aligns with this statement, without too much additional verbosity. Thus he noted that "in the same way and manner as the prayer of the division of the letter *Mem*, heals pain in the right arm, so also the praying of the eight verses of the letter *Ayin*, will cure pain in the left arm and hand."[159] We again find different applications of this section of the hundred-and-nineteenth Psalm in a variant recension of the *Shimmush Tehillim*. In this regard, an individual who is confronted by someone who intends to assault him/her, or one who wishes to make an accurate judgement, is instructed to recite the current eight verses nine times, and conclude saying:

יהי רצון מלפניך מלך חי העולמים הצילני מזה
האיש החומסני והוציא לאור משפטי וזכיני בו
כרצוני וכמו כן זכיני לעשות משפט צדק

Transliteration:
> *Y'hi ratzon mil'fanecha melech chai ha'olamim hatzileini mizeh ha'ish hachom'seini v'hotzi l'or mish'pati v'zakeini bo kir'tzoni uk'mo chein zakeini la'asot mish'pat tzedek.*

Translation:
> May it be your will, Living King of the worlds, to rescue me from this man which is oppressing me, and bring my judgment to light, and in this grant me merit in accordance with my will, and make me worthy to fulfill the right of justice.[160]

פ (*Pei*) Verses 129–136: These verses are employed to clear the left nostril.[161] They are said elsewhere to be "for one who has a swollen/blocked left nostril (sinusitis)."[162] In this regard, we read in the standard printed edition of the *Shimmush Tehillim*, that "to blow the left nostril," the current set of eight verses should be whispered over oil, and this substance applied as an ointment.[163] However, in a variant recension of this text, this portion of the current psalm is whispered ten times over the said segment of the nose.[164] According to Selig "the prayer of this division, will prove of the same effect in the case of a boil or swelling on the left side of the nose, and the proceedings in both cases [right and left] must be the same to effect a cure."[165] In yet another version of the *Shimmush Tehillim* we find these eight verses listed to those who wish to do penance and good deeds, and to silence discussion of the calamities of others. In this regard, the current eight verses are recited nine times.[166]

Other than these applications, it should be noted that the following Divine Name construct, employed for the purpose of "Opening the Heart," i.e. improving learning and memory skills in a child, was derived from *Psalm 119:130*:

$$\text{פְּדֶךְ יֵבְפֶ תַבְיְ}$$
$$\text{רִיתָ חַרָא מֶנַאיִם}$$

To achieve the said result, the six portions of this Divine Name construct are copied once a day over five consecutive days on the surface of a single apple. They are written, as it were, in columns around the apple. Following this action, the current verse, reading פתח דבריך יאיר מבין פתיים (*peitach d'varecha ya'ir meivin p'tayim*—"The opening of Thy words giveth light; it giveth understanding unto the simple"), is whispered in the ear of the said child, and the procedure concluded with the following prayer-incantation directed at certain "Spirit Intelligences" (Angels), one of which (*Potah*) is said to be "in charge of forgetting":

המלאכים הקדושים הממונים על פתיחת הלב
שתפתחו לבו של זה הנער [....name of recipient....]

ללמוד התורה והחכמה והדעת וכל מה דילמד
יליף וכל מה דיליף יזכור ולא ישכח מלבו לעולם
בכח אלו השמות למדיאל זבדיאל [זכריאל]
יְדִכֵרַנְיֵאל ובשם הגדול פּוֹתָה הממונה על השכחה
אמן אמן אמן סלה סלה סלה סלה

Transliteration:

Ham'lachim hak'doshim ham'munim al p'tichat halev shetif't'chu libo shel zeh hana'ar [....name of recipient....] lil'mod hatorah v'hachoch'mah v'habinah v'hada'at v'chol mah dil'mad yalif v'chol mah d'yalif yiz'kor v'lo yishakach m'libo l'olam b'ko'ach eilu hashemot Lamadi'el Zav'di'el [Zach'ri'el] Yidicheiranei'el ub'shem hagadol Potah ham'muneh al hashich'chah Omein Omein Omein Selah Selah Selah.

Translation:

Holy Messengers in charge of "Opening the Heart," open the heart of this boy [....name of recipient....] to learn *Torah*, and the wisdom, and the understanding, and the knowledge, and everything he learned he will retain, and all what he learned he will remember, and will never forget from his heart, by the power of these Names, *L'madi'el Zav'di'el [Zach'ri'el] Yidicheiranei'el*, and in the great Name of *Potah* who is in charge of forgetting, *Amen Amen Amen Selah Selah Selah*.

The action is concluded with the apple being consumed by the child. We are told the vowels employed in writing the Divine Names are not from the said verse, but are purportedly seven vowel points derived from the first three words of *Psalm 119:18* reading גַּל עֵינַי וְאַבִּיטָה (*gal einai v'abitah*—literally "open my eyes, and I see").[167]

צ (*Tzadi*) Verses 137–144: It is said this set of eight verses is employed to destroy[168] or lose enemies.[169] Whilst this portion of the current psalm is absent in the standard published version of the *Shimmush Tehillim*, a variant recension of this text maintains it is utilised against an ailment of the right foot. In this regard, the said verses are whispered over oil, and the said bodily part anointed with it.[170] We are informed elsewhere that the current section of *Psalm 119* is "for legal trials and sentencing." In this regard the said verses are recited twenty-four times prior to a trial and sentencing.[171] This aligns with instructions shared in one recension of the *Shimmush Tehillim* in which we are informed that to accept a judgement, and to direct a judgement "to its truth," the current eight verses should be enunciated twenty-four times. In this instance, the action is concluded with the following prayer-incantation:

אל ברוך ומבורך בפי כל חי לפניך באתי שתצדיקני
בצדקתיך כי כל צדק ומשפט מכון כסאיך חסד
ורחמים יקדמו פניך (Psalm 89:15) אמן נצח סלה

Transliteration:
> *El baruch um'vorach b'fi chol chai l'fanecha bati shetatz'dikeini b'tzid'katecha ki kol tzedek umish'pat m'chon kis'echa chesed v'rachamim y'kad'mu fanecha (Psalm 89:15) Omein Netzach Selah.*

Translation:
> *El*, blessed and blessed in the mouth of all living things, I came before you, so that you accept (the verdict) with your righteousness, for all "righteousness and justice are the foundation of Thy throne; mercy and compasion go before Thee." (*Psalm 89:15*) *Amen* Eternal *Selah*.[172]

Godfrey Selig expressed similar sentiments in his German/English version of the *Shimmush Tehillim*, saying that "since it frequently happens that persons in an official station are induced, through misrepresentations and other circumstances, to give a wrong and unjust decision, even against their better knowledge and desire, they are kindly advised to pray the eight verses of this letter, three times devoutly before giving their decision, at the same time asking the help of the Judge of all Judges, to enlighten their minds."[173]

ק (*Kof*) Verses 145–152: This section of the current psalm is enunciated for "the left leg/foot,"[174] for "weakness of the left leg,"[175] and "for one who has pain in his left foot/leg."[176] In this regard, we are instructed in the *Shimmush Tehillim* to whisper the eight verses over rose oil, with which to anoint the afflicted left leg/foot.[177] According to Selig "the mysterious operation of this division....relates to the cure of a dangerous and painful injury at the left leg. These eight verses should be pronounced in a low and conjuring voice over a quantity of rose-oil and the injury anointed with the oil.[178] Much of this statement is again absent in any of the primary versions of the *Shimmush Tehillim*.

Elsewhere we find the current portion of *Psalm 119* recommended "for anger,"[179] and it has also been suggested that *Psalm 119:145* should be uttered with great intent "if you should get lost on the road."[180] Interestingly enough, a variant version of the *Shimmush Tehillim* noted that one who wishes "to go from town to town, and also to have his fast accepted," should enunciate the current eight verses twelve times, and then conclude with the following prayer-incantation:

רם רם רם רם שמעיאל ענאל חי שמע תפלתי
והצילני מכל צרה ויגון ואם להלך מעיר לעיר אנא
יהוה אלהים אלהי הצבאות הוציאני מהעיר הזאת
לשמחה ולשלום ורוח והצלחה ולברכה וחיים
ולשלום בשמך הנכבד והנורא אמן אמן אמן נצח סלה

Transliteration:

> *Ram Ram Ram Ram Shemi'el Ana'el Chai sh'ma t'filati v'hatzi'leini mikol tzarah v'yagon v'im l'halech m'ir l'ir ana YHVH Elohim elohei hatz'va'ot hotzi'ani meiha'ir hazot l'sim'chah ul'shalom v'ru'ach v'hatz'lachah v'liv'racha v'chayim ul'shalom b'shim'cha hanich'bad v'hanora Omein Omein Omein Netzach Selah.*

Translation:

> *Ram* [Lofty] *Ram Ram Ram Shemi'el An'el Chai* [Living], hear my prayer and deliver me from every affliction and sorrow, and when going from city to city. Please *YHVH Elohim*, God of hosts, bring me out of this city to joy, peace, prosperity, prosperity, blessings, life and peace, with your honored and awesome name. *Amen Amen Amen* Eternal *Selah*.[181]

In conclusion, it should be noted that רָאָה (*Ra'ah*), the sixty-ninth tri-letter portion of "The Name of Seventy-two Names," is directly aligned with *Psalm 119:145*.[182]

ר (*Resh*) Verses 153–160: This section of the current psalm is enunciated "for the right ear,"[183] "for weakness of the right ear,"[184] or "for one who has pain in his right ear.[185] In this regard, instruction in the *Shimmush Tehillim* pertains to reading the current eight verses over onion water ("a crushed onion" in a variant recension), and to place a single drop in the afflicted right ear.[186] In his German/English version of this text, Godfrey Selig wrote "are you burdened with a painful, constantly running boil in the right ear, pronounce the eight verses of the division of the letter *Resh*, in a low and conjuring voice, over onion-water or juice, and let one drop run into the ear, when you will experience immediate relief.[187] Whilst boils are not specifically referenced in the *Shimmush Tehillim*, there is no doubt that the said eight verses are meant to impact any ailment of the said ear.

A different recension of this text noted that reciting the current portion of *Psalm 119* is good in ensuring that not a single word of *Torah* studies is forgotten. The same source further maintains it is equally good for dispelling pursuers and haters, i.e. enemies. In this regard, the current eight verses are recited thirty times, and the action concluded with the following prayer-incantation:

מחום אחום אחום אל שוכן מרום תן לי לב טוב
שלא אשכח מאומה מלמודי ותבריח כל אויבי ושונאי
וריבה את יריבי לחם את לוחמי (*Psalm 35:1*) והכניעם
והשפילם ועשה בהם משפט

Transliteration:
> *Machus Achus Achus El shochen marom tein li lev tov*
> *sh'lo esh'kach m'umah m'limudi v'tav'ri'ach kol oiy'vai*
> *uson'ai v'rivah et y'rivai l'cham et lochamai (Psalm 35:1)*
> *v'hach'ni'eim v'hash'pileim v'aseh b'hem mish'pat.*

Translation:
> *Machus Achus Achus*, God who dwells on high, give me a good heart, so that I shall not forget anything of my studies,

and you shall drive out all my enemies and my haters, and "Strive with them that strive with me; fight against them that fight against me," (*Psalm 35:1*) and subdue them, humble them and do them justice.[188]

(*Shin*) Verses 161–168: These verses are said to be "for the head,"[189] or for an individual who suffers ailments of the head, e.g. headaches.[190] In this regard, we are informed in the *Shimmush Tehillim* that the current verses should be spoken over olive oil (six times according to a variant recension), and this substance rubbed directly on the painful locale on the head.[191] Godfrey Selig's pronouncements on this magical application of these verses reads "against severe and burning headache speak the division of this letter, in a low conjuring voice, three times over pure olive oil, and anoint the place where the pain is the most severe."[192]

We are informed elsewhere that this portion of *Psalm 119* is employed "against the fear of an enemy."[193] Excepting this single reference, I have not seen this application mentioned anywhere else. However, one recension of the *Shimmush Tehillim* noted that this section of the current psalm is utilised "to make peace between those who are fighting or because your prosecutors will strike you." In this regard, it is recited seven times, each time concluding with the following prayer-incantation:

שמע תפלתי ושמרני מרודפי לבל יפגשוני בדרך
זו אמן אמן אמן נצח סלה

Transliteration:
> *Sh'ma t'filati v'sham'reini m'rod'fai l'val yif'g'shoni b'derech zo Omein Omein Omein Netzach Selah.*

Translation:
> Hear my prayer and protect me from my pursuers, lest they meet me on this road. *Amen Amen Amen* Eternal *Selah*.[194]

(*Tav*) Verses 169–176: The concluding eight verses of the current psalm are said to be "for the left ear,"[195] "for weakness of the left ear,"[196] or "for one who has pain in his left ear."[197] Repeating the earlier listed instructions applicable to the right ear, the *Shimmush Tehillim* instructs the current verses to be said over onion water, a single drop of which is to be located inside the afflicted left ear.[198] Selig, whose focus is here again on boils, wrote "the last division of this Psalm, should be used in the same manner as the division of the letter *Resh*, that is, it should be spoken over onion-water, and by its use a boil in the left ear may be cured."[199]

A different source maintains this portion of *Psalm 119* should be read twenty-one times for success,[200] and a variant version of the *Shimmush Tehillim* notes it should be recited nine times to be saved from magic spells. The latter is followed by reciting the following prayer incantation:

אהיה פץ יהו אל שדי שתברכני ותעזרני ותשלח
ברכה בכל מעשה ידי כתיב כי יהוה אלהיך ברכך
בכל מעשה ידיך ידע לכתך את המדבר הגדול הזה
זה ארבעים שנה יהוה אלהיך עמך לא חסרת דבר
(Deuteronomy 2:7) עזרנו בשם יהוה עושה שמים וארץ
יהי חסדך יהוה עלינו כאשר ייחלנו לך סלה נצח סלה

Transliteration:

> *Eh'yeh Patz Yaho El Shadai sh'tavaricheini v'ta'az'reini v'tish'lach b'rachah b'chol ma'aseh yadai k'tiv ki YHVH elohe'cha beirach'cha b'chol ma'aseih yadecha yada lech't'cha et hamid'bar hagadol hazeh zeh ar'ba'im shana YHVH elohecha im'cha lo chasar'ta davar (Deuteronomy 2:7) az'reinu b'shem YHVH oseh shamayim v'aretz y'hi chas'd'cha YHVH aleinu k'asher yichal'nu lach Selah Netzach Selah.*

Translation:

> *Eh'yeh Patz Yaho El Shadai*, so that you bless me, help me and send blessings in everything I do with my hands, as it is written "For *YHVH* thy God hath blessed thee in all the work of thy hand; He hath known thy walking through this great wilderness; these forty years *YHVH* thy God hath been with thee; thou hast lacked nothing." (*Deuteronomy 2:7*) Help us in the name of *YHVH*, maker of heaven and earth. May your grace be upon us, *YHVH*, as we await you. *Amen* Eternal *Selah*.[201]

It has been suggested that the current portion of *Psalm 119* is "for one who has pain in his arms and sides,"[202] but this is incorrect. In this regard, we are informed in the *Shimmush Tehillim* that an individual who is suffering pain and paralysis in the arms, one side, and soles of the feet, should work the "tried and tested" procedure of reciting the verses of this psalm in the ש"ב ת"א (*Atbash*) order: א (*Alef*): verses 1–8; ת (*Tav*): verses 169–176; ב (*Bet*): verses 9–16; ש (*Shin*): verses 161–168; ג (*Gimel*): verses 17–24; ר (*Resh*): verses 153–160; ד (*Dalet*): verses 25–32; ק (*Kof*): verses 145–152; ה (*Heh*): verses 33–40; צ (*Tzadi*): verses 137–144; ו (*Vav*): verses 41–48; פ (*Peh*): verses 129–136; ז (*Zayin*): verses 49–56; ע (*Ayin*): verses 121–128; ח (*Chet*): verses 57–64; ס (*Samech*): verses 113–120; ט (*Tet*): verses 65–72; נ (*Nun*): verses 105–112; י (*Yod*): verses 73–80; מ (*Mem*): verses 97–104; כ (*Kaf*): verses 81–88; ל (*Lamed*): verses 89–104.[203] Other than noting that "it is stated at the end of this Psalm, that whosoever is afflicted with a tearing pain in both arms, in the sides, and in the legs at one and the same time," Selig's German/English translation is here in full agreement with the Hebrew edition of the *Shimmush Tehillim*.[204]

It would seem that very little use is again made of the current psalm in Christian Magic. In this regard, I have seen *Psalm 119:105* included in a Christian amulet employed against snakebite,[205] and in the *"Livre d'Or"* the current psalm is recited seven times, an incredible task considering its size, and written down, following which the writing is perfumed with mastic, and carried on the person of an individual requiring protection "from all infirmities."[206]

PSALM 120

[1] שיר המעלות אל יהוה‬אהדוני‬אהדונהי בצרתה לי
קראתי ויענני
[2] יהוה‬אהדוני‬אהדונהי הצילה נפשי משפת שקר
מלשון רמיה
[3] מה יתן לך ומה יסיף לך לשון רמיה
[4] חצי גבור שנונים עם גחלי רתמים
[5] אויה לי כי גרתי משך שכנתי עם אהלי קדר
[6] רבת שכנה לה נפשי עם שונא שלום
[7] אני שלום וכי אדבר המה למלחמה

Transliteration:

[1] *shir hama'alot el YHVH batzaratah li karati vaya'aneini*

[2] *YHVH hatzilah naf'shi mis'fat sheker milashon r'miyah*

[3] *mah yitein l'cha umah yosif lach lashon r'miyah*

[4] *chitzei gibor sh'nunim im gachalei r'tamim*

[5] *oyah li ki gar'ti meshech shachan'ti im oholei keidar*

[6] *rabat shach'nah lah naf'shi im sonei shalom*

[7] *ani shalom v'chi adabeir heimah lamil'chamah*

Translation:

[1] A Song of Ascents. In my distress I called unto *YHVH*, and He answered me.

[2] *YHVH*, deliver my soul from lying lips, from a deceitful tongue.

[3] What shall be given unto thee, and what shall be done more unto thee, thou deceitful tongue?

[4] Sharp arrows of the mighty, with coals of broom.

[5] Woe is me, that I sojourn with Meshech, that I dwell beside the tents of Kedar!

[6] My soul hath full long had her dwelling with him that hateth peace.

[7] I am all peace; but when I speak, they are for war.

Psalm 120 is the first of fifteen psalms each of which bears the superscription שיר המעלות (*shir hama'alot*—"A Song of Ascents [or degrees]"). These fifteen psalms are believed to align with the fifteen מעלות (*ma'alot*—"favours") which the Divine One granted the Israelites following the exodus out of Egypt, and "which culminated with the building of the Temple."[1] These "favours" are further understood to correspond to the fifteen steps in the Holy Temple, which "led from the court of the women to the court of the Israelites,"[2] and to the fifteen words of the magnificent "Priestly Blessing"[3] [*Numbers 6:24–28*] reading:

יברכך יהוה וישמרך

יאר יהוה פניו אליך ויחנך

יסע יהוה פניו אליך וישם לך שלום

Transliteration:

Y'varech'cha YHVH v'yishm'recha

Ya'eir YHVH panav eilecha vichuneka

Yisa YHVH panav eilecha v'yasem l'cha shalom

Translation:

YHVH bless thee, and keep thee,

YHVH make His face to shine upon thee, and be gracious unto thee,

YHVH lift up His countenance upon thee, and give thee peace.

We are informed that just as the Divine One "blesses us with fifteen words," we compliment this blessing with fifteen expressions of praise,[4] i.e. שיר ושבחה (*shir ush'vachah*—"song and adulation"), הלל וזמרה (*haleil v'zim'rah*—"glorification and singing"), עז וממשלה (*oz umem'shalah*—"strength and rulership"), נצח גדלה וגבורה (*netzach g'dulah ug'vurah*—"endurance, greatness and courage"), תהלה ותפארת (*t'hilah v'tif'eret*—"praise and splendour"), קדשה ומלכות (*k'dushah umal'chut*—"sanctification and kingship"), ברכות והודאות (*b'rachot v'hoda'ot*—"blessings and acknowledgement [gratitude]"). Thus the figure fifteen is said to reference "the highest degree attainable in praising God."[5] It has been suggested that the term "ascents" might pertain to "an internal spiritual/ psychological ascent, requiring the person to search his soul and raise himself up to greater religious heights."[6] It should be noted that the number fifteen is further considered significant, because this figure is the *gematria* (numerical value) of the Divine Name יָהּ (*Yah*) [י = 10 + ה = 5 = 15].[7]

In Jewish worship, the fifteen "Song of Ascents" psalms are read at every Sabbath *Min'chah* service (afternoon prayers) over the period commencing with the first Sabbath following *Sukkot* (Festival of Booths), and concluding with the Sabbath prior to *Pesach* (Festival of Passover).[8] *Psalm 120* is also one of a number in this set of psalms, which are recited in times of trouble and tragedy.[9] In this regard, we are reminded that "the source of distress is the treacherous organs of speech, lips, and tongue,"[10] and in ancient times it was believed that those who indulged in evil gossip and slander, i.e. לְשׁוֹן רְמִיָּה (*lashon r'miyah*—"a deceitful tongue") referenced in the first and second verse of the current psalm, will suffer the punishment of leprosy.[11] However, *Psalm 120* also references שָׁלוֹם (*shalom*—"peace"), and in this regard this psalm is recommended in *Practical Kabbalah* for the purpose of establishing peace,[12] especially "for peace with one's friend."[13]

About those individuals who delight in spreading rumours, slander, and falsehood, it is maintained in the "*Book of Psalms*": שָׁנְנוּ לְשׁוֹנָם כְּמוֹ נָחָשׁ חֲמַת עַכְשׁוּב תַּחַת שְׂפָתֵימוֹ (*shan'nu l'shonam k'mo nachash chamat ach'shuv tachat sh'fateimo* —"They have sharpened their tongue like a serpent; vipers' venom is under their lips") [*Psalm 140:4*]. In my estimation, it is highly probable that this perception, as well as the call to be saved "from lying lips, from a deceitful tongue" in the second verse of the current psalm, are the primary reasons why the *Shimmush Tehillim* maintains *Psalm 120* should be recited seven times upon seeing a snake or a scorpion.[14] In this regard, Godfrey Selig appears to have lost the plot in his German/English version of the *Shimmush Tehillim*. He maintains that *Psalm 120* should be repeated prior to appearing before a judge, which will ensure that "you will receive grace and favour."[15] There is no reference to this application in any of the surviving recensions of the *Shimmush Tehillim* that I am aware of. Furthermore, when it comes to the earlier mentioned enunciation of the current psalm against snakes and scorpions, Selig depicts a scenario which is equally absent in the primary Hebrew versions of this text. Thus he wrote that "if a traveler should find himself in a forest infested with many poisonous snakes, scorpions and other poisonous reptiles as may easily happen, and thus be exposed to danger, let him pray this Psalm as soon as he comes in sight of the forest seven times, and he will be able to proceed on his journey without any harm."[16]

There are again a variety of applications of the hundred-and-twentieth Psalm, which are not listed in the *Shimmush Tehillim*. Thus, considering the earlier remarks about a venemous tongue, I have seen the current psalm suggested against verbal abuse, as well as to be saved from evil and slanderous libel, defamation, and gossip. This psalm is further recited to encourage humility, and is recommended to victims of wrongdoing. It should also be kept in mind that all fifteen "Song of Ascents" psalms (*120–134*) are enunciated to elevate your spirit to the Divine One; when visiting the graves of loved ones; and to alleviate the plight of women suffering the constraints of religious marriages (עגונות [*Agunot*]). Lastly, as far as individual verses are concerned, it should be noted that *Psalm 120:2* is directly affiliated with הההּ (*Hahah*), the forty-first tri-letter portion of the "Name of Seventy-two Names."[17]

The Byzantine Christian magical manuscripts noted that an individual who wishes "to walk about" in front of his or her enemies, should pronounce *Psalm 120* over water which was not exposed to sunlight. Following this action, a portion of the liquid is consumed, and the face and chest washed with the remainder.[18] In the "*Livre d'Or*" we find this psalm utilised to negatively impact enemies. In this regard, the practitioner is instructed to recite it seven times over the water in which a woman bathed on a Saturday. The said fluid is afterwards sprinkled over the entrance of the enemy, whom it is said "will flee and perish."[19]

PSALM 121

[1] שיר למעלות אשא עיני אל ההרים מאין יבא
עזרי

[2] עזרי מעם יהוה‎אדני‎אהדונהי עשה שמהים וארץ

[3] אל יתן למוט רגלך אל ינום שמרך

[4] הנה לא ינום ולא יישן שומר ישראל

[5] יהוה‎אדני‎אהדונהי שמרך יהוה‎אדני‎אהדונהי צלך על
יד ימינך

[6] יומם השמש לא יככה וירח בלילה

[7] יהוה‎אדני‎אהדונהי ישמרך מכל רע ישמר את נפשך

[8] יהוה‎אדני‎אהדונהי ישמר צאתך ובואך מעתה ועד
עולם

Transliteration:

[1] *shir lama'alot esa einai el heharim mei'ayin yavo ez'ri*
[2] *ez'ri mei'im YHVH oseih shamayim va'aretz*
[3] *al yitein lamot rag'lecha al yanum shom'recha*
[4] *hinei lo yanum v'lo yishan shomeir yis'ra'el*
[5] *YHVH shom'recha YHVH tzil'cha al yad y'minecha*
[6] *yomam hashemesh lo yakekah v'yarei'ach balailah*
[7] *YHVH yish'mor'cha mikol ra yish'mor et naf'shecha*
[8] *YHVH yish'mor tzeit'cha uvo'echa mei'atah v'ad olam*

Translation:

[1] A Song of Ascents. I will lift up mine eyes unto the mountains: from whence shall my help come?

[2] My help cometh from *YHVH*, who made heaven and earth.

[3] He will not suffer thy foot to be moved; He that keepeth thee will not slumber.

[4] Behold, He that keepeth Israel doth neither slumber nor sleep.

[5] *YHVH* is thy keeper; *YHVH* is thy shade upon thy right hand.

[6] The sun shall not smite thee by day, nor the moon by night.

[7] *YHVH* shall keep thee from all evil; He shall keep thy soul.

[8] *YHVH* shall guard thy going out and thy coming in, from this time forth and for ever.

Psalm 121, the second of the fifteen "Songs of Ascents," is said to be "one of the most famous and frequently used psalms in all rites, probably due to its simple language, its encouraging theme, and its wide applicability."[1] As noted earlier, it is recited with the other "Songs of Ascents" at every Sabbath *Min'chah* service (afternoon prayers) over the period commencing with the first Sabbath following *Sukkot* (Festival of Booths), and concluding with the Sabbath prior to *Pesach* (Festival of Passover).[2] In Sefardic tradition the current psalm is also recited on *Yom Kippur* ("Day of Atonement"),[3] and in Sefardic rites *Psalms 121–124* are enunciated during the Sabbath *Shacharit* (Morning Prayer Service). As far as the current psalm is concerned, it was suggested that the reference to "the moon by night" in verse 6, is probably the reason why this psalm is included in the monthly הלבנה ברכת (*Bir'kat Hal'vanah*—"the Blessing of the Moon"),[4] and vocalised at the conclusion of evening services in the Yemenite and Sefard-Chasidic rites.[5] It is said that "the recitation of this psalm when embarking on a journey and, in the Italian rite, after the reading of the *Shema* before retiring for the night attests to its popularity and use in times of worry, uncertainty, and liminality."[6]

This is likely to be the basis for *Psalm 121* being also recommended to individuals who have to travel alone at night.[7] In this regard, the *Shimmush Tehillim* maintains the current psalm should be recited seven times.[8] Godfrey Selig holds the same opinion, with some thoughts on the outcome. Thus he noted that one who is "compelled to travel alone by night," should "pray this Psalm reverently seven times," which will ensure safety "from all accidents and evil occurrences."[9] We are told that *Psalm 121* "is an excellent tool for protecting against threats that come in the night,"[10] and a variant recension of the *Shimmush Tehillim* maintained that "it is good to recite seven times on the way, and also in every affliction."[11] In terms of the latter application, we are informed that whoever suffers from fears generally, should read the earlier addressed "*Vihi No'am Prayer*" three times every morning and evening, and conclude by reading *Psalm 121* three times.[12]

Elsewhere, this psalm is employed for quite a different purpose whilst "on the road," which is probably not as useful today when travel routes are determined by global positioning satellite systems. In this regard, we are informed that those intending to undertake journeys, should carry two or three stones from outside their own homes. If it should happen that they reach a fork in a road, and are unsure which path to follow, a stone should be placed on each track, and the current psalm recited thereafter. It is said that, "a stone will jump," which indicates "the course you must follow."[13]

It should be noted that the current psalm is also resorted to for protection from harm, especially in times of trouble.[14] It is often enunciated in synagogues at the conclusion of services, when Jewish communities are faced with circumstances of crises and great danger.[15] The safeguarding qualities of this psalm is emphasised particularly in its extensive use in Hebrew amulets. In this regard, I noted elsewhere that it is sometimes written in a *Menorah* format, and included in *Shiviti* plaques and *Kameot* (Hebrew amulets), as indicated below:[16]

The current psalm is not only vocalised in an audible manner, but features also, both in full and an abbreviated format, in *Kameot* which are carried as a call for help and protection.[17] In this respect, consider the following standard abbreviation of this psalm with vowel points:[18]

שְׁלָא עָאֶה מֵיעָ עֲמִי עֹשָׁוָ אַיְלַ רַאֲיָ שֹׁהִל יָוְי
שַׁיְי שֹׁיְצ עַיָי יֹהַל יָוְב יַיְמָ רָיְא נַיְי צֵיְם עַוְע

Transliteration:

> *Shila'e Ei'ehe Mei'a'e Emiy' Oshava Ayila Ra'aya Shohilo Yav'yi Shoyiy' Shoy'tzi Ayay' Yohalo Yav'va Yiyimi Rayi'e Nay'yi Tzei'umei Av'o*

Regarding its application, I noted elsewhere that "individuals who wake at night in states of fear and trembling with their imagination running wild, should write the full abbreviation of *Psalm 121* on parchment. The Hebrew letters should be written with great care, as if every letter is a garment of some special being, at the same time imagining them streaming with Divine Light. Afterwards the writing should be rubbed off with rose petals and seven pepper corns inside water. Then the individuals must consume some of this liquid, and rub the remainder on their bodies."[19] Whilst we are addressing the night-time protective powers of the current psalm, we should consider the application of this psalm against the "Evil Eye," and especially to safeguard pregnant mothers and their offspring against the wiles of *Lilit*, the notorious night demoness, who is predisposed to harming mothers and killing infants. In some communities this unique protection commences with a *"Shir Lama'alot"* amulet suspended on the wall of the birth locale, on the arrival of the pregnant mother.[20] Such items comprise *Psalm 121*, or selected verses therefrom, Divine/Angelic Names, additional verses from Holy Writ suited to its purpose, and sometimes incorporate the names of the Primordial Ancestors, as well as those of the Hebrew Patriarchs and Matriarchs, as indicated in the following amulet:

We are told that items such as these serve "as a safeguard for the mother etc., both during the birth itself so that it will proceed normally and easily, and also during the following days, so that they will survive for a long life."[21] Whilst numerous amulets of this kind were printed and distributed in East European Jewish communities, the *Chamsa* (popularly *"Hamsa"*) and other metal amulets were, and still are, more popular in Sefardic communities. In this regard, we are told that following the birth of infants, visitors "would often bring gifts of amulets to ward off evil spirits," and that "Yemenite Jews, for example, would hang a *hamsikah*, an amulet shaped like outstretched hands, over the crib to protect the child. It often contained Psalm 121, because of the verse, 'The sun will not strike you by day, nor the moon by night (Psalm 121:6)'."[22] Curiously enough, this verse resulted in this psalm being recommended against sunstroke (heatstroke),[23] and the influence of the moon, i.e. being psychologically impacted by "lunar forces." We are also informed that "metallic amulets, inscribed with this psalm were worn by men as well as women at all times and became an article of decoration."[24]

It should be noted that the important Divine Name עשצי״י (*Ash'tzei*; also vocalised *Oshotziyiyi*), which is often included in

Hebrew birth amulets, was derived from the letters immediately succeeding the five appearances of the Ineffable Name in *Psalm 121*, i.e. ע (*Ayin*) verse 2; ש (*Shin*) and צ (*Tzadi*) verse 5; and the two letters י (*Yod*) respectively from verses 7 and 8. As noted elsewhere, "the power of this Divine Name is said to be vast and mighty,"[25] i.e. subduing demonic forces, restraining the mouth that curses, protection against the Evil Eye, and enemies in general, support during pregnancy, as well as precluding miscarriage and infant mortality.[26] We are informed that the *gematria* (numerical value) of עששציי (*Ash'tzei* [ע = 70 + ש = 300 + צ = 90 + י = 10 + י = 10 = 480]) is equal to that of ליל׳ת (*Lilit* [ל = 30 + י = 10 + ל = 30 + י = 10 + ת = 400 = 480]). The "secret" here is said to be protection of the *"B'rit Milah"* (Holy Covenant [circumcised penis]) against impurities and spontaneous seminal flow, i.e. nocturnal emissions.[27] As indicated below, this Divine Name is sometimes conjoined with the "magic square of the third order," i.e. the so-called "Saturn Square," and included in an amulet to protect and support a woman in labour:

׳	׳	צ	ש	ע
׳	ד	ט	ב	ש
צ	ג	ה	ז	צ
ש	ח	א	ו	׳
ע	ש	צ	׳	׳

The said threefold "Magic Square" is located centrally, and enclosed on all four sides by the Name *Ash'tzei*. As noted elsewhere, the one who writes this amulet is required to purify himself in a *Mikveh* (ritual bath). Afterwards the *Kamea* is written on *Kosher* parchment or paper, the letters inscribed in the manner of those employed in the writing of a *Torah* scroll. When completed, the amulet is placed between two sheets of paper, and

located in the bed near the pregnant woman.[28] The Divine Name
עשציי (*Ash'tzei*) is sometimes conjoined with a companion
Divine Name מלכהך (*Melachaheicha*), which was derived from
the concluding letters of the Hebrew words preceding the five
appearances of the Ineffable Name in *Psalm 121*. It has been
indicated that the combined *gematria* of the עשציי מלכהך
(*Ash'tzei Melachaheicha*) Divine Name combination [ע = 70 + ש
= 300 + צ = 90 + י = 10 + י = 10 + מ = 40 + ל = 30 + כ = 20 +
ה = 5 + כ = 20 = 595] equates with the full spelling of the letters
comprising the name לילית (*Lilit* [ל = 30 + מ = 40 + ד = 4 + י
= 10 + ו = 6 + ד = 4 + ל = 30 + מ = 40 + ד = 4 + י = 10 + ו =
6 + ד = 4 + ת = 400 + א = 1 + ו = 6 = 595]).[29] This equation is
considered to be an affirmation of the power of this Divine Name
combination to protect mothers and infants. However, the
עשציי מלכהך (*Ash'tzei Melachaheicha*) Divine Name
combination is also employed in a procedure to protect a residence
against burglars. As noted elsewhere, the practitioner is advised "to
collect five small stones from a road, which have to be washed
until they are thoroughly cleansed."[30] Following this action, *Psalm
121* is enunciated five times over the stones, whilst keeping the
mind focused on the עשציי מלכהך (*Ash'tzei Melachaheicha*)
Divine Name combination. The procedure is concluded with the
practitioner climbing onto the roof of the residence, or property to
be protect, and casting the four stones respectively in the four
directions, doing so with all his or her might. The fifth stone is
kept in a box inside the protected property. We are told this action
will both cancel and exhaust the power of thieves who intend to
invade a personal space.[31]

    In conclusion I wish to focus on a unique amulet
comprising a combination of the Divine Names אהיה (*Eh'yeh*),
יהוה (*YHVH*), and אדני (*Adonai*), as well as certain phrases
from *Psalm 20:3*, and *Psalm 121:7–8*, all carefully intertwined into
the following powerful magical unit, which I have addressed in
some detail in a previous volume:[32]

The vowel points included in this Divine Name construct, are exactly those accompanying the letters in the words they were derived from. In transliteration these read:

Top Row: *Eyiyiyi H'sh'sh'sh' Yelamama H'ch'r'r'*
Middle Row: *Yo'echatzei Heiz'mi'ei Var'chat' Heichal'cha*
Bottom Row: *Amira'u Doko'avo Nadeyi'eh Y'sh'sh'cha*

To decipher the hidden Divine Names and Hebrew phrases, you have to read the first letter in each box (starting with the right letter in the top right box, then reading from right to left the rightmost letter in each box), followed by all the second letters, then the third letters, and concluding the procedure with the fourth letters. The hidden phrases are:

1.   Reading the first letter in each box:
      Upper Row: אהיה—*Eh'yeh*
      Middle Row: יהוה—*YHVH*
      Lower Row: אדני—*Adonai*
2.   Reading the second letter in each box:
      ישלח עזרך מקדש
      Yis'lach Ez'recha Mikodesh (Psalm 20:3)
3.   Reading the third letter in each box:
      ישמרך מכל רע י"ש
      Yish'mar'cha mikol ra Y"Sh (Psalm 121:7)
4.   Reading the fourth letter in each box:
      ישמר צאתך ובאך
      Yish'mor Tzeit'cha Uvo'echa (Psalm 121:8)

In translation these Divine Names and biblical phrases read "*Ehyeh YHVH Adonai*, may he send you help from (his) holiness, may he keep you from all evil, Blessed be His Name, may He guard your going out and your coming in." This amazing Divine Name construct is said to be a protection against malevolent forces and disease generally, and will guard the bearer against attack and abduction.[33] It is written on deerskin parchment, paper, or inscribed on a silver metal square to be worn on the upper arm. In the instance of it being written on parchment, it could be located inside a special *Kame'a* holder which is carried around the neck as a pendant. I have shared the use of this remarkable Divine Name construct as a "protection incantation" in a previous volume of this series of texts on Jewish Magic.[34]

By complete contrast, *Psalm 121* is enunciated for "finding a mate."[35] Other than this, the current psalm is prescribed against illness and for healing in general; for all manner of trouble and distress; and when individuals are in need of Divine protection, or Divine aid and support. Thus it is one of the psalms recited when there is a crisis in Israel, and it is further enunciated for justice and peace. In conclusion, this psalm was suggested for recitation during times of mourning; when in need for comfort; and equally to those who seek a "spiritual return," i.e. תשובה (*teshuvah*— "repentance and atonement." In conclusion, it should be noted that *Psalm 121:5, 7* and *8* are respectively associated directly with היי (*Hayi*), מיך (*Mich*) and וול (*Veval*), the seventy-first, forty-second, and forty-third, tri-letter portions of the "Name of Seventy-two Names."[36]

Psalm 121 is employed to a much lesser extent in Christian Magic. It is referenced in the Byzantine Christian magical manuscripts for the purpose of ensuring a residence is blessed. In this regard, it is copied conjointly with *Psalm 122* on four pieces of paper, which are afterwards buried "in the four quarters of your house."[37] It is said this will ensure that "you will have a blessing from God and savior."[38] Elsewhere, in the "*Livre d'Or*," it is employed to facilitate invisibility. In this regard, the individual who wishes to appear invisible to anybody, is instructed to collect dust from underneath his/her feet, and then to read the current psalm over it. A portion of the dust is afterwards poured on his/her own head, and the remainder thrown into the face of the other party, which we are told will result in invisibility.[39]

PSALM 122

[1] שיר המעלות לדוד שמחתי באמרים יל בית
יהוﬣﬞﬤﬞﬥﬦﬡאהדונהי נלך
[2] עמדות היו רגלינו בשעריך ירושלם
[3] ירושלם הבנויה כעיר שחברה לה יחדו
[4] ששם עלו שבטים שבטי יה עדות לישראל
להדות לשם יהוﬣﬞﬡאהדונהי
[5] כי שמה ישבו כסאות למשפט כסאות לבית
דוד
[6] שאלו שלום ירושלם ישליו אהביך
[7] יהי שלום בחילך שלוה בארמנותיך
[8] למען אחי ורעי אדברה נא שלום בך
[9] למען בית יהוﬣﬞﬡאהדונהי אלהינו אבקשה
טוב לך

Transliteration:

[1] *shir hama'alot l'david samach'ti b'om'rim li beit YHVH neileich*

[2] *om'dot hayu rag'leinu bish'arayich y'rushalam*

[3] *y'rushalam hab'nuyah k'ir shechub'rah lah yach'dav*

[4] *shesham alu sh'vatim shiv'tei Yah eidut l'yis'ra'el l'hodot l'shem YHVH*

[5] *ki shamah yash'vu chis'ot l'mish'pat kis'ot l'veit david*

[6] *sha'alu sh'lom y'rushalam yish'layu ohavayich*

[7] *y'hi shalom b'cheileich shal'vah b'ar'm'notayich*

[8] *l'ma'an achai v'rei'ai adab'rah na shalom bach*

[9] *l'ma'an beit YHVH eloheinu avak'shah tov lach*

Translation:

[1] A Song of Ascents; of David. I rejoiced when they said unto me: 'Let us go unto the house of *YHVH*.'

[2] Our feet are standing within thy gates, O Jerusalem;

[3] Jerusalem, that art builded as a city that is compact together;

[4] Whither the tribes went up, even the tribes of *Yah*, as a testimony unto Israel, to give thanks unto the name of *YHVH*.

[5] For there were set thrones for judgment, the thrones of the house of David.

[6] Pray for the peace of Jerusalem; may they prosper that love thee.

[7] Peace be within thy walls, and prosperity within thy palaces.

[8] For my brethren and companions' sakes, I will now say: 'Peace be within thee.'

[9] For the sake of the house of *YHVH* our God I will seek thy good.

Psalm 122 is the third of the fifteen "Songs of Ascents" psalms, which we noted are enunciated at every Sabbath *Min'chah* service (afternoon prayers) over the period commencing with the Sabbath following *Sukkot* (Festival of Booths), and ending with the Sabbath prior to *Pesach* (Festival of Passover).[1] The current psalm is one of four psalms [*Psalms 121–124*] recited on Sabbath mornings in the Yemenite and Sefard-Chasidic Rites.[2] *Psalm 122* is further recommended in "A Modern Orthodox rabbinic manual" for recitation with *Psalms 121* and *126* at *Bat Mitz'vah* ceremonies, i.e. the coming of age ceremonies for Jewish girls.[3]

As far as the magical applications of the current psalm are concerned, it has been recommended for recitation against individuals who managed to escape enslavement.[4] However, this is erroneous, since this use is applicable to *Psalm 123*. The current psalm is mainly recommended for recitation prior to meeting an individual of great importance,[5] "a high potentate,"[6] or "powerful person."[7] In this regard, the *Shimmush Tehillim* noted, "when you go near a great man, recite the psalm thirteen times (three times in several published versions), and you will be well received, and furthermore, pray it in the synagogue and you will be blessed."[8] Godfrey Selig's German/English translation of this text reads "If you are about to address a man high in station, repeat this Psalm thirteen times beforehand, and you will be received graciously and find favour. Also, pray this Psalm each time that you are present in church, and you will obtain a blessing."[9]

A variant recension of the *Shimmush Tehillim* recommends the current psalm to an individual who is learning *Torah,* also to one who is seeking mercy and favour in the eyes of a king or prince, and to an individual who will be entering a synagogue, or who intends going into a city. In this instance, the said individual is instructed to enunciate this psalm seven times with associated Divine/Angelic Names, the latter being:

חנה חניאל רחמיאל אהביאל צדקיאל
אוריאל ברכיאל בואל אופניאל

Transliteration:

> *Chanah Chani'el Rach'mi'el Ahavi'el Tzad'ki'el Ori'el Baraki'el Bo'el Ofani'el.*

The procedure is concluded by uttering the following prayer-incantation:

יהי רצון מלפניכם השמות הקדושים שתתנו אותי
לחן ולחסד ולרחמים יהי רצון מלפניך יהוה אלהי
שתצליחני וברכני ותיישר אורחותי ותתן ברכה
בכל מעשה ידי אמן נצח סלה

Transliteration:

> *Y'hi ratzon milif'neichem hashemot hak'doshim shetit'nu oti l'chen ul'chesed ul'rachamim y'hi ratzon mil'fanecha YHVH elohai she'tatz'licheini ubar'cheini utiyasher or'chotai v'titein b'racha b'chol ma'aseih yadai Omein Netzach Selah.*

Translation:

> May it be your will, you Holy Names, that you give me mercy, favour and compassion. May it be pleasing to you, *YHVH* my God, that you grant me success and bless me, and you shall straighten my ways, and you shall bless all the works of my hands. *Amen* Eternal *Selah.*[10]

It should be noted that *Psalm 122* is also proposed for success in general,[11] and the capitals of the words of *Psalm 122:1* were conjoined in the Divine Name construct שהלשבלבין which is included in amulets for success.[12] Furthermore, whilst, as said, *Psalm 122* is suggested for recitation prior to meeting an individual of great authority, e.g. princes, kings, rulers, etc., I have seen it recommended for enunciation prior to addressing superiors. The current psalm is also suggested for fidelity to religion, justice and righteousness, and is recommended for recitation in the synagogue. Lastly, this psalm is vocalised for the well-being of Jerusalem, and is also one of the psalms employed against diseases of the eyes.

I again found little use of *Psalm 122* in Christian Magic. As noted earlier, this psalm is listed in Byzantine Magical Manuscripts in conjunction with the previous one, for the purpose of ensuring the blessing of a home.[13] The "*Libre D'or*" maintains that reading the first five verses of this psalm will guarantee victory over an enemy.[14]

PSALM 123

[1] שִׁיר הַמַּעֲלוֹת אֵלֶיךָ נָשָׂאתִי אֶת עֵינַי הַיֹּשְׁבִי
בַּשָּׁמָיִם
[2] הִנֵּה כְעֵינֵי עֲבָדִים אֶל יַד אֲדוֹנֵיהֶם כְּעֵינֵי
שִׁפְחָה אֶל יַד גְּבִרְתָּהּ כֵּן עֵינֵינוּ אֶל יְהֹוָהאדניאהדונהי
אֱלֹהֵינוּ עַד שֶׁיְּחָנֵּנוּ
[3] חָנֵּנוּ יְהֹוָהאדניאהדונהי חָנֵּנוּ כִּי רַב שָׂבַעְנוּ בוּז
[4] רַבַּת שָׂבְעָה לָּהּ נַפְשֵׁנוּ הַלַּעַג הַשַּׁאֲנַנִּים הַבּוּז לִגְאֵיוֹנִים

Transliteration:

[1] *shir hama'alot eilecha nasati et einai hayosh'vi bashamayim*

[2] *hineih ch'einei avadim el yad adoneihem k'einei shif'chah el yad g'vir'tah ken eineinu el YHVH eloheinu ad shey'choneinu*

[3] *choneinu YHVH choneinu ki rav sava'nu vuz*

[4] *rabat sav'ah lah naf'sheinu hala'ag hasha'ananim habuz lig'eiyonim*

Translation:

[1] A Song of Ascents. Unto Thee I lift up mine eyes, O Thou that art enthroned in the heavens.

[2] Behold, as the eyes of servants unto the hand of their master, as the eyes of a maiden unto the hand of her mistress; so our eyes look unto *YHVH*, our God, until He be gracious unto us.

[3] Be gracious unto us, *YHVH*, be gracious unto us; for we are full sated with contempt.

[4] Our soul is full sated with the scorning of those that are at ease, and with the contempt of the proud oppressors.

Psalm 123 is the fourth of the fifteen "Songs of Ascents" psalms enunciated at every Sabbath *Min'chah* service (afternoon prayers) over the period commencing with the Sabbath following *Sukkot* (Festival of Booths), and concluding with the Sabbath prior to *Pesach* (Festival of Passover).[1] As indicated, this psalm is one of four [*Psalms 121–124*], recited on Sabbath mornings in the Yemenite and Sefard-Chasidic Rites,[2] and it is one of the psalms which are enunciated as a call to the Divine One "in time of trouble, and/or thank Him for saving the speaker."[3] Ironically, the magical application of the current psalm pertains to causing trouble and discomfort for those amongst our fellow humankind who attempted to escape enslavement. In this regard, *Psalm 122* is employed to retrieve a "runaway slave."[4] The practitioner is instructed to engrave the names of the slave and his "master" on a leaden plate, and it is said "he will return."[5] There is no indication as to what should be done with the current psalm, but it is probably also engraved on the said leaden plate. Godfrey Selig repeated these details in his German/English translation of the *Shimmush Tehillim*, adding that the writing could be done "on a leaden or tin plate."[6]

We are informed "this use is probably motivated by verse 2, which mentions slaves and masters; indeed, the third through fifth words of that verse, taken out of context, could be understood as alluding to the return of 'slaves to the hand of their masters'."[7] Conditions of slavery, human trafficking, forced labour, etc., are utterly deplorable, and must be condemned in the strongest possible manner. It is tragic that this situation is still very common in the 21st century. A much better application of the current psalm is listed in a variant recension of the *Shimmush Tehillim*, i.e. the ability to utter prayers without any hindrance. In this regard, the practitioner is instructed to recite *Psalm 123*, concluding with the following prayer-incantation which include associated Divine Names:

יהו יהו יהו יהו יהו אל רחום וחנון חוסה ורחם
עלי ותן לי יכולת להתפלל לפניך בלא שום עכוב
ואכבדה מהודך אשר נתת לנביאים כאמור כבד
את יהוה מהוניך (*Proverbs 3:9*) בשם צור יהוה מלך
עולם ועד יהיה הדבר לי אני [.... personal name ....]
אמן נצח סלה

Transliteration:

Yaho Yaho Yaho Yaho el rachum v'chanun chusah v'rachem alai v'ten li y'cholet l'hit'palel l'fanecha b'li shum ikuv v'chab'dah m'hod'cha asher natata l'n'vi'im k'amur kabeid et YHVH meihonecha (Proverbs 3:9) b'shem Tzur YHVH melech olam va'ed yih'yeh hadavar hazeh li ani [....personal name ....] Omein Netzach Selah

Translation:

> *Yaho Yaho Yaho Yaho*, merciful and gracious God, spare and have compassion on me, and grant me the ability to pray before you without any hindrance, and I will glorify you in your splendour which you gave to the prophets, as it is said "Honour *YHVH* with thy substance" (*Proverbs 3:9*). In the Name *Tzur* ("Rock") *YHVH*, eternal King. Let this be my word, me [....personal name....] *Amen* Eternal *Selah*.[8]

Psalm 123 is erroneously recommended to individuals who "travel by ship."[9] In·this regard, *Psalm 124* is employed for this purpose. However, the current psalm is also recommended in "unofficial" sources for support against enemies; protection against wild, dangerous and savage beasts; against diseases of the blood; to maintain chastity; and to increase trust in the Divine One.

In Christian Magic the Byzantine Magical Manuscripts recommends the current psalm to one who wishes to become friends with a chosen individual. In this regard, it is said that "if you consider him a friend," the current psalm should be enunciated "in his name each day."[10] By contrast, the *"Livre d'Or"* maintains that reading *Psalm 123* seven times, will result in the Divine One allowing you to "overcome those who wish to cause some violence against you."[11]

PSALM 124

[1] שיר המעלות לדוד לולי יהוה^{אדני}אהדונהי שהיה
לנו יאמר נא ישראל

[2] לולי יהוה^{אדני}אהדונהי שהיה לנו בקום עלינו אדם

[3] אזי חיים בלעונו בחרות אפם בנו

[4] אזי המים שטפונו נחלה עבר על נפשנו

[5] אזי עבר על נפשנו המים הזידונים

[6] ברוך יהוה^{אדני}אהדונהי שלא נתננו טרף לשניהם

[7] נפשנו כצפור נמלטה מפח יוקשים הפח נשבר
ואנחנו נמלטנו

[8] עזרנו בשם יהוה^{אדני}אהדונהי עשה שמים וארץ

Transliteration:

[1] *shir hama'alot l'david lulei YHVH shehayah lanu yomar na yis'ra'el*

[2] *lulei YHVH shehayah lanu b'kum aleinu adam*

[3] *azai chayim b'la'unu bacharot apam banu*

[4] *azai hamayim sh'tafunu nach'lah avar al naf'sheinu*

[5] *azai avar al naf'sheinu hamayim hazeidonim*

[6] *baruch YHVH shelo n'tananu teref l'shineihem*

[7] *naf'sheinu k'tzipor nim'l'tah mipach yok'shim hapach nish'bar va'anach'nu nim'lat'nu*

[8] *ez'reinu b'shem YHVH oseih shamayim va'aretz*

Translation:

[1] A Song of Ascents; of David. 'If it had not been *YHVH* who was for us', let Israel now say;

[2] 'If it had not been *YHVH* who was for us, when men rose up against us,

[3] Then they had swallowed us up alive, when their wrath was kindled against us;

[4] Then the waters had overwhelmed us, the stream had gone over our soul;

[5] Then the proud waters had gone over our soul.'

[6] Blessed be *YHVH*, who hath not given us as a prey to their teeth.

[7] Our soul is escaped as a bird out of the snare of the fowlers; the snare is broken, and we are escaped.

[8] Our help is in the name of *YHVH*, who made heaven and earth.

Psalm 124 is the fifth of the fifteen "Songs of Ascents" psalms which we noted are pronounced at every Sabbath *Min'chah* service (afternoon prayers) over the period commencing with the Sabbath following *Sukkot* (Festival of Booths), and ending with the Sabbath preceding *Pesach* (Festival of Passover).[1] This psalm is likewise recited conjointly with *Psalms 121–123* on Sabbath mornings in the Yemenite and Sefard-Chasidic Rites,[2] and is also enunciated weekdays prior to the "Psalm of the Day" in the Sefard-Chasidic rites. In Yemenite rites it is vocalised during the Festival of *Purim*.[3]

In terms of magical applications, it would seem the expression "raging waters" (translated "proud waters") in *Psalm 124:5*, is the source of this psalm being recited prior to crossing a river or when travelling by ship.[4] In this regard, Selig wrote in his German/English version of the *Shimmush Tehillim* "if you are about to cross a swollen stream, or undertake a journey by water, pray this Psalm before entering the ship, and then you may commence your journey without fear."[5] In a variant recension of the *Shimmush Tehillim* the current psalm is recommended "for a pleasant voice." In this regard, the practitioner is instructed to recite the psalm, then enunciate *Song of Songs 2:14* ten times. This verse reads:

יונתי בחגוי הסלע בסתר המדהגה הראיני את
מראיך השמיעיני את קולך כי קולך ערב ומראך
נאוה [*Song of Songs 2:14*]

Transliteration:
> *Yonati b'chag'vei hasela b'seiter hamad'reigah har'ini et mar'ayich hash'mi'ini et koleich ki kolech areiv umar'eich naveh. (Song of Songs 2:14)*

Translation:
> "my dove, that art in the clefts of the rock, in the covert of the cliff, let me see thy countenance, let me hear thy voice; for sweet is thy voice, and thy countenance is comely."
> *Song of Songs 2:14)*

Conclude this procedure with the following prayer incantation:

אנא אל נא עזרני נא ותן לי קול נעימה ויפה
לבל יחר גרוני ולבל יפסוק קולי לשורר ולזמר
לפניך אמן אמן אמן סלה סלה סלה סלה

Transliteration:

> *Ana el na az'reini na v'ten li kol n'ima v'yafeh l'bal yichar g'roni ul'bal yif'sok koli l'shorer ul'zamer l'fanecha Omein Omein Omein Selah Selah Selah.*

Translation:

> Please God, please help me, and give me a pleasant and beautiful voice, so that my throat does not get hoarse, and my voice does not stop singing, and making music before you. *Amen Amen Amen Selah Selah Selah.*[6]

Whilst, as we noted, *Psalm 124* is officially utilised in Jewish Magic for travel over water, it has also been suggested for finding a mate.[7] It is popularly employed against abuse, malice, threats and oppression. In this regard, it is recited for the Jewish Nation and Judaism. It is one of the psalms recited for the well-being of the Land of Israel, and is also amongst the selected psalms enunciated specifically when there is a crisis in Israel. Other than that, the current psalm is said to be for honesty and honest people, and is vocalised to express gratitude.[8]

In Christian magic the Byzantine Magical Manuscripts maintains this psalm to be "for a ship, if it harbors evil men, or a corsair."[9] In this regard, it is noted "if there is an exile or murderer or thief (on board) and (the ship) is in danger of being destroyed, repeat the same Psalm seven times over water and sprinkle the boat, and the sea will calm. If against a skiff or a corsair, repeat the Psalm facing (it) seven times, and let them beseech God, and [the user] will get help."[10] The same source recommends a verse from the current psalm against a "paroxysm," i.e. convulsion, etc. In this regard, it suggests boiling eggs from a black hen in wine, and writing on it specific expressions from the Christian liturgy conjointly with the name of the Christian saviour. An egg is consumed by the patient whenever he/she suffers the said affliction, and the action concluded by reciting *Psalm 124:8*.[11] Other than this, the *"Livre d'Or"* instructs the recitation of the current psalm in order to "find your path."[12] It also maintains that reciting the psalm over a cup of water, which has never been exposed to sunlight, afterwards sprinkling the psalm with the water, and burying it inside a residence, will bring luck.[13] In conclusion it should be noted that in the "*Key of Solomon*" the current psalm is enunciated with *Psalms 72* and *117* over parchment to ensure its "efficacy and strength."[14]

PSALM 125

[1] שיר המעלות הבטחים ביהואהדונהי כהר
ציון לא ימוט לעולם ישב

[2] ירושלם הרים סביב לה ויהואהדונהי סביב
לעמו מעתה ועד עולם

[3] כי לא ינוח שבט הרשע על גורל הצדיקים
למען לא ישלחו הצדיקים בעולתה ידיהם

[4] היטיבה יהואהדונהי לטובים ולישרים בלבותם

[5] והמטים עקלקלותם יוליכם יהואהדונהי את
פעלי האון שלום על ישראל

Transliteration:

[1] *shir hama'alot habot'chim baYHVH k'har tziyon lo yimot l'olam yeisheiv*

[2] *yerushalam harim saviv lah vaYHVH saviv l'amo mei'atah v'ad olam*

[3] *ki lo yanu'ach sheivet haresha al goral hatzadikim l'ma'an lo yish'l'chu hatzadikim b'av'latah y'deihem*

[4] *heitivah YHVH latovim v'lisharim b'libotam*

[5] *v'hamatim akal'kalotam yolicheim YHVH et po'alei ha'aven shalom al yis'ra'el*

Translation:

[1] A Song of Ascents. They that trust in *YHVH* are as mount Zion, which cannot be moved, but abideth for ever.

[2] As the mountains are round about Jerusalem, so *YHVH* is round about His people, from this time forth and for ever.

[3] For the rod of wickedness shall not rest upon the lot of the righteous; that the righteous put not forth their hands unto iniquity.

[4] Do good, *YHVH*, unto the good, and to them that are upright in their hearts.

[5] But as for such as turn aside unto their crooked ways, *YHVH* will lead them away with the workers of iniquity. Peace be upon Israel.

Psalm 125 is the sixth of the fifteen "Songs of Ascents" psalms which we noted are pronounced at every Sabbath *Min'chah* service (afternoon prayers) during the period starting with the Sabbath after *Sukkot* (Festival of Booths), and concluding with the Sabbath prior to *Pesach* (Festival of Passover).[1] It is employed in *Practical Kabbalah* against enemies.[2] We are informed in the *Shimmush Tehillim* that an individual who is setting out on the road, and is confronted by enemies, should hold salt in his/her hand, and recite this psalm seven times.[3] A variant recension of the *Shimmush Tehillim* maintains the psalm should be recited over the salt.[4] The same recension maintains the salt should be cast in front of the enemy,[5] a statement reiterated elsewhere, in which the practitioner is instructed "to throw the salt in front of your enemy, but not on him."[6] As expected, Selig's German/English translation of the *Shimmush Tehillim* displays additional verbiage which is once again entirely absent in primary Hebrew sources. Thus he wrote "if you are compelled to travel in a country, where you have avowed enemies whom you have reason to fear on account of threatened injury to yourself, then take, before entering the country, both your hands full of salt, pronounce this Psalm seven times over it, and scatter it into the air toward the four quarters of the globe, and by so doing, not one of your enemies will be able to bring any harm against you."[7] Be that as it may, we are informed "that the general topics of this psalm—trusting God and asking for His help —justify this popular use."[8]

In terms of further magical uses, we are told *Psalm 125* is recited "for Jerusalem,"[9] and it is employed in abbreviated format in conjunction with *Deuteronomy 28:10*, in an amulet which is said to have the power to overcome barrenness.[10] In this regard, the capitals of the words comprising the current psalm were conjoined in the following Divine Name construct:

שהה בכצ ליל ייה
סלו סלמ ועב ליש העג
הלל יהב יהי לוב ועי
יאפ השעי

The writing is concluded by adding the following Divine Name construct formulated from the initials of the words in *Deuteronomy 28:10*:

וכע הכשי נע ומ

Four copies of this amulet are prepared and buried (or hidden) in the four corners of the residence of the barren woman, and it is said that, with the support of the Divine One, she will conceive.[11] In conclusion, besides its use as a protection against enemies on the road, or when travelling in enemy territory, *Psalm 125* is enunciated to increase trust in the Divine One, and also in support of exiles and refugees.

In Christian Magic the "*Livre d'Or*" recommends the current psalm to be written and attached "to a sick man," and it maintains "he will have relief immediately."[12] The same source added that burying the psalm "in front of your door" will bring good fortune.[13] In conclusion, it should be noted that in the "*Key of Solomon*" the perimeter of the "*Third Pentacle of Jupiter*" is inscribed with *Psalm 125:1.*[14]

PSALM 126

[1] שיר המעלות בשוב יהוהאדני־אהדונהי את שיבת
ציון היינו כחלמים
[2] אז ימלא שחיק פינו ולשוננו רנה אז יאמרו
בגוים הגדיל יהוהאדני־אהדונהי לעשות עם אלה
[3] הגדיל יהוהאדני־אהדונהי לעשות עמנו היינו
שמחים
[4] שובה יהוהאדני־אהדונהי את שביתנו כאפיקים
בנגב
[5] הזרעים בדמעה ברנה יקצרו
[6] הלוך ילך ובכה נשא משך הזרע בא יבא ברנה
נשא אלמתיו

Transliteration:

[1] *shir hama'alot b'shuv YHVH et shivat tziyon hayinu k'chol'mim*

[2] *az yimalei s'chok pinu ul'shoneinu rinah az yom'ru vagoyim hig'dil YHVH la'asot im eileh*

[3] *hig'dil YHVH la'asot imanu hayinu sh'meichim*

[4] *shuvah YHVH et sh'viteinu ka'afikim banegev*

[5] *hazor'im b'dim'ah b'rinah yik'tzoru*

[6] *haloch yeileich uvachoh nosei meshech hazara bo yavo v'rinah nosei alumotav*

Translation:

[1] A Song of Ascents. When *YHVH* brought back those that returned to Zion, we were like unto them that dream.
[2] Then was our mouth filled with laughter, and our tongue with singing; then said they among the nations: '*YHVH* hath done great things with these.'
[3] *YHVH* hath done great things with us; we are rejoiced.
[4] Turn our captivity, *YHVH*, as the streams in the dry land.
[5] They that sow in tears shall reap in joy.
[6] Though he goeth on his way weeping that beareth the measure of seed, he shall come home with joy, bearing his sheaves.

Psalm 126 is the seventh of the fifteen "Songs of Ascents" psalms, which we noted are enunciated at every Sabbath *Min'chah* service (afternoon prayers) over the period commencing with the Sabbath following *Sukkot* (Festival of Booths), and concluding with the Sabbath prior to *Pesach* (Festival of Passover).[1] The current psalm is recited in the Ashkenazic and Sefard-Chasidic rites on the Sabbath and Festivals prior to saying Grace after Meals,[2] and it is spoken by some Ashkenazi, Sefardi, and Sefard-Chasidic Jewry at the end of the weekday *Arvit* (the evening prayer service).[3] It is vocalised on the day of the New Moon,[4] and also after the evening circumambulations (*Hakafot*) on *Simchat Torah*, "in order to conclude the rejoicing with a psalm of redemption."[5] *Psalm 126* is further recited in the Yemenite and Italian rites on תשעה באב (*Tishah b'Av*—"Ninth of Av"),[6] an extremely sad fast day of mourning marking the calamities which befell the Jewish nation over the last two millennia. In this regard, it is said *Psalm 126* is enunciated towards the conclusion of the Afternoon Prayer service "as a promise for times in which happiness will replace mourning."[7] This psalm was also recommended in a modern Orthodox rabbinic manual for recitation conjointly with *Psalms 121* and *122* at *Bat Mitz'vah* ceremonies.[8]

In Jewish Magic the current psalm is recommended to women whose children die.[9] The *Shimmush Tehillim* recommends the preparation of four copies of an amulet comprising this psalm, as well as the Angelic Names סנוי, סנסנוי and סמנלגף (*Sanoi, San'sanoi* and *Seman'gelof*) "in the last line," which should be located in the four corners of the house.[10] A variant recension maintains they should be suspended inside the residence.[11] I have addressed the listed Spirit Intelligences in some detail elsewhere in this series of texts on *Practical Kabbalah*.[12] Regarding this application of the current psalm, it is one of the rare instances in which Godfrey Selig's German/English translation of the *Shimmush Tehillim* aligns with the primary recensions of this text without too much additional interpolation and variation.[13] It has been noted that this magical application "probably builds on the last two verses of the psalm, which, invoking the theme of fertility and seed, speak of a movement over time from tears to joy."[14] Gershom Scholem noted that "amulets written for women who used to lose their children customarily included Psalm 126," and that this psalm was later replaced by *Psalm 121*.[15] However, it should be kept in mind that both psalms are currently employed to protect the newborn and infants against the wiles of the demoness *Lilit* and other evil forces.

Psalm 126 is listed for a very different purpose in a variant recension of the *Shimmush Tehillim*. In this regard, it is recommended "for someone who has had a bad dream," and who is instructed to recite this psalm, as well as saying the following prayer-incantation:

חהו חהי חהו חהו **אל שדי** אני שלך וחלומותי
שלך יהי רצון מלפניך שתצילני מכל חלום רע
והנחם על הרעה אשר חשבת לעשות לעבדך בן
אמתיך (*Psalm 116:16*) והצילני מחלומות הרעים
ותהפכם מקללה לברכה כאשר הפכת קללת בלעם
הרשע לברכה על ישראל עמך כן הפוך החלום
הזה אם רע הוא לברכה ולטובה ואם טוב הוא
חזקיהו ואמצהו כחלומות יוסף הצדיק אמן אמן
אמן סלה סלה

Transliteration:

Chaho Chahi Chaho Chaho El Shadai ani shel'cha v'chalomotai shel'cha y'hi ratzon mil'fanecha shetatzileini mikol chalom ra v'hanachem al hara'ah asher chashav't' la'asot l'av'd'cha ben amatecha (Psalm 116:16) v'hatzi'leini michalomot hara'im v'tahaf'chem mik'lalah liv'rachah k'asher hafach'ta k'lalat bil'am harasha liv'rachah al yis'ra'el am'cha kein hafoch hachalom hazeh im ra hu liv'rachah ul'tovah v'im tov hu chaz'keihu v'am'tzeihu kachalomot yosef hatzadik Omein Omein Omein Selah Selah.

Translation:

Chaho Chahi Chaho Chaho El Shadai, I am yours and my dreams are yours. May it be your will to save me from every bad dream. Consider the evil you thought you would do to "Thy servant, the son of Thy handmaid," (*Psalm 116:16*), and save me from the bad dreams, and turn them from a curse into a blessing. As you turned the curse of Balaam the wicked into a blessing on Israel your people, so turn this dream, if it is evil, into a blessing and for good. And if it is good, strengthen and confirm it, like the dreams of Joseph the Righteous. *Amen Amen Amen Selah Selah.*[16]

Other than guarding infants and children from death, the current psalm is employed for the protection of children generally, and to ensure conception. It is further used against insomnia, and is said to be good for a residence. In fact, *Psalm 126:6* is recommended as an incantation for the home. In conclusion, it should be noted that the current psalm is amongst those enunciated to end the exile of the Jewish People.

Psalm 126 and *127* are referenced conjointly in the Byzantine Christian magical manuscripts, in which you are instructed to recite them over flour. We are told this will preclude you from losing any, and it is further said "you will have a blessing from God."[17] In the *"Livre d'Or"* the focus is on seed. This work recommends the current psalm to be read seven times over seed, which should then be planted forthwith. In this regard, it is noted that the blessing of the Divine One "will be upon the seeds and upon the field."[18] Lastly, the current psalm is one of the earlier mentioned set of nineteen listed in the *"Key of Solomon,"* i.e. *Psalms 8, 15, 22, 46, 47, 49, 51, 53, 68, 72, 84, 102, 110, 113, 126, 130, 131,* 133, and 139, which are enunciated over the wax from which ritual candles are manufactured.[19]

PSALM 127

[1] שיר המעלות לשלמה אם יהוה אם יהוהאדני־יאהדונהי לא
יבנה בית שוא עמלו בוניו בו אם יהוהאדני־יאהדונהי
לא ישמר עיר שוא שקד שומר
[2] שוא לכם משכימי קום מאחי שבת אכלי לחם
העצבים כן יתן לידידו שנא
[3] הנה נחלת יהוהאדני־יאהדונהי בנים שכר פרי הבטן
[4] כחצים ביד גבור כן בני הנעורים
[5] אשרי הגבר אשר מלא את אשפתו מהם לא יבשו
כי ידברו את אויבים בשער

Transliteration:

[1] *shir hama'alot lish'lomoh im YHVH lo yiv'neh vayit
shav am'lu vonav bo im YHVH lo yish'mor ir shav shakad
shomeir*

[2] *shav lachem mash'kimei kum m'acharei shevet och'lei
lechem ha'atzavim kein yitein lidido sheina*

[3] *hineih nachalat YHVH banim sachar p'ri habaten*

[4] *k'chitzim b'yad gibor kein b'nei han'urim*

[5] *ash'rei hagever asher milei et ash'pato meihem lo
yeivoshu ki y'dab'ru et oy'vim basha'ar*

Translation:

[1] A Song of Ascents; of Solomon. Except *YHVH* build
the house, they labour in vain that build it; except *YHVH*
keep the city, the watchman waketh but in vain.

[2] It is vain for you that ye rise early, and sit up late, ye
that eat the bread of toil; so He giveth unto His beloved in
sleep.

[3] Lo, children are a heritage of *YHVH*; the fruit of the
womb is a reward.

[4] As arrows in the hand of a mighty man, so are the
children of one's youth.

[5] Happy is the man that hath his quiver full of them; they
shall not be put to shame, when they speak with their
enemies in the gate.

Psalm 127 is the eighth of the fifteen "Songs of Ascents" psalms,
which we noted are enunciated at every Sabbath *Min'chah* service

(afternoon prayers) over the period commencing with the Sabbath following *Sukkot* (Festival of Booths), and concluding with the Sabbath prior to *Pesach* (Festival of Passover).[1] Regarding the current psalm, tradition has it that the High Priest, who was forbidden to sleep on the night of *Yom Kippur* ("Day of Atonement"), would be kept awake by the young priests who would snap their fingers at him, and "engage him in various ways until the time would arrive to slaughter the daily offering." One of these ways was to recite *Psalm 127:1* reading "Except *YHVH* build the house, they labour in vain that build it; except *YHVH* keep the city, the watchman waketh but in vain." [*TB Yoma 19b*]

    Psalms 127 and *128* were suggested in a Modern Orthodox rabbinic manual for recitation at a baby girl's naming celebration,[2] and in Jewish Magic the current psalm is said to be for a baby who has just been born.[3] The *Jewish Encyclopedia* maintains this psalm to be "for protection"[4] with no reference to infants. One source stated that it is for a peaceful birth experience, and noted that in this instance *Psalm 22* should be read to the woman, and *Psalm 127* to the newborn.[5] The same source commented that the current psalm is for the protection of crying infants, and further observed that it should be recited with the *"Ribono Shel Olam"* prayer.[6] It also stated this psalm is enunciated to support the education of the child,[7] which aligns with the opinion that it is "for children's success."[8]

    The *Shimmush Tehillim* stresses the current psalm to be for protecting children. In this regard, it maintains the psalm should be copied and located on the newborn, an action which is said to be "good for protection."[9] In his German/English version of the *Shimmush Tehillim*, Selig rephrased this application, instructing the practitioner to "write this Psalm upon pure parchment, place this amulet in a clean bag, and hang it about the neck of a newborn son immediately after birth, and no evil will ever befall him afterward."[10] We are informed "this use was probably motivated by the references both to God as a watchman [in the psalm] (v. 1) and to youngsters (vv. 3–4)."[11] Whilst *Psalm 127* is mainly employed to protect infants, the following Divine Name construct, formulated from the concluding letters of the words of this psalm, is said to have the power to protect women against infertility (barrenness) and miscarriage:[12]

רְתֹה מְהָא הֶתָא וָוו מְהָא
רְרָא דְרָא מֵיִם יֵתִ מְמֵן נוֹא
הֵתֹה מְרִי נְמֵד רְנִי מִיר
רְאֵת וּמָא וִיו תְמֵר

The vowel-points included in the Divine Name construct are those associated with the glyphs in the psalm. It should be noted that the current psalm is employed for a very different purpose in a variant recension of the *Shimmush Tehillim*, i.e. "to disparage lying words spoken against you," or plainly to halt the "Evil Tongue."[13] In this regard, an individual who is the target of such falsehood, is instructed to copy this psalm, as well as an accompanying prayer-incantion, on kosher parchment. The latter usually references deerskin, but a clean sheet of good quality white paper will suffice equally well. When completed, the writing is located inside a cover, which is often a plain leather envelope, and then suspended on the left arm. The prayer-incantation reads:

אֲמַתִיאֵל וַורִיאֵל אתם השמות הקדושים עשו לי בקשתי
[....delineate the falsehood....] וסתמו פי דוברי שקר עלי
כאשר אמר הכתוב כי יסכר פי דוברי שקר (*Psalm 63:12*)
בשם בוראי אדוניכם אמן אמן אמן סלה סלה סלה סלה

Transliteration:
Amitei'el Vav'ri'el atem hashemot hak'doshim asu li bakashati v'sit'mu pi dov'rei sheker alai [....delineate the falsehood....] *k'asher amar hakatuv ki yisacheir pi dov'rei shaker* (*Psalm 63:12*) *b'shem borei adoneichem Omein Omein Omein Selah Selah Selah.*

Translation:
Amitei'el Vav'ri'el, you Holy Names, grant me my request, and shut the mouths of those who lie about me [....delineate the falsehood....], as the scripture says "for the mouth of them that speak lies shall be stopped." (*Psalm 63:12*) In the Name of my Creator, your Lord. *Amen Amen Amen Selah Selah Selah.*[14]

Besides its use to protect the newborn against evil, *Psalm 127* is recited for a happy retirement and old age. It is also said to be good for the home. In this regard, the earlier mentioned version of *"The Book of Abramelin the Mage,"* maintains that a building can be ensured to remain standing, by writing the opening phrase of *Psalm 127:1* on seven "unhewn fieldstones." They are located in seven different locales on the foundations of the building, and a little rice is placed on each stone. The rice is then lit, and allowed to finish smoking, following which the practitioner is instructed to build and work in the name of the Divine One, "for then the foundations are well-laid, of that you may be sure."[15] Be that as it may, the current psalm has been further recommended against pride, and it is again one of the psalms enunciated for the well-being of the Land of Israel.[16]

In Christian Magic it would seem the current psalm was recommended to men who suffers erectile dysfunction due to magical enchantment. In this regard, it is suggested in the *"Livre d'Or"* to copy the current psalm and certain magical characters with a mixture of saffron and rosewater, which is afterwards perfumed with "wood of aloe." Following this action, this item is tied "to the thigh of the enchanted husband," and the psalm read "seven times over a glass of wine," which is afterwards consumed by the said husband. We are told the spell "will be destroyed immediately." [17]

PSALM 128

[1] שיר המעלות אשרי כל ירא יהוהאדני־אהדונהי
ההלך בדרכיו
[2] יגיע כפיך כי תאכל אשריך וטוב לך
[3] אשתך כגפן פריה בירכתי ביתך בניך כשתלי
זיתים סביב לשלחנך
[4] הנה כי כן יברך גבר ירא יהוהאדני־אהדונהי
[5] יברכך יהוהאדני־אהדונהי מציון וראה בטוב
ירושלם כל ימי חייך
[6] וראה בנים לבניך שלום על ישראל

Transliteration:
[1] *shir hama'alot ash'rei kol y'rei YHVH haholeich
bid'rachav*
[2] *y'gi'a kapecha ki tocheil ash'recha v'tov lach*
[3] *esh't'cha k'gefen poriyah b'yar'k'tei veitecha banecha
kish'tilei zeitim saviv l'shul'chanecha*
[4] *hineih chi chein y'vorach gaver y'rei YHVH*
[5] *y'varech'cha YHVH mitziyon ur'eih b'tuv y'rushalam
kol y'mei chayecha*
[6] *ur'eih vanim l'vanecha shalom al yis'ra'eil*
Translation:
[1] A Song of Ascents. Happy is every one that feareth
YHVH, that walketh in His ways.
[2] When thou eatest the labour of thy hands, happy shalt
thou be, and it shall be well with thee.
[3] Thy wife shall be as a fruitful vine, in the innermost
parts of thy house; thy children like olive plants, round
about thy table.
[4] Behold, surely thus shall the man be blessed that feareth
YHVH.
[5] *YHVH* bless thee out of Zion; and see thou the good of
Jerusalem all the days of thy life;
[6] And see thy children's children. Peace be upon Israel!

Psalm 128 is the ninth in the set of fifteen "Songs of Ascents"
psalms, which is said at every Sabbath *Min'chah* service (afternoon
prayers) over the period starting with the Sabbath after *Sukkot*

(Festival of Booths), and ending with the Sabbath before *Pesach* (Festival of Passover).[1] The current psalm is enunciated in the Ashkenazic and Sefard–Chasidic rites on Saturday night at the conclusion of *Arvit* (the evening prayer service), i.e. at the start of a new week.[2] We are told that since this psalm "emphasizes the dignity of labor," the reason for reciting it on this occasion is to encourage individuals to conduct themselves with honesty in all their endeavours. It is said that if they maintain this stance, they "will merit happiness in this life and good in the hereafter."[3]

It is worth noting that some communities include *Psalm 128* in the bedtime prayer,[4] and the current psalm is recognised as a wedding psalm by both Jews and Christians. In fact, this psalm is said to be a "marriage psalm" for men. In this regard, we are told that Rabbi Yosef Yechiel Mechel Lebovits, the Nikolsburg-Monsey Rebbe, suggested it as "a *tikkun* for getting married."[5] It is one of the psalms held in very high regard, and is recommended for recitation every day.[6] Rabbi Lebovits is said to have likewise prescribed *Psalm 128* for daily recitation.[7] As in the case of *Psalm 67*, the current one is sometimes included in *Shiviti* plaques and Hebrew amulets in the form of a *Menorah*, i.e. the sacred seven-branched candelabrum, as indicated below:[8]

Be that as it may, in some Sefardi communities the current psalm is read at the conclusion of the מִילָה בְּרִית סֵדֶר (*Seder Brit Milah*), i.e. the circumcision service,[9] and likewise at the conclusion of the הַבַּת זֶבֶד סֵדֶר (*Seder Zeved Habat*—"naming a daughter").[10] We are told the latter ceremony became "more common among other Jews as well."[11] *Psalm 128*, indicated to be "for having children,"[12] should be considered the "birth psalm" *per excellence*. In Jewish Magic it is recited for pregnant women,[13] or "for the fetus" according to one commentator.[14] *Psalm 128:3* is likewise recommended for a pregnant woman.[15]

However, the current psalm is enunciated to encourage pregnancy, as well as for protection during pregnancy.[16] In this regard, one procedure maintained that the husband should recite *Psalm 128:3* to his wife "on the night of submersion (in the ritual bath [*Mikveh*]) and pre-mating," and the couple is further advised to "give charity in the merit of the soul of Rabbi Meir Baal Hanes ('Master of Miracles')], may his memory protect us."[17] Elsewhere the capitals of the first eight words of *Psalm 128:3* which read

אֶשְׁתְּךָ כְּגֶפֶן פֹּרִיָּה בְּיַרְכְּתֵי בֵיתֶךָ בָּנֶיךָ כִּשְׁתִלֵי זֵיתִים

(*esh't'cha k'gefen poriyah b'yar'k'tei veitecha banecha kish'tilei zeitim*—"Thy wife shall be as a fruitful vine, in the innermost parts of thy house; thy children like olive plants"), are conjoined in the Divine Name construct בְּכִזֵי אֶכִפֹבְּבֵ (*Ekifov'bei Bakizei*). It is whispered in the right ear of a woman by her partner prior to sexual intercourse, and it is said that, God willing, she will fall pregnant.[18] The same source lists the initials and concluding letters of each word of *Psalm 128* conjoined in the the following Divine Name construct, which is included in an amulet meant to counteract infertility, as well as to protect pregnant women against miscarriage:[19]

שַׁר הַת אַי כָּל יָא יְה הַךְ בּוֹ
יַע כַּךְ כִּי תֹל אַךְ וּב לְךָ אָךְ
בֵּן פֹּה בִּי בֶּךְ בָּךְ כִּי זֶם סָב
לֵךְ הֹה כִּי כֵן יַךְ גַּר יָא יְה
יַךְ יְה מֶן וֹה בַּב יֵם כֹּל יְי
חַךְ וֹה בָּם לֵךְ שֵׁם עַל יַל

The *Shimmush Tehillim* recommends the current psalm to be written on kosher parchment, which is afterwards worn around the neck by women for a successful pregnancy.[20] Godfrey Selig rephrased these instructions in his German/English version of this text, saying "write this Psalm upon clean parchment, and hang it upon a pregnant woman, when she and the fruit of her body will always be secure from unlucky accidents, and she will have a fortunate confinement."[21] We are told that this application of the current psalm "is based probably on the mention of a fruitful wife and children in verse 3 and the reference to grandchildren in verse 6."[22] Whatever the case may be, a very different use is listed in a variant recension of the *Shimmush Tehillim* in which we read that anyone wishing "to go for a *Mitzvah*," i.e. fulfilling a "religious obligation (commandment)," should pray this psalm in conjunction with the following prayer-incantation.

בשם יהוה אלהי ישראל חנוך ואליהו גבורי אל
חזקים היו ולא טעמו טעם מיתה הלכו ביום
ובלילה גם בים גם ביבשה ולא חוזקו יהי רצון
מלפניך אלהי השמים כשם שהלכו ולא הוזקו כך
אני אלך ולא אנזק לא היום ולא לעולם בשם
ארגי מרגי נרגי סרגי אמן אמן אמן סלה סלה
סלה

Transliteration:

> *B'shem YHVH elohei yisra'el chanoch v'eliyahu giburei el chazakim hayu v'lo ta'amu ta'am mitah hal'chu b'yom ub'lailah gam b'yam gam b'yavashah v'lo chuz'ku y'hi ratzon mil'faneicha elohei hashamayim k'sheim shehal'chu v'lo huz'ku kach ani eilech v'lo enazeik lo hayom v'lo l'olam b'shem Ar'gi Mar'gi Nar'gi Sar'gi Omein Omein Omein Selah Selah Selah.*

Translation:

> In the name of *YHVH* God of Israel. Enoch and Elijah were mighty heroes of God, and they did not taste death, they went on day and night, both at sea and on land, and they were not detained. May it be your will, God of the heavens, that as they went and were not detained, so may I go and not be harmed, not today and not ever. In the Name *Ar'gi Mar'gi Nar'gi Sar'gi Amen Amen Amen Selah Selah Selah.*[23]

As noted, *Psalm 128* is recommended to individuals who are seeking a marriage partner, as well as wanting a safe and fortunate pregnancy. I have also seen verses from the current psalm employed in a procedure shared in *"The Book of Abramelin the Mage"* for couples who are infertile. The jury is still out as to whether this text is of Jewish or Christian origin. Whatever the case may be, it instructs "a barren couple" to pick an olive branch comprising a twig with exactly seven leaves, doing so before sunrise. The branch is fumigated with incense, and then inscribed "on the right side" with the opening phrase in *Psalm 128:1*, and on the opposite side with the concluding phrase of the said verse. The same is done with the seven leaves, following which the branch is again fumigated with incense, and then placed on the pillow of the bed of the couple. Following this action, *Psalm 128:3* is engraved on gold, silver, or pure wax, fumigated, and suspended around the husband's neck.[24]

It should be noted that the current psalm is also recommended in unofficial sources, to those who find themselves in times of trouble and perilous situations, and is further enunciated against malice. In this regard, the initials of the words comprising *Psalm 128:1* were formulated into the Divine Name construct שׁאהיּיכּהב, which is included in amulets for general protection.[25] The current psalm is also employed against illness and for healing in general; recited for honesty and honest people; and to increase trust in the Divine One. It should also be noted that *Psalm 128:4* is directly aligned with הרי (*Hari*), the fifteenth tri-letter portion of the "Name of Seventy-two Names."[26]

Psalm 128 is listed conjointly with *Psalm 56* in the Byzantine Christian magical manuscripts, to aid children who suffer and are overwhelmed by fear. The said source recommends the preparation of an amulet by writing these psalms, which is afterwards worn as an amulet by the fearful infant.[27] In addressing the magical use of the current psalm in Christian Magic, the focus in the *"Livre d'Or"* is very different. It suggests copying *Psalm 128:1–3* as an amulet which is buried "at the root of a vine." We are told this will ensure "the vineyard will bear fruit." This text further maintains that this psalm "is also good for sight."[28]

PSALM 129

[1] שיר המעלות רבת צררוני מנעורי יאמר
נא ישראל

[2] רבת צררוני מנעורי גם לא יכלו לי

[3] על גבי חרשו חרשים האריכו למעניתם

[4] יהוהאהדונהיאהדונהי צדיק קצץ עבות רשעים

[5] יבשו ויסגו אחור כל שנאי ציון

[6] יהיו כחציר גגות שקדמת שלף יבש

[7] שלא מלא כפו קוצר וחצנו מעמר

[8] ולא אמרו העברים ברכת יהוהאהדונהיאהדונהי
אליכם ברכנו אתכם בשם יהוהאהדונהיאהדונהי

Transliteration:

[1] *shir hama'alot rabat tz'raruni min'urai yomar na yis'ra'el*

[2] *rabat tz'raruni min'urai gam lo yach'lu li*

[3] *al gabi char'shu chor'shim he'erichu l'ma'anitam*

[4] *YHVH tzadik kitzeitz avot r'sha'im*

[5] *yeivoshu v'yisogu achor kol son'ei tziyon*

[6] *yih'yu kachatzir gagot shekad'mat shalaf yaveish*

[7] *shelo milei chapo kotzeir v'chitz'no m'ameir*

[8] *v'lo am'ru ha'ov'rim bir'kat YHVH aleichem beirach'nu et'chem b'shem YHVH*

Translation:

[1] A Song of Ascents. 'Much have they afflicted me from my youth up', let Israel now say;

[2] 'Much have they afflicted me from my youth up; but they have not prevailed against me.

[3] The plowers plowed upon my back; they made long their furrows.

[4] *YHVH* is righteous; He hath cut asunder the cords of the wicked.'

[5] Let them be ashamed and turned backward, all they that hate Zion.

[6] Let them be as the grass upon the housetops, which withereth afore it springeth up;

[7] Wherewith the reaper filleth not his hand, nor he that bindeth sheaves his bosom.

[8] Neither do they that go by say: 'The blessing of *YHVH* be upon you; we bless you in the name of *YHVH*.

Psalm 129 is the tenth in the set of fifteen "Songs of Ascents" psalms, which is enunciated at every Sabbath *Min'chah* service (afternoon prayers) over the period commencing with the Sabbath after *Sukkot* (Festival of Booths), and concluding with the Sabbath before *Pesach* (Festival of Passover).[1] In *Practical Kabbalah* this psalm is said in to be "for a *Mitzvah*," i.e. for the performance of a religious commandment.[2] In this regard, the *Shimmush Tehillim* maintains it should be recited every day.[3] Godfrey Selig sidelined the performance of religious precepts, which is intrinsic to the magical application of the current psalm as delineated in the *Shimmush Tehillim*. Thus he noted, in his German/English translation of this text, that "whoever accustoms himself to repeat the Psalm daily after the morning prayer, will finally prepare himself to live piously and virtuously, and will be able to carry out many remunerative and good works."[4]

A variant recension of the *Shimmush Tehillim* indicates the current psalm to be "good to pray against the wicked."[5] I have also seen *Psalm 129* recommended for the revelation and certitude of secret things; for peace of soul; and for praise of the Divine One; and for protection against enemies. Curiously enough, it was also suggested for rheumatism.

The use of this psalm in Christian Magic appears to be very sparse. The "*Livre d'Or*" noted that it should be written "on a blade of grass" which is afterwards rinsed in water. This psalm-infused water is afterwards sprinkled in a residence, and this is said will ensure the premises are rid of malevolent spirit forces.[6]

PSALM 130

[1] שיר המעלות ממעמקים קראתיך יהוהאהדונהי

[2] אדני שמעה בקולי תהיינה אזניך קשבות לקול
תחנוני

[3] אם עונות תשמר יה אדני מי יעמד

[4]a כי עמך הסליחה למען תורא

[5] קויתי יהוהאהדונהי קותה נפשי ולדברו הוחלתי

[6] נפשי לאדני משמרים לבקר שמרים לבקר

[7] יחל ישראל אל יהוהאהדונהי כי עם יהוהאהדונהי
החסד והרבה עמו פדות

[8] והוא יפדה את ישראל מכל עונתיו

Transliteration:

[1] *shir hama'alot mima'amakim k'raticha YHVH*

[2] *adonai shim'ah v'koli tih'yenah oz'necha kashuvot l'kol tachanunai*

[3] *im avonot tish'mor Yah adonai mi ya'amod*

[4] *ki im'cha has'lichah l'ma'an tivarei*

[5] *kiviti YHVH kiv'tah naf'shi v'lid'varo hochal'ti*

[6] *naf'shi ladonai mishom'rim laboker shom'rim laboker*

[7] *yacheil yis'ra'eil el YHVH ki im YHVH hachesed v'har'beih imo f'dut*

[8] *v'hu yif'deh et yis'ra'eil mikol avonotav*

Translation:

[1] A Song of Ascents. Out of the depths have I called Thee, *YHVH*.

[2] *Adonai*, hearken unto my voice; let Thine ears be attentive to the voice of my supplications.

[3] If Thou, *Yah*, shouldest mark iniquities, *Adonai*, who could stand?

[4] For with Thee there is forgiveness, that Thou mayest be feared.

[5] I wait for *YHVH*, my soul doth wait, and in His word do I hope.

[6] My soul waiteth for *Adonai*, more than watchmen for the morning; yea, more than watchmen for the morning.

[7] O Israel, hope in *YHVH*; for with *YHVH* there is mercy, and with Him is plenteous redemption.
[8] And He will redeem Israel from all his iniquities.

Psalm 130 is the eleventh of fifteen "Songs of Ascents" psalms, which are enunciated at every Sabbath *Min'chah* service (afternoon prayers) over the period commencing with the Sabbath after *Sukkot* (Festival of Booths), and ending with the Sabbath before *Pesach* (Festival of Passover).¹ This is a penitential psalm which is recited throughout the year on Mondays and Thurdays, as part of תחנון (*Tachanun*), i.e. the "Supplication" service in the Italian rite,² and it features prominently over the *Rosh Hashanah/Yom Kippur* ("New Year"/"Day of Atonement") period. In this regard, it is uttered during the *Tash'lich* (תשליך—"cast off") ceremony which is usually performed on the afternoon of the first day of *Rosh Hashanah* (New Year). *Tash'lich* is an atonement ceremony during which worshippers cast their personal sins "upon the waters," the latter being a flowing body of water, i.e. a river, lake, etc.² The current psalm is further vocalised in *Shacharit* (Morning Prayer Service) over עשרת ימי תשובה (*Aseret Y'mei T'shuvah*—"Ten Days of Repentance"), i.e. the ten days commencing with *Rosh Hashanah* (New Year) and concluding with *Yom Kippur* (Day of Atonement).³ It is frequently recited in times of crisis,⁴ and is one of the psalms enunciated for the Land of Israel. It is also recommended for chanting at a cemetery, i.e. at the anniversary of the death of an individual.⁵

Psalm 130 is recommended to individuals who wish to travel by boat.⁶ However, we are informed the current psalm is employed "to escape from guards,"⁷ or "escape arrest by the night watchman."⁸ In this regard, it is maintained in the *Shimmush Tehillim* that individuals who wish to enter a city unnoticed, should whisper the psalm facing "the four corners of the world," i.e. in the four directions, in order to cause the city guards to fall into a deep sleep.⁹ It has been suggested that "the reference to guards in verse 6 may motivate this use."¹⁰ In his German/English translation of the *Shimmush Tehillim*, Selig resorted to excessive dramatisation of this application, giving it a military slant with business undertones which is absent in the primary Hebrew text. Thus he wrote "if you are living in a besieged city, to and from which no one can go without danger, and if you have urgent business, so that you feel constrained to venture on a journey, then, just as you are about to leave the city, pray this Psalm in a low and adjuring voice, toward the four quarters of the earth, and then you will be able to pass all the sentries without being seen or harmed. A heavy sleep will overcome them, so that they will not be conscious of your presence."[11]

A variant recension of the *Shimmush Tehillim* lists a very different application of *Psalm 130*, noting that "it is good for one who climbs into an underground pit,"[12] or a cave for that matter. The said individual is instructed to recite the psalm in conjunction with the following prayer-incantation:

מלכי אלהי יחד שמך בעולמך שכלל היכלך רפא מזבחך
פדה עמך שמח עדתך קבץ נפוצתם קרב ביאת משיחך
יהוה למען שמך למען ימיניך יהוה עשה למענך לא
למעני למען אחלץ אני [....insert personal name....] ידידך
הושיעה ימינך וענני (*Psalm 108 :7*)

Transliteration:

Mal'ki elohai yacheid shim'cha b'olomecha shach'leil heichalecha rofei miz'b'checha p'deih amecha s'mach adatecha kabeitz nifutzotam k'reiv bi'at m'shichecha YHVH l'ma'an shim'cha l'ma'an y'minecha YHVH aseih l'ma'an'cha lo l'ma'ani l'ma'an achaleitz ani [....insert personal name....] y'didecha hoshi'ah y'min'cha va'aneini (Psalm 108 :7)

Translation:

My King, my God, your name is singular in your world. Build your palace, restore your altar, redeem your people, let your people rejoice, gather their scattering, draw near to the coming of your Messiah *YHVH*, for the sake of your Name, for the sake of your righteousness, *YHVH*, act for your sake, not for my sake, that I may be saved, I [....insert personal name....] your beloved, "save with Thy right hand, and answer me." (*Psalm 108 :7*)[13]

Psalm 130 has been recommended against pride and stupidity, i.e. foolhardiness and irresponsibility, though this application really pertains to the following psalm. In fact, the current psalm is said to be for holiness. In this regard, it is enunciated by those who have committed and are burdened with a sin. Hence it is uttered for תשובה (*Teshuvah*—"spiritual return," i.e. atonement, and as a prayer for forgiveness. It is also recommended to individuals who are in need of Divine aid, support, and Divine Protection. Thus it is recited against threats, as well as for protection in perilous situations and in times of trouble. It is further employed for diseases of, or pain in, the eyes, and against illness, as well as for healing, in general.

In Christian Magic the "*Livre d'Or*" maintains the "four corners" theme mentioned in terms of the previous psalm. In the current instance, practitioners are instructed to write *Psalm 130* conjointly with *Psalm 109* on four cards, which are to be buried in the "four corners of a field or a house," and it is said "blessings will be upon them."[14] Other than this, it is worth noting that this psalm is one of nineteen listed in the "*Key of Solomon*," which are recited over the wax from which ritual candles are manufactured. The complete set is *Psalms 8, 15, 22, 46, 47, 49, 51, 53, 68, 72, 84, 102, 110, 113, 126, 130, 131, 133,* and *139*.[15] The current psalm is also one of seven, i.e. *Psalms 3, 9, 31 42, 60, 51* and *130,* which are employed in the "*Key of Solomon*" for the consecration of "the needle and other iron instruments."[16]

PSALM 131

[1] שיר המעלות לדוד יהוהאהדניהאדני לא גבה לבי
ולא רמו עיני ולא הלכתי בגדלות ובנפלאות ממני
[2] אם לא שויתי ודוממתי נפשי כגמל עלי אמו
כגמל עלי נפשי
[3] יחל ישראל אל יהוהאהדניהאדני מעתה ועד עולם

Transliteration:

[1] *shir hama'alot l'david YHVH lo gavah libi v'lo ramu einai v'lo hilach'ti big'dolot uv'nif'la'ot mimeni*

[2] *im lo shiviti v'domam'ti naf'shi k'gamul alei imo kagamul alai naf'shi*

[3] *yacheil yis'ra'eil el YHVH mei'atah v'ad olam*

Translation:

[1] A Song of Ascents; of David. *YHVH*, my heart is not haughty, nor mine eyes lofty; neither do I exercise myself in things too great, or in things too wonderful for me.

[2] Surely I have stilled and quieted my soul; like a weaned child with his mother; my soul is with me like a weaned child.

[3] O Israel, hope in *YHVH* from this time forth and for ever.

Psalm 131 is the twelfth of fifteen "Songs of Ascents" psalms, which are enunciated at every Sabbath *Min'chah* service (afternoon prayers) over the period commencing with the Sabbath after *Sukkot* (Festival of Booths), and concluding with the Sabbath before *Pesach* (Festival of Passover).[1] We are told that this psalm is recited "for the proud,"[2] "against the proud,"[3] "against undue presumption,"[4] or "for helping one who is haughty to moderate his arrogance."[5] In this regard, the *Shimmush Tehillim* advised those who are so afflicted with exaggerated pride, that they are unable to reach "the straight middle ground," to regularly recite the current psalm three times a day.[6] Godfrey Selig reiterated this application with interpolations which are absent in primary versions of *Shimmush Tehillim*. Thus he wrote "he who is so strongly possessed of the evil spirit of pride that he regards all other people with scorn, but who, upon sober reflection, desires to occupy a middle path, if his intolerable pride would only permit him, is advised to pray this Psalm reverently three times daily, after the morning and evening prayer. His pride will receive a certain check."[7] We are informed that "this use is no doubt motivated by the opening verse of this psalm."[8] However, besides acting against pride, haughtiness, and insolence, the current psalm is also enunciated for atonement/repentance, as well as to increase trust in the Divine One. It is further recited to encourage refreshing sleep, and for the protection of paupers and beggars. It is also worth keeping in mind that *Psalm 131:3* is directly aligned with מוּם (*Mum*), the seventy-second tri-letter portion of the "Name of Seventy-two Names."[9]

The employment of *Psalm 131* for a "good sleep," is also maintained in Christian Magic. In this regard, the *"Livre d'Or"* instructs the practitioner to copy the psalm, which is afterwards attached to the right arm. We are informed that this will preclude one from having bad dreams.[10] The current psalm is also one of the nineteen mentioned in the *"Key of Solomon,"* which are recited over the wax from which ritual candles are manufactured. The complete set comprises *Psalms 8, 15, 22, 46, 47, 49, 51, 53, 68, 72, 84, 102, 110, 113, 126, 130, 131,* 133, and 139.[11]

PSALM 132

[1] שיר המעלות זכור יהו‎אדני‎אהדונהי לדוד את כל ענותו

[2] אשר נשבע ליהו‎אדני‎אהדונהי נדר לאביר יעקב

[3] אם אבא באהל ביתי אם אעלה על ערש יצועי

[4] אם אתן שנת לעיני לעפעפי תנומה

[5] עד אמצא מקום ליהו‎אדני‎אהדונהי משכנות לאביר יעקב

[6] הנה שמענוה באפרתה מצאנוה בשדי יער

[7] נבואה למשכנותיו נשתחוה להדם רגליו

[8] קומה יהו‎אדני‎אהדונהי למנוחתך אתה וארון עזך

[9] כהניך ילבשו צדק וחסידיך ירננו

[10] בעבור דוד עבדך אל תשב פני משיחך

[11] נשבע יהו‎אדני‎אהדונהי לדוד אמת לא ישוב ממנה מפרי בטנך אשית לכסא לך

[12] אם ישמרו בניך בריתי ועדתי זו אלמדם גם בניהם עדי עד ישבו לכסא לך

[13] כי בחר יהו‎אדני‎אהדונהי בציון אוה למושב לו

[14] זאת מנוחתי עדי עד פה אשב כי אותיה

[15] צידה ברך אברך אביוניה אשביע לחם

[16] וכהניה אלביש ישע וחסידיה רנן ירננו

[17] שם אצמיח קרן לדוד ערכתי נר למשיחי

[18] אויביו אלביש בשת ועליו יציץ נזרו

Transliteration:
[1] *shir hama'alot z'chor YHVH l'david et kol unoto*
[2] *asher nish'ba laYHVH nadar la'avir ya'akov*
[3] *im avo b'ohel beiti im e'eleh al eres y'tzu'ai*
[4] *im etein sh'nat l'einai l'af'apai t'numah*
[5] *ad em'tza makom laYHVH mish'kanot la'avir ya'akov*
[6] *hineih sh'ma'anuha b'ef'ratah m'tzanuha bish'dei ya'ar*
[7] *navo'ah l'mish'k'notav nish'tachaveh lahadom rag'lav*
[8] *kumah YHVH lim'nuchatecha atah va'aron uzecha*
[9] *kohanecha yil'b'shu tzedek vachasidecha y'raneinu*

[10] *ba'avur david av'decha al tasheiv p'nei m'shichecha*
[11] *nish'ba YHVH l'david emet lo yashuv mimenah mip'ri vit'n'cha ashit l'chisei lach*
[12] *im yish'm'ru vanecha b'riti v'eidoti zo alam'deim gam b'neihem adei ad yeish'vu l'chisei lach*
[13] *ki vachar YHVH b'tziyon ivah l'moshav lo*
[14] *zot m'nuchati adei ad poh eisheiv ki ivitiha*
[15] *tzeidah bareich avareich ev'yoneha as'bi'a lachem*
[16] *v'chohaneha al'bish yesha vachasideha ranein y'raneinu*
[17] *sham atz'mi'ach keren l'david arach'ti neir lim'shichi*
[18] *oy'vav al'bish boshet v'alav yatzitz niz'ro*

Translation:

[1] A Song of Ascents. *YHVH*, remember unto David all his affliction;

[2] How he swore unto *YHVH*, and vowed unto the Mighty One of Jacob:

[3] 'Surely I will not come into the tent of my house, nor go up into the bed that is spread for me;

[4] I will not give sleep to mine eyes, nor slumber to mine eyelids;

[5] Until I find out a place for *YHVH*, a dwelling-place for the Mighty One of Jacob.'

[6] Lo, we heard of it as being in Ephrath; we found it in the field of the wood.

[7] Let us go into His dwelling-place; let us worship at His footstool.

[8] Arise, *YHVH*, unto Thy resting-place; Thou, and the ark of Thy strength.

[9] Let Thy priests be clothed with righteousness; and let Thy saints shout for joy.

[10] For Thy servant David's sake turn not away the face of Thine anointed.

[11] *YHVH* swore unto David in truth; He will not turn back from it: 'Of the fruit of thy body will I set upon thy throne.

[12] If thy children keep My covenant and My testimony that I shall teach them, their children also for ever shall sit upon thy throne.'

[13] For *YHVH* hath chosen Zion; He hath desired it for His habitation:

[14] 'This is My resting-place for ever; here will I dwell; for I have desired it.

[15] I will abundantly bless her provision; I will give her needy bread in plenty.

[16] Her priests also will I clothe with salvation; and her saints shall shout aloud for joy.

[17] There will I make a horn to shoot up unto David, there have I ordered a lamp for Mine anointed.

[18] His enemies will I clothe with shame; but upon himself shall his crown shine.'

Psalm 132 is the thirteenth of fifteen "Songs of Ascents" psalms, which are enunciated at every Sabbath *Min'chah* service (afternoon prayers) over the period starting with the Sabbath after *Sukkot* (Festival of Booths), and ending with the Sabbath before *Pesach* (Festival of Passover).[1] *Psalm 132:8–10* are amongst the verses recited in the synagogue when the *Torah* scroll is returned to the Ark, and verses 9 and 10 are amongst those enunciated in the Sefardic liturgy when the Ark is opened to remove the *Torah* scroll.[2] We are told that "these verses were recited by Solomon when he wanted to bring the ark (of the covenant) into the Temple and the gates held fast together."[3] Considering the sentiments expressed in this psalm, it should come as no surprise that it is enunciated for redemption, and the rebuilding of the Temple in Jerusalem.[4]

According to some commentators the current psalm is for individuals who wish "to break an oath,"[5] whilst others say it is enunciated "to keep oaths."[6] The *Jewish Encyclopedia* maintains it is recited "on fulfilling a rash vow,"[7] and elsewhere this psalm is said to be "for helping one who is quick to swear" an oath.[8] In this regard, we are informed in the *Shimmush Tehillim* that an invidual who broke an oath, would be able to keep it if this psalm is spoken every day.[9] As usual, Godfrey Selig greatly embelished these details in his German/English version of the *Shimmush Tehillim*, saying "if you have sworn to perform anything punctually, and notwithstanding your oath you neglect to perform your obligation, and in this manner have perjured himself, you should, in order to avoid a future crime of a similar kind, pray this Psalm daily with profound reverence."[10] Be that as it may, a variant recension of the *Shimmush Tehillim* instructs those who wish to keep an oath, to vocalise *Psalm 132* twenty-five times, each time concluding with the following prayer-incantation:

קיימיאל שבעתיאל אתם מלאכים קדושים עשו
רצוני ובקשתי בשם אל מלך אלהי עולם תנו לי
כח וגבורה לקיים שבועתי זו בעגלא ובזמן קריב
אמן אמן אמן סלה סלה סלה סלה

Transliteration:
> *Keimi'el Shav'ati'el atem malachim k'doshim osu r'tzoni ub'kashati b'shem el melech elohei olam t'nu li ko'ach v'g'vurah l'kayeim sh'vu'ati zu b'agala uviz'man kariv Omein Omein Omein Selah Selah Selah.*

Translation:
> *Kimi'el Shava'ti'el*, you holy angels, do my will and my request, in the name of *El*, King, eternal God, grant me strength and power to keep this vow of mine, in a speedily and timely manner. *Amen Amen Amen Selah Selah Selah.*[11]

In line with the "oath keeping" application of this psalm, I have seen the current psalm employed for punctuality. It is also enunciated for Jewish unity, universal brotherhood, and peace. It is worth noting that *Psalm 132:13* is directly aligned with חבו (*Chavu*), the sixty-eighth tri-letter portion of the "Name of Seventy-two Names."[12]

Psalm 132 is employed for a very different purpose in Christian Magic. In this regard, fishermen are instructed in the "*Livre d'Or*" to copy *Psalm 132:1–15*, and attach the writing to fishing nets in order to ensure a great catch. It is further maintained that some of the fish will have certain listed magical characters on them.[13]

PSALM 133

‎[1] שיר המעלות לדוד הנה מה טוב ומה נעים
‎שבת אחים גם יחד
‎[2] כשמן הטוב על הראש ירד על הזקן זקן אהרן
‎שירד על פי מדותיו
‎[3] כטל חרמון שירד על הררי ציון כי שם צוה
‎יהוה אדני אהדונהי את הברכה חיים עד העולם

Transliteration:

[1] *shir hama'alot l'david hineih mah tov umah na'im shevet achim gam yachad*

[2] *kashemen hatov al harosh yoreid al hazakan z'kan aharon sheyoreid al pi midotav*

[3] *k'tal cher'mon sheyoreid al har'rei tziyon ki sham tzivah YHVH et hab'rachah chayim ad ha'olam*

Translation:

[1] A Song of Ascents; of David. Behold, how good and how pleasant it is for brethren to dwell together in unity!

[2] It is like the precious oil upon the head, coming down upon the beard; even Aaron's beard, that cometh down upon the collar of his garments;

[3] Like the dew of Hermon, that cometh down upon the mountains of Zion; for there *YHVH* commanded the blessing, even life for ever.

Psalm 133 is the fourteenth of fifteen "Songs of Ascents" psalms, which are enunciated at every Sabbath *Min'chah* service (afternoon prayers) over the period starting with the Sabbath after *Sukkot* (Festival of Booths), and ending with the Sabbath before *Pesach* (Festival of Passover).[1] The theme of friendship, love, and brotherhood, with special reference to the main phrase of the first verse which features in the acclaimed Hebrew song "*Hineih Ma Tov*" ("Behold, how good"), guaranteed the global popularity of this psalm. In this regard, it is worth noting the practice of inscribing this very brief psalm on decorative plaques, which are often displayed in Christian homes. Similar items, comprising verses from holy writ, can likewise be found in Jewish homes, as indicated in the following detail from a spectacular *Shiviti* amulet in the Magnes collection:[2]

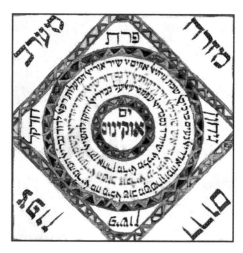

The concentric circles encompassing the centre of the image, comprise the words of *Psalm 133:1–2* intertwined with Angelic Names in the following manner:

[1] (Outer Circle) שִׁיר **אוֹרוּאֵל** הַמַּעֲלוֹת **רְפָאֵל** לְדָוִד
גַּבְרִיאֵל הִנֵּה **נוּרִיאֵל** מַה **מִיכָאֵל** טוֹב **מֶטַטְרוֹן** וּמַה
אַדְרִיאֵל נָעִים **בַּרִיאֵל** שֶׁבֶת **גֵּוְיָתִיאֵל** אַחִים
(Central Circle) גַּם **דוֹרְשֵׁיאֵל** יַחַד [2] **הֲדַרִיאֵל** כַּשֶּׁמֶן
(**הַדְרִיאֵל**) **וַעֲדִיאֵל** הַטּוֹב **זוֹכְרִיאֵל** עַל **חַנִיאֵל** הָרֹאשׁ **טוּבִילְאֵל**
(**טוּבִיאֵל**) יָרַד **יְקוּתִיאֵל**
(Inner Circle) עַל **כַּבִּירִיאֵל** הַזָּקָן **לְהַטִּיאֵל** זְקַן אַהֲרֹן
מֶדִיאֵל **מַלְכִּיאֵל** שֶׁיּוֹרֵד **נִסְגָדִיאֵל** עַל [עָנָן] פִּין [מִדוֹתָיו]
סָרָעִיאֵל

Transliteration:
(Outer Circle) [1] *Shir **Ori'el** hama'alot **Rafa'el** l'david*
***Gavri'el** hineih **Nuri'el** mah **Micha'el** tov **Metatron** umah*
***Ad'ri'el** na'im **Bari'el** shevat **Gev'yati'el** achim*
(Central Circle) *gam **Dor'shei'el** yachad* [2] ***Hadari'el***
(***Had'ri'el***) *kashemen **Vei'di'el** hatov **Zoch'ri'el** al*
Chani'el** ha'rosh **Tubil'el** (Tubi'el) yoreid **Yekuti'el
(Inner Circle) *al **Kabiri'el** hazakan **Lahati'el** z'kan aharon*
***Medi'el** **Mal'chi'el** sheyoreid **Nis'gudi'el** al pi midotav*
Sarai'el

In the corners of the inner square, are the names of the four Edenic Rivers: פישון (*Pishon*); גיחון (*Gichon*); חדקל (*Chedekel*); פרת (*Frat*), whilst in the corners of the external square are located the four directions: מזרח (*Mizrach*—"East"); מערב (*Ma'arav*— "West"); צפון (*Tzafon*—"North"); דרום (Darom—*South*"). The very centre of the image reads: י (*Yam*—"Sea"); אוקינוס (*Okinos [Okeanos]*—"Ocean" [Greek]).

It is said *Psalm 133:1* is likely the inspiration for the recitation of this psalm in *Practical Kabbalah* for the purpose of strengthening the bond of love between lovers, as well as between friends.[3] We are told that *Psalm 133* is enunciated "to inspire friendship";[4] "to cultivate love from those whom you love";[5] and generally "for friendship and love."[6] In this regard, we are informed in the *Shimmush Tehillim*, "to maintain the love of lovers and connect with friends, all should keep this psalm always on their lips."[7] Godfrey Selig noted in his German/English translation of this text, that "whoever prays this Psalm daily, will not only retain the love and friendship of his friends, but he will also gain many more friends."[8]

Interestingly enough, *Psalm 133:1*, senza the opening expression, is listed in *"The Book of Abramelin the Mage"* for the very purpose of maintaining a friendship between two friends. In this regard, the practitioner is instructed to collect dew before dawn, which is afterwards mixed with honey. This substance is used to write the said verse inside a glass or silver bowl, and the remainder imbibed by the said friends. This procedure is said to be particularly powerful if it is enacted seven times.[9] The current psalm is employed in a similar manner in Jewish "love magic." In this regard, we are told that love and happiness can be encouraged between a husband and a wife, by the couple writing *Psalm 133* inside a new dish, the latter being something like a large soup plate. The writing is afterwards dissolved by pouring wine, brandy, or any prefered alcoholic beverage into the vessel, and the action concluded with the couple consuming this "psalm infused" liquid whilst reciting the psalm.[10] It was further suggested that the said dish should afterwards be located inside the residence in a locale where it is easily visible, and that the couple should enjoy as much sex as they want, as often as they can.

A variant recension of the *Shimmush Tehillim* recommends the current psalm to an individual who joins forces with a companion to succeed. In this regard, the psalm is enunciated three times, and the action concluded by uttering the following prayer-incantation:

אל אל יה יה השם הגדול הגבור והנורא
העזוז האמיץ החזק האדיר שתצליח דרכי עם
חבירי ותישר אורחותי [....name of recipient....]
ותמלא משאלותי ותעשה חפצי ביום הזה מעתה
ועד עולם אמן אמן אמן סלה סלה סלה סלה

Transliteration:

> *El El Yah Yah hashem hagadol hagibor v'hanora he'azuz he'amitz hechazak ha'adir shetatz'li'ach dar'kai im [....name of recipient....] chaveiri v'tiyasher or'chotai ut'malei mish'alotai v'ta'aseh chef'tzi b'yom hazeh mei'atah v'ad olam Omein Omein Omein Selah Selah Selah.*

Translation:

> *El El Yah Yah*, the great, powerful, awesome, strong, courageous, fierce, and mighty Name, that you find ways for [....name of recipient....], my companion, to succeed, and straighten my ways, and fulfill my wishes, and carry out my desire this day, from now unto eternity. *Amen Amen Amen Selah Selah Selah.*[11]

In Christian Magic *Psalms 133* and *134* are dealt with conjointly in the Byzantine Christian magical manuscripts, in which we are told that these psalms should be copied for a man or woman who cannot sleep at night, or a child who has "terrors from the heart or from any cause of terror or pain." In terms of the infant, it is noted that the psalms should be copied on a Sunday "with musk and rose oil and saffron," and "the names of the seven holy children of Ephesus" should be written on an olive leaf. These writings are afterwards placed on the pillow of the child.[12] In the "*Livre d'Or*" we find *Psalm 133* employed for a purpose more aligned with its use in Jewish Magic. In this regard, those who seek "to be welcomed everywhere," are instructed to copy this psalm, "read it seven times over good rose oil," and rub it on the face.[13] In conclusion, it should be noted that the current psalm is also one of the nineteen listed in the *"Key of Solomon,"* for enunciation over the wax from which ritual candles are manufactured. The complete set comprises *Psalms 8, 15, 22, 46, 47, 49, 51, 53, 68, 72, 84, 102, 110, 113, 126, 130, 131,* 133, and 139.[14]

PSALM 134

[1] שִׁיר הַמַּעֲלוֹת הִנֵּה בָּרֲכוּ אֶת יְהֹוָה‎אדניאהדונהי
כָּל עַבְדֵי יְהֹוָה‎אדניאהדונהי הָעֹמְדִים בְּבֵית
יְהֹוָה‎אדניאהדונהי בַּלֵּילוֹת
[2] שְׂאוּ יְדֵכֶם קֹדֶשׁ וּבָרֲכוּ אֶת יְהֹוָה‎אדניאהדונהי
[3] יְבָרֶכְךָ יְהֹוָה‎אדניאהדונהי מִצִּיּוֹן עֹשֵׂה שָׁמַיִם
וָאָרֶץ

Transliteration:

[1] *shir hama'alot hineih barachu et YHVH kol av'dei YHVH ha'om'dim b'veit YHVH baleilot*
[2] *s'u y'deichem kodesh uvar'chu et YHVH*
[3] *y'varech'cha YHVH mitziyon oseih shamayim va'aretz*

Translation:

[1] A Song of Ascents. Behold, bless ye *YHVH*, all ye servants of *YHVH*, that stand in the house of *YHVH* in the night seasons.
[2] Lift up your hands to the sanctuary, and bless ye *YHVH*.
[3] *YHVH* bless thee out of Zion; even He that made heaven and earth.

Psalm 134 is the last of the fifteen "Songs of Ascents" psalms, which are enunciated at every Sabbath *Min'chah* service (afternoon prayers) over the period commencing with the Sabbath after *Sukkot* (Festival of Booths), and concluding with the Sabbath before *Pesach* (Festival of Passover).[1] In certain Ashkenazi, Sefardi, and Sefard–Chasidic communities, it is recited at the commencement of the weekday *Arvit* (evening prayer service).[2] We are informed that this psalm is good to recite prior to studying.[3] In this regard, it was noted that the current psalm aids an individual "with his learning."[4] Thus Godfrey Selig noted in his German/English version of the *Shimmush Tehillim* that this psalm "should be repeated by every learned man, and especially by every student before entering college."[5] However, in this instance the term "learning/studying" pertains to "*Torah* study."[6] Elsewhere this term was misread, and hence it was said that this psalm is for studying the *Talmud*.[7] I should think it would be applicable in both biblical and Talmudic studies.

It should be noted that whilst the magical application of *Psalm 134*, is included in the modern Hebrew editions of the *Shimmush Tehillim*, it is absent in some of the earlier publications. In one recension of this text this psalm is recommended to those who prefer studying *Torah* at night,[8] i.e. from midnight to daybreak. It was suggested "that this may reflect the claim in *TB Menachot 110a* that verse 1's reference to those 'who stand nightly in the house of the Lord' alludes to scholars who study Torah in the nighttime."[9] The mentioned recension of the *Shimmush Tehillim* suggests the current psalm should be enunciated conjointly with the following prayer-incantation prior to commencing the said nighttime *Torah* studies:

יהי רצון מלפניך יהוה אלהי האל הגדול הגבור
והנורא (*Nehemiah 9:32*) והקדוש שמך שתברך
את מעשי ידי ותצליחני ללמוד בזו הלילה ובכל
שאר הלילות ולא אבטל מדברי תורתך ותטיב
אחריתי וסופי ומברכותיך יבורך בית עבדך לעולם
ובך חסיתי (*Psalm 32:8*) כי עליך עיני (*II Samuel 7:29*)
ואל אשוב מלפניך ריקם מעתה ועד עולם (*Psalm 7:2*)
אמן נצח סלה

Transliteration:

> *Y'hi ratzon mil'fanecha YHVH elohai ha'el hagadol hagibor v'hanora (Nehemiah 9:32) v'hakadosh shim'cha shet'varech et ma'asei yadai v'tatz'licheini lil'mod b'zu halailah ub'chol sha'ar haleilot v'lo avatel m'div'rei toratecha v'teitiv ach'riti v'sofi umibir'chotecha y'vorach beit av'd'cha l'olam (II Samuel 7:29) ki alecha eini (Psalm 32:8) ub'cha chasiti (Psalm 7:2) v'al eshov mil'fanecha reikam mei'atah v'ad olam Omein Netzach Selah.*

Translation:

> May it be your will *YHVH*, my God, "the great, mighty, and awesome God" (*Nehemiah 9:32*), and holy, blessed is your name, that you may see the works of my hands, and you will enable me to study this night, and all the other nights, and I will not neglect the words of your *Torah*, and let my last days and my end be good, "and through your blessing let the house of your servant be blessed for

ever"(*II Samuel 7:29*), "for my eye is upon you" (*Psalm 32:8*) and "in you have I taken refuge" (*Psalm 7:2*), and I will not return empty-handed before you, from now unto eternity. *Amen Eternal Selah.*[10]

Besides its recitation when committing to intense *Torah* study, *Psalm 134* is said to sharpen and increase intelligence. It is also employed for rain and good wind, and especially for the protection of people and animals. Other than that, it is enunciated for justice and just people, as well as for punishment.

As noted earlier, *Psalms 133* and *134* are addressed conjointly in the Byzantine Christian magical manuscripts, and are written down for sleep.[11] The *"Livre d'Or"* instructs practitioners to recite the current psalm seven times in the morning and at night, in order to increase their goods.[12] In the *"Key of Solomon"* it is one of the psalms enunciated during the construction of "pentacles," the full compliment being *Psalms 8, 21, 27, 32, 29, 51*, and *134*.[13] It is also part of four psalms, i.e. *Psalms 72, 82, 134* and *64*, which are uttered for the "perfuming" of the silk cloth in which "the instruments of art" are wrapped when not in use.[14]

PSALM 135

[1] הללו יה הללו את שם יהוה הללו
עבדי יהוה

[2] שעמדים בבית יהוה בחצרות בית
אלהינו

[3] הללו יה כי טוב יהוה זמרו לשמו
כי נעים

[4] כי יעקב בחר לו יה ישראל לסגלתו

[5] כי אני ידעתי כי גדול יהוה
ואדנינו מכל אלהים

[6] כל אשר חפץ יהוה עשה בשמים
ובארץ בימים וכל תהמות

[7] מעלה נשאים מקצה הארץ ברקים למטר
עשה מוצא רוח מאוצרתיו

[8] שהכה בכורי מצרים מאדם עד בהמה

[9] שלח אתות ומפתים בתוככי מצרים
בפרעה ובכל עבדיו

[10] שהכה גוים רבים והרג מלכים עצומים

[11] לסיחון מלך האמרי ולעוג מלך הבשן
ולכל ממלכות כנען

[12] ונתן ארצם נחלה נחלה לישראל עמו

[13] יהוה שמך לעולם יהוה
זכרך לדר ודר

[14] כי ידין יהוה עמו ועל עבדיו
יתנחם

[15] עצבי הגוים כסף וזהב מעשה ידי אדם

[16] פה להם ולא ידברו עינים להם ולא יראו

[17] אזנים להם ולא יאזינו אף אין יש רוח בפיהם

[18] כמוהם יהיו עשיהם כל אשר בטח בהם

[19] בית ישראל ברכו את יהוה בית
אהרן ברכו את יהוה

[20] בית הלוי ברכו את יהוה יראי
יהוה ברכו את יהוה

[21] בָּרוּךְ יְהוָֹה אֲדֹנָי אֲהדוּנהי מִצִּיּוֹן שֹׁכֵן יְרוּשָׁלַ͏ִם
הַלְלוּ יָהּ

Transliteration:

[1] *hal'lu Yah hal'lu et shem YHVH hal'lu av'dei YHVH*

[2] *she'om'dim b'veit YHVH b'chatz'rot beit eloheinu*

[3] *hal'lu Yah ki tov YHVH zam'ru lish'mo ki na'im*

[4] *ki ya'akov bachar lo Yah yis'ra'eil lis'gulato*

[5] *ki ani yada'ti ki gadol YHVH va'adoneinu mikol elohim*

[6] *kol asher chafeitz YHVH asah bashamayim uva'aretz bayamim v'chol t'homot*

[7] *ma'aleh n'si'im mik'tzeih ha'aretz b'rakim lamatar osah motzei ru'ach mei'otz'rotav*

[8] *shehikah b'chorei mitz'rayim mei'adam ad b'heimah*

[9] *shalach otot umof'tim b'tocheichi mitz'rayim b'far'oh uv'chol avadav*

[10] *shehikah goyim rabim v'harag m'lachim atzumim*

[11] *l'sichon melech ha'emori ul'og melech habashan ul'chol mam'l'chot k'na'an*

[12] *v'natan ar'tzam nachalah nachalah l'yis'ra'eil amo*

[13] *YHVH shim'cha l'olam YHVH zich'r'cha l'dor vador*

[14] *ki yadin YHVH amo v'al avadav yit'necham*

[15] *atzabei hagoyim kesef v'zahav ma'aseih y'dei adam*

[16] *peh lahem v'lo y'dabeiru einayim lahem v'lo yir'u*

[17] *oz'nayim lahem v'lo ya'azinu af ein yesh ru'ach b'fihem*

[18] *k'mohem yih'yu oseihem kol asher botei'ach bahem*

[19] *beit yis'ra'eil bar'chu et YHVH beit aharon bar'chu et YHVH*

[20] *beit haleivi bar'chu et YHVH yir'ei YHVH bar'chu et YHVH*

[21] *baruch YHVH mitziyon shochein y'rushalam hal'lu Yah*

Translation:

[1] Hallelujah. Praise ye the name of *YHVH*; give praise, O ye servants of *YHVH*,

[2] Ye that stand in the house of *YHVH*, in the courts of the house of our God.

[3] Praise ye *Yah*, for *YHVH* is good; sing praises unto His name, for it is pleasant.

[4] For *Yah* hath chosen Jacob unto Himself, and Israel for His own treasure.

[5] For I know that *YHVH* is great, and that our Lord is above all gods.

[6] Whatsoever *YHVH* pleased, that hath He done, in heaven and in earth, in the seas and in all deeps;

[7] Who causeth the vapours to ascend from the ends of the earth; He maketh lightnings for the rain; He bringeth forth the wind out of His treasuries.

[8] Who smote the first-born of Egypt, both of man and beast.

[9] He sent signs and wonders into the midst of thee, O Egypt, upon Pharaoh, and upon all his servants.

[10] Who smote many nations, and slew mighty kings:

[11] Sihon king of the Amorites, and Og king of Bashan, and all the kingdoms of Canaan;

[12] And gave their land for a heritage, a heritage unto Israel His people.

[13] *YHVH*, Thy name endureth for ever; thy memorial, *YHVH*, throughout all generations.

[14] For *YHVH* will judge His people, and repent Himself for His servants.

[15] The idols of the nations are silver and gold, the work of men's hands.

[16] They have mouths, but they speak not; eyes have they, but they see not;

[17] They have ears, but they hear not; neither is there any breath in their mouths.

[18] They that make them shall be like unto them; yea, every one that trusteth in them.

[19] O house of Israel, bless ye *YHVH*; O house of Aaron, bless ye *YHVH*;

[20] O house of Levi, bless ye *YHVH*; ye that fear *YHVH*, bless ye *YHVH*.

[21] Blessed be *YHVH* out of Zion, who dwelleth at Jerusalem. Hallelujah.

Psalm 135 is recited in *Shacharit* (Morning Prayer Service) on *Shabbat* and festivals. In this regard, we are informed that "it serves as a preface to *Psalm 136* which follows immediately in the service."[1] It was suggested that the current psalm "entered the liturgy because it preceded *Psalm 136*, the Great *Hallel*, which was attributed with mystical powers by the kabbalists."[2] However, it has been noted that *Psalm 135* "is most fitting for the Sabbath because it extols the justice and the loving-kindness of God as revealed in nature and history."[3] Nevertheless, *Psalms 135* and *136* are often viewed conjointly, since they are understood to be a pair of psalms, each of which is referencing the occupation of Canaan as narrated in the biblical book of "Exodus."[4] Keep in mind that the current psalm is reserved for the first day of *Pesach* (Festival of Passover), and *Psalm 136* for the last day.[5]

A major theme of the current psalm is the recognition of the sovereignty of the Divine One over other deities. In this regard, the psalmist maintains "the idols of the nations" to be "silver and gold." Whether referencing items such as effigies constructed from these metals, or their measure in terms of monetary value, it is certainly true that over the millennia of bartering amongst humankind, many have made a "god" of their money, and yet in years to come many more would gladly give their souls away for even the smell of money. A dear friend once exclaimed that the last bit of water on this planet would run out of the "golden faucet," and everybody will run for the gold! Whatever it may be referencing, the "idols" statement inspired the recommendation of *Psalm 135* to individuals who contemplates heresy and idolatry.[6]

Elsewhere we are informed that the current psalm is "for repentance and amendment."[7] In this regard, the *Shimmush Tehillim* instructs individuals who wish "to affect complete repentance,"[8] to recite the current psalm every day after *Shacharit*, *Min'chah*, and *Ma'ariv* (*Arvit*), i.e. the morning, afternoon, and evening prayer services, and it is said that "a true spirit will be renewed in his innermost being."[9] Selig repeated these details with some variation in his German/English translation of the *Shimmush Tehillim*, stating that "whoever is desirous of repenting sincerely from sin, and of consecrating his life to the service of God, should pray this Psalm daily after the morning and evening prayers, and then his heart and spirit will be daily renewed, and he will become more closely united with God from day to day."[10]

A variant recension of the *Shimmush Tehillim* maintains it is good to recite the current psalm with the following prayer-incantation, doing so every day over the "Days of Repentance," i.e.

the ten days between *Rosh Hashanah* (New Year) and *Yom Kippur* (Day of Atonement):

פתחיאל שמעיאל קשוביה אדוניאל יופיאל
יהואל אתם מלאכים קדושים השמיעו תחנתי לפני
הבורא שאני מתחנן על עונותי לפני הבורא יתברך
שמו שיקבלני בתשובה שלימה לפניו ויקבל ברצון
תעניתי ותפלותי ויכנסו לפני כסא כבודו אמן סלה

Transliteration:

> *Petachi'el Shemi'el Kashuv'yah Adoni'el Yofi'el Yeho'el*
> *atem mal'achim k'doshim hash'mi'u t'chinati lif'nei*
> *haborei she'ani mit'chanein al ovonotai lif'nei haborei*
> *yit'barach sh'mo shikab'leini b't'shuvah sh'leimah l'fanav*
> *vikabeil b'ratzon t'aniti ut'filotai vikan'su lif'nei kisei*
> *k'vodo Omein Selah.*

Translation:

> *Petachi'el Shemi'el Kashuv'yah Adoni'el Yofi'el Yeho'el*
> you holy angels, bring my supplications before the Creator,
> for I bow down for my transgressions before the Creator,
> praised be his Name, that he may receive me in complete
> repentance before him, and he should accept my fasting
> and my prayers kindly, and let them gather before the
> throne of his glory. *Amen Selah.* [11]

This psalm has been suggested for recitation in the synagogue, and is one of the psalms uttered when visiting the graves of loved ones.

Practical applications of *Psalm 135* appears to be scarce in Christian Magic. The *"Livre d'Or"* suggests that those who are ill should recite it "seven times over some good oil," which is afterwards rubbed on the face.[12] The same source recommends placing a "tuff stone," i.e. a rock formed from volcanic ash, in wine at night, following which the current psalm is enunciated whilst bathing the eyes of the afflicted individual with this liquid. The said text guarantees both actions will facilitate healing.[13] Other than this, the *"Key of Solomon"* includes the second phrase of *Psalm 135:16* in the perimeter of the *"Sixth Pentacle of the Sun."*[14]

PSALM 136

[1] הודו ליהוה‎אהדונהי כי טוב כי לעולם חסדו

[2] הודו לאלהי האלהים כי לעולם חסדו

[3] הודו לאדני האדנים כי לעולם חסדו

[4] לעשה נפלאות גדלות לבדו כי לעולם חסדו

[5] לעשה השמים בתבונה כי לעולם חסדו

[6] לרקע הארץ על המים כי לעולם חסדו

[7] לעשה אורים גדלים כי לעולם חסדו

[8] את השמש לממשלת ביום כי לעולם חסדו

[9] את הירח וכוכבים לממשלות בלילה כי לעולם חסדו

[10] למכה מצרים בבכוריהם כי לעולם חסדו

[11] ויוצא ישראל מתוכם כי לעולם חסדו

[12] ביד חזקה ובזרוע נטויה כי לעולם חסדו

[13] לגזר ים סוף לגזרים כי לעולם חסדו

[14] והעביר ישראל בתוכו כי לעולם חסדו

[15] ונער פרעה וחילו בים סוף כי לעולם חסדו

[16] למוליך עמו במדבר כי לעולם חסדו

[17] למכה מלכים גדלים כי לעולם חסדו

[18] ויהרג מלכים אדירים כי לעולם חסדו

[19] לסיחון מלך האמרי כי לעולם חסדו

[20] ולעוג מלך הבשן כי לעולם חסדו

[21] ונתן ארצם לנחלה כי לעולם חסדו

[22] נחלה לישראל עבדו כי לעולם חסדו

[23] שבשפלנו זכר לנו כי לעולם חסדו

[24] ויפרקנו מצרינו כי לעולם חסדו

[25] נתן לחם לכל בשר כי לעולם חסדו

[26] הודו לאל השמים כי לעולם חסדו

Transliteration:
[1] *hodu laYHVH ki tov ki l'olam chas'do*
[2] *hodu leilohei ha'elohim ki l'olam chas'do*
[3] *hodu la'adonei ha'adonim ki l'olam chas'do*
[4] *l'oseih nif'la'ot g'dolot l'vado ki l'olam chas'do*

[5] *l'oseih hashamayim bit'vunah ki l'olam chas'do*
[6] *l'roka ha'aretz al hamayim ki l'olam chas'do*
[7] *l'oseih orim g'dolim ki l'olam chas'do*
[8] *et hashemesh l'mem'shelet bayom ki l'olam chas'do*
[9] *et hayarei'ach v'chochavim l'mem'sh'lot balailah ki l'olam chas'do*
[10] *l'makeih mitz'rayim biv'choreihem ki l'olam chas'do*
[11] *vayotzei yis'ra'eil mitocham ki l'olam chas'do*
[12] *b'yad chazakah uviz'ro'a n'tuyah ki l'olam chas'do*
[13] *l'gozeir yam suf lig'zarim ki l'olam chas'do*
[14] *v'he'evir yis'ra'eil b'tocho ki l'olam chas'do*
[15] *v'ni'eir par'oh v'cheilo v'yam suf ki l'olam chasdo*
[16] *l'molich amo bamid'bar ki l'olam chas'do*
[17] *l'makeih m'lachim g'dolim ki l'olam chas'do*
[18] *vayaharog m'lachim adirim ki l'olam chas'do*
[19] *l'sichon melech ha'emori ki l'olam chas'do*
[20] *ul'og melech habashan ki l'olam chas'do*
[21] *v'natan ar'tzam l'nachalah ki l'olam chas'do*
[22] *nachalah l'yis'ra'eil av'do ki l'olam chas'do*
[23] *sheb'shif'leinu zachar lanu ki l'olam chas'do*
[24] *vayif'r'keinu mitzareinu ki l'olam chas'do*
[25] *notein lechem l'chol basar ki l'olam chas'do*
[26] *hodu l'el hashamayim ki l'olam chas'do*

Translation:

[1] O give thanks unto *YHVH*, for He is good, for His mercy endureth for ever.

[2] O give thanks unto the God of gods, for His mercy endureth for ever.

[3] O give thanks unto the Lord of lords, for His mercy endureth for ever.

[4] To Him who alone doeth great wonders, for His mercy endureth for ever.

[5] To Him that by understanding made the heavens, for His mercy endureth for ever.

[6] To Him that spread forth the earth above the waters, for His mercy endureth for ever.

[7] To Him that made great lights, for His mercy endureth for ever;

[8] The sun to rule by day, for His mercy endureth for ever;

[9] The moon and stars to rule by night, for His mercy endureth for ever.

[10] To Him that smote Egypt in their first-born, for His mercy endureth for ever;

[11] And brought out Israel from among them, for His mercy endureth for ever;

[12] With a strong hand, and with an outstretched arm, for His mercy endureth for ever.

[13] To Him who divided the Red Sea in sunder, for His mercy endureth for ever;

[14] And made Israel to pass through the midst of it, for His mercy endureth for ever;

[15] But overthrew Pharaoh and his host in the Red Sea, for His mercy endureth for ever.

[16] To Him that led His people through the wilderness, for His mercy endureth for ever.

[17] To Him that smote great kings; for His mercy endureth for ever;

[18] And slew mighty kings, for His mercy endureth for ever.

[19] Sihon king of the Amorites, for His mercy endureth for ever;

[20] And Og king of Bashan, for His mercy endureth for ever;

[21] And gave their land for a heritage, for His mercy endureth for ever;

[22] Even a heritage unto Israel His servant, for His mercy endureth for ever.

[23] Who remembered us in our low estate, for His mercy endureth for ever;

[24] And hath delivered us from our adversaries, for His mercy endureth for ever.

[25] Who giveth food to all flesh, for His mercy endureth for ever.

[26] O give thanks unto the God of heaven, for His mercy endureth for ever.

Psalm 136, termed the הלל הגדול (*Halel Hagadol*—"Great *Halel* [Praise]*") in the *Talmud* [*TB Pesachim 118a*], is enunciated during

Shacharit (Morning Prayer Service) on *Shabbat.*[1] It is also recited during festivals, and is the psalm of the last day of *Pesach.*[2] We are reminded that this psalm "includes the praise of God from the aspect of creation and of miracles,"[3] and it was said that the twenty-six verses of this psalm align with "the twenty-six generations (from Adam until Moses) that the Holy One, blessed be He, created in His world."[4] It was further noted that these twenty-six verses correspond to the *gematria* (numerical value) of the Ineffable Name [י = 10 + ה = 5 + ו = 6 + ה = 5 = 26],[5] In this regard, we are informed that *Psalm 136* is termed *Halel Hagadol* ("Great *Halel*"), because "*YHVH* is great, and highly to be praised" (*Psalm 145:3*).[6] However, it should be noted that some consider *Psalms 135* and *136* to comprise the "*Great Halel*" conjointly, and these two psalms are amongst nine, i.e. *Psalms 19, 34, 90, 91, 135, 136, 33, 92* and *93*, which are enunciated on *Shabbat*, though not during the week. We are informed that "these Psalms have been interpreted as expressing three 'fundamental concepts embodied in the Sabbath': Creation; the Exodus from Egypt; and the Sabbath (i.e., World to Come)."[7]

Whilst the previous psalm is employed "to affect complete repentance," *Psalm 136* is enunciated in *Practical Kabbalah* for the purpose of confessing personal wickedness.[8] Thus it has been said that this psalm is uttered "when one feels the need to atone for sins done with malice and forethought, probably because it mentions God's grace or love (חסד [*Chesed*]) at the end of each verse."[9] In this regard, Godfrey Selig noted in his German/English translation of the *Shimmush Tehillim* that "whosoever desires, on account of wilful sins and transactions, to make a penitent confession of his misdeeds, should pray this Psalm beforehand, and then make this confession with an humble and broken heart and with great reverence."[10] Be that as it may, one source maintains this recitation should be done on the second day of *Pesach* (Passover).[11] However, a variant recension of the *Shimmush Tehillim* shares a very different application of the current psalm, i.e. complete protection.[12] To affect this aim, the practitioner is instructed to enunciate the following unique prayer-incantation. It incorporates the conjunction of the twenty-six verses of the current psalm with associated Divine or Angelic Names, a further set of ten Angelic Names, as well as a concluding statement of intent:

[1] **הודואל** הודו ליהוה כי טוב כי לעולם חסדו

[2] **יאהדונהי** הודו לאלהי האלהים [3] **אדני**

הודו לאדני האדנים [4] **יאהדונה** לעושה נפלאות

גדלות לבדו [5] **אלהים** לעושה השמים בתבונה

[6] **אל** יה לרוקע הארץ על המים [7] והו לעושה

אורים גדלים [8] **שמשיאל** את השמש לממשלת

ביום [9] **צבאות** את הירח וכוכבים לממשלות

בלילה [10] **נעורירון** למכה מצרים בבכוריהם

[11] **מיכאל** ויוצא ישראל מתוכם [12] **גבריאל**

ביד חזקה ובזרוע נטויה [13] **אוריאל** לגזר ים

סוף לגזרים [14] **רפאל** והעביר ישראל בתוכו

[15] **נוריאל** וניער פרעה וחילו בים סוף [16] **אל**

שדי למוליך עמו במדבר [17] **אהיה** למכה

מלכים גדלים [18] **אני** ויהרג מלכים אדירים

[19] **קצפיאל** לסיחון מלך האמרי [20] **סמאל**

ולעוג מלך הבשן [21] **חפציאל** ונתן ארצם

לנחלה [22] **נחליאל** נחלה לישראל עבדו

[23] **זכריאל** שבשפלנו זכר לנו [24] **חאליאל**

ויפרקנו מצרינו [25] **צדקיאל** נותן לחם לכל

בשר [26] **פרנסיאל** הודו לאל השמים חסדיאל

מיכאל השר הגדול הממונה על שרים גדולים

גבריאל על שרי האומות

חסדיאל הממונה על שרי החסד

ענאל הממונה על הנחלים ועל הצועקים

ארמוניאל הממונה על האדם ועל הנפשות

צוריאל הממונה על יצירת הולד

מפתחיאל הממונה על מפתיח רחמים

ברכיאל הממונה על מעשה בני אדם

סוד־יאל הממונה שבו יודע תעלומות בני אדם
צפצפיאל היושב תחת כסא הכבוד ונותן שירה
וזמרה בפי דהמלאכים המשרתים כנגד כסא הכבוד ֗
כדבר שנאמר שרפים עומדים ממעל לו (Isaiah 6:2)
כל אלה השמות ישמרו אותי בצאתי ובבואי בבית
ובחוץ בלכתי ובשבתי בשכבי ובקומי אותי ואת
כל ביתי וכל אשר יש לי מעתה ועד עולם אמן
אמן אמן סלה סלה סלה סלה

Transliteration:

[1] **Hodu'el** *hodu laYHVH ki tov ki l'olam chas'do* [2] **Y'ahodovanaheiyo** *(Yahadonahi) hodu leilohei ha'elohim* [3] **Adonai** *hodu la'adonei ha'adonim* [4] **Y'ahodovanahei** *(Yahadonah') l'oseih nif'la'ot g'dolot l'vado* [5] **Elohim** *l'oseih hashamayim bit'vonah* [6] **El Yah** *l'roka ha'aretz al hamayim* [7] **Vaho** *l'oseih orim g'dolim* [8] **Sham'shi'el** *et hashemesh l'mem'shelet bayom* [9] **Tz'va'ot** *et hayarei'ach v'chochavim l'mem'sh'lot balailah* [10] **N'avurayeirivun** *(N'oriron) l'makeih mitz'rayim biv'choreihem* [11] **Micha'el** *vayotzei yis'ra'eil mitocham* [12] **Gavri'el** *b'yad chazakah uviz'ro'a n'tuyah* [13] **Ori'el** *l'gozeir yam suf lig'zarim* [14] **Rafa'el** *v'he'evir yis'ra'eil b'tocho* [15] **Nuri'el** *v'ni'eir par'oh v'cheilo v'yam suf* [16] **El Shadai** *l'molich amo bamid'bar* [17] **Eh'yeh** *l'makeih m'lachim g'dolim* [18] **Ani** *vayaharog m'lachim adirim* [19] **Katz'pi'el** *(Kitz'pi'el) l'sichon melech ha'emori* [20] **Sama'el** *ul'og melech habashon* [21] **Cheif'tzi'el** *v'natan ar'tzam l'nachalah* [22] **Nach'li'el** *nachalah l'yis'ra'eil av'do* [23] **Zachari'el** *sheb'shif'leinu zachar lanu* [24] **Ch'ali'el** *vayif'r'keinu mitzareinu* [25] **Tzad'ki'el** *notein lechem l'chol basar* [26] **Par'nasi'el** *hodu l'el hashamayim ki l'olam chas'do* **Chas'di'el**.

Micha'el *hasar hagadol ham'muneh al sarim g'dolim.*

Gavri'el *al sarei ha'umot.*

Chas'di'el *ham'muneh al sarei hachesed.*

Ana'el *ham'muneh al han'chalim v'al hatzo'akim.*

Ar'moni'el *ham'muneh al ha'adam v'al han'fashot.*

Tzuri'el *ham'muneh al y'tzirat hav'lad.*

Maf'teichi'el ham'muneh al maf'tei'ach rachamim.
Bar'ki'el ham'muneh al ma'aseih b'nei adam.
Sodi'el ham'muneh shebo yodei'a ta'alumot b'nei adam.
Tzaf'tz'fi'el hayoshev tachat kisei hakavod v'noten shirah
v'zim'rah b'fi hamalachim ham'shar'tim k'neged kisei
kavod kadavar shene'emar s'rafim om'dim mima'al lo
(*Isaiah 6:2*) kol eileh hashemot yish'm'ru oti b'tzeiti
ub'vo'i b'bayit ubachuts b'lech'ti ub'shiv'ti b'shoch'vi
uv'kumi oti v'et kol beiti v'chol asher yeish li mei'atah
v'ad olam Omein Omein Omein Selah Selah Selah.

Translation:

[1] **Hodu'el**, give thanks unto *YHVH*, for He is good, for His mercy endureth for ever. [2] **Yahadonahi** (*Y'ahodovanaheiyo*), give thanks unto the God of gods. [3] **Adonai**, give thanks unto the Lord of lords [4] **Y'ahodovanahei** (*Yahadonah'*), to Him who alone doeth great wonders. [5] **Elohim**, to Him that by understanding made the heavens. [6] **El Yah**, to Him that spread forth the earth above the waters, [7] **Vaho**, to Him that made great lights, [8] **Sham'shi'el**, the sun to rule by day. [9] **Tz'va'ot** ["hosts"], the moon and the stars to rule by night, [10] **N'avurayeirivun** (*N'oriron*), to Him that smote Egypt in their first-born, [11] **Micha'el**, and brought out Israel from among them, [12] **Gavri'el**, with a strong hand, and with an outstretched arm, [13] **Ori'el**, to Him who divided the Red Sea in sunder, [14] **Rafa'el**, and made Israel to pass through the midst of it, [15] **Nuri'el**, but overthrew Pharaoh and his host in the Red Sea, [16] **El Shadai**, to Him that led His people through the wilderness, [17] **Eh'yeh** ["I am"], to Him that smote great kings, [18] **Ani** ["I"], and slew mighty kings, [19] **Katz'pi'el** (*Kitz'pi'el*), Sihon king of the Amorites. [20] **Sama'el**, and Og king of Bashan, [21] **Cheif'tzi'el**, and gave their land for a heritage, [22] **Nach'li'el**, even a heritage unto Israel His servant, [23] **Zachari'el**, who remembered us in our low estate, [24] **Ch'ali'el**, and hath delivered us from our adversaries, [25] **Tzad'ki'el**, who giveth food to all flesh, [26] **Par'nasi'el**, give thanks unto the God of heaven, for His mercy endureth for ever **Chas'di'el**.

Micha'el, the great prince, set over the great princes.
Gavri'el, over the princes of the nations.
Chas'di'el, who is set above the princes of mercy (grace).
Ana'el, set over streams and over protesters (screamers).
Ar'moni'el, who is set over men and over souls.
Tzuri'el, posited on the education of the child.
Maf'teichi'el, who is set over the Key of Mercy.
Bar'ki'el, who is set above the deeds of men.
Sodi'el, who is posited to know the secrets of men with him.
Tzaf'tz'fi'el, who sits under the throne of glory, putting song and praise into the mouths of the angels who minister opposite the throne of glory, as it is said "above Him stood the *serafim*" (*Isaiah 6:2*). All these names will protect me when I go out and when I come in and out of the house, when I go and when I rest, when I lie down and when I get up, me and all my house and everything I have, from now unto eternity. *Amen Amen Amen Selah Selah Selah.*

Psalm 136 is also recommended to individuals who wish to express gratitude,[13] e.g. gratitude to the Divine One for good fortune, etc. It is further enunciated in support of refugees, and is one of the psalms employed for the well-being of the Land of Israel.[14]

In Christian Magic the current psalm is recited to defeat an enemy. In this regard, the psalm is read in front of the door of the said adversary.[15]

PSALM 137

‏[1] עַל נַהֲרוֹת בָּבֶל שָׁם יָשַׁבְנוּ גַּם בָּכִינוּ בְּזָכְרֵנוּ אֶת
צִיּוֹן
‏[2] עַל עֲרָבִים בְּתוֹכָהּ תָּלִינוּ כִּנֹּרוֹתֵינוּ
‏[3] כִּי שָׁם שְׁאֵלוּנוּ שׁוֹבֵינוּ דִּבְרֵי שִׁיר וְתוֹלָלֵינוּ
שִׂמְחָה שִׁירוּ לָנוּ מִשִּׁיר צִיּוֹן
‏[4] אֵיךְ נָשִׁיר אֶת שִׁיר יְהוָהאֲדֹנָיאֲדֹנִי עַל אַדְמַת נֵכָר
‏[5] אִם אֶשְׁכָּחֵךְ יְרוּשָׁלָםִ תִּשְׁכַּח יְמִינִי
‏[6] תִּדְבַּק לְשׁוֹנִי לְחִכִּי אִם לֹא אֶזְכְּרֵכִי אִם לֹא אַעֲלֶה
אֶת יְרוּשָׁלַםִ עַל רֹאשׁ שִׂמְחָתִי
‏[7] זְכֹר יְהוָהאֲדֹנָיאֲדֹנִי לִבְנֵי אֱדוֹם אֵת יוֹם יְרוּשָׁלָםִ
הָאֹמְרִים עָרוּ עָרוּ עַד הַיְסוֹד בָּהּ
‏[8] בַּת בָּבֶל הַשְּׁדוּדָה אַשְׁרֵי שֶׁיְשַׁלֶּם לָךְ אֶת גְּמוּלֵךְ
שֶׁגָּמַלְתְּ לָנוּ
‏[9] אַשְׁרֵי שֶׁיֹּאחֵז וְנִפֵּץ אֶת עֹלָלַיִךְ אֶל הַסָּלַע

Transliteration:

[1] *al naharot bavel sham yashav'nu gam bachinu b'zoch'reinu et tziyon*

[2] *al aravim b'tochah talinu kinoroteinu*

[3] *ki sham sh'eilunu shoveinu div'rei shir v'tolaleinu sim'chah shiru lanu mishir tziyon*

[4] *eich nashir et shir YHVH al ad'mat neichar*

[5] *im esh'kacheich y'rushalam tish'kach y'mini*

[6] *tid'bak l'shoni l'chiki im lo ez'k'reichi im lo a'aleh et y'rushalam al rosh sim'chati*

[7] *z'chor YHVH liv'nei edom et yom y'rushalam ha'om'rim aru aru ad hay'sod bah*

[8] *bat bavel hash'dudah ash'rei shey'shalem lach et g'muleich shegamal't lanu*

[9] *ash'rei sheyocheiz v'nipeitz et olalayich el hasala*

Translation:

[1] By the rivers of Babylon, there we sat down, yea, we wept, when we remembered Zion.

[2] Upon the willows in the midst thereof we hanged up our harps.

[3] For there they that led us captive asked of us words of song, and our tormentors asked of us mirth: 'Sing us one of the songs of Zion.'

[4] How shall we sing *YHVH*'s song in a foreign land?

[5] If I forget thee, O Jerusalem, let my right hand forget her cunning.

[6] Let my tongue cleave to the roof of my mouth, if I remember thee not; if I set not Jerusalem above my chiefest joy.

[7] Remember, *YHVH*, against the children of Edom the day of Jerusalem; who said: 'Rase it, rase it, even to the foundation thereof.'

[8] O daughter of Babylon, that art to be destroyed; happy shall he be, that repayeth thee as thou hast served us.

[9] Happy shall he be, that taketh and dasheth thy little ones against the rock.

Psalm 137 is a mournful lament recollecting the tragedy of the Babylonian exile, yet Jewish people have continued to suffer prejudice, vilification, and have been ostracized virtually continuously over the last two millennia. We are reminded that "a verse in the psalm that has been on the lips of the Jews throughout their long exile is 'If I forget you, O Jerusalem, let my right hand forget its skill' (*Psalm 137:5*)."[1] It should therefore come as no surprise that the current psalm was reserved for *Tisha B'av*,[2] the day set aside for the commemoration of the destruction of the First and Second Temples in Jerusalem. It is also recited weekdays prior to הַמָּזוֹן בְּרְכַּת (*Birkat Hamazon*—"Prayer-blessing after Meals").[3] This custom is based on the statement in the *Zohar* [*Terumah 157b*] that "One who delight at his table and enjoys that food should be mindful and concerned about the holiness of the Holy Land and the Temple of the King that has been destroyed because the sadness he feels at his table in the midst of that joy and feasting there, the blessed Holy One considers him to have rebuilt His house and to have rebuilt those ruins of the Temple. Happy is his share!"[4] However, on *Shabbat* and during festivals *Psalm 137* is replaced by *Psalm 126*, since it is understood that the sadness of the current psalm "would remove the joy of the Sabbath and holidays,"[5] when "the hope of redemption" is invoked.[6] Yet, it is this very factor of "redemption" associated with *Psalm 137*, which led to Rabbi Nachman of Bratslav including it in the set of ten "healing psalms" of the previously addressed הָתִּיקוּן הַכְּלָלִי (*ha-Tikun ha-K'lali*—"The Comprehensive Rectification").[7]

We are told that *Psalm 137* is employed to ward off or remove enmity.[8] In this regard, the *Shimmush Tehillim* maintains this psalm "is good to recite to overcome hatred."[9] Godfrey Selig noted in his German/English version of this text that "the praying of this Psalm, it is said, will root out of the heart the most inveterate hate, envy, and malice."[10] However, whilst this psalm is employed in *Practical Kabbalah* to eradicate hatred, a variant recension of the *Shimmush Tehillim* shares a procedure in which the current psalm is applied for the very opposite purpose of instilling hatred, in this instance between lovers.[11] As noted before, procedures of this nature have no place in this series of texts on Jewish Magic. Be that as it may, besides being enunciated to eradicate malice, the current psalm is also employed to encourage humility, and is further recited for Jerusalem.[12] In this regard, it should be noted that *Psalm 137:1* inspired the Rastafari song "*By the Rivers of Babylon*."[13] Since its first release in 1970, it was popularised by pop groups like "The Melodians" and "Boney M.," as well as by singers like Bob Marley, Linda Ronstadt, and others who performed this blockbuster song to an ecstatic "sing-along" listenership of many millions around the world.

As far as the magical application of individual verses is concerned, *Psalm 137:7* is employed in an unique procedure to support a woman who is suffering a difficult labour. In this regard, the said verse is enunciated thirteen times in her right ear, followed by uttering the expression צֵא צֵא צֵא (*Tzei Tzei Tzei*—literally "out out out") three times in the same manner. Afterwards the practitioner takes a glass of fresh water, bless it, then consume some of it, and offer the remainder to the woman.[14]

Psalm 137:7 is likewise employed for a successful birth in Christian Magic, as indicated in a number of anonymous Byzantine medical codices.[15] Elsewhere, we find the current psalm utilised in an amulet to preclude a woman from suffering excessive menstrual blood-loss. In this regard, the "*Livre d'Or*" instructs *Psalm 137:1—7* to be written "with a woman's menstrual blood, along with the names of her husband and her mother," which is afterwards perfumed with myrrh," and located in a wax sealed vial, which is to be buried in a Eastwards flowing stream. In conclusion, the psalm is read "seven times over it in the name of the woman and her husband," and, it is said, "the loss of blood will cease and the blood will flow no longer."[16]

PSALM 138

[1] לדוד אודך בכל לבי נגד אלהים אזמרך

[2] אשתחוה אל היכל קדשך ואודה את שמך על
חסדך ועל אמתך כי הגדלת על כל שמך אמרתך

[3] ביום קראתי ותענני תרהבני בנפשי עז

[4] יודוך יהוה‎אדניאהדונהי כל מלכי ארץ כי שמעו
אמרי פיך

[5] וישירו בדרכי יהוה‎אדניאהדונהי כי גדול כבוד
יהוה‎אדניאהדונהי

[6] כי רם יהוה‎אדניאהדונהי ושפל יראה וגבה ממרחק
יידע

[7] אם אלך בקרב צרה תחיני על אף איבי תשלח
ידך ותושיעני ימינך

[8] יהוה‎אדניאהדונהי יגמר בעדי יהוה‎אדניאהדונהי חסדך
לעולם מעשי ידיך אל תרף

Transliteration:

[1] *l'david od'cha v'chol libi neged elohim azam'reka*
[2] *esh'tachaveh el heichal kod'sh'cha v'odeh et sh'mecha
al chas'd'cha v'al amitecha ki hig'dal'ta al kol shim'cha
im'ratecha*
[3] *b'yom karati vata'aneini tar'hiveini v'naf'shi oz*
[4] *yoducha YHVH kol mal'chei aretz ki sham'u im'rei
ficha*
[5] *v'yashiru b'dar'chei YHVH ki gadol k'vod YHVH*
[6] *ki ram YHVH v'shafal yir'eh v'gavoha mimer'chak
y'yeida*
[7] *im eileich b'kerev tzarah t'chayeini al af oy'vai
tish'lach yadecha v'toshi'eini y'minecha*
[8] *YHVH yig'mor ba'adi YHVH chas'd'cha l'olam
ma'asei yadecha al teref*

Translation:

[1] A Psalm of David. I will give Thee thanks with my
whole heart, in the presence of *Elohim* will I sing praises
unto Thee.
[2] I will bow down toward Thy holy temple, and give
thanks unto Thy name for Thy mercy and for Thy truth; for
Thou hast magnified Thy word above all Thy name.

[3] In the day that I called, Thou didst answer me; Thou didst encourage me in my soul with strength.
[4] All the kings of the earth shall give Thee thanks, *YHVH*, for they have heard the words of Thy mouth.
[5] Yea, they shall sing of the ways of *YHVH*; for great is the glory of *YHVH*.
[6] For though *YHVH* be high, yet regardeth He the lowly, and the haughty He knoweth from afar.
[7] Though I walk in the midst of trouble, Thou quickenest me; Thou stretchest forth Thy hand against the wrath of mine enemies, and Thy right hand doth save me.
[8] *YHVH* will accomplish that which concerneth me; Thy mercy, *YHVH*, endureth for ever; forsake not the work of Thine own hands.

Psalms 138 does not feature in any Jewish liturgy, despite single verses being recited at certain moments in synagogal worship. However, the current psalm is traditionally employed to express thanks and gratitude to the Divine One.[1] Its application in Jewish Magic is also fairly minimal. We are informed that this psalm is enunciated to eliminate personal pride and arrogance.[2] However, whilst it is not included in every published version of the *Shimmush Tehillim*, this psalm is mainly said to be good to recite for love or friendship.[3] In this regard, a variant recension of the said text offers a somewhat more complex procedure for the same purpose. In this instance the individual working this procedure, is instructed to write the current psalm and his personal name with the blood of a dove on a piece of sheepskin. The writing is afterwards dissolved in wine, and this beverage given to whomsoever he wishes to fall in love with him, and the action concluded with the following prayer-incantation:

אהביאל ידידיאל חביבאל אתם המלאכים
הקדושים עשו רצוני ומשאלות לבי ושימו אהבה
עזה ביני ובין [....name of recipient....] אמן אמן אמן
סלה סלה סלה

Transliteration:
Ahavi'el Yedidei'el Chaviv'el atem ham'lachim hak'doshim asu r'tzoni umish'alot libi v'simu ahavah azah

beini ubein [....name of recipient....] *Omein Omein Omein Selah Selah Selah*

Translation:

Ahavi'el Yedidei'el Chaviv'el, holy angels fulfill my will and the desires of my heart, and put a strong love between me and [....name of recipient....] *Amen Amen Amen Selah Selah Selah.*[4]

Psalm 138 is primarily employed for the purpose of receiving, engendering, and increasing love, as well as increasing and maintaining friends and friendship. It is also enunciated for all manner of troubles and distress, as well as "to improve the quality of humanity." This psalm was further suggested to individuals who wish to comprehend the "Occult Sciences," and, curiously enough, to those who intend travelling by air.

An individual who is incarcerated is advised in Christian Magic to recite the current psalm seven times over rose water, which is afterwards rubbed on his/her face. The said individual is further instructed to copy the psalm, and to attach it to his/her arm, and this is said to result in this person being delivered from imprisonment.[5]

PSALM 139

[1] למנצח לדוד מזמור **יהוה**אדני־יאהדונהי חקרתני
ותדע

[2] **אתה** ידעת שבתי וקומי בנתה לרעי מרחוק

[3] **ארחי** ורבעי זרית וכל דרכי הסכנתה

[4] כי **אין** מלה בלשוני הן **יהוה**אדני־יאהדונהי ידעת
כלה

[5] **אחור** וקדם צרתני ותשת עלי כפכה

[6] **פליאה** דעת ממני נשגבה לא אוכל לה

[7] **אנה** אלך מרוחך ואנה מפניך אברח

[8] **אם** אסק שמים שם אתה ואציעה שאול הנך

[9] **אשא** כנפי שחר אשכנה באחרית ים

[10] **גם** שם ידך תנחני ותאחזני ימינך

[11] **ואמר** אך חשך ישופני ולילה אור בעדני

[12] **גם** חשך לא יחשיך ממך ולילה כיום יאיר
כחשיכה כאורה

[13] **כי** אתה קנית כליתי תסכני בבטן אמי

[14] **אודך** על כי נוראות נפליתי נפלאים מעשיך
ונפשי ידעת מאד

[15] **לא** נכחד עצמי ממך אשר עשיתי בסתר
רקמתי בתחתיות ארץ

[16] **גלמי** ראו עיניך ועל ספרך כלם יכתבו
ימים יצרו ולו אחד בהם

[17] **ולי** מה יקרו רעיך אל מה עצמו ראשיהם

[18] **אספרם** מחול ירבון הקיצתי ועודי עמך

[19] **אם** תקטל אלוה רשע ואנשי דמים סורו מני

[20] **אשר** יאמרך למזמה נשוא לשוא עריך

[21] **הלוא** משנא**י**ך **יהוה**אדני־יאהדונהי אשנא
ובתקוממיך אתקוטט

[22] **תכלית** שנאה שנאתים לאויבים היו לי

[23] **חקרני** אל ודע לבבי בחנני ודע שרעפי

[24] **וראה** אם דרך עצב בי ונחני בדרך עולם

Transliteration:

[1] *lam'natzei'ach l'david miz'mor YHVH chakar'tani vateida*

[2] *atah yada'ta shiv'ti v'kumi ban'tah l'rei'i meirachok*

[3] *or'chi v'riv'i zeirita v'chol d'rachai his'kan'tah*

[4] *ki ein milah bil'shoni hein YHVH yada'ta chulah*

[5] *achor vakedem tzar'tani vatashet alai kapechah*

[6] *p'li'ah da'at mimeni nis'g'vah lo uchal lah*

[7] *anah eileich meiruchecha v'anah mipanecha ev'rach*

[8] *im esak shamayim sham atah v'atzi'ah sh'ol hineka*

[9] *esa chan'fei shachar esh'k'nah b'acharit yam*

[10] *gam sham yad'cha tan'cheini v'tochazeini y'minecha*

[11] *va'omar ach choshech y'shufeini v'lailah or ba'adeini*

[12] *gam choshech lo yach'shich mimeka v'lailah kayom ya'ir kachasheicha ka'orah*

[13] *ki atah kanita chil'yotai t'sukeini b'veten imi*

[14] *od'cha al ki nora'ot nif'leiti nif'la'im ma'asecha v'naf'shi yoda'at m'od*

[15] *lo nich'chad otz'mi mimeka asher useiti vaseiter rukam'ti b'tach'tiyot aretz*

[16] *gol'mi ra'u einecha v'al sif'r'cha kulam yikateivu yamim yutzaru v'lo echad bahem*

[17] *v'li mah yak'ru rei'echa el meh atz'mu rasheihem*

[18] *es'p'reim meichol yir'bun hekitzoti v'odi imach*

[19] *im tik'tol eloha rasha v'an'shei damim suru meni*

[20] *asher yom'rucha lim'zimah nasu lashav arecha*

[21] *halo m'san'echa YHVH es'na uvit'kom'mecha et'kotat*

[22] *tach'lit sin'ah s'neitim l'oy'vim hayu li*

[23] *hok'reini el v'da l'vavi b'choneini v'da sar'apai*

[24] *ur'eih im derech otzev bi un'cheini b'derech olam*

Translation:

[1] For the Leader. A Psalm of David. *YHVH*, Thou hast searched me, and known me.

[2] Thou knowest my downsitting and mine uprising, Thou understandest my thought afar off.

[3] Thou measurest my going about and my lying down, and art acquainted with all my ways.

[4] For there is not a word in my tongue, but, lo, *YHVH*, Thou knowest it altogether.

[5] Thou hast hemmed me in behind and before, and laid Thy hand upon me.

[6] Such knowledge is too wonderful for me; too high, I cannot attain unto it.

[7] Whither shall I go from Thy spirit? or whither shall I flee from Thy presence?

[8] If I ascend up into heaven, Thou art there; if I make my bed in the nether-world, behold, Thou art there.

[9] If I take the wings of the morning, and dwell in the uttermost parts of the sea;

[10] Even there would Thy hand lead me, and Thy right hand would hold me.

[11] And if I say: 'Surely the darkness shall envelop me, and the light about me shall be night';

[12] Even the darkness is not too dark for Thee, but the night shineth as the day; the darkness is even as the light.

[13] For Thou hast made my reins; Thou hast knit me together in my mother's womb.

[14] I will give thanks unto Thee, for I am fearfully and wonderfully made; wonderful are Thy works; and that my soul knoweth right well.

[15] My frame was not hidden from Thee, when I was made in secret, and curiously wrought in the lowest parts of the earth.

[16] Thine eyes did see mine unformed substance, and in Thy book they were all written—even the days that were fashioned, when as yet there was none of them.

[17] How weighty also are Thy thoughts unto me, O God! How great is the sum of them!

[18] If I would count them, they are more in number than the sand; were I to come to the end of them, I would still be with Thee.

[19] If Thou but wouldest slay the wicked, O God—depart from me therefore, ye men of blood;

[20] Who utter Thy name with wicked thought, they take it for falsehood, even Thine enemies—

[21] Do not I hate them, *YHVH*, that hate Thee? And do not I strive with those that rise up against Thee?

[22] I hate them with utmost hatred; I count them mine enemies.

[23] Search me, O God, and know my heart, try me, and know my thoughts;
[24] And see if there be any way in me that is grievous, and lead me in the way everlasting.

Psalm 139 is said to have been composed by the primordial ancestor Adam.[1] Whilst it is not included in Jewish liturgies, it is listed in Dr. Seligmann Baer's *Siddur Avodat Yisra'el* as the psalm of *Shabbat Bereishit*,[2] i.e. the Sabbath of a new beginning. This is the first Sabbath after שמחת תורה (*Simchat Torah*— "Rejoicing with the *Torah*"), which marks the beginning of a new cycle at the conclusion of the Jewish New Year celebrations.[3] The current psalm is noted in Jewish Magic to be good for the purpose of reawakening love between husband and wife.[4] This psalm is not included in every published Hebrew edition of the *Shimmush Tehillim*, but it does feature in the manuscripts of this text.[5] In one of these the current psalm is dealt with in a somewhat more complex manner. In this instance, the procedure of establishing love between spouses, necessitates copying the psalm with the name of the man, this being done with the blood of a white dove, or white hen, on calf skin. As in the case of the previous psalm, the writing is dissolved, this time in plain clean water, and the liquid afterwards consumed by the couple. The procedure is concluded with the following prayer-incantation:

דרוריאל חבושיאל אתם שמות הקדושים עשו
בקשתי זאת ל[....name of recipient....] ושתהיה
אהבה בין איש [....name of husband....] ובין אישתו
[....name of wife....] אמן סלה

Transliteration:
D'rori'el Chavushi'el atem shemot hak'doshim asu b'kashati zot l'[....name of recipient....] v'shitih'yeh ahavah bein ish [....name of husband....] ubein ish'to [....name of wife....] Omein Selah.

Translation:
D'rori'el Chavushi'el, holy names, grant this my request for [....name of recipient....], and there will be love between the man [....name of husband....] and his woman [....name of wife....]. Amen Selah.[6]

Besides being used to establish and preserve marital love, the current psalm is recommended as a plea for divine guidance, and is also enunciated during a birth.[7] I have further seen it recommended against malice, to be saved from slander and gossip, as well as against witchcraft and bewitchment.

In Christian Magic *Psalms 139, 140* and *141* are referenced conjointly in the Byzantine Christian magical manuscripts for establishing peace between friends following a quarrel. In this regard, the said psalms are enunciated seven times over water, and the liquid disposed of at the homes of the friends, and, it is said, harmony will be restored.[8] By contrast, the *"Livre d'Or"* maintains *Psalm 139* should be enunciated seven times a day, in order for the Divine One to "make you contrite with true penitence from your bawdiness and from adultery," and to save you.[9] The current psalm is also one of nineteen mentioned in the *"Key of Solomon,"* i.e. *Psalms 8, 15, 22, 46, 47, 49, 51, 53, 68, 72, 84, 102, 110, 113, 126, 130, 131,* 133, and 139, which are enunciated over the wax from which ritual candles are manufactured.[10]

PSALM 140

[1] למנצח מזמור לדוד

[2] חלצני יהוה^{אדני}־אהדונהי מאדם רע מאיש חמסים
תנצרני

[3] אשר חשבו רעות בלב כל יום יגורו מלחמות

[4] שננו לשונם כמו נחש חמת עכשוב תחת שפתימו
סלה

[5] שמרני יהוה^{אדני}־אהדונהי מידי רשע מאיש חמסים
תנצרני אשר חשבו לדחות פעמי

[6] טמנו גאים פח לי וחבלים פרשו רשת ליד מעגל
מקשים שתו יל סלה

[7] אמרתי ליהוה^{אדני}־אהדונהי אלי אתה האזינה
יהוה^{אדני}־אהדונהי קול תחנוני

[8] יהוה^{אדני}־אהדונהי אדני עז ישועתי סכתה לראשי
ביום נשק

[9] אל תתן יהוה^{אדני}־אהדונהי מאויי רשע זממו אל
תפק ירומי סלה

[10] ראש מסבי עמל שפתימו יכסמו

[11] ימוטו עליהם גחלים באש יפלם במהמרות
בל יקומו

[12] איש לשון בל יכון בארץ איש חמס רע
יצודנו למדחפת

[13] ידעתי כי יעשה יהוה^{אדני}־אהדונהי דין עני
משפט אבינים

[14] אך צדיקים יודו לשמך ישבו ישרים את פניך

Transliteration:

[1] *lam'natzei'ach miz'mor l'david*

[2] *chal'tzeini YHVH mei'adam ra mei'ish chamasim tin'tz'reini*

[3] *asher chash'vu ra'ot b'leiv kol yom yaguru mil'chamot*

[4] *shan'nu l'shonam k'mo nachash chamat ach'shuv tachat s'fateimo selah*

[5] *shom'reini YHVH midei rasha mei'ish chamasim tin'tz'reini asher chash'vu lid'chot p'amai*

[6] *tam'nu gei'im pach li va'chavalim par'su reshet l'yad ma'gal mok'shim shatu li selah*
[7] *amar'ti laYHVH eili atah ha'azinah YHVH kol tachanunai*
[8] *YHVH adonai oz y'su'ati sakotah l'roshi b'yom nashek*
[9] *al titein YHVH ma'avayei rasha z'mamo al tafeik yarumu selah*
[10] *rosh m'sibai amal s'fateimo y'chaseimo*
[11] *yimotu aleihem gechalim ba'eish yapileim b'mahamorot bal yakumu*
[12] *ish lashon bal yikon ba'aretz ish chamas ra y'tzudenu l'mad'cheifot*
[13] *yada'ti ki ya'aseh YHVH din ani mish'pat ev'yonim*
[14] *ach tzadikim yodu lish'mecha yeish'vu y'sharim et panecha*

Translation:

[1] For the Leader. A Psalm of David.
[2] Deliver me, *YHVH*, from the evil man; preserve me from the violent man;
[3] Who devise evil things in their heart; every day do they stir up wars.
[4] They have sharpened their tongue like a serpent; vipers' venom is under their lips. *Selah*
[5] Keep me, *YHVH*, from the hands of the wicked; preserve me from the violent man; who have purposed to make my steps slip.
[6] The proud have hid a snare for me, and cords; they have spread a net by the wayside; they have set gins for me. *Selah*
[7] I have said unto *YHVH*: 'Thou art my God'; give ear, *YHVH*, unto the voice of my supplications.
[8] *YHVH Adonai*, the strength of my salvation, who hast screened my head in the day of battle,
[9] Grant not, *YHVH*, the desires of the wicked; further not his evil device, so that they exalt themselves. *Selah*
[10] As for the head of those that compass me about, let the mischief of their own lips cover them.
[11] Let burning coals fall upon them; let them be cast into the fire, into deep pits, that they rise not up again.

[12] A slanderer shall not be established in the earth; the violent and evil man shall be hunted with thrust upon thrust.
[13] I know that *YHVH* will maintain the cause of the poor, and the right of the needy.
[14] Surely the righteous shall give thanks unto Thy name; the upright shall dwell in Thy presence.

Psalms 140—143 are said to "form a unity in that they are all personal prayers for deliverance against enemies."[1] As in the case of the previous two psalms, the current one does not feature in Jewish liturgies. However, in the Conservative *Siddur Lev Shalem* it is listed with *Psalms 120, 121,* and *130* for recitation "in times of tragedy."[2] Little use is also made of *Psalm 140* in *Practical Kabbalah,* and, as in the case of the previous psalm, it is likewise employed to improve relations between a man and his spouse. It is also one of the psalms which does not appear in every edition of the *Shimmush Tehillim.* However, it is enunciated in Jewish Magic for the purpose of eliminating hatred between marriage partners.[3] Whilst the current action simply demands the recitation of the psalm to affect the sought-after consequence of removing enmity, a variant recension of the *Shimmush Tehillim* listed the current psalm for the opposite, and very noxious purpose of provoking hatred between a husband and wife.[4] As noted before, such baneful actions have no place in this series of texts on Jewish Magic. It is worth noting that other than removing outright hostility between cohabitants, the current psalm has also been recommended to simply remove plain bad feelings between a man and his wife, as well as to increase respect amongst humans generally. It is also recited against anxiety caused by enemies, as well as against flattery. In conclusion, it is worth noting that *Psalm 140:2* is direcly affiliated with רדי (*Yeret*), the twenty-seventh tri-letter portion of the "Name of Seventy-two Names."[5]

As indicated earlier, *Psalms 139, 140* and *141* are referenced conjointly in the Byzantine Christian magical manuscripts in order to establish peace between quarreling friends,[6] and the said manuscripts further list the current psalm for recitation against blasphemy.[7] We also find the current psalm recommended in Christian Magic to individuals suffering from venemous tongues. The "*Livre d'Or*" maintains that one who has imbibed poison, could be saved by enunciating *Psalm 140:1—4* "seven times in the evening and seven times in the morning," over a period of seven days. In this regard, the practitioner is instructed to maintain a chaste disposition.[8]

PSALM 141

[1] מזמור לדוד יהוהאדני־יאהדונהי קראתיך חושה
לי האזינה קולי בקראי לך

[2] תכון תפלתי קטרת לפניך משאת כפי מנחת
ערב

[3] שיתה יהוהאדני־יאהדונהי שמרה לפי נצרה על דל
שפתי

[4] אל תט לבי לדבר רע להתעולל עללות ברשע
את אישים פעלי און ובל אלחם במנעמיהם

[5] יהלמני צדיק חסד ויוכיחני שמן ראש אל יני
ראשי כי עוד ותפלתי ברעותיהם

[6] נשמטו בידי סלע שפטיהם ושמעו אמרי כי נעמו

[7] כמו פלח ובקע בארץ נפזרו עצמינו לפי שאול

[8] כי אליך יהוהאדני־יאהדונהי אדני עיני בכה חסיתי
אל תער נפשי

[9] שמרני מידי פח יקשו לי ומקשות פעלי און

[10] יפלו במכמריו רשעים יחד אנכי עד אעבור

Transliteration:

[1] *miz'mor l'david YHVH k'raticha chushah li ha'azinah koli b'kor'i lach*

[2] *tikon t'filati k'toret l'fanecha mas'at kapai min'chat arev*

[3] *shitah YHVH sham'rah l'fi nitz'rah al dal s'fatai*

[4] *al tat libi l'davar ra l'hit'oleil alilot b'resha et ishim po'alei aven uval el'cham b'man'ameihem*

[5] *yehel'meini tzadik chesed v'yochicheini shemen rosh al yani roshi ki od ut'filati b'ra'oteihem*

[6] *nish'm'tu videi sela shof'teihem v'sham'u amarai ki na'eimu*

[7] *k'mo folei'ach uvokei'a ba'aretz nif'z'ru atzameinu l'fi sh'ol*

[8] *ki eilecha YHVH adonai einai b'chah chasiti al t'ar naf'shi*

[9] *shom'reini midei fach yak'shu li umok'shot po'alei aven*

[10] *yip'lu v'mach'morav r'sha'im yachad anochi ad e'evor*

Translation:

[1] A Psalm of David. *YHVH*, I have called Thee; make haste unto me; give ear unto my voice, when I call unto Thee.

[2] Let my prayer be set forth as incense before Thee, the lifting up of my hands as the evening sacrifice.

[3] Set a guard, *YHVH*, to my mouth; keep watch at the door of my lips.

[4] Incline not my heart to any evil thing, to be occupied in deeds of wickedness with men that work iniquity; and let me not eat of their dainties.

[5] Let the righteous smite me in kindness, and correct me; oil so choice let not my head refuse; for still is my prayer because of their wickedness.

[6] Their judges are thrown down by the sides of the rock; and they shall hear my words, that they are sweet.

[7] As when one cleaveth and breaketh up the earth, our bones are scattered at the grave's mouth.

[8] For mine eyes are unto Thee, *YHVH Adonai*; in Thee have I taken refuge, O pour not out my soul.

[9] Keep me from the snare which they have laid for me, and from the gins of the workers of iniquity.

[10] Let the wicked fall into their own nets, whilst I withal escape.

Psalm 141 is enunciated in the Yemenite rite every day after the weekday *Min'chah* (afternoon prayers), and the second verse is recited by Mizrachi Jews at the commencement of the afternoon service.[1] This psalm is associated with *Psalm 140* in several ways, the most obvious said to be "the fear of the destructive power of speech."[2] However, whilst the previous psalm addressed the "Evil Tongue," the current one deals with guarding the lips. Verily it has been said that "death and life are in the power of the tongue, and those who love it will eat its fruits." [*Proverbs 18:21*] In this regard, it should be kept in mind that many wars past, and many more yet to come, were and will be fought over speech. The foundation of "evil speech" is often envy and resentment, i.e. the

"Evil Eye," and we are informed that *Psalm 141:4* "is a talisman against various bodily openings being invaded by, or being the source for, the evil spirits of jealous envy that would then cause a person to cast an evil eye upon someone else."[3]

We are told in Jewish Magic that the current psalm is good to recite for pain in the heart (heartache),[4] or for heart-disease.[5] It has been suggested that the reference to "my heart" in the fourth verse "may be the reason for this suggestion, but it is not clear whether this relates to physical or to emotional suffering."[6] This is probably why Godfrey Selig interpreted the expression "pain in the heart" quite differently in his German/English version of the *Shimmush Tehillim*, in which he noted that "whoever is often oppressed with heartfelt fears should pray this Psalm frequently."[7] Nothing even remotely similar is mentioned regarding the current psalm in the said text. It has been observed that "since the next three psalms are designated, according to *Shimmush Tehillim*, as remedies for various physical illnesses, it seems plausible that this applies also to our psalm,"[8] and this is indeed the case as far as the magical application of the current psalm is concerned. In this regard, an amuletic application of *Psalm 141* for ailments of the heart is listed in a variant recension of the *Shimmush Tehillim*. Here the practitioner is instructed to write the psalm on kosher parchment, suspend it on the left arm, and to conclude with the following prayer-incantation:

[....name of recipient....] ברקותיאל טופניאל תשיבו לב

ורפאוהו בשם יהוה צבאות אמן אמן אמן סלה סלה

סלה

Transliteration:
> *Bar'kuti'el Tuf'ni'el tashivu lev* [....name of recipient....]
> *urafa'eihu b'shem YHVH Tz'vaot Omein Omein Omein Selah Selah Selah.*

Translation:
> *Bar'kuti'el Tuf'ni'el* restore the heart of [....name of recipient....], and heal it in the name of *YHVH* of Hosts. *Amen Amen Amen Selah Selah Selah.*[9]

Other than these applications, *Psalm 141* is said to be one of the psalms traditionally recited when a woman is suffering a difficult labour.[10] I have also seen it recommended against enemies in unofficial sources, and it is likewise applied for this purpose in Christian Magic. In this regard, the *"Livre d'Or"* informs those who should chance upon "scoundrels," to recite *Psalm 141* seven times, which is said will facilitate being "delivered from them through the aid of God."[11]

PSALM 142

‎[1] מַשְׂכִּיל לְדָוִד בִּהְיוֹתוֹ בַמְּעָרָה תְפִלָּה
‎[2] קוֹלִי אֶל יְהוָהאדני־יאהדונהי אֶזְעָק קוֹלִי אֶל
‎יְהוָהאדני־יאהדונהי אֶתְחַנָּן
‎[3] אֶשְׁפֹּךְ לְפָנָיו שִׂיחִי צָרָתִי לְפָנָיו אַגִּיד
‎[4] בְּהִתְעַטֵּף עָלַי רוּחִי וְאַתָּה יָדַעְתָּ נְתִיבָתִי
‎בְּאֹרַח זוּ אֲהַלֵּךְ טָמְנוּ פַח לִי
‎[5] הַבֵּיט יָמִין וּרְאֵה וְאֵין לִי מַכִּיר אָבַד מָנוֹס
‎מִמֶּנִּי אֵין דּוֹרֵשׁ לְנַפְשִׁי
‎[6] זָעַקְתִּי אֵלֶיךָ יְהוָהאדני־יאהדונהי אָמַרְתִּי אַתָּה
‎מַחְסִי חֶלְקִי בְּאֶרֶץ הַחַיִּים
‎[7] הַקְשִׁיבָה אֶל רִנָּתִי כִּי דַלּוֹתִי מְאֹד הַצִּילֵנִי
‎מֵרֹדְפַי כִּי אָמְצוּ מִמֶּנִּי
‎[8] הוֹצִיאָה מִמַּסְגֵּר נַפְשִׁי לְהוֹדוֹת אֶת שְׁמֶךָ בִּי
‎יַכְתִּרוּ צַדִּיקִים כִּי תִגְמֹל עָלָי

Transliteration:

[1] *mas'kil l'david bih'yoto vam'arah t'filah*

[2] *koli el YHVH ez'ak koli el YHVH et'chanan*

[3] *esh'poch l'fanav sichi tzarati l'fanav agid*

[4] *b'hit'ateif alai ruchi v'atah yada'ta n'tivati b'orach zu ahaleich tam'nu fach li*

[5] *habeit yamin ur'eih v'ein li makir avad manos mimeni ein doreish l'naf'shi*

[6] *za'ak'ti eilecha YHVH amar'ti atah mach'si chel'ki b'eretz hachayim*

[7] *hak'shivah el rinati ki daloti m'od hatzileini meirod'fai ki am'tzu mimeni*

[8] *hotzi'ah mimas'geir naf'shi l'hodot et sh'mecha bi yach'tiru tzadikim ki tig'mol alai*

Translation:

[1] Maschil of David, when he was in the cave; a Prayer.

[2] With my voice I cry unto *YHVH*; with my voice I make supplication unto *YHVH*.

[3] I pour out my complaint before Him, I declare before Him my trouble;

[4] When my spirit fainteth within me—Thou knowest my path—in the way wherein I walk have they hidden a snare for me.

[5] Look on my right hand, and see, for there is no man that knoweth me; I have no way to flee; no man careth for my soul.

[6] I have cried unto Thee, *YHVH*; I have said: 'Thou art my refuge, my portion in the land of the living.'

[7] Attend unto my cry; for I am brought very low; deliver me from my persecutors; for they are too strong for me.

[8] Bring my soul out of prison, that I may give thanks unto Thy name; the righteous shall crown themselves because of me; for Thou wilt deal bountifully with me.

Psalm 142 is a prayer for deliverance which is linked to the previous two psalms by a common theme, which is said to be that the Divine One "protects those who are oppressed and in need."[1] The current psalm does not feature in Jewish worship, except again in the Yemenite rite, when it is enunciated with *Psalm 141* at the conclusion of the weekday *Min'chah* (afternoon prayers), "probably just as a continuation of the previous psalm."[2] This psalm is recommended to individuals who suffer pain and illness in the thighs,[3] whilst others claim it to be good for lumbago, i.e. severe pain in the lower back.[4] The current psalm does not appear in every published version of the *Shimmush Tehillim*, but in those editions and manuscripts in which it is included, it is said to be good to recite for ailments of the lower legs, i.e. shins and calves.[5] A variant recension of this text instructs those who suffer from a medical condition in the lower legs, to write *Psalm 142* with the name of the sufferer on the skin of a cat. The writing is afterwards suspended on the left foot of the recipient, and the action concluded with the following prayer-incantation:

בהרקיאל טהניאל רפאו [....name of recipient....]

מחליו ויקל מעליו חליו משוקיו בעגלא ובזמן קריב

אמן אמן סלה

Transliteration:

Bahar'ki'el Tahani'el (?) *r'fa'o* [....name of recipient....] *m'chol'yo v'yakel mei'alav chol'yo m'shukav b'agala uviz'man kariv Omein Omein Selah.*

Translation:

> *Bahar'ki'el Tahani'el* (?), heal [....name of recipient....]
> from his disease, and the disease in his legs should become
> easier for him, speedily and shortly. *Amen Amen Selah.*[6]

The same recension further maintains the current psalm is good to
say "in every affliction." This should be done evenings and
mornings with the following prayer-incantation:

יהי רצון מלפניך יהוה אלהי שתצילני מן הצרה
הזאת כשם שהצלת את דוד שהתפלל לפניך במערה
מפני שאול בשם אזבונה תורכוסיה

Transliteration:

> *Y'hi ratzon mil'fanecha YHVH elohai shetatzileini min
> hatzarah hazot k'shem sheheitzal'ta et david shehit'palel
> l'fanecha b'ma'arah mip'nei sha'ul b'shem Az'bunah
> [Azbugah (?)] Tor'chus'yah.*

Translation:

> May it be your will, *YHVH* my God, to deliver me from
> this affliction, just as you delivered David, who prayed
> before you in the cave regarding Saul. In the name
> *Az'bunah [Azbugah (?)] Tor'chus'yah.*[7]

A very different use is made of *Psalm 142:8*, which is included in
the following amulet to strengthen an infant during a difficult
childbirth:[8]

As I stated elsewhere,[9] this amulet was formulated in the following manner:

1.   Take a kosher scroll, i.e. clean parchment or paper, and write the threefold "magic square," i.e. the one associated with the planet Saturn, doing so in exact numerical order in the centre of the page.
2.   Continue by writing the three columns of letter/number combinations comprising the "magic square," respectively directly above, to the right, and to the left of the said square.
3.   Copy the *Digrammaton* (יה—*Yah*), the *gematria* of which [י = 10 + ה = 5 = 15] is equal to the numerical value of each row, column, and diagonal of the "magic square," is located directly below.
4.   Commencing at the bottom, and writing from right to left, encircle the central *chotam* (seal) with the words of *Psalm 142:8*.
5.   Conclude by ensuring that the amulet is placed with the writing against the stomach of the woman in labour.

Moses Zacutto commented that this amulet was tried and tested.[10] As noted elsewhere, I have seen this amulet tied in the very same manner to the solar plexus of individuals (both adults and children), in order to "strengthen" the wearers in times of great trouble and stress.[11] In this regard, it should be noted that *Psalm 142* is recommended for recitation against disasters generally, especially against those of the unforseen kind. In fact, the current psalm has been employed against threats, for protection in perilous situations, and in times of trouble.[12] It is enunciated for a large variety of purposes in "unofficial sources," i.e. it is uttered for the safety and well-being of places (locales), and is one of the psalms narrated when there is a crisis in the Land of Israel.[13] It is further recited for captives, against fierce persecution, and for all manner of distress, including anxiety caused by enemies. This psalm is also enunciated against abandonment, when feeling forsaken, and in support of the masses.

       On a more personal note, *Psalm 142* is recommended to individuals who seek honest love, and is suggested to men for marriage. It is enunciated for choice in life, and success in business. Religionists and others who feel the need to do penance, will find the current psalm recommended for atonement and penitence. As far as physical health is concerned, we noted that this psalm is mainly for illness of the thighs and lower legs, but it is also employed for illness and healing in general.

Similarly to the enunciation of the current psalm for captives in Jewish Magic, *Psalm 142* is recommended in Christian Magic to those who are incarcerated. In this regard, the psalm is spoken up to the phrase "bring my soul out of prison" [verse 8], This is done seven times in the morning, and likewise in the evening. It is said that with the "Grace of God," the captives will be freed.[14]

PSALM 143

‎[1] מזמור לדוד יהוה‏אדני‏אהדונהי שמע תפלתי האזינה אל תחנוני באמנתך ענני בצדקתך

‎[2] ואל תבוא במשפט את עבדך כי לא יצדק לפניך כל חי

‎[3] כי רדף אויב נפשי דכא לארץ חיתי הושבני במחשכים כמתי עולם

‎[4] ותתעטף עלי רוחי בתוכי ישתומם לבי

‎[5] זכרתי ימים מקדם הגיתי בכל פעלך במעשה ידיך אשוחח

‎[6] פרשתי ידי אליך נפשי כארץ עיפה לך סלה

‎[7] מהר ענני יהוה‏אדני‏אהדונהי כלתה רוחי אל תסתר פניך ממני ונמשלתי עם ירדי בור

‎[8] השמיעני בבקר חסדך כי בך בטחתי הודיעני דרך זו אלך כי אליך נשאתי נפשי

‎[9] הצילני מאיבי יהוה‏אדני‏אהדונהי אליך כסתי

‎[10] למדני לעשות רצונך כי אתה אלוהי רוחך טובה תנחני בארץ מישור

‎[11] למען שמך יהוה‏אדני‏אהדונהי תחיני בצדקתך תוציא מצרה נפשי

‎[12] ובחסדך תצמית איבי והאבדת כל צררי נפשי כי אני עבדך

Transliteration:

[1] *miz'mor l'david YHVH sh'mah t'filati ha'azinah el tachanunai be'emunat'cha aneini b'tzid'katecha*

[2] *v'al tavo v'mish'pat et av'decha ki lo yitz'dak l'fanecha chol chai*

[3] *ki radaf oyeiv naf'shi dika la'aretz chayati hoshivani v'machashakim k'meitei olam*

[4] *vatit'ateif alai ruchi b'tochi yish'tomeim libi*

[5] *zachar'ti yamim mikedem hagiti v'chol po'olecha b'ma'aseih yadecha asochei'ach*

[6] *peiras'ti yadai eilecha naf'shi k'eretz ayeifah l'cha selah*

[7] *maheir aneini YHVH kal'tah ruchi al tas'teir panecha mimeni v'nim'shal'ti im yor'dei vor*

[8] *hash'mi'eini vaboker chas'decha ki v'cha vatach'ti hodi'eini derech zu eileich ki eilecha nasati naf'shi*

[9] *hatzileini mei'oy'vai YHVH eilecha chisiti*

[10] *lam'deini la'asot r'tzonecha ki atah elohai ruchacha tovah tan'cheini b'eretz mishor*

[11] *l'ma'an shim'cha YHVH t'chayeini b'tzid'kat'cha totzi mitzarah naf'shi*

[12] *uv'chas'd'cha tatz'mit oy'vai v'ha'avad'ta kol tzorarei naf'shi ki ani av'decha*

Translation:

[1] A Psalm of David. *YHVH*, hear my prayer, give ear to my supplications; in Thy faithfulness answer me, and in Thy righteousness.

[2] And enter not into judgment with Thy servant; for in Thy sight shall no man living be justified.

[3] For the enemy hath persecuted my soul; he hath crushed my life down to the ground; he hath made me to dwell in darkness, as those that have been long dead.

[4] And my spirit fainteth within me; my heart within me is appalled.

[5] I remember the days of old; I meditate on all Thy doing; I muse on the work of Thy hands.

[6] I spread forth my hands unto Thee; my soul thirsteth after Thee, as a weary land. *Selah*

[7] Answer me speedily, *YHVH*, my spirit faileth; hide not Thy face from me; lest I become like them that go down into the pit.

[8] Cause me to hear Thy lovingkindness in the morning, for in Thee do I trust; cause me to know the way wherein I should walk, for unto Thee have I lifted up my soul.

[9] Deliver me from mine enemies, *YHVH*; with Thee have I hidden myself.

[10] Teach me to do Thy will, for Thou art my God; let Thy good spirit lead me in an even land.

[11] For Thy name's sake, *YHVH*, quicken me; in Thy righteousness bring my soul out of trouble.

[12] And in Thy mercy cut off mine enemies, and destroy all them that harass my soul; for I am Thy servant.

Psalm 143 is not included in any Jewish liturgy. However, it is said that there was a tradition in which individuals were expected to recite this psalm as well as the following one on their deathbeds.[1] The current psalm is enunciated in Jewish Magic for ailments of the arms.[2] In this regard, Godfrey Selig noted in his German/English version of the *Shimmush Tehillim* that reciting this psalm "will remove tearing pains in the arms."[3] In a variant recension of the said text, we are told that *Psalm 143* is good for answering prayer, getting out of trouble, and for diseases of the arms. In this regard, the practitioner is instructed to write the psalm with the personal name of the recipient on calfskin parchment. This item is afterwards suspended on the right arm, and the procedure concluded with the following prayer-incantation:

הרקיאל והואל אתם מלאכים קדושים שלחו
רפואה שלימה ל[....name of recipient....] ורפאו
חולי של זרועותיו בעגלא ובזמן קריב אמן סלה

Transliteration:

> *Har'ki'el Veho'el atem malachim k'doshim shel'chu r'fu'ah sh'leimah l'[....name of recipient....] v'rif'u choli shel z'ro'otav b'agala uviz'man kariv Omein Selah.*

Translation:

> *Har'ki'el* and *Veho'el*, holy angels, send full healing to [....name of recipient....], and heal the ailment of his arms speedily and timeously. *Amen Selah.*[4]

I have seen *Psalm 143* recommended for public disasters; protection in perilous situations, and in times of trouble; to halt wars; and for peace. Other than that, it is recited for the "fruits of the earth"; the fecundity of animals; and for the home. It is further suggested to those who suffer confusion in their religious beliefs. It is further recommended against illness, as well as for healing in general. In this regard, the initials of the first eight words of *Psalm 143:1* were conjoined in the Divine Name construct מל ישתהאת, which is included in amulets against epilepsy.[5]

The current psalm is listed in the Byzantine Christian magical manuscripts against catalepsy.[6] The same manuscripts recommend this psalm "for a plague of hail," and when an individual is "disturbed by enemies."[7] According to the "*Livre d'Or*," writing and reading *Psalm 143:1—9* will aid in being freed from prison, and it is said to have the same effect "if you are in any kind of difficulty."[8]

PSALM 144

‫[1] לדוד ברוך יהוה‪אדני‬‪אהדונהי‬ צורי המלמד ידי לקרב אצבעותי למלחמה‬

‫[2] חסדי ומצודתי משגבי ומפלטי לי מגני ובו חסיתי הרודד עמי תחתי‬

‫[3] יהוה‪אדני‬‪אהדונהי‬ מה אדם ותדעהו בן אנוש ותחשבהו‬

‫[4] אדם להבל דמה ימיו כצל עובר‬

‫[5] יהוה‪אדני‬‪אהדונהי‬ הט שמיך ותרד גע בהרים ויעשנו‬

‫[6] ברוק ברק ותפיצם שלח חציך ותהמם‬

‫[7] שלח ידיך ממרום פצני והצילני ממים רבים מיד בני נכר‬

‫[8] אשר פיהם דבר שוא וימינם ימין שקר‬

‫[9] אלהים שיר חדש אשירה לך בנבל עשור אזמרה לך‬

‫[10] הנותן תשועה למלכים הפוצה את דוד עבדו מחרב רעה‬

‫[11] פצני והצילני מיד בני נכר אשר פיהם דבר שוא וימינם ימין שקר‬

‫[12] אשר בנינו כנטעים מגדלים בנעוריהם בנותינו כזוית מחטבות תבנית היכל‬

‫[13] מזוינו מלאים מפיקים מזן אל זן צאוננו מאליפות מרבבות בחוצותינו‬

‫[14] אלופינו מסבלים אין פרץ ואין יוצאת ואין צוחה ברחבתינו‬

‫[15] אשרי העם שככה לו אשרי העם שיהוה‪אדני‬‪אהדונהי‬ אלהיו‬

Transliteration:

[1] *l'david baruch YHVH tzuri ham'lameid yadai lak'rav etz'b'otai lamil'chamah*

[2] *chas'di um'tzudati mis'gabi um'fal'ti li magini uvo chasiti harodeid ami tach'tai*

[3] *YHVH mah adam vateida'eihu ben enosh vat'chash'veihu*

[4] *adam lahevel damah yamav k'tzeil oveir*

[5] *YHVH hat shamecha v'teireid ga beharim v'ye'eshanu*

[6] *b'rok barak ut'fitzeim sh'lach chitzecha ut'humeim*

[7] *sh'lach yadecha mimarom p'tzeini v'hatzileini mimayim rabim miyad b'nei neichar*

[8] *asher pihem diber shav viminam y'min shaker*

[9] *Elohim shir chadash ashirah lach b'neivel asor azam'rah lach*

[10] *hanotein t'shu'ah lam'lachim hapotzeh et david av'do meicherev ra'ah*

[11] *p'tzeini v'hatzileini miyad b'nei neichar asher pihem diber shav viminam y'min shaker*

[12] *asher baneinu kin'ti'im m'gudalim bin'ureihem b'noteinu ch'zaviyot m'chutavot tav'nit heichal*

[13] *m'zaveinu m'lei'im m'fikim mizan el zan tzoneinu ma'alifot m'rubavot b'chutzoteinu*

[14] *alufeinu m'subalim ein peretz v'ein yotzeit v'ein tz'vachah bir'chovoteinu*

[15] *ash'rei ha'am shekachah lo ash'rei ha'am sheYHVH elohav*

Translation:

[1] A Psalm of David. Blessed be *YHVH* my Rock, who traineth my hands for war, and my fingers for battle;

[2] My lovingkindness, and my fortress, my high tower, and my deliverer; my shield, and He in whom I take refuge; who subdueth my people under me.

[3] *YHVH*, what is man, that Thou takest knowledge of him? or the son of man, that Thou makest account of him?

[4] Man is like unto a breath; his days are as a shadow that passeth away.

[5] *YHVH*, bow Thy heavens, and come down; touch the mountains, that they may smoke.

[6] Cast forth lightning, and scatter them; send out Thine arrows, and discomfit them.

[7] Stretch forth Thy hands from on high; rescue me, and deliver me out of many waters, out of the hand of strangers;

[8] Whose mouth speaketh falsehood, and their right hand is a right hand of lying.

[9] *Elohim*, I will sing a new song unto Thee, upon a psaltery of ten strings will I sing praises unto Thee;

[10] Who givest salvation unto kings, who rescuest David Thy servant from the hurtful sword.

[11] Rescue me, and deliver me out of the hand of strangers, whose mouth speaketh falsehood, and their right hand is a right hand of lying.

[12] We whose sons are as plants grown up in their youth; whose daughters are as corner-pillars carved after the fashion of a palace;

[13] Whose garners are full, affording all manner of store; whose sheep increase by thousands and ten thousands in our fields;

[14] Whose oxen are well laden; with no breach, and no going forth, and no outcry in our broad places;

[15] Happy is the people that is in such a case. Yea, happy is the people whose God is *YHVH*.

Psalm 144 is enunciated in Jewish liturgies on a Saturday night prior to *Arvit* (evening prayer service).[1] We are informed that the reason for saying psalms before the Saturday evening service is "to escort the departing Shabbos with song, just as it was welcomed with song when it arrived the day before."[2] As noted earlier, the Sabbath is perceived to be one of the personifications of the *Shechinah*, i.e. the "Feminine Aspect of Divinity." It is further maintained that reciting the current psalm, as well as *Psalm 67* on this occasion, is "because *Psalm 144* is considered to be protective....and *Psalm 67* has forty-nine words," the latter aligning with the forty-nine Sabbaths in a year, and equally with the forty-nine days of "*Sefirat ha-Omer*" (Counting of the Sheaves [of wheat]),[3] i.e. seven weeks of "intensive psycho-spiritual self examination and adjustment of ones personal being towards a mindful fulfilment of the most ideal existence on this planet, i.e. relating Self (Centre) to כל (*Kol*— 'All'), the 'Whole of Creation' (Circumference)."[4]

We are informed that *Psalm 144* is generally recommended for a broken hand.[5] The *Jewish Encyclopedia* maintains the current psalm is employed "to heal a fractured or dislocated hand,"[6] and elsewhere the psalm is said to be for a broken arm.[7] In this regard,

Godfrey Selig noted in his German/English translation of the *Shimmush Tehillim* that "when any one breaks an arm this Psalm should be prayed, and the perfect cure of the arm cannot be delayed or interrupted by untoward circumstances."[8] However, whilst the current psalm is again not included in all published versions of the *Shimmush Tehillim*, the application of the current psalm for a fractured hand is shared in some editions, as well as in primary manuscripts.[9] A variant recension of this text asserts this psalm should be written with the personal name of the injured individual, as well as the following prayer-incantation, directly on the fractured hand:

שברירִיאל נגפִיאל אתם שמות נקִיים הקלו מעל
[....name of recipient....] חליו אמן אמן אמן סלה סלה

Transliteration:
> *Shab'riri'el Nag'fi'el atem shemot n'kiyim heikalu mei'al* [....name of recipient....] *chol'yo Omein Omein Omein Selah Selah.*

Translation:
> *Shab'riri'el Nag'fi'el*, you pure names lighten the plight of [....name of recipient....], *Amen Amen Amen Selah Selah.*[10]

The *Shimmush Tehillim* further maintains that this psalm is good for protection against מזיקים (*Mazikim*—"Harmful Spirits") and שדים (*Shedim*—"Evil Spirits").[11] On this point, it was noted that *Psalm 144* is for "protection against danger and demons,"[12] and it was said that this dual function of the current psalm, "can be explained on the basis of mentioning hands and fingers (v. 1) and thanking God for being a shield and a shelter (v. 2)."[13] *Psalm 144* is put to exactly such use in the earlier mentioned recension of "*The Book of Abramelin the Mage.*" In this regard, we are told that an individual who was chased into mountains by enemies who are pursuing him/her, and from whom there is no escape, should remove his/her shoes, turn to face in the direction from whence the enemies are coming, raise his/her eyes heavenwards, and utter *Psalm 144:5—6* seven times. Following this action, the said individual is instructed to throw the left shoe in the direction via which he/she is seeking to escape, or "run boldly in that direction," and having taken seven steps, to cast the right shoe over the head behind him/her without a backward glance. Then continue with confidence that there will be a miraculous escape from the enemies.[14]

As far as single verses are concerned, the initials of the words comprising *Psalm 144:2* were conjoined into the Divine Name construct חומו למו חדעת, which is included in an amulet "for protection at sea."[15] *Psalm 144:14* is employed in a very unique magical procedure, which is meant to impact the newly born in a specific manner. In this instance, the following Divine Name construct was formulated from the capitals of the first eight words of the verse, with an additional א (*Alef*), as well as the first three letters of the concluding word, all of which are intertwined with the four appearances of the Ineffable Name in the psalm:

$$\text{יְאַהְמְוָאָה יַאְהַפֱוּוֹה יְיֶהֱוֱוֹצֶה יְבֶהֱרְוֹחֶה}$$

The vowels associated with the four appearances of the Ineffrable Name, are said to be those traditionally associated with the first four *Sefirot*, i.e. *Keter* to *Chesed*. In terms of this Divine Name construct being employed to impact the newborn, the practitioner is instruct to create a small breast-shaped silver container, with an opening at its back. The said Divine Name construct is written on deerskin parchment, and located inside this recepticle, which is then held to the lips of the infant to briefly suck on, prior to him/her being suckled by the mother. It is said that "it will be shown with supreme grace that the child will be steadfast in his faith, and will not at all succumb to boredom."[16]

In Christian Magic it is noted in the "*Livre d'Or*" that reciting *Psalm 144*, and afterwards carrying certain magical symbols, will ensure victory in battles. The same text maintains the psalm is beneficial when copied on the hip of a woman in labour, and that reciting *Psalm 144:1—7* will ensure an individual is saved in a shipwreck.[17]

PSALM 145

[1] תהלה לדוד **ארוממך** אלוהי המלך **ואברכה** שמך לעולם ועד

[2] בכל יום **אברכך** ואהללה שמך לעולם ועד

[3] גדול **יהוה**אדני·יאהדונהי ומהלל **מאד** ולגדלתו **אין** חקר

[4] דור לדור ישבח מעשיך וגבורתיך יגידו

[5] הדר כבוד הודך ודברי **נפלאתיך** אשיחה

[6] ועזוז נוראתיך יאמרו וגדולתך **אספרנה**

[7] זכר רב **טובך** יביעו וצדקתך ירננו

[8] חנון ורחום **יהוה**אדני·יאהדונהי **ארך** אפים **וגדל** חסד

[9] טוב **יהוה**אדני·יאהדונהי לכל ורחמיו על כל מעשיו

[10] יודוך **יהוה**אדני·יאהדונהי כל מעשיך וחסידיך יברכוכה

[11] כבוד מלכותך יאמרו וגבורתך ידברו

[12] להודיע לבני **האדם** גבורתיו וכבוד הדר מלכותו

[13] מלכותך מלכות כל עלמים וממשלתך בכל דור ודר

[14] סומך **יהוה**אדני·יאהדונהי לכל הנפלים **וזוקף** לכל הכפופים

[15] עיני כל **אליך** ישברו ואתה נותן להם את **אכלם** בעתו

[16] **פותח את** ידך ומשביע לכל חי רצון

[17] צדיק **יהוה**אדני·יאהדונהי בכל דרכיו וחסיד בכל מעשיו

[18] קרוב **יהוה**אדני·יאהדונהי לכל קראיו לכל **אשר** יקראהו באמת

[19] רצון יראיו יעשה ואת שועתם ישמע ויושיעם

[20] שומר **יהוה**אדני·יאהדונהי·את כל אהביו ואת כל הרשעים ישמיד

[21] תהלת יהוהאדני־אהדוני־יאהדונהי ידבר פי ויברך כל בשר
שם קדשו לעולם ועד

Transliteration:

[1] *t'hilah l'david aromim'cha elohai hamelech va'avar'cha shim'cha l'olam va'ed*

[2] *b'chol yom avar'cheka va'ahal'lah shim'cha l'olam va'ed*

[3] *gadol YHVH um'hulal m'od v'lig'dulato ein cheiker*

[4] *dor l'dor y'shabach ma'asecha ug'vurotecha yagidu*

[5] *hadar k'vod hodecha v'div'rei nif'l'otecha asichah*

[6] *ve'ezuz nor'otecha yomeiru ug'dulat'cha asap'renah*

[7] *zicher rav tuv'cha yabi'u v'tzid'kat'cha y'raneinu*

[8] *chanun v'rachum YHVH erech apayim ug'dol chased*

[9] *tov YHVH lakol v'rachamav al kol ma'asav*

[10] *yoducha YHVH kol ma'asecha vachasidecha y'var'chuchah*

[11] *k'vod mal'chut'cha yomeiru ug'vurat'cha y'dabeiru*

[12] *l'hodi'a liv'nei ha'adam g'vurotav uch'vod hadar mal'chuto*

[13] *mal'chut'cha malchut kol olamim umem'shel't'cha b'chol dor vador*

[14] *someich YHVH l'chol hanof'lim v'zokeif l'chol hak'fufim*

[15] *einei chol eilecha y'sabeiru v'atah notein lahem et och'lam b'ito*

[16] *potei'ach et yadecha umas'bi'a l'chol chai ratzon*

[17] *tzadik YHVH b'chol d'rachav v'chasid b'chol ma'asav*

[18] *karov YHVH l'chol kor'av l'chol asher yik'ra'uhu ve'emet*

[19] *r'tzon y'rei'av ya'aseh v'et shav'atam yish'ma v'yoshi'eim*

[20] *shomeir YHVH et kol ohavav v'eit kol har'sha'im yash'mid*

[21] *t'hilat YHVH y'daber pi vivareich kol basar shem kod'sho l'olam va'ed*

Translation:

[1] A Psalm of praise; of David. I will extol Thee, my God, O King; and I will bless Thy name for ever and ever.

[2] Every day will I bless Thee; and I will praise Thy name for ever and ever.

[3] Great is *YHVH*, and highly to be praised; and His greatness is unsearchable.

[4] One generation shall laud Thy works to another, and shall declare Thy mighty acts.

[5] The glorious splendour of Thy majesty, and Thy wondrous works, will I rehearse.

[6] And men shall speak of the might of Thy tremendous acts; and I will tell of Thy greatness.

[7] They shall utter the fame of Thy great goodness, and shall sing of Thy righteousness.

[8] *YHVH* is gracious, and full of compassion; slow to anger, and of great mercy.

[9] *YHVH* is good to all; and His tender mercies are over all His works.

[10] All Thy works shall praise Thee, *YHVH*; and Thy saints shall bless Thee.

[11] They shall speak of the glory of Thy kingdom, and talk of Thy might;

[12] To make known to the sons of men His mighty acts, and the glory of the majesty of His kingdom.

[13] Thy kingdom is a kingdom for all ages, and Thy dominion endureth throughout all generations.

[14] *YHVH* upholdeth all that fall, and raiseth up all those that are bowed down.

[15] The eyes of all wait for Thee, and Thou givest them their food in due season.

[16] Thou openest Thy hand, and satisfiest every living thing with favour.

[17] *YHVH* is righteous in all His ways, and gracious in all His works.

[18] *YHVH* is nigh unto all them that call upon Him, to all that call upon Him in truth.

[19] He will fulfil the desire of them that fear Him; He also will hear their cry, and will save them.

[20] *YHVH* preserveth all them that love Him; but all the wicked will He destroy.

[21] My mouth shall speak the praise of *YHVH*; and let all flesh bless His holy name for ever and ever.

Psalm 145, a "song of praise," is the last of the acrostic psalms, i.e. those in which the verses are arranged in alphabetical order. However, in the current instance there is no verse commencing with the letter נ (*Nun*). Whilst there is yet much speculation regarding this letter being missing in the current psalm, it is worthwhile considering the observations in the *Sefer Yetzirah* ("Book of Creation") regarding the letter נ (*Nun*). We are informed that the Hebrew month of *Cheshvan*, and the zodiacal sign of *Akrav* (*Scorpio*) were "formed" with this letter.[1] As I noted elsewhere, "the 'missing' verse is said to indicate a sudden fall into error, this being suggested by the 'bent-over' נ (*Nun*). However, the succeeding verse, *Psalm 145:14*, beginning with the letter *Samech* (ס) reads '*YHVH* upholdeth all that fall, and raiseth up all those that are bowed down.' This is said to demonstrate the support of the Almighty, Who will raise the fallen who are 'bent over,' or who are in the condition indicated by נ (*Nun*)."[2] It has been noted that the "contrast between destruction and fall, on the one hand, and construction and essential stability, on the other, is a prominent theme of this month and is revealed through the letter *Nun*."[3] It is further said that, "in its negative aspect," the letter נ (*Nun*) is the capital of the word נפילה (*N'filah*—"fall"), and it is for this reason that "in King David's prayer *Ashrei* (*Psalms 145*), which praises God according to the aleph-beth, the verse of the letter *Nun* does not appear. Instead, the next letter takes over and sings, '*Somech Hashem lechol hanoflim*'—'God supports those who fall'."[4]

Psalms 145 to *150* are included in the collection of psalms termed פְּסוּקֵי דְזִמְרָא (*Pesukei d'Zimra*—"Verses of Song"), and is the first of six psalms which are enunciated every day. These psalms are collectively termed "*Halel* Psalms," since Psalms 146—150 all commence and end with the expression הַלְלוּ יָהּ (*hal'lu Yah*—"Hallelujah"). *Psalm 145* is included in this set due to the root of the word הַלֵּל (*Halel*—"praise") appearing in the first and concluding verse of this psalm.[5] The importance of the current psalm in Jewish worship is borne out by the fact that it is recited three times every day, i.e. in the beginning as well as at the conclusion of *Shacharit* (Morning Prayer Service), and again at the beginning of *Min'chah* (Afternoon Prayer Service).[6] It has been said that these daily repetitions of this psalm "is due to the phrase *l'olam va'ed*, 'forever and ever,' which appears three times in the Psalm."[7] Talmudic teaching noted that anyone who recites *Psalm 145* three times every day, is assured a place in "the world to come,"[8] [*TB Berachot 4b*] and this action is further said to be a "*segulah* for *parnasah*," i.e. a benevolent magical recipe for a good livelihood.[9] *Psalm 145:16*, which speaks of the generosity of the Divine One in satisfying "every living thing with favour," is of particular importance in Jewish Magic. It is said the seven words of this verse pertain to "the seven (*sheva*, שֶׁבַע) qualities (*midot*) upon which the satiety (*sova*, שֹׂבַע) of the world depends."[10]

We are told that "the source of nourishment is connected with the great trait of *Chesed* (kindness),"[11] and that for livelihood the said verse should be enunciated with great *Kavanah* (focused attention and intention) whilst "bearing in mind the meaning of the words."[12] It is further noted that if the words are not uttered with devotion, the verse should be repeated, and the following verses recited to the end of the psalm.[13] Those who follow this custom are told to "concentrate especially on the initials of the three words פּוֹתֵחַ אֶת יָדֶךָ (*potei'ach et yadecha*—'You open your hand'), which form the word פאי (*Pai*), one of the seventy-two names of God that are connected with *parnassah* (livelihood)."[14] It is customary in Sefardic communities to extend the open palm of the hand, when the said words are uttered during the daily recitations of the current psalm.[15] This is done "as a symbolic gesture toward heaven, and as a sign of receiving abundance from above."[16] The same action was recommended to practitioners of *Practical Kabbalah*,[17] and both the capitals as well as the concluding letters of the פּוֹתֵחַ אֶת יָדֶךָ (*potei'ach et yadecha*—"You open your hand") phrase, were formulated into Divine Name constructs, respectively פאי (*Pai* or *Poi*) and חתך (*Chatach*). They are regularly included in amulets for the purpose of charity, and to generate a good income.[18] The latter Divine Name construct was further transformed by means of the א"ת ב"ש (*Atbash*) cipher to read סאל (*Sal*), which we are told is the name of the Spirit Intelligence (angel) in charge of livelihood.[19]

It should be noted that *Psalm 145* is mainly employed in Jewish Magic to counteract fear.[20] In this regard, we are informed in the *Shimmush Tehillim* that this psalm is good for one who is overcome with fear. The said individual who has received a fright, is instructed to recite the current psalm three times, followed by *Psalm 91* which should be enuniated nine times.[21] Reasons are not given for this onset of fear, but that did not prevent Godfrey Selig from concocting his own. As readers have probably realised by now, much of what Selig wrote in his German/English translation of the *Shimmush Tehillim*, is of his own invention. Thus he remarked regarding the current psalm, that "he who fears ghosts and evil spirits, should pray this Psalm in connection with the *144th*, with reverence, for the praying of these Psalms will drive away all ghosts and apparitions instantly."[22]

A variant recension of the *Shimmush Tehillim* maintained the current psalm should be enunciated twice a day in order to open the "gates of mercy."[23] The same recension further recommended *Psalm 145* for healing purposes. In this instance, it is said the psalm should be written on the "skin of an elephant, or on its bones," which is to be suspended around a fractured foot. The practitioner is further instructed to conclude this action with the following prayer-incantation:

רפופיאל ברוכיאל עשו רפואה והצילו

[....name of recipient....] והקילו מעליו חליו זה

אמן אמן סלה סלה

Transliteration:
Rafufi'el (?) *B'ruchi'el asu r'fu'ah v'hatzilu* [....name of recipient....] *v'hakilu mei'alav chol'yo zeh Omein Omein Selah Selah.*

Translation:
Rafufi'el (?) *B'ruchi'el*, give healing and rescue [....name of recipient....], and relieve him from this ailment. *Amen Amen Selah Selah.*[24]

As far as the magical application of single verses is concerned, it should be noted that the initials of the first four words of *Psalm 145:18* were conjoined into the Divine Name construct קילק. It is included in amulets as a call for help.[25] We are also told that דיי (*Riyi*), the twenty-ninth tri-letter portion of the "*Shem Vayisa Vayet*," is an anagram of the first three words of *Psalm 145:19*.[26] It is also worth keeping in mind that *Psalm 145:3, 14* and *17* are respectively associated directly with והו (*Vehu*), נממ (*Nemem*), and יבמ (*Yabam*), i.e. the forty-ninth, fifty-seventh, and seventieth tri-letter portions of the "Name of Seventy-two Names."[27] Other than the listed applications, I have seen *Psalm 145* recommended not only against frightening experiences and being fearful, but to those who suffer fears generally. This psalm is further enunciated in support of orphans, and those who are widowed. It is also recited for strangers; the protection of paupers and beggars; and the release of prisoners. As far as physical health is concerned, the current psalm was said to be good for diseases of, and pain in, the eyes. In conclusion, it was suggested to those individuals who seek a more mindful interaction with their pets, to recite *Psalm 145:9* whenever they are stroking a pet.[28]

    Psalm 145 is employed in the Byzantine Christian magical manuscripts for the purpose of defeating opponents in court. In this regard, it is written and torn up at the door of an opponent, which is coerced to step over it, following which it is said "go to court and you will defeat your enemies."[29] Elsewhere it is said that Christians use this psalms against fever,[30] regarding which Johann Weyer wrote "Another washes his hands with the patient during the rise of the fever and at its onset, he whispers the psalm which begins, 'Exaltabo te Deus meus rex' (Psalm 145)."[31]

PSALM 146

[1] הללו יה הללי נפשי את יהוה‎אדני‎יאהדונהי

[2] אהללה יהוה‎אדני‎יאהדונהי בחיי אזמרה לאלהי בעודי

[3] אל תבטחו בנדיבים בבן אדם שאין לו תשועה

[4] תצא רוחי ישב לאדמתו ביום ההוא אבדו עשתנתיו

[5] אשרי שאל יעקב בעזרו שברו על יהוה‎אדני‎יאהדונהי אלהיו

[6] עשה שמים וארץ את הים ושת כל אשר בם השמר אמת לעולם

[7] עשה משפט לעשוקים נתן לחם לרעבים יהוה‎אדני‎יאהדונהי מתיר אסורים

[8] יהוה‎אדני‎יאהדונהי פקח עורים יהוה‎אדני‎יאהדונהי זקף כפופים יהוה‎אדני‎יאהדונהי אהב צדיקים

[9] יהוה‎אדני‎יאהדונהי שמר את גרים יתום ואלמנה יעודד ודרך רשעים יעות

[10] ימלך יהוה‎אדני‎יאהדונהי לעולם אלהיך ציון לדר ודר הללו יה

Transliteration:

[1] *hal'lu Yah hal'li naf'shi et YHVH*
[2] *ahal'lah YHVH b'chayai azam'rah leilohai b'odi*
[3] *al tiv't'chu vin'divim b'ven adam she'ein lo t'shu'ah*
[4] *teitzei rucho yashuv l'ad'mato bayom hahu av'du esh'tonotav*
[5] *ash'rei she'eil ya'akov b'ez'ro siv'ro al YHVH elohav*
[6] *oseh shamayim va'aretz et chayam v'et kol asher bam hashomeir emet l'olam*
[7] *oseh mish'pat la'ashukim notein lechem lar'eivim YHVH matir asurim*
[8] *YHVH pokei'ach iv'rim YHVH zokeif k'fufim YHVH oheiv tzadikim*
[9] *YHVH shomeir et geirim yatom v'al'manah y'odeid v'derech r'sha'im y'aveit*

[10] *yim'loch YHVH l'olam elohayich tziyon l'dor vador hal'lu Yah*

Translation:

[1] Hallelujah. Praise *YHVH*, O my soul.

[2] I will praise *YHVH* while I live; I will sing praises unto my God while I have my being.

[3] Put not your trust in princes, nor in the son of man, in whom there is no help.

[4] His breath goeth forth, he returneth to his dust; in that very day his thoughts perish.

[5] Happy is he whose help is the God of Jacob, whose hope is in *YHVH* his God,

[6] Who made heaven and earth, the sea, and all that in them is; who keepeth truth for ever;

[7] Who executeth justice for the oppressed; who giveth bread to the hungry. *YHVH* looseth the prisoners;

[8] *YHVH* openeth the eyes of the blind; *YHVH* raiseth up them that are bowed down; *YHVH* loveth the righteous;

[9] *YHVH* preserveth the strangers; He upholdeth the fatherless and the widow; but the way of the wicked He maketh crooked.

[10] *YHVH* will reign for ever, Thy God, O Zion, unto all generations. Hallelujah.

Psalm 146 is the first of five psalms which commence and conclude with the expression *Hallelujah* ("praise *Yah*"), and the second of the set of six "*Halel* Psalms" enunciated daily in praise of the Divine One during the *Pesukei d'Zimrah* ("Verses of Song") portion of *Shacharit* (Morning Prayer Service).[1] In this regard, we are informed that this conforms with the statement in the *Talmud* [*TB Shabbat 188b*] that Rabbi Josei said "may my portion be among those who recite the entire Halel every day."[2] As far as magical applications of the current psalm is concerned, it should be noted that whilst the current psalm is not included in every published version of the *Shimmush Tehillim*, in those in which it does appear, this psalm is said to be good to enunciate when an individual was struck by a sword.[3] Selig heavily inflated this simple instruction in his German/English version of the *Shimmush Tehillim*, stating that "whoever has been dangerously wounded by a sword or other deadly weapon, he shall, during the time he is receiving surgical assistance, pray this Psalm reverently daily, and especially when the wound is being dressed and the bandages renewed, and he will shortly find reason to rejoice in a perfect restoration from his injuries."[4]

A variant recension of the *Shimmush Tehillim* maintains that when an individual was wounded by a sword, blood from the wound should be used to write down the psalm, the name of the injured person, as well as the following prayer-incantation on kosher parchment. This amulet is afterwards suspended around the neck of the said person. The following arrangement of the Angelic Names in the prayer-incantation is my own. In the original manuscript the reduction of the letters comprising the Angelic Name נדריאל (*N'dari'el*) is written in a single line. The prayer-incantation reads:

ברקותיאל טופניאל

נדריאל

דריאל

ריאל

יאל

אל

ל

אתון אותיות הקדוש הקלו מעל [....name of recipient....]
חוליו לבל יכבד עליו עוד אמן אמן אמן סלה סלה

Transliteration:

Bar'kuti'el Tof'ni'el N'dari'el [reduction of the letters of the latter Angelic Name], *aton otiyot hakadosh heikalu mei'al* [....name of recipient....] *chol'yo l'val yich'bad alav od Omein Omein Omein Selah Selah.*

Translation:

Bar'kuti'el Tof'ni'el N'dari'el [reduction of the letters of the latter Angelic Name], you letters of the Holy One, lighten the affliction of [....name of recipient....], so that it will not be a burden on him anymore. *Amen Amen Amen Selah Selah.*[5]

The same recension of the *Shimmush Tehillim* stated the psalm should be recited "with every trust in every word concerning the Holy One, Blessed be He."[6] In this regard, the worshipper is advised to include the following prayer-incantation:

יהי רצון מלפניך יהוה אלהי שתעניני ותרחמיני
כי אין מי שירחם עלי אלא אתה אמן אמן אמן
סלה סלה סלה

Transliteration:

Y'hi ratzon mil'fanecha YHVH elohai shet'aneini v'tarachameini ki ein mi shiyarachem alai ela atah Omein Omein Omein Selah Selah Selah.

Translation:

May it be your will *YHVH* my God, that you answer me and have mercy on me, for no one will have mercy on me but you. *Amen Amen Amen Selah Selah Selah.*

Psalm 146 is recited as a statement of trust, as well as to increase trust in the Divine One. Other than sword wounds, I have seen the current psalm recommended for the healing of all manner of stab and bullet wounds. It is also enunciated for a national force and welfare, as well as for rain.

It would seem little attention is paid to the current psalm in Christian Magic. The reference in the *"Livre d'Or"* equally pertains to matters of healing. In this regard, the psalm is enunciated seven times over oil, which is rubbed on an indisposed individual during a further recitation.[7] The said text also maintains that reading *Psalm 146:1—9*, and then rubbing broken bones with the oil, will ensure that "they will knit back together."[8]

PSALM 147

[1] הללו יה כי טוב זמרה אלהינו כי נעים נאוה
תהלה

[2] בונה ירושלם יהוה‏אדני‏יאהדונהי נדחי ישראל יכנס

[3] הרפא לשבורי לב ומחבש לעצבותם

[4] מונה מספר לכוכבים לכלם שמות יקרא

[5] גדול אדונינו ורב כח לתבונתו אין מספר

[6] מעודד ענוים יהוה‏אדני‏יאהדונהי משפיל רשעים עדי
ארץ

[7] ענו ליהוה‏אדני‏יאהדונהי בתודה זמרו לאלהינו בכנור

[8] המכסה שמים בעבים המכין לארץ מטר המצמיח
הרים חציר

[9] נותן לבהמה לחמה לבני ערב אשר יקראו

[10] לא בגבורת הסוס יחפץ לא בשוקי האיש ירצה

[11] רוצה יהוה‏אדני‏יאהדונהי את יראיו את המיחלים
לחסדו

[12] שבחי ירושלם את יהוה‏אדני‏יאהדונהי הללי אלהיך
ציון

[13] כי חזק בריחי שעריך ברך בניך בקרבך

[14] השם גבולך שלום חלב חטים ישביעך

[15] השלח אמרתו ארץ עד מהרה ירוץ דברו

[16] הנתן שלג כצמר כפור כאפר יפזר

[17] משליך קרחו כפתים לפני קרתו מי יעמד

[18] ישלח דברו וימסם ישב רוחו יזלו מים

[19] מגיד דבריו ליעקב חקיו ומשפטיו לישראל

[20] אל עשה כן לכל גוי ומשפטים בל ידעום
הללו יה

Transliteration:

[1] *hal'lu Yah ki tov zam'rah eloheinu ki na'im navah t'hilah*

[2] *boneih y'rushalam YHVH nid'chei yis'ra'eil y'chaneis*

[3] *harofei lish'vurei leiv um'chabeish l'atz'votam*

[4] *moneh mis'par lakochavim l'chulam sheimot yik'ra*

[5] *gadol adoneinu v'rav ko'ach lit'vunato ein mis'par*

[6] *m'odeid anavim YHVH mash'pil r'sha'im adei aretz*

[7] *enu laYHVH b'todah zam'ru leiloheinu v'chinor*

[8] *ham'chaseh shamayim b'avim hameichin la'aretz matar hamatz'mi'ach harim hatzir*

[9] *notein liv'heimah lach'mah liv'nei oreiv asher yik'ra'u*

[10] *lo vig'vurat hasus yech'patz lo v'shokei ha'ish yir'tzeh*

[11] *rotzeh YHVH et y'rei'av et ham'yachalim l'chas'do*

[12] *shab'chi y'rushalam et YHVH hal'li elohayich tziyon*

[13] *ki chizak b'richei sh'arayich beirach banayich b'kir'beich*

[14] *hasam g'vuleich shalom cheilev chitim yas'bi'eich*

[15] *hasholei'ach im'rato aretz ad m'heirah yarutz d'varo*

[16] *hanotein sheleg katzamer k'for ka'eifer y'fazeir*

[17] *mash'lich kar'cho ch'fitim lif'nei karato mi ya'amod*

[18] *yish'lach d'varo v'yam'seim yasheiv rucho yiz'lu mayim*

[19] *magid d'varav l'ya'akov chukav umish'patav l'yis'ra'eil*

[20] *lo asah chein l'chol goi umish'patim bal y'da'um hal'lu Yah*

Translation:

[1] Hallelujah; for it is good to sing praises unto our God; for it is pleasant, and praise is comely.

[2] *YHVH* doth build up Jerusalem, He gathereth together the dispersed of Israel;

[3] Who healeth the broken in heart, and bindeth up their wounds.

[4] He counteth the number of the stars; He giveth them all their names.

[5] Great is our Lord, and mighty in power; His understanding is infinite.

[6] *YHVH* upholdeth the humble; He bringeth the wicked down to the ground.

[7] Sing unto *YHVH* with thanksgiving, sing praises upon the harp unto our God;

[8] Who covereth the heaven with clouds, who prepareth rain for the earth, who maketh the mountains to spring with grass.

[9] He giveth to the beast his food, and to the young ravens which cry.

[10] He delighteth not in the strength of the horse; He taketh no pleasure in the legs of a man.

[11] *YHVH* taketh pleasure in them that fear Him, in those that wait for His mercy.

[12] Glorify *YHVH*, O Jerusalem; praise thy God, O Zion.

[13] For He hath made strong the bars of thy gates; He hath blessed thy children within thee.

[14] He maketh thy borders peace; He giveth thee in plenty the fat of wheat.

[15] He sendeth out His commandment upon earth; His word runneth very swiftly.

[16] He giveth snow like wool; He scattereth the hoar-frost like ashes.

[17] He casteth forth His ice like crumbs; who can stand before His cold?

[18] He sendeth forth His word, and melteth them; He causeth His wind to blow, and the waters flow.

[19] He declareth His word unto Jacob, His statutes and His ordinances unto Israel.

[20] He hath not dealt so with any nation; and as for His ordinances, they have not known them. Hallelujah

Psalm 147 is the second of five psalms which commence and conclude with the expression *Hallelujah* ("praise *Yah*"), and the third of the set of six "*Halel* Psalms" enunciated daily in the *Pesukei d'Zimrah* ("Verses of Song") portion of *Shacharit* (Morning Prayer Service).[1] In Jewish Magic this psalm is recommended to an individual who was bitten by a snake.[2] As in the case of the previous psalm, the current one does not feature in every published version of the *Shimmush Tehillim*, however in those in which it is listed it is recommended for snake bite.[3] In this regard, Selig maintains in his German/English translation of this text, that the current psalm is "for the cure of dangerous and deadly wounds, bites, stings of a salamander, lizard, snake, scorpion or other poisonous reptile, the earnest prayer of this Psalm is said to possess the same power of healing as the former Psalm, already described."[4]

A variant recension of the *Shimmush Tehillim* instructs an individual who suffered a bite from a serpent, to acquire milk from four women, wheat flour from four mills, and four eggs that were laid on a Thursday. A cake is then prepared from these ingredients, and the current psalm, as well as the "Name of Seventy-two Names," written on it with the blood of the snakebite victim. There is also an associated prayer-incantation which reads:

תמנייה יעשייה דרייה אל רחום וחנון שלח רפואה

אמן אמן אמן [....name of recipient...] שלימה לזה האיש

סלה סלה סלה

Transliteration:

Tamaniyah Ya'ashi'yah Dar'yah el rachum v'chanun sh'lach r'fu'ah sh'leimah l'zeh ha'ish [....name of recipient...] *Omein Omein Omein Selah Selah Selah.*

Translation:

Tamaniyah Ya'ashi'yah Dar'yah, merciful and gracious God, send full healing to this man [....name of recipient...] *Amen Amen Amen Selah Selah Selah.*[5]

It should be obvious that, unless the individual in question received professional medical attention forthwith, he/she will expire long before the necessary milk from four women, or wheat flour from four different mills can be found, what to say work the remainder of this crazy "magical" rigmarole! Elsewhere we find *Psalm 147* employed in conjunction with the following psalm, to quench a fire.[6] I referenced this application under *Psalm 148*, since the latter psalm pertains specifically to putting out fires. As far as the magical uses of individual verses are concerned, it should be noted that the capitals of the five words of *Psalm 147:3* were conjoined in the Divine Name construct הללול, which is employed in amulets for heart ailments.[7] Other than this, *Psalm 147:11* is directly affiliated with ייי (*Yeyay*), the twenty-second tri-letter portion of the "Name of Seventy-two Names."[8]

The biblical psalms are renumbered and verses rearranged in Christian bibles. In this regard, *Psalm 147* is divided into two with verses 1—11 listed as *Psalm 146*, and verses 12—20 being *Psalm 147*. Many nonsensical reasons have been given for the rearrangement of the Hebrew scriptures, e.g. there is no hard and fast rule regarding the numbering of the psalms, and the rearrangement enhances their intelligibility. I hardly think Christians would have tolerated the same done to their "New Testament." Be that as it may, *Psalm 147:1—10*, listed *Psalm 146* in the Christian scriptures, are employed in Christian Magic for healing purposes. In this regard, the *"Livre d'Or"* maintains that reciting *Psalm 146:1—3* seven times over oil, and rubbing the body of the indisposed with this substance, will ensure healing.[9] The same text further maintains that reading this psalm prior to sharing "anything with anyone," will ensure the "shared portion will be good."[10] On the other hand, practitioners are instructed in the *"Livre d'Or"* to write *Psalm 147:11—20*, the latter being considered to be *Psalm 147* proper in Christian bibles, with a mixture of saffron and rosewater. Following this action, we are told that it should be perfumed with "wood of aloe," and then buried "at the foundations of a house." It is said that the blessings of the Divine One will be present when a building is erected on these foundations.[11]

PSALM 148

[1] הללו יה הללו את יהוה‎אדני‎יאהדונהי מן השמים
הללוהו במרומים

[2] הללוהו כל מלאכיו הללוהו כל צבאיו

[3] הללוהו שמש וירח הללוהו כל כוכבי אור

[4] הללוהו שמי השמים והמים אשר מעל השמים

[5] יהללו את שם יהוה‎אדני‎יאהדונהי כי הוא צוה
ונבראו

[6] ויעמידם לעד לעולם חק נתן ולא יעבור

[7] הללו את יהוה‎אדני‎יאהדונהי מן הארץ תנינים וכל
תהמות

[8] אש וברד שלג וקיטור רוח סערה עשה דברו

[9] ההרים וכל גבעות עץ פרי וכל ארזים

[10] החיה וכל בהמה רמש וצפור כנף

[11] מלכי ארץ וכל לאמים שרים וכל שפטי ארץ

[12] בחורים וגם בתולות זקנים עם נערים

[13] יהללו את שם יהוה‎אדני‎יאהדונהי כי נשגב שמו
לבדו הודו על ארץ ושמים

[14] וירם קרן לעמו תהלה לכל חסידיו לבני
ישראל עם קרבו הללו יה

Transliteration:

[1] *hal'lu Yah hal'lu et YHVH min hashamayim hal'luhu bam'romim*

[2] *hal'luhu chol mal'achav hal'luhu kol tz'va'av*

[3] *hal'luhu shemesh v'yarei'ach hal'luhu kol koch'vei or*

[4] *hal'luhu sh'mei hashamayim v'hamayim asher mei'al hashamayim*

[5] *y'hal'lu et shem YHVH ki hu tzivah v'niv'ra'u*

[6] *vaya'amideim la'ad l'olam chok natan v'lo ya'avor*

[7] *hal'lu et YHVH min ha'aretz taninim v'chol t'homot*

[8] *esh uvarad sheleg v'kitor ru'ach s'arah osah d'varo*

[9] *heharim v'chol g'va'ot eitz p'ri v'chol arazim*

[10] *hachayah v'chol b'heimah remes v'tzipor kanaf*

[11] *mal'chei eretz v'chol l'umim sarim v'chol shof'tei aretz*

[12] *bachurim v'gam b'tulot z'keinim im n'arim*
[13] *y'hal'lu et shem YHVH ki nis'gav sh'mo l'vado hodo al eretz v'shamayim*
[14] *vayarem keren l'amo t'hilah l'chol chasidav liv'nei yis'ra'eil am k'rovo hal'lu Yah*

Translation:

[1] Hallelujah. Praise ye *YHVH* from the heavens; praise Him in the heights.

[2] Praise ye Him, all His angels; praise ye Him, all His hosts.

[3] Praise ye Him, sun and moon; praise Him, all ye stars of light.

[4] Praise Him, ye heavens of heavens, and ye waters that are above the heavens.

[5] Let them praise the name of *YHVH*; for He commanded, and they were created.

[6] He hath also established them for ever and ever; He hath made a decree which shall not be transgressed.

[7] Praise *YHVH* from the earth, ye sea-monsters, and all deeps;

[8] Fire and hail, snow and vapour, stormy wind, fulfilling His word;

[9] Mountains and all hills, fruitful trees and all cedars;

[10] Beasts and all cattle, creeping things and winged fowl;

[11] Kings of the earth and all peoples, princes and all judges of the earth;

[12] Both young men and maidens, old men and children;

[13] Let them praise the name of *YHVH*, for His name alone is exalted; His glory is above the earth and heaven.

[14] And He hath lifted up a horn for His people, a praise for all His saints, even for the children of Israel, a people near unto Him. Hallelujah.

Psalm 148 is the third of five psalms which commence and conclude with the expression *Hallelujah* ("praise *Yah*"), and the fourth of the set of six "*Halel* Psalms" enunciated daily in the *Pesukei d'Zimrah* ("Verses of Song") portion of *Shacharit* (Morning Prayer Service).[1] Verses 1 to 6, referencing the heavenly and angelic praises for the Divine One, are pronounced during

ברכת הלבנה (*Birkat haLevanah*), the monthly "Consecration of the Moon" ceremony.[2] Verses 13 and 14 are recited in the Synagogue when the *Torah* scroll is returned to the ark.[3] In Jewish Magic the current psalm is spoken against a fire.[4] The *Shimmush Tehillim* noted that this psalm is good to block a fire from causing serious damage.[5] Godfrey Selig addressed *Psalms 148* and *149* conjointly in his German/English translation of the *Shimmush Tehillim*, stating "these two Psalms are said to possess the desirable virtue of checking fire, when they are prayed in childlike trust on the unfailing help of the Almighty."[6] *Psalms 147* and *148* are also referenced conjointly for the purpose of extinguishing a fire. In this instance the practitioner is instructed to recite *Exodus 3:2* reading והנה הסנה בער באש והסנה איננו אכל, (*v'hineih has'neh bo'eir ba'esh v'has'neh einenu ukal*—"and, behold, the bush burned with fire, and the bush was not consumed"), as well as the said psalms.[7]

One commentator maintained that in the current instance the term "fire" is referencing a "fever." Hence he noted that the current psalm is good to recite against a fever, lest it destroys an indisposed individual.[8] A variant recension of the *Shimmush Tehillim* indeed recommends *Psalm 148* against fevers. In this regard, the psalm, the name of the sufferer, as well as an associated prayer-incantation, are all written down, and the writing suspended around the neck of the afflicted individual. The prayer incantation reads:

אֵלְיַי אֵלָה אֵל חַי הָעֵל זה [....name of recipient...]
כן יתקלקלו חליו ושריפתו של אש באבר
[....name of recipient...] וירפא מהרה אמן אמן
אמן סלה

Transliteration:
Eiliyai Eileh El Chai ha'el zeh [....name of recipient...] *ken yit'kal'k'lu chol'yo us'reifato shel esh b'ever* [....name of recipient...] *virapei m'heirah Omein Omein Selah Selah.*

Translation:
Eiliyai Eilah El Chai ("Living God") raise [....name of recipient...], destroy his sickness, and the burning of fever (fire) in the body of [....name of recipient...], and heal him speedily, *Amen Amen Amen Selah.*[9]

The current psalm is recommended in less "official sources" for recitation by those who find themselves in nature, and also as an offering of praise to the Divine One.

In Christian Magic we are informed in the *"Livre d'Or"* that reciting *Psalm 148* seven times a day in a residence, will rid the locale of a demon, "and the house will be full of blessings."[10] The same source maintains this psalm to be equally "good for a sick woman." In this regard, it is said the afflicted individual will be healed, if the practitioner recites the psalm over "pure oil," which is afterwards rubbed on her body.[11]

PSALM 149

‏[1] הללו יה שירו ליהוה‏אדני‏אהדונהי שיר חדש
תהלתו בקהל חסידים
‏[2] ישמח ישראל בעשיו בני ציון יגילו במלכם
‏[3] יהללו שמו במחול בתף וכנור יזמרו לו
‏[4] כי רוצה יהוה‏אדני‏אהדונהי בעמו יפאר ענוים
בישועה
‏[5] יעלזו חסידים בכבוד ירננו על משכבותם
‏[6] רוממות אל בגרונם וחרב פיפיות בידם
‏[7] לעשות נקמה בגוים תוכחות בל אמים
‏[8] לאסר מלכיהם בזקים ונכבדיהם בכבלי
ברזל
‏[9] לעשות בהם משפט כתוב הדר הוא לכל
חסידיו הללו יה

Transliteration:

[1] *hal'lu Yah shiru laYHVH shir chadash t'hilato bik'hal chasidim*
[2] *yis'mach yis'ra'eil b'osav b'nei tzion yagilu v'mal'kam*
[3] *y'hal'lu sh'mo v'machol b'tof v'chinor y'zam'ru lo*
[4] *ki rotzeh YHVH b'amo y'fa'eir anavim bishu'ah*
[5] *ya'l'zu chasidim b'chavod y'ran'nu al mish'k'votam*
[6] *rom'mot el big'ronam v'cherev pifiyot b'yadam*
[7] *la'asot n'kamah bagoyim tocheichot bal umim*
[8] *le'sor mal'cheihem b'zikim v'nich'b'deihem b'chav'lei var'zel*
[9] *la'asot bahem mish'pat katuv hadar hu l'chol chasidav hal'lu Yah*

Translation:

[1] Hallelujah. Sing unto *YHVH* a new song, and His praise in the assembly of the saints.
[2] Let Israel rejoice in his Maker; let the children of Zion be joyful in their King.
[3] Let them praise His name in the dance; let them sing praises unto Him with the timbrel and harp.
[4] For *YHVH* taketh pleasure in His people; He adorneth the humble with salvation.

[5] Let the saints exult in glory; let them sing for joy upon their beds.
[6] Let the high praises of God be in their mouth, and a two-edged sword in their hand;
[7] To execute vengeance upon the nations, and chastisements upon the peoples;
[8] To bind their kings with chains, and their nobles with fetters of iron;
[9] To execute upon them the judgment written; He is the glory of all His saints. Hallelujah.

Psalm 149 is the fourth of five psalms which commence and conclude with the expression *Hallelujah* ("praise *Yah*"), and the fifth of the set of six "*Halel* Psalms" recited daily in the *Pesukei d'Zimrah* ("Verses of Song") portion of *Shacharit* (Morning Prayer Service).[1] We are told that this psalm is enunciated along with the previous one, "simply because it follows that psalm."[2] As in the case of *Psalm 148*, the current one is equally employed in Jewish Magic against fire.[3] In this instance, the purpose is to prevent a fire from spreading.[4] In this regard, some maintain this psalm should be recited three times.[5] As we have seen with the previous psalm, a commentator again maintained the term "fire" to be referencing a "fever," the spread of which is being halted by the magical application of the current psalm.[6] He noted that the term אֵשׁ (*Esh*) can mean either "fire" or a "fever," and suggested the latter to be applicable in the current instance. He further interpreted the expression "fire of *Geihinom*" to be a raging fever, the said expression having been referenced in this manner a variant recension of the *Shimmush Tehillim*.[7] In this regard, we are told that *Psalm 149* "is good against the fire of *Geihinom*, lest it spread any further." In the said recension the raging fever ("fire of *Geihinom*") is curbed, by writing the psalm on kosher parchment conjointly with the following prayer-incantation,:

נוריאל שרפיאל רפאל ישעיאל אתם מלאכים
קדושים שלחו לזה במהרה והצילו אותו פן יחמיר
עליו חליו משרפת אש גיהנום אשר בא עליו מאת
השם אלהי ואל יקשה עליו יותר ואל תרבה עליו

שריפה כבתוב ויתפלל משה אל יהוה ותשקע האש

וכתוב אשם אשום אשום הוא אשם אשום אשם ליהוה (*Numbers 11:2*)

ליהוה אשם אשום אשם הוא אשום הוא (*Leviticus 5:19*)

אשם בשם רופא האמת יהיה רפואה שלימה

ל[....name of recipient....] מקדחת שורפת זה אמן אמן

אמן סלה סלה סלה ברוך יהוה לעולם אמן ואמן

Transliteration:

Nuri'el Serafi'el Rafa'el Yishayi'el atem malachim k'doshim shel'chu l'zeh bim'heirah v'hatzilu oto pen yach'mir alav chol'yo mis'reifat esh geihinom asher ba alav mei'at hashem elohei v'al yak'sheh alav yoter v'al tar'beh alav s'reifah k'katuv v'yit'paleil mosheh el YHVH vatish'ka ha'esh (Numbers 11:2) v'katuv asham hu ashom asham laYHVH (Leviticus 5:19) laYHVH asham ashom asham hu hu asham b'shem rofei ha'emet yih'yeh r'fu'ah sh'leimah l'[....name of recipient....] mikadachat sorefet zeh Omein Omein Omein Selah Selah Selah baruch YHVH l'olam Omein v'Omein.

Translation:

Nuri'el Serafi'el Rafa'el Yishayi'el, holy angels, send to this one speedily, and save him, lest his illness worsens from the burning fire (fever) of *Geihinom*, which has come upon him from *Hashem*, my God, and do not make it harder on him, and do not increase the fire over him, as it is written "and Moses prayed unto *YHVH*, and the fire abated." (*Numbers 11:2*), and it is written "it is a guilt-offering—he is certainly guilty before *YHVH*" (*Leviticus 5:19*) "before YHVH guilty he certainly is, a guilt-offering it is" (inversion of *Leviticus 5:19*), in the name of Healer of Truth, there will be complete healing for [....name of recipient....] from this burning fever. *Amen Amen Amen Selah Selah Selah*, blessed be *YHVH* eternally. *Amen* and *Amen*.[8]

In conclusion it should be noted that the current psalm is also enunciated against tyranny, and was further recommended to strengthen faith. In this regard, the "fire" association of this psalm in Jewish Magic, may perhaps be understood to pertain to the "fervour of faith."

Psalm 149 is employed in Christian Magic for healing purposes. In this regard, we are informed in the *"Livre d'Or"* that, as in the case of the previous psalm, reciting the current psalm over oil, which is afterwards rubbed on the body of an indisposed woman, will ensure her return to normal health.[9]

PSALM 150

[1] הללו יה הללו אֵל בקדשו הללוהו ברקיע עזו
[2] הללוהו בגבורתיו הללוהו כרב גדלו
[3] הללוהו בתקע שופר הללוהו בנבל וכנור
[4] הללוהו בתף ומחול הללוהו במנים ועוגב
[5] הללוהו בצלצלי שמע הללוהו בצלצלי תרועה
[6] כל הנשמה תהלל יה הללו יה

Transliteration:
[1] *hal'lu Yah hal'lu El b'kod'sho hal'luhu bir'kiya uzo*
[2] *hal'luhu vig'vurotav hal'luhu k'rov gud'lo*
[3] *hal'luhu b'teika shofar hal'luhu b'neivel v'chinor*
[4] *hal'luhu v'tof umachol hal'luhu b'minim v'ugav*
[5] *hal'luhu v'tzil'tz'lei shama hal'luhu b'tzil'tz'lei t'ru'ah*
[6] *kol han'shamah t'haleil Yah hal'lu Yah*

Translation:
[1] *Hallelujah.* Praise *El* in His sanctuary; praise Him in the firmament of His power.
[2] Praise Him for His mighty acts; praise Him according to His abundant greatness.
[3] Praise Him with the blast of the horn; praise Him with the psaltery and harp.
[4] Praise Him with the timbrel and dance; praise Him with stringed instruments and the pipe.
[5] Praise Him with the loud-sounding cymbals; praise Him with the clanging cymbals.
[6] Let every thing that hath breath praise *Yah. Hallelujah.*

Psalm 150 is delineated "a symphony of praise" for the Divine One.[1] It is the fifth of the five psalms which commence and conclude with the expression *Hallelujah* ("praise *Yah*"), and the last of the set of six "*Halel* Psalms" recited daily in the *Pesukei d'Zimrah* ("Verses of Song") portion of *Shacharit* (Morning Prayer Service).[2] It is also enunciated on *Rosh Hashanah* (New Year), and at ברכת הלבנה (*Birkat Halevanah*), the monthly "Consecration of the Moon."[3] It is maintained in Kabbalistic writings that the ten expressions of praise in the current psalm, commencing with הללו אֵל בקדשו (*hal'lu El b'kod'sho*—"Praise *El* in His sanctuary") and concluding with הַלְלוּהוּ בְּצִלְצְלֵי (*hal'luhu b'tzil'tz'lei*—"praise Him with the clanging cymbals"), align with the Ten *Sefirot* in direct order.[4] It is also said that the term הלל (*Halel*—"praise") "occurs thirteen times in the psalm, the number corresponding to the Thirteen Attributes of Mercy manifested by God's loving-kindness."[5] It was further noted that the expression הללו (*Halelu*) "appears in the psalm twelve times, corresponding to the twelve months of the year,"[6] and this is one of the reasons given for the recitation of *Psalm 150* during the monthly "Blessing of the Moon."[7]

The praise of the Divine One expressed in *Psalm 150*, indicates the manner of its application in Jewish Magic, i.e. to thank and praise the Divine One in all His actions.[8] Godfrey Selig upheld a very different reason for uttering the current psalm in his verbose and flawed German/English version of the *Shimmush Tehillim*. In this regard, he maintained that "this happy Psalm of Praise should be uttered by every God-fearing, thankful being, after having escaped a great danger, or received a peculiar grace in answer to a prayer to the Lord of Hosts, and it should be repeated with a thankful heart to His praise and glory."[9] Whilst there is no indication in any of the primary recensions of the *Shimmush Tehillim* regarding *Psalm 150* being specifically enunciated after having survived a great danger, one commentator noted that this psalm is for "general thanksgiving.[10] It is also noted in one recension of the *Shimmush Tehillim*, that "this psalm is good for answering prayer before the Creator," as well as to offer praise "for the abundance of miracles and mighty deeds, which He does every day."[11] In this regard, the practitioner is instructed to recite *Psalm 150*, and conclude with the following prayer-incantation:

חפניאל שוניאל טופיאל טורניאל יה יה יה
שם אל חי לך אני מתענה ומתפלל על כל הטובות
הנפלאות והנסים שעשית לי ועל כן יבורך שמך
לעולם ועד אמן אמן אמן אמן סלה סלה סלה סלה

Transliteration:

Chaf'ni'el Shoni'el Tofi'el Tur'ni'el Yah Yah Yah shem El Chai l'cha ani mit'aneh umit'palel al kol hatovot hanif'la'ot v'hanisim she'asita li v'al kein y'vorach shim'cha l'olam va'ed Omein Omein Omein Selah Selah Selah.

Translation:

Chaf'ni'el Shoni'el Tofi'el Tur'ni'el Yah Yah Yah in the name *El Chai*, for you I fast and pray for all that is good, the miracles, and the wonders you have prepared for me, and therefore may your Name be blessed forever and ever. *Amen Amen Amen Selah Selah Selah.*[12]

The current psalm is also recommended for musicians, and as a meditation. In this regard, it is worth considering a unique introspective exercise based on the opening phrase of *Psalm 150:6*. This very simple meditation, which could be worked at any time anywhere, and in all circumstances, has a direct and most beneficial mental, emotional, and physical impact on all who made it an integral part of their daily lives. In this regard, the practitioner should maintain a calm and relaxed disposition, and then recite the words כל הנשמה תהלל יה (*kol han'shamah t'haleil Yah*—"Let every thing that hath breath praise *Yah*"), doing so twice over a slow, comfortable breathing cycle, i.e. once during inhalation, and once during exhalation. The peace, serenity, and healing inspired by this practice is truly remarkable, especially when faced with the stress of daily existence on this planet.[13]

In Christian Magic the "*Livre d'Or*" maintains that the recitation of *Psalm 150* "seven times over wheat and over oil," each time followed by "a little prayer," will multiply these substances with Divine support. It is further noted that this should be done during the Waxing Moon, and preferably when "the Signs were in their ascendancy at the same time."[14] The Byzantine Magical Manuscripts recommend *Psalms 147—150* for "paroxysm," noting that "it is useful to say them on seven mornings: Sunday, Tuesday, Thursday, Saturday, Monday, Wednesday, and Friday."[15] Elsewhere we find *Psalm 150:6* written conjointly with *Luke 16:29* and *Psalm 68:1* on "virgin parchment," and located in the four corners of a residence "to drive away spirits that are haunting a house."[16]

. ...They looked and searched and when they opened the door where the two barrels stood....they saw Yossele the golem pouring the water. This prompted a great deal of laughter in the house and the Maharal too began laughing... ... .

Epilogue:
Psalms & Psalm Societies

The "*Sefer Shimmush Tehillim*" concludes with the recommendation of five biblical verses, specifically *Psalms 121:2, 55:23, 37:37, 37:3*, and *Isaiah 12:2*, which it maintains "are suitable and good for a man to get used to."[1] Throughout this work I have focused mainly on the application of single psalms in *Practical Kabbalah*. However, the biblical psalms are very often enunciated collectively for a variety of purposes. In this regard, a friend remarked that "reciting psalms is a serious business in Judaism!" As one might expect, this is not restricted to the synagogue, or to formal religious occasions. In fact, it has been noted that "the recital of the whole Book of Psalms is widespread, whether as an act of piety by saintly individuals, or by groups of unlearned people,"[2] and that "there are any number of private occasions when individual Psalms or groups of them are read."[3] In this regard, chanting a selection of psalms either before or after the morning prayer service, is a very commonplace daily action in traditional Jewish communities, and the entire compliment of biblical psalms is enunciated in full every month.[4] In Jewish Communities, some very pious worshippers have memorised the entire Book of Psalms, and many have joined small groups termed חברות תהלים (*Chev'rot Tehillim*), i.e. "Psalm Societies," which are devoted to enunciating the said biblical text every week.[5] This is usually done in the following order:

Sunday: *Psalms 1–29* Monday: *Psalms 30–50*
Tuesday: *Psalms 51–72* Wednesday: *Psalms 73–89*
Thursday: *Psalms 90–106* Friday: *Psalms 107–119*
Shabbat: *Psalms 120–150*.[6]

"Psalm Societies" have been in existence for several centuries. They continue to be established, and are still functioning in many parts of the world.[7] Two such groups are devoted to reciting the 150 biblical psalms every single day at the Western Wall,[8] and in Jerusalem a street was named "*Chevrat Tehillim*" in honour of

405

those who recite psalms for peace in Israel.[9] Considering the extent of the Jewish diaspora, it is to be expected that "Psalm societies" have on occasion surfaced in unexpected locales and circumstances. A fascinating 19th century document delineates the actions of one such group comprising thirty-two Russian Jewish soldiers. They are said to have served with "dignity, loyalty, and courage" in the army of Tsar Alexander II, "while at the same time remaining loyal members of the Jewish community."[10] It is not surprising to find Jewish soldiers reciting the biblical psalms, especially in times of trouble and great danger. We are informed that "during the Yom Kippur War of October 1973, thousands of copies of *Sefer Tehillim* (Book of Psalms) were distributed to Israeli troops at the front,"[11] and it is further said that "faith in the power of the Psalms has invaded even the most secular Jewish consciousness."[12] In this regard, we are told that a rabbi who was a soldier in the tank division in Israel during the October War, "was reading through the Psalms for comfort in this terrifying situation. His words were picked up on the intercome and the other soldiers asked him what he was reading. When he said it was the Psalms, these 'secular' Israelis said: 'Don't keep them to yourself!' and he carried on reading them out loud."[13]

As indicated throughout this study, the believe in the power of the biblical psalms, resulted in their extensive application for a great variety of "magical purposes," and this unique resource is still impacting the lives of many Jews, and non-Jews for that matter, to this very day. As mentioned earlier, there is little difference between mainstream religionists seeking "miracles," and esotericists believing in the power of "Jewish Magic" aka "*Practical Kabbalah.*"[14] It has been said that "the possibility of communication between systems concerning wonders or unusual events rests upon the distinction at hand,"[15] to which I added that "the distinction between 'miracles' and 'magic' is but a question of deciding who are 'insiders' and who are 'outsiders'."[16] This is said to connote "the simple judgment that what my side does is a miracle; and by the way, it works; what your side does is magic, whether or not it works."[17] However, this issue takes an interesting turn when the supposed dividing line between the "miraculous" and the "magical" starts to blur, as it often does in the hands of ultra-orthodox Rabbis, and other mainstream religionists, who liberally share שֵׁמוֹת (*Shemot*—"Divine Names"), סְגוּלוֹת (*Segulot*—"Magical Recipes"), קְמֵעוֹת (*Kameot*—"amulets"), רְפוּאוֹת (*Refuot*—"Magical Cures"), etc.

This is not the exclusive domain of certain selected Rabbis living in centuries past, like the acclaimed *Ba'alei Shem* ("Masters of the Name"), i.e. the East European "Jewish Sorcerers," and other purveyors of *Practical Kabbalah,* but also of a number of contemporary religious figures such as the late Rabbi Yitzchak Kaduri, who was a most revered Charedi Rabbi. He shared unique blessings, amulets, and "magical remedies" with literally thousands of clients, who visited him in search of solutions to what appeared to be insurmountable difficulties. In this regard, the magical application of the biblical psalms was, and still is, absolutely central. We are told that "another custom that is still widely practiced (especially in ultra-Orthodox communities) involves the recitation of the entire Book of Psalms by a group of people (very often women), either daily or on Sabbath afternoons," and that this is typically "performed on behalf of an individual (or various individuals) in crisis, usually someone with a serious illness."[18] However, it is also customary amongst such groups to enunciate selected psalms, in order to benefit individuals and groups who are faced with overwhelming circumstances in their daily lives. In this regard, it is impossible to include a complete inventory, especially when there are differences of opinion regarding the exact set of psalms to be chanted for any given purpose. Hence I am including here the following brief survey, referencing only some of the requirements for successful human survival on this planet, i.e. protection, health, wealth, love, and happiness.

ALL PURPOSE (Marriage, Children, Happiness, Fulfillment, Peace of Mind, etc.):
> *Psalms 3, **6**, **13**, 16, **20**, 22, 23, **27**, 32, 41, 42, 51, 56, 59, 70, 77, 86, 88, **90**, **102**, **121**, 128, **130**, 137, **142**, 143* and *150.* We are told this is "a good general list for times of need (of course, any part of it is fine)," and that "some of the most powerful ones are in bold."[19]

CHILDBIRTH:
> *Psalms 1, 4, 5, 8, 57, 93, 108* and *142.* For an easy birth

and also for a normal pregnancy (recite every day during pregnancy). [reported in the name of Rabbi Chaim Kanievsky].[20]

Psalms 4, 5, 8, 20, 35, 57, 93, 108 and *142*. For a healthy birth.

Psalms 90—93 or *112—150* (recite during confinement).

BAD CULTURE:

Psalms 90—101. To ensure offspring do not mix with the wrong crowd. [reported in the name of Rabbi Asher Freund].[21]

EVIL EYE (jealousy, resentment, etc.):

Psalms 122, 131 and *133*. To guard against the Evil Eye, say on the first night of the "Counting of the Omer."[22]

FEAR (terror):

Psalm 20:10 (three times) followed by *Psalm 53*. Hold a Hebrew Bible, and say שם פחדו פחד [*sham pachadu fachad*— "There are they in great fear"] (*Psalm 53:6*), then tap on the Bible twice, and say *Psalm 41:4* (three times). Recite the ויהי נועם prayer (*Psalm 90/91*). Conclude by saying, in direct order and in reverse, the opening phrase from the blessing for healing in the *Amidah* prayer reading: רפאנו יהוה ונרפא הושיענו ונושעה כי תהילתנו אתה [*r'fa'einu Adonai v'neirafei hoshi'einu v'nivashei'ah ki t'hilateinu atah*—"Heal us *Hashem* and we will be healed, save us and we will be saved, for you are our praise"].[23]

GOOD FORTUNE (rectification of loss of luck and success due to misdeeds and the "Evil Inclination" [greed/desire to receive]):

Psalms 30, 139, 1, 121, 103, 67, 23, 148, 6, 105, 33, 27, 90—91, 4, 20, 29, 16 and *38*. (recite before daybreak).[24]

GRATITUDE & PRAISE:

Psalms 145—150: To express gratitude and/or Praise to the Divine One.

Psalms 9, 21, 57, 95, 116 and *138*.[25]

HOME (protection against Evil Spirits):
Psalms 120—134: "On the dedication of a house which has been inhabited by evil spirits"[26]

ILLNESS:
Psalms 6, 30 and *142* (to be said after daily prayers).[27]
Psalms 6, 10, 30 and *41.*[28]
Psalms 20, 30, 121, 130 and *142.*[29]
Psalms 90—108, 20, 38, 41, 86 and *118.*[30]
Psalms 6, 9, 13, 16—18, 20, 22, 23, 25, 30—33, 37—39, 41, 49, 55, 56, 69, 86, 88, 90, 91, 102—104, 107, 116, 118, 142, 143 and/or 148.[31]

LIVELIHOOD:
Psalms 1—150 (recite all psalms without interruption). For individuals who suffer difficulties with livelihood, and/or other problems.[32]
Psalms 23, 104, 128 and *145.* "When one is looking for work, or needs greater financial stability."[33]
Psalms 25, 49, 80, 88, 90, 96, 98, 106, 137 and 140 (recite every day).[34]

LOVE (for finding a life partner [*Shidduch*]):
Psalms 32, 38, 70 and *124.*[35]
Psalms 32,38,70,71 and 124.[36]
Psalms 31, 32, 70, 72 and *124* (recite for forty days). [reported in the name of Rabbi Yitzchak Kaduri].[37]
Psalms 32, 38, 70, 71 and *124.*[38]
Psalms 32, 38, 70, 71, 121 and *124.*[39]

PROTECTION:
Psalms 72, 108, 111, 119 letter ˋ (*Yod*), *139* and *140.*[40]
Psalms 13, 20, 79, 80, 83, 91, 121, 130 and *142.* "For Israel, Protection, and Danger to Jewish People."[41]

RAIN:
Psalms 17, 25, 32, 86, 103, 105, 108, 120, 121, 123, 124, 130 and *136.*[42]

RESCUE (*Yeshu'ot*):
>Psalms *4, 5, 8, 20* (seven times), *37, 57, 93, 108* (for all manner of deliverance) [reported in the name of Rabbi Moshe Yaakov Ravikov HaCohen, "the Holy Shoemaker"].[43]

SEXUAL RELATIONS (at various times):
>*Psalms 32, 38* and *70.*[44]

SUCCESS:
>*Psalms 57, 112* and *122.*[45]
>*Psalms 4, 17, 63, 65,116, 137, 138* and *150.* [reported in the name of Rabbi Boruch of Medzhybizh].[46]
>*Psalms 6—8, 13, 28, 38, 57, 65* and *69* (recite every day).[47]
>*Psalms 6—8, 13, 28, 38, 57, 65, 69, 71, 72, 108, 111,139, 140,* as well as *Psalm 119* letter ' (*Yod*) (recite every day).[48]

SUPPORT IN DIFFICULT TIMES:
>*Psalms 16, 20, 25, 26, 38, 54, 81, 85—87, 102, 130* and *142.*[49]

This concludes the "*The Book of Magical Psalms.*" I pray this tome will be meaningful, and of good service to all who peruse its pages.

. ...'Look here,' he told his wife, 'you found yourself some water carrier for Passover!' He immediately ran to the golem, took the bucket from him, and said, 'Enough! That's quite enough!'.... Because of that incident, a popular saying spread through Prague. When someone wanted to criticize a workman's shoddy labor, he would say, 'You're fit to be a watchmaker like Yossele the golem is fit for water carrying.'... ... ."

Index of Magical Applications

1. General

Affliction [against every]: **[Part 3]** 121
Affliction & the Afflicted: **[Part 1]** 38; **[Part 3]** 102; 119:41–48 [ר (*Vav*)]

Bad Incidents [to be rescued from]: **[Part 2]** 46:8
Bad Things & Circumstances [against]: **[Part 1]** 26; 30; **[Part 2]** 67

Danger [protection against any type of]: **[Part 2]** 49:6; 77
Danger & Suffering [to be set aside]: **[Part 3]** 90:17
Dangerous Circumstances [to escape from]: **[Part 3]** 91:10
Difficult Circumstances [salvation in]: **[Part 3]** 91:15–16
Disaster [generally against]: **[Part 2]** 48; 57; **[Part 3]** 106; 142
Disasters [public]: **[Part 1]** 16; **[Part 2]** 45; **[Part 3]** 143
Disasters [unforseen]: **[Part 1]** 40; **[Part 3]** 106; 142

Everything [for]: **[Part 1]** 9; 25; 32:7; 39; **[Part 3]** 91:10–16

Grievous Circumstances [a call for help in]: **[Part 2]** 67

Harm [protection from]: **[Part 3]** 121
Help [a call for]: **[Part 1]** 16:8; 19:15; 20:2; 20:10; 27:7; 30:11; 34:8; 41:4; **[Part 2]** 46:8; 46:12; 67; 67:1–2; 86:3; **[Part 3]** 91:9; 91:11; 91:15; 102:2; 115:11

Injuries & Damage [of every kind]: **[Part 1]** 14; 17:8; **[Part 2]** 68; **[Part 3]** 101; 118
Injury [against suffering]: **[Part 2]** 67
Invisibility [to see & not be seen]: **[Part 1]** 31:21; **[Part 3]** 91

Liberty [for true]: **[Part 2]** 71
Life & Rescue: **[Part 1]** 31
Lost Keys [finding]: **[Part 1]** 16

Need [to be saved from every]: **[Part 2]** 42; 86:9

411

Odours [against bad]: **[Part 2]** 84
Open Doors [in spite of a lost key]: **[Part 1]** 24

Praise: **[Part 1]** 8; 19; 33; **[Part 2]** 65; **[Part 3]** 100; 104; 113; 114; 117; 150
Protection [complete/total]: **[Part 3]** 136
Protection [general]: **[Part 1]** 32:7; **[Part 2]** 48; 67; **[Part 3]** 90; 91
Protection [of people]: **[Part 3]** 134
Prosperity [general]: **[Part 2]** 67
Purpose & Need [for any]: **[Part 1]** 4
Redstring [preparation]: **[Part 1]** 33
Respect [general]: **[Part 2]** 78

Safety [general]: **[Part 2]** 67
Secret Things [revelation & certitude of]: **[Part 1]** 16; 31; **[Part 3]** 129
Suffering: **[Part 1]** 38; 39; **[Part 3]** 90:17; 102

Temporal affairs & Trouble [of every kind]: **[Part 1]** 22; 25
Troublesome Situations [for protection in]: **[Part 2]** 67

2. Health, Healing & General Physical Well-being

Anaemia: **[Part 1]** 21; 37; **[Part 2]** 72
Afflictions (recurring): **[Part 3]** 96
Arm [pain in the left arm]: **[Part 3]** 119:121–128 [ע (*Ayin*)]
Arm [pain in the right arm]: **[Part 3]** 119:97–104 [מ (*Mem*)]
Arm [for a broken]: **[Part 3]** 144
Arms [for ailments of the]: **[Part 3]** 143
Asthma: **[Part 1]** 3:9

Backache: **[Part 1]** 3
Bites: **[Part 1]** 21; 31
Blood [diseases]: **[Part 1]** 6; **[Part 3]** 123
Body [against trembling of the]: **[Part 3]** 119:1–8 [א (*Alef*)]
Body [emaciated from severe illnesses]: **[Part 2]** 84
Body [pains in the upper]: **[Part 3]** 119:57–64 [ח (*Chet*)]
Bones [diseases]: **[Part 1]** 6:3-4; 21; 31:11; 33; 34:21; 38:11; **[Part 3]** 101
Bones [broken or disintegrating due to severe illness]: **[Part 2]** 89
Broken limbs: **[Part 1]** 37

Cancer: [Part 1] 37
Chest [diseases of]: [Part 1] 21; [Part 2] 72
Chicken-pox [protection against]: [Part 3] 106:30
Cold [or common influensa]: [Part 3] 147
Constipation [to alleviate]: [Part 1] 31:10
Convalescence: [Part 2] 65
Cure [for the gift of a]: [Part 3] 102

Deafness [loss of hearing]: [Part 1] 37
Diarrhea [to alleviate]: [Part 1] 31:10
Digestive Tract [ailments of]: [Part 1] 31:10
Disease [protection from all]: [Part 3] 106:30
Diseases [general]: [Part 1] 29; [Part 2] 87; [Part 3] 106:30; 114
Diseases [serious or incurable]: [Part 1] 9; 21; [Part 2] 88; [Part 3] 90; 91
Dizziness [against]: [Part 3] 119
Dumb [for the]: [Part 1] 38

Ear [ailments of, pain or a boil in the left]: [Part 3] 119:169–176 [ת (*Tav*)]
Ear [ailments of, pain or a boil in the right]: [Part 3] 119:153–160 [ר (*Resh*)]
Ears [diseases of or problems with the]: [Part 2] 93; 113
Energy [for]: [Part 2] 43; [Part 3] 91
Epidemics [against]: [Part 2] 43; 51; [Part 3] 91; 91:3–4; 91:10; 96; 98; 106:30; 109:6 [see also *Plagues*]
Epilepsy: [Part 1] 16; 37; 78; [Part 3] 91:5 & 10; 102:2; 143:1
Eye [illness in the left (catarrh)]: [Part 3] 119:25–32 [ד (*Dalet*)]
Eye [pain in & recovery of the left]: [Part 3] 119:25–32 [ד (*Dalet*)]
Eye [illness in the right (catarrh)]: [Part 3] 119:17–24 [ג (*Gimel*)]
Eye [pain in & recovery of the right]: [Part 3] 119:17–24 [ג (*Gimel*)]
Eye [weakness in the right]: [Part 3] 119:17–24 [ג (*Gimel*)]
Eyes [diseases of or pain in the]: [Part 1] 6; 10; 12; 13; 37; [Part 3] 113; 119:49–56 [ז (*Zayin*)]; 122; 130; 145;

Fatigue [languor/lethargy]: [Part 1] 31; [Part 3] 101
Feet [problems with]: [Part 2] 82

Fever [against]: **[Part 1]** 8:2; 13; 15; 16; 17; 18; 19; 34; 37; **[Part 2]** 49; 67; 68; 78; **[Part 3]** 90:17; 148; 149
Fever [against chronic or incurable]: **[Part 2]** 49; 50; 67; **[Part 3]** 106 (perpetual fever); 107
Fever [to cure]: **[Part 3]** 105 (a four-day fever); 106 (a three-day); 107 (a one-day or two-day fever)
Food Poisoning [to alleviate]: **[Part 1]** 31:10

Gangrene: **[Part 1]** 37

Haemorrhage or Loss of Blood [to halt]: **[Part 1]** 1:1–3; **[Part 2]** 51:3
Hand [for a broken]: **[Part 3]** 144
Hand [for weakness, pain & ailments of the left]: **[Part 3]** 119:121–128 [ע (*Ayin*)]
Hand [for weakness, pain & ailments of the right]: **[Part 3]** 119:97–104 [מ (*Mem*)]
Hands [diseases of the]: **[Part 3]** 113
Head [against diseases of the]: **[Part 2]** 67; **[Part 3]** 119:161–168 [ש (*Shin*)]
Headaches [brought on by stress]: **[Part 2]** 57
Headaches & Pains in the Head [against]: **[Part 1]** 2; 3; 7; **[Part 3]** 119:161–168 [ש (*Shin*)]
Heal & Empower: **[Part 3]** 109:18; 109:19
Healing [to facilitate]: **[Part 2]** 67; 69:7; **[Part 3]** 90–91
Health [for good]: **[Part 3]** 104
Hearing [for good]: **[Part 3]** 91
Heart [ailments & problems]: **[Part 1]** 13; 21; 31:11; 34:19; 38:11; **[Part 2]** 44; 45; 51:12; 62:9; 72; **[Part 3]** 93; 101; 141; 147:3
Hip [pain in the]: **[Part 3]** 119:65–72 [ט (*Tet*)]

Illness [against being plagued with]: **[Part 2]** 89; **[Part 3]** 106:30
Illness [against the effects of]: **[Part 2]** 89
Illness [to be cured of an]: **[Part 3]** 119:73–80 [י (*Yod*)]
Illness & Healing [in general]: **[Part 1]** 4; 6; 6:1–4; 7; 9; 10; 13; 16; 18; 20; 23; 25; 27; 29; 30; 30:3; 31; 32; 33; 34:18; 37; 38; 39; 41; **[Part 2]** 42; 49; 51; 55; 69; 81; 84; 85; 86; 88; **[Part 3]** 91; 94; 100; 102; 103; 104; 105; 106:30; 107; 108; 109; 110; 116; 118; 119; 121; 128; 130; 142; 143; 145

Nostril [for a blocked, painful, or boil in the left]: **[Part 3]** 119:129–136 [**פ** (*Peh*)]

Nostril [for a blocked, painful, or boil in the right]: **[Part 3]** 119:81–88 [**כ** (*Kaf*)]

Pain [for every]: **[Part 3]** 91:10–16
Pains [general]: **[Part 2]** 77
Paralysis: **[Part 2]** 50; **[Part 3]** 94; 107; 118
Pestilence (Plague) [to relieve citizens of a city from a]: **[Part 3]** 98
Physical Strength [to be empowered in]: **[Part 3]** 112
Plagues (Epidemics/Pandemics) [to be saved & protected from]: **[Part 1]** 33; **[Part 2]** 86 **[Part 3]** 90; 91; 91:3–4; 91:10; 96; 106:30; 109:6 [see also *Epidemics*]
Prostate (for healing of the): **[Part 3]** 105:41–45

Recovery [of patients]: **[Part 2]** 89
Rheumatism: **[Part 1]** 15; 31; **[Part 3]** 129

Shoulders [pain in the]: **[Part 1]** 3
Sickly to work without fatigue [to allow the]: **[Part 3]** 89
Sinusitis: **[Part 3]** 119:81–88 [**כ** (*Kaf*)]; 119:129–136 [**פ** (*Peh*)]
Sight [for good]: **[Part 3]** 91
Skin [ailments of]: **[Part 1]** 38:4
Smallpox [protection against]: **[Part 3]** 106:30
Spine [diseases of the]: **[Part 3]** 106
Spleen [against disorders of the]: **[Part 3]** 119:49–56 [**ז** (*Zayin*)]
Sportsmen: **[Part 1]** 17; **[Part 3]** 92
Stomach [diseases of]: **[Part 1]** 13; 21
Stomach [for the upper]: **[Part 3]** 119:57–64 [**ח** (*Chet*)]
Sunstroke (Heatstroke): **[Part 3]** 121

Teeth [against diseases of the]: **[Part 3]** 119:49–56 [z (*Zayin*)]
Toothache [pains in teeth & gums]: **[Part 1]** 3
Thighs [pain in the]: **[Part 3]** 142
Throat [pains in]: **[Part 1]** 2; **[Part 2]** 68; **[Part 3]** 113
Tuberculosis: **[Part 1]** 3:9

Voice [preservation of]: **[Part 1]** 32; **[Part 2]** 68

3. Mental & Emotional Well-being

Uplifted [to be]: **[Part 1]** 8; 19; 24; **[Part 2]** 47; 48

Vanity [against]: **[Part 1]** 11; 30; **[Part 2]** 93; 100; 118

4. Sleep & Dreams

Dream Question (*She'elat Chalom*) [receiving answers in]: **[Part 1]** 4:2; 12; 13; 23; 39; **[Part 2]** 42
Dreams [against bad & demonic]: **Part 3]** 90; 91:5; 126
Dreams [problems with]: **[Part 2]** 51:13
Dreams [interpretation of & help in understanding]: **[Part 2]** 42

Incubi [against male sexual night demons]: **[Part 3]** 90
Insomnia [inability to sleep]: **[Part 1]** 4; **[Part 2]** 62; 76; **[Part 3]** 90; 101; 126

Night Spirits/Demons (*Lilits*) [against]: **[Part 3]** 90; 126
Nightmares: **[Part 1]** 30:3; **[Part 3]** 90; 91:5

Sleep [protection against evil during]: **[Part 3]** 91
Sleep [to encourage refreshing]: **[Part 3]** 131
Sleep [when waking in states of fear & trembling]: **[Part 3]** 121
Succubae [against female sexual night demons]: **[Part 3]** 90

Waking [(magical alarm clock) to wake at specific times: **[Part 2]** 57:9

5. Intelligence, Study, Memory, Speech & Secret Sciences

Ignorance [against]: **[Part 1]** 17; **[Part 3]** 104; 106
Intelligence [to awaken]: **[Part 1]** 16; 19; 19:8–10
Intelligence [to sharpen & increase]: **[Part 1]** 16; 19; 19:8–10; 22; **[Part 2]** 54; **[Part 3]** 91; 118; 134
Intuition: **[Part 1]** 16

Knowledge [to retain]: **[Part 3]** 119:9–16 [ב (*Bet*)]; 119: 57–64 [ח (*Chet*)]; 105–112 [נ (*Nun*)]

Language [gift of]: **[Part 2]** 80
Learning [to aid with]: **[Part 3]** 134

Memory [for a good]: **[Part 1]** 12; 19; 19:8–10; **[Part 3]** 119:9–16 [בּ *(Bet)*]; 119:105

Memory [not to lose]: **[Part 3]** 119:9–16 [בּ *(Bet)*]
Memory [to improve]: **[Part 3]** 119:9; 119: 57–64 [ח *(Chet)*]

Occult Intrigues: **[Part 1]** 25
Occult Sciences [to comprehend the]: **[Part 2]** 50; **[Part 3]** 138

Preaching (sermons/lectures): **[Part 1]** 34
Preaching (to crowds): **[Part 3]** 119:25–32 [ד *(Dalet)*]

Recollection [to encourage good]: **[Part 3]** 119:9–16 [בּ *(Bet)*]; 119: 57–64 [ח *(Chet)*]; 119:105

Sciences [human]: **[Part 1]** 18; **[Part 3]** 93; 118
Sources [discovery of]: **[Part 2]** 73; **[Part 3]** 103; 113
Speech [to acquire the gift of]: **[Part 2]** 50; **[Part 3]** 110
Speakers [to be heard by every listener]: **[Part 2]** 77
Speaking [in public]: **[Part 3]** 119:25–32 [ד *(Dalet)*]
Study [love of]: **[Part 1]** 30; 31
Study [to be recited prior to]: **[Part 3]** 119:49; 134
Success [in studying & learning]: **[Part 1]** 25; **[Part 3]** 134

Thought & Contemplation [for]: **[Part 2]** 51:12

Will [force of]: **[Part 1]** 30; **[Part 2]** 50
Wisdom [to encourage]: **[Part 1]** 19

6. Journeys & Travel

Accidents [protection against & during chariot & motor-vehicle]: **[Part 1]** 36:7

Bridges [when crossing]: **[Part 3]** 91

Detours: **[Part 1]** 11
Direction [to determine the right]: **[Part 3]** 121

7. Success

8. Career, Trade, Transactions, Financial Success
Livelihood, Good Fortune & Charity

9. Food, Agriculture, Plant Growth, Fisheries, Animal Husbandry & Nature

Water [against life-threatening danger from]: **[Part 1]** 2; 26; **[Part 3]** 93:4
Water [against destruction by]: **[Part 2]** 69; 76
Water or Fire [to be saved from]: **[Part 2]** 76
Wells/Boreholes [to draw water from]: **[Part 3]** 90
Wind [for a good]: **[Part 3]** 106; 134

10. Human Interaction, Friendship, Brotherhood, & Reconciliation

Alliances [to establish]: **[Part 3]** 107

City [when entering a]: **[Part 2]** 82–83
City (New Environment) [to conquer a strange & to be kindly received in a]: **[Part 1]** 27; **[Part 2]** 82–83
Commitments [to keep]: **[Part 3]** 119: 57–64 [ח (*Chet*)]
Companion [to appease a]: **[Part 2]** 85
Companions [to succeed]: **[Part 3]** 133
Conquer [to overcome with personal strength]: **[Part 3]** 112
Crowds & Passersby [when gazing at]: **[Part 1]** 35:18

Deception [against]: **[Part 3]** 90
Dignitaries & Authorities [before waiting on]: **[Part 3]** 92; 122
Difficult People [against]: **[Part 2]** 80
Divisive Individuals [against]: **[Part 3]** 94

Enemies [reconciliation with]: **[Part 1]** 9; 28; **[Part 3]** 110
Enemies [to establish peace between]: **[Part 3]** 98; 110
Enemies [turning into friends]: **[Part 1]** 9; 16
Errors [saving friends from]: **[Part 2]** 80, 81
Exploitation [against being taken advantage of]: **[Part 1]** 35

Favour & Grace [of princes, magistrates & authorities]: **[Part 1]** 5; 20:6; 34; **[Part 2]** 71; 72; 78
Favour [to find]: **[Part 1]** 1:3; 4; 5; 8; **[Part 2]** 42; 47; 67; 71; 72; 85; **[Part 3]** 119
Favour [with all men]: **[Part 1]** 14; 15; **[Part 2]** 47; 67; **[Part 3]** 119:73–80 [י (*Yod*)]
Fellow Humans [to be loved & respected by]: **[Part 2]** 47
Friend [to reconcile with an long standing]: **[Part 2]** 85

Friends [for more]: **[Part 3]** 111
Friends [to be received favourably]: **[Part 1]** 34
Friends [to connect with]: **[Part 3]** 133
Friends [to find favour in the eyes of]: **[Part 2]** 85
Friends [to strengthen the bond of love between]: **[Part 3]** 111; 133
Friends & Friendship [to increase & maintain]: **[Part 3]** 111; 133;
138
Friendships [against false]: **[Part 2]** 54
Friendship [generally to inspire]: **[Part 3]** 111; 133

Grace, Favour & Loving-kindness: **[Part 2]** 72
Grace & Favour [in the eyes of God & Man]: **[Part 2]** 67; **[Part 3]**
119:73–80 [י (*Yod*)]
Grace, Favour & Mercy [in the eyes of all people]: **[Part 2]** 51:14;
72
Grace & Mercy [to receive]: **[Part 1]** 20:5; 20:6; 32; **[Part 2]** 72;
[Part 3] 106
Greatness [to ascend in]: **[Part 3]** 92

Harm [protection from]: **[Part 1]** 3; 5; 7; 14; 20; 23; 27; 31; 35; 40;
[Part 2] 48; 55; 59; 69; 70; **[Part 3]** 91; 102; 119; 121

Heartless Individuals [protection against]: **[Part 2]** 88
High Office [to ascend to]: **[Part 3]** 92
Higher Official or Ruler [to become a]: **[Part 3]** 92
Higher Official or Ruler [to defeat a]: **[Part 3]** 92
Honours [to attain high]: **[Part 3]** 92
Humanity [to improve the quality of]: **[Part 3]** 138
Humiliation [against]: **[Part 1]** 22
Hurt [against being]: **[Part 1]** 35; 41; **[Part 2]** 55
Hurt [by perverted individuals]: **[Part 1]** 8

Kings [to be rescued from evil]: **[Part 1]** 18; 38; 39
King or Ruling Authority [to appear before a]: **[Part 3]** 119:41–48
[ו (*Vav*)]; 122
Kings, Judges & Ruling Authorities [to be saved from]: **[Part 1]** 40;

Love [for love generally]: **[Part 3]** 133

Love [to cultivate from loved ones]: **[Part 3]** 133
Maintaining Self [before a spiritual/temporal authority]: **[Part 1]** 21; 21:2
Masses [for the]: **[Part 3]** 142
Mercy/Compassion [to request]: **[Part 1]** 12; 32; **[Part 3]** 119:41–48 [ו (*Vav*)]; 119:73–80 [י (*Yod*)]

Oath [to keep an]: **[Part 3]** 132
Officials [to deal kindly with the populace]: **[Part 3]** 102

Peace [to establish & maintain between people]: **[Part 3]** 98
Perseverance [for]: **[Part 2]** 61
Promises [to keep/fulfill]: **[Part 3]** 119:1–8 [א (*Alef*)]

Respect [to increase human]: **[Part 3]** 140
Ruler [to cause anger against an individual]: **[Part 3]** 119:41–48 [ו (*Vav*)]
Ruler/Governor [to inspire fear of a]: **[Part 3]** 119:41–48 [ו (*Vav*)]
Ruler/Governor [to intimidate a]: **[Part 3]** 119:41–48 [ו (*Vav*)]
Ruler/Governor [to threaten a]: **[Part 3]** 119:41–48 [ו (*Vav*)]
Rulers [when appearing before]: **[Part 1]** 21; 40; **[Part 3]** 119:41–48 [ו (*Vav*)]; 122

Social Menaces [against]: **[Part 3]** 94
Strangers [for]: **[Part 3]** 145
Suspicion [to ward off]: **[Part 3]** 119:73–80 [י (*Yod*)]

Truth [when veracity is doubted]: **[Part 1]** 14

Universal Brotherhood: **[Part 1]** 32; **[Part 2]** 45; 71; 75; **[Part 3]** 132
Vows [to keep/fulfill]: **[Part 3]** 119: 57–64 [ח (*Chet*)]

Well Received [to be]: **[Part 1]** 15
Words [fearing not being heard]: **[Part 1]** 14

11. Relationships, Love, Marriage, Family & Homes

Sorrow [resulting from the dissolution of a relationship]: **[Part 2]** 42
Soul Mate [finding a]: **[Part 2]** 68
Spouse [against harshness of a]: **[Part 1]** 10; 11

Wedding [on day of]: **[Part 1]** 19
Wife [for one who hates her husband]: **[Part 2]** 46
Wife/Husband [against an evil & abusive spouse]: **[Part 2]** 45; 46
Woman [against an angry]: **[Part 2]** 45

12. Pregnancy, Childbirth & Children

Barren Women [for]: **[Part 1]** 36; **[Part 3]** 102; 103; 112; 125; 127
Birth (confinement) [for protection during & a peaceful]: **[Part 3]** 121; 127

Childbirth [difficult confinement or dangerous delivery]: **[Part 1]** 1; 1:1–3; 19; 19:6; 26; **[Part 2]** 46:8 **[Part 3]** 100
Childbirth [during confinement]: **[Part 1]** 1–4; 20; 21–24; 22; 32:7; 33; **[Part 2]** 47; 72; 86; **[Part 3]** 104; 121; 139
Childbirth [to strengthen infants during confinement]: **[Part 3]** 142:8
Childlessness [against]: **[Part 3]** 103
Children [for crying]: **[Part 1]** 8; 9; 34:8–9; 41:5; **[Part 3]** 111; 111:1; 127
Children [for retarded]: **[Part 1]** 15
Children [for sick]: **[Part 1]** 8; 9
Children [for the success of]: **[Part 3]** 127; 128
Children [on taking to school]: **[Part 3]** 119
Children [protection of]: **[Part 1]** 35; **[Part 2]** 70; **[Part 3]** 113; 114; 126; 127; 147
Children [protection of the newborn against evil]: **[Part 3]** 127
Children [restoring health of]: **[Part 1]** 9
Children [to have]: **[Part 3]** 102; 103; 128
Children [to support the education of]: **[Part 3]** 127
Circumcision [on the day]: **[Part 1]** 12
Conception [to ensure]: **[Part 1]** 36; **[Part 3]** 101; 112; 126;

Delivery of a Child [successful]: **[Part 1]** 19; 20
Delivery of a Premature Child [successful]: **[Part 1]** 41

Evil Eye [protection of women during childbirth against the]: **[Part 2]** 67; **[Part 3]** 106:30; 121
Evil Spirits [to ward off following birth]: **[Part 3]** 106:30; 121; 126

Fear [during labour]: **[Part 2]** 76

Infants [to ward off evil spirits following birth]: **[Part 3]** 106:30 121; 126; 127

Infertility (sterility) [to counteract]: **[Part 3]** 112; 127; 128

Learning & Memory [to improve skills in children]: **[Part 3]** 119:130
Lilit [protection of women during childbirth against the demoness]: **[Part 2]** 67; **[Part 3]** 121; 126

Menstruation [to bring on]: **[Part 3]** 103
Miscarriage [against]: **[Part 1]** 1; 1:1–3; 32; 33; 33:1; **[Part 2]** 67:5–8; 69; **[Part 3]** 91:10; 91:10–16; 121; 127; 128
Miscarriage [for a woman to fall pregnant again following a]: **[Part 2]** 79
Miscarriage [to recover from a]: **[Part 2]** 55:9; 68
Mothers & Infants [protection against harm/safeguarding]: **[Part 3]** 121

Newborn [for protection of the]: **[Part 3]** 127; 128

Offspring [to engender pure and holy]: **[Part 3]** 115:12

Pregnancy [for a fortunate]: **[Part 3]** 128; 128:3
Pregnancy [for a successful]: **[Part 3]** 128; 128:3
Pregnancy [protection during]: **[Part 3]** 128
Pregnancy [to cause]: **[Part 1]** 5; 33; **[Part 2]** 69; **[Part 3]** 128
Pregnancy [to ensure a safe]: **[Part 1]** 1; 4; 8; 20; 33; 35; **[Part 2]** 57; **[Part 3]** 93; 108; 114; 128
Pregnant Woman [to cast out an evil spirit from a]: **[Part 2]** 76
Premature Delivery [against]: **[Part 1]** 1; 1:1–3 **[Part 3]** 127

Rebellious Children [to instill obedience in]: **[Part 1]** 23

Unborn [against possible afflictions of the]: **[Part 2]** 67:5–8

Witches [to save a mother from]: **[Part 3]** 91:5 & 10
Woman in labour [support for]: **[Part 1]** 20; **[Part 3]** 121

13. Dying, Death, Orphans, Old Age & Life Extension

Cemetery [for recitation at a]: **[Part 2]** 72; **[Part 3]** 119; 130
Children [for a woman whose offspring died]: **[Part 1]** 33
Children [against the loss of]: **[Part 1]** 20; **[Part 2]** 69

Death [against an unnatural & strange]: **[Part 1]** 13 (good for one day); 32:7
Death [against a sudden, violent, unusual, or unexpected]: **[Part 3]** 116
Death [at an anniversary (*Yahrtzeit*)]: **[Part 3]** 130
Death [fear of]: **[Part 1]** 38; **[Part 2]** 48; 54
Death [for a good]: **[Part 1]** 17; 38
Death [for natural]: **[Part 3]** 113
Death [protecting infants & children from]: **[Part 1]** 33; **[Part 3]** 126
Deceased [for the]: **[Part 3]** 119

Elderly [to support the]: **[Part 2]** 70; 71; **[Part 3]** 113

Funeral [on the day]: **[Part 1]** 23; 91; **[Part 3]** 119

Gravesites [protecting against demonic impact]: **[Part 1]** 91; **[Part 3]** 119

Life [for a long]: **[Part 1]** 23; **[Part 2]** 61
Longevity: **[Part 1]** 23; **[Part 2]** 61; **[Part 3]** 90; 91:15–16; 92

Mourning [during times of]: **[Part 1]** 23; 27; **[Part 2]** 49; **[Part 3]** 91; 121

Old Age [beset by]: **[Part 2]** 70; 71;
Old Age & Retirement [happy]: **[Part 1]** 29; 30; **[Part 2]** 70; 71; 77; 89; **[Part 3]** 91; 127

Opening the Heart [improving learning & memory skills in children]: **[Part 3]** 119:130
Orphans: **[Part 1]** 26; 34; **[Part 2]** 67; 81; **[Part 3]** 145

Parents [loss of]: **[Part 1]** 20

Visiting the Graves [of loved ones]: **[Part 1]** 25; 34; **[Part 3]** 111; 112; 119; 120–134; 135; 144–150

Widows/Widowers: **[Part 1]** 34; **[Part 2]** 67; **[Part 3]** 145

14. Religion & Spirituality

Accounting of the Soul [*Chesh'bon Hanefesh*]: **[Part 1]** 15
Afterlife (World to Come): **[Part 3]** 145
Atonement/Repentance [תשובה—*teshuvah* (spiritual return)]: **[Part 1]** 6; 15; 20; 25; 32; 38; **[Part 2]** 47; 51; 62; 86; **[Part 3]** 90; 116; 121; 130; 131; 135; 142

Baptism/Impurity [against being tricked into]: **[Part 2]** 95
Baptism [against compulsory]: **[Part 2]** 73
Beit Hamikdash (the Holy Temple) [to build]: **[Part 2]** 42; 43
Blasphemy [against]: **[Part 1]** 14; 23; **[Part 3]** 113
Blessed [for your coming & going to be]: **[Part 3]** 108
Boredom [to not succumb to]: **[Part 3]** 144

Candle-lighting [with]: **[Part 1]** 18:29
Celestial Accusers [to be recited from *Rosh Hashanah* (New Year) onwards to strip]: **[Part 1]** 27
Christian Priests [for public disputes with]: **[Part 3]** 115
Commitments [to keep]: **[Part 3]** 119: 57–64 [ח (*Chet*)]
Confession [penitent]: **[Part 3]** 136
Confused Religiously: **[Part 1]** 25; **[Part 3]** 143
Controlled Daydream [(*She'elah b'Hakitz*) divinatory answers to queries whilst fully awake]: **[Part 2]** 51
Conversion [against forced]: **[Part 2]** 73

Debates [to be victorious in religious]: **[Part 3]** 115
Divine Aid & Support [in need of]: **[Part 2]** 70; **[Part 3]** 91; 121; 130

Good spirits [loyalty of]: **[Part 1]** 26; **[Part 2]** 85; **[Part 3]** 98; 102
Good Year [to be recited from *Rosh Hashanah* (New Year) onwards to ensure a]: **[Part 1]** 27
Gratitude [to the Divine One]: **[Part 1]** 9; 18; **[Part 2]** 65; 68; **[Part 3]** 116;136
Gratitude [for success & prosperity]: **[Part 2]** 65; **[Part 3]** 147
Greatness of the Divine One [compared to the smallness of humankind, to consider]: **[Part 3]** 90
Guidance [for Divine]: **[Part 3]** 139

Hands [after washing]: **[Part 1]** 23; **[Part 2]**
Hands [with washing]: **[Part 1]** 26:6; **[Part 2]**
Heresy (זרה עבודה—*Avodah Zarah*) [for protection against engaging in]: **[Part 2]** 80; **[Part 3]** 113; 135
Heretics [to silence]: **[Part 3]** 118
Heretics [when arguing with]: **[Part 3]** 115
Holiness [for]: **[Part 3]** 130

Idolaters [for religious disputes against]: **[Part 3]** 115
Idolatry (אלילים עבודת—*Avodat Elilim*): **[Part 2]** 80; 81; **[Part 3]** 113
Impurity/Baptism [against being tricked into]: **[Part 2]** 95
Israel [for crisis in]: **[Part 1]** 20; **[Part 2]** 83; **[Part 3]** 121; 124; 130; 142

Jerusalem [for the well-being of]: **[Part 2]** 87; **[Part 3]** 122; 125
Jewish Nation [for the]: **[Part 2]** 53; 74; 83; **[Part 3]** 124
Jewish Unity: **[Part 3]** 132
Judaism: **[Part 2]** 53; 74; 83; **[Part 3]** 124

Land of Israel [for the well-being of the]: **[Part 2]** 74; 79; 83 **[Part 3]** 124; 127; 136

Meal [reciting before the blessing of a]: **[Part 1]** 23
Meditation [whilst walking]: **[Part 2]** 86:11
Meditations: **[Part 1]** 16:8; **[Part 2]** 80; **[Part 3]** 150
Mercy [request for Divine]: **[Part 1]** 32; **[Part 2]** 89; **[Part 3]** 98; 102
Miracles [to witness great]: **[Part 3]** 92

15. Malevolent Spirit Forces, Ghosts & Evil Spells

Angels [for protection against possible injury during exorcism]: **[Part 1]** 31:19

Demonic Attack [against]: **[Part 1]** 3; 3:2–9; **[Part 3]** 91
Demonic Forces [protection against]: **[Part 3]** 90; 91; 106:30; 110:6; 121; 144
Demonic Forces [protection of new residence against]: **[Part 3]** 119
Demonic Forces [to defeat]: **[Part 1]** 32:7; **[Part 3]** 94.1
Demonic Obsession [against]: **[Part 1]** 10; 21
Demonic Possession [against]: **[Part 2]** 66; **[Part 3]** 90; 91
Demonic Practices [against]: **[Part 3]** 105
Demons [to slay]: **[Part 1]** 15; **Part 3]** 104
Dibuk [to rid an individual of a demon or a]: **[Part 3]** 91

Evil [protection against & freedom from all]: **[Part 1]** 30; 36; **[Part 2]** 55; **[Part 3]** 91; 106:30
Evil [security from]: **[Part 1]** 17; **[Part 3]** 91; 106:30
Evil [to be saved from all]: **[Part 2]** 46:8; **[Part 3]** 91; 106:30
Evil [to fear no]: **[Part 1]** 12
Evil Powers [causing fever]: **[Part 1]** 8:2
Evil Spells [to counteract & be saved from]: **[Part 2]** 59; 67; 78; **[Part 3]** 91; 91:11; 105; 169–176 [ת *(Tav)*]
Evil Spirits [against fear of]: **[Part 3]** 145
Evil Spirits [protection against & to avert attacks from]: **[Part 1]** 5; 5:8; 10:17; 11; 15; 19; 24; 29; 39:2; 40; **[Part 2]** 67; 68; **[Part 3]** 90; 91; 91:5–6; 101; 106:30; 110:6; 144
Evil Spirits [to cast out]: **[Part 1]** 5:8; 10; 15; 29; 30:12; **[Part 2]** 50:21; 66; 86
Evil Spirits [freedom from]: **[Part 1]** 24; 40
Evil Spirits [to cause them to flee]: **[Part 3]** 90; 90–91; 91; 94.1

Ghosts [against fear of]: **[Part 3]** 145
Ghosts [protection against all]: **[Part 2]** 50; **[Part 3]** 90
Harmful Forces [to kill, drive away, or distance oneself from]: **[Part 3]** 104; 110:6
Harmful Spirits [protection against all]: **[Part 2]** 50; **[Part 3]** 106:30; 110:6; 121; 144
Haunted Houses: **[Part 2]** 47; **[Part 3]** 90

16. Hatred, Jealousy, Evil Eye, Enemies,
Adversity & Animosity

Enemies [to subdue known or secret]: **[Part 2]** 53; 54; 54:6; 55; 55:9

Enemies [to subjugate]: **[Part 2]** 79

Enemies/Robbers [when hiding in fear of being discovered by]: **[Part 2]** 54

Enemy [against an affliction by an]: **[Part 2]** 71; **[Part 3]** 109

Enemy [against fear of an]: **Part 3]** 161–168 [שׁ (*Shin*)]

Enmity [to overcome]: **Part 3]** 136

Envy [against]: **[Part 3]** 137

Evil Decrees & Evil Tidings [against]: **[Part 1]** 36

Evil Eye (*Ayin Hara*) [against & to avert the]: **[Part 1]** 5; 5:8; 20; 20:3; 31; 32; **[Part 2]** 71; **[Part 3]** 106:30; 119:113–120 [ס (*Samech*)]; 121; 141:4

Evil People [not to envy]: **[Part 1]** 37

Evil People [protection against]: **[Part 1]** 11; 38; **[Part 3]** 94; 106:30

Evil People [to frighten & drive away]: **[Part 1]** 94.1

Evil Plans/Machinations [to avert]: **[Part 3]** 119:81–88 [כ (*Kaf*)]

Fugitive [when fleeing from enemies]: **[Part 2]** 57

Hate [against]: **[Part 3]** 137

Hate [for haters to depart]: **[Part 1]** 7

Hate [to rid oneself of]: **[Part 3]** 137

Haters [for those who have]: **[Part 2]** 74; **[Part 3]** 109

Haters [to defeat]: **[Part 2]** 79

Haters [to dispel]: **[Part 3]** 119:153–160 [ר (*Resh*)]

Haters [to exact retribution on]: **[Part 3]** 94

Haters [to frighten]: **[Part 2]** 48; 53; **[Part 3]** 94.1

Haters [to kill]: **[Part 2]** 79

Haters [to subjugate]: **[Part 2]** 79

Haters [to transform into lovers]: **[Part 2]** 78:9

Hatred [against]: **[Part 1]** 10; 25:19; 30; 35; **[Part 3]** 137

Hostilility [against inimicality/quarreling]: **[Part 2]** 54

Intimidation [against]: **[Part 1]** 7; **[Part 3]** 119:153–160 [ר (*Resh*)]

Jealousy & Resentment [against]: **[Part 1]** 20; **[Part 2]** 51; **[Part 3]** 106:30; 111 [see also *Evil Eye*]

Malice [against]: [**Part 1**] 5; 30; 34; [**Part 2**] 52; 53; 54; 62; [**Part 3**] 100; 106:30; 118; 124; 128; 137; 139
Malediction [against unmerited]: [**Part 2**] 61

Peace [to establish with enemies]: [**Part 1**] 16; 28; [**Part 3**] 110
Peace [to establish between enemies/combatants]: [**Part 3**] 98; 161–168 [ש (*Shin*)]
Plots [protection against wicked]: [**Part 2**] 46:8
Prosecutors [to avert being struck by]: [**Part 3**] 161–168 [ש (*Shin*)]
Pursuers (Stalkers) [to dispel]: [**Part 3**] 119:153–160 [ר (*Resh*)]

Sabotage [against]: [**Part 2**] 68:2
Subterfuge [against]: [**Part 2**] 68:2

Temptation [against lies from enemies leading an individual into]: [**Part 1**] 64
Traitors [to subjugate & destroy]: [**Part 2**] 75
Trouble [to be saved/rescued from]: [**Part 2**] 54:9; 71:9
Trouble & Danger [against]: [**Part 1**] 20; 25; 26; 26:8; [**Part 3**] 91; 94

Wicked [against the]: [**Part 3**] 129
Wicked [to subjugate & destroy the]: [**Part 2**] 75

17. Slander, Falsehood & Wrongdoing

Accused Unjustly [to clear a group of people]: [**Part 2**] 60

Bad Language: [**Part 1**] 5; [**Part 2**] 63; [**Part 3**] 90; 119
Busybodies [against mischievous]: [**Part 1**] 35

Confession [of sins & transgressions]: [**Part 2**] 51; [**Part 3**] 136

Defamation, Slander & Gossip [against & to be saved from]: [**Part 1**] 4; 14; 31; 37; 38, 39; [**Part 2**] 51; 52; 56; 62; 64; 71; [**Part 3**] 90; 101; 108; 118; 119; 120; 139

Evil & Slanderous Libel [against]: [**Part 1**] 36; [**Part 3**] 119; 120; 127
Evil Doers [for the annihilation of]: [**Part 1**] 36

Evil Undertakings [to withdraw from]: **[Part 3]** 119:49–56 [ז (*Zayin*)]

Falsehoods [against spreading]: **[Part 2]** 52
Forgiveness [of errors & transgressions]: **[Part 1]** 16; 31; 37; **[Part 2]** 50; 72; 75; **[Part 3]** 94; 102; 117; 118

Lies [against]: **[Part 1]** 11; 33; **[Part 2]** 52; 57; **[Part 3]** 108; 115

Meddling [against (in the affairs of others)]: **[Part 2]** 52

Sin [after committing & being burdened with]: **[Part 1]** 25; 32; **[Part 2]** 51; **[Part 3]** 130
Sin [to refrain from]: **[Part 3]** 119:33–40 [ה (*Heh*)]
Sins [atonement for]: **[Part 2]** 75
Sins [forgiveness of]: **[Part 2]** 62; 75
Sin [to discourage transgression]: **[Part 1]** 12
Sinner [to avoid becoming a]: **[Part 2]** 79
Sinners [for]: **[Part 2]** 44
Slanderers & Slander [for deliverance from]: **[Part 3]** 101; 119; 127
Slandered Falsely [for an individual who is]: **[Part 3]** 117; 119; 127

Tongue [binding an evil]: **[Part 1]** 31; 31:19; **[Part 3]** 127
Transgressions [atonement for]: **[Part 2]** 75; **[Part 3]** 103; 113

Unjust Accusations [against]: **[Part 1]** 7; 17; 25
Unjust Denunciations [against]: **[Part 2]** 68

Wicked Men [against]: **[Part 1]** 11; **[Part 3]** 129
Wrongdoing [victim of]: **[Part 1]** 39; **[Part 2]** 64; **[Part 3]** 120

18. Robbery, Theft & Common Criminality
Criminals [to halt gangs of]: **[Part 2]** 48
Criminals [to locate]: **[Part 1]** 35
Criminals [to repent]: **[Part 2]** 73

Robbers & Bandits [to flee]: **[Part 1]** 18:1
Robbers & Brigands [to escape]: **[Part 2]** 50

Theft, Thieves & Robbers [protection against]: **[Part 1]** 5; 7; 11; 18:1; 26; 36; **[Part 2]** 50; 54; 61; 67; 68; **[Part 3]** 97:2; 147
Thiefs [to discover identity of]: **[Part 1]** 16; 29; 77:15; 78
Thiefs [to halt burglars before harm & to cause repentance of]: **[Part 1]** 15

19. Justice, Legal Matters, Law Suits & Judgment
Court of Law [in a]: **[Part 1]** 20; **[Part 2]** 55
Court of Law [against enemies in a]: **[Part 1]** 7; 38:14–15

Injustice [against]: **[Part 3]** 100

Judge [appearing before a]: **[Part 1]** 5; **[Part 2]** 43
Judge [finding favour from a]: **[Part 3]** 119:89–96 [ל *(Lamed)*]
Judge [to be recited before sitting in judgement]: **[Part 2]** 76
Judgement [for good]: **[Part 1]** 20
Judgement [for wrongful or unfavourable]: **[Part 1]** 7; 12; 25; 38; **[Part 2]** 51; 70
Judgement [to accept a]: **[Part 3]** 119:137–144 [צ *(Tzadi)*]
Judgement [to ensure a truthful]: **[Part 3]** 119:137–144 [צ *(Tzadi)*]
Judgement [to nullify negative]: **[Part 3]** 119: 89–96 [ל *(Lamed)*]
Judges & Tribunals [to support]: **[Part 3]** 93
Judicial Matters [general]: **[Part 1]** 20
Justice [for just people]: **[Part 2]** 81; **[Part 3]** 105; 111; 121; 134

Lawsuit [for support in a]: **[Part 3]** 93
Lawsuit [success in a]: **[Part 1]** 7; 35; 38:14–15; **[Part 2]** 73; **[Part 3]** 93; 119:25–32 [ד *(Dalet)*]; 109:7
Lawsuit [to secure victory in a]: **[Part 3]** 93; 119: 89–96 [ל *(Lamed)*]; 109:7
Lawsuit [winning against the unrighteous, quarrelsome & vengeful]: **[Part 1]** 35; 38:14–15

Perjury: **[Part 2]** 62

Trials & Sentencing: **[Part 1]** 12; **[Part 3]** 119:137–144 [צ *(Tzadi)*]

20. Punishment, Vengeance & Imprisonment

21. Anger, Rage, Belligerence, Violence, War & Peace

Oppressed [for those who are]: **[Part 1]** 9; 35; **[Part 3]** 93; 109
Oppressors [against]: **[Part 1]** 35; 37; **[Part 2]** 58; 79; **[Part 3]** 109

Peace: **[Part 1]** 36; **[Part 2]** 45; 46; 71; 75; **[Part 3]** 119; 121; 132; 143; 147
Perilous Situations & Times of Trouble [protection in]: **[Part 1]** 4; 6; 7; 9; 13; 16; 18; 20; 20:3; 23; 25; 26; 27; 29; 30; 31; 32; 33; 37; 38; 39; 41; **[Part 2]** 42; 49; 51; 54; 55; 56; 67; 69; 71; 81; 85; 86; 87; **[Part 3]** 91; 94; 100; 102–105 (recited individually or collectively); 107; 109; 110; 116; 118; 119; 121; 128; 130; 142; 143
Perils [against all]: **[Part 1]** 11
Persecution [against fierce]: **[Part 1]** 7; 34; 36; **[Part 2]** 54; 67; 70; **[Part 3]** 142
Persecution [safety from]: **[Part 1]** 11; 12; **[Part 2]** 68; **[Part 3]** 101
Prisoners of War [to free]: **[Part 2]** 43

Rage [alleviate personal]: **[Part 1]** 31

Siege [for Divine Intervention during a]: **[Part 2]** 47
Slavery [against]: **[Part 3]** 104
Slaves [to free]: **[Part 2]** 54
Slaves [to retrieve runaway]: **[Part 3]** 123
Soldiers [safety for]: **[Part 2]** 60
Sword [when struck with a knife, sharp instrument, bullet, or with a]: **[Part 3]** 146

Threats [against]: **[Part 1]** 30; 38; **[Part 2]** 53; 74; 83; 85; 86; **[Part 3]** 102; 124; 130; 142
Threats [at night]: **[Part 3]** 121
Torment [against]: **[Part 1]** 3
Troop Commander [protection of a]: **[Part 2]** 47
Troops [to strengthen]: **[Part 2]** 47
Tyranny [against]: **[Part 1]** 2; **[Part 2]** 57; 58; 75; 88; **[Part 3]** 149
Violence [for protection in conditions of great]: **[Part 2]** 68:2
Violence [when incited to commit]: **[Part 2]** 62

War [before going to]: **[Part 2]** 60
War [for protection & safety in conditions of]: **[Part 2]** 68:2; 83; 83:14

". ... ...but Perele, the Maharal's wife, peace upon her, could not resist making use of Yossele (Yosef) the golem a day before Passover Eve to help her with holiday preparations. Unbeknownst to the Maharal, she motioned to the golem to fetch water and fill up the two large barrels that stood in a special room that had already been cleaned and made ready for Passover....Yossele quickly seized the yoke and the two buckets and dashed off to the well to bring water. But no one was around to notice what he was up to....In short, Yossele the golem did not have the faintest idea when to stop fetching water.

Because no one told him to stop, he kept on bringing water and pouring it into the barrels, even though they were already full....When members of the household noticed the water suddenly gushing on the floor of the house, they became frightened and astounded. 'Water! Water!" they began shouting....

They looked and searched and when they opened the door where the two barrels stood....they saw Yossele the golem pouring the water. This prompted a great deal of laughter in the house and the Maharal too began laughing.

'Look here,' he told his wife, "you found yourself some water carrier for Passover!" He immediately ran to the golem, took the bucket from him, and said, 'Enough! That's quite enough!'.... Because of that incident, a popular saying spread through Prague. When someone wanted to criticize a workman's shoddy labor, he would say, 'You're fit to be a watchmaker like Yossele the golem is fit for water carrying.'... ... ."

— Yudl Rosenberg
(The Golem and the Wondrous
Deeds of the Maharal of Prague)

REFERENCES
&
BIBLIOGRAPHY

INTRODUCTION

1. **Gray, W.G.:** *An Outlook on Our Inner Western Way,* the Sangreal Sodality Press, Johannesburg 2008.
2. **Tzadok, A. bar:** *Walking in Fire: Classical Torah/Kabbalistic Meditations, Practices & Prayers,* Kosher Torah Publishers, Tarzana 2007.
    —*Protection from Evil: Exposing & Neutralizing Harmful Spiritual Forces in Light of Torah & Kabbalah,* Kosher Torah Publishers 2010.
    —*Aliens, Angels and Demons: Extraterrestrial Life in Judaism/Kabbalah & Its Vital Relevance for Modern Times,* The Kosher Torah School 2017.
    —*Protection From Evil: Exposing & Neutralizing Harmful Spiritual Forces in Light of Torah and Kabbalah,* The Kosher Torah School 2020.
    —*Let There Be....KNOWING: Using the Prophetic Kabbalah & Ma'aseh Merkava to Expand the Powers of the Mind/Soul,* The Kosher Torah School 2021.
    —*Using the Holy Names of God: Developing Psychic Abilities, Using the Secret Codes Within the Torah,* Kosher Torah School 2022.
3. **Swart, J.G.:** *The Book of Immediate Magic—Part 1,*
4. *Ibid.*
5. *Ibid.*
6. *Ibid.*
7. *Ibid.*

CHAPTER 5

Psalm 90

1.   Nemoy, L., Lieberman, S. & Wolfson, H.A.: *The Midrash on Psalms (Midrash Tehillim)*, Vol. 2, Yale University Press, New Haven 1959.
2.   Cohen, A.: *The Psalms*, Soncino Press 1945.
      Gruber, M.I.: *Rashi's Commentary on Psalms*, Jewish Publication Society, Philadelphia 2007.
      Schmutzer, A.J. & Howard, D.M.: *The Psalms: Language for All Seasons of the Soul*, Moody Publishers, Chicago 2014.
3.   Nemoy, L., Lieberman, S. & Wolfson, H.A.: *The Midrash on Psalms (Midrash Tehillim)*, Vol. 2, *Op. Cit.*
      Simon, U.: *Four Approaches to the Book of Psalms: From Saadiah Gaon to Abraham Ibn Ezra*, State University of New York Press, Albany 1991.
4.   Nulman, M.: *The Encyclopedia of Jewish Prayer*, Jason Aronson, Northvale 1993.
      Rosenberg, A.S.: *Jewish Liturgy as a Spiritual System: a Prayer-by-Prayer Explanation of the Nature and Meaning of Jewish Worship*, Jason Aronson Inc., Northvale 1997.
5.   *Ibid.*
6.   *Ibid.*
7.   *Ibid.*
8.   Singer, I. & Adler, C.: *The Jewish Encyclopedia: A Descriptive Record of the History, Religion, Literature and Customs of the Jewish People from the Earliest Times to the Present Day*, Funk & Wagnalls Company, New York & London 1901–1906.
      Le Livre des Psaumes Hébreu-Français et Phonétique: Traduction Français et Transcription Phonétique du Livre des Psaumes. Prières pour les malades, la subsistance. Prières prononcées sur la tombe des tsadikim, hachkavot, différents kaddich, allumage des bougies. Message du Ramban et autre prières, Nouvelle Edition, Editions Sinai, Tel Aviv 2006.
      Ronen, D.: *Tehilim Kavvanot ha-Lev*, Machon Shirah Chadashah, Petah Tikva 2013.
      Azulai, H.Y.D.: *Sefer Tehillim Sha'arei Rachamim: im Segulot v'Tefilot ha'Chida*, Agudat Zichron Rachamim, Jerusalem 1997.
9.   Kimchi, D. ben Y.: *Sefer Tehillim: im Perush Rabbi David Kimchi*, Amsterdam 1731.

Sefer Shimmush Tehillim, Éliás Békéscsaba Klein, Budapest.

Seder Tefilot Tikun Ezra: kolel tefilot kol hashanah, Taubstummen Instituts Druckerei, Wien 1815.

Grünwald, M.: *Ueber den Einfluss der Psalmen auf die Katholische Liturgie, mit steter Rücksichtnahme auf die Talmudisch-Midraschische Literatur*, Commissions-Verlag von J. Kauffmann, Frankfurt am Main 1891.

Refuah v'Chayim m'Yerushalayim im Shimush Tehilim, Defus Yehudah vi-Yerushalayim, Jerusalem 1931.

Landsberg, M.: *Sefer Tehillim im Peirush Rashi Metzudat David Metzudat Tziyon v'alav sovev Peirush Divrei Mosheh*, S.D. Friedman, Brooklyn 2015.

Brauner, R.: *Synopsis of Sefer Shimush Tehillim, containing protections against numerous calamities: attributed to Rav Hai Gaon*, Reuven Brauner sixth edition, Raanana 2012.

Rebiger, B.: *Sefer Shimmush Tehillim: Buch vom magischen Gebrauch der Psalmen, Edition, Übersetzung und Kommentar*, TSAJ 137, Mohr Siebeck, Tübingen 2010.

Hai ben Sherira Gaon & Varady, A.N.: *Shimush Tehillim (the Theurgical Use of Psalms)*, document shared on Creative Commons Attribution-ShareAlike (CC BY-SA) 4.0 International, May 4th 2015.

10. *Ibid.*
11. *Ibid.*
12. **Selig, G.:** *Sepher Schimmusch Tehillim. Oder: Gebrauch der Psalme zum leiblichen Wohl der Menschen*, Johann Andreas Kunze, Berlin 1788/ Verlag E. Schubert, Bilfingen 1972.

—Secrets of the Psalms: A Fragment of the Practical Kabala, with Extracts from other Kabalistic writings, as translated by the author, Dorene, Arlington 1929.

The Sixth and Seventh Books of Moses or, Moses' Magical Spirit-art, known as the Wonderful Arts of the Old Wise Hebrews, taken from the Mosaic books of the Cabala and the Talmud, for the good of mankind. Translated from the German, word for word, according to Old Writings, with Numerous Engravings, The Arthur Westbrook Co., 1870.

Peterson, J.H.: *The Sixth and Seventh Books of Moses or Moses' Magical Spirit-Art: Known as the Wonderful Arts of the Old Wise Hebrews, Taken from the Mosaic Books of the Kabbalah and the Talmud, for the Good of Mankind*, Ibis Press, Newburyport 2008.

13. *Ibid.*
14. **Brauner, R.:** *Synopsis of Sefer Shimush Tehillim, Op. Cit.*

457

15. **Rebiger, B.:** *Sefer Shimmush Tehillim, Op. Cit.*
16. *Ibid.*
17. **Singer, I. & Adler, C.:** *The Jewish Encyclopedia, Op. Cit.*
18. **Beinish, B.:** *Amtachat Binyamin,* Hotza'at Backal, Jerusalem 1966.
   Harari, Y.: *Between Magic and Practical Kabbalah: The Shema as a Performative Praxis,* in Benovitz, N. & Mevorah, D.: *Hear, O Israel: The Magic of the Shema,* The Israel Museum, Jerusalem 2021.
19. **Swart, J.G.:** *The Book of Sacred Names,* The Sangreal Sodality Press, Johannesburg 2011.
   —*The Book of Seals & Amulets,* The Sangreal Sodality Press, Johannesburg 2014.
   —*The Book of BImmediate Magic—Part 1,* The Sangreal Sodality Press, Johannesburg 2015.
20. *Ibid.*
21. **Feldman, Y.Y.:** *Tehillim Eis Ratzon: A Time of Favor,* Feldheim Publishers, Jerusalem & New York 2004.
22. *Ibid.*
23. **Zacutto, M.:** *Shorshei ha-Shemot,* Hotzaat Nezer Shraga, Jerusalem 1999.
24. *Ibid.*
25. **Freedman, H. & Simon, M.:** *Midrash Rabbah: Exodus,* Soncino Press, London 1939.
   Sharfman, B.: *The Rabbinical Council Manual of Holiday and Sabbath Sermons,* Rabbinical Council Press, New York 1957.
   Bleich, D. & Scherman, N.: *Bircas haChammah,* Mesorah Publications, Brooklyn 1980.
   Nulman, M.: *The Encyclopedia of Jewish Prayer, Op. Cit.*
   Assaf, D.: *Kaddish: Its Origins, Meanings and Laws,* Maimonides Research Institute, Haifa, 2003.
26. **Weintraub, S.Y.:** *Healing of Soul, Healing of Body: Spiritual Leaders Unfold the Strength & Solace in Psalms,* Jewish Light Publishing, Woodstock 2002.
27. **Schrire, T.:** *Hebrew Amulets,* Routledge & Kegan Paul, London 1966.
   Davis, E. & Frenkel, D.A.: *Ha-Kami'a ha-Ivri: Mikra'i Refu'i Kelali im Tatzlumim v'Iyurim Rabim,* Machon l'Mada'e ha-Yahadut, Jerusalem 1995.
   Green, A.: *Judaic Artifacts: Unlocking the Secrets of Judaic Charms and Amulets,* Astrolog Publishing House, Hod Hasharon 2004.

28. *Ibid.*
29. **Eliram (Amslam), S.:** *Sefer Segulot, Terufot u'Mazalot,* Eliram–Sifre Kodesh, Jerusalem 2002.
30. **Keller, I.:** *Prosper Our Hands,* https://www.irwinkeller.com/ itzikswell/2022/3/5/prosper-our-hands.
31. **Swart, J.G.:** *The Book of Seals & Amulets, Op. Cit.*
32. **Rosenberg, Y.:** *Rafael ha-Malach,* Asher Klein, Jerusalem 2000.
33. *Ibid.*
34. *Ibid.*
35. **Swart, J.G.:** *The Book of Seals & Amulets, Op. Cit.*
36. *Ibid.*
    Wasserfall, R.R.: *Women and Water: Menstruation in Jewish Life and Law,* Bandeis University Press, Hanover 1999.
    Philip, T.S.: *Menstruation and Childbirth in the Bible: Fertility and Impurity,* Peter Lang Publishing Inc., New York 2006.
37. **Swart, J.G.:** *The Book of Seals & Amulets, Op. Cit.*
38. *Ibid.*
    Rosenberg, Y.: *Rafael ha-Malach, Op. Cit.*
39. **Rankine, D. & Barron, P.H.:** *The Book of Gold: A 17th Century Magical Grimoire of Amulets, Charms, Prayers, Sigils and Spells using the Biblical Psalms of King David,* Avalonia, London 2010.
    Marty, J. & MacParthy, F.: *Usage Mago-Théurgiques des Psaumes: Selon la Kabbala Judaique et Chrétienne: Sefer Shimoush Théhilim & Le Livre d'Or,* Sesheta Publications, Brestot 2018.
40. *Ibid.*
41. *Ibid.*

Psalm 91

1. **Nemoy, L., Lieberman, S. & Wolfson, H.A.:** *The Midrash on Psalms* (*Midrash Tehillim*), Vol. 2, *Op. Cit.*
   Simon, U.: *Four Approaches to the Book of Psalms, Op. Cit.*
   Cohen, A.: *The Psalms, Op. Cit.*
   Gruber, M.I.: *Rashi's Commentary on Psalms, Op. Cit.*
   Schmutzer, A.J. & Howard, D.M.: *The Psalms: Language for All Seasons of the Soul, Op. Cit.*
2. **Townsend, J.T.:** *Midrash Tanhuma: S. Buber Recension,* Ktav Publishing House, Jersey City 1989–2003.
3. **Singer, S.:** *The Authorised Daily Prayer Book of the United Hebrew Congregations of the British Commonwealth of Nations,* Eyre and Spottiswoode Ltd., London 1962.

Siddur Kol Yaakov, edited Bitton, D., Sephardic Heritage Foundation Inc., New York 1985.

Baruch, S.Z. ben & Mangel, N.: *Siddur Tehillat Hashem al pi Nusach ha-Ari Zal with English Translation, Annotated Edition*, Merkoz L'inyonei Chinuch Inc., Brooklyn 2003.

Churba, A.: *Siddur Keter Shelomo: Complete Weekday and Shabbat Siddur with linear English translation according to the customs of Aram Soba*, Congregation Shaare Rachamim, Brooklyn 2011.

Scherman, N. & Zlotowitz, G.: *Siddur Kol Sim'chah: The Artscroll Sephardic Siddur*, The Schottenstein Edition, Mesorah Publications, Brooklyn 2019.

4. **Chajes, J.H.**: *Between Worlds: Dybbuks, Exorists, and Early Modern Judaism*, University of Pennsylvania Press, Philadelphia 2003.

   Henze, M.: *Psalm 91 in Premodern Interpretation and at Qumran* in **M. Henze, M. (ed.)**: *Biblical Interpretation at Qumran*, Grand Rapids 2005.

   Harari, Y.: *Jewish Magic before the Rise of Kabbalah*, Wayne State University Press, Detroit 2017.

   Vreugdenhil, G.C.: *Psalm 91 and Demonic Menace*, Brill, Leiden, 2020.

5. **Nulman, M.**: *The Encyclopedia of Jewish Prayer*, Op. Cit.
6. *Ibid.*
7. *Ibid.*

   Trachtenberg, J.: *Jewish Magic and Superstition: A Study in Folk Religion*, Behrman's Jewish Book House Publishers, New York 1939.

8. **Zaleski, P. & Zaleski, C.**: *Prayer: A History*, Houghton Mifflin Company, Boston & New York 2005.

9. **Schmid, D.**: *Jüdische Amulette aus Osteuropa – Phänomene, Rituale, Formensprache*, Dissertation, Universität Wien, Vienna 2012.

10. **Kanarfogel, E.**: *Peering Through the Lattices: Mystical, Magical, and Pietistic Dimensions in the Tosafist Period*, Wayne State University Press, Detroit 2000.

11. **Nulman, M.**: *The Encyclopedia of Jewish Prayer*, Op. Cit.
12. *Ibid.*
13. *Ibid.*
14. *Ibid.*
15. *The Zohar*, transl. D.C. Matt (Pritzker edition Vol. 1), Stanford University Press, Stanford 2003.
16. **Nulman, M.**: *The Encyclopedia of Jewish Prayer*, Op. Cit.

17. *Ibid.*
18. *Ibid.*
19. **Trachtenberg, J.:** *Jewish Magic and Superstition, Op. Cit.*
20. **Swart, J.G.:** *The Book of Magical Psalms—Part 1*, The Sangreal Sodality Press, Johannesburg 2021.
21. **Zaleski, P. & Zaleski, C.:** *Prayer: A History, Op. Cit.*
22. **Klein, M.:** *A Time to Be Born: Customs and Folklore of Jewish Birth*, The Jewish Publication Society, Philadelphia 2000.
23. **Dobrinsky, H.C.:** *A Treasury of Sephardic laws and customs: the ritual practices of Syhrian, Moroccan, Judeo-Spanish and Spanish and Portuguese Jews of North America*, Yeshiva University Press, New York 1986.
24. **Trachtenberg, J.:** *Jewish Magic and Superstition, Op. Cit.*
25. **Nulman, M.:** *The Encyclopedia of Jewish Prayer, Op. Cit.*
26. **Perles, J.:** *Die Berner Handschrift Kleinen Aruch* in *Jubelschrift zum Siebzigsten Geburtstage des Prof. Dr. H. Graetz*, S. Schottlaender, Breslau 1887.
    Trachtenberg, J.: *Jewish Magic and Superstition, Op. Cit.*
    Nulman, M.: *The Encyclopedia of Jewish Prayer, Op. Cit.*
27. **Kimchi, D. ben Y.:** *Sefer Tehillim, Op. Cit.*
    Sefer Shimmush Tehillim, Op. Cit.
    Seder Tefilot Tikun Ezra, Op. Cit.
    Grünwald, M.: *Ueber den Einfluss der Psalmen auf die Katholische Liturgie, Op. Cit.*
    Singer, I. & Adler, C.: *The Jewish Encyclopedia, Op. Cit.*
    Le Livre des Psaumes Hébreu-Français et Phonétique, Op. Cit.
    Azulai, H.Y.D.: *Sefer Tehillim Sha'arei Rachamim, Op. Cit.*
    Refuah v'Chayim m'Yerushalayim im Shimush Tehilim, Op. Cit.
    Rebiger, B.: *Sefer Shimmush Tehillim, Op. Cit.*
    Brauner, R.: *Synopsis of Sefer Shimush Tehillim. Op. Cit.*
    Landsberg, M.: *Sefer Tehillim im Peirush Rashi, Op. Cit.*
    Ronen, D.: *Tehilim Kavvanot ha-Lev, Op. Cit.*
    Hai ben Sherira Gaon & Varady, A.N.: *Shimush Tehillim* (*the Theurgical Use of Psalms*), *Op. Cit.*
    Trachtenberg, J.: *Jewish Magic and Superstition, Op. Cit.*
    Dennis, G.W.: *The Encyclopedia of Jewish Myth, Magic and Mysticism*, Llewellyn Publications, Woodbury 2007.
28. **Kaplan, A.:** *The Torah Anthology: Deuteronomy III, Gratitude & discipline*, Moznaim Publishing Company, New York 1977.
29. **Kimchi, D. ben Y.:** *Sefer Tehillim, Op. Cit.*
    Sefer Shimmush Tehillim, Op. Cit.
    Seder Tefilot Tikun Ezra, Op. Cit.
    Grünwald, M.: *Ueber den Einfluss der Psalmen auf die Katholische Liturgie, Op. Cit.*

Singer, I. & Adler, C.: *The Jewish Encyclopedia, Op. Cit.*
Le Livre des Psaumes Hébreu-Français et Phonétique, Op. Cit.
Azulai, H.Y.D.: *Sefer Tehillim Sha'arei Rachamim, Op. Cit.*
Refuah v'Chayim m'Yerushalayim im Shimush Tehilim, Op. Cit.
Rebiger, B.: *Sefer Shimmush Tehillim, Op. Cit.*
Ronen, D.: *Tehilim Kavvanot ha-Lev, Op. Cit.*
Brauner, R.: *Synopsis of Sefer Shimush Tehillim. Op. Cit.*
Landsberg, M.: *Sefer Tehillim im Peirush Rashi, Op. Cit.*
Hai ben Sherira Gaon & Varady, A.N.: *Shimush Tehillim* (*the Theurgical Use of Psalms*), *Op. Cit.*

30. Trachtenberg, J.: *Jewish Magic and Superstition, Op. Cit.*
31. *Ibid.*
32. Dennis, G.W.: *The Encyclopedia of Jewish Myth, Magic and Mysticism, Op. Cit.*
33. Blau, L.: *Das Altjüdische Zauberwesen*, Budapest 1898.
    Trachtenberg, J.: *Jewish Magic and Superstition, Op. Cit.*
34. Nulman, M.: *The Encyclopedia of Jewish Prayer, Op. Cit.*
35. Davies, J.: *Death, Burial, and Rebirth in the Religions of Antiquity*, Routledge, London 1999.
    Breed, B.: *Reception of the Psalms: The Example of Psalm 91*, in Brown, W.P.: *The Oxford Handbook of the Psalms*, Oxford University Press, Oxford & New York 2014
    Jütte, R.: *The Jewish Body: A History*, transl. Bredeck, E., University of Pennsylvania Press, Philadelphia 2021.]
36. Klein, I.: *A Guide to Jewish Religious Practice,* The Jewish Theological Seminary of America, New York & Jerusalem 1992.
    Eisenberg, R.L.: *The JPS Guide to Jewish Traditions*, The Jewish Publication Society, Philadelphia 2004.
37. Frojimovics, K.; Kmoróczy, G.; Pusztai, V. & Strbik, A.: *Jewish Budapest: Monuments, Rites, History*, Central University Press, Budapest 1999.
38. Nulman, M.: *The Encyclopedia of Jewish Prayer, Op. Cit.*
39. *Ibid.*
40. Scholem, G.G.: *On the Kabbalah and Its Symbolism*, Schocken Books, New York 1972.
41. Sobel, Z. & Beit-Hallahmi, B.: *Jewishness and Judaism in Contemporary Israel*, State University of New York Press, New York 1991.
42. Swart, J.G.: *The Book of Magical Psalms—Part 2*, The Sangreal Sodality Press, Johannesburg 2022.
43. Trachtenberg, J.: *Jewish Magic and Superstition, Op. Cit.*
44. Nulman, M.: *The Encyclopedia of Jewish Prayer, Op. Cit.*
    Rossoff, D.: *Safed: The Mystical City*, Sha'ar Books, Jerusalem 1991.

Schwartz, H.: *Tree of Souls: The Mythology of Judaism*, Oxford University Press, Oxford & New York 2004.

45. Scholem, G.G.: *On the Kabbalah and Its Symbolism*, *Op. Cit.*
Sobel, Z. & Beit-Hallahmi, B.: *Jewishness and Judaism in Contemporary Israel*, *Op. Cit.*
Feldman, E.: *Biblical and Post-Biblical Defilement and Mourning: Law as Theology*, Yeshiva University Press, New York 1977.

46. Heilman, S.C.: *When a Jew Dies: The Ethnography of a Bereaved Son*, University of California Press, Berkeley, Los Angeles & London 2001.

47. *Ibid.*

48. *Ibid.*

49. *Ibid.*

50. Rossoff, D.: *Safed: The Mystical City*, *Op. Cit.*

51. Singer, I. & Adler, C.: *The Jewish Encyclopedia*, *Op. Cit.*

52. Montgomery, J.A.: *Aramaic Incantation Texts from Nippur*, University Museum, University of Philadelphia, Pennsylvania1913.
Schiffmann, L.H. & Swartz, M.D.: *Hebrew and Aramaic Incantation Texts from the Cairo Genizah*, Sheffield Academic Press Ltd., Sheffield 1992.
Naveh, J. & Shaked, S.: *Magic Spells and Formulae: Aramaic Incantations of Late Antiquity*, The Magnes Press, Jerusalem 1993.

53. Kimchi, D. ben Y.: *Sefer Tehillim*, *Op. Cit.*
Sefer Shimmush Tehillim, *Op. Cit.*
Seder Tefilot Tikun Ezra, *Op. Cit.*
Le Livre des Psaumes Hébreu-Français et Phonétique, *Op. Cit.*
Grünwald, M.: *Ueber den Einfluss der Psalmen auf die Katholische Liturgie*, *Op. Cit.*
Refuah v'Chayim m'Yerushalayim im Shimush Tehilim, *Op. Cit.*
Landsberg, M.: *Sefer Tehillim im Peirush Rashi*, *Op. Cit.*
Rebiger, B.: *Sefer Shimmush Tehillim*, *Op. Cit.*
Hai ben Sherira Gaon & Varady, A.N.: *Shimush Tehillim* (*the Theurgical Use of Psalms*), *Op. Cit.*

54. *Ibid.*

55. Selig, G.: *Sepher Schimmusch Tehillim*, *Op. Cit.*
The Sixth and Seventh Books of Moses, *Op. Cit.*
Peterson, J.H.: *The Sixth and Seventh Books of Moses*, *Op. Cit.*

56. Swart, J.G.: *The Book of Self Creation*, The Sangreal Sodality Press, Johannesburg 2021.
—*The Book of Sacred Names*, *Op. Cit.*

463

—The Book of Seals & Amulets, *Op. Cit.*
—The Book of Immediate Magic—Part 1, *Op. Cit.*
—The Book of Immediate Magic—Part 2, The Sangreal Sodality Press, Johannesburg 2018.
—The Book of Magical Psalms—Part 1, *Op. Cit.*
—The Book of Magical Psalms—Part 2, The Sangreal Sodality Press, Johannesburg 2022.

57. **Harari, Y.**: *Between Magic and Practical Kabbalah: The Shema as a Performative Praxis*, in Benovitz, N. & Mevorah, D.: *Hear, O Israel: The Magic of the Shema*, The Israel Museum, Jerusalem 2021.

58. **Gikatilla, J.**: *Gates of Light: Sha'are Orah*, transl. Avi Weinstein, Alta Mira Press, Walnut Creek 1998.

59. **Rebiger, B.**: *Sefer Shimmush Tehillim, Op. Cit.*

60. *Ibid.*

61. **Vukosavović, F.**: *Angels and Demons: Jewish Magic through the Ages*, Bible Lands Museum Jerusalem, Jerusalem 2010.
Swart, J.G.: *The Book of Seals & Amulets, Op. Cit.*

62. **Ba'al Shem, E.; Ba'al-Shem, J. & Hillel, M.**: *Sefer Toldot Adam, Op. cit.*

63. **Swart, J.G.**: *The Book of Sacred Names, Op. Cit.*
—The Book of Seals & Amulets, Op. Cit.

64. **Ochanah, R. ben C.**: *Sefer Mareh ha-Yeladim*, Yerid ha-Sefarim, Jerusalem 1990.

65. **Swart, J.G.**: *The Book of Seals & Amulets, Op. Cit.*
Zacutto, M.: *Shorshei ha-Shemot, Op. Cit.*

66. **Feldman, Y.Y.**: *Tehillim Eis Ratzon, Op. Cit.*

67. **Rebiger, B.**: *Sefer Shimmush Tehillim, Op. Cit.*

68. *Ibid.*

69. **Schrire, T.**: *Hebrew Amulets, Op. Cit.*
Green, A.: *Judaic Artifacts, Op. Cit.*

70. **Swart, J.G.**: *The Book of Seals & Amulets, Op. Cit.*
—The Book of Immediate Magic—Part 1, Op. Cit.

71. **Swart, J.G.**: *The Book of Sacred Names, Op. Cit.*
Hoffman, L.A.: *My People's Passover Haggadah: Traditional Texts, Modern Commentaries*, Jewish Lights Publishing, Woodstock 2008.

72. **Gumbiner, A.A.**: *Sefer Magen Avraham*, Amsterdam 1732.

73. **Swart, J.G.**: *The Book of Sacred Names, Op. Cit.*
Kanarfogel, E.: *Peering Through the Lattices: Mystical, Magical, and Pietistic Dimensions in the Tosafist Period*, Wayne State University Press, Detroit 2000.

74. **Swart, J.G.:** *The Book of Seals & Amulets, Op. Cit.*
    Zacutto, M.: *Shorshei ha-Shemot, Op. Cit.*
75. **Swart, J.G.:** *Ibid.*
76. *Ibid.*
    —*The Book of Sacred Names, Op. Cit.*
    —*The Book of Immediate Magic—Part 1, Op. Cit.*
77. **Swart, J.G.:** *The Book of Sacred Names, Op. Cit.*
78. **Zacutto, M.:** *Shorshei ha-Shemot, Op. Cit.*
79. **Swart, J.G.:** *The Book of Sacred Names, Op. Cit.*
    —*The Book of Immediate Magic—Part 1, Op. Cit.*
80. *Ibid.*
81. *Ibid.*
    Zacutto, M.: *Shorshei ha-Shemot, Op. Cit.*
82. *Ibid.*
83. **Swart, J.G.:** *The Book of Immediate Magic—Part 1, Op. Cit.*
84. *Ibid.*
    Zacutto, M.: *Shorshei ha-Shemot, Op. Cit.*
85. *Ibid.*
    Swart, J.G.: *The Book of Seals & Amulets, Op. Cit.*
86. **Swart, J.G.:** *The Book of Sacred Names, Op. Cit.*
    —*The Book of Immediate Magic—Part 1, Op. Cit.*
87. **Swart, J.G.:** *The Book of Seals & Amulets, Op. Cit.*
    Zacutto, M.: *Shorshei ha-Shemot, Op. Cit.*
88. *Ibid.*
89. **Zaleski, P. & Zaleski, C.:** *Prayer: A History, Op. Cit.*
90. **Trachtenberg, J.:** *Jewish Magic and Superstition, Op. Cit.*
    Nulman, M.: *The Encyclopedia of Jewish Prayer, Op. Cit.*
91. **Swart, J.G.:** *The Book of Self Creation, Op. Cit.*
    —*The Book of Seals & Amulets, Op. Cit.*
92. *Ibid.*
93. *Ibid.*
94. **Chajes, J.H.:** *Between Worlds, Op. Cit.*
95. **Gutmacher, E.:** *Tzaf'nat Pane'ah*, Brody 1875
    Schwartz, H.: *Lilith's Cave. Jewish Tales of the Supernatural*, Harper & Row Publishers, San Francisco 1988.
96. *Ibid.*
97. **Zacutto, M.:** *Shorshei ha-Shemot, Op. Cit.*
98. **Bos, G.:** *Hayyim Vital's "Practical Kabbalah and Alchemy": A Seventeenth Century Book of Secrets*, in *The Journal of Jewish Thought and Philosophy 4*, Koninklijke Brill NV, Leiden & Boston 1994.
99. **Braun, M.A.:** *The Heschel Tradition: The Life and Teachings of Rabbi Abraham Joshua Heschel of Apt*, Jason Aronson 1997.

465

Itshakov, I.: *Order of Chanukah with Songs and Blessings after Meals*, Ben Israel Inc., Flushing 2022.

100. Wertheim, A.: *Law and Custom in Hasidism*, transl. Himelstein, S., Ktav Publishing House Inc., Hoboken 1992.
101. Keller, I.: *Prosper Our Hands, Op. Cit.*
102. Selig, G.: *Sepher Schimmusch Tehillim, Op. Cit.*
     The Sixth and Seventh Books of Moses, Op. Cit.
     Peterson, J.H.: *The Sixth and Seventh Books of Moses, Op. Cit.*
     Lecouteux, C.: *Dictionary of Ancient Magic Words and Spells from Abraxas to Zoar*, transl. Graham, J.E., Inner Traditions, Rochester & Toronto 2014.
103. *Ibid.*
104. Peterson, J.H.: *The Sixth and Seventh Books of Moses, Op. Cit.*
105. Zacutto, M.: *Shorshei ha-Shemot, Op. cit.*
106. Peterson, J.H.: *The Sixth and Seventh Books of Moses, Op. Cit.*
107. *Ibid.*
     Selig, G.: *Sepher Schimmusch Tehillim, Op. Cit.*
     The Sixth and Seventh Books of Moses, Op. Cit.
108. *Ibid.*
109. Trachtenberg, J.: *Jewish Magic and Superstition, Op. Cit.*
110. Singer, I. & Adler, C.: *The Jewish Encyclopedia, Op. Cit.*
111. Rubin, S.: *Geschichte des Aberglaubens: Aus dem Hebräischen Übersetzt*, transl. J. Stern, E. Thiele, Leipzig 1888.
112. *Ibid.*
113. Brauner, R.: *Synopsis of Sefer Shimush Tehillim. Op. Cit.*
114. Swart, J.G.:*The Book of Sacred Names, Op. Cit.*
     Zacutto, M.: *Shorshei ha-Shemot, Op. Cit.*
115. Zacutto, M.: *Ibid.*
     Yitz'chaki, Y.: *Lachash v'Kamia: Segulot, Chalomot, Kelalot uV'rachot, Tzim'chei Mar'pe uRefu'ot*, Keter, Jerusalem 1995.
     Green, A.: *Judaic Artifacts, Op. Cit.*
116. Zacutto, M.: *Ibid.*
117. *Ibid.*
     Swart, J.G.:*The Book of Sacred Names, Op. Cit.*
118. Swart, J.G.:*The Book of Magical Psalms—Part 2, Op. Cit.*
119. Swart, J.G.:*The Book of Sacred Names, Op. Cit.*
     Zacutto, M.: *Shorshei ha-Shemot, Op. Cit.*
120. Davis, E. & Frenkel, D.A.: *Ha-Kami'a ha-Ivri, Op. Cit.*
     Green, A.: *Judaic Artifacts, Op. Cit.*
121. *Ibid.*
122. Rosenberg, Y.: *Rafael ha-Malach, Op. Cit.*
     Schrire, T.: *Hebrew Amulets, Op. Cit.*
     Green, A.: *Judaic Artifacts, Op. Cit.*

123. **Vreugdenhil, G.C.:** *Psalm 91 and Demonic Menace, Op. Cit.*
124. **Zacutto, M.:** *Shorshei ha-Shemot, Op. Cit.*
     Swart, J.G.: *The Book of Seals & Amulets, Op. Cit.*
125. *Ibid.*
     Schrire, T.: *Hebrew Amulets, Op. Cit.*
     Green, A.: *Judaic Artifacts, Op. Cit.*
126. **Singer, I. & Adler, C.:** *The Jewish Encyclopedia, Op. Cit.*
127. **Davis, E. & Frenkel, D.A.:** *Ha-Kami'a ha-Ivri, Op. Cit.*
     Green, A.: *Judaic Artifacts, Op. Cit.*
128. **Ba'al Shem, E.; Ba'al-Shem, J. & Hillel, M.:** *Sefer Toldot Adam*, Machon Bnei Yishaschar, Jerusalem 1994.
     Zacutto, M.: *Shorshei ha-Shemot, Op. Cit.*
129. **Schrire, T.:** *Hebrew Amulets, Op. Cit.*
     Davis, E. & Frenkel, D.A.: *Ha-Kami'a ha-Ivri, Op. Cit.*
     Green, A.: *Judaic Artifacts, Op. Cit.*
130. **Swart, J.G.:** *The Book of Seals & Amulets, Op. Cit.*
131. **Zacutto, M.:** *Shorshei ha-Shemot, Op. Cit.*
132. **Ba'al Shem, E.; Ba'al-Shem, J. & Hillel, M.:** *Sefer Toldot Adam, Op. Cit.*
133. **Zacutto, M.:** *Shorshei ha-Shemot, Op. Cit.*
     Swart, J.G.: *The Book of Sacred Names, Op. Cit.*
134. **Davis, E. & Frenkel, D.A.:** *Ha-Kami'a ha-Ivri, Op. Cit.*
     Green, A.: *Judaic Artifacts, Op. Cit.*
135. **Zacutto, M.:** *Shorshei ha-Shemot, Op. Cit.*
136. **Davis, E. & Frenkel, D.A.:** *Ha-Kami'a ha-Ivri, Op. Cit.*
     Green, A.: *Judaic Artifacts, Op. Cit.*
137. *Sefer Raziel ha-Malach*, Amsterdam 1701.
138. **Swart, J.G.:** *The Book of Seals & Amulets, Op. Cit.*
139. *Ibid.*
140. **Bischoff, E.:** *Die Kabbalah,: Einführung in die Jüdische Mystik und Geheimwissenschaft*, Th. Grieben's Verlag (L. Fernau), Leipzig 1917.
     Wallis Budge, E.A.: *Amulets and Talismans*, University Books, New York 1968.
141. **Davis, E. & Frenkel, D.A.:** *Ha-Kami'a ha-Ivri, Op. Cit.*
     Green, A.: *Judaic Artifacts, Op. Cit.*
     Schrire, T.: *Hebrew Amulets, Op. Cit.*
142. *Ibid.*
143. **Swart, J.G.:** *The Book of Immediate Magic—Part 1, Op. Cit.*
144. **Vital, Chaim:** *Sefer Etz Chayim*, quoted in Ariel, D.S.: *The Mystic Quest*, Schocken Books Inc., New York 1992.
145. **Luzzatto, M. Chaim:** *General Principles of the Kabbalah*, New York 1970.

146. **Green, A.:** *Ehyeh: A Kabbalah for Tomorrow*, Jewish Lights Publishing, Woodstock 2011.
147. **Zacutto, M.:** *Shorshei ha-Shemot, Op. Cit.*
148. *Ibid.*
149. **Davis, E. & Frenkel, D.A.:** *Ha-Kami'a ha-Ivri, Op. Cit.*
     Green, A.: *Judaic Artifacts, Op. Cit*
150. *Ibid.*
151. *Ibid.*
     Shachar, I.: *Jewish Tradition in Art: The Feuchtwanger Collection of Judaica*, transl. R Grafman, The Israel Museum, Jerusalem 1981.
152. **Zacutto, M.:** *Shorshei ha-Shemot, Op. Cit.*
153. *Ibid.*
154. **Bruyn, T. de:** *Making Amulets Christian: Artefacts, Scribes, and Contexts*, Oxford University Press, Oxford 2017.
155. **Meyer, M.W. & Smith, R.:** *Ancient Christian Magic: Coptic Texts of Ritual Power*, Princeton University Press, Princeton 1994.
156. **Bruyn, T. de:** *Making Amulets Christian, Op. Cit.*
157. **Betz, H.D.:** *The Greek Magical Papyri in Translation: Including the Demotic Spells*, The University of Chicago Press, Chicago & London 1986.
158. **Breed, B.:** *Reception of the Psalms, Op. Cit.*
     Kraus, T.J.: *"He That Dwelleth In the Help of the Highest": Septuagint Psalm 90 and the Iconographic Program on Byzantine Armbands*, in **Evans, C.A. & Zacharias, H.D.:** *Jewish and Christian Scriture as Artifact and Canon*, T. & T. Clark, London 2009.
159. **Prentice, W.K.:** *Magical Formulae on Lintels of the Christian Period in Syria*, in *American Journal of Archeology and of the History of the Fine Arts* 10, Archeological Institute of America, New York 1906.
160. **Trzcionka, S.:** *Magic and the Supernatural in Fourth Century Syria*, Routledge, London & New York 2007.
161. *Ibid.*
     Prentice, W.K.: *Magical Formulae on Lintels of the Christian Period in Syria, Op. Cit.*
162. **Breed, B.:** *Reception of the Psalms, Op. Cit.*
163. **Zellmann-Rohrer, M.:** *"Psalms Useful for Everything": Byzantine and Post-Byzantine Manuals for the Amuletic Use of the Psalter,* Dumbarton Oaks Research Library and Collection, Washington 2019.

164. Strabus, F.; Lyra, Nicholas of; Burgensus, P.; Toringus, M.; Feuardent, F.; Dadré, J.; Cuilly, J. de: *Bibliorum Sacrorum cum Glossa Ordinaria*, Ioannes Baptista Regnauld et Societas Bibliopolarum Parisiensium, Lugduni 1589.

165. **Breed, B.:** *Reception of the Psalms, Op. Cit.*

166. *Ibid.*
      Bar-Koni, T.: *Livre des Scolies* (*Recension d'Urmiah*), transl. Hespel, R., E. Peeters, Louvain 1984.

167. **Breed, B.:** *Ibid.*
      Rittgers, R.: *Protestants and the Plague: The Case of the 1562/63 Pest in Nurnburg*, in Mormando, F. &Vorcester, T.: *Piety and Plague: From Byzantium to the Baroque*, Truman State University Press, Kirksville 2007.

168. **Spurgeon, C.H.:** *The Treasury of David: containing an Original Exposition of the Book of Psalms Vol. IV*, Funk & Wagnalls, New York 1885.

169. **Jenkins, P.:** *He Will Save You from the Deadly Pestilence: The Many Lives of Psalm 91*, Oxford University Press, Oxford & New York 2023.

170. *Ibid.*

171. *Ibid.*

172. **Breed, B.:** *Reception of the Psalms, Op. Cit.*
      Jenkins, P.: *The New Faces of Christianity: Believing the Bible in the Global South*, Oxford University Press, Oxford & New York 2006.

173. **Breed, B.:** *Ibid.*

174. **Skinner, S. & Rankine, D.:** *A Collection of Magical Secrets: taken from Peter de Abano, Cornelius Agrippa and from other famous Occult Philosophers, and a Treatise of Mixed Cabalah which comprises the Angelic Art taken from Hebrew Sages*, Avalonia, London 2009.

175. *Ibid.*

176. *Ibid.*

177. *Ibid.*

178. *Ibid.*

179. **Lecouteux, C.:** *Dictionary of Ancient Magic Words and Spells from Abraxas to Zoar, Op. Cit.*

180. **Smith, R.:** *The Coptic Book of Ritual Power from Leiden, in* **Meyer, M.W. & Smith, R.:** *Ancient Christian Magic: Coptic Texts of Ritual Power*, Harper San Francisco, San Francisco 1994.
      Bruyn, T. de: *Making Amulets Christian: Artefacts, Scribes, and Contexts*, Oxford University Press, Oxford & New York 2017.

181. **Rankine, D. & Barron, P.H.:** *The Book of Gold, Op. Cit.*
Marty, J. & MacParthy, F.: *Usage Mago-Théurgiques des Psaumes, Op. Cit.*
182. *Ibid.*
183. **Mathers, S.L. Macgregor:** *Key of Solomon the King: Clavicula Salomonis*, Routledge & Kegan Paul, London 1974.
184. *Ibid.*

Psalm 92

1. *The Zohar*, transl. D.C. Matt (Pritzker edition Vol. 5), Stanford University Press, Stanford 2009.
2. **Nemoy, L., Lieberman, S. & Wolfson, H.A.:** *The Midrash on Psalms (Midrash Tehillim)*, Vol. 2, *Op. Cit.*
3. *Ibid.*
   Pirke d'Rabbi Eliezer: The Chapters of Rabbi Eliezer the Great, transl. G. Friedlander, Sepher Hermon Press, New York 1916.
4. **Ginsburg, E.K.:** *The Sabbath in the Classical Kabbalah*, State University of New York Press, Albany 1989.
   Matt, D.C.: *Zohar Annotated and Explained*, SkyLight Paths Publishing, Woodstock 2002.
   Fishbane, E.: *The Sabbath Soul: Mystical Reflections on the Transformative Power of Holy Time*, Jewish Lights Publishing, Woodstock 2012.
5. **Swart, J.G.:** *The Book of Self Creation, Op. Cit.*
   —*The Book of Sacred Names, Op. Cit.*
   —*The Book of Seals & Amulets, Op. Cit.*
   —*The Book of Immediate Magic—Part 1, Op. Cit.*
   —*The Book of Immediate Magic—Part 2, Op. Cit.*
   —*The Book of Magical Psalms—Part 1, Op. Cit.*
   —*The Book of Magical Psalms—Part 2, Op. Cit.*
6. *Pirke d'Rabbi Eliezer, Op. Cit.*
7. **Marcus, Y.B.:** *Book of Psalms with Commentary from the Talmud, Midrash, Kabbalah, Classic Commentators, and the Chasidic Masters*, Kehot Publication Society, Brooklyn, New York 2016.
8. **Hoffman, L.A.:** *My People's Prayer Book: Traditional Prayers, Modern Commentaries: Vol. 8—Kabbalat Shabbat (Welcoming Shabbat in the Synagogue)*, Jewish Lights Publishing, Woodstock 2005.
9. **Nemoy, L., Lieberman, S. & Wolfson, H.A.:** *The Midrash on Psalms (Midrash Tehillim)*, Vol. 2, *Op. Cit.*
   Simon, U.: *Four Approaches to the Book of Psalms, Op. Cit.*
   Cohen, A.: *The Psalms, Op. Cit.*
   Gruber, M.I.: *Rashi's Commentary on Psalms, Op. Cit.*

Schmutzer, A.J. & Howard, D.M.: *The Psalms: Language for All Seasons of the Soul*, Op. Cit.

10. Hoffman, L.A.: *My People's Prayer Book: Vol. 8*, Op. Cit.

11. *Ibid.*

12. Nulman, M.: *The Encyclopedia of Jewish Prayer*, Op. Cit.
Rosenberg, A.S.: *Jewish Liturgy as a Spiritual System*, Op. Cit.

13. *Ibid.*
Eisenstein, J.D.: *Otzar Yisrael*, Vol. 3, Pardes Publishing House, New York 1951.

14. Feldman, Y.Y.: *Tehillim Eis Ratzon*, Op. Cit.

15. Singer, I. & Adler, C.: *The Jewish Encyclopedia*, Op. Cit.

16. *Le Livre des Psaumes Hébreu-Français et Phonétique*, Op. Cit.
Azulai, H.Y.D.: *Sefer Tehillim Sha'arei Rachamim*, Op. Cit.

17. Brauner, R.: *Synopsis of Sefer Shimush Tehillim*. Op. Cit.

18. Kimchi, D. ben Y.: *Sefer Tehillim*, Op. Cit.
Sefer Shimmush Tehillim, Op. Cit.
Seder Tefilot Tikun Ezra, Op. Cit.
Grünwald, M.: *Ueber den Einfluss der Psalmen auf die Katholische Liturgie*, Op. Cit.
Refuah v'Chayim m'Yerushalayim im Shimush Tehilim, Op. Cit.
Landsberg, M.: *Sefer Tehillim im Peirush Rashi*, Op. Cit.
Rebiger, B.: *Sefer Shimmush Tehillim*, Op. Cit.
Hai ben Sherira Gaon & Varady, A.N.: *Shimush Tehillim* (*the Theurgical Use of Psalms*), Op. Cit.

19. Rebiger, B.: *Ibid.*

20. *Ibid.*
Kimchi, D. ben Y.: *Sefer Tehillim*, Op. Cit.
Sefer Shimmush Tehillim, Op. Cit.
Seder Tefilot Tikun Ezra, Op. Cit.
Refuah v'Chayim m'Yerushalayim im Shimush Tehilim, Op. Cit.
Landsberg, M.: *Sefer Tehillim im Peirush Rashi*, Op. Cit.
Hai ben Sherira Gaon & Varady, A.N.: *Shimush Tehillim* (*the Theurgical Use of Psalms*), Op. Cit.

21. *Ibid.*

22. Rebiger, B.: *Sefer Shimmush Tehillim*, Op. Cit.

23. *Ibid.*
Kimchi, D. ben Y.: *Sefer Tehillim*, Op. Cit.
Sefer Shimmush Tehillim, Op. Cit.
Seder Tefilot Tikun Ezra, Op. Cit.
Refuah v'Chayim m'Yerushalayim im Shimush Tehilim, Op. Cit.
Landsberg, M.: *Sefer Tehillim im Peirush Rashi*, Op. Cit.

Hai ben Sherira Gaon & Varady, A.N.: *Shimush Tehillim* (*the Theurgical Use of Psalms*), *Op. Cit.*

24. **Rebiger, B.**: *Sefer Shimmush Tehillim, Op. Cit.*
25. *Ibid.*

Kimchi, D. ben Y.: *Sefer Tehillim, Op. Cit.*
Sefer Shimmush Tehillim, Op. Cit.
Seder Tefilot Tikun Ezra, Op. Cit.
Refuah v'Chayim m'Yerushalayim im Shimush Tehilim, Op. Cit.
Landsberg, M.: *Sefer Tehillim im Peirush Rashi, Op. Cit.*
Hai ben Sherira Gaon & Varady, A.N.: *Shimush Tehillim* (*the Theurgical Use of Psalms*), *Op. Cit.*

26. *The Prayer Meditations of Alexander Susskind of Grodno*, in **Jacobs, L.**: *The Schocken Book of Jewish Mystical Testimonies*, Schocken Books, New York 1976.
27. **Selig, G.**: *Sepher Schimmusch Tehillim, Op. Cit.*
The Sixth and Seventh Books of Moses, Op. Cit.
Peterson, J.H.: *The Sixth and Seventh Books of Moses, Op. Cit.*
28. **Rebiger, B.**: *Sefer Shimmush Tehillim, Op. Cit.*
29. **Zacutto, M.**: *Shorshei ha-Shemot, Op. Cit.*
30. *Ibid.*
Swart, J.G.: *The Book of Sacred Names, Op. Cit.*
31. **Swart, J.G.**: *The Book of Seals & Amulets, Op. Cit.*
32. **Skinner, S. & Rankine, D.**: *A Collection of Magical Secrets, Op. cit.*
33. **Rankine, D. & Barron, P.H.**: *The Book of Gold, Op. Cit.*
Marty, J. & MacParthy, F.: *Usage Mago-Théurgiques des Psaumes, Op. Cit.*

Psalm 93

1. **Hoffman, L.A.**: *My People's Prayer Book: Vol. 8, Op. Cit.*
2. *Ibid.*
3. *Ibid.*
Berger, K.E.: *Tradition, Interpretation, and Change: Developments in the Liturgy of Medieval and Early Modern Ashkenaz*, Hebrew Union College Press, Cincinnati 2019.
4. *Ibid.*
5. *Ibid.*
6. *Ibid.*
7. **Nulman, M.**: *The Encyclopedia of Jewish Prayer, Op. Cit.*
8. **Nemoy, L., Lieberman, S. & Wolfson, H.A.**: *The Midrash on Psalms* (*Midrash Tehillim*), Vol. 2, *Op. Cit.*

Simon, U.: *Four Approaches to the Book of Psalms*, *Op. Cit.*

Cohen, A.: *The Psalms*, *Op. Cit.*

Gruber, M.I.: *Rashi's Commentary on Psalms*, *Op. Cit.*

Schmutzer, A.J. & Howard, D.M.: *The Psalms: Language for All Seasons of the Soul*, *Op. Cit.*

9.   Nulman, M.: *The Encyclopedia of Jewish Prayer*, *Op. Cit.*

10. *Ibid.*

11. Berlin, A.; Brettler, M.Z. & Fishbane, M.A.: *The Jewish Study Bible: featuring The Jewish Publication Society Tanakh Translation: Torah, Nevi'im Kethuvim*, Oxford University Press, New York 2004.

Rosenberg, A.S.: *Jewish Liturgy as a Spiritual System*, *Op. Cit.*

12. Nulman, M.: *The Encyclopedia of Jewish Prayer*, *Op. Cit.*

13. *Ibid.*

Jacobson, B.S.: *The Sabbath Service: An Exposition and Analysis of Its Structure, Contents, Language and Ideas*, Sinai Publishing, Tel Aviv 1981.

14. Singer, I. & Adler, C.: *The Jewish Encyclopedia*, *Op. Cit.*

15. Kimchi, D. ben Y.: *Sefer Tehillim*, *Op. Cit.*

Sefer Shimmush Tehillim, *Op. Cit.*

Seder Tefilot Tikun Ezra, *Op. Cit.*

Le Livre des Psaumes Hébreu-Français et Phonétique, *Op. Cit.*

Azulai, H.Y.D.: *Sefer Tehillim Sha'arei Rachamim*, *Op. Cit.*

Grünwald, M.: *Ueber den Einfluss der Psalmen auf die Katholische Liturgie*, *Op. Cit.*

Refuah v'Chayim m'Yerushalayim im Shimush Tehilim, *Op. Cit.*

Rebiger, B.: *Sefer Shimmush Tehillim*, *Op. Cit.*

Brauner, R.: *Synopsis of Sefer Shimush Tehillim. Op. Cit.*

Landsberg, M.: *Sefer Tehillim im Peirush Rashi*, *Op. Cit.*

Ronen, D.: *Tehilim Kavvanot ha-Lev*, *Op. Cit.*

Hai ben Sherira Gaon & Varady, A.N.: *Shimush Tehillim* (*the Theurgical Use of Psalms*), *Op. Cit.*

16. Selig, G.: *Sepher Schimmusch Tehillim*, *Op. Cit.*

The Sixth and Seventh Books of Moses, *Op. Cit.*

Peterson, J.H.: *The Sixth and Seventh Books of Moses*, *Op. Cit.*

17. Zacutto, M.: *Shorshei ha-Shemot*, *Op. Cit.*

18. *Ibid.*

Swart, J.G.: *The Book of Sacred Names*, *Op. Cit.*

—*The Book of Immediate Magic—Part 1*, *Op. Cit.*

19. Swart, J.G.: *The Book of Seals & Amulets*, *Op. Cit.*

20. Swart, J.G.:*The Book of Magical Psalms—Part 1*, *Op. Cit.*

21. Zacutto, M.: *Shorshei ha-Shemot*, *Op. Cit.*

Swart, J.G.: *The Book of Sacred Names*, *Op. Cit.*

473

22.   **Rankine, D. & Barron, P.H.:** *The Book of Gold, Op. Cit.*
    Marty, J. & MacParthy, F.: *Usage Mago-Théurgiques des Psaumes, Op. Cit.*

Psalm 94

1.   **Nulman, M.:** *The Encyclopedia of Jewish Prayer, Op. Cit.*
2.   **Nemoy, L., Lieberman, S. & Wolfson, H.A.:** *The Midrash on Psalms (Midrash Tehillim)*, Vol. 2, *Op. Cit.*
    Simon, U.: *Four Approaches to the Book of Psalms, Op. Cit.*
    Cohen, A.: *The Psalms, Op. Cit.*
    Gruber, M.I.: *Rashi's Commentary on Psalms, Op. Cit.*
    Schmutzer, A.J. & Howard, D.M.: *The Psalms: Language for All Seasons of the Soul, Op. Cit.*
3.   **McCann, J.C.:** *The Shape and Shaping of the Psalter: Psalms in Their Literary Context,* in **Brown, W.P.:** *The Oxford Handbook of the Psalms, Op. Cit.*
4.   **Singer, I. & Adler, C.:** *The Jewish Encyclopedia, Op. Cit.*
    Le Livre des Psaumes Hébreu-Français et Phonétique, Op. Cit.
    Azulai, H.Y.D.: *Sefer Tehillim Sha'arei Rachamim, Op. Cit.*
    Ronen, D.: *Tehilim Kavvanot ha-Lev, Op. Cit.*
5.   **Brauner, R.:** *Synopsis of Sefer Shimush Tehillim. Op. Cit.*
6.   **Kimchi, D. ben Y.:** *Sefer Tehillim, Op. Cit.*
    Sefer Shimmush Tehillim, Op. Cit.
    Seder Tefilot Tikun Ezra, Op. Cit.
    Grünwald, M.: *Ueber den Einfluss der Psalmen auf die Katholische Liturgie, Op. Cit.*
    Landsberg, M.: *Sefer Tehillim im Peirush Rashi, Op. Cit.*
    Rebiger, B.: *Sefer Shimmush Tehillim, Op. Cit.*
    Hai ben Sherira Gaon & Varady, A.N.: *Shimush Tehillim (the Theurgical Use of Psalms), Op. Cit.*
7.   **Rebiger, B.:** *Ibid.*
8.   **Kimchi, D. ben Y.:** *Sefer Tehillim, Op. Cit.*
    Sefer Shimmush Tehillim, Op. Cit.
    Seder Tefilot Tikun Ezra, Op. Cit.
    Grünwald, M.: *Ueber den Einfluss der Psalmen auf die Katholische Liturgie, Op. Cit.*
    Landsberg, M.: *Sefer Tehillim im Peirush Rashi, Op. Cit.*
    Rebiger, B.: *Sefer Shimmush Tehillim, Op. Cit.*
    Hai ben Sherira Gaon & Varady, A.N.: *Shimush Tehillim (the Theurgical Use of Psalms), Op. Cit.*
9.   **Selig, G.:** *Sepher Schimmusch Tehillim, Op. Cit.*
    The Sixth and Seventh Books of Moses, Op. Cit.
    Peterson, J.H.: *The Sixth and Seventh Books of Moses, Op. Cit.*

10. *Ibid.*
11. **Rebiger, B.:** *Sefer Shimmush Tehillim, Op. Cit.*
12. **Zacutto, M.:** *Shorshei ha-Shemot, Op. Cit.*
    Swart, J.G.: *The Book of Sacred Names, Op. Cit.*
    —*The Book of Immediate Magic—Part 1, Op. Cit.*
13. *Ibid.*
14. **Swart, J.G.:** *The Book of Sacred Names, Op. Cit.*
    —*The Book of Immediate Magic—Part 1, Op. Cit.*
15. *Ibid.*
    Zacutto, M.: *Shorshei ha-Shemot, Op. Cit.*
16. **Rankine, D. & Barron, P.H.:** *The Book of Gold, Op. Cit.*
    Marty, J. & MacParthy, F.: *Usage Mago-Théurgiques des Psaumes, Op. Cit.*

Psalm 95

1. **Nemoy, L., Lieberman, S. & Wolfson, H.A.:** *The Midrash on Psalms* (*Midrash Tehillim*), Vol. 2, *Op. Cit.*
   Simon, U.: *Four Approaches to the Book of Psalms, Op. Cit.*
   Cohen, A.: *The Psalms, Op. Cit.*
   Gruber, M.I.: *Rashi's Commentary on Psalms, Op. Cit.*
   Schmutzer, A.J. & Howard, D.M.: *The Psalms: Language for All Seasons of the Soul, Op. Cit.*
2. **Berger, K.E.:** *Tradition, Interpretation, and Change, Op. Cit.*
3. **Nulman, M.:** *The Encyclopedia of Jewish Prayer, Op. Cit.*
4. *Ibid.*
   Hoffman, L.A.: *My People's Prayer Book: Vol. 8, Op. Cit.*
   Olitzky, K.M.: *An Encyclopedia of American Synagogue Ritual,* Greenwood Press, Westport & London 2000.
   Green, A.: *These are the Words: A Vocabulary of Jewish Spiritual Life,* Jewish Lights Publishing, Woodstock 2012.
5. **Nulman, M.:** *The Encyclopedia of Jewish Prayer, Op. Cit.*
6. **Hoffman, L.A.:** *My People's Prayer Book: Vol. 8, Op. Cit.*
7. **Berger, K.E.:** *Tradition, Interpretation, and Change, Op. Cit.*
8. **Singer, I. & Adler, C.:** *The Jewish Encyclopedia, Op. Cit.*
9. *Le Livre des Psaumes Hébreu-Français et Phonétique, Op. Cit.*
   Azulai, H.Y.D.: *Sefer Tehillim Sha'arei Rachamim, Op. Cit.*
   Ronen, D.: *Tehilim Kavvanot ha-Lev, Op. Cit.*
   Kimchi, D. ben Y.: *Sefer Tehillim, Op. Cit.*
   Sefer Shimmush Tehillim, Op. Cit.
   Seder Tefilot Tikun Ezra, Op. Cit.
   Grünwald, M.: *Ueber den Einfluss der Psalmen auf die Katholische Liturgie, Op. Cit.*

Rebiger, B.: *Sefer Shimmush Tehillim, Op. Cit.*
Brauner, R.: *Synopsis of Sefer Shimush Tehillim. Op. Cit.*
Landsberg, M.: *Sefer Tehillim im Peirush Rashi, Op. Cit.*
Ronen, D.: *Tehilim Kavvanot ha-Lev, Op. Cit.*
Hai ben Sherira Gaon & Varady, A.N.: *Shimush Tehillim* (*the Theurgical Use of Psalms*), *Op. Cit.*
10. *Ibid.*
11. Rebiger, B.: *Sefer Shimmush Tehillim, Op. Cit.*
12. Selig, G.: *Sepher Schimmusch Tehillim, Op. Cit.*
    The Sixth and Seventh Books of Moses, Op. Cit.
    Peterson, J.H.: *The Sixth and Seventh Books of Moses, Op. Cit.*
13. *Ibid.*
14. Rebiger, B.: *Sefer Shimmush Tehillim, Op. Cit.*
15. *Ibid.*
16. Feldman, Y.Y.: *Tehillim Eis Ratzon, Op. Cit.*
17. Zacutto, M.: *Shorshei ha-Shemot, Op. Cit.*
    Swart, J.G.: *The Book of Sacred Names, Op. Cit.*
18. Rankine, D. & Barron, P.H.: *The Book of Gold, Op. Cit.*
    Marty, J. & MacParthy, F.: *Usage Mago-Théurgiques des Psaumes, Op. Cit.*

Psalm 96

1. Feuer, A.Ch. & Scherman, N.: *Sefer Tehillim: a New Translation with a Commentary Anthologized from Talmudic, Midrashic, and Rabbinic sources*, Mesorah Publications, Brooklyn 1985.
   Gillingham, S.: *Psalms Through the Centuries, Volume 3*, John Wiley & Sons Ltd., Chichester & Hoboken 2012.
   Angley, J.: *Ephod of God*, Covenant Books Inc., La Vergne 2020.
2. Gillingham, S.: *Psalms Through the Centuries, Volume 3, Op. Cit.*
3. McCann, J.C.: *The Shape and Shaping of the Psalter: Psalms in Their Literary Context*, in Brown, W.P.: *The Oxford Handbook of the Psalms, Op. Cit.*
4. *Ibid.*
5. Nemoy, L., Lieberman, S. & Wolfson, H.A.: *The Midrash on Psalms* (*Midrash Tehillim*), Vol. 2, *Op. Cit.*
   Nulman, M.: *The Encyclopedia of Jewish Prayer, Op. Cit.*
6. *Ibid.*
7. Kimchi, D. ben Y.: *Sefer Tehillim, Op. Cit.*
   Sefer Shimmush Tehillim, Op. Cit.
   Seder Tefilot Tikun Ezra, Op. Cit.

Singer, I. & Adler, C.: *The Jewish Encyclopedia, Op. Cit.*
Le Livre des Psaumes Hébreu-Français et Phonétique, Op. Cit.
Azulai, H.Y.D.: *Sefer Tehillim Sha'arei Rachamim, Op. Cit.*
Refuah v'Chayim m'Yerushalayim im Shimush Tehilim, Op. Cit.
Rebiger, B.: *Sefer Shimmush Tehillim, Op. Cit.*
Ronen, D.: *Tehilim Kavvanot ha-Lev, Op. Cit.*
Brauner, R.: *Synopsis of Sefer Shimush Tehillim. Op. Cit.*
Landsberg, M.: *Sefer Tehillim im Peirush Rashi, Op. Cit.*
Hai ben Sherira Gaon & Varady, A.N.: *Shimush Tehillim* (*the Theurgical Use of Psalms*), *Op. Cit.*

8. Rebiger, B.: *Sefer Shimmush Tehillim, Op. Cit.*
9. *Ibid.*
10. Selig, G.: *Sepher Schimmusch Tehillim, Op. Cit.*
    The Sixth and Seventh Books of Moses, Op. Cit.
    Peterson, J.H.: *The Sixth and Seventh Books of Moses, Op. Cit.*
11. *Ibid.*
12. Barkai, R.: *Jewish Treatises on the Black Death* (*1350–1500*): *A Preliminary Study*, in **French, R.; Arrizabalaga, J.; Cunningham, A. & Garcia-Ballester, L.**: *Medicine from the Black Death to the French Disease*, Routledge, Oxon & New York 2019.
13. *Ibid.*
14. Rebiger, B.: *Sefer Shimmush Tehillim, Op. Cit.*
15. Weintraub, S.Y.: *From the Depths: The Use of Psalms*, in **Friedman, D.A.**: *Jewish Pastoral Care: A Practical Handbook from Traditional and Contemporary Sources*, Jewish Lights Publishing, Woodstock 2015.
16. *Ibid.*
17. Rankine, D. & Barron, P.H.: *The Book of Gold, Op. Cit.*
    Marty, J. & MacParthy, F.: *Usage Mago-Théurgiques des Psaumes, Op. Cit.*

Psalm 97

1. Feuer, A.Ch. & Scherman, N.: *Sefer Tehillim, Op. Cit.*
    Gillingham, S.: *Psalms Through the Centuries, Volume 3, Op. Cit.*
2. Angley, J.: *Ephod of God, Op. Cit.*
3. Nulman, M.: *The Encyclopedia of Jewish Prayer, Op. Cit.*
4. Metzger, B.M. & David, M.: *The Oxford Companion to the Bible*, Oxford University Press, Oxford & New York 1993.
5. Hubbard, E.: *Selected Writings of Elbert Hubbard: His Mintage of Wisdom coined from a Life of Love, Laughter and Work*, Vol. 4, W. H. Wise & Company, New York 1923.

6. **Swart, J.G.:** *The Book of Self Creation, Op. Cit.*
7. **Schwartz, H.:** Tree of Souls: The Mythology of Judaism, Oxford University Press, Oxford & New York 2004.
8. **Hoffman, L.A.:** *All These Vows: Kol Nidre*, Jewish Lights Publishing, Vermont 2011.
9. **Kimchi, D. ben Y.:** *Sefer Tehillim, Op. Cit.*
    Sefer Shimmush Tehillim, Op. Cit.
    Seder Tefilot Tikun Ezra, Op. Cit.
    Grünwald, M.: *Ueber den Einfluss der Psalmen auf die Katholische Liturgie, Op. Cit.*
    Singer, I. & Adler, C.: *The Jewish Encyclopedia, Op. Cit.*
    Le Livre des Psaumes Hébreu-Français et Phonétique, Op. Cit.
    Azulai, H.Y.D.: *Sefer Tehillim Sha'arei Rachamim, Op. Cit.*
    Refuah v'Chayim m'Yerushalayim im Shimush Tehilim, Op. Cit.
    Rebiger, B.: *Sefer Shimmush Tehillim, Op. Cit.*
    Ronen, D.: *Tehilim Kavvanot ha-Lev, Op. Cit.*
    Brauner, R.: *Synopsis of Sefer Shimush Tehillim. Op. Cit.*
    Landsberg, M.: *Sefer Tehillim im Peirush Rashi, Op. Cit.*
    Hai ben Sherira Gaon & Varady, A.N.: *Shimush Tehillim (the Theurgical Use of Psalms), Op. Cit.*
10. *Ibid.*
11. **Rebiger, B.:** *Sefer Shimmush Tehillim, Op. Cit.*
12. **Selig, G.:** *Sepher Schimmusch Tehillim, Op. Cit.*
    The Sixth and Seventh Books of Moses, Op. Cit.
    Peterson, J.H.: *The Sixth and Seventh Books of Moses, Op. Cit.*
13. **Rebiger, B.:** *Sefer Shimmush Tehillim, Op. Cit.*
14. **Zacutto, M.:** *Shorshei ha-Shemot, Op. Cit.*
    Swart, J.G.: *The Book of Sacred Names, Op. Cit.*
15. **Schrire, T.:** *Hebrew Amulets, Op. Cit.*
    Green, A.: *Judaic Artifacts, Op. Cit.*
16. **Henein, N.H. & Banquis, T.:** *La Magie par les Psaumes: Édition et Traduction d'un Manuscrit Arabe Chrétien d'Égypte*, Bibliothèque d'Études Coptes 12, Cairo 1985.
    Hansen, N.B.: *Ancient Execration Magic in Coptic and Islamic Egypt*, in **Mirecki, P. & Meyer, M.:** *Magic and Ritual in the Ancient World*, Koninklijke Brill NV, Leiden 2002.
17. **Rankine, D. & Barron, P.H.:** *The Book of Gold, Op. Cit.*
    Marty, J. & MacParthy, F.: *Usage Mago-Théurgiques des Psaumes, Op. Cit.*

Psalm 98

1. **Feuer, A.Ch. & Scherman, N.:** *Sefer Tehillim, Op. Cit.*
   Gillingham, S.: *Psalms Through the Centuries, Volume 3, Op. Cit.*
   Angley, J.: *Ephod of God, Op. Cit.*
2. *Ibid.*
3. *Ibid.*
4. **Swart, J.G.:** *The Book of Self Creation, Op. Cit.*
5. **Nulman, M.:** *The Encyclopedia of Jewish Prayer, Op. Cit.*
6. **Kimchi, D. ben Y.:** *Sefer Tehillim, Op. Cit.*
   Sefer Shimmush Tehillim, Op. Cit.
   Seder Tefilot Tikun Ezra, Op. Cit.
   Grünwald, M.: *Ueber den Einfluss der Psalmen auf die Katholische Liturgie, Op. Cit.*
   Le Livre des Psaumes Hébreu-Français et Phonétique, Op. Cit.
   Azulai, H.Y.D.: *Sefer Tehillim Sha'arei Rachamim, Op. Cit.*
   Refuah v'Chayim m'Yerushalayim im Shimush Tehilim, Op. Cit.
   Rebiger, B.: *Sefer Shimmush Tehillim, Op. Cit.*
   Ronen, D.: *Tehilim Kavvanot ha-Lev, Op. Cit.*
   Brauner, R.: *Synopsis of Sefer Shimush Tehillim. Op. Cit.*
   Landsberg, M.: *Sefer Tehillim im Peirush Rashi, Op. Cit.*
   Hai ben Sherira Gaon & Varady, A.N.: *Shimush Tehillim (the Theurgical Use of Psalms), Op. Cit.*
7. **Singer, I. & Adler, C.:** *The Jewish Encyclopedia, Op. Cit.*
8. **Selig, G.:** *Sepher Schimmusch Tehillim, Op. Cit.*
   The Sixth and Seventh Books of Moses, Op. Cit.
   Peterson, J.H.: *The Sixth and Seventh Books of Moses, Op. Cit.*
9. **Kimchi, D. ben Y.:** *Sefer Tehillim, Op. Cit.*
   Sefer Shimmush Tehillim, Op. Cit.
   Seder Tefilot Tikun Ezra, Op. Cit.
   Grünwald, M.: *Ueber den Einfluss der Psalmen auf die Katholische Liturgie, Op. Cit.*
   Refuah v'Chayim m'Yerushalayim im Shimush Tehilim, Op. Cit.
   Rebiger, B.: *Sefer Shimmush Tehillim, Op. Cit.*
   Landsberg, M.: *Sefer Tehillim im Peirush Rashi, Op. Cit.*
   Hai ben Sherira Gaon & Varady, A.N.: *Shimush Tehillim (the Theurgical Use of Psalms), Op. Cit.*
10. **Selig, G.:** *Sepher Schimmusch Tehillim, Op. Cit.*
    The Sixth and Seventh Books of Moses, Op. Cit.
    Peterson, J.H.: *The Sixth and Seventh Books of Moses, Op. Cit.*
11. **Rebiger, B.:** *Sefer Shimmush Tehillim, Op. Cit.*

12. *Ibid.*
13. *Ibid.*
14. **Feldman, Y.Y.:** *Tehillim Eis Ratzon*, *Op. Cit.*
15. **Eliram (Amslam), S.:** *Sefer Segulot, Terufot u'Mazalot, Op. Cit.*
16. **Feldman, Y.Y.:** *Tehillim Eis Ratzon*, *Op. Cit.*
17. **Eliram (Amslam), S.:** *Sefer Segulot, Terufot u'Mazalot, Op. Cit.*
18. **Swart, J.G.:** *The Book of Magical Psalms—Part 1, Op. Cit.*
19. **Zacutto, M.:** *Shorshei ha-Shemot, Op. Cit.*
    Swart, J.G.: *The Book of Sacred Names, Op. Cit.*
20. **Luijendijk, A.:** *Forbidden Oracles? The Gospel of the Lots of Mary*, Mohr Siebeck, Tübingen 2014.
    Meyer, M.W. & Smith, R.: *Ancient Christian Magic, Op. Cit.*
21. **Rankine, D. & Barron, P.H.:** *The Book of Gold, Op. Cit.*
    Marty, J. & MacParthy, F.: *Usage Mago-Théurgiques des Psaumes, Op. Cit.*

Psalm 99

1. **Nulman, M.:** *The Encyclopedia of Jewish Prayer, Op. Cit.*
2. **Feuer, A.Ch. & Scherman, N.:** *Sefer Tehillim, Op. Cit.*
   Gillingham, S.: *Psalms Through the Centuries, Volume 3, Op. Cit.*
   Angley, J.: *Ephod of God, Op. Cit.*
3. **Hoffman, L.A.:** *My People's Prayer Book: Vol. 8, Op. Cit.*
4. *Le Livre des Psaumes Hébreu-Français et Phonétique, Op. Cit.*
   Azulai, H.Y.D.: *Sefer Tehillim Sha'arei Rachamim, Op. Cit.*
   Refuah v'Chayim m'Yerushalayim im Shimush Tehilim, Op. Cit.
   Rebiger, B.: *Sefer Shimmush Tehillim, Op. Cit.*
   Ronen, D.: *Tehilim Kavvanot ha-Lev, Op. Cit.*
   Brauner, R.: *Synopsis of Sefer Shimush Tehillim. Op. Cit.*
   Landsberg, M.: *Sefer Tehillim im Peirush Rashi, Op. Cit.*
5. **Selig, G.:** *Sepher Schimmusch Tehillim, Op. Cit.*
   The Sixth and Seventh Books of Moses, Op. Cit.
   Peterson, J.H.: *The Sixth and Seventh Books of Moses, Op. Cit.*
6. **Rebiger, B.:** *Sefer Shimmush Tehillim, Op. Cit.*
7. **Rankine, D. & Barron, P.H.:** *The Book of Gold, Op. Cit.*
   Marty, J. & MacParthy, F.: *Usage Mago-Théurgiques des Psaumes, Op. Cit.*
8. **Deissmann, A.:** *Bible Studies: Contributions chiefly from Papyri and Inscriptions to the History of the Language, the Literature, and the Religion of Hellenistic Judaism and Primitive Christianity*, transl. Grieve, A., T. & T. Clark, Edinburgh 1901.

Psalm 100

1. **Feuer, A.Ch. & Scherman, N.:** *Sefer Tehillim, Op. Cit.*
   Gillingham, S.: *Psalms Through the Centuries, Volume 3, Op. Cit.*
   Angley, J.: *Ephod of God, Op. Cit.*
2. **Fields, H.J.:** *B'chol L'vavcha: With All Your Heart: a Commentary on the Prayer Book*, Central Conference of American Rabbis, New York 2021.
3. **Baumol, A.:** *The Poetry of Prayer: Tehillim in Tefillah*, Gefen Publishing House, Jerusalem & New York 2009.
4. **Brauner, R.:** *Synopsis of Sefer Shimush Tehillim. Op. Cit.*
5. **Baumol, A.:** *The Poetry of Prayer, Op. Cit.*
6. **Feldman, Y.Y.:** *Tehillim Eis Ratzon, Op. Cit.*
7. **Rebiger, B.:** *Sefer Shimmush Tehillim, Op. Cit.*
8. *Ibid.*
9. *Le Livre des Psaumes Hébreu-Français et Phonétique, Op. Cit.*
   Azulai, H.Y.D.: *Sefer Tehillim Sha'arei Rachamim, Op. Cit.*
   Singer, I. & Adler, C.: *The Jewish Encyclopedia, Op. Cit.*
   Ronen, D.: *Tehilim Kavvanot ha-Lev, Op. Cit.*
   Brauner, R.: *Synopsis of Sefer Shimush Tehillim. Op. Cit.*
10. **Selig, G.:** *Sepher Schimmusch Tehillim, Op. Cit.*
    The Sixth and Seventh Books of Moses, Op. Cit.
    Peterson, J.H.: *The Sixth and Seventh Books of Moses, Op. Cit.*
11. **Kimchi, D. ben Y.:** *Sefer Tehillim, Op. Cit.*
    Sefer Shimmush Tehillim, Op. Cit.
    Seder Tefilot Tikun Ezra, Op. Cit.
    Grünwald, M.: *Ueber den Einfluss der Psalmen auf die Katholische Liturgie, Op. Cit.*
    Refuah v'Chayim m'Yerushalayim im Shimush Tehilim, Op. Cit.
    Rebiger, B.: *Sefer Shimmush Tehillim, Op. Cit.*
    Landsberg, M.: *Sefer Tehillim im Peirush Rashi, Op. Cit.*
    Hai ben Sherira Gaon & Varady, A.N.: *Shimush Tehillim (the Theurgical Use of Psalms), Op. Cit.*
12. **Rebiger, B.:** *Ibid.*
13. **Selig, G.:** *Sepher Schimmusch Tehillim, Op. Cit.*
    The Sixth and Seventh Books of Moses, Op. Cit.
    Peterson, J.H.: *The Sixth and Seventh Books of Moses, Op. Cit.*
14. **Rebiger, B.:** *Sefer Shimmush Tehillim, Op. Cit.*
15. **Mykoff, M.:** *Likutei Moharan*, Vols. 12–13, Breslov Research Institute, New York & Jerusalem 2008.
    Klein, M.: *A Time to Be Born, Op. Cit.*

16. **Mykoff, M.:** *Ibid.*
17. *Ibid.*
18. **Zacutto, M.:** *Shorshei ha-Shemot, Op. cit.*
    Swart, J.G.: *The Book of Sacred Names, Op. Cit.*
19. **Rankine, D. & Barron, P.H.:** *The Book of Gold, Op. Cit.*
    Marty, J. & MacParthy, F.: *Usage Mago-Théurgiques des Psaumes, Op. Cit.*

Psalm 101

1. *Le Livre des Psaumes Hébreu-Français et Phonétique, Op. Cit.*
   Azulai, H.Y.D.: *Sefer Tehillim Sha'arei Rachamim, Op. Cit.*
   Singer, I. & Adler, C.: *The Jewish Encyclopedia, Op. Cit.*
   Ronen, D.: *Tehilim Kavvanot ha-Lev, Op. Cit.*
   Brauner, R.: *Synopsis of Sefer Shimush Tehillim. Op. Cit.*
2. **Kimchi, D. ben Y.:** *Sefer Tehillim, Op. Cit.*
   Sefer Shimmush Tehillim, Op. Cit.
   Seder Tefilot Tikun Ezra, Op. Cit.
   Grünwald, M.: *Ueber den Einfluss der Psalmen auf die Katholische Liturgie, Op. Cit.*
   Refuah v'Chayim m'Yerushalayim im Shimush Tehilim, Op. Cit.
   Rebiger, B.: *Sefer Shimmush Tehillim, Op. Cit.*
   Landsberg, M.: *Sefer Tehillim im Peirush Rashi, Op. Cit.*
3. **Selig, G.:** *Sepher Schimmusch Tehillim, Op. Cit.*
   The Sixth and Seventh Books of Moses, Op. Cit.
   Peterson, J.H.: *The Sixth and Seventh Books of Moses, Op. Cit.*
4. **Rebiger, B.:** *Sefer Shimmush Tehillim, Op. Cit.*
5. *Ibid.*
6. **Zellmann-Rohrer, M.:** *Psalms Useful for Everything, Op. Cit.*
7. *Ibid.*
8. *Ibid.*
9. **Rankine, D. & Barron, P.H.:** *The Book of Gold, Op. Cit.*
   Marty, J. & MacParthy, F.: *Usage Mago-Théurgiques des Psaumes, Op. Cit.*
10. *Ibid.*

Psalm 102

1. **Nulman, M.:** *The Encyclopedia of Jewish Prayer, Op. Cit.*
2. *Ibid.*
   Greenwald, Z.: *Shaarei Halachah: A Summary of Laws for Jewish Living,* Feldheim Publishers, Jerusalem & New York 2000; **Gold, A.:** *Yom Kippur Katan Service,* Mesorah Publications Ltd., Brooklyn 2002.

482

3. **Feldman, Y.Y.:** *Tehillim Eis Ratzon*, *Op. Cit.*
4. **Singer, I. & Adler, C.:** *The Jewish Encyclopedia*, *Op. Cit.*
5. *Le Livre des Psaumes Hébreu-Français et Phonétique, Op. Cit.*
    Azulai, H.Y.D.: *Sefer Tehillim Sha'arei Rachamim*, *Op. Cit.*
    Ronen, D.: *Tehilim Kavvanot ha-Lev*, *Op. Cit.*
    Brauner, R.: *Synopsis of Sefer Shimush Tehillim. Op. Cit.*
6. **Kimchi, D. ben Y.:** *Sefer Tehillim, Op. Cit.*
    Sefer Shimmush Tehillim, Op. Cit.
    Seder Tefilot Tikun Ezra, Op. Cit.
    Grünwald, M.: *Ueber den Einfluss der Psalmen auf die Katholische Liturgie, Op. Cit.*
    Refuah v'Chayim m'Yerushalayim im Shimush Tehilim, Op. Cit.
    Rebiger, B.: *Sefer Shimmush Tehillim, Op. Cit.*
    Landsberg, M.: *Sefer Tehillim im Peirush Rashi, Op. Cit.*
    Hai ben Sherira Gaon & Varady, A.N.: *Shimush Tehillim (the Theurgical Use of Psalms), Op. Cit.*
7. **Rebiger, B.:** *Ibid.*
8. **Selig, G.:** *Sepher Schimmusch Tehillim, Op. Cit.*
    The Sixth and Seventh Books of Moses, Op. Cit.
    Peterson, J.H.: *The Sixth and Seventh Books of Moses, Op. Cit.*
9. *Ibid.*
10. **Feldman, Y.Y.:** *Tehillim Eis Ratzon*, *Op. Cit.*
11. **Rebiger, B.:** *Sefer Shimmush Tehillim, Op. Cit.*
12. **Zacutto, M.:** *Shorshei ha-Shemot, Op. cit.*
13. *Ibid.*
14. **Azulai, H.J.D.:** *Sefer Tehilim im Gerem ha'Ma'alot*, Livorno 1856.
    Palagi, H. ben Y.: *Sefer Tehilim im peirush Hakatuv L'chaim*, Livorno 1861.
15. **Feldman, Y.Y.:** *Tehillim Eis Ratzon*, *Op. Cit.*
16. **Davis, E. & Frenkel, D.A.:** *Ha-Kami'a ha-Ivri*, *Op. Cit.*
    Green, A.: *Judaic Artifacts*, *Op. Cit.*
17. **Rankine, D. & Barron, P.H.:** *The Book of Gold, Op. Cit.*
    Marty, J. & MacParthy, F.: *Usage Mago-Théurgiques des Psaumes, Op. Cit.*
18. **Mathers, S.L. Macgregor:** *Key of Solomon the King, Op. Cit.*

Psalm 103

1. **Nulman, M.:** *The Encyclopedia of Jewish Prayer*, *Op. Cit.*
    Hoffman, L.A.: *My People's Prayer Book: Vol. 8*, *Op. Cit.*
2. **Singer, I. & Adler, C.:** *The Jewish Encyclopedia*, *Op. Cit.*
3. **Kimchi, D. ben Y.:** *Sefer Tehillim, Op. Cit.*

Sefer Shimmush Tehillim, Op. Cit.
Seder Tefilot Tikun Ezra, Op. Cit.
Grünwald, M.: *Ueber den Einfluss der Psalmen auf die Katholische Liturgie, Op. Cit.*
Le Livre des Psaumes Hébreu-Français et Phonétique, Op. Cit.
Azulai, H.Y.D.: *Sefer Tehillim Sha'arei Rachamim, Op. Cit.*
Refuah v'Chayim m'Yerushalayim im Shimush Tehilim, Op. Cit.
Rebiger, B.: *Sefer Shimmush Tehillim, Op. Cit.*
Ronen, D.: *Tehilim Kavvanot ha-Lev, Op. Cit.*
Brauner, R.: *Synopsis of Sefer Shimush Tehillim. Op. Cit.*
Landsberg, M.: *Sefer Tehillim im Peirush Rashi, Op. Cit.*
Hai ben Sherira Gaon & Varady, A.N.: *Shimush Tehillim (the Theurgical Use of Psalms), Op. Cit.*
4. *Ibid.*
5. **Selig, G.:** *Sepher Schimmusch Tehillim, Op. Cit.*
    The Sixth and Seventh Books of Moses, Op. Cit.
    Peterson, J.H.: *The Sixth and Seventh Books of Moses, Op. Cit.*
6. *Ibid.*
7. **Rebiger, B.:** *Sefer Shimmush Tehillim, Op. Cit*
8. **Feldman, Y.Y.:** *Tehillim Eis Ratzon, Op. Cit.*
9. **Davis, E. & Frenkel, D.A.:** *Ha-Kami'a ha-Ivri, Op. Cit.*
    Green, A.: *Judaic Artifacts, Op. Cit.*
10. **Zacutto, M.:** *Shorshei ha-Shemot, Op. Cit.*
    Swart, J.G.: *The Book of Sacred Names, Op. Cit.*
11. **Zellmann-Rohrer, M.:** *Psalms Useful for Everything, Op. Cit.*
12. **Rankine, D. & Barron, P.H.:** *The Book of Gold, Op. Cit.*
    Marty, J. & MacParthy, F.: *Usage Mago-Théurgiques des Psaumes, Op. Cit.*
13. **Skinner, S. & Rankine, D.:** *A Collection of Magical Secrets, Op. Cit.*

Psalm 104

1. **Scherman, N.:** *Siddur Sukat David: The Complete Artscroll Siddur*, Mesorah Publications, Brooklyn 1985.
    Wertheim, A.: *Law and Custom in Hasidism*, Ktav Publishing House Inc., Hoboken 1992.
    Klein, I.: *A Guide to Jewish Religious Practice, Op. Cit.*
    Nulman, M.: *The Encyclopedia of Jewish Prayer, Op. Cit.*
    Rutman, J.Y.: *Jewish Prayers to an Evolutionary God: Science in the Siddur*, Joel Yehudah Rutman 2017.
2. **Nulman, M.:** *Ibid.*
3. **Scherman, N.:** *Siddur Sukat David: The Complete Artscroll Siddur, Op. Cit.*
    Wertheim, A.: *Law and Custom in Hasidism*, Ktav Publishing

House Inc., Hoboken 1992.

Klein, I.: *A Guide to Jewish Religious Practice, Op. Cit.*

Nulman, M.: *The Encyclopedia of Jewish Prayer, Op. Cit.*

Rutman, J.Y.: *Jewish Prayers to an Evolutionary God: Science in the Siddur, Op. Cit.*

4. **Nulman, M.:** *Ibid.*

5. *Ibid.*

6. *Ibid.*

7. *Ibid.*

8. *Ibid.*

Berkowitz, H.: *Kiddush or Sabbath Sentiment in the Home,* Henry Berkowitz, Philadelphia 1898.

9. **Rosenzweig, F. & Glatzer, N.N.:** *Franz Rosenzweig: His Life and Thought,* Jewish Publication Society of America, Philadelphia 1953.

10. **Nulman, M.:** *The Encyclopedia of Jewish Prayer, Op. Cit.*

11. **Tziyon, R.:** *Beit Imi: Edut mitoch ha-bayit p'nimah al chayeha ha-mufla'im shel imi ha-Rabanit Bat Sheva Ester Kanevsky,* Mishpachat Tzion, Bnei Brak 2017.

12. **Singer, I. & Adler, C.:** *The Jewish Encyclopedia, Op. Cit.*

13. *Le Livre des Psaumes Hébreu-Français et Phonétique, Op. Cit.*

Azulai, H.Y.D.: *Sefer Tehillim Sha'arei Rachamim, Op. Cit.*

Ronen, D.: *Tehilim Kavvanot ha-Lev, Op. Cit.*

14. **Brauner, R.:** *Synopsis of Sefer Shimush Tehillim. Op. Cit.*

15. **Kimchi, D. ben Y.:** *Sefer Tehillim, Op. Cit.*

Refuah v'Chayim m'Yerushalayim im Shimush Tehilim, Op. Cit.

Rebiger, B.: *Sefer Shimmush Tehillim, Op. Cit.*

Landsberg, M.: *Sefer Tehillim im Peirush Rashi, Op. Cit.*

16. **Selig, G.:** *Sepher Schimmusch Tehillim, Op. Cit.*

The Sixth and Seventh Books of Moses, Op. Cit.

Peterson, J.H.: *The Sixth and Seventh Books of Moses, Op. Cit.*

17. **Zacutto, M.:** *Shorshei ha-Shemot, Op. Cit.*

Swart, J.G.: *The Book of Sacred Names, Op. Cit.*

18. *Ibid.*

19. *Ibid.*

20. **Zellmann-Rohrer, M.:** *Psalms Useful for Everything, Op. Cit.*

21. **Hansen, N.B.:** *Ancient Execration Magic in Coptic and Islamic Egypt,* in **Mirecki, P. & Meyer, M.:** *Magic and Ritual in the Ancient World, Op. Cit.*

22. *Ibid.*

23. **Doutté, E.:** *Magie et Religion dans l'Afrique du Nord,* Adolphe Jourdan, Alger 1909.

24. **Rankine, D. & Barron, P.H.:** *The Book of Gold, Op. Cit.*

485

Marty, J. & MacParthy, F.: *Usage Mago-Théurgiques des Psaumes, Op. Cit.*

25. *Ibid.*

Psalm 105

1. **Gillingham, S.:** *Psalms Through the Centuries, Volume 3, Op. Cit.*
2. **Rosenberg, A.S.:** *Jewish Liturgy as a Spiritual System: A Prayer-by-Prayer Explanation of the Nature and Meaning of Jewish Worship*, Rowen & Littlefield Publishers Inc., Lanham, New York & Oxford 2004.
3. **Chacham, A.:** *The Bible: Psalms with the Jerusalem Commentary*, Vol. 3, Mosad Harav Kook, Jerusalem 2003.
4. **Nulman, M.:** *The Encyclopedia of Jewish Prayer, Op. Cit.*
   Feuer, A.Ch. & Scherman, N.: *Sefer Tehillim, Op. Cit.*
   Friedland, E.L.: *Were Our Mouths Filled With Song: Studies in Liberal Jewish Liturgy*, Hebrew Union College Press, Cincinatti 1997.
5. **Swart, J.G.:** *The Book of Magical Psalms—Part 2, Op. Cit.*
6. **Kimchi, D. ben Y.:** *Sefer Tehillim, Op. Cit.*
   Sefer Shimmush Tehillim, Op. Cit.
   Seder Tefilot Tikun Ezra, Op. Cit.
   Azulai, H.Y.D.: *Sefer Tehillim Sha'arei Rachamim, Op. Cit.*
   Refuah v'Chayim m'Yerushalayim im Shimush Tehilim, Op. Cit.
   Rebiger, B.: *Sefer Shimmush Tehillim, Op. Cit.*
   Ronen, D.: *Tehilim Kavvanot ha-Lev, Op. Cit.*
   Landsberg, M.: *Sefer Tehillim im Peirush Rashi, Op. Cit.*
   Hai ben Sherira Gaon & Varady, A.N.: *Shimush Tehillim (the Theurgical Use of Psalms), Op. Cit.*
7. **Singer, I. & Adler, C.:** *The Jewish Encyclopedia, Op. Cit.*
   Brauner, R.: *Synopsis of Sefer Shimush Tehillim. Op. Cit.*
8. **Brauner, R.:** *Ibid.*
   Le Livre des Psaumes Hébreu-Français et Phonétique, Op. Cit.
9. **Rebiger, B.:** *Sefer Shimmush Tehillim, Op. Cit.*
10. *Le Livre des Psaumes Hébreu-Français et Phonétique, Op. Cit.*
11. **Selig, G.:** *Sepher Schimmusch Tehillim, Op. Cit.*
    The Sixth and Seventh Books of Moses, Op. Cit.
    Peterson, J.H.: *The Sixth and Seventh Books of Moses, Op. Cit.*
12. *Ibid.*
13. **Rebiger, B.:** *Sefer Shimmush Tehillim, Op. Cit.*
14. **Davis, A.:** *The Metsudah Tehillim: A New Linear Tehillim with English Translation and Notes*, Ktav Publishing House, Hoboken, New Jersey 1983.
15. **Zacutto, M.:** *Shorshei ha-Shemot, Op. Cit.*
    Swart, J.G.: *The Book of Sacred Names, Op. Cit.*
16. **Zacutto, M.:** *Shorshei ha-Shemot, Op. Cit.*

17. *Ibid.*
18. *Ibid.*
19. **Weintraub, S.Y.**: *From the Depths: The Use of Psalms*, in **Friedman, D.A.**: *Jewish Pastoral Care*, *Op. Cit.*
20. *Ibid.*
21. **Zellmann-Rohrer, M.**: *Psalms Useful for Everything, Op. Cit.*
22. **Rankine, D. & Barron, P.H.**: *The Book of Gold*, *Op. Cit.*
   Marty, J. & MacParthy, F.: *Usage Mago-Théurgiques des Psaumes, Op. Cit.*
23. **Mathers, S.L. Macgregor**: *Key of Solomon the King*, *Op. Cit.*

Psalm 106

1. **Chacham, A.**: *The Bible*, Vol. 3, *Op. Cit.*
2. **Nulman, M.**: *The Encyclopedia of Jewish Prayer*, *Op. Cit.*
   Feuer, A.Ch. & Scherman, N.: *Sefer Tehillim, Op. Cit.*
   Friedland, E.L.: *Were Our Mouths Filled With Song, Op. Cit.*
3. **Nulman, M.**: *The Encyclopedia of Jewish Prayer, Op. Cit.*
4. **Kimchi, D. ben Y.**: *Sefer Tehillim, Op. Cit.*
   Azulai, H.Y.D.: *Sefer Tehillim Sha'arei Rachamim, Op. Cit.*
   Refuah v'Chayim m'Yerushalayim im Shimush Tehilim, Op. Cit.
   Rebiger, B.: *Sefer Shimmush Tehillim, Op. Cit.*
   Ronen, D.: *Tehilim Kavvanot ha-Lev, Op. Cit.*
   Landsberg, M.: *Sefer Tehillim im Peirush Rashi, Op. Cit.*
   Hai ben Sherira Gaon & Varady, A.N.: *Shimush Tehillim* (*the Theurgical Use of Psalms*), *Op. Cit.*
5. **Singer, I. & Adler, C.**: *The Jewish Encyclopedia, Op. Cit.*
   Brauner, R.: *Synopsis of Sefer Shimush Tehillim. Op. Cit.*
6. **Rebiger, B.**: *Sefer Shimmush Tehillim, Op. Cit.*
7. *Le Livre des Psaumes Hébreu-Français et Phonétique, Op. Cit.*
8. **Kimchi, D. ben Y.**: *Sefer Tehillim, Op. Cit.*
   Refuah v'Chayim m'Yerushalayim im Shimush Tehilim, Op. Cit.
   Rebiger, B.: *Sefer Shimmush Tehillim, Op. Cit.*
   Landsberg, M.: *Sefer Tehillim im Peirush Rashi, Op. Cit.*
9. **Rebiger, B.**: *Ibid.*
10. *Sefer Shimmush Tehillim, Op. Cit.*
    Seder Tefilot Tikun Ezra, Op. Cit.
    Grünwald, M.: *Ueber den Einfluss der Psalmen auf die Katholische Liturgie, Op. Cit.*
    Hai ben Sherira Gaon & Varady, A.N.: *Shimush Tehillim* (*the Theurgical Use of Psalms*), *Op. Cit.*
11. **Selig, G.**: *Sepher Schimmusch Tehillim, Op. Cit.*
    The Sixth and Seventh Books of Moses, Op. Cit.
    Peterson, J.H.: *The Sixth and Seventh Books of Moses, Op. Cit.*

12. **Rebiger, B.:** *Sefer Shimmush Tehillim, Op. Cit.*
13. **Davis, E. & Frenkel, D.A.:** *Ha-Kami'a ha-Ivri, Op. Cit.*
    Green, A.: *Judaic Artifacts, Op. Cit.*
14. **Swart, J.G.:** *The Book of Seals & Amulets, Op. Cit.*
15. **Shachar, I.:** *Jewish Tradition in Art, Op. Cit.*
    Davis, E. & Frenkel, D.A.: *Ha-Kami'a ha-Ivri, Op. Cit.*
    Green, A.: *Judaic Artifacts, Op. Cit.*
16. *Ibid.*
    Zacutto, M.: *Shorshei ha-Shemot, Op. Cit.*
    Rosenberg, Y.: *Rafael ha-Malach, Op. Cit.*
    Heschel, A.Y.: *Shemirot uSegulot Niflot, Op. Cit.*
    Palagi, C.: *Refuah v'Chayim, Op. cit.*
    Schrire, T.: *Hebrew Amulets, Op. cit.*
17. *Ibid.*
18. Wellcome Library, London.
19. **Swart, J.G.:** *The Book of Seals & Amulets, Op. Cit.*
20. *MS Heb. A 19*, Wellcome Library, London.
21. **Swart, J.G.:** *The Book of Sacred Names, Op. Cit.*
    —*The Book of Seals & Amulets, Op. Cit.*
22. **Zacutto, M.:** *Shorshei ha-Shemot, Op. Cit.*
    Swart, J.G.: *The Book of Seals & Amulets, Op. Cit.*
23. *Ibid.*
24. *Ibid.*
25. *Ibid.*
26. *Ibid.*
27. **Zacutto, M.:** *Shorshei ha-Shemot, Op. Cit.*
    Swart, J.G.: *The Book of Sacred Names, Op. Cit.*
28. **Skinner, S. & Rankine, D.:** *A Collection of Magical Secrets, Op. Cit.*
29. **Rankine, D. & Barron, P.H.:** *The Book of Gold, Op. Cit.*
    Marty, J. & MacParthy, F.: *Usage Mago-Théurgiques des Psaumes, Op. Cit.*

CHAPTER 6

Psalm 107

1. **Nulman, M.:** *The Encyclopedia of Jewish Prayer*, *Op. Cit.*
2. *Ibid.*
3. *Ibid.*
4. *Ibid.*
5. *Ibid.*
6. *Ibid.*

   Greenberg, B.: *How to Run a Traditional Jewish Household*, Simon & Schuster Inc., New York 1983.

   Henkin, Y.: *Responsa on Contemporary Jewish Women's Issues*, KTAV Publishing House, New Jersey 2003.

   Berkovits, R.: *Hilkhot Nashim: Kaddish, Birkat Hagomel, Megillah*, Maggid Books, New Milford 2018.
7. **Feldman, Y.Y.:** *Tehillim Eis Ratzon, Op. Cit.*
8. **Kimchi, D. ben Y.:** *Sefer Tehillim, Op. Cit.*

   Azulai, H.Y.D.: *Sefer Tehillim Sha'arei Rachamim, Op. Cit.*

   Refuah v'Chayim m'Yerushalayim im Shimush Tehilim, Op. Cit.

   Rebiger, B.: *Sefer Shimmush Tehillim, Op. Cit.*

   Ronen, D.: *Tehilim Kavvanot ha-Lev, Op. Cit.*

   Landsberg, M.: *Sefer Tehillim im Peirush Rashi, Op. Cit.*
9. **Singer, I. & Adler, C.:** *The Jewish Encyclopedia, Op. Cit.*
10. **Brauner, R.:** *Synopsis of Sefer Shimush Tehillim. Op. Cit.*

    Le Livre des Psaumes Hébreu-Français et Phonétique, Op. Cit.
11. **Selig, G.:** *Sepher Schimmusch Tehillim, Op. Cit.*

    The Sixth and Seventh Books of Moses, Op. Cit.

    Peterson, J.H.: *The Sixth and Seventh Books of Moses, Op. Cit.*
12. **Rebiger, B.:** *Sefer Shimmush Tehillim, Op. Cit.*
13. **Selig, G.:** *Sepher Schimmusch Tehillim, Op. Cit.*

    The Sixth and Seventh Books of Moses, Op. Cit.

    Peterson, J.H.: *The Sixth and Seventh Books of Moses, Op. Cit.*
14. **Rebiger, B.:** *Sefer Shimmush Tehillim, Op. Cit.*
15. **Zacutto, M.:** *Shorshei ha-Shemot, Op. Cit.*
16. *Ibid.*
17. *Ibid.*
18. **Swart, J.G.:** *The Book of Magical Psalms—Part 2, Op. Cit.*
19. **Zacutto, M.:** *Shorshei ha-Shemot, Op. Cit.*
20. **Rankine, D. & Barron, P.H.:** *The Book of Gold, Op. Cit.*

    Marty, J. & MacParthy, F.: *Usage Mago-Théurgiques des Psaumes, Op. Cit.*
21. **Mathers, S.L. Macgregor:** *Key of Solomon the King, Op. Cit.*

Psalm 108

1. *Le Livre des Psaumes Hébreu-Français et Phonétique, Op. Cit.*
    Azulai, H.Y.D.: *Sefer Tehillim Sha'arei Rachamim, Op. Cit.*
    Ronen, D.: *Tehilim Kavvanot ha-Lev, Op. Cit.*
    Feldman, Y.Y.: *Tehillim Eis Ratzon, Op. Cit.*
2. **Brauner, R.:** *Synopsis of Sefer Shimush Tehillim. Op. Cit.*
3. **Kimchi, D. ben Y.:** *Sefer Tehillim, Op. Cit.*
    Sefer Shimmush Tehillim, Op. Cit.
    Seder Tefilot Tikun Ezra, Op. Cit.
    Grünwald, M.: *Ueber den Einfluss der Psalmen auf die Katholische Liturgie, Op. Cit.*
    Refuah v'Chayim m'Yerushalayim im Shimush Tehilim, Op. Cit.
    Rebiger, B.: *Sefer Shimmush Tehillim, Op. Cit.*
    Landsberg, M.: *Sefer Tehillim im Peirush Rashi, Op. Cit.*
    Hai ben Sherira Gaon & Varady, A.N.: *Shimush Tehillim (the Theurgical Use of Psalms), Op. Cit.*
4. **Selig, G.:** *Sepher Schimmusch Tehillim, Op. Cit.*
    The Sixth and Seventh Books of Moses, Op. Cit.
    Peterson, J.H.: *The Sixth and Seventh Books of Moses, Op. Cit.*
5. **Kimchi, D. ben Y.:** *Sefer Tehillim, Op. Cit.*
    Sefer Shimmush Tehillim, Op. Cit.
    Seder Tefilot Tikun Ezra, Op. Cit.
    Grünwald, M.: *Ueber den Einfluss der Psalmen auf die Katholische Liturgie, Op. Cit.*
    Hai ben Sherira Gaon & Varady, A.N.: *Shimush Tehillim (the Theurgical Use of Psalms), Op. Cit.*
6. *Refuah v'Chayim m'Yerushalayim im Shimush Tehilim, Op. Cit.*
    Rebiger, B.: *Sefer Shimmush Tehillim, Op. Cit.*
    Landsberg, M.: *Sefer Tehillim im Peirush Rashi, Op. Cit.*
7. **Selig, G.:** *Sepher Schimmusch Tehillim, Op. Cit.*
    The Sixth and Seventh Books of Moses, Op. Cit.
    Peterson, J.H.: *The Sixth and Seventh Books of Moses, Op. Cit.*
8. **Rebiger, B.:** *Sefer Shimmush Tehillim, Op. Cit.*
9. **Zacutto, M.:** *Shorshei ha-Shemot, Op. Cit.*
10. **Singer, I. & Adler, C.:** *The Jewish Encyclopedia, Op. Cit.*
11. **Feldman, Y.Y.:** *Tehillim Eis Ratzon, Op. Cit.*
12. **Zellmann-Rohrer, M.:** *Psalms Useful for Everything, Op. Cit.*
13. **Rankine, D. & Barron, P.H.:** *The Book of Gold, Op. Cit.*
    Marty, J. & MacParthy, F.: *Usage Mago-Théurgiques des Psaumes, Op. Cit.*

Psalm 109

1. **Card, M.:** *A Sacred Sorrow: Reaching Out to God in the Lost Language of Lament*, NavPress, Colorado Springs 2005.

2. **Dennis, G.W.:** *The Encyclopedia of Jewish Myth, Magic and Mysticism, Op. Cit.*
3. **Chajes, J.H.:** *Between Worlds, Op. Cit.*
4. *Ibid.*
5. *Ibid.*
6. *Ibid.*
7. *Ibid.*
8. *Ibid.*
9. **Singer, I. & Adler, C.:** *The Jewish Encyclopedia, Op. Cit.*
10. **Azulai, H.Y.D.:** *Sefer Tehillim Sha'arei Rachamim, Op. Cit.*
    Ronen, D.: *Tehilim Kavvanot ha-Lev, Op. Cit.*
    Brauner, R.: *Synopsis of Sefer Shimush Tehillim. Op. Cit.*
11. *Le Livre des Psaumes Hébreu-Français et Phonétique, Op. Cit.*
12. **Kimchi, D. ben Y.:** *Sefer Tehillim, Op. Cit.*
    Sefer Shimmush Tehillim, Op. Cit.
    Seder Tefilot Tikun Ezra, Op. Cit.
    Rebiger, B.: *Sefer Shimmush Tehillim, Op. Cit.*
    Hai ben Sherira Gaon & Varady, A.N.: *Shimush Tehillim (the Theurgical Use of Psalms), Op. Cit.*
13. **Selig, G.:** *Sepher Schimmusch Tehillim, Op. Cit.*
    The Sixth and Seventh Books of Moses, Op. Cit.
    Peterson, J.H.: *The Sixth and Seventh Books of Moses, Op. Cit.*
14. *Refuah v'Chayim m'Yerushalayim im Shimush Tehilim, Op. Cit.*
    Rebiger, B.: *Sefer Shimmush Tehillim, Op. Cit.*
    Landsberg, M.: *Sefer Tehillim im Peirush Rashi, Op. Cit.*
15. *Ibid.*
    Kimchi, D. ben Y.: *Sefer Tehillim, Op. Cit.*
    Sefer Shimmush Tehillim, Op. Cit.
    Seder Tefilot Tikun Ezra, Op. Cit.
    Hai ben Sherira Gaon & Varady, A.N.: *Shimush Tehillim (the Theurgical Use of Psalms), Op. Cit.*
    Selig, G.: *Sepher Schimmusch Tehillim, Op. Cit.*
    The Sixth and Seventh Books of Moses, Op. Cit.
    Peterson, J.H.: *The Sixth and Seventh Books of Moses, Op. Cit.*
16. *Refuah v'Chayim m'Yerushalayim im Shimush Tehilim, Op. Cit.*
    Landsberg, M.: *Sefer Tehillim im Peirush Rashi, Op. Cit.*
    Kimchi, D. ben Y.: *Sefer Tehillim, Op. Cit.*
    Sefer Shimmush Tehillim, Op. Cit.
    Seder Tefilot Tikun Ezra, Op. Cit.
    Hai ben Sherira Gaon & Varady, A.N.: *Shimush Tehillim (the Theurgical Use of Psalms), Op. Cit.*
17. **Rebiger, B.:** *Sefer Shimmush Tehillim, Op. Cit.*

18.   **Selig, G.:** *Sepher Schimmusch Tehillim, Op. Cit.*
      The Sixth and Seventh Books of Moses, Op. Cit.
      Peterson, J.H.: *The Sixth and Seventh Books of Moses, Op. Cit.*
19.   **Rebiger, B.:** *Sefer Shimmush Tehillim, Op. Cit.*
20.   **Feldman, Y.Y.:** *Tehillim Eis Ratzon, Op. Cit.*
21.   **Zacutto, M.:** *Shorshei ha-Shemot, Op. Cit.*
22.   *Ibid.*
23.   *Ibid.*
24.   *Ibid.*
25.   *Ibid.*
26.   *Ibid.*
27.   *Ibid.*
28.   *Ibid.*
29.   **Zacutto, M.:** *Shorshei ha-Shemot, Op. Cit.*
      Swart, J.G.: *The Book of Sacred Names, Op. Cit.*
30.   **Kropp, A.M.:** *Ausgewählte Koptische Zaubertexte.* 3 Volumes,
      La Fondation Égyptologique Reine Élisabeth, Brussels 1931.
      Hansen, N.B.: *Ancient Execration Magic in Coptic and Islamic
      Egypt,* in **Mirecki, P. & Meyer, M.:** *Magic and Ritual in the
      Ancient World, Op. Cit.*
31.   *Ibid.*
32.   **Rankine, D. & Barron, P.H.:** *The Book of Gold, Op. Cit.*
      Marty, J. & MacParthy, F.: *Usage Mago-Théurgiques des
      Psaumes, Op. Cit.*
33.   **Mathers, S.L. Macgregor:** *Key of Solomon the King, Op. Cit.*

Psalm 110

1.   **Singer, I. & Adler, C.:** *The Jewish Encyclopedia, Op. Cit.*
2.   **Kimchi, D. ben Y.:** *Sefer Tehillim, Op. Cit.*
      Sefer Shimmush Tehillim, Op. Cit.
      Seder Tefilot Tikun Ezra, Op. Cit.
      Grünwald, M.: *Ueber den Einfluss der Psalmen auf die
      Katholische Liturgie, Op. Cit.*
      Le Livre des Psaumes Hébreu-Français et Phonétique, Op. Cit.
      Azulai, H.Y.D.: *Sefer Tehillim Sha'arei Rachamim, Op. Cit.*
      Refuah v'Chayim m'Yerushalayim im Shimush Tehilim, Op. Cit.
      Rebiger, B.: *Sefer Shimmush Tehillim, Op. Cit.*
      Ronen, D.: *Tehilim Kavvanot ha-Lev, Op. Cit.*
      Brauner, R.: *Synopsis of Sefer Shimush Tehillim. Op. Cit.*
      Landsberg, M.: *Sefer Tehillim im Peirush Rashi, Op. Cit.*
      Hai ben Sherira Gaon & Varady, A.N.: *Shimush Tehillim (the
      Theurgical Use of Psalms), Op. Cit.*

3. **Tirshom, J. ben E.:** *Shoshan Yesod Olam* in *Collectanea of Kabbalistic and Magical Texts*, Bibliothèque de Genève: Comites Latentes 145, Genève.

4. **Selig, G.:** *Sepher Schimmusch Tehillim, Op. Cit.*
    The Sixth and Seventh Books of Moses, Op. Cit.

5. **Peterson, J.H.:** *The Sixth and Seventh Books of Moses, Op. Cit.*

6. *Ibid.*
    Tirshom, J. ben E.: *Shoshan Yesod Olam, Op. Cit.*
    Kimchi, D. ben Y.: *Sefer Tehillim, Op. Cit.*
    Sefer Shimmush Tehillim, Op. Cit.
    Seder Tefilot Tikun Ezra, Op. Cit.
    Grünwald, M.: *Ueber den Einfluss der Psalmen auf die Katholische Liturgie, Op. Cit.*
    Refuah v'Chayim m'Yerushalayim im Shimush Tehilim, Op. Cit.
    Rebiger, B.: *Sefer Shimmush Tehillim, Op. Cit.*
    Landsberg, M.: *Sefer Tehillim im Peirush Rashi, Op. Cit.*
    Hai ben Sherira Gaon & Varady, A.N.: *Shimush Tehillim (the Theurgical Use of Psalms), Op. Cit.*
    Selig, G.: *Sepher Schimmusch Tehillim, Op. Cit.*
    The Sixth and Seventh Books of Moses, Op. Cit.

7. **Rebiger, B.:** *Sefer Shimmush Tehillim, Op. Cit.*

8. *Ibid.*

9. **Zacutto, M.:** *Shorshei ha-Shemot, Op. Cit.*

10. *Ibid.*

11. *Ibid.*

12. *Ibid.*

13. *Ibid.*

14. **Samuel, G.:** *The Kabbalah Handbook: A Concise Encyclopedia of Terms and Concepts in Jewish Mysticism*, Jeremy P. Tarcher/Penguin, New York 2007.

15. **Zacutto, M.:** *Shorshei ha-Shemot, Op. Cit.*

16. *Ibid.*

17. *Ibid.*

18. **Schrire, T.:** *Hebrew Amulets, Op. Cit.*
    Green, A.: *Judaic Artifacts, Op. Cit.*

19. *Ibid.*

20. **Zellmann-Rohrer, M.:** *Psalms Useful for Everything, Op. Cit.*

21. *Ibid.*

22. **Rankine, D. & Barron, P.H.:** *The Book of Gold, Op. Cit.*
    Marty, J. & MacParthy, F.: *Usage Mago-Théurgiques des Psaumes, Op. Cit.*

23. **Mathers, S.L. Macgregor:** *Key of Solomon the King, Op. Cit.*

24. *Ibid.*

Psalm 111

1. **Gillingham, S.:** *Psalms Through the Centuries, Volume 3, Op. Cit.*
2. *Ibid.*
3. *Ibid.*
4. *Ibid.*
5. **Swart, J.G.:** *The Book of Sacred Names, Op. Cit.*
6. **Gelbard, S.P.:** *Rite and Reason: 1050 Jewish Customs and Their Sources,* Volume 1, transl. Bulman, R.N., Mifal Rashi Publications, Petach Tikvah 1998.
7. **Wertheim, A.:** *Law and Custom in Hasidism,* transl. Himelstein, S., *Op. Cit.*
8. **Nulman, M.:** *The Encyclopedia of Jewish Prayer, Op. Cit.*
9. **Tirshom, J. ben E.:** *Shoshan Yesod Olam, Op. Cit.*
   Kimchi, D. ben Y.: *Sefer Tehillim, Op. Cit.*
   Le Livre des Psaumes Hébreu-Français et Phonétique, Op. Cit.
   Azulai, H.Y.D.: *Sefer Tehillim Sha'arei Rachamim, Op. Cit.*
   Singer, I. & Adler, C.: *The Jewish Encyclopedia, Op. Cit.*
   Refuah v'Chayim m'Yerushalayim im Shimush Tehilim, Op. Cit.
   Rebiger, B.: *Sefer Shimmush Tehillim, Op. Cit.*
   Ronen, D.: *Tehilim Kavvanot ha-Lev, Op. Cit.*
   Brauner, R.: *Synopsis of Sefer Shimush Tehillim. Op. Cit.*
   Landsberg, M.: *Sefer Tehillim im Peirush Rashi, Op. Cit.*
10. **Selig, G.:** *Sepher Schimmusch Tehillim, Op. Cit.*
    The Sixth and Seventh Books of Moses, Op. Cit.
    Peterson, J.H.: *The Sixth and Seventh Books of Moses, Op. Cit.*
11. **Rebiger, B.:** *Sefer Shimmush Tehillim, Op. Cit.*
12. **Feldman, Y.Y.:** *Tehillim Eis Ratzon, Op. Cit.*
13. **Lipshitz, S. ben Y.Y.:** *Segulot Yisrael,* Kahn & Fried, Munkatch 1905.
    Eliram (Amslam), S.: *Sefer Segulot, Terufot u'Mazalot, Op. Cit.*
14. **Zacutto, M.:** *Shorshei ha-Shemot, Op. Cit.*
15. **Davis, E. & Frenkel, D.A.:** *Ha-Kami'a ha-Ivri, Op. Cit.*
    Green, A.: *Judaic Artifacts, Op. Cit.*
16. **Zacutto, M.:** *Shorshei ha-Shemot, Op. Cit.*
    Swart, J.G.: *The Book of Sacred Names, Op. Cit.*
17. **Zellmann-Rohrer, M.:** *Psalms Useful for Everything, Op. Cit.*
18. **Rankine, D. & Barron, P.H.:** *The Book of Gold, Op. Cit.*
    Marty, J. & MacParthy, F.: *Usage Mago-Théurgiques des Psaumes, Op. Cit.*

494

Psalm 112

1. **Feldman, Y.Y.:** *Tehillim Eis Ratzon*, *Op. Cit.*
2. **Kimchi, D. ben Y.:** *Sefer Tehillim, Op. Cit.*
   Azulai, H.Y.D.: *Sefer Tehillim Sha'arei Rachamim*, *Op. Cit.*
   Singer, I. & Adler, C.: *The Jewish Encyclopedia*, *Op. Cit.*
   Refuah v'Chayim m'Yerushalayim im Shimush Tehilim, Op. Cit.
   Rebiger, B.: *Sefer Shimmush Tehillim, Op. Cit.*
   Ronen, D.: *Tehilim Kavvanot ha-Lev, Op. Cit.*
   Landsberg, M.: *Sefer Tehillim im Peirush Rashi, Op. Cit.*
3. *Le Livre des Psaumes Hébreu-Français et Phonétique, Op. Cit.*
4. **Brauner, R.:** *Synopsis of Sefer Shimush Tehillim. Op. Cit.*
5. **Selig, G.:** *Sepher Schimmusch Tehillim, Op. Cit.*
   The Sixth and Seventh Books of Moses, Op. Cit.
   Peterson, J.H.: *The Sixth and Seventh Books of Moses, Op. Cit.*
6. **Rebiger, B.:** *Sefer Shimmush Tehillim, Op. Cit.*
7. **Rankine, D. & Barron, P.H.:** *The Book of Gold, Op. Cit.*
   Marty, J. & MacParthy, F.: *Usage Mago-Théurgiques des Psaumes, Op. Cit.*
8. **Mathers, S.L. Macgregor:** *Key of Solomon the King, Op. Cit.*

Psalm 113

1. **Nulman, M.:** *The Encyclopedia of Jewish Prayer*, *Op. Cit.*
   Hoffman, L.A. & Arnow, D.: *My People's Passover Haggadah*, *Op. Cit.*
   deClaissé-Walford, N.L.: *Wisdom Commentary: Psalms Books 4–5*, Liturgical Press, Collegeville 2020.
2. **Atkinson, D.:** *A Light for the Pathway: Exploring the Psalms*, Wipf & Stock, Eugene 2021.
3. **Hoffman, L.A. & Arnow, D.:** *My People's Passover Haggadah*, *Op. Cit.*
4. *Ibid.*
5. *Ibid.*
6. *Ibid.*
7. **Swart, J.G.:** *The Book of Immediate Magic—Part 2*, *Op. Cit.*
8. **Hoffman, L.A. & Arnow, D.:** *My People's Passover Haggadah*, *Op. Cit.*
   Goodman, P.: *The Sukkot and Simhat Torah Anthology*, The Jewish Publication Society of America, Philadelphia 1973.
   —*The Hanukkah Anthology*, The Jewish Publication Society of America, Philadelphia 1976.
   —*The Shavuot Anthology*, The Jewish Publication Society of America, Philadelphia 1991.

Kohn, D.: *Jewish Faqs: An Internet Rabbi's Answers to Frequently asked Questions about Judaism*, Xlibris Corporation, Bloomington 2009.

9.   *Le Livre des Psaumes Hébreu-Français et Phonétique, Op. Cit.*
     Azulai, H.Y.D.: *Sefer Tehillim Sha'arei Rachamim, Op. Cit.*

10. **Singer, I. & Adler, C.:** *The Jewish Encyclopedia, Op. Cit.*

11. **Kimchi, D. ben Y.:** *Sefer Tehillim, Op. Cit.*
     Sefer Shimmush Tehillim, Op. Cit.
     Seder Tefilot Tikun Ezra, Op. Cit.
     Grünwald, M.: *Ueber den Einfluss der Psalmen auf die Katholische Liturgie, Op. Cit.*
     Refuah v'Chayim m'Yerushalayim im Shimush Tehilim, Op. Cit.
     Rebiger, B.: *Sefer Shimmush Tehillim, Op. Cit.*
     Brauner, R.: *Synopsis of Sefer Shimush Tehillim. Op. Cit.*
     Landsberg, M.: *Sefer Tehillim im Peirush Rashi, Op. Cit.*
     Hai ben Sherira Gaon & Varady, A.N.: *Shimush Tehillim (the Theurgical Use of Psalms), Op. Cit.*

12. **Selig, G.:** *Sepher Schimmusch Tehillim, Op. Cit.*
     The Sixth and Seventh Books of Moses, Op. Cit.
     Peterson, J.H.: *The Sixth and Seventh Books of Moses, Op. Cit.*

13. **Rebiger, B.:** *Sefer Shimmush Tehillim, Op. Cit.*

14. **Weintraub, S.Y.:** *From the Depths: The Use of Psalms*, in **Friedman, D.A.:** *Jewish Pastoral Care, Op. Cit.*

15. **Zacutto, M.:** *Shorshei ha-Shemot, Op. Cit.*

16. **Zellmann-Rohrer, M.:** *Psalms Useful for Everything, Op. Cit.*

17. **Clelland, S. & Paul Ferguson, P.:** *Book II of the Sacred Magic of Abramelin the Mage: An English Translation Based on a Newly Discovered Manuscript*, in **Fanger, C., Ostling, M., & Zwissler, L.:** *Magic, Ritual, and Witchcraft*, Vol. 18 No. 3, University of Pennsylvania Press, Pennsylvania 2023.

18. *Ibid.*

19. *Ibid.*

20. **Rankine, D. & Barron, P.H.:** *The Book of Gold, Op. Cit.*
     Marty, J. & MacParthy, F.: *Usage Mago-Théurgiques des Psaumes, Op. Cit.*

21. *Ibid.*

22. **Skinner, S. & Rankine, D.:** *A Collection of Magical Secrets, Op. Cit.*

23. **Mathers, S.L. Macgregor:** *Key of Solomon the King, Op. Cit.*

24. *Ibid.*

Psalm 114

1.   **deClaissé-Walford, N.L.:** *Wisdom Commentary: Psalms Books 4–5, Op. cit.*

2:     *Ibid.*

3.   *Ibid.*

4.   **Hoffman, L.A. & Arnow, D.**: *My People's Passover Haggadah, Op. Cit.*
    Goodman, P.: *The Sukkot and Simhat Torah Anthology, Op. Cit.*
    —*The Hanukkah Anthology, Op. Cit.*
    —*The Shavuot Anthology, Op. Cit.*
    Kohn, D.: Jewish Faqs, *Op. Cit.*

5.   *Le Livre des Psaumes Hébreu-Français et Phonétique, Op. Cit.*
    Azulai, H.Y.D.: *Sefer Tehillim Sha'arei Rachamim, Op. Cit.*
    Ronen, D.: *Tehilim Kavvanot ha-Lev, Op. Cit.*

6.   **Singer, I. & Adler, C.**: *The Jewish Encyclopedia, Op. Cit.*
    Brauner, R.: *Synopsis of Sefer Shimush Tehillim. Op. Cit.*

7.   **Kimchi, D. ben Y.**: *Sefer Tehillim, Op. Cit.*
    Sefer Shimmush Tehillim, Op. Cit.
    Seder Tefilot Tikun Ezra, Op. Cit.
    Grünwald, M.: *Ueber den Einfluss der Psalmen auf die Katholische Liturgie, Op. Cit.*
    Refuah v'Chayim m'Yerushalayim im Shimush Tehilim, Op. Cit.
    Rebiger, B.: *Sefer Shimmush Tehillim, Op. Cit.*
    Landsberg, M.: *Sefer Tehillim im Peirush Rashi, Op. Cit.*
    Hai ben Sherira Gaon & Varady, A.N.: *Shimush Tehillim (the Theurgical Use of Psalms), Op. Cit.*

8.   **Selig, G.**: *Sepher Schimmusch Tehillim, Op. Cit.*
    The Sixth and Seventh Books of Moses, Op. Cit.
    Peterson, J.H.: *The Sixth and Seventh Books of Moses, Op. Cit.*

9.   **Kimchi, D. ben Y.**: *Sefer Tehillim, Op. Cit.*
    Sefer Shimmush Tehillim, Op. Cit.
    Seder Tefilot Tikun Ezra, Op. Cit.
    Grünwald, M.: *Ueber den Einfluss der Psalmen auf die Katholische Liturgie, Op. Cit.*
    Refuah v'Chayim m'Yerushalayim im Shimush Tehilim, Op. Cit.
    Rebiger, B.: *Sefer Shimmush Tehillim, Op. Cit.*
    Landsberg, M.: *Sefer Tehillim im Peirush Rashi, Op. Cit.*
    Hai ben Sherira Gaon & Varady, A.N.: *Shimush Tehillim (the Theurgical Use of Psalms), Op. Cit.*

10.   **Selig, G.**: *Sepher Schimmusch Tehillim, Op. Cit.*
    The Sixth and Seventh Books of Moses, Op. Cit.
    Peterson, J.H.: *The Sixth and Seventh Books of Moses, Op. Cit.*

11.   **Rebiger, B.**: *Sefer Shimmush Tehillim, Op. Cit.*

12.   *Ibid.*

13.   **Zacutto, M.**: *Shorshei ha-Shemot, Op. Cit.*

14.   **Gikatilla, J.**: *Gates of Light: Sha'are Orah, Op. Cit.*

497

15. **Horowitz, I.:** *Isaiah Horowitz: The Generations of Adam*, transl. M. Krassen, Paulist Press, Mahwah 1996.
16. **Zacutto, M.:** *Shorshei ha-Shemot, Op. Cit.*
17. **Rosenberg, Y.:** *Rafael ha-Malach, Op. cit.*
    Davis, E. & Frenkel, D.A.: *Ha-Kami'a ha-Ivri, Op. Cit.*
    Green, A.: *Judaic Artifacts, Op. Cit.*
18. **Rankine, D. & Barron, P.H.:** *The Book of Gold, Op. Cit.*
    Marty, J. & MacParthy, F.: *Usage Mago-Théurgiques des Psaumes, Op. Cit.*

Psalm 115

1. **Nulman, M.:** *The Encyclopedia of Jewish Prayer, Op. Cit.*
   Hoffman, L.A. & Arnow, D.: *My People's Passover Haggadah, Op. Cit.*
   deClaissé-Walford, N.L.: *Wisdom Commentary: Psalms Books 4–5, Op. Cit.*
2. **Yeivin, I.:** *The Division into Sections in the Book of Psalms*, in *Textus:A Journal on Textual Criticism of the Hebrew Bible*, Vol. 7 (1), Koninklijke Brill NV, Leiden 1969.
   Breuer, M.: *The Book of Psalms: Corrected According to the Text and Masorah of the Aleppo Codex and its Associated Manuscripts*, Rav Kook Institute, Jerusalem 1990.
   Jerusalem Crown: The Bible of the Hebrew University of Jerusalem, N. Ben-Zvi, Jerusalem 2000.
   Brettler, M.Z.: *A Jewish Historical-Critical Commentary on Psalms: Psalm 114 as an Example*, in *Hebrew Bible and Ancient Israel*, Vol. 5 (4), Mohr-Siebeck, Tübingen 2016.
3. MS. Heb. D. 33, Hebrew Manuscripts, Bodleian Library, Oxford.
4. **Sander, P.J.:** *Alternate Delimitations in the Hebrew and Greek Psalters: A Theological Analysis*, Mohr Siebeck, Tübingen 2020.
5. **Brenton, L.C.L:** *The Septuagint with Apocrypha: Greek and English*, Zondervan Publishing House, Grand Rapids 1972.
6. *Latin Vulgate Bible*, American Bible Society/HarperCollins Publishers Limited, New York 1991.
7. **Flint, P.W.:** *Unrolling the Dead Sea Psalm Scrolls*, in **Brown, W.P.:** *The Oxford Handbook of the Psalms*, Oxford University Press, Oxford & New York 2014.
   Sander, P.J.: *Alternate Delimitations in the Hebrew and Greek Psalters, Op. Cit.*
8. **Elliger, K. & Rudolph, W.:** *Biblia Hebraica Stuttgartensia*, Deutsche Bibelgesellschaft, Stuttgart 1997.

9. **Sander, P.J.:** *Alternate Delimitations in the Hebrew and Greek Psalters, Op. Cit.*

10. **Ben Chayim, J.:** *Second Edition of the Rabbinic Bible* (the editio princeps) Bomberg, Venice 1524–25.
The Second Rabbinic Bible of 1525, Lasting Legacy Books, Federal Way 2016.

11. **Kittel, R.; P. Kahle, P. & Alt, A.:** *Biblia Hebraica*, Würtembergische Bibelanstalt, Stuttgart 1937.
Sander, P.J.: *Alternate Delimitations in the Hebrew and Greek Psalters, Op. Cit.*

12. *Le Livre des Psaumes Hébreu-Français et Phonétique, Op. Cit.*
Azulai, H.Y.D.: *Sefer Tehillim Sha'arei Rachamim, Op. Cit.*
Ronen, D.: *Tehilim Kavvanot ha-Lev, Op. Cit.*

13. **Singer, I. & Adler, C.:** *The Jewish Encyclopedia, Op. Cit.*

14. **Kimchi, D. ben Y.:** *Sefer Tehillim, Op. Cit.*
Sefer Shimmush Tehillim, Op. Cit.
Seder Tefilot Tikun Ezra, Op. Cit.
Grünwald, M.: *Ueber den Einfluss der Psalmen auf die Katholische Liturgie, Op. Cit.*
Refuah v'Chayim m'Yerushalayim im Shimush Tehilim, Op. Cit.
Rebiger, B.: *Sefer Shimmush Tehillim, Op. Cit.*
Brauner, R.: *Synopsis of Sefer Shimush Tehillim. Op. Cit.*
Landsberg, M.: *Sefer Tehillim im Peirush Rashi, Op. Cit.*
Hai ben Sherira Gaon & Varady, A.N.: *Shimush Tehillim* (the Theurgical Use of Psalms), *Op. Cit.*

15. **Selig, G.:** *Sepher Schimmusch Tehillim, Op. Cit.*
The Sixth and Seventh Books of Moses, Op. Cit.
Peterson, J.H.: *The Sixth and Seventh Books of Moses, Op. Cit.*

16. **Rebiger, B.:** *Sefer Shimmush Tehillim, Op. Cit.*

17. **Davis, E. & Frenkel, D.A.:** *Ha-Kami'a ha-Ivri, Op. Cit.*
Green, A.: *Judaic Artifacts, Op. Cit.*

18. **Swart, J.G.:** *The Book of Sacred Names, Op. Cit.*

19. **Zacutto, M.:** *Shorshei ha-Shemot, Op. Cit.*

20. **Rankine, D. & Barron, P.H.:** *The Book of Gold, Op. Cit.*
Marty, J. & MacParthy, F.: *Usage Mago-Théurgiques des Psaumes, Op. Cit.*

Psalm 116

1. **Eisenberg, R.L.:** *The JPS Guide to Jewish Traditions, Op. Cit.*
Robinson, G.: *Essential Judaism: Updated Edition: A Complete Guide to Beliefs, Customs and Rituals*, Atria Paperback, New York & London 2016;

2. **Nulman, M.:** *The Encyclopedia of Jewish Prayer, Op. Cit.*

3.   **Azulai, H.Y.D.:** *Sefer Tehillim Sha'arei Rachamim, Op. Cit.*
     Ronen, D.: *Tehilim Kavvanot ha-Lev, Op. Cit.*
4.   *Le Livre des Psaumes Hébreu-Français et Phonétique, Op. Cit.*
5.   **Brauner, R.:** *Synopsis of Sefer Shimush Tehillim. Op. Cit.*
6.   *Ibid.*
     Kimchi, D. ben Y.: *Sefer Tehillim, Op. Cit.*
     Sefer Shimmush Tehillim, Op. Cit.
     Seder Tefilot Tikun Ezra, Op. Cit.
     Grünwald, M.: *Ueber den Einfluss der Psalmen auf die Katholische Liturgie, Op. Cit.*
     Singer, I. & Adler, C.: *The Jewish Encyclopedia, Op. Cit.*
     Refuah v'Chayim m'Yerushalayim im Shimush Tehilim, Op. Cit.
     Rebiger, B.: *Sefer Shimmush Tehillim, Op. Cit.*
     Landsberg, M.: *Sefer Tehillim im Peirush Rashi, Op. Cit.*
     Hai ben Sherira Gaon & Varady, A.N.: *Shimush Tehillim (the Theurgical Use of Psalms), Op. Cit.*
7.   **Selig, G.:** *Sepher Schimmusch Tehillim, Op. Cit.*
     The Sixth and Seventh Books of Moses, Op. Cit.
     Peterson, J.H.: *The Sixth and Seventh Books of Moses, Op. Cit.*
8.   **Rebiger, B.:** *Sefer Shimmush Tehillim, Op. Cit.*
9.   **Feldman, Y.Y.:** *Tehillim Eis Ratzon, Op. Cit.*
10. **Klein, M.:** *A Time to Be Born, Op. Cit.*
     Falk, S. & Judson, D.: *The Jewish Pregnancy Book: A Resource for the Soul, Body & Mind during Pregnancy, Birth & the First Three Months,* Jewish Lights Publishing, Woodstock 2004.
11. **Shachar, I.:** *Jewish Tradition in Art, Op. Cit.*
     Green, A.: *Judaic Artifacts, Op. Cit.*
     Swart, J.G.: *The Book of Seals & Amulets, Op. Cit.*
12. **Zacutto, M.:** *Shorshei ha-Shemot, Op. Cit.*
     Swart, J.G.: *The Book of Sacred Names, Op. Cit.*
13. **Rankine, D. & Barron, P.H.:** *The Book of Gold, Op. Cit.*
     Marty, J. & MacParthy, F.: *Usage Mago-Théurgiques des Psaumes, Op. Cit.*
14. **Mathers, S.L. Macgregor:** *Key of Solomon the King, Op. Cit.*

Psalm 117

1.   **Nulman, M.:** *The Encyclopedia of Jewish Prayer, Op. Cit.*
     deClaissé-Walford, N.L.: *Wisdom Commentary: Psalms Books 4–5, Op. Cit.*
2.   **deClaissé-Walford, N.L.:** *Ibid.*
3.   **Singer, I. & Adler, C.:** *The Jewish Encyclopedia, Op. Cit.*
     Ronen, D.: *Tehilim Kavvanot ha-Lev, Op. Cit.*

4.   *Le Livre des Psaumes Hébreu-Français et Phonétique, Op. Cit.*
5.   **Kimchi, D. ben Y.:** *Sefer Tehillim, Op. Cit.*
      Azulai, H.Y.D.: *Sefer Tehillim Sha'arei Rachamim, Op. Cit.*
      Sefer Shimmush Tehillim, Op. Cit.
      Seder Tefilot Tikun Ezra, Op. Cit.
      Grünwald, M.: *Ueber den Einfluss der Psalmen auf die Katholische Liturgie, Op. Cit.*
      Refuah v'Chayim m'Yerushalayim im Shimush Tehilim, Op. Cit.
      Rebiger, B.: *Sefer Shimmush Tehillim, Op. Cit.*
      Landsberg, M.: *Sefer Tehillim im Peirush Rashi, Op. Cit.*
      Hai ben Sherira Gaon & Varady, A.N.: *Shimush Tehillim (the Theurgical Use of Psalms), Op. Cit.*
6.   **Brauner, R.:** *Synopsis of Sefer Shimush Tehillim. Op. Cit.*
7.   **Selig, G.:** *Sepher Schimmusch Tehillim, Op. Cit.*
      The Sixth and Seventh Books of Moses, Op. Cit.
      Peterson, J.H.: *The Sixth and Seventh Books of Moses, Op. Cit.*
8.   **Rankine, D. & Barron, P.H.:** *The Book of Gold, Op. Cit.*
      Marty, J. & MacParthy, F.: *Usage Mago-Théurgiques des Psaumes, Op. Cit.*
9.   *Ibid.*
10.   **Mathers, S.L. Macgregor:** *Key of Solomon the King, Op. Cit.*
11.   *Ibid.*
12.   *Ibid.*

Psalm 118

1.   **Ben Levi, R.:** *Romance of the Hebrew Calendar*, Xlibris Corporation, Bloomington 2013.
2.   *Ibid.*
3.   **Nulman, M.:** *The Encyclopedia of Jewish Prayer, Op. Cit.*
4.   *Ibid.*
5.   **Fairweather, W. & Sutherland Black, J.:** The First Book of Maccabees with Introduction and Notes, C.J. Clay & Sons, London 1897.
      Abrahams, I.: *A Companion to the Authorized Daily Prayer Book*, Sepher-Hermon Press Inc., New York 1966.
6.   **Nulman, M.:** *The Encyclopedia of Jewish Prayer, Op. Cit.*
7.   *Ibid.*
      Birnbaum, P.: *ha-Siddur ha-Shalem* (The Daily Prayer Book), 1949.
      Abrahams, I.: *A Companion to the Authorized Daily Prayer Book, Op. Cit.*
      Scherman, N.: *Siddur Sukat David: The Complete Artscroll Siddur, Op. Cit.*

501

Scherman, N. & Zlotowitz, G.: *Siddur Kol Sim'chah: The Artscroll Sephardic Siddur, Op. Cit.*

8.   **Nulman, M.:** *The Encyclopedia of Jewish Prayer, Op. Cit.*

9.   *Ibid.*

Tcechenov, Landa, A. of: *Seder Tefillah-Tzeluta D'Avraham,* Vol. 1, Va'ad Lehotza'at Sifrei Admur Mi-Tcechenov, Tel Aviv 1958—1961.]

10.   **Nulman, M.:** *The Encyclopedia of Jewish Prayer, Op. Cit.*

11.   **Swart, J.G.:** *The Book of Magical Psalms—Part 1, Op. Cit.*

12.   **Scherman, N. & Zlotowitz, M.:** *Machzor Beit Yosef: The Complete ArtScroll Machzor—Sukkot,* Mesorah Publications Ltd., Brooklyn 1987.

13.   **Nulman, M.:** *The Encyclopedia of Jewish Prayer, Op. Cit.*

14.   *Ibid.*

15.   **Kimchi, D. ben Y.:** *Sefer Tehillim, Op. Cit.*
      Azulai, H.Y.D.: *Sefer Tehillim Sha'arei Rachamim, Op. Cit.*
      Refuah v'Chayim m'Yerushalayim im Shimush Tehilim, Op. Cit.
      Rebiger, B.: *Sefer Shimmush Tehillim, Op. Cit.*
      Ronen, D.: *Tehilim Kavvanot ha-Lev, Op. Cit.*
      Landsberg, M.: *Sefer Tehillim im Peirush Rashi, Op. Cit.*

16.   *Le Livre des Psaumes Hébreu-Français et Phonétique, Op. Cit.*

17.   **Singer, I. & Adler, C.:** *The Jewish Encyclopedia, Op. Cit.*
      Brauner, R.: *Synopsis of Sefer Shimush Tehillim. Op. Cit.*

18.   **Selig, G.:** *Sepher Schimmusch Tehillim, Op. Cit.*
      The Sixth and Seventh Books of Moses, Op. Cit.
      Peterson, J.H.: *The Sixth and Seventh Books of Moses, Op. Cit.*

19.   **Rebiger, B.:** *Sefer Shimmush Tehillim, Op. Cit.*

20.   **Kimchi, D. ben Y.:** *Sefer Tehillim, Op. Cit.*
      Sefer Shimmush Tehillim, Op. Cit.
      Seder Tefilot Tikun Ezra, Op. Cit.
      Refuah v'Chayim m'Yerushalayim im Shimush Tehilim, Op. Cit.
      Rebiger, B.: *Sefer Shimmush Tehillim, Op. Cit.*
      Landsberg, M.: *Sefer Tehillim im Peirush Rashi, Op. Cit.*
      Hai ben Sherira Gaon & Varady, A.N.: *Shimush Tehillim (the Theurgical Use of Psalms), Op. Cit.*

21.   **Rebiger, B.:** *Ibid.*

22.   **Zacutto, M.:** *Shorshei ha-Shemot, Op. Cit.*

23.   **Swart, J.G.:** *The Book of Sacred Names, Op. Cit.*
      —The Book of Seals & Amulets, Op. Cit.
      —The Book of Immediate Magic—Part 1, Op. Cit.

24.   **Zacutto, M.:** *Shorshei ha-Shemot, Op. Cit.*

25.   *Ibid.*

26. **Trachtenberg, J.:** *Jewish Magic and Superstition*, *Op. Cit.*
27. **Zacutto, M.:** *Shorshei ha-Shemot*, *Op. Cit.*
28. **Davis, E. & Frenkel, D.A.:** *Ha-Kami'a ha-Ivri*, *Op. Cit.*
    Green, A.: *Judaic Artifacts*, *Op. Cit.*
29. *Ibid.*
30. **Zacutto, M.:** *Shorshei ha-Shemot*, *Op. Cit.*
31. *Ibid.*
    Swart, J.G.: *The Book of Sacred Names*, *Op. Cit.*
32. *Ibid.*
33. **Weintraub, S.Y.:** *From the Depths: The Use of Psalms*, in **Friedman, D.A.:** *Jewish Pastoral Care*, *Op. Cit.*
34. **Rankine, D. & Barron, P.H.:** *The Book of Gold*, *Op. Cit.*
    Marty, J. & MacParthy, F.: *Usage Mago-Théurgiques des Psaumes*, *Op. Cit.*

Psalm 119

1. **Scherman, N. & Zlotowitz, M.:** *Machzor Beit Yosef: The Complete ArtScroll Machzor—Rosh Hashanah*, Mesorah Publications Ltd., Brooklyn 1985.
2. **Nulman, M.:** *The Encyclopedia of Jewish Prayer*, *Op. Cit.*
3. *Ibid.*
4. *Ibid.*
    Eisenberg, R.L.: *The JPS Guide to Jewish Traditions*, *Op. Cit.*
5. *Ibid.*
6. **Swart, J.G.:** *The Book of Sacred Names*, *Op. Cit.*
    —*The Book of Seals & Amulets*, *Op. Cit.*
    —*The Book of Immediate Magic—Part 1*, *Op. Cit.*
    —*The Book of Magical Psalms—Part 1*, *Op. Cit.*
7. **Nulman, M.:** *The Encyclopedia of Jewish Prayer*, *Op. Cit.*
8. **Sher, A.A. & Scher, A.:** *Sefer Beneh Bet'cha: hil'chot nidah ut'vilah*, A. Scher, Brooklyn 2015.
9. **Kadden, B.B. & Kadden, B.:** *Teaching Jewish Life Cycle: Traditions and Activities*, A.R.E. Publishing, Inc., Denver 1997.
    Goldberg, H.E.: *Jewish Passages: Cycles of Jewish Life*, University of California Press, Berkeley, Los Angeles & London 2003.
10. *Ibid.*
    Scherman, N.: *Siddur Sukat David: The Complete Artscroll Siddur*, *Op. Cit.*
    Weber, V.L.: *Tradition!: Celebration and Ritual in Jewish Life*, Hugh Lauter Levin Associates Inc., Fairfield 2000.
11. **Nulman, M.:** *The Encyclopedia of Jewish Prayer*, *Op. Cit.*

503

12.   **Rashkow, I.N.**: *The Healing Power of Judaism*, in **Ellens, J.H.**: *The Healing Power of Spirituality: How Faith Helps Humans Thrive*, Vol. 1, Praeger/ABC-CLIO, Santa Barbara 2010.

13.   *Ibid.*
        Nulman, M.: *The Encyclopedia of Jewish Prayer*, *Op. Cit.*
        Eisenberg, R.L.: *The JPS Guide to Jewish Traditions*, *Op. Cit.*

14.   **Swart, J.G.**:*The Book of Magical Psalms—Part 1*, *Op. Cit.*

15.   **Nulman, M.**: *The Encyclopedia of Jewish Prayer*, *Op. Cit.*

16.   *Ibid.*
        Dobrinsky, H.C.: *A Treasury of Sephardic Laws and Customs*, *Op. Cit.*

17.   *Ibid.*

18.   **Levy, Y.**: *Journey Through Grief: A Sephardic Manual for the Bereaved and Their Community*, KTAV Publishing House, Inc., Jersey City 2003.

19.   *Ibid.*

20.   **Dennis, G.W.**: *The Encyclopedia of Jewish Myth, Magic and Mysticism*, *Op.*

21.   **Singer, I. & Adler, C.**: *The Jewish Encyclopedia*, *Op. Cit.*

22.   *Ibid.*

23.   *Ibid.*

24.   **Feldman, Y.Y.**: *Tehillim Eis Ratzon*, *Op. Cit.*

25.   **Eliram (Amslam), S.**: *Sefer Segulot, Terufot u'Mazalot*, *Op. Cit.*

26.   **Lipshitz, S. ben Y.Y.**: *Segulot Yisrael*, *Op. Cit.*

27.   *Ibid.*

28.   *Ibid.*

29.   **Eliram (Amslam), S.**: *Sefer Segulot, Terufot u'Mazalot*, *Op. Cit.*

30.   *Ibid.*

31.   **Hayman, A.P.**: *Sefer Yesira*, Mohr Siebeck, Tübingen 2004.

32.   **Raz, Uri**: *Shimmush Tehilim & Sepher Yetzira*, Message #3685, Concepts of Kabbalah Yahoo egroup, 6 May 2005.

33.   **Brauner, R.**: *Synopsis of Sefer Shimush Tehillim*. *Op. Cit.*

34.   **Kimchi, D. ben Y.**: *Sefer Tehillim*, *Op. Cit.*
        Sefer Shimmush Tehillim, *Op. Cit.*
        Seder Tefilot Tikun Ezra, *Op. Cit.*
        Grünwald, M.: *Ueber den Einfluss der Psalmen auf die Katholische Liturgie*, *Op. Cit.*
        Refuah v'Chayim m'Yerushalayim im Shimush Tehilim, *Op. Cit.*
        Rebiger, B.: *Sefer Shimmush Tehillim*, *Op. Cit.*
        Landsberg, M.: *Sefer Tehillim im Peirush Rashi*, *Op. Cit.*
        Hai ben Sherira Gaon & Varady, A.N.: *Shimush Tehillim (the Theurgical Use of Psalms)*, *Op. Cit.*

35. **Selig, G.:** *Sepher Schimmusch Tehillim, Op. Cit.*
The Sixth and Seventh Books of Moses, Op. Cit.
Peterson, J.H.: *The Sixth and Seventh Books of Moses, Op. Cit.*
36. **Kimchi, D. ben Y.:** *Sefer Tehillim, Op. Cit.*
Le Livre des Psaumes Hébreu-Français et Phonétique, Op. Cit.
Azulai, H.Y.D.: *Sefer Tehillim Sha'arei Rachamim, Op. Cit.*
Sefer Shimmush Tehillim, Op. Cit.
Seder Tefilot Tikun Ezra, Op. Cit.
Grünwald, M.: *Ueber den Einfluss der Psalmen auf die Katholische Liturgie, Op. Cit.*
Refuah v'Chayim m'Yerushalayim im Shimush Tehilim, Op. Cit.
Rebiger, B.: *Sefer Shimmush Tehillim, Op. Cit.*
Brauner, R.: *Synopsis of Sefer Shimush Tehillim. Op. Cit.*
Ronen, D.: *Tehilim Kavvanot ha-Lev, Op. Cit.*
Landsberg, M.: *Sefer Tehillim im Peirush Rashi, Op. Cit.*
Hai ben Sherira Gaon & Varady, A.N.: *Shimush Tehillim (the Theurgical Use of Psalms), Op. Cit.*
37. **Selig, G.:** *Sepher Schimmusch Tehillim, Op. Cit.*
The Sixth and Seventh Books of Moses, Op. Cit.
Peterson, J.H.: *The Sixth and Seventh Books of Moses, Op. Cit.*
38. **Rebiger, B.:** *Sefer Shimmush Tehillim, Op. Cit.*
39. *Le Livre des Psaumes Hébreu-Français et Phonétique, Op. Cit.*
40. **Kimchi, D. ben Y.:** *Sefer Tehillim, Op. Cit.*
Azulai, H.Y.D.: *Sefer Tehillim Sha'arei Rachamim, Op. Cit.*
Sefer Shimmush Tehillim, Op. Cit.
Seder Tefilot Tikun Ezra, Op. Cit.
Grünwald, M.: *Ueber den Einfluss der Psalmen auf die Katholische Liturgie, Op. Cit.*
Refuah v'Chayim m'Yerushalayim im Shimush Tehilim, Op. Cit.
Rebiger, B.: *Sefer Shimmush Tehillim, Op. Cit.*
Ronen, D.: *Tehilim Kavvanot ha-Lev, Op. Cit.*
Landsberg, M.: *Sefer Tehillim im Peirush Rashi, Op. Cit.*
Hai ben Sherira Gaon & Varady, A.N.: *Shimush Tehillim (the Theurgical Use of Psalms), Op. Cit.*
41. **Brauner, R.:** *Synopsis of Sefer Shimush Tehillim. Op. Cit.*
42. **Rebiger, B.:** *Sefer Shimmush Tehillim, Op. Cit.*
43. *Ibid.*
44. **Zacutto, M.:** *Shorshei ha-Shemot, Op. Cit.*
45. *Ibid.*
46. **Eliram (Amslam), S.:** *Sefer Segulot, Terufot u'Mazalot, Op. Cit.*
47. **Brauner, R.:** *Synopsis of Sefer Shimush Tehillim. Op. Cit.*

48. **Kimchi, D. ben Y.**: *Sefer Tehillim, Op. Cit.*
Sefer Shimmush Tehillim, Op. Cit.
Seder Tefilot Tikun Ezra, Op. Cit.
Grünwald, M.: *Ueber den Einfluss der Psalmen auf die Katholische Liturgie, Op. Cit.*
Refuah v'Chayim m'Yerushalayim im Shimush Tehilim, Op. Cit.
Rebiger, B.: *Sefer Shimmush Tehillim, Op. Cit.*
Landsberg, M.: *Sefer Tehillim im Peirush Rashi, Op. Cit.*
Hai ben Sherira Gaon & Varady, A.N.: *Shimush Tehillim (the Theurgical Use of Psalms), Op. Cit.*
49. *Ibid.*
50. **Rebiger, B.**: *Sefer Shimmush Tehillim, Op. Cit.*
51. **Selig, G.**: *Sepher Schimmusch Tehillim, Op. Cit.*
The Sixth and Seventh Books of Moses, Op. Cit.
Peterson, J.H.: *The Sixth and Seventh Books of Moses, Op. Cit.*
52. **Azulai, H.Y.D.**: *Sefer Tehillim Sha'arei Rachamim, Op. Cit.*
Ronen, D.: *Tehilim Kavvanot ha-Lev, Op. Cit.*
53. *Le Livre des Psaumes Hébreu-Français et Phonétique, Op. Cit.*
54. **Brauner, R.**: *Synopsis of Sefer Shimush Tehillim. Op. Cit.*
55. **Kimchi, D. ben Y.**: *Sefer Tehillim, Op. Cit.*
Sefer Shimmush Tehillim, Op. Cit.
Seder Tefilot Tikun Ezra, Op. Cit.
Grünwald, M.: *Ueber den Einfluss der Psalmen auf die Katholische Liturgie, Op. Cit.*
Refuah v'Chayim m'Yerushalayim im Shimush Tehilim, Op. Cit.
Rebiger, B.: *Sefer Shimmush Tehillim, Op. Cit.*
Landsberg, M.: *Sefer Tehillim im Peirush Rashi, Op. Cit.*
Hai ben Sherira Gaon & Varady, A.N.: *Shimush Tehillim (the Theurgical Use of Psalms), Op. Cit.*
56. **Selig, G.**: *Sepher Schimmusch Tehillim, Op. Cit.*
The Sixth and Seventh Books of Moses, Op. Cit.
Peterson, J.H.: *The Sixth and Seventh Books of Moses, Op. Cit.*
57. **Rebiger, B.**: *Sefer Shimmush Tehillim, Op. Cit.*
58. **Zacutto, M.**: *Shorshei ha-Shemot, Op. Cit.*
59. *Ibid.*
60. **Rebiger, B.**: *Sefer Shimmush Tehillim, Op. Cit.*
61. **Zacutto, M.**: *Shorshei ha-Shemot, Op. Cit.*
62. **Kimchi, D. ben Y.**: *Sefer Tehillim, Op. Cit.*
Le Livre des Psaumes Hébreu-Français et Phonétique, Op. Cit.
Azulai, H.Y.D.: *Sefer Tehillim Sha'arei Rachamim, Op. Cit.*
Sefer Shimmush Tehillim, Op. Cit.
Seder Tefilot Tikun Ezra, Op. Cit.
Grünwald, M.: *Ueber den Einfluss der Psalmen auf die Katholische Liturgie, Op. Cit.*

Refuah v'Chayim m'Yerushalayim im Shimush Tehilim, Op. Cit.
Rebiger, B.: *Sefer Shimmush Tehillim, Op. Cit.*
Ronen, D.: *Tehilim Kavvanot ha-Lev, Op. Cit.*
Landsberg, M.: *Sefer Tehillim im Peirush Rashi, Op. Cit.*
Hai ben Sherira Gaon & Varady, A.N.: *Shimush Tehillim (the Theurgical Use of Psalms), Op. Cit.*
63. **Brauner, R.:** *Synopsis of Sefer Shimush Tehillim. Op. Cit.*
64. **Rebiger, B.:** *Sefer Shimmush Tehillim, Op. Cit.*
65. *Ibid.*
Kimchi, D. ben Y.: *Sefer Tehillim, Op. Cit.*
Sefer Shimmush Tehillim, Op. Cit.
Seder Tefilot Tikun Ezra, Op. Cit.
Grünwald, M.: *Ueber den Einfluss der Psalmen auf die Katholische Liturgie, Op. Cit.*
Refuah v'Chayim m'Yerushalayim im Shimush Tehilim, Op. Cit.
Rebiger, B.: *Sefer Shimmush Tehillim, Op. Cit.*
Landsberg, M.: *Sefer Tehillim im Peirush Rashi, Op. Cit.*
Hai ben Sherira Gaon & Varady, A.N.: *Shimush Tehillim (the Theurgical Use of Psalms), Op. Cit.*
66. **Lipshitz, S. ben Y.Y.:** *Segulot Yisrael, Op. Cit.*
67. **Selig, G.:** *Sepher Schimmusch Tehillim, Op. Cit.*
The Sixth and Seventh Books of Moses, Op. Cit.
Peterson, J.H.: *The Sixth and Seventh Books of Moses, Op. Cit.*
68. **Rebiger, B.:** *Sefer Shimmush Tehillim, Op. Cit.*
69. **Singer, I. & Adler, C.:** *The Jewish Encyclopedia, Op. Cit.*
70. **Kimchi, D. ben Y.:** *Sefer Tehillim, Op. Cit.*
Le Livre des Psaumes Hébreu-Français et Phonétique, Op. Cit.
Azulai, H.Y.D.: *Sefer Tehillim Sha'arei Rachamim, Op. Cit.*
Sefer Shimmush Tehillim, Op. Cit.
Seder Tefilot Tikun Ezra, Op. Cit.
Grünwald, M.: *Ueber den Einfluss der Psalmen auf die Katholische Liturgie, Op. Cit.*
Refuah v'Chayim m'Yerushalayim im Shimush Tehilim, Op. Cit.
Rebiger, B.: *Sefer Shimmush Tehillim, Op. Cit.*
Brauner, R.: *Synopsis of Sefer Shimush Tehillim. Op. Cit.*
Ronen, D.: *Tehilim Kavvanot ha-Lev, Op. Cit.*
Landsberg, M.: *Sefer Tehillim im Peirush Rashi, Op. Cit.*
Hai ben Sherira Gaon & Varady, A.N.: *Shimush Tehillim (the Theurgical Use of Psalms), Op. Cit.*
71. **Rebiger, B.:** *Ibid.*
72. **Eliram (Amslam), S.:** *Sefer Segulot, Terufot u'Mazalot, Op. Cit.*

73.   **Kimchi, D. ben Y.:** *Sefer Tehillim, Op. Cit.*
Sefer Shimmush Tehillim, Op. Cit.
Seder Tefilot Tikun Ezra, Op. Cit.
Grünwald, M.: *Ueber den Einfluss der Psalmen auf die Katholische Liturgie, Op. Cit.*
Refuah v'Chayim m'Yerushalayim im Shimush Tehilim, Op. Cit.
Rebiger, B.: *Sefer Shimmush Tehillim, Op. Cit.*
Brauner, R.: *Synopsis of Sefer Shimush Tehillim. Op. Cit.*
Landsberg, M.: *Sefer Tehillim im Peirush Rashi, Op. Cit.*
Hai ben Sherira Gaon & Varady, A.N.: *Shimush Tehillim (the Theurgical Use of Psalms), Op. Cit.*
74.   **Rebiger, B.:** *Sefer Shimmush Tehillim, Op. Cit.*
75.   *Ibid.*
76.   **Selig, G.:** *Sepher Schimmusch Tehillim, Op. Cit.*
The Sixth and Seventh Books of Moses, Op. Cit.
Peterson, J.H.: *The Sixth and Seventh Books of Moses, Op. Cit.*
77.   **Rebiger, B.:** *Sefer Shimmush Tehillim, Op. Cit.*
78.   **Lipshitz, S. ben Y.Y.:** *Segulot Yisrael, Op. Cit.*
79.   **Azulai, H.Y.D.:** *Sefer Tehillim Sha'arei Rachamim, Op. Cit.*
80.   *Le Livre des Psaumes Hébreu-Français et Phonétique, Op. Cit.*
81.   **Ronen, D.:** *Tehilim Kavvanot ha-Lev, Op. Cit.*
82.   **Rebiger, B.:** *Sefer Shimmush Tehillim, Op. Cit.*
83.   *Ibid.*
Kimchi, D. ben Y.: *Sefer Tehillim, Op. Cit.*
Sefer Shimmush Tehillim, Op. Cit.
Seder Tefilot Tikun Ezra, Op. Cit.
Grünwald, M.: *Ueber den Einfluss der Psalmen auf die Katholische Liturgie, Op. Cit.*
Refuah v'Chayim m'Yerushalayim im Shimush Tehilim, Op. Cit.
Brauner, R.: *Synopsis of Sefer Shimush Tehillim. Op. Cit.*
Landsberg, M.: *Sefer Tehillim im Peirush Rashi, Op. Cit.*
Hai ben Sherira Gaon & Varady, A.N.: *Shimush Tehillim (the Theurgical Use of Psalms), Op. Cit.*
84.   *Ibid.*
85.   **Rebiger, B.:** *Sefer Shimmush Tehillim, Op. Cit.*
86.   **Selig, G.:** *Sepher Schimmusch Tehillim, Op. Cit.*
The Sixth and Seventh Books of Moses, Op. Cit.
Peterson, J.H.: *The Sixth and Seventh Books of Moses, Op. Cit.*
87.   **Rebiger, B.:** *Sefer Shimmush Tehillim, Op. Cit.*
88.   *Ibid.*
89.   **Zacutto, M.:** *Shorshei ha-Shemot, Op. Cit.*
90.   *Ibid.*
91.   **Rebiger, B.:** *Sefer Shimmush Tehillim, Op. Cit.*
92.   *Ibid.*

93. **Kimchi, D. ben Y.:** *Sefer Tehillim, Op. Cit.*
Azulai, H.Y.D.: *Sefer Tehillim Sha'arei Rachamim, Op. Cit.*
Sefer Shimmush Tehillim, Op. Cit.
Seder Tefilot Tikun Ezra, Op. Cit.
Grünwald, M.: *Ueber den Einfluss der Psalmen auf die Katholische Liturgie, Op. Cit.*
Refuah v'Chayim m'Yerushalayim im Shimush Tehilim, Op. Cit.
Rebiger, B.: *Sefer Shimmush Tehillim, Op. Cit.*
Ronen, D.: *Tehilim Kavvanot ha-Lev, Op. Cit.*
Landsberg, M.: *Sefer Tehillim im Peirush Rashi, Op. Cit.*
Hai ben Sherira Gaon & Varady, A.N.: *Shimush Tehillim (the Theurgical Use of Psalms), Op. Cit.*
94. *Le Livre des Psaumes Hébreu-Français et Phonétique, Op. Cit.*
95. **Brauner, R.:** *Synopsis of Sefer Shimush Tehillim. Op. Cit.*
96. **Kimchi, D. ben Y.:** *Sefer Tehillim, Op. Cit.*
Azulai, H.Y.D.: *Sefer Tehillim Sha'arei Rachamim, Op. Cit.*
Sefer Shimmush Tehillim, Op. Cit.
Seder Tefilot Tikun Ezra, Op. Cit.
Grünwald, M.: *Ueber den Einfluss der Psalmen auf die Katholische Liturgie, Op. Cit.*
Refuah v'Chayim m'Yerushalayim im Shimush Tehilim, Op. Cit.
Rebiger, B.: *Sefer Shimmush Tehillim, Op. Cit.*
Ronen, D.: *Tehilim Kavvanot ha-Lev, Op. Cit.*
Landsberg, M.: *Sefer Tehillim im Peirush Rashi, Op. Cit.*
Hai ben Sherira Gaon & Varady, A.N.: *Shimush Tehillim (the Theurgical Use of Psalms), Op. Cit.*
97. **Brauner, R.:** *Synopsis of Sefer Shimush Tehillim. Op. Cit.*
98. **Kimchi, D. ben Y.:** *Sefer Tehillim, Op. Cit.*
Azulai, H.Y.D.: *Sefer Tehillim Sha'arei Rachamim, Op. Cit.*
Sefer Shimmush Tehillim, Op. Cit.
Seder Tefilot Tikun Ezra, Op. Cit.
Grünwald, M.: *Ueber den Einfluss der Psalmen auf die Katholische Liturgie, Op. Cit.*
Refuah v'Chayim m'Yerushalayim im Shimush Tehilim, Op. Cit.
Rebiger, B.: *Sefer Shimmush Tehillim, Op. Cit.*
Ronen, D.: *Tehilim Kavvanot ha-Lev, Op. Cit.*
Landsberg, M.: *Sefer Tehillim im Peirush Rashi, Op. Cit.*
Hai ben Sherira Gaon & Varady, A.N.: *Shimush Tehillim (the Theurgical Use of Psalms), Op. Cit.*
99. **Rebiger, B.:** *Ibid.*
100. **Selig, G.:** *Sepher Schimmusch Tehillim, Op. Cit.*
The Sixth and Seventh Books of Moses, Op. Cit.
Peterson, J.H.: *The Sixth and Seventh Books of Moses, Op. Cit.*

101. **Rebiger, B.:** *Sefer Shimmush Tehillim, Op. Cit.*
102. *Ibid.*
103. **Singer, I. & Adler, C.:** *The Jewish Encyclopedia, Op. Cit.*
104. **Zacutto, M.:** *Shorshei ha-Shemot, Op. Cit.*
105. *Le Livre des Psaumes Hébreu-Français et Phonétique, Op. Cit.*
106. **Azulai, H.Y.D.:** *Sefer Tehillim Sha'arei Rachamim, Op. Cit.*
     Brauner, R.: *Synopsis of Sefer Shimush Tehillim. Op. Cit.*
     Ronen, D.: *Tehilim Kavvanot ha-Lev, Op. Cit.*
107. **Kimchi, D. ben Y.:** *Sefer Tehillim, Op. Cit.*
     Sefer Shimmush Tehillim, Op. Cit.
     Seder Tefilot Tikun Ezra, Op. Cit.
     Grünwald, M.: *Ueber den Einfluss der Psalmen auf die Katholische Liturgie, Op. Cit.*
     Refuah v'Chayim m'Yerushalayim im Shimush Tehilim, Op. Cit.
     Rebiger, B.: *Sefer Shimmush Tehillim, Op. Cit.*
     Landsberg, M.: *Sefer Tehillim im Peirush Rashi, Op. Cit.*
     Hai ben Sherira Gaon & Varady, A.N.: *Shimush Tehillim* (*the Theurgical Use of Psalms*), *Op. Cit.*
108. **Selig, G.:** *Sepher Schimmusch Tehillim, Op. Cit.*
     The Sixth and Seventh Books of Moses, Op. Cit.
     Peterson, J.H.: *The Sixth and Seventh Books of Moses, Op. Cit.*
109. **Rebiger, B.:** *Sefer Shimmush Tehillim, Op. Cit.*
110. *Le Livre des Psaumes Hébreu-Français et Phonétique, Op. Cit.*
     Azulai, H.Y.D.: *Sefer Tehillim Sha'arei Rachamim, Op. Cit.*
     Ronen, D.: *Tehilim Kavvanot ha-Lev, Op. Cit.*
111. **Kimchi, D. ben Y.:** *Sefer Tehillim, Op. Cit.*
     Sefer Shimmush Tehillim, Op. Cit.
     Seder Tefilot Tikun Ezra, Op. Cit.
     Grünwald, M.: *Ueber den Einfluss der Psalmen auf die Katholische Liturgie, Op. Cit.*
     Refuah v'Chayim m'Yerushalayim im Shimush Tehilim, Op. Cit.
     Landsberg, M.: *Sefer Tehillim im Peirush Rashi, Op. Cit.*
     Hai ben Sherira Gaon & Varady, A.N.: *Shimush Tehillim* (*the Theurgical Use of Psalms*), *Op. Cit.*
112. **Rebiger, B.:** *Sefer Shimmush Tehillim, Op. Cit.*
113. **Selig, G.:** *Sepher Schimmusch Tehillim, Op. Cit.*
     The Sixth and Seventh Books of Moses, Op. Cit.
     Peterson, J.H.: *The Sixth and Seventh Books of Moses, Op. Cit.*
114. **Rebiger, B.:** *Sefer Shimmush Tehillim, Op. Cit.*
115. **Zacutto, M.:** *Shorshei ha-Shemot, Op. Cit.*
116. **Swart, J.G.:** *The Book of Sacred Names, Op. Cit.*
117. *Ibid.*
     Swart, J.G.: *The Book of Seals & Amulets, Op. Cit.*
     —*The Book of Immediate Magic—Part 1, Op. Cit.*

118. **Zacutto, M.:** *Shorshei ha-Shemot, Op. Cit.*
119. *Ibid.*
  Swart, J.G.: *The Book of Sacred Names, Op. Cit.*
120. **Vital, Ch.:** *Sefer haPe'ulot : Refu'ot, Segulot, Kabbalah Ma'asit, Kimiyah: noda'a gam b'shem: Sefer Kabbalah Ma'asit, Sefer haRefu'ot, Refu'ot v'Segulot*, Jerusalem 2009.
121. *Ibid.*
122. **Zacutto, M.:** *Shorshei ha-Shemot, Op. Cit.*
  Swart, J.G.: *The Book of Sacred Names, Op. Cit.*
123. **Kimchi, D. ben Y.:** *Sefer Tehillim, Op. Cit.*
  Azulai, H.Y.D.: *Sefer Tehillim Sha'arei Rachamim, Op. Cit.*
  Sefer Shimmush Tehillim, Op. Cit.
  Seder Tefilot Tikun Ezra, Op. Cit.
  Grünwald, M.: *Ueber den Einfluss der Psalmen auf die Katholische Liturgie, Op. Cit.*
  Refuah v'Chayim m'Yerushalayim im Shimush Tehilim, Op. Cit.
  Rebiger, B.: *Sefer Shimmush Tehillim, Op. Cit.*
  Ronen, D.: *Tehilim Kavvanot ha-Lev, Op. Cit.*
  Landsberg, M.: *Sefer Tehillim im Peirush Rashi, Op. Cit.*
  Hai ben Sherira Gaon & Varady, A.N.: *Shimush Tehillim (the Theurgical Use of Psalms), Op. Cit.*
124. *Ibid.*
125. **Selig, G.:** *Sepher Schimmusch Tehillim, Op. Cit.*
  The Sixth and Seventh Books of Moses, Op. Cit.
  Peterson, J.H.: *The Sixth and Seventh Books of Moses, Op. Cit.*
126. *Le Livre des Psaumes Hébreu-Français et Phonétique, Op. Cit.*
127. **Rebiger, B.:** *Sefer Shimmush Tehillim, Op. Cit.*
128. **Zacutto, M.:** *Shorshei ha-Shemot, Op. Cit.*
  Swart, J.G.: *The Book of Sacred Names, Op. Cit.*
  —*The Book of Immediate Magic—Part 1, Op. Cit.*
129. **Azulai, H.Y.D.:** *Sefer Tehillim Sha'arei Rachamim, Op. Cit.*
130. *Le Livre des Psaumes Hébreu-Français et Phonétique, Op. Cit.*
  Ronen, D.: *Tehilim Kavvanot ha-Lev, Op. Cit.*
131. **Brauner, R.:** *Synopsis of Sefer Shimush Tehillim. Op. Cit.*
132. **Kimchi, D. ben Y.:** *Sefer Tehillim, Op. Cit.*
  Sefer Shimmush Tehillim, Op. Cit.
  Seder Tefilot Tikun Ezra, Op. Cit.
  Grünwald, M.: *Ueber den Einfluss der Psalmen auf die Katholische Liturgie, Op. Cit.*
  Refuah v'Chayim m'Yerushalayim im Shimush Tehilim, Op. Cit.
  Rebiger, B.: *Sefer Shimmush Tehillim, Op. Cit.*
  Landsberg, M.: *Sefer Tehillim im Peirush Rashi, Op. Cit.*
  Hai ben Sherira Gaon & Varady, A.N.: *Shimush Tehillim (the Theurgical Use of Psalms), Op. Cit.*

133. Selig, G.: *Sepher Schimmusch Tehillim, Op. Cit.*
     The Sixth and Seventh Books of Moses, Op. Cit.
     Peterson, J.H.: *The Sixth and Seventh Books of Moses, Op. Cit.*
134. Rebiger, B.: *Sefer Shimmush Tehillim, Op. Cit.*
135. Azulai, H.Y.D.: *Sefer Tehillim Sha'arei Rachamim, Op. Cit.*
136. *Le Livre des Psaumes Hébreu-Français et Phonétique, Op. Cit.*
137. Kimchi, D. ben Y.: *Sefer Tehillim, Op. Cit.*
     Sefer Shimmush Tehillim, Op. Cit.
     Seder Tefilot Tikun Ezra, Op. Cit.
     Grünwald, M.: *Ueber den Einfluss der Psalmen auf die Katholische Liturgie, Op. Cit.*
     Refuah v'Chayim m'Yerushalayim im Shimush Tehilim, Op. Cit.
     Rebiger, B.: *Sefer Shimmush Tehillim, Op. Cit.*
     Brauner, R.: *Synopsis of Sefer Shimush Tehillim. Op. Cit.*
     Landsberg, M.: *Sefer Tehillim im Peirush Rashi, Op. Cit.*
     Hai ben Sherira Gaon & Varady, A.N.: *Shimush Tehillim (the Theurgical Use of Psalms), Op. Cit.*
138. Selig, G.: *Sepher Schimmusch Tehillim, Op. Cit.*
     The Sixth and Seventh Books of Moses, Op. Cit.
     Peterson, J.H.: *The Sixth and Seventh Books of Moses, Op. Cit.*
139. Rebiger, B.: *Sefer Shimmush Tehillim, Op. Cit.*
140. Azulai, H.Y.D.: *Sefer Tehillim Sha'arei Rachamim, Op. Cit.*
     Ronen, D.: *Tehilim Kavvanot ha-Lev, Op. Cit.*
141. *Le Livre des Psaumes Hébreu-Français et Phonétique, Op. Cit.*
142. Kimchi, D. ben Y.: *Sefer Tehillim, Op. Cit.*
     Sefer Shimmush Tehillim, Op. Cit.
     Seder Tefilot Tikun Ezra, Op. Cit.
     Grünwald, M.: *Ueber den Einfluss der Psalmen auf die Katholische Liturgie, Op. Cit.*
     Refuah v'Chayim m'Yerushalayim im Shimush Tehilim, Op. Cit.
     Rebiger, B.: *Sefer Shimmush Tehillim, Op. Cit.*
     Brauner, R.: *Synopsis of Sefer Shimush Tehillim. Op. Cit.*
     Landsberg, M.: *Sefer Tehillim im Peirush Rashi, Op. Cit.*
     Hai ben Sherira Gaon & Varady, A.N.: *Shimush Tehillim (the Theurgical Use of Psalms), Op. Cit.*
143. Selig, G.: *Sepher Schimmusch Tehillim, Op. Cit.*
     The Sixth and Seventh Books of Moses, Op. Cit.
     Peterson, J.H.: *The Sixth and Seventh Books of Moses, Op. Cit.*
144. *Le Livre des Psaumes Hébreu-Français et Phonétique, Op. Cit.*
     Azulai, H.Y.D.: *Sefer Tehillim Sha'arei Rachamim, Op. Cit.*
     Ronen, D.: *Tehilim Kavvanot ha-Lev, Op. Cit.*
145. Brauner, R.: *Synopsis of Sefer Shimush Tehillim. Op. Cit.*

146. **Kimchi, D. ben Y.:** *Sefer Tehillim, Op. Cit.*
Sefer Shimmush Tehillim, Op. Cit.
Seder Tefilot Tikun Ezra, Op. Cit.
Grünwald, M.: *Ueber den Einfluss der Psalmen auf die Katholische Liturgie, Op. Cit.*
Refuah v'Chayim m'Yerushalayim im Shimush Tehilim, Op. Cit.
Rebiger, B.: *Sefer Shimmush Tehillim, Op. Cit.*
Landsberg, M.: *Sefer Tehillim im Peirush Rashi, Op. Cit.*
Hai ben Sherira Gaon & Varady, A.N.: *Shimush Tehillim (the Theurgical Use of Psalms), Op. Cit.*
147. **Selig, G.:** *Sepher Schimmusch Tehillim, Op. Cit.*
The Sixth and Seventh Books of Moses, Op. Cit.
Peterson, J.H.: *The Sixth and Seventh Books of Moses, Op. Cit.*
148. **Rebiger, B.:** *Sefer Shimmush Tehillim, Op. Cit.*
149. **Eliram (Amslam), S.:** *Sefer Segulot, Terufot u'Mazalot, Op. Cit.*
150. **Zacutto, M.:** *Shorshei ha-Shemot, Op. Cit.*
Swart, J.G.: *The Book of Sacred Names, Op. Cit.*
—*The Book of Immediate Magic—Part 1, Op. Cit.*
151. *Le Livre des Psaumes Hébreu-Français et Phonétique, Op. Cit.*
Azulai, H.Y.D.: *Sefer Tehillim Sha'arei Rachamim, Op. Cit.*
Ronen, D.: *Tehilim Kavvanot ha-Lev, Op. Cit.*
Brauner, R.: *Synopsis of Sefer Shimush Tehillim. Op. Cit.*
152. **Kimchi, D. ben Y.:** *Sefer Tehillim, Op. Cit.*
Sefer Shimmush Tehillim, Op. Cit.
Seder Tefilot Tikun Ezra, Op. Cit.
Grünwald, M.: *Ueber den Einfluss der Psalmen auf die Katholische Liturgie, Op. Cit.*
Refuah v'Chayim m'Yerushalayim im Shimush Tehilim, Op. Cit.
Rebiger, B.: *Sefer Shimmush Tehillim, Op. Cit.*
Landsberg, M.: *Sefer Tehillim im Peirush Rashi, Op. Cit.*
Hai ben Sherira Gaon & Varady, A.N.: *Shimush Tehillim (the Theurgical Use of Psalms), Op. Cit.*
153. **Selig, G.:** *Sepher Schimmusch Tehillim, Op. Cit.*
The Sixth and Seventh Books of Moses, Op. Cit.
Peterson, J.H.: *The Sixth and Seventh Books of Moses, Op. Cit.*
154. **Rebiger, B.:** *Sefer Shimmush Tehillim, Op. Cit.*
155. **Azulai, H.Y.D.:** *Sefer Tehillim Sha'arei Rachamim, Op. Cit.*
Ronen, D.: *Tehilim Kavvanot ha-Lev, Op. Cit.*
156. *Le Livre des Psaumes Hébreu-Français et Phonétique, Op. Cit.*
157. **Brauner, R.:** *Synopsis of Sefer Shimush Tehillim. Op. Cit.*
158. **Kimchi, D. ben Y.:** *Sefer Tehillim, Op. Cit.*
Sefer Shimmush Tehillim, Op. Cit.

Seder Tefilot Tikun Ezra, Op. Cit.

Grünwald, M.: *Ueber den Einfluss der Psalmen auf die Katholische Liturgie, Op. Cit.*

Refuah v'Chayim m'Yerushalayim im Shimush Tehilim, Op. Cit.

Rebiger, B.: *Sefer Shimmush Tehillim, Op. Cit.*

Landsberg, M.: *Sefer Tehillim im Peirush Rashi, Op. Cit.*

Hai ben Sherira Gaon & Varady, A.N.: *Shimush Tehillim (the Theurgical Use of Psalms), Op. Cit.*

159. **Selig, G.:** *Sepher Schimmusch Tehillim, Op. Cit.*

The Sixth and Seventh Books of Moses, Op. Cit.

Peterson, J.H.: *The Sixth and Seventh Books of Moses, Op. Cit.*

160. **Rebiger, B.:** *Sefer Shimmush Tehillim, Op. Cit.*

161. *Le Livre des Psaumes Hébreu-Français et Phonétique, Op. Cit.*

Azulai, H.Y.D.: *Sefer Tehillim Sha'arei Rachamim, Op. Cit.*

Ronen, D.: *Tehilim Kavvanot ha-Lev, Op. Cit.*

162. **Brauner, R.:** *Synopsis of Sefer Shimush Tehillim. Op. Cit.*

163. **Kimchi, D. ben Y.:** *Sefer Tehillim, Op. Cit.*

Sefer Shimmush Tehillim, Op. Cit.

Seder Tefilot Tikun Ezra, Op. Cit.

Grünwald, M.: *Ueber den Einfluss der Psalmen auf die Katholische Liturgie, Op. Cit.*

Refuah v'Chayim m'Yerushalayim im Shimush Tehilim, Op. Cit.

Landsberg, M.: *Sefer Tehillim im Peirush Rashi, Op. Cit.*

Hai ben Sherira Gaon & Varady, A.N.: *Shimush Tehillim (the Theurgical Use of Psalms), Op. Cit.*

164. **Rebiger, B.:** *Sefer Shimmush Tehillim, Op. Cit.*

165. **Selig, G.:** *Sepher Schimmusch Tehillim, Op. Cit.*

The Sixth and Seventh Books of Moses, Op. Cit.

Peterson, J.H.: *The Sixth and Seventh Books of Moses, Op. Cit.*

166. **Rebiger, B.:** *Sefer Shimmush Tehillim, Op. Cit.*

167. **Zacutto, M.:** *Shorshei ha-Shemot, Op. Cit.*

168. **Azulai, H.Y.D.:** *Sefer Tehillim Sha'arei Rachamim, Op. Cit.*

Ronen, D.: *Tehilim Kavvanot ha-Lev, Op. Cit.*

169. *Le Livre des Psaumes Hébreu-Français et Phonétique, Op. Cit.*

170. **Rebiger, B.:** *Sefer Shimmush Tehillim, Op. Cit.*

171. **Eliram (Amslam), S.:** *Sefer Segulot, Terufot u'Mazalot, Op. Cit.*

172. **Rebiger, B.:** *Sefer Shimmush Tehillim, Op. Cit.*

173. **Selig, G.:** *Sepher Schimmusch Tehillim, Op. Cit.*

The Sixth and Seventh Books of Moses, Op. Cit.

Peterson, J.H.: *The Sixth and Seventh Books of Moses, Op. Cit.*

174. **Azulai, H.Y.D.:** *Sefer Tehillim Sha'arei Rachamim, Op. Cit.*

Ronen, D.: *Tehilim Kavvanot ha-Lev, Op. Cit.*

175. *Le Livre des Psaumes Hébreu-Français et Phonétique, Op. Cit.*
176. **Brauner, R.:** *Synopsis of Sefer Shimush Tehillim. Op. Cit.*
177. **Kimchi, D. ben Y.:** *Sefer Tehillim, Op. Cit.*
Sefer Shimmush Tehillim, Op. Cit.
Seder Tefilot Tikun Ezra, Op. Cit.
Grünwald, M.: *Ueber den Einfluss der Psalmen auf die Katholische Liturgie, Op. Cit.*
Refuah v'Chayim m'Yerushalayim im Shimush Tehilim, Op. Cit.
Rebiger, B.: *Sefer Shimmush Tehillim, Op. Cit.*
Landsberg, M.: *Sefer Tehillim im Peirush Rashi, Op. Cit.*
Hai ben Sherira Gaon & Varady, A.N.: *Shimush Tehillim (the Theurgical Use of Psalms), Op. Cit.*
178. **Selig, G.:** *Sepher Schimmusch Tehillim, Op. Cit.*
The Sixth and Seventh Books of Moses, Op. Cit.
Peterson, J.H.: *The Sixth and Seventh Books of Moses, Op. Cit.*
179. **Eliram (Amslam), S.:** *Sefer Segulot, Terufot u'Mazalot, Op. Cit.*
180. *Ibid.*
181. **Rebiger, B.:** *Sefer Shimmush Tehillim, Op. Cit.*
182. **Zacutto, M.:** *Shorshei ha-Shemot, Op. Cit.*
Swart, J.G.: *The Book of Sacred Names, Op. Cit.*
—*The Book of Immediate Magic—Part 1, Op. Cit.*
183. **Azulai, H.Y.D.:** *Sefer Tehillim Sha'arei Rachamim, Op. Cit.*
Ronen, D.: *Tehilim Kavvanot ha-Lev, Op. Cit.*
184. *Le Livre des Psaumes Hébreu-Français et Phonétique, Op. Cit.*
185. **Brauner, R.:** *Synopsis of Sefer Shimush Tehillim. Op. Cit.*
186. **Kimchi, D. ben Y.:** *Sefer Tehillim, Op. Cit.*
Sefer Shimmush Tehillim, Op. Cit.
Seder Tefilot Tikun Ezra, Op. Cit.
Grünwald, M.: *Ueber den Einfluss der Psalmen auf die Katholische Liturgie, Op. Cit.*
Refuah v'Chayim m'Yerushalayim im Shimush Tehilim, Op. Cit.
Rebiger, B.: *Sefer Shimmush Tehillim, Op. Cit.*
Landsberg, M.: *Sefer Tehillim im Peirush Rashi, Op. Cit.*
Hai ben Sherira Gaon & Varady, A.N.: *Shimush Tehillim (the Theurgical Use of Psalms), Op. Cit.*
187. **Selig, G.:** *Sepher Schimmusch Tehillim, Op. Cit.*
The Sixth and Seventh Books of Moses, Op. Cit.
Peterson, J.H.: *The Sixth and Seventh Books of Moses, Op. Cit.*
188. **Rebiger, B.:** *Sefer Shimmush Tehillim, Op. Cit.*
189. **Azulai, H.Y.D.:** *Sefer Tehillim Sha'arei Rachamim, Op. Cit.*
Ronen, D.: *Tehilim Kavvanot ha-Lev, Op. Cit..*

190. **Kimchi, D. ben Y.:** *Sefer Tehillim, Op. Cit.*
Sefer Shimmush Tehillim, Op. Cit.
Seder Tefilot Tikun Ezra, Op. Cit.
Grünwald, M.: *Ueber den Einfluss der Psalmen auf die Katholische Liturgie, Op. Cit.*
Refuah v'Chayim m'Yerushalayim im Shimush Tehilim, Op. Cit.
Rebiger, B.: *Sefer Shimmush Tehillim, Op. Cit.*
Brauner, R.: *Synopsis of Sefer Shimush Tehillim. Op. Cit.*
Landsberg, M.: *Sefer Tehillim im Peirush Rashi, Op. Cit.*
Hai ben Sherira Gaon & Varady, A.N.: *Shimush Tehillim (the Theurgical Use of Psalms), Op. Cit.*
191. *Ibid.*
192. **Selig, G.:** *Sepher Schimmusch Tehillim, Op. Cit.*
The Sixth and Seventh Books of Moses, Op. Cit.
Peterson, J.H.: *The Sixth and Seventh Books of Moses, Op. Cit.*
193. *Le Livre des Psaumes Hébreu-Français et Phonétique, Op. Cit.*
194. **Rebiger, B.:** *Sefer Shimush Tehillim, Op. Cit.*
195. **Azulai, H.Y.D.:** *Sefer Tehillim Sha'arei Rachamim, Op. Cit.*
Ronen, D.: *Tehilim Kavvanot ha-Lev, Op. Cit.*
196. *Le Livre des Psaumes Hébreu-Français et Phonétique, Op. Cit.*
197. **Brauner, R.:** *Synopsis of Sefer Shimush Tehillim. Op. Cit.*
198. **Kimchi, D. ben Y.:** *Sefer Tehillim, Op. Cit.*
Sefer Shimmush Tehillim, Op. Cit.
Seder Tefilot Tikun Ezra, Op. Cit.
Grünwald, M.: *Ueber den Einfluss der Psalmen auf die Katholische Liturgie, Op. Cit.*
Refuah v'Chayim m'Yerushalayim im Shimush Tehilim, Op. Cit.
Rebiger, B.: *Sefer Shimmush Tehillim, Op. Cit.*
Brauner, R.: *Synopsis of Sefer Shimush Tehillim. Op. Cit.*
Landsberg, M.: *Sefer Tehillim im Peirush Rashi, Op. Cit.*
Hai ben Sherira Gaon & Varady, A.N.: *Shimush Tehillim (the Theurgical Use of Psalms), Op. Cit.*
199. **Selig, G.:** *Sepher Schimmusch Tehillim, Op. Cit.*
The Sixth and Seventh Books of Moses, Op. Cit.
Peterson, J.H.: *The Sixth and Seventh Books of Moses, Op. Cit.*
200. **Eliram (Amslam), S.:** *Sefer Segulot, Terufot u'Mazalot, Op. Cit.*
201. **Rebiger, B.:** *Sefer Shimmush Tehillim, Op. Cit.*
202. **Brauner, R.:** *Synopsis of Sefer Shimush Tehillim. Op. Cit.*
203. **Kimchi, D. ben Y.:** *Sefer Tehillim, Op. Cit.*
Sefer Shimmush Tehillim, Op. Cit.
Seder Tefilot Tikun Ezra, Op. Cit.

Grünwald, M.: *Ueber den Einfluss der Psalmen auf die Katholische Liturgie, Op. Cit.*
Refuah v'Chayim m'Yerushalayim im Shimush Tehilim, Op. Cit.
Rebiger, B.: *Sefer Shimmush Tehillim, Op. Cit.*
Landsberg, M.: *Sefer Tehillim im Peirush Rashi, Op. Cit.*
Hai ben Sherira Gaon & Varady, A.N.: *Shimush Tehillim* (*the Theurgical Use of Psalms*), *Op. Cit.*

204. **Selig, G.:** *Sepher Schimmusch Tehillim, Op. Cit.*
The Sixth and Seventh Books of Moses, Op. Cit.
Peterson, J.H.: *The Sixth and Seventh Books of Moses, Op. Cit.*

205. **Meyer, M.W. & Smith, R.:** *Ancient Christian Magic, Op. Cit.*
Mirecki, P. & Meyer, M.: *Ancient Magic & Ritual Power*, Brill Academic Publishers Inc., Boston & Leiden 2001.

206. **Rankine, D. & Barron, P.H.:** *The Book of Gold, Op. Cit.*
Marty, J. & MacParthy, F.: *Usage Mago-Théurgiques des Psaumes, Op. Cit.*

Psalm 120

1. **Nulman, M.:** *The Encyclopedia of Jewish Prayer, Op. Cit.*
2. *Ibid.*
3. *Ibid.*
4. *Ibid.*
5. *Ibid.*
6. **Baumol, A.:** *The Poetry of Prayer, Op. Cit.*
7. **Nulman, M.:** *The Encyclopedia of Jewish Prayer, Op. Cit.*
8. *Ibid.*
Klein, I.: *A Guide to Jewish Religious Practice, Op. Cit.*
9. **Berlin, A.:** *The JPS Bible Commentary: Psalms 120–150*, University of Nebraska Press, Lincoln 2023.
10. *Ibid.*
11. *Ibid.*
12. *Le Livre des Psaumes Hébreu-Français et Phonétique, Op. Cit.*
Azulai, H.Y.D.: *Sefer Tehillim Sha'arei Rachamim, Op. Cit.*
Ronen, D.: *Tehilim Kavvanot ha-Lev, Op. Cit.*
Feldman, Y.Y.: *Tehillim Eis Ratzon, Op. Cit.*
13. **Berlin, A.:** *The JPS Bible Commentary: Psalms 120–150, Op. Cit.*
14. **Kimchi, D. ben Y.:** *Sefer Tehillim, Op. Cit.*
Sefer Shimmush Tehillim, Op. Cit.
Seder Tefilot Tikun Ezra, Op. Cit.
Grünwald, M.: *Ueber den Einfluss der Psalmen auf die Katholische Liturgie, Op. Cit.*

Singer, I. & Adler, C.: *The Jewish Encyclopedia, Op. Cit.*
Refuah v'Chayim m'Yerushalayim im Shimush Tehilim, Op. Cit.
Rebiger, B.: *Sefer Shimmush Tehillim, Op. Cit.*
Landsberg, M.: *Sefer Tehillim im Peirush Rashi, Op. Cit.*
Hai ben Sherira Gaon & Varady, A.N.: *Shimush Tehillim (the Theurgical Use of Psalms), Op. Cit.*

15.   Selig, G.: *Sepher Schimmusch Tehillim, Op. Cit.*
The Sixth and Seventh Books of Moses, Op. Cit.
Peterson, J.H.: *The Sixth and Seventh Books of Moses, Op. Cit.*

16.   *Ibid.*

17.   Swart, J.G.: *The Book of Sacred Names, Op. Cit.*
—*The Book of Immediate Magic—Part 1, Op. Cit.*

18.   Zellmann-Rohrer, M.: *Psalms Useful for Everything, Op. Cit.*

19.   Rankine, D. & Barron, P.H.: *The Book of Gold, Op. Cit.*
Marty, J. & MacParthy, F.: *Usage Mago-Théurgiques des Psaumes, Op. Cit.*

Psalm 121

1.   Berlin, A.: *The JPS Bible Commentary: Psalms 120–150, Op. Cit.*

2.   Nulman, M.: *The Encyclopedia of Jewish Prayer, Op. Cit.*
Klein, I.: *A Guide to Jewish Religious Practice, Op. Cit.*

3.   Nulman, M.: *Ibid.*

4.   Berlin, A.: *The JPS Bible Commentary: Psalms 120–150, Op. Cit.*

5.   *Ibid.*

6.   *Ibid.*

7.   *Le Livre des Psaumes Hébreu-Français et Phonétique, Op. Cit.*
Azulai, H.Y.D.: *Sefer Tehillim Sha'arei Rachamim, Op. Cit.*
Singer, I. & Adler, C.: *The Jewish Encyclopedia, Op. Cit.*
Ronen, D.: *Tehilim Kavvanot ha-Lev, Op. Cit.*

8.   Kimchi, D. ben Y.: *Sefer Tehillim, Op. Cit.*
Sefer Shimmush Tehillim, Op. Cit.
Seder Tefilot Tikun Ezra, Op. Cit.
Grünwald, M.: *Ueber den Einfluss der Psalmen auf die Katholische Liturgie, Op. Cit.*
Refuah v'Chayim m'Yerushalayim im Shimush Tehilim, Op. Cit.
Rebiger, B.: *Sefer Shimmush Tehillim, Op. Cit.*
Brauner, R.: *Synopsis of Sefer Shimush Tehillim. Op. Cit.*
Landsberg, M.: *Sefer Tehillim im Peirush Rashi, Op. Cit.*
Hai ben Sherira Gaon & Varady, A.N.: *Shimush Tehillim (the Theurgical Use of Psalms), Op. Cit.*

9. Selig, G.: *Sepher Schimmusch Tehillim, Op. Cit.*
    The Sixth and Seventh Books of Moses, Op. Cit.
    Peterson, J.H.: *The Sixth and Seventh Books of Moses, Op. Cit.*
10. Dennis, G.W.: *The Encyclopedia of Jewish Myth, Magic and Mysticism, Op.*
11. Rebiger, B.: *Ibid.*
12. Eliram (Amslam), S.: *Sefer Segulot, Terufot u'Mazalot, Op. Cit.*
13. Lipshitz, S. ben Y.Y.: *Segulot Yisrael, Op. Cit.*
14. Feldman, Y.Y.: *Tehillim Eis Ratzon, Op. Cit.*
15. Berlin, A.: *The JPS Bible Commentary: Psalms 120–150, Op. Cit.*
16. Swart, J.G.: *The Book of Seals & Amulets, Op. Cit.*
17. *Ibid.*
    Sefer Shimmush Tehillim, Op. cit.
    Zacutto, M.: *Shorshei ha-Shemot, Op. Cit.*
    Schrire, T.: *Hebrew Amulets, Op. Cit.*
    Shachar, I.: *Jewish Tradition in Art, Op. Cit.*
    Davis, E. & Frenkel, D.A.: *Ha-Kami'a ha-Ivri, Op. Cit.*
    Green, A.: *Judaic Artifacts, Op. Cit.*
    Peursen, W.T. van & Dyk, J.W.: *Tradition and Innovation in Biblical Interpretation: Studies presented to Professor Eep Talstra on the Occasion of his Sixty-Fifth Birthday*, Koninklijke Brill NV, Leiden 2011.
18. Zacutto, M.: *Ibid.*
19. Swart, J.G.: *The Book of Seals & Amulets, Op. Cit.*
20. Schrire, T.: *Hebrew Amulets, Op. Cit.*
    Klein, M.: *A Time to Be Born, Op. Cit.*
    Holtzberg, A.Y.: *Kovetz Minhagim: An Anthology of Chabad-Lubavitch Customs regarding Pregnancy, Childbirth, Circumcision, Redemption of the Firstborn, and the Birth of Girls*, transl. Neubort, S., Kehot Publication Society, Brooklyn 2012.
21. *Ibid.*
22. Kadden, B.B. & Kadden, B.: *Teaching Jewish Life Cycle, Op. Cit.*
23. Schrire, T.: *Hebrew Amulets, Op. Cit.*
    Swart, J.G.: *The Book of Seals & Amulets, Op. Cit.*
24. *Ibid.*
25. Zacutto, M.: *Shorshei ha-Shemot, Op. Cit.*
    Swart, J.G.: *The Book of Seals & Amulets, Op. Cit.*
26. *Ibid.*
    —*The Book of Immediate Magic—Part 1, Op. Cit.*

519

27. **Zacutto, M.:** *Shorshei ha-Shemot, Op. Cit.*
    Swart, J.G.: *The Book of Seals & Amulets, Op. Cit.*
28. **Ba'al Shem, E.; Ba'al-Shem, J. & Hillel, M.:** *Sefer Toldot Adam, Op. Cit.*
    Rosenberg, Y.: *Rafael ha-Malach, Op. Cit.*
    Davis, E. & Frenkel, D.A.: *Ha-Kami'a ha-Ivri, Op. Cit.*
    Green, A.: *Judaic Artifacts, Op. Cit.*
    Schmid, D.: *Jüdische Amulette aus Osteuropa, Op. Cit.*
29. **Swart, J.G.:** *The Book of Seals & Amulets, Op. Cit.*
    Zacutto, M.: *Shorshei ha-Shemot, Op. Cit.*
30. **Swart, J.G.:** *Ibid.*
31. *Ibid.*
    Zacutto, M.: *Shorshei ha-Shemot, Op. Cit.*
32. **Swart, J.G.:** *The Book of Sacred Names, Op. Cit.*
33. **Zacutto, M.:** *Shorshei ha-Shemot, Op. Cit.*
34. **Swart, J.G.:** *The Book of Sacred Names, Op. Cit.*
35. **Feldman, Y.Y.:** *Tehillim Eis Ratzon, Op. Cit.*
36. **Zacutto, M.:** *Shorshei ha-Shemot, Op. Cit.*
    Swart, J.G.: *The Book of Sacred Names, Op. Cit.*
    —*The Book of Immediate Magic—Part 1, Op. Cit.*
37. **Zellmann-Rohrer, M.:** *Psalms Useful for Everything, Op. Cit.*
38. *Ibid.*
39. **Rankine, D. & Barron, P.H.:** *The Book of Gold, Op. Cit.*
    Marty, J. & MacParthy, F.: *Usage Mago-Théurgiques des Psaumes, Op. Cit.*

Psalm 122

1. **Nulman, M.:** *The Encyclopedia of Jewish Prayer, Op. Cit.*
2. **Berlin, A.:** *The JPS Bible Commentary: Psalms 120–150, Op. Cit.*
3. *Ibid.*
4. **Azulai, H.Y.D.:** *Sefer Tehillim Sha'arei Rachamim, Op. Cit.*
   Ronen, D.: *Tehilim Kavvanot ha-Lev, Op. Cit.*
5. *Le Livre des Psaumes Hébreu-Français et Phonétique, Op. Cit.*
6. **Singer, I. & Adler, C.:** *The Jewish Encyclopedia, Op. Cit.*
7. **Berlin, A.:** *The JPS Bible Commentary: Psalms 120–150, Op. Cit.*
8. *Ibid.*
   Kimchi, D. ben Y.: *Sefer Tehillim, Op. Cit.*
   Sefer Shimmush Tehillim, Op. Cit.
   Seder Tefilot Tikun Ezra, Op. Cit.
   Refuah v'Chayim m'Yerushalayim im Shimush Tehilim, Op. Cit.
   Rebiger, B.: *Sefer Shimmush Tehillim, Op. Cit.*

Brauner, R.: *Synopsis of Sefer Shimush Tehillim. Op. Cit.*

Landsberg, M.: *Sefer Tehillim im Peirush Rashi, Op. Cit.*

Hai ben Sherira Gaon & Varady, A.N.: *Shimush Tehillim (the Theurgical Use of Psalms), Op. Cit.*

9. **Selig, G.:** *Sepher Schimmusch Tehillim, Op. Cit.*
    The Sixth and Seventh Books of Moses, Op. Cit.
    Peterson, J.H.: *The Sixth and Seventh Books of Moses, Op. Cit.*

10. **Rebiger, B.:** *Sefer Shimmush Tehillim, Op. Cit.*

11. **Feldman, Y.Y.:** *Tehillim Eis Ratzon, Op. Cit.*

12. **Rosenberg, Y.:** *Rafael ha-Malach, Op. Cit.*
    Davis, E. & Frenkel, D.A.: *Ha-Kami'a ha-Ivri, Op. Cit.*
    Green, A.: *Judaic Artifacts, Op. Cit.*

13. **Zellmann-Rohrer, M.:** *Psalms Useful for Everything, Op. Cit.*

14. **Rankine, D. & Barron, P.H.:** *The Book of Gold, Op. Cit.*
    Marty, J. & MacParthy, F.: *Usage Mago-Théurgiques des Psaumes, Op. Cit.*

Psalm 123

1. **Nulman, M.:** *The Encyclopedia of Jewish Prayer, Op. Cit.*

2. **Berlin, A.:** *The JPS Bible Commentary: Psalms 120–150, Op. Cit.*

3. *Ibid.*

4. *Le Livre des Psaumes Hébreu-Français et Phonétique, Op. Cit.*
    Singer, I. & Adler, C.: *The Jewish Encyclopedia, Op. Cit.*
    Brauner, R.: *Synopsis of Sefer Shimush Tehillim. Op. Cit.*
    Ronen, D.: *Tehilim Kavvanot ha-Lev, Op. Cit.*

5. **Kimchi, D. ben Y.:** *Sefer Tehillim, Op. Cit.*
    Sefer Shimmush Tehillim, Op. Cit.
    Seder Tefilot Tikun Ezra, Op. Cit.
    Grünwald, M.: *Ueber den Einfluss der Psalmen auf die Katholische Liturgie, Op. Cit.*
    Refuah v'Chayim m'Yerushalayim im Shimush Tehilim, Op. Cit.
    Rebiger, B.: *Sefer Shimmush Tehillim, Op. Cit.*
    Landsberg, M.: *Sefer Tehillim im Peirush Rashi, Op. Cit.*
    Hai ben Sherira Gaon & Varady, A.N.: *Shimush Tehillim (the Theurgical Use of Psalms), Op. Cit.*

6. **Selig, G.:** *Sepher Schimmusch Tehillim, Op. Cit.*
    The Sixth and Seventh Books of Moses, Op. Cit.
    Peterson, J.H.: *The Sixth and Seventh Books of Moses, Op. Cit.*

7. **Berlin, A.:** *The JPS Bible Commentary: Psalms 120–150, Op. Cit.*

8. **Rebiger, B.:** *Sefer Shimmush Tehillim, Op. Cit.*

521

9.   **Azulai, H.Y.D.:** *Sefer Tehillim Sha'arei Rachamim, Op. Cit.*
         Ronen, D.: *Tehilim Kavvanot ha-Lev, Op. Cit.*
10.   **Zellmann-Rohrer, M.:** *Psalms Useful for Everything, Op. Cit.*
11.   **Rankine, D. & Barron, P.H.:** *The Book of Gold, Op. Cit.*
         Marty, J. & MacParthy, F.: *Usage Mago-Théurgiques des Psaumes, Op. Cit.*

Psalm 124

1.   **Nulman, M.:** *The Encyclopedia of Jewish Prayer, Op. Cit.*
2.   **Berlin, A.:** *The JPS Bible Commentary: Psalms 120–150, Op. Cit.*
3.   *Ibid.*
4.   **Kimchi, D. ben Y.:** *Sefer Tehillim, Op. Cit.*
         Le Livre des Psaumes Hébreu-Français et Phonétique, Op. Cit.
         Azulai, H.Y.D.: *Sefer Tehillim Sha'arei Rachamim, Op. Cit.*
         Sefer Shimmush Tehillim, Op. Cit.
         Seder Tefilot Tikun Ezra, Op. Cit.
         Grünwald, M.: *Ueber den Einfluss der Psalmen auf die Katholische Liturgie, Op. Cit.*
         Singer, I. & Adler, C.: *The Jewish Encyclopedia, Op. Cit.*
         Refuah v'Chayim m'Yerushalayim im Shimush Tehilim, Op. Cit.
         Rebiger, B.: *Sefer Shimmush Tehillim, Op. Cit.*
         Brauner, R.: *Synopsis of Sefer Shimush Tehillim. Op. Cit.*
         Landsberg, M.: *Sefer Tehillim im Peirush Rashi, Op. Cit.*
         Hai ben Sherira Gaon & Varady, A.N.: *Shimush Tehillim (the Theurgical Use of Psalms), Op. Cit.*
         Berlin, A.: *The JPS Bible Commentary: Psalms 120–150, Op. Cit.*
5.   **Selig, G.:** *Sepher Schimmusch Tehillim, Op. Cit.*
         The Sixth and Seventh Books of Moses, Op. Cit.
         Peterson, J.H.: *The Sixth and Seventh Books of Moses, Op. Cit.*
6.   **Rebiger, B.:** *Sefer Shimmush Tehillim, Op. Cit.*
7.   **Feldman, Y.Y.:** *Tehillim Eis Ratzon, Op. Cit.*
8.   *Ibid.*
9.   **Zellmann-Rohrer, M.:** *Psalms Useful for Everything, Op. Cit.*
10.   *Ibid.*
11.   *Ibid.*
12.   **Rankine, D. & Barron, P.H.:** *The Book of Gold, Op. Cit.*
         Marty, J. & MacParthy, F.: *Usage Mago-Théurgiques des Psaumes, Op. Cit.*
13.   *Ibid.*
14.   **Mathers, S.L. Macgregor:** *Key of Solomon the King, Op. Cit.*

Psalm 125

1. **Nulman, M.:** *The Encyclopedia of Jewish Prayer, Op. Cit.*
   Berlin, A.: *The JPS Bible Commentary: Psalms 120–150, Op. Cit.*
2. *Le Livre des Psaumes Hébreu-Français et Phonétique, Op. Cit.*
   Singer, I. & Adler, C.: *The Jewish Encyclopedia, Op. Cit.*
   Ronen, D.: *Tehilim Kavvanot ha-Lev, Op. Cit.*
3. **Kimchi, D. ben Y.:** *Sefer Tehillim, Op. Cit.*
   Sefer Shimmush Tehillim, Op. Cit.
   Seder Tefilot Tikun Ezra, Op. Cit.
   Refuah v'Chayim m'Yerushalayim im Shimush Tehilim, Op. Cit.
   Rebiger, B.: *Sefer Shimmush Tehillim, Op. Cit.*
   Brauner, R.: *Synopsis of Sefer Shimush Tehillim. Op. Cit.*
   Landsberg, M.: *Sefer Tehillim im Peirush Rashi, Op. Cit.*
   Hai ben Sherira Gaon & Varady, A.N.: *Shimush Tehillim (the Theurgical Use of Psalms), Op. Cit.*
4. **Rebiger, B.:** *Ibid.*
5. *Ibid.*
6. **Eliram (Amslam), S.:** *Sefer Segulot, Terufot u'Mazalot, Op. Cit.*
7. **Selig, G.:** *Sepher Schimmusch Tehillim, Op. Cit.*
   The Sixth and Seventh Books of Moses, Op. Cit.
   Peterson, J.H.: *The Sixth and Seventh Books of Moses, Op. Cit.*
8. **Berlin, A.:** *The JPS Bible Commentary: Psalms 120–150, Op. Cit.*
9. **Feldman, Y.Y.:** *Tehillim Eis Ratzon, Op. Cit.*
10. **Zacutto, M.:** *Shorshei ha-Shemot, Op. Cit.*
11. *Ibid.*
12. **Rankine, D. & Barron, P.H.:** *The Book of Gold, Op. Cit.*
    Marty, J. & MacParthy, F.: *Usage Mago-Théurgiques des Psaumes, Op. Cit.*
13. *Ibid.*
14. **Mathers, S.L. Macgregor:** *Key of Solomon the King, Op. Cit.*

Psalm 126

1. **Nulman, M.:** *The Encyclopedia of Jewish Prayer, Op. Cit.*
   Berlin, A.: *The JPS Bible Commentary: Psalms 120–150, Op. Cit.*
2. *Ibid.*
   Magonet, J.: *A Rabbi Reads the Psalms*, SCM Press, London 1994.
3. **Nulman, M.:** *The Encyclopedia of Jewish Prayer, Op. Cit.*

4. **Vishny, P.H.:** *The Siddur Companion*, Devora Publishing Company, Jerusalem 2005.
5. **Nulman, M.:** *The Encyclopedia of Jewish Prayer, Op. Cit.*
6. *Ibid.*
7. **Berlin, A.:** *The JPS Bible Commentary: Psalms 120–150, Op. Cit.*
8. *Ibid.*
9. *Le Livre des Psaumes Hébreu-Français et Phonétique, Op. Cit.*
    Azulai, H.Y.D.: *Sefer Tehillim Sha'arei Rachamim, Op. Cit.*
    Singer, I. & Adler, C.: *The Jewish Encyclopedia, Op. Cit.*
    Ronen, D.: *Tehilim Kavvanot ha-Lev, Op. Cit.*
    Brauner, R.: *Synopsis of Sefer Shimush Tehillim. Op. Cit.*
10. **Kimchi, D. ben Y.:** *Sefer Tehillim, Op. Cit.*
    Sefer Shimmush Tehillim, Op. Cit.
    Seder Tefilot Tikun Ezra, Op. Cit.
    Refuah v'Chayim m'Yerushalayim im Shimush Tehilim, Op. Cit.
    Rebiger, B.: *Sefer Shimmush Tehillim, Op. Cit.*
    Landsberg, M.: *Sefer Tehillim im Peirush Rashi, Op. Cit.*
    Hai ben Sherira Gaon & Varady, A.N.: *Shimush Tehillim (the Theurgical Use of Psalms), Op. Cit.*
11. **Rebiger, B.:** *Ibid.*
12. **Swart, J.G.:** *The Book of Seals & Amulets, Op. Cit.*
13. **Selig, G.:** *Sepher Schimmusch Tehillim, Op. Cit.*
    The Sixth and Seventh Books of Moses, Op. Cit.
    Peterson, J.H.: *The Sixth and Seventh Books of Moses, Op. Cit.*
14. **Berlin, A.:** *The JPS Bible Commentary: Psalms 120–150, Op. Cit.*
15. **Scholem, G.:** *Kabbalah*, Quadrangle/New York Times Book Co., New York 1974.
16. **Rebiger, B.:** *Sefer Shimmush Tehillim, Op. Cit.*
17. **Zellmann-Rohrer, M.:** *Psalms Useful for Everything, Op. Cit.*
18. **Rankine, D. & Barron, P.H.:** *The Book of Gold, Op. Cit.*
    Marty, J. & MacParthy, F.: *Usage Mago-Théurgiques des Psaumes, Op. Cit.*
19. **Mathers, S.L. Macgregor:** *Key of Solomon the King, Op. Cit.*

Psalm 127

1. **Nulman, M.:** *The Encyclopedia of Jewish Prayer, Op. Cit.*
    Berlin, A.: *The JPS Bible Commentary: Psalms 120–150, Op. Cit.*
2. **Berlin, A.:** *Ibid.*
3. *Le Livre des Psaumes Hébreu-Français et Phonétique, Op. Cit.*
    Azulai, H.Y.D.: *Sefer Tehillim Sha'arei Rachamim, Op. Cit.*

Ronen, D.: *Tehilim Kavvanot ha-Lev, Op. Cit.*
Brauner, R.: *Synopsis of Sefer Shimush Tehillim. Op. Cit.*
4. Singer, I. & Adler, C.: *The Jewish Encyclopedia, Op. Cit.*
5. Eliram (Amslam), S.: *Sefer Segulot, Terufot u'Mazalot, Op. Cit.*
6. *Ibid.*
7. *Ibid.*
8. Feldman, Y.Y.: *Tehillim Eis Ratzon, Op. Cit.*
9. Kimchi, D. ben Y.: *Sefer Tehillim, Op. Cit.*
    Sefer Shimmush Tehillim, Op. Cit.
    Seder Tefilot Tikun Ezra, Op. Cit.
    Refuah v'Chayim m'Yerushalayim im Shimush Tehilim, Op. Cit.
    Rebiger, B.: *Sefer Shimmush Tehillim, Op. Cit.*
    Landsberg, M.: *Sefer Tehillim im Peirush Rashi, Op. Cit.*
    Hai ben Sherira Gaon & Varady, A.N.: *Shimush Tehillim (the Theurgical Use of Psalms), Op. Cit.*
10. Selig, G.: *Sepher Schimmusch Tehillim, Op. Cit.*
    The Sixth and Seventh Books of Moses, Op. Cit.
    Peterson, J.H.: *The Sixth and Seventh Books of Moses, Op. Cit.*
11. Berlin, A.: *The JPS Bible Commentary: Psalms 120–150, Op. Cit.*
12. Zacutto, M.: *Shorshei ha-Shemot, Op. Cit.*
13. Rebiger, B.: *Sefer Shimmush Tehillim, Op. Cit.*
14. *Ibid.*
15. Clelland, S. & Paul Ferguson, P.: *Book II of the Sacred Magic of Abramelin the Mage, Op. Cit.*
16. Feldman, Y.Y.: *Tehillim Eis Ratzon, Op. Cit.*
17. Rankine, D. & Barron, P.H.: *The Book of Gold, Op. Cit.*
    Marty, J. & MacParthy, F.: *Usage Mago-Théurgiques des Psaumes, Op. Cit.*

Psalm 128

1. Nulman, M.: *The Encyclopedia of Jewish Prayer, Op. Cit.*
    Berlin, A.: *The JPS Bible Commentary: Psalms 120–150, Op. Cit.*
2. *Ibid.*
3. Nulman, M.: *The Encyclopedia of Jewish Prayer, Op. Cit.*
4. Berlin, A.: *The JPS Bible Commentary: Psalms 120–150, Op. Cit.*
5. Spiegel, J.: *Dancing with Angels: Jewish Kabbalah Meditation from Torah to Self-improvement to Prophecy*, electronic text published online 2006.
6. Grünwald, M.: *Ueber den Einfluss der Psalmen auf die Katholische Liturgie, Op. Cit.*

7.   **Spiegel, J.:** *Dancing with Angels, Op. Cit.*
8.   **Swart, J.G.:** *The Book of Seals & Amulets, Op. Cit.*
9.   **Nulman, M.:** *The Encyclopedia of Jewish Prayer, Op. Cit.*
      Berlin, A.: *The JPS Bible Commentary: Psalms 120–150, Op. Cit.*
10. *Ibid.*
11. **Berlin, A.:** *Ibid.*
      Lavie, A.: *A Jewish Woman's Prayer Book,* Spiegel & Grau, New York 2008.
12. **Feldman, Y.Y.:** *Tehillim Eis Ratzon, Op. Cit.*
13. *Le Livre des Psaumes Hébreu-Français et Phonétique, Op. Cit.*
      Azulai, H.Y.D.: *Sefer Tehillim Sha'arei Rachamim, Op. Cit.*
      Singer, I. & Adler, C.: *The Jewish Encyclopedia, Op. Cit.*
      Brauner, R.: *Synopsis of Sefer Shimush Tehillim. Op. Cit.*
14. **Ronen, D.:** *Tehilim Kavvanot ha-Lev, Op. Cit.*
15. **Rosenberg, Y.:** *Rafael ha-Malach, Op. Cit.*
16. **Eliram (Amslam), S.:** *Sefer Segulot, Terufot u'Mazalot, Op. Cit.*
17. *Ibid.*
18. **Zacutto, M.:** *Shorshei ha-Shemot, Op. Cit.*
19. *Ibid.*
20. **Kimchi, D. ben Y.:** *Sefer Tehillim, Op. Cit.*
      Sefer Shimmush Tehillim, Op. Cit.
      Seder Tefilot Tikun Ezra, Op. Cit.
      Refuah v'Chayim m'Yerushalayim im Shimush Tehilim, Op. Cit.
      Rebiger, B.: *Sefer Shimmush Tehillim, Op. Cit.*
      Landsberg, M.: *Sefer Tehillim im Peirush Rashi, Op. Cit.*
      Hai ben Sherira Gaon & Varady, A.N.: *Shimush Tehillim (the Theurgical Use of Psalms), Op. Cit.*
21. **Selig, G.:** *Sepher Schimmusch Tehillim, Op. Cit.*
      The Sixth and Seventh Books of Moses, Op. Cit.
      Peterson, J.H.: *The Sixth and Seventh Books of Moses, Op. Cit.*
22. **Berlin, A.:** *The JPS Bible Commentary: Psalms 120–150, Op. Cit.*
23. **Rebiger, B.:** *Sefer Shimmush Tehillim, Op. Cit.*
24. **Clelland, S. & Paul Ferguson, P.:** *Book II of the Sacred Magic of Abramelin the Mage, Op. Cit.*
25. **Davis, E. & Frenkel, D.A.:** *Ha-Kami'a ha-Ivri, Op. Cit.*
      Green, A.: *Judaic Artifacts, Op. Cit.*
26. **Zacutto, M.:** *Shorshei ha-Shemot, Op. Cit.*
      Swart, J.G.: *The Book of Sacred Names, Op. Cit.*
      —*The Book of Immediate Magic—Part 1, Op. Cit.*
27. **Zellmann-Rohrer, M.:** *Psalms Useful for Everything, Op. Cit.*

28. Rankine, D. & Barron, P.H.: *The Book of Gold, Op. Cit.*
Marty, J. & MacParthy, F.: *Usage Mago-Théurgiques des Psaumes, Op. Cit.*

Psalm 129

1. **Nulman, M.:** *The Encyclopedia of Jewish Prayer, Op. Cit.*
Berlin, A.: *The JPS Bible Commentary: Psalms 120–150, Op. Cit.*
2. *Le Livre des Psaumes Hébreu-Français et Phonétique, Op. Cit.*
Azulai, H.Y.D.: *Sefer Tehillim Sha'arei Rachamim, Op. Cit.*
Singer, I. & Adler, C.: *The Jewish Encyclopedia, Op. Cit.*
Ronen, D.: *Tehilim Kavvanot ha-Lev, Op. Cit.*
3. **Kimchi, D. ben Y.:** *Sefer Tehillim, Op. Cit.*
Sefer Shimmush Tehillim, Op. Cit.
Seder Tefilot Tikun Ezra, Op. Cit.
Grünwald, M.: *Ueber den Einfluss der Psalmen auf die Katholische Liturgie, Op. Cit.*
Refuah v'Chayim m'Yerushalayim im Shimush Tehilim, Op. Cit.
Rebiger, B.: *Sefer Shimmush Tehillim, Op. Cit.*
Landsberg, M.: *Sefer Tehillim im Peirush Rashi, Op. Cit.*
Hai ben Sherira Gaon & Varady, A.N.: *Shimush Tehillim (the Theurgical Use of Psalms), Op. Cit.*
4. **Selig, G.:** *Sepher Schimmusch Tehillim, Op. Cit.*
The Sixth and Seventh Books of Moses, Op. Cit.
Peterson, J.H.: *The Sixth and Seventh Books of Moses, Op. Cit.*
5. **Rebiger, B.:** *Sefer Shimmush Tehillim, Op. Cit.*
Berlin, A.: *The JPS Bible Commentary: Psalms 120–150, Op. Cit.*
6. **Rankine, D. & Barron, P.H.:** *The Book of Gold, Op. Cit.*
Marty, J. & MacParthy, F.: *Usage Mago-Théurgiques des Psaumes, Op. Cit.*

Psalm 130

1. **Nulman, M.:** *The Encyclopedia of Jewish Prayer, Op. Cit.*
Berlin, A.: *The JPS Bible Commentary: Psalms 120–150, Op. Cit.*
2. **Berlin, A.:** *Ibid.*
3. *Ibid.*
Nulman, M.: *The Encyclopedia of Jewish Prayer, Op. Cit.*
4. **Berlin, A.:** *The JPS Bible Commentary: Psalms 120–150, Op. Cit.*
Feldman, Y.Y.: *Tehillim Eis Ratzon, Op. Cit.*

5.   *Ibid.*

6.   *Le Livre des Psaumes Hébreu-Français et Phonétique, Op. Cit.*
        Azulai, H.Y.D.: *Sefer Tehillim Sha'arei Rachamim, Op. Cit.*
        Ronen, D.: *Tehilim Kavvanot ha-Lev, Op. Cit.*
        Berlin, A.: *The JPS Bible Commentary: Psalms 120–150, Op. Cit.*

7.   **Brauner, R.:** *Synopsis of Sefer Shimush Tehillim. Op. Cit.*

8.   **Singer, I. & Adler, C.:** *The Jewish Encyclopedia, Op. Cit.*

9.   **Kimchi, D. ben Y.:** *Sefer Tehillim, Op. Cit.*
        Sefer Shimmush Tehillim, Op. Cit.
        Seder Tefilot Tikun Ezra, Op. Cit.
        Grünwald, M.: *Ueber den Einfluss der Psalmen auf die Katholische Liturgie, Op. Cit.*
        Refuah v'Chayim m'Yerushalayim im Shimush Tehilim, Op. Cit.
        Rebiger, B.: *Sefer Shimmush Tehillim, Op. Cit.*
        Landsberg, M.: *Sefer Tehillim im Peirush Rashi, Op. Cit.*
        Hai ben Sherira Gaon & Varady, A.N.: *Shimush Tehillim (the Theurgical Use of Psalms), Op. Cit.*

10.   **Berlin, A.:** *The JPS Bible Commentary: Psalms 120–150, Op. Cit.*

11.   **Selig, G.:** *Sepher Schimmusch Tehillim, Op. Cit.*
        The Sixth and Seventh Books of Moses, Op. Cit.
        Peterson, J.H.: *The Sixth and Seventh Books of Moses, Op. Cit.*

12.   **Rebiger, B.:** *Sefer Shimmush Tehillim, Op. Cit.*

13.   *Ibid.*

14.   **Rankine, D. & Barron, P.H.:** *The Book of Gold, Op. Cit.*
        Marty, J. & MacParthy, F.: *Usage Mago-Théurgiques des Psaumes, Op. Cit.*

15.   **Mathers, S.L. Macgregor:** *Key of Solomon the King, Op. Cit.*

16.   *Ibid.*

Psalm 131

1.   **Nulman, M.:** *The Encyclopedia of Jewish Prayer, Op. Cit.*
        Berlin, A.: *The JPS Bible Commentary: Psalms 120–150, Op. Cit.*

2.   **Ronen, D.:** *Tehilim Kavvanot ha-Lev, Op. Cit.*

3.   *Le Livre des Psaumes Hébreu-Français et Phonétique, Op. Cit.*
        Azulai, H.Y.D.: *Sefer Tehillim Sha'arei Rachamim, Op. Cit.*

4.   **Singer, I. & Adler, C.:** *The Jewish Encyclopedia, Op. Cit.*

5.   **Brauner, R.:** *Synopsis of Sefer Shimush Tehillim. Op. Cit.*

6.   **Kimchi, D. ben Y.:** *Sefer Tehillim, Op. Cit.*
        Sefer Shimmush Tehillim, Op. Cit.

Seder Tefilot Tikun Ezra, Op. Cit.
Grünwald, M.: *Ueber den Einfluss der Psalmen auf die Katholische Liturgie, Op. Cit.*
Refuah v'Chayim m'Yerushalayim im Shimush Tehilim, Op. Cit.
Rebiger, B.: *Sefer Shimmush Tehillim, Op. Cit.*
Landsberg, M.: *Sefer Tehillim im Peirush Rashi, Op. Cit.*
Hai ben Sherira Gaon & Varady, A.N.: *Shimush Tehillim (the Theurgical Use of Psalms), Op. Cit.*

7. **Selig, G.:** *Sepher Schimmusch Tehillim, Op. Cit.*
The Sixth and Seventh Books of Moses, Op. Cit.
Peterson, J.H.: *The Sixth and Seventh Books of Moses, Op. Cit.*

8. **Berlin, A.:** *The JPS Bible Commentary: Psalms 120–150, Op. Cit.*

9. **Zacutto, M.:** *Shorshei ha-Shemot, Op. Cit.*
Swart, J.G.: *The Book of Sacred Names, Op. Cit.*
—The Book of Immediate Magic—Part 1, Op. Cit.

10. **Rankine, D. & Barron, P.H.:** *The Book of Gold, Op. Cit.*
Marty, J. & MacParthy, F.: *Usage Mago-Théurgiques des Psaumes, Op. Cit.*

11. **Mathers, S.L. Macgregor:** *Key of Solomon the King, Op. Cit.*

Psalm 132

1. **Nulman, M.:** *The Encyclopedia of Jewish Prayer, Op. Cit.*
Berlin, A.: *The JPS Bible Commentary: Psalms 120–150, Op. Cit.*

2. **Nulman, M.:** *Ibid.*

3. *Ibid.*

4. **Feldman, Y.Y.:** *Tehillim Eis Ratzon, Op. Cit.*

5. **Azulai, H.Y.D.:** *Sefer Tehillim Sha'arei Rachamim, Op. Cit.*
Ronen, D.: *Tehilim Kavvanot ha-Lev, Op. Cit.*

6. *Le Livre des Psaumes Hébreu-Français et Phonétique, Op. Cit.*

7. **Singer, I. & Adler, C.:** *The Jewish Encyclopedia, Op. Cit.*

8. **Brauner, R.:** *Synopsis of Sefer Shimush Tehillim. Op. Cit.*

9. **Kimchi, D. ben Y.:** *Sefer Tehillim, Op. Cit.*
Sefer Shimmush Tehillim, Op. Cit.
Seder Tefilot Tikun Ezra, Op. Cit.
Grünwald, M.: *Ueber den Einfluss der Psalmen auf die Katholische Liturgie, Op. Cit.*
Refuah v'Chayim m'Yerushalayim im Shimush Tehilim, Op. Cit.
Rebiger, B.: *Sefer Shimmush Tehillim, Op. Cit.*
Landsberg, M.: *Sefer Tehillim im Peirush Rashi, Op. Cit.*
Hai ben Sherira Gaon & Varady, A.N.: *Shimush Tehillim (the Theurgical Use of Psalms), Op. Cit.*

529

10. **Selig, G.:** *Sepher Schimmusch Tehillim, Op. Cit.*
    The Sixth and Seventh Books of Moses, Op. Cit.
    Peterson, J.H.: *The Sixth and Seventh Books of Moses, Op. Cit.*
11. **Rebiger, B.:** *Sefer Shimmush Tehillim, Op. Cit.*
12. **Zacutto, M.:** *Shorshei ha-Shemot, Op. Cit.*
    Swart, J.G.: *The Book of Sacred Names, Op. Cit.*
    —*The Book of Immediate Magic—Part 1, Op. Cit.*
13. **Rankine, D. & Barron, P.H.:** *The Book of Gold, Op. Cit.*
    Marty, J. & MacParthy, F.: *Usage Mago-Théurgiques des Psaumes, Op. Cit.*

Psalm 133

1. **Nulman, M.:** *The Encyclopedia of Jewish Prayer, Op. Cit.*
   Berlin, A.: *The JPS Bible Commentary: Psalms 120–150, Op. Cit.*
2. **Manuscript 74.0.01:** *Shiviti amulet dedicated to Rachel and Mosheh Avraham Sassoon* (India, 19th century), The Magnes Collection of Jewish Art and Life at the University of California, Berkeley.
3. **Tirshom, J. ben E.:** *Shoshan Yesod ha-Olam* in *Collectanea of Kabbalistic and Magical Texts*, Bibliothèque de Genève: Comites Latentes 145, Genève.
   Brauner, R.: *Synopsis of Sefer Shimush Tehillim. Op. Cit.*
4. *Le Livre des Psaumes Hébreu-Français et Phonétique, Op. Cit.*
5. **Azulai, H.Y.D.:** *Sefer Tehillim Sha'arei Rachamim, Op. Cit.*
   Ronen, D.: *Tehilim Kavvanot ha-Lev, Op. Cit.*
6. **Singer, I. & Adler, C.:** *The Jewish Encyclopedia, Op. Cit.*
7. **Kimchi, D. ben Y.:** *Sefer Tehillim, Op. Cit.*
   Sefer Shimmush Tehillim, Op. Cit.
   Seder Tefilot Tikun Ezra, Op. Cit.
   Grünwald, M.: *Ueber den Einfluss der Psalmen auf die Katholische Liturgie, Op. Cit.*
   Refuah v'Chayim m'Yerushalayim im Shimush Tehilim, Op. Cit.
   Rebiger, B.: *Sefer Shimmush Tehillim, Op. Cit.*
   Landsberg, M.: *Sefer Tehillim im Peirush Rashi, Op. Cit.*
   Hai ben Sherira Gaon & Varady, A.N.: *Shimush Tehillim* (*the Theurgical Use of Psalms*), *Op. Cit.*
8. **Selig, G.:** *Sepher Schimmusch Tehillim, Op. Cit.*
   The Sixth and Seventh Books of Moses, Op. Cit.
   Peterson, J.H.: *The Sixth and Seventh Books of Moses, Op. Cit.*
9. **Clelland, S. & Paul Ferguson, P.:** *Book II of the Sacred Magic of Abramelin the Mage, Op. Cit.*

10. Lipshitz, S. ben Y.Y.: *Segulot Yisrael, Op. Cit.*
    Eliram (Amslam), S.: *Sefer Segulot, Terufot u'Mazalot, Op. Cit.*
11. Rebiger, B.: *Sefer Shimmush Tehillim, Op. Cit.*
12. Zellmann-Rohrer, M.: *Psalms Useful for Everything, Op. Cit.*
13. Rankine, D. & Barron, P.H.: *The Book of Gold, Op. Cit.*
    Marty, J. & MacParthy, F.: *Usage Mago-Théurgiques des Psaumes, Op. Cit.*
14. Mathers, S.L. Macgregor: *Key of Solomon the King, Op. Cit.*

Psalm 134

1. Nulman, M.: *The Encyclopedia of Jewish Prayer, Op. Cit.*
   Berlin, A.: *The JPS Bible Commentary: Psalms 120–150, Op. Cit.*
2. *Ibid.*
3. Kimchi, D. ben Y.: *Sefer Tehillim, Op. Cit.*
   Le Livre des Psaumes Hébreu-Français et Phonétique, Op. Cit.
   Azulai, H.Y.D.: *Sefer Tehillim Sha'arei Rachamim, Op. Cit.*
   Refuah v'Chayim m'Yerushalayim im Shimush Tehilim, Op. Cit.
   Rebiger, B.: *Sefer Shimmush Tehillim, Op. Cit.*
   Landsberg, M.: *Sefer Tehillim im Peirush Rashi, Op. Cit.*
   Hai ben Sherira Gaon & Varady, A.N.: *Shimush Tehillim (the Theurgical Use of Psalms), Op. Cit.*
4. Brauner, R.: *Synopsis of Sefer Shimush Tehillim. Op. Cit.*
5. Selig, G.: *Sepher Schimmusch Tehillim, Op. Cit.*
   The Sixth and Seventh Books of Moses, Op. Cit.
   Peterson, J.H.: *The Sixth and Seventh Books of Moses, Op. Cit.*
6. Rebiger, B.: *Sefer Shimmush Tehillim, Op. Cit.*
   Berlin, A.: *The JPS Bible Commentary: Psalms 120–150, Op. Cit.*
7. Ronen, D.: *Tehilim Kavvanot ha-Lev, Op. Cit.*
8. Rebiger, B.: *Sefer Shimmush Tehillim, Op. Cit.*
9. Berlin, A.: *The JPS Bible Commentary: Psalms 120–150, Op. Cit.*
10. Rebiger, B.: *Sefer Shimmush Tehillim, Op. Cit.*
11. Zellmann-Rohrer, M.: *Psalms Useful for Everything, Op. Cit.*
12. Rankine, D. & Barron, P.H.: *The Book of Gold, Op. Cit.*
    Marty, J. & MacParthy, F.: *Usage Mago-Théurgiques des Psaumes, Op. Cit.*
13. Mathers, S.L. Macgregor: *Key of Solomon the King, Op. Cit.*
14. *Ibid.*

Psalm 135

1. **Nulman, M.:** *The Encyclopedia of Jewish Prayer, Op. Cit.*
   Berlin, A.: *The JPS Bible Commentary: Psalms 120–150, Op. Cit.*
2. **Rosenberg, A.S.:** *Jewish Liturgy as a Spiritual System, Op. Cit.*
3. **Nulman, M.:** *The Encyclopedia of Jewish Prayer, Op. Cit.*
4. **Gillingham, S.:** *Psalms Through the Centuries, Volume 3, Op. Cit.*
5. **Hoffman, L.A.:** *My People's Prayer Book: Vol. 8, Op. Cit.*
6. *Le Livre des Psaumes Hébreu-Français et Phonétique, Op. Cit.*
   Azulai, H.Y.D.: *Sefer Tehillim Sha'arei Rachamim, Op. Cit.*
   Ronen, D.: *Tehilim Kavvanot ha-Lev, Op. Cit.*
7. **Singer, I. & Adler, C.:** *The Jewish Encyclopedia, Op. Cit.*
8. **Brauner, R.:** *Synopsis of Sefer Shimush Tehillim. Op. Cit.*
9. *Ibid.*
   Kimchi, D. ben Y.: *Sefer Tehillim, Op. Cit.*
   Sefer Shimmush Tehillim, Op. Cit.
   Seder Tefilot Tikun Ezra, Op. Cit.
   Grünwald, M.: *Ueber den Einfluss der Psalmen auf die Katholische Liturgie, Op. Cit.*
   Refuah v'Chayim m'Yerushalayim im Shimush Tehilim, Op. Cit.
   Rebiger, B.: *Sefer Shimmush Tehillim, Op. Cit.*
   Landsberg, M.: *Sefer Tehillim im Peirush Rashi, Op. Cit.*
   Hai ben Sherira Gaon & Varady, A.N.: *Shimush Tehillim (the Theurgical Use of Psalms), Op. Cit.*
10. **Selig, G.:** *Sepher Schimmusch Tehillim, Op. Cit.*
    The Sixth and Seventh Books of Moses, Op. Cit.
    Peterson, J.H.: *The Sixth and Seventh Books of Moses, Op. Cit.*
11. **Rebiger, B.:** *Sefer Shimmush Tehillim, Op. Cit.*
12. **Rankine, D. & Barron, P.H.:** *The Book of Gold, Op. Cit.*
    Marty, J. & MacParthy, F.: *Usage Mago-Théurgiques des Psaumes, Op. Cit.*
13. *Ibid.*
14. **Mathers, S.L. Macgregor:** *Key of Solomon the King, Op. Cit.*

Psalm 136

1. **Nulman, M.:** *The Encyclopedia of Jewish Prayer, Op. Cit.*
   Hoffman, L.A. & Arnow, D.: *My People's Passover Haggadah, Op. Cit.*
2. *Ibid.*
3. **Nulman, M.:** *The Encyclopedia of Jewish Prayer, Op. Cit.*
4. *Ibid.*

5. *Ibid.*
6. *Ibid.*
7. **Vishny, P.H.:** *The Siddur Companion, Op. Cit.*
8. **Kimchi, D. ben Y.:** *Sefer Tehillim, Op. Cit.*
   Azulai, H.Y.D.: *Sefer Tehillim Sha'arei Rachamim, Op. Cit.*
   Sefer Shimmush Tehillim, Op. Cit.
   Seder Tefilot Tikun Ezra, Op. Cit.
   Refuah v'Chayim m'Yerushalayim im Shimush Tehilim, Op. Cit.
   Rebiger, B.: *Sefer Shimmush Tehillim, Op. Cit.*
   Brauner, R.: *Synopsis of Sefer Shimush Tehillim. Op. Cit.*
   Ronen, D.: *Tehilim Kavvanot ha-Lev, Op. Cit.*
   Landsberg, M.: *Sefer Tehillim im Peirush Rashi, Op. Cit.*
   Hai ben Sherira Gaon & Varady, A.N.: *Shimush Tehillim (the Theurgical Use of Psalms), Op. Cit.*
9. **Berlin, A.:** *The JPS Bible Commentary: Psalms 120–150, Op. Cit.*
10. **Selig, G.:** *Sepher Schimmusch Tehillim, Op. Cit.*
    The Sixth and Seventh Books of Moses, Op. Cit.
    Peterson, J.H.: *The Sixth and Seventh Books of Moses, Op. Cit.*
11. **Grünwald, M.:** *Ueber den Einfluss der Psalmen auf die Katholische Liturgie, Op. Cit.*
12. **Rebiger, B.:** *Sefer Shimmush Tehillim, Op. Cit.*
13. **Feldman, Y.Y.:** *Tehillim Eis Ratzon, Op. Cit.*
14. *Ibid.*
15. **Rankine, D. & Barron, P.H.:** *The Book of Gold, Op. Cit.*
    Marty, J. & MacParthy, F.: *Usage Mago-Théurgiques des Psaumes, Op. Cit.*

Psalm 137

1. **Nulman, M.:** *The Encyclopedia of Jewish Prayer, Op. Cit.*
2. **Hoffman, L.A.:** *My People's Prayer Book: Vol. 8, Op. Cit.*
3. **Nulman, M.:** *The Encyclopedia of Jewish Prayer, Op. Cit.*
   Vishny, P.H.: *The Siddur Companion, Op. Cit.*
4. **Matt, D.C.:** *The Zohar*, Pritzker edition Vol. 5, Stanford University Press, Stanford 2009.
5. **Nulman, M.:** *The Encyclopedia of Jewish Prayer, Op. Cit.*
6. **Vishny, P.H.:** *The Siddur Companion, Op. Cit.*
7. **Swart, J.G.:** *The Book of Magical Psalms—Part 2, Op. Cit.*
8. *Le Livre des Psaumes Hébreu-Français et Phonétique, Op. Cit.*
   Azulai, H.Y.D.: *Sefer Tehillim Sha'arei Rachamim, Op. Cit.*
   Singer, I. & Adler, C.: *The Jewish Encyclopedia, Op. Cit.*
   Brauner, R.: *Synopsis of Sefer Shimush Tehillim. Op. Cit.*
   Ronen, D.: *Tehilim Kavvanot ha-Lev, Op. Cit.*

9.   **Tirshom, J. ben E.:** *Shoshan Yesod ha-Olam, Op. Cit.*
       Kimchi, D. ben Y.: *Sefer Tehillim, Op. Cit.*
       Azulai, H.Y.D.: *Sefer Tehillim Sha'arei Rachamim, Op. Cit.*
       Sefer Shimmush Tehillim, Op. Cit.
       Seder Tefilot Tikun Ezra, Op. Cit.
       Grünwald, M.: *Ueber den Einfluss der Psalmen auf die Katholische Liturgie, Op. Cit.*
       Refuah v'Chayim m'Yerushalayim im Shimush Tehilim, Op. Cit.
       Rebiger, B.: *Sefer Shimmush Tehillim, Op. Cit.*
       Brauner, R.: *Synopsis of Sefer Shimush Tehillim. Op. Cit.*
       Ronen, D.: *Tehilim Kavvanot ha-Lev, Op. Cit.*
       Landsberg, M.: *Sefer Tehillim im Peirush Rashi, Op. Cit.*
       Hai ben Sherira Gaon & Varady, A.N.: *Shimush Tehillim (the Theurgical Use of Psalms), Op. Cit.*
10.   **Selig, G.:** *Sepher Schimmusch Tehillim, Op. Cit.*
       The Sixth and Seventh Books of Moses, Op. Cit.
       Peterson, J.H.: *The Sixth and Seventh Books of Moses, Op. Cit.*
11.   **Rebiger, B.:** *Sefer Shimmush Tehillim, Op. Cit.*
12.   **Feldman, Y.Y.:** *Tehillim Eis Ratzon, Op. Cit.*
13.   **Dowe, B. & McNaughton, T.:** *By the Rivers of Babylon*, Al Gallico Music Corp: Ackee Music Inc., Los Angeles 1978.
14.   **Zacutto, M.:** *Shorshei ha-Shemot, Op. Cit.*
15.   **Zellmann-Rohrer, M.:** *Psalms Useful for Everything, Op. Cit.*
16.   **Rankine, D. & Barron, P.H.:** *The Book of Gold, Op. Cit.*
       Marty, J. & MacParthy, F.: *Usage Mago-Théurgiques des Psaumes, Op. Cit.*

Psalm 138

1.   **Feldman, Y.Y.:** *Tehillim Eis Ratzon, Op. Cit.*
       Weintraub, S.Y.: *From the Depths: The Use of Psalms*, in **Friedman, D.A.:** *Jewish Pastoral Care, Op. Cit.*
2.   *Le Livre des Psaumes Hébreu-Français et Phonétique, Op. Cit.*
       Azulai, H.Y.D.: *Sefer Tehillim Sha'arei Rachamim, Op. Cit.*
       Ronen, D.: *Tehilim Kavvanot ha-Lev, Op. Cit.*
       Berlin, A.: *The JPS Bible Commentary: Psalms 120–150, Op. Cit.*
3.   **Tirshom, J. ben E.:** *Shoshan Yesod ha-Olam, Op. Cit.*
       Kimchi, D. ben Y.: *Sefer Tehillim, Op. Cit.*
       Singer, I. & Adler, C.: *The Jewish Encyclopedia, Op. Cit.*
       Refuah v'Chayim m'Yerushalayim im Shimush Tehilim, Op. Cit.
       Rebiger, B.: *Sefer Shimmush Tehillim, Op. Cit.*
       Brauner, R.: *Synopsis of Sefer Shimush Tehillim. Op. Cit.*
       Landsberg, M.: *Sefer Tehillim im Peirush Rashi, Op. Cit.*

Hai ben Sherira Gaon & Varady, A.N.: *Shimush Tehillim (the Theurgical Use of Psalms), Op. Cit.*
Selig, G.: *Sepher Schimmusch Tehillim, Op. Cit.*
The Sixth and Seventh Books of Moses, Op. Cit.
Peterson, J.H.: *The Sixth and Seventh Books of Moses, Op. Cit.*
4. Rebiger, B.: *Sefer Shimmush Tehillim, Op. Cit.*
5. Rankine, D. & Barron, P.H.: *The Book of Gold, Op. Cit.*
Marty, J. & MacParthy, F.: *Usage Mago-Théurgiques des Psaumes, Op. Cit.*

Psalm 139

1. Braude, W.G.: *The Midrash on Psalms* (2 Vols), New Haven: Yale University Press, New Haven 1987.
2. Baer, S.: *Siddur Avodat Yisrael*, Hotza'ot Or Torah, Tel Aviv 1957.
3. Robinson, G.: *Essential Judaism, Op. Cit.*
4. *Le Livre des Psaumes Hébreu-Français et Phonétique, Op. Cit.*
Kimchi, D. ben Y.: *Sefer Tehillim, Op. Cit.*
Azulai, H.Y.D.: *Sefer Tehillim Sha'arei Rachamim, Op. Cit.*
Singer, I. & Adler, C.: *The Jewish Encyclopedia, Op. Cit.*
Refuah v'Chayim m'Yerushalayim im Shimush Tehilim, Op. Cit.
Rebiger, B.: *Sefer Shimmush Tehillim, Op. Cit.*
Brauner, R.: *Synopsis of Sefer Shimush Tehillim. Op. Cit.*
Ronen, D.: *Tehilim Kavvanot ha-Lev, Op. Cit.*
Landsberg, M.: *Sefer Tehillim im Peirush Rashi, Op. Cit.*
Hai ben Sherira Gaon & Varady, A.N.: *Shimush Tehillim (the Theurgical Use of Psalms), Op. Cit.*
Selig, G.: *Sepher Schimmusch Tehillim, Op. Cit.*
The Sixth and Seventh Books of Moses, Op. Cit.
Peterson, J.H.: *The Sixth and Seventh Books of Moses, Op. Cit.*
5. Rebiger, B.: *Sefer Shimmush Tehillim, Op. Cit.*
6. *Ibid.*
7. Feldman, Y.Y.: *Tehillim Eis Ratzon, Op. Cit.*
8. Zellmann-Rohrer, M.: *Psalms Useful for Everything, Op. Cit.*
9. Rankine, D. & Barron, P.H.: *The Book of Gold, Op. Cit.*
Marty, J. & MacParthy, F.: *Usage Mago-Théurgiques des Psaumes, Op. Cit.*
10. Mathers, S.L. Macgregor: *Key of Solomon the King, Op. Cit.*

Psalm 140

1. Gillingham, S.: *Psalms Through the Centuries, Volume 3, Op. Cit.*

2. **Berlin, A.**: *The JPS Bible Commentary: Psalms 120–150, Op. Cit.*

3. *Le Livre des Psaumes Hébreu-Français et Phonétique, Op. Cit.*
Kimchi, D. ben Y.: *Sefer Tehillim, Op. Cit.*
Azulai, H.Y.D.: *Sefer Tehillim Sha'arei Rachamim, Op. Cit.*
Singer, I. & Adler, C.: *The Jewish Encyclopedia, Op. Cit.*
Refuah v'Chayim m'Yerushalayim im Shimush Tehilim, Op. Cit.
Rebiger, B.: *Sefer Shimmush Tehillim, Op. Cit.*
Brauner, R.: *Synopsis of Sefer Shimush Tehillim. Op. Cit.*
Ronen, D.: *Tehilim Kavvanot ha-Lev, Op. Cit.*
Landsberg, M.: *Sefer Tehillim im Peirush Rashi, Op. Cit.*
Hai ben Sherira Gaon & Varady, A.N.: *Shimush Tehillim (the Theurgical Use of Psalms), Op. Cit.*
Selig, G.: *Sepher Schimmusch Tehillim, Op. Cit.*
The Sixth and Seventh Books of Moses, Op. Cit.
Peterson, J.H.: *The Sixth and Seventh Books of Moses, Op. Cit.*

4. **Rebiger, B.**: *Sefer Shimmush Tehillim, Op. Cit.*

5. **Zacutto, M.**: *Shorshei ha-Shemot, Op. Cit.*
Swart, J.G.: *The Book of Sacred Names, Op. Cit.*
—The Book of Immediate Magic—Part 1, Op. Cit.

6. **Zellmann-Rohrer, M.**: *Psalms Useful for Everything, Op. Cit.*

7. *Ibid.*

8. **Rankine, D. & Barron, P.H.**: *The Book of Gold, Op. Cit.*
Marty, J. & MacParthy, F.: *Usage Mago-Théurgiques des Psaumes, Op. Cit.*

Psalm 141

1. **Berlin, A.**: *The JPS Bible Commentary: Psalms 120–150, Op. Cit.*

2. **Gillingham, S.**: *Psalms Through the Centuries, Volume 3, Op. Cit.*

3. **Koltuv, B.B.**: *Amulets, Talismans, and Magical Jewelry: A Way to the Unseen, Ever-present, Almighty God*, Nicolas-Hays, Berwick 2005.

4. *Le Livre des Psaumes Hébreu-Français et Phonétique, Op. Cit.*
Kimchi, D. ben Y.: *Sefer Tehillim, Op. Cit.*
Azulai, H.Y.D.: *Sefer Tehillim Sha'arei Rachamim, Op. Cit.*
Sefer Shimmush Tehillim, Op. Cit
Seder Tefilot Tıkun Ezra, Op. Cit.
Refuah v'Chayim m'Yerushalayim im Shimush Tehilim, Op. Cit.
Rebiger, B.: *Sefer Shimmush Tehillim, Op. Cit.*
Brauner, R.: *Synopsis of Sefer Shimush Tehillim. Op. Cit.*

Ronen, D.: *Tehilim Kavvanot ha-Lev*, *Op. Cit.*

Landsberg, M.: *Sefer Tehillim im Peirush Rashi*, *Op. Cit.*

Hai ben Sherira Gaon & Varady, A.N.: *Shimush Tehillim* (*the Theurgical Use of Psalms*), *Op. Cit.*

5. Brauner, R.: *Ibid.*

Singer, I. & Adler, C.: *The Jewish Encyclopedia*, *Op. Cit.*

6. Berlin, A.: *The JPS Bible Commentary: Psalms 120–150*, *Op. Cit.*

7. Selig, G.: *Sepher Schimmusch Tehillim*, *Op. Cit.*

The Sixth and Seventh Books of Moses, *Op. Cit.*

Peterson, J.H.: *The Sixth and Seventh Books of Moses*, *Op. Cit.*

8. Berlin, A.: *The JPS Bible Commentary: Psalms 120–150*, *Op. Cit.*

9. Rebiger, B.: *Sefer Shimmush Tehillim*, *Op. Cit.*

10. Weisberg, C.: *Expecting Miracles: Finding Meaning and Spirituality in Pregnancy Through Judaism*, Urim Publications, Jerusalem & New York 2004.

11. Rankine, D. & Barron, P.H.: *The Book of Gold*, *Op. Cit.*

Marty, J. & MacParthy, F.: *Usage Mago-Théurgiques des Psaumes*, *Op. Cit.*

Psalm 142

1. Gillingham, S.: *Psalms Through the Centuries, Volume 3*, *Op. Cit.*

2. Berlin, A.: *The JPS Bible Commentary: Psalms 120–150*, *Op. Cit.*

3. *Le Livre des Psaumes Hébreu-Français et Phonétique*, *Op. Cit.*

Brauner, R.: *Synopsis of Sefer Shimush Tehillim. Op. Cit.*

Hai ben Sherira Gaon & Varady, A.N.: *Shimush Tehillim* (*the Theurgical Use of Psalms*), *Op. Cit.*

Selig, G.: *Sepher Schimmusch Tehillim*, *Op. Cit.*

The Sixth and Seventh Books of Moses, *Op. Cit.*

Peterson, J.H.: *The Sixth and Seventh Books of Moses*, *Op. Cit.*

4. Singer, I. & Adler, C.: *The Jewish Encyclopedia*, *Op. Cit.*

Brauner, R.: *Synopsis of Sefer Shimush Tehillim. Op. Cit.*

Hai ben Sherira Gaon & Varady, A.N.: *Shimush Tehillim* (*the Theurgical Use of Psalms*), *Op. Cit.*

5. Kimchi, D. ben Y.: *Sefer Tehillim*, *Op. Cit.*

Azulai, H.Y.D.: *Sefer Tehillim Sha'arei Rachamim*, *Op. Cit.*

Refuah v'Chayim m'Yerushalayim im Shimush Tehilim, *Op. Cit.*

Rebiger, B.: *Sefer Shimmush Tehillim*, *Op. Cit.*

Brauner, R.: *Synopsis of Sefer Shimush Tehillim. Op. Cit.*

Ronen, D.: *Tehilim Kavvanot ha-Lev, Op. Cit.*
Landsberg, M.: *Sefer Tehillim im Peirush Rashi, Op. Cit.*
Hai ben Sherira Gaon & Varady, A.N.: *Shimush Tehillim (the Theurgical Use of Psalms), Op. Cit.*
6.   Rebiger, B.: *Ibid.*
7.   *Ibid.*
8.   Zacutto, M.: *Shorshei ha-Shemot, Op. Cit.*
9.   Swart, J.G.: *The Book of Seals & Amulets, Op. Cit.*
10. Zacutto, M.: *Shorshei ha-Shemot, Op. Cit.*
11. Swart, J.G.: *The Book of Seals & Amulets, Op. Cit.*
12. Feldman, Y.Y.: *Tehillim Eis Ratzon, Op. Cit.*
13. *Ibid.*
14. Rankine, D. & Barron, P.H.: *The Book of Gold, Op. Cit.*
     Marty, J. & MacParthy, F.: *Usage Mago-Théurgiques des Psaumes, Op. Cit.*

Psalm 143

1.   Berlin, A.: *The JPS Bible Commentary: Psalms 120–150, Op. Cit.*
2.   *Le Livre des Psaumes Hébreu-Français et Phonétique, Op. Cit.*
     Kimchi, D. ben Y.: *Sefer Tehillim, Op. Cit.*
     Azulai, H.Y.D.: *Sefer Tehillim Sha'arei Rachamim, Op. Cit.*
     Sefer Shimmush Tehillim, Op. Cit.
     Seder Tefilot Tikun Ezra, Op. Cit.
     Singer, I. & Adler, C.: *The Jewish Encyclopedia, Op. Cit.*
     Grünwald, M.: *Ueber den Einfluss der Psalmen auf die Katholische Liturgie, Op. Cit.*
     Refuah v'Chayim m'Yerushalayim im Shimush Tehilim, Op. Cit.
     Rebiger, B.: *Sefer Shimmush Tehillim, Op. Cit.*
     Brauner, R.: *Synopsis of Sefer Shimush Tehillim. Op. Cit.*
     Ronen, D.: *Tehilim Kavvanot ha-Lev, Op. Cit.*
     Landsberg, M.: *Sefer Tehillim im Peirush Rashi, Op. Cit.*
     Hai ben Sherira Gaon & Varady, A.N.: *Shimush Tehillim (the Theurgical Use of Psalms), Op. Cit.*
3.   Selig, G.: *Sepher Schimmusch Tehillim, Op. Cit.*
     The Sixth and Seventh Books of Moses, Op. Cit.
     Peterson, J.H.: *The Sixth and Seventh Books of Moses, Op. Cit.*
4.   Rebiger, B.: *Sefer Shimmush Tehillim, Op. Cit.*
5.   Davis, E. & Frenkel, D.A.: *Ha-Kami'a ha-Ivri, Op. Cit.*
     Green, A.: *Judaic Artifacts, Op. Cit.*
6.   Zellmann-Rohrer, M.: *Psalms Useful for Everything, Op. Cit.*
7.   *Ibid.*
8.   Rankine, D. & Barron, P.H.: *The Book of Gold, Op. Cit.*

Marty, J. & MacParthy, F.: *Usage Mago-Théurgiques des Psaumes, Op. Cit.*

Psalm 144

1. **Nulman, M.:** *The Encyclopedia of Jewish Prayer, Op. Cit.*]
2. **Welcz, I. & Sonnenfeld, J.H. ben A.S.:** *When Erev Pesach falls on Shabbos: A Compendium of Laws and Customs pertaining to Preparations and Conduct when Erev Pesach falls on a Shabbos,* Shmuel Mordechi Wolner and Nesivos Bais Yakov, New York 2008.
3. *Ibid.*
4. **Swart, J.G.:** *The Book of Immediate Magic—Part 2, Op. Cit.*
5. *Le Livre des Psaumes Hébreu-Français et Phonétique, Op. Cit.*
   Azulai, H.Y.D.: *Sefer Tehillim Sha'arei Rachamim, Op. Cit.*
   Ronen, D.: *Tehilim Kavvanot ha-Lev, Op. Cit.*
6. **Singer, I. & Adler, C.:** *The Jewish Encyclopedia, Op. Cit.*
7. **Brauner, R.:** *Synopsis of Sefer Shimush Tehillim. Op. Cit.*
   Hai ben Sherira Gaon & Varady, A.N.: *Shimush Tehillim (the Theurgical Use of Psalms), Op. Cit.*
8. **Selig, G.:** *Sepher Schimmusch Tehillim, Op. Cit.*
   The Sixth and Seventh Books of Moses, Op. Cit.
   Peterson, J.H.: *The Sixth and Seventh Books of Moses, Op. Cit.*
9. **Kimchi, D. ben Y.:** *Sefer Tehillim, Op. Cit.*
   Refuah v'Chayim m'Yerushalayim im Shimush Tehilim, Op. Cit.
   Rebiger, B.: *Sefer Shimmush Tehillim, Op. Cit.*
   Landsberg, M.: *Sefer Tehillim im Peirush Rashi, Op. Cit.*
10. **Rebiger, B.:** *Sefer Shimmush Tehillim, Op. Cit.*
11. *Ibid.*
    Kimchi, D. ben Y.: *Sefer Tehillim, Op. Cit.*
    Refuah v'Chayim m'Yerushalayim im Shimush Tehilim, Op. Cit.
    Landsberg, M.: *Sefer Tehillim im Peirush Rashi, Op. Cit.*
12. **Brauner, R.:** *Synopsis of Sefer Shimush Tehillim. Op. Cit.*
    Hai ben Sherira Gaon & Varady, A.N.: *Shimush Tehillim (the Theurgical Use of Psalms), Op. Cit.*
13. **Berlin, A.:** *The JPS Bible Commentary: Psalms 120–150, Op. Cit.*
14. **Clelland, S. & Paul Ferguson, P.:** *Book II of the Sacred Magic of Abramelin the Mage, Op. Cit.*
15. **Schrire, T.:** *Hebrew Amulets, Op. Cit.*
    Green, A.: *Judaic Artifacts, Op. Cit.*
16. **Zacutto, M.:** *Shorshei ha-Shemot, Op. Cit.*
17. **Rankine, D. & Barron, P.H.:** *The Book of Gold, Op. Cit.*
    Marty, J. & MacParthy, F.: *Usage Mago-Théurgiques des Psaumes, Op. Cit.*

Psalm 145

1. **Blumenthal, D.:** *Understanding Jewish Mysticism: A Source Reader*, Volume I, *Op. cit.*
   Kaplan, A.: *Sefer Yetzirah: The Book of Creation In Theory and Practice*, Samuel Weiser Inc., *Op. cit.*
   Hyman, A.P.: *Sefer Yesira*, Mohr Siebeck, Tübingen 2004.
2. **Swart, J.G.:** *The Book of Sacred Names, Op. Cit.*
3. **Glazerson, M.:** *Above the Zodiac: Astrology in Jewish Thought*, Jason Aronson Inc., Northvale & Jerusalem 1997.
4. *Ibid.*
5. **Berlin, A.:** *The JPS Bible Commentary: Psalms 120–150, Op. Cit.*
6. **Magonet, J.:** *A Rabbi Reads the Psalms, Op. Cit.*
   Nulman, M.: *The Encyclopedia of Jewish Prayer, Op. Cit.*
   Vishny, P.H.: *The Siddur Companion, Op. Cit.*
   Berlin, A.: *The JPS Bible Commentary: Psalms 120–150, Op. Cit.*
7. **Vishny, P.H.:** *Ibid.*
8. **Nulman, M.:** *The Encyclopedia of Jewish Prayer, Op. Cit.*
   Herrmann, K.: *Jewish Mysticism in the Geonic Period: The Prayer of Rav Hamnuna Sava* in **Shaked, S.:** *Officina Magica: Essays on the Practice of Magic in Antiquity*, Koninklijke Brill NV, Leiden & Boston 2005.
   Berlin, A.: *The JPS Bible Commentary: Psalms 120–150, Op. Cit.*
9. **Chamui, A.:** *Devek Me'Ach*, Yarid ha-Sefarim, Jerusalem 2005.
10. **Glazerson, M.:** *Building Blocks of the Soul: Studies on the Letters and Words of the Hebrew Language*, Jason Aronson Inc., Northvale 1997.
11. *Ibid.*
12. **Nulman, M.:** *The Encyclopedia of Jewish Prayer, Op. Cit.*
13. *Ibid.*
14. **Glazerson, M.:** *Building Blocks of the Soul: Studies on the Letters and Words of the Hebrew Language*, Jason Aronson Inc., Northvale 1997.
15. *Ibid.*
16. **Nulman, M.:** *The Encyclopedia of Jewish Prayer, Op. Cit.*
17. **Eliram (Amslam), S.:** *Sefer Segulot, Terufot u'Mazalot, Op. Cit.*
18. **Zacutto, M.:** *Shorshei ha-Shemot, Op. cit.*
    Schrire, T.: *Hebrew Amulets, Op. cit.*
    Nachmiyas, B.: *Chamsa: Kameot, Emunot, Minhagim u'Refu'ah Amamit ba'Ir ha'Atikah Yerushalayim*, Modan, Tel Aviv 1996.

Davis, E. & Frenkel, D.A.: *Ha-Kami'a ha-Ivri, Op. Cit.*
Green, A.: *Judaic Artifacts, Op. Cit.*
Swart, J.G.: *The Book of Seals & Amulets, Op. Cit.*
—*The Book of Immediate Magic—Part 1, Op. Cit.*

19. Glazerson, M.: *Building Blocks of the Soul, Op. Cit.*
20. *Le Livre des Psaumes Hébreu-Français et Phonétique, Op. Cit.*
    Azulai, H.Y.D.: *Sefer Tehillim Sha'arei Rachamim, Op. Cit.*
    Ronen, D.: *Tehilim Kavvanot ha-Lev, Op. Cit.*
    Singer, I. & Adler, C.: *The Jewish Encyclopedia, Op. Cit.*
21. Kimchi, D. ben Y.: *Sefer Tehillim, Op. Cit.*
    Sefer Shimmush Tehillim, Op. Cit.
    Seder Tefilot Tikun Ezra, Op. Cit.
    Grünwald, M.: *Ueber den Einfluss der Psalmen auf die Katholische Liturgie, Op. Cit.*
    Refuah v'Chayim m'Yerushalayim im Shimush Tehilim, Op. Cit.
    Rebiger, B.: *Sefer Shimmush Tehillim, Op. Cit.*
    Brauner, R.: *Synopsis of Sefer Shimush Tehillim. Op. Cit.*
    Landsberg, M.: *Sefer Tehillim im Peirush Rashi, Op. Cit.*
    Hai ben Sherira Gaon & Varady, A.N.: *Shimush Tehillim (the Theurgical Use of Psalms), Op. Cit.*
22. Selig, G.: *Sepher Schimmusch Tehillim, Op. Cit.*
    The Sixth and Seventh Books of Moses, Op. Cit.
    Peterson, J.H.: *The Sixth and Seventh Books of Moses, Op. Cit.*
23. Rebiger, B.: *Sefer Shimmush Tehillim, Op. Cit.*
24. *Ibid.*
25. Davis, E. & Frenkel, D.A.: *Ha-Kami'a ha-Ivri, Op. Cit.*
    Green, A.: *Judaic Artifacts, Op. Cit.*
26. Zacutto, M.: *Shorshei ha-Shemot, Op. Cit.*
    Swart, J.G.: *The Book of Sacred Names, Op. Cit.*
    —*The Book of Immediate Magic—Part 1, Op. Cit.*
27. *Ibid.*
    Swart, J.G.: *The Book of Immediate Magic—Part 1, Op. Cit.*
28. Weintraub, S.Y.: *From the Depths: The Use of Psalms*, in Friedman, D.A.: *Jewish Pastoral Care, Op. Cit.*
29. Zellmann-Rohrer, M.: *Psalms Useful for Everything, Op. Cit.*
30. Grünwald, M.: *Ueber den Einfluss der Psalmen auf die Katholische Liturgie, Op. Cit.*
31. Weier, J.: *Histoire Disputes et Discours des Illusions et Impostures des Diables, des Magiciens Infames, Sorcieres et Empoisonners*, Vol. 2, A. Delahave et Lecrosnier, Paris 1885.
    Lecouteux, C.: *Dictionary of Ancient Magic Words and Spells from Abraxas to Zoar, Op. Cit.*

Psalm 146

1. **Nulman, M.:** *The Encyclopedia of Jewish Prayer, Op. Cit.*
   Berlin, A.: *The JPS Bible Commentary: Psalms 120–150, Op. Cit.*
   Hoffman, L.A.: *My People's Prayer Book,* Volume 3, *P'sukei D'zimrah* (Morning Psalms), Turner Publishing Company, La Vergne 2013.
2. *Ibid.*
3. *Le Livre des Psaumes Hébreu-Français et Phonétique, Op. Cit.*
   Kimchi, D. ben Y.: *Sefer Tehillim, Op. Cit.*
   Azulai, H.Y.D.: *Sefer Tehillim Sha'arei Rachamim, Op. Cit.*
   Singer, I. & Adler, C.: *The Jewish Encyclopedia, Op. Cit.*
   Refuah v'Chayim m'Yerushalayim im Shimush Tehilim, Op. Cit.
   Rebiger, B.: *Sefer Shimmush Tehillim, Op. Cit.*
   Brauner, R.: *Synopsis of Sefer Shimush Tehillim. Op. Cit.*
   Ronen, D.: *Tehilim Kavvanot ha-Lev, Op. Cit.*
   Landsberg, M.: *Sefer Tehillim im Peirush Rashi, Op. Cit.*
   Hai ben Sherira Gaon & Varady, A.N.: *Shimush Tehillim (the Theurgical Use of Psalms), Op. Cit.*
4. **Selig, G.:** *Sepher Schimmusch Tehillim, Op. Cit.*
   The Sixth and Seventh Books of Moses, Op. Cit.
   Peterson, J.H.: *The Sixth and Seventh Books of Moses, Op. Cit.*
5. **Rebiger, B.:** *Sefer Shimmush Tehillim, Op. Cit.*
6. *Ibid.*
7. **Rankine, D. & Barron, P.H.:** *The Book of Gold, Op. Cit.*
   Marty, J. & MacParthy, F.: *Usage Mago-Théurgiques des Psaumes, Op. Cit.*
8. *Ibid.*

Psalm 147

1. **Nulman, M.:** *The Encyclopedia of Jewish Prayer, Op. Cit.*
   Berlin, A.: *The JPS Bible Commentary: Psalms 120–150, Op. Cit.*
2. *Le Livre des Psaumes Hébreu-Français et Phonétique, Op. Cit.*
   Azulai, H.Y.D.: *Sefer Tehillim Sha'arei Rachamim, Op. Cit.*
   Ronen, D.: *Tehilim Kavvanot ha-Lev, Op. Cit.*
   Singer, I. & Adler, C.: *The Jewish Encyclopedia, Op. Cit.*
3. **Kimchi, D. ben Y.:** *Sefer Tehillim, Op. Cit.*
   Refuah v'Chayim m'Yerushalayim im Shimush Tehilim, Op. Cit.
   Rebiger, B.: *Sefer Shimmush Tehillim, Op. Cit.*
   Brauner, R.: *Synopsis of Sefer Shimush Tehillim. Op. Cit.*

Landsberg, M.: *Sefer Tehillim im Peirush Rashi, Op. Cit.*

Hai ben Sherira Gaon & Varady, A.N.: *Shimush Tehillim (the Theurgical Use of Psalms), Op. Cit*

4.   **Selig, G.**: *Sepher Schimmusch Tehillim, Op. Cit.*
The Sixth and Seventh Books of Moses, Op. Cit.
Peterson, J.H.: *The Sixth and Seventh Books of Moses, Op. Cit.*

5.   **Rebiger, B.**: *Sefer Shimmush Tehillim, Op. Cit.*

6.   **Lipshitz, S. ben Y.Y.**: *Segulot Yisrael, Op. Cit.*

7.   **Davis, E. & Frenkel, D.A.**: *Ha-Kami'a ha-Ivri, Op. Cit.*
Green, A.: *Judaic Artifacts, Op. Cit.*

8.   **Zacutto, M.**: *Shorshei ha-Shemot, Op. Cit.*
Swart, J.G.: *The Book of Sacred Names, Op. Cit.*
—*The Book of Immediate Magic—Part 1, Op. Cit.*

9.   **Rankine, D. & Barron, P.H.**: *The Book of Gold, Op. Cit.*
Marty, J. & MacParthy, F.: *Usage Mago-Théurgiques des Psaumes, Op. Cit.*

10.   *Ibid.*

11.   *Ibid.*

Psalm 148

1.   **Nulman, M.**: *The Encyclopedia of Jewish Prayer, Op. Cit.*
Berlin, A.: *The JPS Bible Commentary: Psalms 120–150, Op. Cit.*

2.   *Ibid.*

3.   **Nulman, M.**: *The Encyclopedia of Jewish Prayer, Op. Cit.*

4.   *Le Livre des Psaumes Hébreu-Français et Phonétique, Op. Cit.*
Azulai, H.Y.D.: *Sefer Tehillim Sha'arei Rachamim, Op. Cit.*
Ronen, D.: *Tehilim Kavvanot ha-Lev, Op. Cit.*
Singer, I. & Adler, C.: *The Jewish Encyclopedia, Op. Cit.*

5.   **Kimchi, D. ben Y.**: *Sefer Tehillim, Op. Cit.*
Sefer Shimmush Tehillim, Op. Cit.
Seder Tefilot Tikun Ezra, Op. Cit.
Grünwald, M.: *Ueber den Einfluss der Psalmen auf die Katholische Liturgie, Op. Cit.*
Refuah v'Chayim m'Yerushalayim im Shimush Tehilim, Op. Cit.
Rebiger, B.: *Sefer Shimmush Tehillim, Op. Cit.*
Brauner, R.: *Synopsis of Sefer Shimush Tehillim. Op. Cit.*
Landsberg, M.: *Sefer Tehillim im Peirush Rashi, Op. Cit.*
Hai ben Sherira Gaon & Varady, A.N.: *Shimush Tehillim (the Theurgical Use of Psalms), Op. Cit.*

6.   **Selig, G.**: *Sepher Schimmusch Tehillim, Op. Cit.*
The Sixth and Seventh Books of Moses, Op. Cit.
Peterson, J.H.: *The Sixth and Seventh Books of Moses, Op. Cit.*

7. **Lipshitz, S. ben Y.Y.:** *Segulot Yisrael, Op. Cit.*
8. **Rebiger, B.:** *Sefer Shimmush Tehillim, Op. Cit.*
9. *Ibid.*
10. **Rankine, D. & Barron, P.H.:** *The Book of Gold, Op. Cit.*
    Marty, J. & MacParthy, F.: *Usage Mago-Théurgiques des Psaumes, Op. Cit.*
11. *Ibid.*

Psalm 149

1. **Nulman, M.:** *The Encyclopedia of Jewish Prayer, Op. Cit.*
    Berlin, A.: *The JPS Bible Commentary: Psalms 120–150, Op. Cit.*
2. **Berlin, A.:** *Ibid.*
3. **Singer, I. & Adler, C.:** *The Jewish Encyclopedia, Op. Cit.*
4. *Le Livre des Psaumes Hébreu-Français et Phonétique, Op. Cit.*
    Kimchi, D. ben Y.: *Sefer Tehillim, Op. Cit.*
    Azulai, H.Y.D.: *Sefer Tehillim Sha'arei Rachamim, Op. Cit.*
    Sefer Shimmush Tehillim, Op. Cit.
    Seder Tefilot Tikun Ezra, Op. Cit.
    Grünwald, M.: *Ueber den Einfluss der Psalmen auf die Katholische Liturgie, Op. Cit.*
    Refuah v'Chayim m'Yerushalayim im Shimush Tehilim, Op. Cit.
    Rebiger, B.: *Sefer Shimmush Tehillim, Op. Cit.*
    Ronen, D.: *Tehilim Kavvanot ha-Lev, Op. Cit.*
    Landsberg, M.: *Sefer Tehillim im Peirush Rashi, Op. Cit.*
5. **Brauner, R.:** *Synopsis of Sefer Shimush Tehillim. Op. Cit.*
    Hai ben Sherira Gaon & Varady, A.N.: *Shimush Tehillim (the Theurgical Use of Psalms), Op. Cit.*
6. **Rebiger, B.:** *Sefer Shimmush Tehillim, Op. Cit.*
7. *Ibid.*
8. *Ibid.*
9. **Rankine, D. & Barron, P.H.:** *The Book of Gold, Op. Cit.*
    Marty, J. & MacParthy, F.: *Usage Mago-Théurgiques des Psaumes, Op. Cit.*

Psalm 150

1. **Berlin, A.:** *The JPS Bible Commentary: Psalms 120–150, Op. Cit.*
2. *Ibid.*
    Nulman, M.: *The Encyclopedia of Jewish Prayer, Op. Cit.*
3. *Ibid.*
4. **Friedman, B. ben Y.:** *Sefer Mekor Hatefilot,* Friedman, Mishkoltz 1935.

5.   **Nulman, M.:** *The Encyclopedia of Jewish Prayer, Op. Cit.*
       Kimchi, D. ben Y.: *Sefer Tehillim, Op. Cit.*
6.   **Nulman, M.:** *Ibid.*
7.   *Ibid.*
8.   *Le Livre des Psaumes Hébreu-Français et Phonétique, Op. Cit.*
       Kimchi, D. ben Y.: *Sefer Tehillim, Op. Cit.*
       Azulai, H.Y.D.: *Sefer Tehillim Sha'arei Rachamim, Op. Cit.*
       Sefer Shimmush Tehillim, Op. Cit.
       Seder Tefilot Tikun Ezra, Op. Cit.
       Grünwald, M.: *Ueber den Einfluss der Psalmen auf die Katholische Liturgie, Op. Cit.*
       Singer, I. & Adler, C.: *The Jewish Encyclopedia, Op. Cit.*
       Refuah v'Chayim m'Yerushalayim im Shimush Tehilim, Op. Cit.
       Rebiger, B.: *Sefer Shimmush Tehillim, Op. Cit.*
       Ronen, D.: *Tehilim Kavvanot ha-Lev, Op. Cit.*
       Landsberg, M.: *Sefer Tehillim im Peirush Rashi, Op. Cit.*
       Hai ben Sherira Gaon & Varady, A.N.: *Shimush Tehillim (the Theurgical Use of Psalms), Op. Cit.*
9.   **Selig, G.:** *Sepher Schimmusch Tehillim, Op. Cit.*
       The Sixth and Seventh Books of Moses, Op. Cit.
       Peterson, J.H.: *The Sixth and Seventh Books of Moses, Op. Cit.*
10.   **Brauner, R.:** *Synopsis of Sefer Shimush Tehillim. Op. Cit.*
11.   **Rebiger, B.:** *Sefer Shimmush Tehillim, Op. Cit.*
12.   *Ibid.*
13.   **Weintraub, S.Y.:** *From the Depths: The Use of Psalms,* in **Friedman, D.A.:** *Jewish Pastoral Care, Op. Cit.*
14.   **Rankine, D. & Barron, P.H.:** *The Book of Gold, Op. Cit.*
       Marty, J. & MacParthy, F.: *Usage Mago-Théurgiques des Psaumes, Op. Cit.*
15.   **Zellmann-Rohrer, M.:** *Psalms Useful for Everything, Op. Cit.*
16.   **Scot, R.:** *Discoverie of Witchcraft,* Book XII, Elliot Stock, London 1886.
       Lecouteux, C.: *Dictionary of Ancient Magic Words and Spells from Abraxas to Zoar, Op. Cit.*

EPILOGUE: PSALMS & PSALM SOCIETIES

1.   **Kimchi, D. ben Y.:** *Sefer Tehillim, Op. Cit.*
      Sefer Shimmush Tehillim, Op. Cit.
      Seder Tefilot Tikun Ezra, Op. Cit.
      Refuah v'Chayim m'Yerushalayim im Shimush Tehilim, Op. Cit.
      Rebiger, B.: *Sefer Shimmush Tehillim, Op. Cit.*
      Hai ben Sherira Gaon & Varady, A.N.: *Shimush Tehillim (the Theurgical Use of Psalms), Op. Cit.*
2.   *Encyclopedia Judaica*, Vol. 13, The Macmillan Company, New York 1971.
3.   **Magonet, J.:** *A Rabbi Reads the Psalms, Op. Cit.*
4.   **Berlin, A.:** *The JPS Bible Commentary: Psalms 120–150, Op. Cit.*
5.   **Doren, M. van & Samuel, M.:** *The Book of Praise: Dialogues on the Psalms*, John Day Company, New York 1975.
      Posner, R.: *Jewish Liturgy: Prayer and Synagogue Service Through the Ages*, Keter Publishing House, Jerusalem 1975.
6.   **Berlin, A.:** *The JPS Bible Commentary: Psalms 120–150, Op. Cit.*
7.   *Ibid.*
      Encyclopedia Judaica, Vol. 13, *Op. Cit.*
      Posner, R.: *Jewish Liturgy, Op. Cit.*
      Doren, M. van & Samuel, M.: *The Book of Praise Op. Cit.*
      Magonet, J.: *A Rabbi Reads the Psalms, Op. Cit.*
      Nadav, M. & Rosman, M.J.: *The Jews of Pinsk, 1506 to 1880*, Stanford University Press, Stanford 2008.
8.   *Ibid.*
9.   **Eisenberg, R.L.:** *The Streets of Jerusalem: Who, What, Why*, Devora Publishing Company, Jerusalem & New York 2006.
10.   **Medding, P.Y. & The Institute of Contemporary Jewry, the Hebrew University of Jerusalem:** *A New Jewry? America Since the Second World War*, Studies in Contemporary Jewry Vol. 8, Oxford University Press, Oxford & New York 1992.
11.   **Doren, M. van & Samuel, M.:** *The Book of Praise Op. Cit.*
12.   **Magonet, J.:** *A Rabbi Reads the Psalms, Op. Cit.*
13.   *Ibid.*
14.   **Swart, J.G.:** *The Book of Immediate Magic—Part 1, Op. Cit.*
15.   **Neusner, J.; Frerichs, E.S. & Flesher, P.V.M.:** *Religion, Science, and Magic: In Concert and in Conflict*, Oxford University Press, New York 1989.

16. **Swart, J.G.:** *The Book of Immediate Magic—Part 1*, *Op. Cit.*
17. **Neusner, J.; Frerichs, E.S. & Flesher, P.V.M.:** *Religion, Science, and Magic*, *Op. Cit.*
18. **Berlin, A.:** *The JPS Bible Commentary: Psalms 120–150*, *Op. Cit.*
19. **Rosenfeld, D.:** *Recommended Tehillim (Psalms) for Israel, Protection, & More*, *Op. Cit.*
20. *Segulot* (*Spiritual Tips*) *for a Healthy and Easy Birth*, https://meshiv.co.il/en/shelot_vetshuvot/segulot-spiritual-tips-for-a- healthy-and-easy-birth/
21. *The Tehillim Chapters Orders for Different Problems*, https://meshiv.co.il/tefilot/tehillim-chapters-for-different-problems/
22. **Eliram (Amslam), S.:** *Sefer Segulot, Terufot u'Mazalot*, *Op. Cit.*
23. **Azulai, H.Y.D.:** *Sefer Avodat haKodesh*, M'Ain HaChochmah, Jerusalem 1956.
    Lipshitz, S. ben Y.Y.: *Segulot Yisrael*, *Op. Cit.*
24. **Chamui, A.:** *Sefer Yamlit Nafsho*, Y. Cohen, Jerusalem 1990.
25. *Tehillim for All*, https://www.tehillimforall.com/tehillim/collections/tehillim-for-personal-requests/tehillim-to-express-gratitude/
26. **Singer, I. & Adler, C.:** *The Jewish Encyclopedia*, *Op. Cit.*
27. *Segulos for Refu'ah*, Tzohar Journal Issue 4, Tzohar, Lod 2016.
28. **Eliram (Amslam), S.:** *Sefer Segulot, Terufot u'Mazalot*, *Op. Cit.*
29. **Rosenfeld, D.:** *Recommended Tehillim (Psalms) for Israel, Protection, & More*, https://aish.com/recommended-tehillim-psalms-lists/
30. **Polish, D.F.:** *Bringing the Psalms to Life: How to Understand and Use the Book of Psalms*, Jewish Lights Publishing, Woodstock 2001.
    Rashkow, I.N.: *The Healing Power of Judaism*, in **Ellens, J.H.:** *The Healing Power of Spirituality: How Faith Helps Humans Thrive*, Vol. 1, Praeger/ABC-CLIO, Santa Barbara 2010.
31. **Strassfeld, S. & Strassfeld, M.:** *The Third Jewish Catalog*, The Jewish Publication Society, Philadelphia 1980.
32. **Koretz. P. of:** *Sefer Imrei Pinchas haShalem*, 2 Volumes, Elimelech Elazar Frankel, Bnei Brak 2003.
33. **Rosenfeld, D.:** *Recommended Tehillim (Psalms) for Israel, Protection, & More*, *Op. Cit.*
    Tehillim for All, https://www.tehillimforall.com/tehillim/collections/tehillim-for-personal-requests/tehillim-for-financial-help/

34. **Eliram (Amslam), S.:** *Sefer Segulot, Terufot u'Mazalot, Op. Cit.*
35. **Lipshitz, S. ben Y.Y.:** *Segulot Yisrael, Op. Cit.*
36. **Rosenberg, Y.:** *Rafael ha-Malach, Op. Cit.*
    Bahbout, Eliyahu: *Segulot (mystical virtues) for finding a Shiduch,* https://meshiv.co.il/en/shelot_vetshuvot/virtues-for-finding-a-match/
37. *Ibid.*
38. **Eliram (Amslam), S.:** *Sefer Segulot, Terufot u'Mazalot, Op. Cit.*
39. *Tehillim for All,* https://www.tehillimforall.com/tehillim/collections/tehillim-for-personal-requests/tehillim-to-find-ones-spouse/
40. **Lipshitz, S. ben Y.Y.:** *Segulot Yisrael, Op. Cit.*
41. **Rosenfeld, D.:** *Recommended Tehillim (Psalms) for Israel, Protection, & More, Op. Cit.*
42. **Polish, D.F.:** *Bringing the Psalms to Life, Op. Cit.*
43. *The Tehillim Chapters Orders for Different Problems, Op. Cit.*
44. **Eliram (Amslam), S.:** *Sefer Segulot, Terufot u'Mazalot, Op. Cit.*
45. *The Tehillim Chapters Orders for Different Problems, Op. Cit.*
46. *Ibid.*
47. **Lipshitz, S. ben Y.Y.:** *Segulot Yisrael, Op. Cit.*
48. **Eliram (Amslam), S.:** *Sefer Segulot, Terufot u'Mazalot, Op. Cit.*
49. *Tehillim for All,* https://www.tehillimforall.com/tehillim/collections/tehillim-for-personal-requests/tehillim-for-help-in-hard-times/

also published by The Sangreal Sodality Press

Shadow Tree Series
Volume 1

THE BOOK OF SELF CREATION

Jacobus G. Swart

'The Book of Self Creation' is a study guide for all who seek Divinity within, and who prefer to steer the courses of their lives in a personal manner. The doctrines and techniques addressed in this book will aid practitioners in the expansion of their personal consciousness and spiritual evolution. Combining the principles and teachings of Practical Kabbalah and the Western Mystery Tradition, this book offers step by step instructions on the conscious creation of physical life circumstances, such being always in harmony with the mind-set of the practitioner.

The 'Shadow Tree Series' comprises a unique collection of Western Esoteric studies and practices which Jacobus G. Swart, spiritual successor to William G. Gray and co-founder of the Sangreal Sodality, actuated and taught over a period of forty years. He commenced his journey into the domain of Jewish Mysticism in the early 1970's investigating mainstream Kabbalah, later diversifying into the magical mysteries of Practical Kabbalah. He equally expanded his personal perspectives of the Western Magical Tradition under the careful tutelage of the celebrated English Kabbalist William G. Gray.

ISBN 978-0-620-65589-7 *Paperback*

also published by The Sangreal Sodality Press

Shadow Tree Series
Volume 2

THE BOOK OF
SACRED NAMES

Jacobus G. Swart

'The Book of Sacred Names' is a practical guide into the meditational and magical applications of ancient Hebrew Divine Names. Perpetuating the tenets of traditional Kabbalists who recognised the fundamental bond between 'Kabbalah' and 'Magic,' Jacobus Swart offers step by step instructions on the deliberate and conscious control of personal life circumstances, by means of the most cardinal components of Kabbalistic doctrines and techniques—Divine Names!

The material addressed in this tome derives from the extensive primary literature of '"Practical Kabbalah",' much of which is appearing in print for the first time in English translation.

The 'Shadow Tree Series' comprises a unique collection of Western Esoteric studies and practices which Jacobus Swart, spiritual successor to William G. Gray and co-founder of the Sangreal Sodality, has actuated and taught over a period of forty years. Having commenced his Kabbalah studies in Safed in the early 1970's, he later broadened his 'kabbalistic horizons' under the careful guidance of the famed English Kabbalist William G. Gray.

ISBN 978-0-620-50702-8   *Paperback*

also published by The Sangreal Sodality Press

Shadow Tree Series
Volume 3

THE BOOK OF
SEALS & AMULETS

Jacobus G. Swart

Having introduced a 'nuts and bolts' insight into the inner
workings of Ceremonial Magic and "Practical Kabbalah" in 'The
Book of Self Creation' and 'The Book of Sacred Names,' Jacobus
Swart unfolds further magical resources in 'The Book of Seals &
Amulets.' This tome comprises a comprehensive investigation into
the meaning and relevance of Celestial Alphabets, Magical Seals,
Magic Squares, Divine and Angelic Names, etc., as well as their
employment in Hebrew Amulets in order to benefit personal well-
being in a most significant manner.

Continuing the standards set in the earlier volumes of this
series, Jacobus Swart offers detailed instruction on the contents
and construction of Hebrew Amulets. He again consulted the
enormous array of relevant primary Hebrew literature, large
sections of which are available to an English readership for the
first time.

The 'Shadow Tree Series' comprises a unique collection of
Western Esoteric studies and practices which Jacobus G. Swart,
spiritual successor to William G. Gray and co-founder of the
Sangreal Sodality, actuated and taught over a period of forty years.
He commenced his Kabbalah odyssey in Safed in the early 1970's
studying the doctrines of Lurianic Kabbalah. He also incorporated
the teachings of his late mentor, the celebrated English Kabbalist
William G. Gray, in his personal Kabbalistic worldview.

ISBN 978-0-620-59698-5   *Paperback*

also published by The Sangreal Sodality Press

Shadow Tree Series
Volume 4

THE BOOK OF
IMMEDIATE MAGIC - PART 1

Jacobus G. Swart

'The Book of Immediate Magic' perpetuates the fundamental tenets of 'Self Creation' in which it is maintained that the 'Centre' establishes the 'Circumference,' and that personal reality is emanated in harmony with personal 'Will.' Hence this tome comprises an enhancement and expansion of the magical doctrines of Kabbalah Ma'asit ('Practical Kabbalah') addressed in the first three volumes of this 'Shadow Tree Series' of Jewish Magical texts. Jacobus Swart claims that working 'Immediate Magic' is neither impossible when we fully understand that consciousness is just one vast ocean, and that thoughts are the waves we make in it. It is all a matter of coordinating consciousness.

The 'Shadow Tree Series' comprises a unique collection of Western Esoteric studies and practices which Jacobus G. Swart, spiritual successor to William G. Gray and co-founder of the Sangreal Sodality, has actuated and taught over a period of forty years. He commenced his journey into the domain of Jewish Mysticism in the early 1970's investigating mainstream Kabbalah, later diversifying into the magical mysteries of Practical Kabbalah. He equally expanded his personal perspectives of the Western Magical Tradition under the careful tutelage of the celebrated English Kabbalist William G. Gray.

ISBN 978-0-620-69313-4   *Paperback*

Shadow Tree Series
Volume 4

THE BOOK OF
IMMEDIATE MAGIC - PART 2

Jacobus G. Swart

'The Book of Immediate Magic' perpetuates the fundamental tenets of 'Self Creation' in which it is maintained that the 'Centre' establishes the 'Circumference,' and that personal reality is emanated in harmony with personal 'Will.' Hence this tome comprises an enhancement and expansion of the magical doctrines of *Kabbalah Ma'asit* (*'Practical Kabbalah'*) addressed in the first three volumes of this 'Shadow Tree Series' of Jewish Magical texts. Jacobus Swart claims that working 'Immediate Magic' is neither impossible when we fully understand that consciousness is just one vast ocean, and that thoughts are the waves we make in it. It is all a matter of coordinating consciousness.

    As in the case of all the previous volumes, the current text is dealing with the topic of the 'magical' in this Tradition. In this regard, Jacobus Swart again consulted an array of primary Hebrew literature, major portions of which are being made accessible in translation to an English readership.

    The 'Shadow Tree Series' comprises a unique collection of Western Esoteric studies and practices which Jacobus G. Swart, spiritual successor to William G. Gray and co-founder of the Sangreal Sodality, has actuated and taught over a period of forty years. He commenced his journey into the domain of Jewish Mysticism in the early 1970's investigating mainstream Kabbalah, later diversifying into the magical mysteries of Practical Kabbalah. He equally expanded his personal perspectives of the Western Magical Tradition under the careful tutelage of the celebrated English Kabbalist William G. Gray.

ISBN 978-0-620-69313-4   *Paperback*

also published by The Sangreal Sodality Press

Shadow Tree Series
Volume 5

THE BOOK OF
MAGICAL PSALMS - PART 1

Jacobus G. Swart

Countless individuals all over the world are chanting the *'Psalms of David'* every hour of every day, which makes the *'Book of Psalms'* the most practically applied text in the Hebrew Bible. In this regard this biblical text is reckoned amongst the greatest and most popular works of 'Jewish Magic,' its popularity being due to the Psalms addressing the loftiest "realms of spirit," the lowliest aspects of human existence, and everything in between. They offer ready-made prayers, supplications, and incantations for all to express what is in their hearts and minds. Furthermore, considered to be Divinely inspired, the Psalms comprise a direct link between a 'human mouth' and a 'Divine Ear'!

The material addressed in *'The Book of Magical Psalms'* derives from the extensive primary literature of 'Practical Kabbalah,' much of which is shared in this tome for the first time in English translation. This definitive study includes the magical use of the biblical *'Book of Psalms'* for every conceivable purpose in prayers, incantations, adjurations, and Hebrew amulets.

The 'Shadow Tree Series' comprises a unique collection of Western Esoteric studies and practices which Jacobus G. Swart, spiritual successor to William G. Gray and co-founder of the Sangreal Sodality, has actuated and taught over a period of forty years. He commenced his journey into the domain of Jewish Mysticism in the early 1970's investigating mainstream Kabbalah, later diversifying into the magical mysteries of Practical Kabbalah. He equally expanded his personal perspectives of the Western Magical Tradition under the careful tutelage of the celebrated English Kabbalist William G. Gray.

ISBN 978-0-620-93176-2   *Paperback*

also published by The Sangreal Sodality Press

Shadow Tree Series
Volume 5

THE BOOK OF
MAGICAL PSALMS - PART 2

Jacobus G. Swart

Countless individuals all over the world are chanting the *'Psalms of David'* every hour of every day, which makes the *'Book of Psalms'* the most practically applied text in the Hebrew Bible. In this regard this biblical text is reckoned amongst the greatest and most popular works of 'Jewish Magic,' its popularity being due to the Psalms addressing the loftiest "realms of spirit," the lowliest aspects of human existence, and everything in between. They offer ready-made prayers, supplications, and incantations for all to express what is in their hearts and minds. Furthermore, considered to be Divinely inspired, the Psalms comprise a direct link between a 'human mouth' and a 'Divine Ear'!

The material addressed in *'The Book of Magical Psalms'* derives from the extensive primary literature of 'Practical Kabbalah,' much of which is shared in this tome for the first time in English translation. This definitive study includes the magical use of the biblical *'Book of Psalms'* for every conceivable purpose in prayers, incantations, adjurations, and Hebrew amulets.

The 'Shadow Tree Series' comprises a unique collection of Western Esoteric studies and practices which Jacobus G. Swart, spiritual successor to William G. Gray and co-founder of the Sangreal Sodality, has actuated and taught over a period of forty years. He commenced his journey into the domain of Jewish Mysticism in the early 1970's investigating mainstream Kabbalah, later diversifying into the magical mysteries of Practical Kabbalah. He equally expanded his personal perspectives of the Western Magical Tradition under the careful tutelage of the celebrated English Kabbalist William G. Gray.

ISBN 978-0-6397-0958-1   *Paperback*

also published by The Sangreal Sodality Press

THE LADDER OF LIGHTS
(OR QABALAH RENOVATA)

William G. Gray

The Tree of Life works in relation to consciousness somewhat like a computer. Data is fed in, stored in associative banks, and then fed out on demand. The difference between the Tree and a computer, however, is that a computer can only produce various combinations of the information that has been programmed into it. The Tree, operating through the intelligent consciousness of living beings, whether embodied in this world or not, acts as a sort of Universal Exchange throughout the entire chain of consciousness sharing its scheme, and the extent of this is infinite and incalculable.

The Tree of Life is a means and not an end. It is not in itself an object for worship or some idol for superstitious reverence. It is a means, a method, a map and a mechanism for assisting the attainment of the single objective common to all creeds, systems, mysteries and religions—namely, the mystical union of humanity and divinity. With this end in view, this book is an aid to whoever desires to climb the Tree of Life.

'.....the most original commentary on basic Kabbalistic knowledge that I have read for God knows how many years.'
Israel Regardie

'.....beautifully presented and set in excellent marching order.....For one new to the subject, this is a fine text and an exceptionally lucid introduction to a veiled and meditative lore which is still being enlarged from year to year.'
Max Freedom Long (*Huna Vistas*)

ISBN 978-0-620-40303-0   *Paperback*

also published by The Sangreal Sodality Press

AN OUTLOOK ON OUR INNER WESTERN WAY

William G. Gray

'*An Outlook on Our Inner Western Way*' is a unique book. This is no dusty, quaint grimoire — it is a sane and simple method of true attainment for those who seek communion with their higher selves.

In this book, William Gray shows simply and lucidly, how to *live* the Western Inner Tradition. Tracing the cosmology of Western magic, he substantiates its vitality and urgency for our future.

William G. Gray is rated one of the most prolific — and controversial — occultists today. Blending keen insight, modern psychological models and an overall sense of practicality, his books have torn at the mouldy veils of so-called occult secrets, laying out a no-non sense foundation by which modern Western humanity may once again regain its precious magical soul.

ISBN 978-0-620-40306-1   *Paperback*

also published by The Sangreal Sodality Press

Sangreal Sodality Series
Volume 1

WESTERN INNER WORKINGS

William G. Gray

The '*Sangreal Sodality Series*' is a home study course comprising the fundamental text books of the Sangreal Sodality, that revives the instrumentality inherent in our western Tradition. The series makes available to us, in our own cultural symbolism, a way to enlightenment that we can practice on a daily basis.

'*Western Inner Workings*' provides a practical framework for the western student's psycho-spiritual development. Each day includes a morning meditation, a mid-day invocation, evening exercises, and a sleep subject. Incorporating symbols that are 'close to home,' these rituals increase consciousness in comfortable increments.

ISBN 978-0-620-40304-7   *Paperback*

also published by The Sangreal Sodality Press

A BEGINNERS GUIDE TO LIVING KABBALAH

William G. Gray

This compendium comprises six Kabbalistic works by William G. Gray, some of which are appearing here in print for the first time. The texts included in this compilation are ranging from the simplest introduction to the Spheres and Paths of the Kabbalistic Tree of Life system, to related meditation techniques and associated ritual magical procedures, to an advanced system of what could be termed 'inter-dimensional spiritual communication.'

The title 'A Beginners Guide to Living Kabbalah' is perhaps somewhat misleading, as this compilation equally contains works of an advanced nature, and the ritual and meditation techniques addressed in this tome, pertain to both beginners as well as advanced practitioners of 'Practical Kabbalah.'

ISBN 978-0-620-42887-3   *Paperback*

also published by The Sangreal Sodality Press

LESSONS LEARNED FROM OCCULT LETTERS

William G. Gray

In this book William G. Gray, the renowned English Kabbalist and Ceremonial Magician, delineated some of the lessons he learned from the letters which passed between himself and Emil Napoleon Hauenstein, his Austrian mentor and friend, whom he affectionately called "E.N.H." Contrary to opinions expressed regarding Emil Napoleon Hauenstein's status as a "Magus," it should be noted that he was nothing of the kind. He classified himself a "mystic," and was a Martinist. Whilst he was an "Initiate" of the well-known French Occultist Papus (Gerard Encausse), he had a particularly poor opinion of ritual magic and never shared a single magical practice with William Gray.

On the other hand, E.N.H. addressed important psycho-spiritual occult principles and doctrines in his letters, and encouraged his young friend to acquire a greater understanding of what it means to be an "Occultist." William Gray gained a clear comprehension that "Goodness, Love, Truth, Kindness, and such Spiritual qualities in us that come direct from God must come *first*. Cleverness, intellectuality, and mental attributes can then be safely developed in the course of time." Since "Occultism is the study and practice of subjects and laws which are beyond the bounds and limitations of ordinary physical or even mental experience," Emil Napoleon Hauenstein directed his young protegé in unfolding a well-regulated "Self," who is in full control of all his personal faculties, whether these be physical, mental, emotional or spiritual. This is of particular importance in understanding, as William Gray noted, that "Occultism is *not* a pastime, it is a Power, a Purpose, a Progress, and a Path"—*a Way of Life!*

ISBN 978-0-620-79024-6   *Paperback*

Made in the USA
Columbia, SC
10 February 2025